Contemporary Slavery and Trafficking in Persons

Global Narratives

Contemporary Slavery and Trafficking in Persons

Global Narratives

Edited by:
Arun Kumar Acharya
Jennifer Bryson Clark
Maria Luisa Martinez Sanchez

MAYA PUBLISHING HOUSE
NEW DELHI-110086

Cataloging in Publication Data--DK

Courtesy: D.K. Agencies (P) Ltd. <docinfo@dkagencies.com>

Contemporary slavery and trafficking in persons : global narratives / edited by Arun Kumar Acharya, Jennifer Bryson Clark, Maria Luisa Martinez Sanchez. -- First edition.
pages cm
Contributed articles.
ISBN 9789391642006

1. Human trafficking. 2. Women--Crimes against. I. Acharya, Arun Kumar, editor. II. Clark, Jenny Bryson, editor. III. Martínez Sánchez, María Luisa, editor.

LCC HQ281.C66 2021 | DDC 345.540255 23

Published by:

MAYA PUBLISHING HOUSE
D-135 Agar Nagar, Prem Nagar III,
Som Bazar Road, New Delhi-110086
Ph.+919910728725
E-mail:mayapublishinghouse27@gmail.com

Contemporary Slavery and Trafficking in Persons: Global Narratives

First Edition 2022

ISBN: 978-93-91642-00-6

PRINTED IN INDIA

Printed at: Unitech Graphic Point, Delhi

Notes on the Editors and Contributors

The Editors

Arun Kumar Acharya, Professor at Sambalpur University, India. Prior to this he was Professor and Researcher at Autonomous University of Nuevo León (UANL), Monterrey, Mexico. He specializes in research on perspectives and implications of internal and international migration with regard to human trafficking. He is founder of the Mexican Centre for Migration and Human Trafficking Studies, Monterrey. Dr. Acharya has published eight books and several journal articles on human trafficking. He also actively participated in the formulation of Mexican anti trafficking law during 2012 and 2014. His book Perspectives of Human Trafficking in Mexico led most of the states of Mexico to reformulate their local trafficking laws. Recently, the World Bank, Washington DC, invited him to deliver a lecture on The Fragility of the Mexican State and Gender Inequality: the Case of Trafficking in Women.

Jennifer Bryson Clark, Associate Professor of Political Science and chair of Women's Studies at South Texas College. Her areas of expertise are forced migration, human trafficking, international political economy and globalization and development. Clark is co-editor of *Haman Trafficking: A Complex Phenomenon of Globalization and Vulnerability* (Routledge, 2015). Her recent research (2015-2016), which was funded by the US Department of State's Office to Monitor and Combat Trafficking in Persons, involved working as part of a team to study trafficking in Central America and along Mexico's eastern migration routes. She is a founding board member of the Rio Grande Anti-Human Trafficking Coalition, and she received the 2009 South Texas Civil Rights Project's Emma Tenayuca award for her work bringing to light the forms of trafficking and coercion that affect women. Clark also teaches classes on Human Trafficking at Oklahoma University

María Luisa Martínez Sánchez, Director of Institute for Social Research at Autonomous University of Nuevo León (UANL), Monterrey, Mexico. She is also Advisory Counsellor of the National Institute of Women (Inmujeres) for the period 2018-2021, and member of the Advisory Group of Civil Society of UN Women Mexico. She has published numerous books and articles in various international journals on migration especially of women and gender violence in Mexico. She is also editor of Trayectoria: Journal of Social Science (Trayectorias. Revista de Ciencias Sociale), published by Autonomous University of Nuevo León (UANL), Monterrey, Mexico.

The Contributors'

Adeleye Lewis Olatunji, researcher, trainer, social entrepreneur, and a Program Analyst with the Canadian Red Cross. He has over a decade of experience in Human Trafficking and Transnational research. He is a doctoral candidate at the University of Abuja, and his research focuses on transnational migration, border administration, and national security. He is also grounded in community and international development programming, Conflicts resolution and Peace building.

Ana Cláudia Ruy Cardia Atchabahian, PhD and Master of Laws from the Pontifical Catholic University of São Paulo. Professor of Private International Law at Mackenzie Presbyterian University. Advisor to the Latin American Branch of the Global Business and Human Rights Scholars Association. Member of the Working Group in Supply Chains and Human

Trafficking of the Uniform Law Commission. Member of the Human Rights Commission of the Brazilian BAR Association (São Paulo branch). Coordinator of the Study Group "Mack DH&E: Human Rights and business" and Coordinator of the Research Group "Invisible People: Prevention and Combat of Internal and International Trafficking in Persons", both from Mackenzie Presbyterian University. Lawyer and human rights and business consultant in São Paulo, Brazil

Carmen Meneses-Falcon, Professor of Social and Cultural Anthropology at Comillas University in Madrid, Spain. She holds a PhD in Anthropology. Her main research interests are health risk behaviours, gender, prostitution and trafficking. In particular, she has carried out research on risk behaviours related to drug use and unprotected sexual relations. Her publications focus on gender differences in different behaviours.

Carmen Monico (Ph.D. Virginia Commonwealth University) is teaching curriculum and elective courses in the Joint Master and PhD Social Work Programs of the North Carolina Agricultural and Technical State University and the University of North Carolina Greensboro. Previously, Monico taught human services and core curriculum courses with a global perspective and in international settings at Elon University, social welfare policy at Smith College, and social justice and social policy at VCU. Monico's scholarship includes bilingual and transnational dissertation on illegal adoptions from Guatemala and has published on intercountry adoption, global migration, and human trafficking, and civic engagement and social accountability jointly with other educators, professionals and students. Monico's scholarship involves serving as an international expert and conducting research and teaching in Guatemala with the Universidad del Valle de Guatemala, as a U.S. Fulbright Scholar. Monico has presented at national and international conferences and seminars, and in numerous educational events and conducted research on teaching and learning, community engagement and human service delivery.

Destin Nurafiati Ristantiis, PhD scholar in international studies at WASEDA University, Japan. Her research interest is transnational organised crime and currently focused on trafficking in persons and illegal fishing. She has also published an article on Regional Governance untuk Memerangi Kejahatan Terorganisir Transnasional: Kerja Sama Penanggulangan Perdagangan Manusia di Wilayah Sub-Mekong dalam Coordinated Mekong MinisterialInitiative against Trafficking (COMMIT), Global & Policy Journal, Vol.8, No. 2, July-December 2020.

Diego Lopez Naranjo, PhD scholar in Political and Social Sciences a Universidad Nacional Autonoma de Mexico (UNAM). His current doctoral dissertation is titled Forced Labour and Involuntary Servitude of Indigenous Women Exploited in the Domestic Sector in the Metropolitan Area of Monterrey' in which he investigates the link between human trafficking, forced labour and domestic work. Besides his research in human trafficking, Lopez Naranjo has published articles regarding poverty: the first one in 2011 (in co-authorship with Alejandro Arreola and Diego Urbina) "The Effect of the Liberalisation of Foreign Trade in Some States of Mexico' in *Revista Comercio Exterior*, Mexico; the second one recently in 2018 (in co-authorship with Jose Raul Luyando) "The Effects of Oil Pollution on the Development of Ejido Communities: the Case of San Juan River' *in Revista Investigacion y Desarrollo*, Colombia.

Haley Cole graduated scholar of Elon University where she received her B.A. in Psychology and Human Service Studies with a minor in Criminal Justice Studies. As a member of the Elon College Fellows program, Cole conducted research under Dr. Monico into Push and Pull factors contributing to human trafficking in North Carolina. During her time at Elon

University, Cole was a Family and Youth Services Intern at the Burlington Housing Authority in Burlington, NC. Here she implemented prevention and intervention tactics to combat youth violence, gang activity, and drug use among public housing residents utilizing relationships with law enforcement, the court system, and local school systems. Cole's research interests focus on violence against women, and criminal justice reform, and the role of intersectionality in these disciplines. Following graduation from Elon University, Cole took a role as a Paralegal at a Civil Rights Law firm in Washington, DC.

Hrushikesh Meher, faculty in Biju Patnaik State Police Academy, Bhubaneswar, Odisha. He teaches Criminology, Human Rights and law to the trainee police officers as well as field officers of different ranks. He has a lot of experiences in rescue operations of Trafficking Children and Women of Odisha in different destination states. He has attended various national seminars and presented his paper on trafficking issues. He has got 17years of field experience as a pragmatic police officer and 3 years teaching experience in Police Academy.

Izabela Zonato Villas Boas, Master student in Political and Economic Law at from Mackenzie Presbyterian University. Master by the International Institute of Legal Sociology in Oñati (Spain). Lato Sensu Graduate Student in Constitutional and Administrative Law at Escola Paulista de Direito. Graduated in Law from Mackenzie Presbyterian University. Member of the Research Group "Invisible People: Prevention and Combat of Internal and International Trafficking in Persons", from Mackenzie Presbyterian University. Member of the Research Committee on Sociology of Law. Academic assistant of Prof. Dr. Ana Cláudia Ruy Cardia Atchabahian at the Faculty of Law of Mackenzie Presbyterian University.

Jennifer Toller Erausquin is a social epidemiologist whose research examines gender, race/ethnicity, and socioeconomic factors as determinants of sexual and reproductive health, with an emphasis on HIV prevention and care engagement.

She earned her undergraduate degree from the University of Michigan and her MPH and PhD from the UCLA Fielding School of Public Health. She was a predoctoral fellow of the California Center for Population Research and the UCLA AIDS Research Training Program, receiving training in demography and epidemiology. She completed a postdoctoral fellowship at the Duke Global Health Institute, with an emphasis on gender, poverty, and health. Dr. Erausquin is currently an Associate Professor in the Department of Public Health Education at the University of North Carolina Greensboro. She co-edited a book, *Global Perspectives on Women's Sexual and Reproductive Health Across the Lifecourse* (Springer, 2018), and has served as a survey development consultant for the UNDP/UNFPA/UNICEF/WHO/World Bank Special Programme of Research, Development and Research Training in Human Reproduction.

Jorge Uroz-Olivares, Professor of Social Policy and of Social Work involving Minors at Comillas University in Madrid. His main lines of research focus on children. In particular, he has performed research and published articles about child abuse and minors in situations of risk.

Magdalena Moreno, graduated Geographer at Buenos Aires University (UBA) and a PhD student at the same university. She currently has a doctoral scholarship granted by the National Scientific and Technical Research Council (CONICET - Argentina). She works at the Center for Geographical Research at the National University of the Center of the Province of Buenos Aires (CIG/IGEHCS/UNCPBA). She is a specialist in Comprehensive Sex Education graduated at Higher Institute of Teaching Staff "Dr. Joaquín V. González"; and Professor of "Comprehensive Sex Education" (ESI) in Prof. and Lic. in Physical Education and Sports at Flores University and the Geography Faculty at Higher Institute of Teaching Staff "Dr. Joaquín V. González". She is a co-creator of the collaborative Map of Geography of Sexualities.

Mannel R. Barragan Codina graduate economist from UANL-Doctoral studies economics from the University of Colorado, USA. Former director of Institute of Social Research, UANL. He has also worked as Chief Coordinator of Management Development in Federal Mexican Government. Currently he is working as a full time Professor at UANL, Mexico.

Norah Hashim Msuya, lecturer at Mzumbe University and Advocate of High Court of Tanzania. Currently, she is doing Postdoctoral Research in School of law at the University of KwaZulu Natal South Africa. She is also a coordinator and founder member of the Tanzania Legal Aid Organization for Women and Children, a non-governmental organization that provides legal assistance and education to women and children in Tanzania. Her academic publications cover a wide range of subjects on trafficking and violence against gender-based violence, including African Culture practices that facilitate trafficking of women and Children as well as human rights perspective on traditional juju oath.

Rachel E. Williams Faller, MPH, is a doctoral student in the Department of Public Health Education at the University of North Carolina Greensboro (UNCG). Her dissertation research focuses on intravenous drug use, mental health, and HIV care engagement. Prior to attending UNCG, she worked for several years as a Public Health Specialist conducting research for government-funded contracts on a variety of health topics at SciMetrika, LLC. Ms. Faller also has experience as a Research Assistant for the North Carolina Institute of Medicine and a Literature Review Specialist for IBM Watson Health. She holds a Master's in Public Health from East Carolina University (Greenville, NC) and a Bachelor of Science in biology from Meredith College (Raleigh, NC).

Introduction

Arun Kumar Acharya and Jennifer Bryson Clark

Trafficking of women and young girls is not a recent phenomenon. In the late 19th Century, feminist activists and scholars brought international attention to the "White Slave trade" of Eastern European women for prostitution in Western Europe. However, recently, it has often described as modern day slavery, has been recognised most momentous issues of twenty first century. First it came to the attention of the International community in the late 1980's and by the beginning of the 21st century it became the subject of renewed international concern and recognized as a serious global problem that needed global responses. The United Nations responded in 2000 with the publication of the UN Convention against Transnational Organized Crime and its Supplementary Protocols.

The Protocol to Prevent, Suppress and Punish Trafficking in Persons, Especially Women and Children (the Palermo Protocol) set out the first definition of human trafficking that is still the benchmark for defining human trafficking today. The Article 3 of the Palermo Protocol defines human trafficking: Trafficking in persons shall mean the recruitment, transportation, transfer, harbouring or receipt of persons, by means of the threat or use of force or other forms of coercion, of abduction, of fraud, of deception, of the abuse of power or of a position of vulnerability or of the giving or receiving of payments or benefits to achieve the consent of a person having control over another person, for the purpose of exploitation. Exploitation shall include, at a minimum, the exploitation of the prostitution of others or other forms of sexual exploitation, forced labour or services, slavery or practices similar to slavery, servitude or the removal of organs. The consent of a victim of trafficking to the intended exploitation set forth in subparagraph (a) of this article shall be irrelevant where any of the means set forth in subparagraph (a) have been used. The recruitment, transportation, transfer, harbouring or receipt of a child for the purpose of exploitation shall be considered 'trafficking in persons' even if this does not involve any of the means set forth in subparagraph (a) have been used. "Child"shall mean any person under 18 years of age.

In a globalized world with increasing polarities of wealth both within and between countries, with an increased demand for cheap labour in developed countries, with increased possibilities for travel and telecommunications broadcasting, and (exaggerated) images of western wealth around the world, those living in relative and absolute poverty tend to migrate in search of a better life (ILO, 2005). This global crime generates billions of dollars in profits for the traffickers. The International Labour Organization (ILO) estimates that around 20.9 million people are victims of forced labour globally. This estimate also includes victims of human trafficking for labour and sexual exploitation; however it is not known that how many of these victims were trafficked (UNODC, 2012).

On the contrary, the 2020 Trafficking in Persons Report given by U.S. Department of State indicates that as many as 27 million men, women, and children are trafficking victims at any given time (U.S. Department of State, 2020). Global report on Trafficking in Personas-2012 indicates that, globally women and girls share around 75 percent among victims of trafficked persons, among which 58 percent used for sexual exploitation and 36 percent exploit for forced labour (UNODC, 2012). Poverty, economic inequality including lack of employment opportunities, gender based discrimination, child marriage, cultural practices, child labour and forced migration including political instability are some of the rooted causes of exploitation. Global systems create conditions that allow trafficking to flourish and as such systematic change is need to understand and analyze profoundly. The objective of this book is to analyze the international narratives on human trafficking to understand in different social, cultural, economic and political context.

List of Tables

List of Figures

Appendix

Contents

CHAPTER I

Dynamics and the Altering Threats in Human Trafficking

Adeleye Lewis Olatunji[1]

Introduction

Trafficking in Persons (TIP) as a subject and phenomenon needs general review and continuous augmentation. This is because as the world advances, so also the scheme, trends, and modus operandi of the syndicate groups; whose main objective is to beat the system. Although, slavery was abolished in the middle of 1800s in many parts of the world, enslavement and exploitation of persons remains intact (Henry, 2016). The issues of TIP keep coming-up in the media, while more national and multilateral legislations are being enacted to re-define TIP more elaborately in a bid to finding more ways to apprehend and prosecute offenders, as well as drawing up programs and working plans to rehabilitate and reintegrate rescued survivors. Many times, the law that prohibits the act itself is very handicapped and thereby melting non-commensurate reaction to the actions of the criminal groups and individuals in different parts of the world. Sometimes the gap presents victims as criminals and criminals as innocents; even in the justice system of the United States of America (Parsons, Cray, Saar, & Vafa, 2014).

Human trafficking has generated multiplicities of phases, identifying these phases, therefore, has become imperative to

1. Canadian Red Cross, Canada.

be able to adequately combat the menace in the 21st century. It is a fact, that the strategies of before, are grossly obsolete; its effects and potencies are constantly being neutralized by the schemes of those in the business. As much as it is important to learn from the past, staying in the past will be largely counter-productive if the global battle against TIP must be won. The need for reevaluation consciousness in the fight against TIP and its attendant effect has become necessary especially in the research environment. Human trafficking is essentially propelled by several factors, including social, economic, cultural and environmental elements. There are numerous root causes to this threat, and the variation changes from one background to another, and also from country to country. Factors influencing TIP are context-specific to particular trafficking arrangements, and to the environment in which they transpire. It would be inadequate and erroneous therefore, to measure global human trafficking happening in different environment with similar index.

More focus on transnational human trafficking is shifting the balance against local or domestic perpetration of violence and injustices against many at-risk groups, several victims are daily exploited in an unprecedented manner without having to migrate or travel from their locations, these class of persons needs as more care and support as others who might have be trafficked across borders. This objective of this chapter is to therefore elucidate on the changing patterns and intricacies that narrows the study of human trafficking, with the aim of arguing for a robust and open approach to human trafficking research and policies. This work will be of great relevance to the Academics, policy formulation, law enforcement, as well as national security agencies, in understanding the changing nature of human trafficking and the threat evaluation it creates to human and national security.

The Challenge

Human trafficking has been identified as one of the major threats to human security in our world (Danailova-Trainor & Belser, 2006); it is seriously ravaging the 21st century, inhibiting the developments of states and institutions. It's a multibillion dollar global trade, generating about $150 Billion annually, with between 25 million and 29 million individuals as commodity worldwide according to the International Organization for Migration (ILO) (International labour Organization, 2014). Myriads of the identified threats of the present age have strong links (or dependencies) to TIP directly or otherwise, and these have further contributed to making the crime more tedious to suppress.

Traditional approaches to preventing trafficking in human beings, to protect and assist trafficked persons and bring criminals to justice have had some small impact on the global phenomenon, but not enough (UNODC/UN.GIFT 2008), especially with the reality that at the minimum, an estimate of 24.9 million people are still being robbed of their freedom and basic human dignity around the world (United States Department of State, 2019), and that higher percentage of instances of sexual exploitation remains local in nature. For instance, in Canada, about 90% instances of exploitation in TIP are local or internal in nature, and not necessarily transnational (Niethammer, 2020). A major challenge with human trafficking centers on the under reported nature of the crime, the earlier statistics were mere guesstimates, which were effective in driving policy and policy makers to see the magnitude of the problem. However, the present data in many institutions around the world, reflects the number of reported incidences or cases of human trafficking; which in itself has the potential to go unreported or evade data-collection processes.

If more impactful efforts must be made in addressing TIP, engaging multi-dimensional and evaluative approaches will be necessary so as to identify processes that are viable and others that need to be quickly re-assessed or changed. The political terrain is not as friendly as it used to be with democracy, national populism championed in the 21st century by political establishment like Donald Trump of the United States of America, Jair Bolsonaro of Brazil, Boris Johnson of the United Kingdom, and many far right political platforms in Europe continues to advocate for anti-people rhetoric and protectionism that criminalizes immigration and free movement (Mounk & Kyle, 2018). Populist regime essentially raises toxic argument suggesting that "Elites and "Outsiders" work against the interests of the "true people" and…since populists are the voice of the "true people, " nothing should stand in their way." (ibid).

Interestingly, issues like migration, climate change, globalization, piracy, electoral violence, terrorism, internal crisis and conflicts, drug trafficking, arms dealing, gangsterism and cultism, and cyber-crime are some of the complicated challenges identified as constituting serious threats to human security in Africa, Asia and other parts of the world; analyzing these threats in all its ramifications has a very strong interdependency and link to the crime of human trafficking, therefore a keen attention to each (and more) of these threats (especially Cyber-Sex trafficking), will undoubtedly limit and ultimately obliterate the antics of syndicate groups perpetrating TIP and Smuggling of Migrants (SOM).

As argued by Parsons et al., specifically addressing commercial sexual exploitation of child (CSEC) faces challenges due to tremendous scarcity of broad and reliable data regarding the scope and description of sexual exploitation of minors. While the progress cannot be ignored, there is still need to reframe how the public perceive the problem of CSEC to reflect the abuse and exploitation of minors as against being viewed as a case of teenage prostitution, and the gap in the justice system as well as the social services structures results in victimization of vulnerable persons, making the identification and rescue of victims of TIP difficult (especially children) (Parsons, Cray, Saar, & Vafa, 2014). Such complexities are intertwined as they strengthen TIP. And ultimately, galvanizing approaches from diverse of national, regional, international and multidisciplinary levels is necessary if progress must be made in addressing the phenomenon.

Reassessing the definition of TIP

"Trafficking in persons" and "human trafficking" have been continuously used as umbrella terms for the act of recruiting, harboring, transporting, providing, or obtaining a person for compelled labor or commercial sex acts through the use of force, fraud, or coercion. While there has not been a universal acceptability to what constitutes human trafficking (Jones, Engstrom, Hilliard, & Diaz, 2007), the Trafficking Victims Protection Act (TVPA) of 2000 (Pub. L. 106-386), as amended, and the Protocol to Prevent, Suppress and Punish Trafficking in Persons, Especially Women and Children, supplementing the United Nations Convention against Transnational Organized Crime (the Palermo Protocol), describe this compelled service using a number of different terms, including involuntary servitude, slavery or practices similar to slavery, debt bondage, and forced labor (Victim of Trafficking and Violence Protection Act 2000[1]; (United Nations Office on Drug and Crime, 2000)). This document largely forms the basis for international and domestic laws or regulations to be created in addressing the nuisance.

1. Available at https://www.govinfo.gov/content/pkg/PLAW-106publ386/pdf/PLAW-106publ386.pdf

In attempting to craft a definition, the Protocol was framed in transnational description as against being in more formidable international nature; under its present circumstances, State parties are at liberty to streamline the instrument, and decide what must be adopted, to what extent, and what must constitutes trafficking based on the peculiarities in its jurisdictional environment (Allain, 2015). The Palermo Protocol is therefore infused or domesticated into the national legal framework of many countries in an inconsistent and defective manner, leading to incongruences in the interpretation of the crime amongst many signatories, and the inherent difficulties in addressing the transnational crime effectively by parties.

The general definition ascribed to TIP or human trafficking is somewhat limited in scope and it is important that the highly contestable elements be reviewed in a way that best capture its representations and meanings. Many organizations are working together to address the challenge of human trafficking through of the multiple approaches of criminal justice, victim support, law enforcement and policy development. The legal and policy approaches remain critical in the global fight against TIP; however, these law and policies are not efficient across global spectrum. Its components are debated and interpreted differently as to what should constitute human trafficking or exploitation, and who should be considered a victim of human trafficking or who should be a criminal prostitute.

The argument of the neo-abolitionist supports the criminalization of human trafficking but also contends that sex work; which is an act of deliberate prostitution should not be criminalize, because it is part of the fundamental human rights of an individual to choose what to do with his sexuality, and what job to do to earn a living. The neo-abolitionist also argues that poverty and migration can never be the factor pushing individuals into prostitution (or sex works) (Coleman, 2016).

Similarly, the lacuna presented by the national policy frameworks continue to allow or overlook the labor exploitation of many migrants, and this situation has become a key global human right concern driving human trafficking in the 21st century, and why it is increasingly becoming difficult for the law enforcement to build strong cases against offenders in courts (DeStefano, 2007). The resistance and misunderstanding surrounding the exertion of sex workers; which might also be rationalized from the sexual or labor exploitation perspectives, generate serious concerns on the human rights of sex workers around the world. In an attempt to seek greater safety or better living condition by migrants, they often find themselves engaging in dangerous informal sectors of the economy; where they are mostly exposed to trauma and threats of labor exploitation. Unfavorable state policy targeting migrants contributes to further dehumanization of migrant sex workers, who often have to surrender to a greater (exploitative) power dynamics in return for protection from the law enforcement, shelter, food and security. Essentially the law that criminalizes sex works and sex workers, keep the work dangerous as it increases the vulnerability and trauma of those in the sector (Kempadoo & Doezema, 2018). In many instances, immigrants and sex workers might fall into the category of victims of labor trafficking, who are also sexually exploited simultaneously, or those used for organ and tissue harvesting, forced marriages, illicit street peddling and begging. The issues of semantics and limitations presented in what constitutes human trafficking continues to be a challenge in human trafficking. The arguments as to what extent the elements of coercion and exploitation, as well as the movement of person (s) across international delimitation for human trafficking to take place continues to generate field disagreement among researchers (Jones, Engstrom, Hilliard, & Diaz, 2007). In the summer (October) of 2013 in the United Kingdom, the police arrested couples suspected of holding three women in bounded slavery for 30 years. The couple were both 67 years at that time and they were arrested for holding three women, a 57 year old from Ireland, a 69 years old from Malaysia and interestingly, another 30 years old Briton, who according to the Metropolitan Police Detective Inspector Kevin Hyland "appears to have been in servitude for her entire life" (Bryan-Low & Flynn, 2013). This is a typical instance, where human trafficking might not involve movement or transportation of persons, because vulnerable individuals can be born into servitude, while others might even be trafficked before birth.

It is therefore a sharp contrast from the established notion of TIP, the 21st century TIP is not limited to acts such as recruiting, harboring, providing, or obtaining (etc.), because individuals are born into slavery as indicative in the story above, and many other situations of baby harvesting and exploitation. It is also very imperative to know that vicious cycle of slavery provides the traffickers (or the slave drivers) double gain; when individuals who are victims of TIP give birth to children, who are further pushed into the cycle of TIP for endless profiteering or exploitation. In Nigeria, Nepal, Ukraine and India, this is another form of booming business, otherwise known as "Baby Factory" (which will be expanded on as we progress) (Daily mail Reporter, 2013); (Roache, 2018). Many scenarios have also presented itself where the trafficked persons are more than willing, largely because of (individual) greed or the situation or circumstances they found themselves. The key issue here is, human trafficking doesn't have to be involuntary; and the fact that (TIP) is voluntary has not in any way, ruled out the magnitude of dehumanization inherent in the crime; the consequence still remains. The incongruence in the definition of human trafficking presents a challenge to the responses of the state and the non-state actors in combatting the crime of human trafficking.

It is therefore not out of place for the academia and the State (and non-state actors) to adopt the observation of the United States TIP report which opines that, "Human trafficking can include, but does not require, movement." (US Department of States). People may be considered trafficking victims regardless of whether they were born into a state of servitude, were transported to the exploitative situation, previously consented to work for a trafficker, or participated in a crime as a direct result of being trafficked. At the heart of this phenomenon is the traffickers' goal of exploiting and enslaving the victims and the myriad of coercive and deceptive practices used to do so" (US-TIP Report 2014); as against the Palermo Protocol (2000) which is somewhat limited in scope and can frustrate prosecutions exercise in many parts of the world.

One key avoidable limitation of the Palermo Protocol (2000) is joining to occupy the pitfall of Male expendability and circumscribed identity construct in the definition of human trafficking, just as indicative in the earlier anti-slavery treaties[1]. This might be probably to reflect the degree of vulnerability present in the crime for women and children, or to facilitate the channeling of resources to the "most deserving" demographics (perceived to be women). This is a stereotypical representation that boxes "the victim" of human trafficking into a specific category, which fundamentally undermine the

1. Earlier treaties such as the "The Convention on the Suppression of White Slave Trade" art 1, which was agreed upon in May 18, 1904 mostly addresses the protection of women and girls, while also construing human trafficking concerns as the exploitation of women and girls. The Convention for the Suppression of the Traffic in Persons and of the Exploitation of the Prostitution of Others of 1950, The International Convention for the Suppression of the Traffic in Women and Children of Full Age arts of October 11, 1933, and the International Convention for the Suppression of the Traffic in Women and Children arts of September 30, 1921, also strengthens the conventional assumption that victims of human trafficking are women and girls (Shoaps, 2013).

victimization of others, who might not typically fall within the identity constructed by the Palermo Protocol (2000). Highlighting *"women and children"* in the document reflects male expendability in the framing of human trafficking, while ceding greater protection to women at the expense of the male victims. Human trafficking concerns are generally constructed as the exploitation of women and girls, and such narrow analysis is an injustice to a wholesome anti-human trafficking drive; which must consider everyone including men, boys, members of the LGBTQ groups as well as women and girls.

Emerging Trajectories

It's been argued at different forum, that TIP thrives largely because of poverty; and as much as this fact cannot be totally discredited, a more dangerous aspect (more inure to poverty) has been ignored. If more attention of caution is not given to complicated international issues like religious beliefs, cultural practices, child psychology and ideologies, its influence on human trafficking will begin to thrive to a dastardlier magnitude. Where poverty has been identified to have played a major role as a pull-factor in developing economies (of Africa, Asia and the middle-east), because every trait and characteristic of a developing economy can induce TIP and SOM (smuggling of migrants); beliefs, religion and ideology, breakdown of the social fabric of families in the society will continue to be a major push-factor ravaging the developed states. The effects of this cadre of TIP (ravaging the developed and the developing world) are more colossal, devious and more impactful in that it visibly undermine the security of the States, especially in the United States; where human trafficking is argued to be one of the worst in the world (Keiper & Chiaramonte, 2019).

More than ever in the global effort to address human trafficking, critical examination of social and political intersections and trajectories are necessary to identify how it might impact on anti-TIP efforts or how it might induce TIP. Many of the efforts of the state at controlling border and transnational migration that further leads to border securitization, pushes vulnerable migrants into the greedy hands of smugglers and human traffickers alike. While humane and safe migration profit the migrants and the states, attitudes of the state in policy development and border securitization is a culprit when also accounting for factors leading to the exploitation and death of migrants at many global dangerous borders, as well as when evaluating factors driving profiteering for smugglers and human traffickers.

The efforts of stakeholders also focus more on sexual exploitation or prostitution of women and children (Hollingsworth, 2003), because they are more vulnerable due to cultural or institutional stereotypes placed on them. Prostitution is a sexual labor, and (except in most civilizations in Europe, South America, India, Canada, Indonesia, Bangladesh, and few others) it is an illicit endeavor that embodies hideous shame which has the potential to keep the victims more entangled in the web of exploitation and control of the trafficking networks. However, prostitution affects every population, not only women and children but also men.

There are increasing evidences pointing to the rape, violation and other forms of exploitation of men (especially boys at tender ages, particularly member of the LGBTQ community), many of the victims are also shameful and could therefore not speak out. The concerns about male prostitutions has been a subject of disapproving public discuss, because male victims are usually marginalized and discriminated against in public debates (JAOUEN, 2016). In the analysis of four classifications of male prostitutes advanced by Donald (Allen, 1980), they were mainly classified as full-time street hustlers, full-time call boys or kept boys, part-time hustlers (usually engaged in other occupation or studies) and those classified as peer-delinquents, who uses prostitution or homosexuality to prosecute greater criminal acts. The psychological background and motive of the male demographics were analyzed and were mostly linked to mental and "deviant identity" of the 'perpetrators' (Davis, 1971), but not much was discussed about the positions of their vulnerabilities, or their connection to male exploitation which may arise from human trafficking. Essentially, the traffickers and the "chicken hawk"; who purchase sex from boys (the chicken) often go unpunished while the victims are arrested and treated as criminals by the law enforcement, since they are seen as run-away kids who ventured into boy-whore world and drugs for survival (Stevens, 1980; Reid & Piquero, 2014).

In terms of services and supports availability to victims of human trafficking, not much is available to male survivors and victims of sexual exploitation unlike the female demographics. And where available, shelter services are not available to male survivors in most cases, which goes to buttress the inherent social myth and stereotypes that only associate female to sexual exploitation and abuses. There is a sense where we must therefore rethink and confront the discriminatory myths in services and support for male victims and survivors in the collective drive to end global human trafficking. Any stereotypical ideology by the mainstream anti-TIP crusade would only further conceal the vicious and destructive landscape of (male) prostitutions and human trafficking.

Shift in dimension and direction

Human trafficking is not limited to the quest for labor and sexual exploitations, understanding the emerging forms of human trafficking involves looking critically into social and political drivers inducing situations of vulnerabilities, leading to displacement, irregular migration and human trafficking. War, violence and civil crisis are major push-factors for displacement, mixed migration and human exploitation. As revealing in many emergent bodies of reports on migration and movement, the nature of migration is essentially shaped by the greater political, social, mass mediatization, and economic alterations, affecting and determining the priorities and policies of nations (Beets & Willekens, 2009; Castle, 2011; Krzyżanowski, Triandafyllidou, & Wodak, 2018).

In many parts of the world (especially in Europe and America), migrants seeking safety and better opportunities are daily confronted with hostility and dehumanization. Between January and September 29th, 2020, an estimate of 652 persons perished in the Mediterranean Sea, 75 deaths of migrants were recorded in Europe, 389 in the Americas, 77 deaths of Migrants in the Middle East, 208 deaths in Asia, 491 deaths recorded in Sub-Saharan Africa, North Africa and the Horn of Africa (IOM, 2020). Within the same period globally, about 3600 survivors of irregular migration were recorded, 1192 migrant died, while 700 others are missing in attempts to move through dangerous frontiers *(ibid)*. According to the International Organization for Migration, between 2014 and September 29, 2020, an estimate of 28, 788 human lives perished in movement. Most of these unfortunate deaths are citizens of poor and developing countries. While much progress has been made in uniting global fronts in trade, technology, export of democracy, and the collective decry for human rights violation of despotic leaders (in the developing countries), the perpetrations of human rights of migrants persist at the borders of the global north, where people are fleeing for safety.

Populist ideologies driven by the far-right media and leaders demonize migrants and label them as terrorists, criminals and subversive elements seeking to undermine the developed countries of the world, thereby justifying the use of unlimited violence and border militarization against the "other". The president of the United States describes migrant with demeaning and negative stratifications such as gangs, rapists, criminals and drug dealers, while also describing migrants as persons from *'shit-hole countries'*, who must be violently repealed away from the US border. Such assertions are to validate extreme border security in order to checkmate the activities of transnational criminal groups and migrants entering the territory of a sovereign state.

The European Union (EU) also engages similar practices to checkmate the activities of smugglers and human traffickers; who are believed to be the ultimate drivers of the EU refugee crisis from their own perspectives, and not the unwholesome situations from migrants' sending states. Border militarization was redesigned by the Trump government and the EU to hypothetically protect the vulnerable migrants from the claws of human traffickers, drug smugglers and other criminal elements at the border. But technically, the migration (and refugee) policies in the receiving countries and the securitization of migration serves the criminal elements, and to the detriment of vulnerable migrants; who are either pushed back to death or into the schemes (or antics) of human traffickers and other transnational criminal groups. Border regime is a construct that was designed to advance the course of inequality, sustain the dichotomy between the rich and the poor countries, while also creating viciousness surrounding national frontiers. Border administration in the present dispensation stimulates socio-economic and jurisdictional gaps that causes poverty and displacement at one end of the trajectory, while motivating irregular mobility of migrants, drugs, munitions, and other illicit monetary transactions across the trajectories.

These alterations are occasioned by globalization, and it effectively impact every aspect of human daily endeavors. We are in the age of information, where access to information, goods, and services are becoming cheap and readily available to an appreciable population of people, largely because of the contracting global delimitations caused by trade, tourism and technology. In the aftermath of the global economic meltdown of 2008, many lives were distorted, leading to increase in the patterns and dimensions of international migration (Beets & Willekens, 2009).

The intrusion of COVID-19, which was first noticed in China in 2019 is also bringing about unpresented economic and public health crisis across the world, with many nations directionless even as this text is being written. The effect of border closure between states might have a short-term effect on migration, but not of human trafficking, because the exploitation of vulnerable demographics does not terminate at international borders, many reports across the world shows that violence and exploitation continues in many homes during the lockdown (Batha & Wulfhorst, 2020; Grierson, 2020; Graham-Harrison, Giuffrida, Smith, & Ford, 2020). According to the United Nations, in three months of lockdown, the world could see around 15 million incidences of abuse globally (Batha & Wulfhorst, 2020), and while 'charges and caution for violence increased by 24% in London' [1], many other countries from China to India, Brazil, Germany, Italy, and Canada continues to record increase in the spate of abuse and violence of vulnerable groups (mostly women and children) (Graham-Harrison, Giuffrida, Smith, & Ford, 2020). A research in the united States of America shows that "domestic violence increase by 12% on the average and by 20% during work hours" with the rate of first time abuse increasing between 16% on the average and 23% during work hours (McCrary & Sanga, 2020). In China also, the rate of domestic violence reportage tripled in February 2020 as compared to 2019 because of the mandated lockdown (Godin, 2020).

The rate of exposure of at-risk groups continues to increase

1. See **Invalid source specified.**. Available from https://www.theguardian.com/society/2020/apr/24/charges-and-cautions-for-domestic-violence-rise-by-24-in-london

dynamically in our world, with huge implication to human trafficking and violent exploitation, where help and services are either limited or completely not available to those in dare need. Government policies and laws in the faces of economic, political, social or even public health situations can create a bad situation for vulnerable groups and individuals. While the state is using social distancing and lockdown policies to increase safety from public health crisis for the people, the same policy continues to isolate others negatively for violence and exploitation. At least one in every three women globally are confronted with physical or sexual violence in their lifetime according to theWorld Health Organization, and many of the victims continues to endure the exploitation of the abusers because of the 'blood' or psychological connections they have with the abusers. Violence and sexual abuses from intimate and close relatives are one of the least reported crime or rights violation in the world, it is the reality of many people in times of 'relative peace, ' but the vulnerability of groups and individuals increases in war and crisis situations (WHO, 2018).

Crisis situation potent double jeopardy for at-risk groups, physical and mental being of women and children are equally violated as they are used either as another battleground or spoil of war. The rate of international migration is increasing exponentially; presently, the number of international migrant is estimated to be around 272 million globally, with about two-third being labour migrants and the remaining others as refugees fleeing violence (IOM, 2019). Major displacement and forced migration situation caused by natural disaster, climate change, political instability, epidemic (or pandemic) and extreme violent conflict creates adversity, trauma, and death for people, but it also creates an avenue for gain for smugglers, warlords and human traffickers. The risk of gender-based-violence specifically heightens in crisis situations, either due to the position of vulnerability of individuals who are forced to move their homes and social networks, or because of lack of power and control by the vulnerable groups. Many of such blur lines must be given attention by researchers, so that efforts can be galvanized to provide support and services for the most vulnerable persons in crisis situations.

In general terms, the West asserts itself as the global anti-TIP force, the United States has been identified by many observers as a major strength limiting the impacts and forces of TIP in the 21st century. The United States Annual Trafficking in Person Report (US-TIP) has been the yardstick through which TIP and its many impacts are measured world globally. The US-TIP Report released in June 2020 (for instance) is the 20th edition of a unique data based approach used by the United States to measure governments, and to also equip them with the needed information in the areas where TIP efforts are lacking. Unfortunately, still, while the US apparatus is the most popular yardstick for measuring the world with regards to its relationship to TIP, the rate of serious forms of human trafficking in the US is one of the highest in the world (Keiper & Chiaramonte, 2019), 90 percent of the local sex trafficking victims in Canada are also Canadian-born (Niethammer, 2020). There are critics challenging the tier 1 ranking for the United States in the 2020 TIP Report, saying the United States does not fully comply with the new standards of the US Congress, as enshrined in the TVPRA 2018, and that it lacks the moral right to evaluate itself. The United States falls short in two key areas (out of three) in the tier ranking evaluation; Prosecution and Protection (Alliance to End Slavery and Trafficking (ATEST), 2020). The report also trivializes the pains experienced by victims of human trafficking as its uses point scoring in evaluating countries on TIP initiatives (Hunt, 2015).

Between June 2003 and June 2013, the FBI rescued more than 2, 700 victims CSEC (Parsons, Cray, Saar, & Vafa, 2014). On the 23rd June 2014; it was reported that the FBI recued 168

Americans children (girls) in a weeklong US-wide operation, the youngest being 11 years old, many of them pulled from hotels, truck stops and homes (The Associated Press, 2014). These children were trafficked across the United States in an internal form of TIP for the purpose of Sex-slavery. In the words of the (former) FBI Director James Comey, he said "These are American children some of the victims were in child welfare system, many of these children have been abandon, often abused and neglected. Many of these traumatized children runs away because they believe that is the best option for them" (ibid). More unfortunate is the fact that some of these children were not reported as missing (persons) also, the bulk of them were recruited by pimps on the streets, bus terminals and from the internet (Cyber Trafficking). Such records of egregious incidences and poor or lack of demonstration of will to prosecute offenders, and protect the vulnerable ones (especially victims and survivors of human trafficking) are the reasons why 'other nations' are placed on either 2nd tier, 2nd tier watchlist or 3rd tier in the annual US-TIP report. This might have been 'forgivable' if it happened in the remotest parts of Africa (or in a 'shit-hole country' as widely claim by President Donald Trump); where access to adequate data and identification systems are grossly lacking, but in the United States; where there seems to be more vigilance and suitable (up-to-date) data and identification systems, it is a pointer to the utmost poignant egregious neglect of the most vulnerable in the American society. And just like America, the highest rates of human trafficking are not transnational in nature, it is rather internal or domestic (under the radial perpetration of injustices). The most at-risk demographics are people in (or coming out) of foster care, people in poverty and people of colors with limited opportunities. Looking inward has never been sacrosanct, all efforts must be channeled at understanding nature of vulnerabilities putting children and persons at risk of exploitation, the political and social exertions by stakeholders must be well balanced in tackling all forms of human exploitation and abuses.

There is a sense where we must leverage on power of data in understanding and addressing the root cause of CSEC globally. Creating effective program and policy is largely contingent on first appreciating the nature, scope and dynamics of the crime, while much progress has been made in data and information gathering pertaining to the nature of transnational trafficking and CSEC, the existing facts are not enough to address domestic trafficking and CSEC. While the human rights, law enforcement and justice approach must be invigorated to punish offenders, it is important to also start exploring the trajectory of mental health and child sexual exploitation. This is because of the increasing incidences of child sex (and familiar) trafficking in many locations of the world. Individuals suffering from pedophilia should be supported to seek help without shaming, also, programs and services that keep them away from minors should be extended to them while helping victims rise above weaknesses that makes adult prey on vulnerable children at home, in schools and in every environment.

Globalization and Exploitation

The success of globalization engendered an extraordinary mobile activity of goods, capital, services and labor across all global frontiers. Trade is graciously eroding the international delimitations of nations, thereby increasing the flow of persons and activities across international boundaries. The increased interconnection for the purpose of economic and commerce, culture, tourism, sports and politics, has further boosted the billion dollars trafficking business in our world. While much study has been done to understand the landscape of emerging markets and capital flow between rich and poor states (Reinhart, 2005; Ahmed & Zlate, 2014), commensurate studies that reflects the magnitude of the problem needs to be done, in order to understand how capital flow to emerging market is also creating exploitative gap for migrants and other at-risk populations. Kelvin (Bales, 2004) argues that modern day slavery of human trafficking can be linked to three unrelated dynamics, the first being the explosive population that pervade the global market with very poor and desperate persons; the second factor is economic globalization and modernized agriculture that renders rural agrarian life archaic and unattractive to younger generations; and the third element as the fast economic change and transformation in many developing economies leading to violence and huge corrupt practices. He further argues that these elements brought about the new slavery; which see large corporations engage human as slaves preparing raw materials to the marketplace for optimum profiteering.

Globalization creates inequality for many people, in many geographical locations, in a world where everything is broadly seen as a product with an economic worth, and a price tag to go with it; and so unfortunately, including invaluable human lives. Globalization presents social researchers the opportunity to look beyond local, national or regional outlooks into global assessment of issues. According to IOM, there are about 272 million globally, and about two-third of the figure are labour migrants (IOM, 2019); who are mostly discriminated against and treated as the 'others' outside of their home countries; where they have less than normal rights and respect. Civic stratification used by the state mostly exclude migrants from several benefits and equal opportunities, social exclusionism makes migrant particularly vulnerable to many forms of exploitation and injustice, especially human trafficking. This can be regarded as an exploitative dimension of globalization; a move that favor the movement and protection of capital flow but not the human rights of vulnerable migrants.

Migration do occur from displacement arising from political instability, civil unrest, militarism, civil armed engagement and natural disasters; which further fuels human trafficking. The destabilization and displacement of population not only increases their vulnerability to exploitation and abuses of human trafficking and forced labor (UNODC, 2008, p. 454), it can induce irregular migration, which also causes the mistreatment of migrants. Migrants run risk of sexual, labor, organ and tissue trafficking, in most cases, migrants are used in sweat shops, prostitution, sex trades, domestic labor, street begging, illegal adoption, terror soft-targets, farm and construction site works, and several other exploitative lifestyles. Tied Visas and the Kafala system are examples of negative policy blueprints for exploitation and abuse of migrant workers around the world. Tied Visa is a limiting visa regime, that ties the immigration status of a migrant to a particular employer, with potential to create a situation of vulnerability where an immigrant worker becomes trapped into exploitative labor or forced labor, with close-to-nothing protection of labor law. This kind of practice is operational in the United Kingdom, Canada, the United States of America and other developed nations. Tied Visa leaves migrant vulnerable to gross abuse of human rights and exploitation, it is classical example of how immigration policy enable servitude and modern slavery.

Few years ago, there was a story of a Filipino immigrant (named Eudocia "Lola" Pulido), who served a family (Tizon family) for 56 years in the United States of America, occasioned by the immigration policy of the United States (Lapinig, 2017). It is difficult to estimate the number of migrants in exploitative servitude around the world, even as UNODC started to identify TIP patterns in 2006 (UNODC, 2009). Between 2015 and 2019, an estimate of 3, 600 survivors of human trafficking were with legal documentation that allowed them work (with H-2A and H-2B visas) in the United States (Polaris, 2020).

Earlier estimates focus more on sexual exploitation involving women and children, however anyone else (especially men) are victims of labor (and sex) trafficking in many parts of the word. About US$99 billion accrued from commercial exploitation, and US$51 billion accrued from involuntary economic exploitations in agriculture, domestic servitude and other forms of labor exploitation (International labour Organization, 2014).

As the case is in the United Kingdom and Canada, the United States have multiple types of visa that enables labor servitude, sexual exploitation and other forms of human trafficking. Tied immigration policy represents a power dynamic that bequeaths unfair employers with a controlling instrument to control and dominate immigrant employees, who are already vulnerable due to the lack of knowledge of the system, customs and environment where they found themselves. Several migrants are also trapped in the Arab world, where the Kafala system is depriving them of freedom and human rights. The system also requires migrant workers to be tied or sponsored by an employer, who is deemed responsible for their resident status or legal stay in the country. The practice sees many domestic workers abused and violated by their bosses; who also confiscate their passports without legal consequences to such exploiters nor any protection to the exploited. There are an estimate of 23 million migrant workers in the Middle East, with about 11 million of them in Saudi Arabia (Thibos & Quirk, 2019), working under one of the most invisible and exploitative system protected by the state. With tied regime orchestrated by immigration policy of states (as indicative of the temporary work visas and the kafala system), migrants are legally and intentionally rendered vulnerable to forced and perilous labor that also facilitate the smooth running of the global economy. Migrants are essentially enslaved by the dual powers of both individual exploitation (from the part of the employers) and institutionalized exploitation (designed by the policy instruments and the civic stratifications of the state).

Apart from the usual dependency and connection existing between human traffickers and smugglers, where the latter depend on the former for supply-chain of persons for sex and labor market, there is another intersection of Smuggling of Migrant (SOM) and TIP, where the process of migrant smuggling can metamorphosize into human trafficking. In general terms, smuggling is concern with crime of exporting or importing of prohibited articles, or the act or an attempt to evade the payment of requisite custom duties on an article, which is considered as a crime against the state. Smuggling of migrant is a transnational criminality concerning the procurement for monetary or other material profit of unlawful access or entry of an individual into a country of which the individual is not a citizen or lawful resident. According to the Article 3, Protocol against the Smuggling of Migrants by Land, Sea and Air (otherwise known as the Smuggling of Migrants Protocol), SOM is the

> "procurement, in order to obtain, directly or indirectly, a financial or other material benefit, of the illegal entry of a person into a State Party of which the person is not a national or a permanent resident." (UNODC, 2003).

Transnational organized criminal elements provide smuggling services to irregular migrants, especially when access and equality to free movement is hampered by the (receiving) state. This services aid migrants to evade international border security, migration guidelines and visa requirements of the state for the profit of the smuggling syndicate, because national borders are progressively getting militarized by the security forces of the state. It is a high profit venture with low risk of detection and punishment (Koser, 2008). Smuggler operative a varied and highly sophisticated services, where document counterfeiting is central to the operation. Most of the methods used by smugglers possess high risk to migrants, who either ends up in jail for violation of the border security of another state, becomes kidnapped and trafficked or sometimes pay the ultimate price in the process (UNODC).

It is therefore incumbent on the research community, policy makers and other stakeholders to continue to reconsider and considerately examine the immediate interconnectedness or attractions that exist between these variables and TIP, to further checkmate its exponential growth and the continuous expansion of the billion dollars business in the 21st century. Organized transnational criminal groups are increasingly leveraging on mass movement of migrant in the recent years for financial gain. The recruitment and smuggling markets are dominated by transnational criminal organizations, which leverages on the precarious and desperate situation of the migrant to raise funds for purchase of drugs, arms and other clandestine operations. An analytical evaluation of the behavior and character of multinational companies (MNC) is also exceptionally germane to addressing human trafficking; the cross-border and diasporic nature of the MNC, their organized nature and the huge investment capacity they possess have some great implications to (the nature of) TIP, and to the effect that such activities are powered by technology and delivered by transportation.

Globalization continues to intrude systems and cultures; it is also ravaging the environment and civilizations. Although, globalization has equally brought about tremendous improvement in the general welfare and quality of life of the people (and their societies), albeit; it has also improved the level of smartness of the organized trafficking rings who constantly leverage on the opportunities provided by trade and tourism, transportation and information technology (social media) to lure and exploit myriads of unsuspecting persons (young and old population) at relatively cheap cost.

In the words of Thomas Friedman, "today globalization is farther, faster, cheaper and deeper" (Krogh & Friedman, 2000); so also are the spate also of the incidences of TIP; it is farther, faster, cheaper and deeper. The consequences of the development are in the faces of the weak, the strong and the mighty nations with generalized symptoms; objectifying and exploitation of persons, human degradation and commoditization of persons at a level the world never imagined. It is purely the demonstration of human callousness, from one person, and to another person. Globalization allows for the imbalanced movement of human capital resources and outsourcing (which further explained why more Africans and Asians are mostly gravitated and trafficked to the west).

Cyber-Sex Trafficking; Effects of Technology and Social Media

The 21st Century is the age of information and big data, principally driven and shaped by the internet. The use of internet technologies and tools are increasingly popular with every aspect of human endeavors, although millions of dollars is being dispensed annually to fight TIP around the world, the internal lacuna relating to the unwholesome use of cyberspace and technology continues to exist, which also does not necessarily require the movement of people to perpetrate exploitation (but can induce massive movement of victims and potential victims of human trafficking). While, the conventional means of human trafficking remains active, cyber technologies present the human trafficking arrangements with greater advantage to exploit and access the attention and privacy of large population of victims concurrently, across geopolitical frontiers (Greiman & Bain, 2013; Latonero, 2012). Massive online technologies are used extensively in the modern era to effect sex and labor trafficking and virtual exploitation across the world. There is urgent need for stricter internet legislation and security in many parts of the planet. The use of internet cannot afford to be unchecked, scrutinized or monitored for the vulnerable demographics, who are the target of internet monsters; praying on the innocence of the child. This is because technology has become a more potent tool in the hands of the human trafficking rings, as much as it is an instrument in the hands of the state and its people.

The cyber space is used by human trafficking networks to lure unsuspecting victims daily for personal gains. Parents and caregivers have the responsibility to monitor the activities of children when using the cyber space. Online classified sites such as facebook, and craigslist are exploited against unsuspecting persons and for the advertisement of sex (Wright, Jones, & Olivares, 2010). In 2012, a young Nigeria graduate student, Cynthia Osokogu (24) was lured from her school in Nassarawa state; a suburb of Abuja (the nations' capital) to the city of Lagos, where she was led to a hotel and was eventually raped to death and stripped of her belongings. Intelligence has it that, late Cynthia had never met any of the culprits in person until her journey to Lagos where she also met her untimely death; she met the criminals that ended her life on "facebook" weeks before her trip (Duthiers, 2012; Awojulugbe, 2017).According to FBI, about 293, 000 youths are at risk of underground sex trade, Most of the pimps and victims in this regard are all Americans (Walker-Rodriguez & Hill, 2011). Similarly in the United Kingdom, at least 1, 400 children were subjected to inglorious sexual servitude in Rotherham, United Kingdom between 1997 and 2013 in a report commissioned by Rotherham Borough Council in August 2014 (BBC, 2014). Vulnerable groups can be easily targeted with cyber technology.

In 2019, the number of global internet users was 4.13 billion through computers and smartphones, getting involved principally in social networking, while the global data traffic is set to surpass 77 exabytes per month in 2022 (Clement,

2020). At least, about half of the American internet users have used online classified sites, where human traffickers also market, recruit, trade and exploit others for criminal purposes (Latonero, 2012). Although, the nature of human trafficking is always clandestine, every interaction between traffickers and victims leaves digital footprints that can be explored by the anti-TIP law enforcement initiatives. 'Data mining, mapping and advance data analytics can be engaged by anti-TIP effort to prevent TIP, arrest and prosecute criminals, rescue victims, and understand the patterns of operation of human trafficking networks for constant planning of all stakeholders (ibid.). while progress in being made in the developed nations with regards to cyber security and analyses, developing states does not have requisite data regarding the online activities of traffickers and the trends of such actions.

Cyber-Sex Trade and the Sanity of the World

As earlier highlighted, Cyber Sex trafficking is an ugly trend bedeviling the 21st century society, the world account for over 40 million in modern day slavery, 25 million in forced labor and 15 million others in forced marriage and about 5million the global sex trade (ILO, 2017, p. 11). This form of dehumanization is connected with individual or group (pimps), who preys on the innocence of the weak and the humiliated of the society, either in the comforts of their homes and offices or having to travel to places, to have the canal knowledge of the minors. The trajectory of sex tourism and cyber technology (internet) is also a force in this regard.

The introduction and continuous advancement of technology, telecommunication and the increasing expansion of internet business has further given child predators another hedge and incentive to lure the unsuspecting minors (boys and girls alike). Pedophilia has been taken to another degree with the emergence of social media; human traffickers go on the social media sites and constantly seek improved new ways to take advantage of the unsuspecting internet user. Telecommunication makes it a less arduous task for syndicate groups and individuals to obtain cheap but valuable information about people and places, while also making connections and interactions between people less cumbersome. Irrespective of distance, location and status, access to people and information are easily achieved. Internet in itself is status insensitive, because it provides people of low status access to high status individuals and their ways of life, while also providing access to children by adults of dissimilar status. The cyber space is status-demystifying. Human traffickers can find out information about places and ways of life of people living in a geographical location in no time, so as to explore such situation (and persons).

The link or connectedness between the new wave of human trafficking and technology is very strong; it is a case of the wrong use of the technology and communication. It is almost impossible for TIP to happen in the 21st century, without recourse to the use of technology; at every stage, from recruitment, transportation, to the final stage of exploitation, technology is actively at play.

Child Pornography

There are instances where unsuspecting individuals (especially poor) minors have been promised offer of better life or fabulous job in the city and eventually they become a puppet on the internet. A child does not have to be transported to be exploited in child rape and pornography. The important TIP clause of movement or transportation from one location to another seldom come to play under these circumstances but does not practically need to; because the element of family bounds, trusts and responsibility can be the underlying factor why victims are easily swayed.

Child rape and pornography is an epidemic whose root causes needs analysis. More and more seemingly normal person are predators, praying on children on the internet. In 2006, a seven-year-old girl was advertised on craigslist for sex in Hamilton, Canada by mother's boyfriend, the child was reported to have been assaulted and exploited by multiple individuals, with image of her circulated on the internet before her rescue by the Hamilton Police (Sharkey, 2016). A total of eight adults; including the mother of the victim, her boyfriend, and six others were charged with sexual assault, sexual interference, making, distribution and possession of (child) pornographic materials (ibid.). The Winnipeg Police also arrested a 29 years old man luring a child online, the man pretended to be a 14 year old boy online, and had been in contact with the victim for around one month when the parents of the victim found out about the lewd (and inappropriate) messages, and called the police (Dacey, 2020). Family members and relations like that of a Father to a Daughter or son, Brother to a Sister, Mother of daughter or son, husband to a wife, aunties and uncles (and others close ties), living under the same roof can be a pimp that commoditize relations and dependents. Under many of these circumstances, the movement or transportation (in the definition of TIP) are hardly present, and the very profitable trading activities and exploitation can be as potent, limitless and actualized occurring within the perimeter of the virtual community. The inherent risk for traffickers on the road, sea, borders, tunnels and air are not present, therefore presenting a win-win position for the pimps.

Cyber Exploitations like child pornography and indecent (sexual or erotic) images are freely accessed everywhere, anywhere and anytime, (especially with the emergence of high-tech mobile devices) it is a global phenomenon affecting every nation in the wake of the 21st century. the higher education environment is not protected from this menace, where many professors and faculty members have been arrested, investigated and charged for sexual criminality against minors. Lori (Handrahan, Child Sex Trafficking in Higher Education, 2017) detailed around 210 professors and staff investigated, or arrested, or (and) prosecuted on CSEC related charges, with many of them looking normal until their arrests. Internet (or telecommunication) has proved to be a veritable tool of advertisement and negotiation for sexual purposes, children of all ages especially girls are advertised (like other commercial goods and services) to intending customers on the internet, for sexual practices. Willing Pimps can therefore make their bookings for a particular victim (or person) before actually coming to have canal knowledge of the individuals either in person or online. A generation of (American) children are specifically being targeted and destroy by child sex abuse, and the global craving for child pornography continues to put children at risk everywhere; including in the developed countries (Handrahan, 2017). Most of the victims are ashamed and grossly embarrassed, with their enslavement; they also become a victim of psychological and physical torture and the resulted effect of such actions are limitless, the victims can become a weapon and eventually suicidal.

Poverty and the Question of Causes

In many fora, poverty is advanced as the principal root-cause of the situation of human trafficking, a common denominator of most victim of child pornography and cybersex activities (and that of their family) are mainly poverty and lack of education (Karlsson, 2003, p. 7; Russell, 2014, p. 536; Unicef U.S.A., 2017; Truong, 2006). Poverty is a multilayered and complicated issue in the social parlance, it involves an array of concerns rather than a particular subject, and can therefore be chunked into meanings and interrelated concepts such as material conditions, economic circumstances and classes, and social relationship or position (Spicker, 2020). Paul (Spicker, 2020) further cluster some meanings together because in practice, such words are difficult to untangle; material Condition of poverty includes depravities related to the standard of living, specific need, and a pattern of deprivation; Economic circumstances includes the lack of resources, economic distance, economic class; while social position of poverty and unacceptable hardship includes social class, social dependency, social exclusivity, lack of basic security and lack of entitlement capacity (Spicker, 2020, p. 17) .

Poverty is a global phenomenon which is relative to a time and a place (Bradshaw, 2011). As advance by Abdullahi et al. (2014), poverty is the incapacitation of human beings to live a reasonable kind of life, a situation where access to basic necessities such as portable water, shelter, food, lack of opportunity to education and gainful employment. It is the inability of people to attain the minimum standard of living, and lack of hope for thc future (Abdullahi, Deribe, & Mustapha, 2014). The challenge of constructing an acceptable poverty line, and classifying those who are poor has always been a contextual issue in the principal methodological analysis of poverty in social science (Foster & Shorrocks, 1988). As also argued by Peter (Schuck, 2017), the immediate causes of poverty are also the effects of poverty, producing complex, tragic feedback loops; accordingly:

> "poverty affects people relatively more than one another, and it has many causes; which could be bad luck, bad choices, family breakdown, educational deficits, dysfunctional and self-reinforcement cultural patterns, social and neighborhood isolation, immigration, discrimination and mass incarceration and economic dislocation among them" (Schuck, 2017, p. 25).

Human trafficking can be construed as a developmental problem largely due to the risk factors and the demographics mostly affected by it; which are the deprived, unemployed, low-income and uneducated individuals. The patriarchal societies allow for the exploitation of gender disparities, caste discrimination, ethnicity and the marginalization of groups in a highly disproportionate world. The fact remains that human trafficking affects everyone, irrespective of income and education. Many educated and privileged individuals are daily violated in homes around the world. The complexities around human trafficking is numerous and intricately connected, weak governance, moral poverty, armed conflict and poor social safety nets, absence of active framework to protect against social discrimination and mistreatment might be some of the causes in general terms, however, over-generalization of causes of human trafficking among different people, places and nations can be ambiguous and misrepresentative. Each environment accommodates different dynamics or multiple of elements that are exclusive to its situation and conditions. Most of the generalized description of poverty relates to the situations in the developing countries of the world, leaving out the complex situations of internal human trafficking in the developed economies such as the United States of America, United Kingdom, Germany, France, Italy, Spain etc. A complete exploration of TIP must accommodate the precipitously altering environment that impacts the trends and patterns of human trafficking at domestic and transnational concentrations.

It is germane to identify the symbiotic effect or dependency that exists between poverty and education; the absence of one of the variables can lead to the presence of the other and it can have chain effects on the sanity of the society and our world. I would argue here that moral poverty linked to social relation of hardship and depravity is the bane of human trafficking, and not the generalized idea of poverty (if any even exist). Essentially, poverty occurs due to many disconcerting social concerns, such as drug addiction, criminality, corruption, family weaknesses and disintegration, domestic violence, poor medical and mental health system, climate change and environmental problems, as well as violent conflict and communal clashes among people. Household and community poverty are huge risk-factor in human trafficking, discrimination, stigma and exclusion can induce human trafficking, also, moral and social poverty can induce parents and guidance to sell or exploit their dependents. Migrants are exceptionally vulnerable abroad, undocumented immigrants are largely forced to endure exploitation in sex trade and labor, many of them enter into inappropriate violence cohabitation and relationships; which might also see them been used in illicit ventures by criminal network groups. The situation of irregularity of migrant is essentially a policy issue of the state, which leads to disenfranchisement, social exclusionism, group marginalization under the supervision of the state. In developing policy framework therefore, the context of individual and group vulnerability must be considered in filling exposure and susceptibility gaps.

The late sage; Nelson Mandela says that "Education is the most powerful weapon which you can use to change the world." Education has therefore become a key tool of sustainable development, and in eradicating or addressing TIP in its entire sphere (especially among children and the adolescents). Education must be given priority or a prime of place. Millions of under-age persons living at locations, houses and work environments all over the world are ironically living in prisons or hell. They are kept in dark rooms, with computers and cameras as working tools, they are made to dress seductively and act the same. Many customers across the globe (even as we speak) are in the cyber-sex marketplace of dark web, were children are mostly exploited, and buyers are difficult to track or identify. Two out of every three children sold for sex in the United States are trafficked on the internet (especially in the dark web) (Kurup, 2020). Some of those who engage in the act, just derives satisfaction in seeing two individual or minors (boys or girls) perform erotic with each other. When taken to the extremes, adult perverts for a reason best known to them want to have canal knowledge of babies for personal satisfaction or due to dangerous cultural practices such as the Virgin Cleansing Phenomena in south Africa (Leclerc-Madlala, 2002) and other parts of the world. Most of the "Commodities" in the Cyber-sex trade are ironically the most vulnerable individuals in our society.

In the developed economies of the West, many young individuals buried in actions and fraternizations on their computers and mobile devices are being brainwashed and recruited into Cyber Sex trafficking; the recruitments started from the internet, cultivated on the internet, and payment for such services are done (through credit cards or wired transfers) with the internet. This form of sexual exploitation as simple as it sounds seems harmless because it is done on the internet, but the effects of such are no less sinister, they have grave implications for the sanity of the child and our society.

The nature of education needed in tackling human trafficking is not just to the uneducated (illiterates), it includes education to the mind of everyone, such that even the most educated can understand the boundaries of immorality that tilts towards human trafficking and violence exploitation. Such education that encourages adult to speak out when suffering from mental stress or inordinate desire for sex or pornographic materials must be reinforced in every institutions, the society must be educated altogether to defend the course of the most vulnerable, and a better way to impact education is to start from the cradle.

Human Trafficking and National Security

Since the September 11 (9/11), 2001 attack in the United States of America, the world has woken to a completely different horizon in the region of civil protection and national security. In an attempt to foster better security and protection of critical infrastructures, more focus has been directed towards other hitherto unlikely and unrelated crimes, that were seen as not connected to constituting threats to national security. TIP is in such category, until recently, states and non-states actors never felt compelled to take a critical look at many trajectories that exists between TIP and SOM, and to the security of the state. now analyst have been able to establish the inherent connections of trafficked persons and smuggled migrants to national security.

In December 16, 2002, President G.W Bush (Jnr.) signed the National Security Directive (NSD) 22[1], giving further credence to the connectedness of TIP to terrorism and public health. TIP became a public policy concern in the United States after this action, with the state poised to address the problem of human trafficking using law enforcements, diplomacy and other tools of the state. To further strengthen the NSD 22, the Congress also supported it with the Intelligence Reform and Terrorism Prevention Act, 2004 (IRTPA), which eventually led to the establishment of the Human Smuggling and Trafficking Centre (HSTC) with the mandate to study and analyze the connectedness of human trafficking, alien smuggling and criminal support of underground terrorist travels (Department of State, 2014). President Barrack Hussein Obama also made issues of TIP a priority in his administration. Globally therefore, States have come to the realization of the implications (directly and otherwise) of TIP and SOM to stability and National Security; its poses human and national security challenges, and essentially, national security should include human security (Pati, 2014).

1. Document available at: https://ctip.defense.gov/Portals/12/Documents/NSPD-22.pdf

There is no empirical evidence showing that TIP is a causative factor in making a state become unstable, however, TIP is indicative of a societal decadence which leads to corruption in governance, and the effects and consequences of corruption is any states is unlimitedly sinister. A good monitoring and vigilance by the border security system can prevent a potential terrorist from accessing critical targets and locations, but the new wave of terrorism is beyond physical; Islamic extremists and fundamentalist have also taken their campaigns into the virtual world, luring millions through different inducements, brainwashing and indoctrinations into joining their campaigns. The victims are this category are not often hungry or in economic poverty but have fallen prey to the antics of criminal networks; who can traffic vulnerable person to prosecute terrorist activities.

Globalization as earlier posited, despite its many attendant opportunities, can also provide opportunities that can, aiding an unstable group of individuals or a subversive organization to disrupt the interest and stability of another. Globalization aids the fostering of economic cooperation among states and multinationals, it also allows for easy productive integrations among nations, unfortunately however, it has also fostered the integration of organized trafficking groups into the global challenging market structures. It has consequently allowed local or domestic criminal rings emerged into more advance criminal groups with attendant global security implications.

Terrorist groups work with organized criminal networks for unwitting recruitments of innocent boys and girls (men and women alike) across the world from both real and virtual worlds (internet) as human shield (Brachman & Warius, 2008) and as soldiers.

Foreigners are continually trafficked and used in the prosecution of criminal activities by al-Qaeda in many parts of the world; especially in the Middle East, in 2006, over 2,

500 foreigners were arrested and later freed by the Pakistani government (Wilkinson, 2006). Many of the foreign fighters were children, trafficked from almost every country in the world; including individuals from the United States, United Kingdom, Canada, France, Germany and others. Apart from being used as soldiers and human shield, many of the trafficked and kidnapped persons were used by the Pakistani Taliban to finance their complex network of criminal gangs and jihadi (Walsh, 2012). There is a growing awareness on the connections between terrorism and organized crime; including human trafficking, signifying a huge threat to global security (UNODC, 2019).

Conclusion

With changing forms and patterns in the activities of human traffickers, and what really constitutes the acts, means and purpose (s) in the 21st century, it is important that scholars continue to augment knowledge of the subject, while also sustaining the drive to discourse the dynamics and the altering threats in human trafficking. The problem is context-based; in that TIP differs according to nation, environment and political will of the actors to tackle the challenge. Although, human trafficking continues to attract global attention in politics, government, media and academics; there are widening gaps that needs to be closed by knowledge. An inclusive methodology to closing gaps become unattainable without the conjunction and cooperation of diverse study areas, knowledge capability and standpoints. Economic, socio-political, gender, historical perspectives must be considered in understanding and developing migration and anti-TIP program and policies of the States. The purpose of this document is to draw the attentions of the interest groups to identifying the inherent emergence and dynamics of the subject of TIP and identify a way of addressing the issues.

BIBLIOGRAPHY

Abdullahi, M., Deribe, M., & Mustapha, S. (2014). An Assessment the Relationship between Human Trafficking and Poverty in Nigeria. *Journal of Humanities and Social Science, 19* (10), 49-52.

Allain, J. (2015). No Effective Trafficking Definition Exists: Domestic Implementation of the Palermo Protocol. In J. Allain, The Law and Slavery (pp. 265-294). Leiden, N.V.: Koninklijke Brill Nijhoff.

Allen, D. M. (1980, October 1). Young male prostitutes: A psychosocial study. *Archives of Sexual Behavior, 9*, 399–426.

Alliance to End Slavery and Trafficking (ATEST). (2020, June 29). *ATEST Challenges Tier 1 Ranking for U.S. in 2020 TIP Report.* Retrieved Septemeber 2020, from Alliance to End Slavery and Trafficking (ATEST): https://endslaveryandtrafficking.org/atest-challenges-tier-1-ranking-for-u-s-in-2020-tip-report/

Bales, K. (2004). *Disposable People: New Slavery in the Global Economy.* Berkeley: University of California Press.

Batha, E., & Wulfhorst, E. (2020, April 30). *UN: 3 months of lockdown could result in 15 million cases of domestic abuse worldwide.* Retrieved July 2020, from World Economic Forum: https://www.weforum.org/agenda/2020/04/coronavirus-women-domestic-abuse/

BBC. (2014, August 26). *Rotherham child abuse scandal: 1, 400 children exploited, report finds*. Retrieved September 2018, from BBC: https://www.bbc.com/news/uk-england-south-yorkshire-28939089

Beets, G., & Willekens, F. (2009). *The Global Economic Crisis and International Migration: An Uncertain Outlook.* Netherlands Interdisciplinary Demographic Institute . The Hague: European Commission.

Brachman, J., & Warius, A. (2008, May 1). Abu Yahya al-Libi's "Human Shields in Modern Jihad". *CTC Sentinel, 1* (6), Available at: https://ufdc.ufl.edu/AA00066699/00006.

Bradshaw, J. (2011). Poverty. In A. Walker, A. Sinfield, & C. Walker, *Fighting poverty, inequality and injustice: A manifesto inspired by Peter Townsend* (Vol. www.jstor.org/stable/j.ctt9qgkb7.10. Accessed 16 July 2020., pp. 91-110). Bristol: Bristol University Press, Policy Press.

Bryan-Low, C., & Flynn, A. (2013, November 21). *Pair in U.K. Arrested After Slavery Rescue: Police Arrest Man, Woman After Charity Tips Off Authorities*. Retrieved June 2020, from The Wall Street Journal: https://www.wsj.com/articles/uk-police-rescue-three-women-allegedly-held-as-slaves-1385047060

Clement, J. (2020, January 7). *Global number of internet users 2005-2019*. Retrieved July 2020, from Statista: https://www.statista.com/statistics/273018/number-of-internet-users-worldwide/

Coleman, S. S. (2016). *The Trafficking Victims Protection Act (TVPA) 2000: A policy analysis.* Long Beach, Califonia: California State University Dissertations Publishing.

Dacey, E. (2020, July 15). *Winnipeg police arrest 29-year-old man accused of luring child online.* Retrieved July 2020, from Global News: https://globalnews.ca/news/7179165/winnipeg-police-to-release-details-on-man-who-lured-child-online/

Daily mail Reporter. (2013, October 1). *The Baby Factory: In a huge Clinic in india, hundreds of women are paid 5, 000 pounds each to have Western Couples babies*. Retrieved September 2014, from Daily Mail U.K: https://www.dailymail.co.uk/news/article-2439977/The-baby-factory-In-huge-clinic-India-hundreds-women-paid-5-000-Western-couples-babies.html

Danailova-Trainor, G., & Belser, P. (2006). *Globalization and the illicit market for human trafficking: an empirical analysis of supply and demand.* Geneva: ILO.

Davis, N. J. (1971). The prostitute: Developing a deviant identity. *Studies in the Sociology of Sex*, 297-332.

Department of State. (2014, April 16). *HUMAN SMUGGLING AND TRAFFICKING CENTER BACKGROUND FACT SHEET.* Retrieved July 2020, from Department of States:

https://2009-2017.state.gov/documents/organization/226462.pdf

DeStefano, A. M. (2007). *The War on Human Trafficking: U.s. Policy Assessed.* Chicago, IL.: Rutgers University Press.

Foster, J. E., & Shorrocks, A. F. (1988, January). Poverty Orderings. *Econometrica, 56* (1), 173-177.

Godin, M. (2020, March 18). *As Cities Around the World Go on Lockdown, Victims of Domestic Violence Look for a Way Out.* Retrieved June 2020, from Time: https://time.com/5803887/coronavirus-domestic-violence-victims/

Graham-Harrison, E., Giuffrida, A., Smith, H., & Ford, L. (2020, March 28). *Lockdowns around the world bring rise in domestic violence.* Retrieved July 2020, from The Guardian: https://www.theguardian.com/society/2020/mar/28/lockdowns-world-rise-domestic-violence

Handrahan, L. (2017, February 14). *Child Sex Trafficking in Higher Education.* Retrieved July 2020, from Midium: https://medium.com/@LoriHandrahan2/professors-staff-arrested-for-trading-in-child-rape-6c39fcf62a9e

Handrahan, L. (2017). *Epidemic: America's Trade in Child Rape.* Walterville, Oregon, U.S.A.: TrineDay.

Henry, N. L. (2016, June 16). *Slavery Abolition Act: United Kingdom [1834].* Retrieved July 2020, from Encyclopædia Britannica: https://www.britannica.com/topic/Slavery-Abolition-Act

Hollingsworth, L. D. (2003, April 1). International adoption among families in the United States: Considerations of social justice. *Social Work, 48* (2), 209-217.

Hunt, L. (2015, July 31). *The Trouble with the US Human Trafficking Report: A focus on annual rankings misses the point.* Retrieved September 2020, from The Diplomat: https://thediplomat.com/2015/07/the-trouble-with-the-us-human-trafficking-report/

ILO. (2017). *Global estimates of modern slavery: Forced labour and forced marriage* . Retrieved from ILO: https://www.ilo.org/

wcmsp5/groups/public/---dgreports/---dcomm/documents/publication/wcms_575479.pdf

International labour Organization. (2014, May 20). *ILO says forced labour generates annual profits of US$ 150 billion.* Retrieved June 2020, from International Labour Organization (ILO): https://www.ilo.org/global/about-the-ilo/newsroom/news/WCMS_243201/lang--en/index.htm

IOM. (2019, November 1). *WORLD MIGRATION REPORT 2020.* Retrieved July 2020, from International Organization for Migration: https://www.un.org/sites/un2.un.org/files/wmr_2020.pdf

IOM. (2020, September 29). *Missing Migrants: Tracking Deaths Along Migratory Routes.* Retrieved September 2020, from Missing Migrants Project: https://missingmigrants.iom.int/

JAOUEN, R. (2016). *Male prostitution, 19th-20th centuries.* Retrieved July 2020, from EHNE: Encyclopédie pour une histoire nouvelle de l'Europe: https://ehne.fr/en/article/gender-and-europe/prostitution-19th-21st-centuries/male-prostitution-19th-20th-centuries

Jones, L., Engstrom, D. W., Hilliard, T., & Diaz, M. (2007, June 1). Globalization and Human Trafficking. *The Journal of Sociology and Social Welfare, 34* (2), 107-122.

Keiper, A., & Chiaramonte, P. (2019, June 23). *Human trafficking in America among worst in world: Report*. Retrieved June 2020, from Fox News: https://www.foxnews.com/us/human-trafficking-in-america-among-worst-in-world-report

Kempadoo, K., & Doezema, J. (2018). *Global Sex Workers: Rights, Resistance, and Redefinition.* New York: Routledge.

Koser, K. (2008, May 6). Why Migrant Smuggling Pays. *International Migration, 46* (2), 4-26.

Krogh, P. F., & Friedman, T. (2000). INTERVIEW: Farther, Faster, Deeper, Cheaper. *Georgetown Journal of International Affairs, 1* (2), 87-93 .

Kurup, N. (2020, July 21). *Sex & Modern Slavery: How sexual predators hide behind dark web to facilitate human trafficking.* Retrieved September 2020, from MEAWW: https://meaww.com/sex-and-modern-slavery-human-child-trafficking-internet-dark-web

Lapinig, C. (2017, June 7). *How U.S. Immigration Law Enables Modern Slavery.* Retrieved September 2020, from The Atlantic: https://www.theatlantic.com/business/archive/2017/06/immigration-law-modern-slavery/529446/

Latonero, M. (2012, April 24). *Human trafficking online: The role of social networking sites and online classifieds.* Retrieved July 2020, from SSRN: https://papers.ssrn.com/sol3/papers.cfm?abstract_id=2045851

Leclerc-Madlala, S. (2002). On The Virgin Cleansing Myth: Gendered Bodies, AIDS and Ethnomedicine. *African Journal of AIDS Research, 1,* 87-95.

McCrary, J., & Sanga, S. (2020, May 28). *The Impact of the Coronavirus Lockdown on Domestic Violence.* Retrieved July 2020, from SSRN: https://papers.ssrn.com/sol3/papers.cfm?abstract_id=3612491

Mounk, Y., & Kyle, J. (2018, December 26). *Ideas: What Populists Do to Democracies.* Retrieved July 2020, from The Atlantic: https://www.theatlantic.com/ideas/archive/2018/12/hard-data-populism-bolsonaro-trump/578878/

Niethammer, C. (2020, February 2). *Cracking the $150 Billion Business of Human Trafficking.* Retrieved June 2020, from Forbes: https://www.forbes.com/sites/carmenniethammer/2020/02/02/cracking-the-150-billion-business-of-human-trafficking/#1b3c88174142

Parsons, C., Cray, A., Saar, M. S., & Vafa, Y. (2014, April 8). *3 Key Challenges in Combating the Sex Trafficking of Minors in the United States.* Retrieved from Center for American Progress: https://www.americanprogress.org/issues/lgbtq-rights/reports/2014/04/08/87293/3-key-challenges-in-combating-the-sex-trafficking-of-minors-in-the-united-states/

Pati, R. (2014, February 1). *Human Trafficking: An Issue of Human and National Security.* Retrieved July 2020, from University of Miami Law School Institutional Repository: https://repository.law.miami.edu/cgi/viewcontent.cgi?article=1057&context=umnsac

Polaris. (2020, June 23). *Labor Trafficking Red Flags in Latest Work Visa Program Changes.* Retrieved September 2020, from Polaris Blog: https://polarisproject.org/blog/2020/06/labor-trafficking-red-flags-in-latest-work-visa-program-changes/

Roache, M. (2018, September 13). *Ukraine's 'baby factories': The human cost of surrogacy.* Retrieved June 2020, from Al jazeera: https://www.aljazeera.com/indepth/features/ukraine-baby-factories-human-cost-surrogacy-180912201251153.html

Schuck, P. H. (2017). *One Nation Undecided: Clear Thinking about Five Hard Issues That Divide Us* (Vols. Available at: https://www.jstor.org/stable/pdf/j.ctvc77jnx.5.pdf?ab_segments=0%252Fbasic_SYC-5187%252Ftest&refreqid=excelsior%3A2e08d411617217ac41dda9b44ad6bfd7). Princeton: Princeton University Press.

Sharkey, J. (2016, November 21). *Child exploitation often disguised as 'child model' ads on Craigslist, says expert.* Retrieved July 2020, from CBC: https://www.cbc.ca/news/canada/kitchener-waterloo/child-exploitation-young-models-online-1.3860055

Shoaps, L. L. (2013). ROOM FOR IMPROVEMENT: PALERMO PROTOCOL AND THE TRAFFICKING VICTIMS PROTECTION ACT. *Lewis & Clark Law Review, 17* (3), 931-972.

Spicker, P. (2020). *"Poverty." The Poverty of Nations: A Relational Perspective* (Vol. Available at www.jstor.org/stable/j.ctvxkn6j8.6.). Bristol: Bristol University Press, Policy Press.

The Associated Press. (2014, July 30). *FBI recovers 168 children from sex traffickers, including some never reported missing.* Retrieved September 2014, from National Post: https://nationalpost.com/news/fbi-recovers-168-children-from-sex-traffickers-including-some-never-reported-missing

Thibos, C., & Quirk, J. (2019). *The Fure of Work.* London: openDemocracy.

United Nations Office on Drug and Crime. (2000, November 15). *United Nations Convention against Transnational Organized Crime and the Protocols Thereto.* Retrieved June 2020, from United Nations Office on Drug and Crime: https://www.unodc.org/unodc/en/organized-crime/intro/UNTOC.html#Fulltext

United States Department of State. (2019, July 1). *Trafficking In Persons Report.* Retrieved September 2020, from United States Department of States: https://www.state.gov/wp-content/uploads/2019/06/2019-Trafficking-in-Persons-Report.pdf

UNODC. (2003, September 29). *United Nations Convention against Transnational Organized Crime and the Protocols Thereto.* Retrieved July 2020, from United Nations Office on Drugs and Crime: https://www.unodc.org/unodc/en/organized-crime/intro/UNTOC.html

UNODC. (2008). *Toolkit to Combat Trafficking in Persons: Global Programme against Trafficking in Human Beings.* Retrieved May 2020, from United Nations Office on Drugs and Crime (UNODC): https://www.unodc.org/documents/human-trafficking/HT_Toolkit08_English.pdf

UNODC. (2009, February 1). *Global Report on Trafficking in persons.* Retrieved May 2020, from United Nations Office on Drugs and Crime (UNODC): https://www.unodc.org/documents/human-trafficking/Global_Report_on_TIP.pdf

UNODC. (2019, March 1). *E4J University Module Series: Organized Crime / Counter-Terrorism (Module 16: Linkages between Organized Crime and Terrorism).* Retrieved July 2020, from UNODC: https://www.unodc.org/e4j/en/organized-crime/module-16/introduction-learning-outcomes.html

UNODC. (n.d.). *Migrant Smuggling.* Retrieved July 2020, from United Nations Office for Drugs and Crime: https://www.unodc.org/unodc/en/human-trafficking/smuggling-of-migrants.html?ref=menuside

US Department of States. (n.d.). *policy Issues; Human Trafficking.* Retrieved June 2020, from U.S. Department of States: https://www.state.gov/policy-issues/human-trafficking/

Walker-Rodriguez, A., & Hill, R. (2011, March 1). *Human Sex Trafficking.* Retrieved May 2020, from FBI Law Enforcement Bulletin (LEB): https://leb.fbi.gov/articles/featured-articles/human-sex-trafficking

Walsh, D. (2012, February 19). *Taliban Gaining More Resources From Kidnapping.* Retrieved July 2020, from The New York Times: https://www.nytimes.com/2012/02/20/world/asia/pakistani-taliban-turn-to-kidnapping-to-finance-operations.html

WHO. (2018, November 23). *Violence against Women.* Retrieved July 2020, from World Health Organization: https://www.who.int/news-room/feature-stories/detail/violence-against-women

Wilkinson, I. (2006, September 15). *US outraged as Pakistan frees Taliban fighters.* Retrieved July 2020, from Telegraph: http://www.telegraph.co.uk/news/main.jhtml?xml=%2Fnews%2F2006%2F09%2F15%2Fwpak15.xml

Wright, D., Jones, L., & Olivares, X. (2010, August 10). *'Craigslist: Site for Sex Slaves' Story Saves Girl's Life.* Retrieved June 2020, from ABC News: https://abcnews.go.com/WN/popular-website-craigslist-outlet-sex-trafficking-child-exploitation/story?id=11367581

CHAPTER II

The Trafficking of Children for the Purpose of Sexual Exploitation in Spain

Jorge Uroz Olivares[1]

Introduction

The trafficking of children for the purpose of sexual exploitation is, undoubtedly, the greatest rights violation of minors that exists and one of the worst forms of abuse and exploitation that children can suffer in this world. According to the data from Eurostat, 23% of the victims of trafficking for the purpose of sexual exploitation in Europe are girls and boys (European Commission, 2018). However, the number of children who are identified as victims of trafficking in Spain is very low. That does not mean that there are not any children who have been the object of trafficking in this country, rather that we have not been capable of identifying them adequately. What we do know is that these data are increasing every year in an alarming fashion. Every day, more children are being used by the human trafficking networks to be sexually exploited.

It is vital that we learn why boys and girls are so attractive for the trafficking networks. To be able to identify the victims, we have to learn the ways in which organized crime is using these minors and to try to see where they can place them for the purpose of sexual exploitation.

The work and intervention of both the state and public bodies is of course essential in the process of identification and

1. Universidad Pontificia Comillas, Madrid- Spain

protection of possible underage victims. The question we must ask is whether it is possible to improve these mechanisms in order to be more efficient at detection. And once identified, are the protection and recovery mechanisms that are used in Spain fulfilling their function? Are the resources that the victims are offered really adequate for their effective protection?

What we understand by the trafficking of minors: the data for child trafficking in Spain

The concept of human trafficking is defined in Article 3 of the Palermo Protocol:

> "Trafficking in persons shall mean the recruitment, transportation, transfer, harbouring or receipt of persons, by means of the threat or use of force or other forms of coercion, of abduction, of fraud, of deception, of the abuse of power or of a position of vulnerability or of the giving or receiving of payments or benefits to achieve the consent of a person having control over another person, for the purpose of exploitation. Exploitation shall include, at a minimum, the exploitation of the prostitution of others or other forms of sexual exploitation, forced labour or services, slavery or practices similar to slavery, servitude or the removal of organs." (UNDOC, 2004, p.42)

In the case of children (anyone under the age of eighteen) who are the object of trafficking, there are differences compared to the trafficking of adults, since it is not necessary to prove that there was threat, the use of force, deception or any of the other forms or means that are included in that definition, in order to consider those children as trafficking victims. Those means must be used when concerning whether to identify adults as victims. However, for children it is only required to demonstrate the recruitment or transportation with the purpose of subjecting them to some type of exploitation for them to be considered a victim of trafficking. That is to say, whether there is consent or not of the minor is not an issue to be able to consider them a trafficking victim (something that is essential in the case of adults).

Spain has become established essentially as a destination country of the trafficking of people, although it is also a transit country of trafficking victims whose final destination is other UE countries (mainly France, UK, Germany and Denmark).

Regarding the number of cases detected, it must be stated that according to the official data, Spain is a country with one of the lowest incidences of child trafficking cases. Between 4 and 7% of detected trafficking cases are of children. This datum is in contrast to the figures provided by the European Union, in which the percentage of child victims of trafficking is 23% (European Commission). Similarly, the data for child trafficking detected throughout the whole world, according to the latest Global Report on Trafficking in Persons from UNDOC, is also 23% (UNDOC, 2018).

In Europe, moreover, that number of child trafficking victims has increased over time: in 2010, the percentage of children trafficked in Europe was 13%, and by 2016 that percentage had risen to 23%. As we can see in Table 1, in Spain that percentage of children identified as trafficking victims has also increased in time, but our figures are noticeably lower than those in Europe and the world.

To be able to explain such a low figure for trafficked minors in Spain, we can find three arguments:

a) There is a lack of detection and identification of child trafficking victims by the Spanish authorities. This is perhaps the best explanation. It is possible that our mechanisms for detecting and identifying potential child trafficking victims are either failing or are not wholly efficient and suitable for what is required. In fact, in the 2019 report on the trafficking of people published by the

U.S. State Department, one of the criticisms made against the Spanish government is the low number of victims identified, a number that is lower than previous years without there being sound reasons to justify it. Among the specific recommendations made to the Spanish state is that the training for proactive identification of victims should be fomented, especially in the case of unaccompanied minors (U.S. State Department, 2019). Similarly, in its latest report on the situation in Spain, GRETA considers that the figures provided by the Spanish government reflect neither the reality nor the real scale of the phenomenon of human trafficking. The main difficulty that GRETA finds in Spain is that there is no comprehensive approach for "detecting" and fighting against trafficking in people (GRETA, 2018).

b) The second explanation lies in the changes that have occurred in the trafficking networks' operating methods. A significant shift is taking place with a move away from the sexual exploitation that happened in clubs and brothels, which are open to the public, to private apartments and houses. It is in the publicly licenced clubs where inspections are made by the state security forces, and where child trafficking victims are detected. However, the shift of sexual exploitation to apartments complicates this inspection work, because the police cannot gain access to them without a judicial order. The trafficking networks are aware of this fact, which makes police investigations, and of course the possible detection of exploited minors, far more difficult.

c) The last explanation for such a low figure in the data concerns the effort that has been made throughout these years, by both public and private entities, in the fight against the trafficking of people for the purpose of sexual exploitation. The authorities state that thanks to that effort, it has been possible to contain the number of cases of trafficking victims, and that we are now seeing the fruits of those measures (Fiscalía General del Estado [Spanish Attorney General], 2016). Without a doubt, Spain has made an effort both in the detection of and in the fight against trafficking, but this is perhaps the least convincing explanation for the low figure. Indeed, in the fight against child trafficking, there is still a long way to go both in the detection of trafficked minors and in their subsequent protection.

TABLE II (A)

Cases of minors in situations of risk or detected as trafficking victims

ORIGIN	2013	2014	2015	2016	2017
Nigeria	4	3	5	7	14
Morocco	-	-	2	-	-
Romania	17	14	12	3	4
Bulgaria	-	1	-	1	-
Spain	4	16	7	-	-
Brazil	-	-	1	1	-
Bolivia	-	-	-	6	-
Ecuador	-	-	-	3	-
Colombia	-	-	-	3	-
Paraguay	7	1	-	-	-
Dominican Republic	2	2	4	-	-
China	2	-	-	-	1
TOTAL	36	36	33	28	19
Percentage of child victims of trafficking	3.58	3.91	6.14	6.3	7.3

Source: Fiscalía General del Estado (2013-2018). Compiled by the author.

* The total number of minors does not correspond to the sum of minors by country, because there are cases for which the nationality is not known.

* Throughout the different years, most Spanish minors have been identified as victims of forced sexual exploitation. Out of the total cases, we can say that the number of child trafficking victims identified is nine.

Profile and characteristics of child trafficking victims

The profile of trafficking for the purpose of sexual exploitation in Spain is essentially female. In 2017, 95% of trafficking cases were women and girls. Correctly speaking, if we are referring to cases of child trafficking victims, then in Spain we should speak about the trafficking of girls for the purpose of sexual exploitation, since 99% of the cases detected are girls rather than boys (their ages are not known as they are not provided in the official data). However, we can reach an approximation of the ages according to the data that Europol provides regarding the girls who are brought into Europe for the purpose of sexual exploitation ranges from 7 to 17 years old, with the majority being between 15 and 17 years of age (Europol, 2018).

Some of the characteristics that the child trafficking victims present are common to all: they are minors with great social and personal vulnerability; they have low levels of education or training; they come from families and social contexts characterized by extreme poverty and need; they have experienced abuse in their families of origin; the motivation for their relocation is the search for a better quality of life in Europe; and the majority tend to be without identity papers or with forged papers. However, other characteristics are much more specific and differ between each case, depending above all on their origin, which also conditions the way in which they have reached Spain. In this regard, we shall speak of five differential groups depending on the children's origin (Table 1):

a) the girls who come from Africa: almost all of them from Nigeria;

b) the girls who come from eastern Europe, mostly Romania;
c) the girls who come from the Americas, above all from three countries: Bolivia, Paraguay and the Dominican Republic.
d) the girls who come from Asia, specifically from China;
e) and lastly, we will discuss the case of Spanish girls.

Sub-Saharan girls: NIGERIA

Nigeria is the country where the second-highest number of minors come from who are used by criminal groups for the purpose of sexual exploitation. Most of the women who come from Nigeria are increasingly younger. The girls tend to be between fifteen and seventeen years old with a growing proportion of thirteen- and fourteen-year-old girls (Save the Children, 2018). There are different forms of recruitment, but all of them are deceived. The traffickers tend to form part of the community where they live and know their relatives. This aspect is crucial for the later extortion and threatening of the victims in order to compel them to work as a prostitute once they reach Spain, in the cases where a family is not involved in the girls' trafficking. The criminal groups, taking advantage of their situation of need, tend to use deception or false promises, promising the family a better life for their daughter, a better education, or even making a job offer for the girl that will later prove to be false.

On other occasions, the traffickers even belong to the extended family of the children. These are cases in which the family itself is involved in the crime of trafficking. The family takes on this situation as a kind of sacrifice for the good of the family and the community. These are families from very poor backgrounds whose traditional customs require the firstborn girl to look after her parents and younger siblings. This tradition will keep the girl sexually exploited without her being able to abandon the activity, as a way of fulfilling her family obligations. Furthermore, in the collective imaginary of Nigerian culture, the fact of sending a daughter to a foreign country means that the family attains greater status in their own community (Women's Link Worldwide, 2014; Save the Children, 2018).

The girls tend to be subjected to a voodoo ritual before leaving Nigeria as a way of guaranteeing that the debt contracted with the traffickers will be paid (between 30, 000 and 80, 000 euros, a debt that they only learn about once they are in Spain), and also to ensure that they will never collaborate with the authorities in the destination country with the aim of deterring them from identifying the traffickers (Dunkerley, 2017; Frontex, 2018).

Girls from eastern Europe: Romania

Romania is the country from where the highest number of trafficking victims identified in Spain come. The contexts in which the criminal groups move are always marked by a situation of poverty and need. Although Romania has improved its economic circumstances as a country in recent years, we need to be aware that the wealth that has been generated has not been distributed equally throughout the country, which means that there are still highly socioeconomically disadvantaged areas. Two of those disadvantaged regions are Muntenia and Moldavia, which is where the highest number of girls come from.

There are cases in which the families are not involved and the only thing they want is for their children to have more opportunities and a better life in an economically developed country. They come deceived with false promises of work or education. It is also usual to find girls who come from broken homes or even from orphanages, girls who do not have the figure of an adult who is concerned and responsible for them, which makes them an easier target to recruit and manipulate for the trafficking networks (Save the Children, 2018).

However, there are many cases in which the girl's family itself is involved and complicit in the crime of trafficking, above all in the cases in which the victim is younger. There are no large organized crime networks behind the trafficking of the girls. Rather, it is orchestrated by family clans or people very close to the family. These families are involved both in the origin and in the destination country, since, on occasions, part of the family resides in Spain (Fundació Surt, 2015).

For older adolescents, the tactic employed is different: that of the "lover boy". This involves an attractive young man, well dressed and with money, who first gets the girls to fall in love with him, so that later he can propose relocating to Spain, either because he lives there or because he promises them work and a better quality of life there with him. This is a very efficient tactic in the case of teenagers, who are very manipulatable emotionally speaking, and who quickly become excited about a better life alongside their prince charming. There are two different modi operandi. In the first, these lover boys are members of a human trafficking network who are provided with all the means necessary to deceive and relocate the girls. The lover boy acts as the middle man in the recruitment process of the minors. Once the girls reach Spain, they are handed over to the criminal organization and do not see or hear from the lover boy again. In the second modality, the lover boy acts on a personal level to sexually exploit the women he "recruits" without a criminal group behind him (Fiscalía General del Estado, 2017). Given that for these women this man is their boyfriend, it is more difficult for them to file a complaint or report him, since they are emotionally tied to the person who is their own trafficker.

Girls from South America and the Caribbean

The number of girls who come from the Americas is noticeably lower when compared to those from Romania or Nigeria. Those who have been found in Spain come mainly from the Dominican Republic and Paraguay, although they also come from other countries, such as Bolivia, Colombia, Ecuador and Brazil. This lower number of girls can be explained because we know that the trafficking of minors from these areas takes place internally in their own countries or also between countries within the Americas. The latest UNDOC report puts the figure at 66% of child victims of trafficking in Central America and the Caribbean, making this one of the highest percentages of child victims of trafficking in the world. This means that the destination of the trafficked children stays within the Americas, from the poorer areas to the richer areas and countries (UNDOC, 2018). Another possible explanation for the lower number of minors coming from the Americas is the method the criminal groups use to relocate the victims to Europe. In most cases, this is by air. The control that is maintained in airports by state security forces entails an added risk for human trafficking networks, which reduces the movement of child victims, unless the minors' families are involved in the crime.

Therefore, when we speak of child victims coming from the Americas, we see that there is always some involvement of the girl's family. In many cases, this recruitment is carried out by the mothers themselves, who are living in Spain, or the girls travel to Spain with the mother's consent to be with close relatives, which makes it easier for the girls to enter the country without raising suspicion. What we can be certain about is that the girls are not aware of the activity they are going to carry out in Spain. They come deceived with offers of work or education (Apramp, 2016).

Asian girls: CHINA

The number of Chinese child victims of trafficking is very low in Spain. In general, Chinese trafficking victims are very difficult to detect and identify. For this reason, we cannot say whether this very low number is due either to the fact that these girls undergo internal trafficking in the country, or that we have not been capable of identifying them. They are in the most hidden sectors of prostitution, mainly destined for Asian clients, which makes their detection even more difficult. What we can see is the huge supply that exists of advertisements or flyers of Asian women who provide services in apartments. An analysis of the prostitution offered by advertisements revealed the lack of protection found in the services provided by Asian women, which led to the conclusion that this was forced prostitution and, moreover, using very young women, in some cases possibly minors (Meneses, Uroz & Rua, 2017).

Spanish girls

According to data provided by the Spanish government, Spanish child victims of trafficking are almost non-existent. Only one case of one girl has been detected in the last five years. Regarding Spanish girls, perhaps what has been found more often up until now are cases of sexual exploitation rather than trafficking. However, there have been studies that warn of the increase in the trafficking of Spanish minors in recent years (Castaño & Pérez, 2017). According to Castaño and Pérez, more and more girls are being recruited in Spain by criminal organizations that, through deception and coercion, relocate them to other places within the country where they are sexually exploited. For this recruitment, these criminal groups use other girls who have the purpose of recruiting other minors in nightclubs, in schools or through social networks. They tend to be adolescents in a situation of vulnerability (broken family, drug addiction, financial difficulties, etc.).

This profile of minors in a situation of risk and vulnerability is what worries us the most. In fact, one method for being able to find girls with the aim of sexually exploiting them is to do so in the youth protection centres, where the most vulnerable girls in the country are to be found. These girls are wards of the state, without emotional support in the form of families or caring adults. The latest investigations in Spain indicate as much: a significant number of sexually exploited girls come from the child protection system itself. This form of recruitment is also taking place in other European Union countries (Dominguez, 2020; Europol, 2018).

The main lure for these girls, who hail from economically needy families, is the possibility of earning fast and easy money. The girls are recruited through other girls who are already being exploited and who mix with them, in places of leisure like nightclubs, or in their schools. Afterwards, the procurers/pimps offer them to clients through social networks, and when they set up a meeting, they transport the minors to the apartments in which the sexual exploitation is carried out. The girls could earn between 50 and 200 euros per job, although, depending on the type of service and the time spent with the clients, this amount could be far higher. The criminal network would keep a percentage of that money (Fernández, 2019).

Modi operandi of the criminal groups that traffic minors

The first question that must be asked is the reason why the criminal groups traffic underage girls when the risk they run is so much higher: the state controls set up to eradicate it have intensified and the sentences imposed for this crime are far greater than for trafficking adult women. The answer to this question is found in two factors: first, due to the characteristics of the girls, and second, due to the demand that exists and the economic gain it entails.

For the criminal groups of traffickers, girls, as possible victims of trafficking, are much more vulnerable and manipulatable than women; girls are more easily led, they also have fewer resources to turn to when faced with these situations, they are scared more easily, and, therefore, give the criminals that exploit them fewer problems. We cannot forget that the aim of the criminal groups is essentially financial. In this regard, moreover, girls have a longer shelf life in terms of being exploited than an adult woman, thus the criminal groups' profits will be higher. In addition, the prices traffickers charge for the different sexual services the girls provide are much higher. This is a type of service that is very different to prostitution in general (having sexual relations with a minor, which is a crime), for which the clients that seek it are willing to pay larger amounts of money. As an example of this, we can give the example of how a criminal organization offered, through the network, the virginity of a minor for the price of 5, 000 euros (Rodríguez, 2017).

The method of transporting and getting girls into Spain is different depending on the particular groups we are referring to. The girls who come from Latin America are brought by plane, some directly to Spain and others via Turkey (since the entry controls in that country are much less strict), from where they then travel to Spain by land (Apramp, 2015). The Chinese girls are also brought by plane, but we have no more details because few cases are known.

The girls who come from Nigeria can follow two routes: they might travel through Niger to Libya, to then go by boat to Malta or Italy, and subsequently to Spain by land; or they might travel through Mali to reach Morocco, from where they move on to Spain by small, open boat or by motorboat. This group endures a very hard journey, not only because of the conditions in which it takes place but because during the journey they are abused and raped by the traffickers, a kind of lesson by which they learn their condition of slavery.

Lastly, the Romanian girls are moved by land, in car or bus from Romania to Spain. They will not learn of the deception until they are already in Spain. Subsequently they are held and controlled by the networks using the emotional bond, in the event that they maintain contact with the supposed boyfriend, or by using threats of violence if that method does not work. On many occasions they are threatened with harm to their families, or with telling their families what they have been working as, as a way of humiliating them (in the event that the family is not involved).

For what purpose do the criminal groups use the minors? Girls can be used by the networks in various senses. The most frequent is that the minors are used as an object of business by the criminal groups by being sexually exploited. The second aspect is not direct exploitation of them, rather they are used to force their mothers to keep working as a prostitute for these criminal groups. If the mothers wish to abandon the network or report their situation to the authorities, the networks can threaten them with the abuse, or even the death, of their children. On occasion, that violence toward the children is carried out even in the presence of the mothers so that the latter remain under the power of the networks without causing problems. This occurs above all with the Nigerian women. This is why many Nigerian women are raped during their journey until they are made pregnant. A mother is willing to endure any degrading treatment if it means that no harm will be done to her children. These children are even occasionally separated from their mothers and looked after by another woman who is a member of the criminal group, which allows the mothers to be able to see their children from time to time.

There is a further reason why minors are used by criminal groups. This concerns using minors to enable the entrance and residence in Spain of the women who generally come from Africa, what the Attorney General's Office has called "niños ancla" ("anchor children") (Spanish Attorney General, 2018). These are children who are used by women who are not their biological mothers as if they were theirs when they move to Spain in order to facilitate their entry and their residence in the country, since they are sent to special protection and reception centres, and thus avoid deportation. After a few days, the women escape from the centre with the children, before much data can be collected regarding the situation of those minors.

Lastly, we have to examine where we can find those girls who are trafficking victims and who are being sexually exploited. What we can assert is that they form part of the most concealed and dark sphere of prostitution. Therefore, it is obvious that it will prove unlikely to find underage girls in public hostess clubs or brothels. The location of these girls will overwhelmingly be in private apartments and houses. In some cases, they may also be found working on the streets, above all when they can pass for being older (girls of sixteen or seventeen years of age who can be confused for eighteen- or nineteen-year-old women). But if a girl can clearly be identified as being a minor, the criminal groups will tend to keep her hidden (in the apartments where the police cannot make inspections as they do in the brothels or on the street, where they can also be detected by aid workers). The method of contacting with clients is online. Through these contacts, the criminal group organizes the meeting of this "client-paedophile" with the minor in the apartments that the network has for these purposes (Europol, 2018).

Identification and protection of child trafficking victims

Identification is one of the greatest difficulties we face when it comes to fighting against the trafficking of minors. We must state that in the case of Spain, this identification can only be made by the National Police.

The main problem in identifying minors is the absence of identity papers that would enable us to establish their age. Most of them come to Spain without papers. There is another group that brings documentation but this is forged in their country. Moreover, in all cases the minors lie about their age, hiding their real age, following the instructions they have been given by the criminal groups, identifying themselves as adults when in reality they are children. Lastly, even in the event that a minor identifies herself as such, the Spanish authorities do not trust her word if there are no official papers with which to check it, because they consider that declaration could be a deception in order to take advantage of the condition of being underage so as to be able to enter into Spain more easily.

When no reliable documentation exists that can prove the girls' age, and the authorities doubt or do not know the age of the possible minor, a medical examination – known as an osteometric test – is conducted to be able to determine it. However, the reliability of this test is questionable, since its margin of error is very high (around two years), and neither does it take into account the cultural variables of development that should be considered. Hence we could be identifying an adult of eighteen years of age as a minor of sixteen. We propose that a more holistic method be used to determine the age of possible minors, in which the psychosocial reports are just as or more important than the medical tests (Defensor del Pueblo, 2011; Meneses, Uroz, Rua, Gortazar & Castaño, 2015; Escorial, Marcos & Perazzo, 2016).

The fact that only the police are qualified to determine the identification of victims can also be a problem and perhaps an explanation of the low identification figures in Spain. Firstly, the criteria for determining what a victim is are much more restrictive for the police than for the NGOs that work with them. There are victims identified by the NGOs who have not been done so by law enforcement in Spain. We should also be aware that the objectives set by the different entities that intervene with victims are different. The main objective of the police is the prosecution of crime and obtaining a formal complaint by the victim, whereas for the social entities (NGOs) the main aim is above all to assist and recover victims. In this regard, it would be more advisable for the identification of victims not to be exclusively the concern of the police; rather, it would make more sense if the identification were carried out by other types of social agents. In fact, among the recommendations that GRETA (2018) makes for Spain regarding the identification of minors, it has stated that it would be advisable for social workers and other agents to be enabled alongside police. Furthermore, the Spanish authorities were requested to improve the identification of victims by adopting a more proactive approach, and at the same time to strengthen and make use of multiple agencies and not only the police, in the process of decision making that leads to the formal identification of victims.

However, the efficient progress that has been made with certain problems related to identification must be pointed out. This concerns the case of "anchor children". To prevent this huge problem in Spain, identification with DNA tests is required to prove the parentage of the supposed parents who cannot truthfully prove that they are. On many occasions this DNA test has been able to reveal the trafficking of minors (Cembrero, 2013).

Lastly, we must discuss the measures of protection of the minors who are identified as trafficking victims. This protection is carried out by the "public system of child protection", which, in Spain, depends on each autonomous community because it is a decentralized competence, and managed, therefore, by the communities and not by the national government.

One of the most significant difficulties of the way Spain's system of child protection functions is the proceedings that take place with the children of female victims of trafficking. Often the system, in its mission to protect possible minors in situations of risk, remove them from their mothers' custody, because when they intervene with a woman they do not see a victim of trafficking but a woman who is working as a prostitute and a child who is in a situation of risk due to being in her care. Even when the women enter the public system by reporting the abuse of their children by the criminal networks, the professionals doubt their word because they believe that it is the mother who mistreats her child and is seeking an excuse to cover her behaviour.

Even accepting that the woman is a trafficking victim, the standpoint of the Spanish authorities is that this fact places the child in a situation of neglect. Thenceforth the administrative process of removing custody is fraught with irregularities and many of these women spend years separated from their children and some never get them back (Women's Link Worldwide, 2017).

Therefore, the children born to potential trafficking victims should also be considered trafficking victims in order to guarantee their effective protection and so as not to violate the rights of these women who, on top of finding themselves in a situation of exploitation, are revictimized by a public system that is supposed to protect them but instead takes away what they prize most in their lives.

In the case of minors who come alone, without identity papers and without any references from family figures, for their protection they are taken to reception centres or child protection centres. When finding minors who have been identified as trafficking victims, the first difficulty we might encounter is the organization of our system itself. In order to guarantee the safety of victims, the girls have to be relocated from one autonomous community to another in order to prevent their being found by the criminal organizations.

However, these powers in Spain are decentralized. When a minor has to be protected, it is always done in the Autonomous Community where they have their residence. Therefore, in the cases of child trafficking victims, in order to be able to carry out this possible relocation, a series of significant administrative difficulties need to be overcome.

A second major difficulty concerns the safety of these minors in the protection centres. The reception centres are not designed to protect the victims of organized crime, and therefore they do not provide sufficient guarantees to protect a minor identified as a trafficking victim. In fact, many of the victims who enter these centres disappear within a few days (Castaño & Pérez, 2017).

The last major difficulty that we observe also concerns the problem of fulfilling the objective of protecting and recovering these minors in these centres. The Framework Protocol for the Protection of Victims of Human Trafficking states that minors should be referred to specialized resources. In Spain, there are not enough specialized resources for child trafficking victims. In our case, we are sending them to non-specialist protection centres for minors in situations of risk. These protection centres are designed for a group of minors with a series of needs that are completely different to those of a child trafficking victim. The protection centres take in minors with vulnerable family situations. But these children have not been through the dramatic situations that a girl who has been trafficked and sexually exploited by a criminal group has experienced. What is evident is that child trafficking victims need specialized psychosocial care, and non-specialist child centres are not able to provide this (Escorial, Marcos & Perazzo, 2016).

Conclusions

Trafficking in people is one of the most lucrative businesses that exist for criminal groups. The evolution of the business of trafficking networks shows us how to a greater extent minors are trafficked for the purpose of sexual exploitation, a tragedy that above all affects girls.

For these criminal groups, girls are a group they can manipulate with greater ease and from whom they can gain greater profits than those they obtain with trafficked women. On occasion these girls are also used by criminal groups as a form of blackmail, extortion or pressure in order to keep their mothers controlled and ensure that they pay the debt they owe them.

The authorities must learn about the new methods of recruitment, transport and sexual exploitation that the networks carry out with minors. The shift of sexual exploitation to apartments and the use of the internet and social networks as forms of business make it much more difficult to detect and protect these girls.

Despite the effort made by Spain in the fight against the trafficking of children, we must continue to advance in those aspects that we need to improve, above all in the identification and protection of these minors.

What is being demanded from many spheres and by all agents involved in this issue is the creation of a comprehensive Law against the Trafficking of Human Beings that approaches the fight against trafficking with the perspective of human rights, and, at the same time, that the Spanish state increase the resources aimed at child trafficking victims, who still do not have specialized resources in this country that effectively guarantee their protection.

BIBLIOGRAPHY

Apramp. 2016. *A pie de calle. Actuaciones con menores víctimas de trata.* https://apramp.org/download/a-pie-de-calle-actuaciones-con-menores-victimas-de-trata/

Defensor del Pueblo. 2012. *La trata de seres humanos en España: Victimas invisibles.* Madrid. Defensor del Pueblo.

Defensor del Pueblo. 2011. *¿Menores o adultos? Procedimientos para la determinación de la edad.*Madrid. Defensor del Pueblo.

Dunkerley A. 2017. Exploring the use of juju in Nigerian human trafficking networks: considerations for criminal investigators. *Police Practice and Research.*http://dx.doi.org/10.1080/15614263.2017.1347786

Castaño, M., Pérez, A. (2017).*Son niños y niñas, son víctimas. Situación de los menores de edad víctimas de trata en España.* Cuadernos para el Debate nº 5, UNICEF. Huygens Editorial. Barcelona

Cembrero, I. (23 November 2013). El ADN revela trata de menores en la inmigración irregular a España. *elpaís.com* https://elpais.com/politica/2013/11/23/actualidad/1385215186_381614.html

Dominguez, I. (26 February 2020). Hay prostitución de menores tuteladas en toda España. *elpaís.com* https://elpais.com/sociedad/2020/02/25/actualidad/1582626784_357382.html

Escorial, A., Marcos, L. and Perazzo, C. 2016. *Infancias Invisibles.* Save the Children España. Madrid

European Commission.2018. *Data collection on trafficking 2018 in human beings in the EU.*Ed. European Union. Belgium.

Europol. 2018. *Criminal networks involved in the trafficking and exploitation of underage victims in the European Union*. The Hague.

Fernandez, R. (7 April 2019). Unas "mamis" de las que no caminar de la mano. *La verdad.es.* https://www.laverdad.es/murcia/mamis-caminar-mano-20190407000721-ntvo.html?ref=https:%2F%2Fwww.google.com%2F

Fiscalía General del Estado. Unidad de extranjería. 2017. *Diligencias de Seguimiento del delito de Trata de Seres Humanos.* https://www.fiscal.es/documents/20142/68753488-1551-7260-2ec2-cebcfa82297c

Fiscalía General del Estado. Unidad de extranjería. 2016. *Diligencias de Seguimiento del delito de Trata de Seres Humanos*. https://www.fiscal.es/web/fiscal/-/extranjeria?cat=36759

Fiscalía General del Estado. Unidad de extranjería. 2015. *Diligencias de Seguimiento del delito de Trata de Seres Humanos*. https://www.fiscal.es/documents/20142/84f83e04-f54e-cf3b-8e42-f27966d90db6

Fiscalía General del Estado. Unidad de extranjería. 2014. *Diligencias de Seguimiento del delito de Trata de Seres Humanos*. https://www.fiscal.es/documents/20142/358f9dbb-ad31-8115-a237-a9016811b64c

Fiscalía General del Estado. Unidad de extranjería. 2013. *Diligencias de Seguimiento del delito de Trata de Seres Humanos*. https://www.fiscal.es/web/fiscal/-/extranjeria?cat=36759

Fiscalía General del Estado. Unidad de extranjería. 2018. Recopilación de conclusiones de las jornadas de fiscales delegados de extranjería sobre menores (años 2009- 2018). https://www.fiscal.es/documents/20142/160400/Recopilaci%C3%B3n+conclusiones+menores+2009-2018.pdf/db37b186-8897-2a85-e108-dcaf64936774?version=1.1

FRONTEX. 2018. *Risk analysis for 2018*. Warsaw. https://frontex.europa.eu/publications/risk-analysis-for-2018-aJ5nJu

Fundació Surt. 2015. *La trata para la explotación sexual de mujeres rumanas en España*.http://www.adoratrius.cat/wpcontent/uploads/2016/09/Informe_trata_mujeres_rumanas_es.pdf

GRETA. 2018. *Report concerning the implementation of the Council of Europe Convention on Action against Trafficking in Human Beings by Spain*.Council of Europe. Strasbourg

Meneses, C., Uroz, J. and Rua, A. 2017. Flyers y anuncios de servicios sexuales en Madrid. *Revista Latina de Comunicación Social*, 72 (2), 145-164. DOI: 10.4185/RLCS, 72-2017-1158

Meneses, C., Uroz, J., Rua, A, Gortazar, C and Castaño, M.J. 2015. *Apoyando a las víctimas de trata*. Ministerio de Sanidad, Servicios Sociales e Igualdad. https://violenciagenero.igualdad.gob.

es/violenciaEnCifras/estudios/investigaciones/2015/pdf/Apoyando_Victimas_Trata.pdf

Proyecto EuroTraGuID. 2013. *Desarrollo de directrices y procedimientos comunes para la detección de víctimas de trata.* https://violenciagenero.igualdad.gob.es/otrasFormas/trata/detectarla/pdf/ManualDirectricesDeteccionTSH.pdf

Rodriguez, C. (11 March 2017). Desmantelada en Marbella una red de prostitución que vendía la virginidad de una menor. *Elmundo.es* https://www.elmundo.es/andalucia/2017/03/11/58c3e52ce2704e46698b45a9.html

Save the Children. 2018. *Piccoli schiavi invisibili.* https://resourcecentre.savethechildren.net/node/15103/pdf/piccoli-schiavi-invisibili-2018_2.pdf

UNDOC. 2004. *United Nations Convention against transnational organized crime and the protocols thereto*. United Nacions. New York

UNDOC. 2018. *Global Report on Trafficking in Persons*. United Nacions. New York

U.S. Department of State. 2019. *Trafficking in persons report*. Washington, D.C. www.state.gov/j/tip

Women's Link Worldwide. 2014. *La trata de mujeres y niñas nigerianas: esclavitud entre fronteras y prejuicios.* https://www.womenslinkworldwide.org/informate/publicaciones/la-trata-de-mujeres-y-ninas-nigerianas-esclavitud-entre-fronteras-y-prejuicios-1

Women's Link Worldwide. 2017. *Madres en las redes de trata. Derechos robados.* https://www.womenslinkworldwide.org/files/a0440874f5037bcc7d6e85aa26f4c76e.pdf

CHAPTER III

Efforts to Address Human Trafficking in East Africa: Developments and Challenges in Kenya, Tanzania and Uganda

Norah Hashim Msuya[1]

Introduction

Trafficking is a global problem, affecting every nation in the world. An estimated 600, 000 to 800, 000 individuals are trafficked across international borders, while millions more trafficked within their own countries each year (Conduct Science, 2020). Human trafficking badly affects individuals in all areas of their lives, as most of the time they are victims of physical, sexual and psychological abuse (Msuya, 2019). Manipulation, violence, torture, deprivation, economic exploitation and abusive working and living conditions take place at different stages of trafficking (Zimmerman et al, 2011). Victims are often traumatised, having been so badly injured that irreparable damage has been done (IOM, 2011). They become severely handicapped and may even die. (Zimmerman, 2006).Moreover, victims of trafficking are often subjected to secondary victimization (Msuya, 2017).

A lot has been done to address human trafficking at the international level. On 15th November 2000, the United Nations (UN) General Assembly adopted the Convention Against Organized Crime, which came into force on 23rd

1. Mzumbe University, Tanzania and Kwa Zulu Natal University, South Africa.

September 2003. In addition, the Protocol to Prevent, Suppress and Punish Trafficking in Persons, Especially Women and Children, known as the "Palermo Protocol", was adopted by the UN to supplement the 2000 Convention. Trafficking in Persons is defined by the Palermo Protocol as "the recruitment, transportation, transfer, harbouring or receipt of persons, by means of the threat or use of force or other forms of coercion or abduction, of fraud, of deception, of the abuse of power or of a position of vulnerability, or of the giving or receiving of payments or benefits to achieve the consent of a person being controlled by another person, for the purpose of exploitation. Exploitation includes, as a minimum, the prostitution of others or other forms of sexual exploitation, forced labour or services, slavery or practice similar to slavery, servitude or the removal of organs" (Article 3 (a)). The Palermo Protocol stipulates further that the use of any of the means described above renders consent by the victim irrelevant, and that the recruitment, transportation, harbouring or receipt of a child for the purposes of exploitations hall be considered "trafficking in persons" even if none of the means described are employed (Article 3 (a)).The Palermo Protocol provided a definition and a guideline for law reform in Africa. Kenya, Tanzania and Uganda have ratified the Palermo Protocol.

Another international instrument which addresses human trafficking is the UN Convention on the Rights of the Child (CRC)of 1990, which is the most widely ratified human rights convention dealing with the specific needs and rights of children. All East African countries have ratified it. The CRC provides specific rights to protection, namely protection from all forms of child abuse, neglect, exploitation and cruelty. Specific to trafficking are Articles 34 and 35 of the CRC, which require state parties to protect children from all forms of sexual exploitation and abuse and take all possible measures to ensure they are not abducted, sold or trafficked. The CRC provisions are augmented by the 2000 Optional Protocol on the sale of children, child prostitution and child pornography. The Protocol to the CRC provides a wide definition of "sale of children" that covers many constituents of child trafficking. Furthermore, the 1999 ILO Convention No.182 on the Prohibition and Immediate Action for the Elimination of the Worst Forms of Child Labour recognizes child trafficking as the worst form of child labour. Tanzania, Kenya and Uganda ratified the ILO Convention as shown in table III (a) below of the list of international instruments ratified by these countries.

TABLE III (A)

List of international Instruments Relating to Human Trafficking, Ratified by Kenya (KZ) Tanzania (TZ) and Uganda (UG).

INTERNATIONAL INSTRUMENT		KN	TZ	UG
ILO Convention 182, Elimination of Worst Forms of Child Labour	Ratification	x	x	x
Optional Protocol to the Convention on the Rights of the Child on the Sale of Children, Child Prostitution and Child Pornography	Signature	x	x	x
	Ratification, Accession (a)		X (a)	X (a)
Optional Protocol to the Convention on the Rights of the Child in Armed Conflict	Signature	x	x	x
	Ratification, Accession (a)	x	X (a)	X (a)
ILO Convention 29, Forced Labour	Ratification	x	x	X
ILO Convention 105, Abolition of Forced Labour	Ratification	x	x	X
African Charter on the Rights and Welfare of the Child	Ratification	x	x	X

Source: United State Department of State, Trafficking in Persons Report (2018)

At the regional level, in 1990 the former Organisation of Africa Union, now the African Union (AU), adopted The African Charter on the Rights and Welfare of the Child containing provisions relevant to combating child trafficking concerning adoption and exploitation. Article 24 of the CRC entails states taking appropriate measures to ensure that inter-city adoption and placement does not result in trafficking or inadequate financial gain for those who try to adopt a child. In addition, Article 29 of the CRC insists that governments must prevent children from being sold, trafficked or abducted, and from being used by kidnappers to beg on the streets.

Other regional efforts have been made to combat trafficking, including enactment of the East Africa Community Anti-Trafficking in Persons Bill of 2016 (EAC-CTIP), which provides a legal framework for the prevention of trafficking persons, the prosecution of perpetrators of such trafficking, the protection of the rights of victims of trafficking and the development of partnerships to co-operate in countering trafficking in the East African Community (EAC).In 2015, the EAC also passed a Resolution to address cross-border human trafficking, to ensure the coordination of an anti-trafficking framework in the region through the EAC-CTIP Bill, which adopted the same definition of human trafficking as the Palermo Protocol, as the objective of Section 3 of the Bill provides a legal framework for the prevention of trafficking, the prosecution of offenders and protection of the rights of victims, and Section 18 (3) recommends a 10-year prison sentence for those involved in human trafficking.

In addition to prosecuting perpetrators of human trafficking, Section 5 of the Bill makes "…corporate bodies, directors, managers, secretaries and other similar officers…" responsible for allowing human trafficking to occur through their negligence. While it specifically provides for the much-overlooked aspect of corporate responsibility for trafficking humans to exploit their labour, it does not cover trafficking for the purpose of conscription into the armed forces nor does not provide for the protection for those conscripted. Although the Bill adopted in 2016 offered a glimmer of hope for the end of human trafficking in the region, it still has significant gaps, the most significant being that no standards have been developed to implement it, a setback to regional cooperation on anti-trafficking. The bill still awaits assent by the East African Heads of State before it becomes law (Offia, 2020b). Human trafficking is recognized as a problem in African countries, with 60% of cases coming from West and Central Africa, and 40% from Southern and East Africa (Rickard, 2019: Africa Economic Development Institute, 2020).The law in Kenya, Tanzania and Uganda, where human trafficking is known to take place, has legally defined and recognized that trafficking in persons is a distinct crime (Offia, 2020b).

The purpose of this chapter is to examine what efforts are being made to address human trafficking in Kenya, Uganda and Tanzania to ensure that trafficking in persons is being effectively addressed. This social-legal study employed the case study method to analyse the responses of Kenya, Uganda and Tanzania to human trafficking, focusing on what steps they have been taking to combat human trafficking, and how effective they have been in preventing it. The chapter begins by discussing the forms of human trafficking that take place there and the victims involved. It then examines the states' obligation to prohibit and prevent human trafficking and identifies the key legislative and administrative measures that Kenya Tanzania and Uganda have taken to protect individuals from trafficking, and the effects of those measures. Finally, it makes suggestions on how best human trafficking can be addressed by these counties.

An Overview of Human trafficking in East Africa

Trafficking in persons has been a complex problem in East Africa for several years (IOM, 2008; Conduct Science, 2020), with Kenya, Tanzania and Uganda reported to be the major destination of those being trafficked as well as the origin (Musinguzi, 2017). They share borders and are surrounded by eight other countries, exposing them to various migration patterns in and out of the country. They join Sudan and Chad in hosting the largest number of refugees in Central and East Africa from the Democratic Republic of Congo, Rwanda and Burundi (Concern Worldwide, 2020). These refugees are often more vulnerable to being trafficked because of poverty and do not realise that it is a crime (Offia, 2020b). Trafficking persons in East Africa is often not only fuelled by the demand for cheap labour, but also by people's willingness to be exploited because of their desperate need to survive (Bello et al., 2020). Therefore, the problem of trafficking often does not begin with the traffickers, but with the circumstances that force victims to seek better living conditions in places that render them vulnerable to exploitation (Bello et al., 2020), which is different from the popular image of trafficked persons being kidnapped or coerced to leave their homes, as some people consciously make the decision to migrate for various reasons.

Two types of trafficking in persons are common in East Africa, internal and external human trafficking (IOM, 2008). Internal trafficking, which is domestic, takes place within a country, usually taking the form of moving people from rural areas to urban centres for exploitative work such as prostitution, forced domestic or factory work, drug peddling, working in plantations and construction companies, or being pick-pockets, barmen/women or waiters (Offia, 2020b). External human trafficking takes the form of moving people from one country to another for the purpose of exploitation, which is similar to the domestic form, but in greater proportion. The demand is greater, but so are the costs and implications. In the case of cross-border trafficking, this usually takes place between countries in the same region or neighbouring countries (Rickard, 2019), which are near, and so not much travelling is involved, although there are instances of continental and intercontinental human trafficking. The push and pull factors of human trafficking are two sides of the same coin, as the cause of one is often the consequence of the other. Thus, the push factor are circumstances or issues that drive or force people into accepting demands that render them susceptible to trafficking, while the pull factor is people's demand for cheap labour by offering a job to those in need, which is dehumanising and exploitative.

Push factors

The prevailing push factors that contribute to trafficking in persons in the eastern part of Africa include the lack of livelihood opportunities for different vulnerable groups, their economic situation, peer pressure, harmful cultural practices and personal and family characteristics (Bello et al., 2020; Conduct Science, 2020).Most trafficked persons are those who are already vulnerable and/or lacking options, due to their characteristics, as opposed to the dynamics in their communities. (ILO, 2006; Kamala et al., 2001). People's lack of livelihood opportunities forces them to leave home in search of a better life somewhere else, making them vulnerable to being captured by traffickers (Bello et al., 2020).

For instance, these victims maybe uneducated, homeless, living on the street, without the prospect of a job, or females and young girls thrown out of their family home due to an unplanned pregnancy (Adepoju, 2005, Pearson, 2003; UNICEF, 2003). Girls who drop out of school, those with poor performance or those who get into trouble are particularly vulnerable (Government of Tanzania, 2001). Some victims who have already been exploited are more vulnerable to being trafficked or re-trafficked (Fitzgibbon, 2003; ILO, 2006), such as domestic workers who are sexually abused by their employers and girls fleeing child marriages (Kamala et al., 2001).

Poverty is reported to be a major cause of trafficking, due to the destitution of parents and their optimistic belief that the promises made by traffickers will come true (Fong, 2004). It is further reported that most women work to provide an income for their families (Kamala et al., 2001). Parents and relatives facilitate the trafficking of their children when their means of making a living fail, in the belief that this will ensure that their children's needs are met (Adepoju, 2005). Women and girls have become more vulnerable as they have fewer livelihood options, they are less likely to have land and capital and they receive lower wages due to harmful cultural practices that discriminate against women (Msuya, 2017). Forced marriage, female genital mutilation and the subordination of women are reported to be amongst the reasons why women and girls are trafficked in Kenya, Tanzania and Uganda (Msuya, 2017), as well as the greed of those involved in human trafficking who want to make a quick profit. The perception that working in urban areas is less laborious and pays more than working in rural areas is widespread (Kamala et al., 2001). The fact that there are much fewer recreational and social opportunities in villages than in towns is another reason why potential victims of trafficking migrate.

As regards family characteristics, those whose families have disintegrated through death, leaving orphans and widows, or divorce, are reported to be more at risk of being trafficked (IOM, 2008).Orphans are more exposed to extreme poverty, putting pressure on them to drop out of school and find work, due to their inability to pay school fees (Adepoju, 2005). At times, due to the death of both parents, children are forced to migrate to live with relatives, who may not protect them from exploitation, although they are meant to care for them (IOM, 2008). Having a large family is also connected to children being trafficked, as they are forced to work to meet the family's economic needs (Adepoju, 2005), because the adults in the family cannot do this on their own (IOM, 2008). Illiteracy also plays a part, as less educated women are more frequently exploited because they have no other ways of making a living and little understanding of the urban way of life (Pearson, 2003).Children and women fleeing the violence they have experienced, with no friends or family to help them, are also regarded as vulnerable (IOM, 2008).

Pull factors

The pull factors of human trafficking in eastern Africa include, but are not limited to, the demand for cheap low-skilled labour, weak border control, economic disparities between developed and developing countries and the effect of globalization (Offia, 2020b). Employers attracted by cheap labour, which is more profitable than less or non-exploitive forms of labour, is considered a major factor. Internationally trafficked victims perceive themselves as irregular immigrants, coming from a different cultural context, which makes them more dependent on the trafficker (Fong, 2004).

Children are the most exploitable as they are less likely to have an adult advocating on their behalf for acceptable working conditions and reasonable pay, particularly for domestic work, and against sexual exploitation (Migiro, 2016). Often the one involved in exploiting is the victim's care giver, which enables the exploiter to take advantage of that position for economic gain (Adepoju, 2003).At the beginning, adult victims depend on the trafficker for accommodation after they have abandoned their resources to migrate and are unfamiliar with the new place (Offia, 2020b), giving the trafficker enormous power over them. In Kenya, Tanzania and Uganda people are trafficked for labour not only in illicit or informal industries but also in regulated types of work, such as in agriculture, mining and the service industry. (Adepoju, 2005; Fong, 2004; Pearson, 2003: USDOS, 2006).

Internal trafficking for domestic work is more prevalent than transnational trafficking in Kenya, Tanzania and Uganda (Pearson, 2003; Adepoju, 2005; Anti-Slavery/ANPPCAN, 2005; Fitzgibbon, 2003; Kibuga, 2000; UNICEF, 2003; United States Department of State, 2006), which is mostly facilitated by victims' friends, intermediaries or even family members, offering assistance with education or securing employment in town centres (Musinguzi, 2017). Underprivileged children from the countryside remain the most vulnerable to trafficking, with girls being more likely to be trafficked to become domestic servants, or sex workers, predominantly at tourist hubs and along the border (Musinguzi, 2017). The research done by UNICEF analysing the reasons behind the high demand for trafficked labour for domestic work, particularly in urban areas, found that working mothers usually need someone to care for their children while they are at work (UNICEF, 2006). The unavailability of low-cost and compliant labour in urban areas to meet the demand for domestic workers has created urban/ rural linkages, which facilitates a less formal type of trafficking for domestic labour (Rickard, 2019). In addition, young virgin girls from disadvantaged village families have been targeted by traffickers, who give their parents or relatives a small amount of money, so that entrepreneurs can have sexual intercourse with these girls, in the belief that having sex with a virgin will make their business prosper (Msuya, 2017).Girls from Uganda are reported to having been trafficked to the United Kingdom for domestic work, girls from Tanzania trafficked to the Middle East and Kenya (UNICEF, 2013), and girls trafficked from Kenyain Europe and North America for the same purpose (United States Department of State, 2006).

Tourism in the coastal regions of Mombasa and Zanzibar also contributes to women being trafficked to work there and subsequently to be sexually exploited (IOM, 2018), due to the existence of unregistered employment agencies, which are also involved in recruiting children from the countryside to work as domestic helpers, where they are subject to exploitation. Adults and children are reportedly being trafficked to other countries within and outside East Africa, including South Africa, Mozambique, Ethiopia, the United Arab Emirates (UAR), Yemen, Saudi Arabia, Oman, Pakistan, China, the United Kingdom, France, the United States and Italy (Offia, 2020). Tanzania has become an attractive destination for those involved in human trafficking due to its stability and its need for forced labour for the mining, agricultural and domestic service sectors. Children are trafficked from Uganda, Kenya, Bangladesh, India, Nepal and Yemen for this reason, and adults are sometimes smuggled in to be sex workers (Obe, 2017).Corruption is considered to be one of the factors fuelling human trafficking in East Africa. Government officials have been reported to turn a blind eye once they have been bribed and supply travel documents, or they demand sex with victims before helping them, and may even be part of a trafficking gang (Obe, 2017), which shows that the demand for sex by people in authority is probably much higher than the need to traffic people to cater for sex tourism in Kenya and Tanzania. In Kenya the demands of the sex industry are huge to the point of pulling women from Sudan, Uganda, Ethiopia and South Asia (United States Department of State, 2006).

On top of that, the army in Kenya is alleged to have trafficked women to provide sexual services for the soldiers (UNICEF, 2005), which is reported to have be done by the British Army stationed close to Nanyuki (UNICEF, 2005). The longstanding conflict between the Ugandan People's Defence Force and the Lords Resistance Army (LRA) has led to a considerable demand for trafficked labour for military service in the region. Although much of this work is for combat duties, the sexual servicing of soldiers and military support personnel is also greatly demanded. The LRA has been condemned for the abduction of children from northern Ugandan, South Sudan and the Democratic Republic of Congo, as well as for the violent means it uses to control its soldiers, many of whom are children, which is a flagrant abuse of their human rights (ILO, 2006). The People's Defence Force has also been reported to have force fully recruited children (Human Rights Watch, 2003).

Other forms of exploitation in East Africa are not viewed exclusively in terms of labour, because women are demanded as "wives" (Pearson, 2003). The traditional practice of forced marriage, involving women or girls migrating to join their new husband, is considered a form of trafficking (Msuya, 2017). Victims of human trafficking are alleged to be used in ritual practices in the region as a whole, but particularly in Kenya (Msuya, 2017: Fitzgibbon, 2003).These practices involve religious leaders, who are reported to use trafficked victims for labour and to use their organs for ritual purposes. (Msuya, 2017).

Measures taken by Kenya, Tanzania and Uganda to combat Human trafficking

Kenya, Tanzania and Uganda have specific anti-trafficking laws. However, combating trafficking is still a challenge due to the ineffective implementation of policies and lack of capacity, even when the legislation is in place (USDOS, 2016). The combination of lack of political will, institutional corruption, and a range of underlying perennial socio-economic problems that these countries are confronted with, have made the fight against human trafficking almost unwinnable (IOM, 2018). Furthermore, trafficking remains under-reported, due to the low level of awareness of citizens of what constitutes trafficking.

The 2019 Global Trafficking in Persons Report released annually by the United States Department of State (USDOS) ranked Kenya, Uganda in Tier 2 while Tanzania on the Tier 2 Watch List. The annual ranking of countries by USDOS, done latterly by the UN Office on Crime and Drugs, is an important source of data on trafficking and a powerful incentive for policy and legislative implementation, as well as modification, in the world. The report usually places countries in one of four tiers, based on the extent of their governments' efforts to comply with the minimum standards for the elimination of trafficking found in Section 108 of the United States Trafficking Victims Protection Act (TVPA) of 2000. Tier 1 is the highest rank, indicating that a government meets the minimum standards provided under Section 108 of TVPA. A country with a Tier 2 rating has not met these standards, but has made significant efforts to do so, followed by Tier 3, which is similar to Tier 2 except that the number of victims trafficked has increased significantly. The last and worst rank is Tier 4, which indicates that a country has not met the minimum standards to eliminate human trafficking, and is not making significant efforts to do so. The 2019 Report places Rwanda on Tier 2 while South Sudan and Burundi are on Tier 3.

Kenya

Reports indicate that Kenya is the more likely destination of trafficked persons in the region than Tanzania and Uganda (RMMS., 2013). Kenya is the main destination of men, women and children trafficked for the purposes of forced labour and sexual exploitation (TIPR, 2019), because it borders Somalia, Ethiopia, South Sudan, Uganda and Tanzania, where the victims are known to come from (TIPR, 2019). Girls and boys are trafficked for commercial sex in the country, especially for sex tourism in Nairobi, Kisumu and on the coast (Offia, 2020b: Kaunga, 2008). Children are also trafficked for sex with people working in areas where mild narcotics are cultivated, in gold mines in western Kenya, by truck drivers on major highways and by fishermen around Lake Victoria (Offia, 2020b).

Legal and illegal employment agencies have been recruiting Kenyans for the United States, Europe, southeast Asia, Lebanon, Saudi Arabia, Qatar, Kuwait, Oman and the UAE (HAART, 2015). Some voluntarily migrate to those places in search of employment, where at times they are exploited in brothels and massage parlours, as domestic slaves, or forced manual labourers (Musinguzi, 2013). Internally displaced persons, living near local trading centres and major highways, are considered to be more vulnerable to trafficking than those living in settled areas (Musinguzi, 2013). Illegal agencies based in Nairobi maintain networks in Uganda and Ethiopia that recruit Rwandan, Ethiopian and Ugandan workers through fraudulent employment offers in the Middle East and Asia (USAID, 2009). The security situation of Kenya's biggest refugee camp, Dadaab, hosting approximately 230, 000 refugees and asylum-seekers, often prevents access by those seeking to provide humanitarian assistance and protection (Daghar, 2020). Some children from Dadaab and Kakuma refugees camps are reported to have been subjected to sex trafficking, and others taken from the camps and forced to work in other places (Crisp, 2000).

A lot of research has reported that poverty, corruption and unemployment are the major reasons why human trafficking continues to persist in Kenya, despite various interventions having taken place (Daghar, 2020: Musinguzi, 2013: USAID, 2009), followed by the ignorance of citizens, advanced technology which helps recruitment, existing laws being too lenient on perpetrators, Kenyans being greedy for money, poor implementation of existing laws, trafficking being a lucrative business, porous border points, the high demand for labour in developed countries and the high illiteracy level of Kenyans. Kenya passed the Trafficking in Persons Act No. 8 of 2010 (CTPA), which came into force in 2012. Prior to this, other laws were relied upon to address claims of the perpetration of crimes of this nature, such as sections of the Penal Code of 1948 (Cap 63), Sexual Offences Act, 2006 (Cap 62 a) and Children 's Act, 2001 (Cap 141), which partially address the issue. The CTPA regards trafficking as 'transporting, transferring, harbouring or receiving another person for the purpose of exploitation' (CTPA, Section 3:1), while exploitation is specified as keeping people in a state of slavery and forced labour with or without their consent. The CTPA provides for a stagnant penalty for the offence of human trafficking (CTPA, Section 2). The offender is liable to be imprisoned for a term of not less than 30 years or to a fine of not less than Ksh. 30 million, or both, and upon subsequent conviction to imprisonment for life. The Sexual Offences Act also imposes severe penalties with regard to trafficking in persons (USDOS, 2019).

Kenya also passed the Victims Protection Act No. 17 of 2014, which states that the purpose of combating human trafficking is to punish traffickers, to protect victims, and to prevent trafficking from occurring. The Act was passed with the main aim of providing protection for victims of such crimes. It seeks to provide victims with better information and support concerning reparation, compensation, special protection for vulnerable victims, and connected purposes. Section 5 of the Victim Protection Act specifically provides for the special protection of victims. However, the issue is that no government structure has been put in place to pursue this goal (USDOS, 2019), which has led to the lack of prosecution of cases as most victims fear for their safety (Musinguzi, 2013). The Victim Protection Act gives victims' advocates the right to address the court and introduce new evidence if the prosecutor does not do so (Section 9 (1)a). This is very weighty for trafficking cases, as it strengthen the prosecution's case. Before operation of the anti-trafficking legislation, advocates representing victims used to sit in court as silent observers (watching brief) and prosecutions were led by police officers, who were reported to be less legally proficient than the victims' advocates (Musinguzi, 2013).

Although the CPTA became law in 2012, there have been very few successful prosecutions because of the high threshold of evidence required to obtain a conviction (Daghar, 2020). Despite the Act providing for such severe penalties upon prosecution and conviction, it seems to have loopholes allowing trafficking in persons to take place (USDOS, 2019). The Act permits a fine in lieu of imprisonment for sex trafficking, apenalty which is not commensurate with that of other serious crimes, such as rape (Daghar, 2020). In addition, sections 14 and 15 of Kenya's Sexual Offences Act of 2006 criminalized the facilitation of 'child sex tourism' and 'child prostitution' and stipulates punishment of no less than 10 years' imprisonment, apenalty that is satisfactorily stringent and corresponds with that provided for other severe offences, such as rape. Chapter 3 of Kenya's Constitution states that a child found in Kenya under eight years old of an unknown nationality is considered a citizen. This has arguably provided a loophole for children to be smuggled into the country at a young age (USDOS, 2019).

For implementation purposes the Act established an Advisory Committee (AC) with the primary function of advising relevant areas of government on activities aimed at combating trafficking and the implementation of preventive, protective and rehabilitative programmes for trafficked persons (Sections 19 & 20). The second AC was reconstituted and gazetted in September 2018 following the end of the first term of the AC, as stipulated in the Counter-Trafficking in Persons Act (Section 19:3). The AC is in charge of coming up with and implementing the national plan of action. The Counter-Trafficking in Persons Act resulted in amendments being made to sections of the Penal Code, the Sexual Offences Act 2006 and the Children Act, 2001 that touch on trafficking (Second Schedule). The AC established the National Plan of Action (NPA) for Combating Human Trafficking and Strategic Framework 2013-2017.

The central aim of this plan of action was to create a national atmosphere of co-operation between national, regional and international stakeholders (NPA, 2017) The plan adopted an approach that involved three measures, the prevention of human trafficking, the protection of the victims and the prosecution of perpetrators through implementing the legal mechanisms (NPA, 2017). The strategy for prevention implemented by the NPA included raising public awareness through campaigns, building the capacity of criminal justice practitioners and reducing fraudulent employment opportunities by monitoring and assessing employment agencies (NPA, 2017). The Ministry of Labour, Social Security and Services also assigned labour attaches to Kenyan missions in Qatar, the UAE and Saudi Arabia to protect citizens employed in these countries (RMMS, 2013).

On the protection side, the NPA adopted a strategy aimed at dealing with rescue, reintegration and rehabilitation. The strategy adopted for protection included printing and disseminating national guidelines for identifying victims, and conducting a national mapping exercise to identify all existing support services available to trafficked persons (HAART, 2015). The NPA is also building the capacity of service providers and other relevant stakeholders, and assessing their education and training needs (HAART, 2015). Training will be given on the methods for combating human trafficking, and experts will be deployed in vulnerable areas or hot spots to identify possible victims and perpetrators of trafficking (HAART, 2015).

Apart from prevention, protection and prosecution, the NPA also aimed to make available the data needed to make reports, to get the Kenya National Bureau of Statistics to incorporate indicators of trafficking in household surveys, and to conduct primary and secondary research on human trafficking in the country. The government has subsequently reviewed the NPA. In recent years, it established the Counter-Trafficking in Persons Secretariat to coordinate and carry out anti-human trafficking activities in Kenya on behalf of the AC (Stop the Traffik, 2016). In 2015, the secretariat, together with the AC, developed the National Referral Mechanism guidelines (NRM), which seek to coordinate a multi-agency response to trafficking in persons in the country. The NRM has been disseminated to and piloted in many counties. Kenya has also established a special police unit to handle human trafficking and to vet public officers handling human trafficking matters UNICEF, 2005). Furthermore, the government has made efforts to curb corruption and create jobs for youths as a solution to the challenges faced in preventing and combating human trafficking in the country (Odhiambo, 2016). Other measures taken by the government to eliminate trafficking include introducing strategic checkpoints for verifying documents, banning travelling at night and to certain destinations, and establishing a fund to empower youth, such as the Uwezo fund (Odhiambo, 2016).

Apart from government efforts, a number of NGOs are operating in the country to support the combating of trafficking, including the Awareness against Human Trafficking organization (HAART), which has focused on preventing trafficking through raising awareness, prosecuting trafficking offenders and protecting victims of human trafficking since 2010. The African Network for the Prevention and Protection of Child Abuse and Neglect (ANPCANN) is another NGO that engages local communities in the fight against human trafficking. It was established in 2007, operating as an anti-child trafficking project mainly in Ethiopia, Kenya, Tanzania and Uganda. In 2015, the Federation of Women Lawyers Kenya (FIDA) established a network with the Women in Law East Africa (WLEA) and the Association of Media Women in Kenya (AMWIK) to help combat trafficking in persons. The network grew to incorporate government ministries, civil society organisations, international organisations and embassies (Stop the Traffik, 2016).

Tanzania

Over the past five years, Tanzania has been reported to be a source, transit and destination country for adults and children trafficked for sex and forced labour, although mainly taking place internally rather than externally (Prefworld, 2018). Tanzania is reported to be leading in terms of the number of victims trafficked in East Africa, as more than 350, 000 people were trafficked internally and externally, and is ranked 33rd out of 167 countries on the list of notorious countries with respect to human trafficking (Kamazima, et al., 2018). In 2008, Tanzania adopted the Anti-Trafficking in Persons Act to combat human trafficking, which mandated stricter investigation and prosecution, and afforded protection to victims of trafficking. This law mirrors much of the UN Protocol, but with a more comprehensive definition of trafficking and specific measures for protecting victims. Before this Actwas made law, Tanzania had no laws specifically criminalizing human trafficking, but this Act criminalizes all forms of trafficking with a sentence of one to 20 years' imprisonment or a fine of five million to one hundred and fifty million shillings, depending on the particular trafficking offence (Section 4:3).

Section 4 (1f) of the Act outlaws coercing, recruiting, and transporting a person by any means "for the purpose of prostitution, pornography, sexual exploitation, forced labour, slavery, involuntary servitude or debt bondage", making these acts a crime. A person may also be guilty of a trafficking offence if he/she"promotes, procures or facilitates the commission of trafficking in persons as per Section 5 (1), which includes creating or distributing "unissued, tampered with or fake certificates, registration or stickers of any government agency" or renting or sub-renting any "house, building or establishment for the purpose of trafficking in persons."Furthermore, the Act establishes "severe trafficking" crimes involving the trafficking of more vulnerable victims, such as the disabled or children, for sexual or labour exploitation, and offences committed by crime syndicates, groups of two or more persons, religious leaders, or other authority figures (6:2).The Act imposes heavier penalties for second-time offenders or criminals involved in multiple trafficking (Section 13).

Tanzania's anti-trafficking law enforcement has improved significantly since the police were given new training and the government generously funded their Anti-Human Trafficking Unit, and due to the increased awareness of trafficking of those enforcing the law (USDOS, 2017).The government has also incorporated information in the standard law enforcement training curriculum on how traffickers target vulnerable victims (USDOS, 2019). With the support of NGOs, the government has trained law enforcers, such as magistrates, judges, prosecutors, police officers, social welfare officers and immigration officers, on anti-trafficking measures (Musinguzi, 2017).Staff of the Anti-Human Trafficking Unit appeared on television and were heard on the radio, talking about human trafficking, and they distributed booklets. These awareness-raising efforts have resulted in a significant increase in the number of leads received by the Unit since 2007.

The Tanzanian police also collaborated with Interpol to locate a Tanzanian victim of trafficking, suspected to be in South Africa, using newly acquired cell phone technology.

Moreover, several government agencies conduct periodic inspections of large employers to detect cases of forced labour in Tanzania mainland and Zanzibar. In 2001, the Ministry of Labour, Employment, and Youth Development (MOL) suspended the registration of all labour recruitment agencies, requiring them to reapply and be properly vetted. In early 2018, the government suspended the travel documents of all departing Tanzanian migrant workers due to its concern over their safety abroad (USDOS, 2019).

This increased the vulnerability to trafficking of intending migrant workers who do not have the legal means to travel abroad for work. This suspension was modified later in the year so that migrant workers, who provided relevant training credentials, a contract with a salary, leave and health care provisions, would get a letter of permission and an exit permit from the MOL (USDOS, 2019). The government also requires employers abroad to deposit some form of security at the Tanzanian embassy in their country to ensure that they will be present when the migrant worker arrives so that the embassy can verify that the worker possesses the proper documents, including the contract and passport (Africa Economic Development Institute, 2020).

However, the Tanzanian law does not forbid all forms of human trafficking, and Zanzibar island, which is part of the country, has a separate legal code from mainland Tanzania (Mbalamwezi, 2016). On the mainland, traffickers can be prosecuted under the existing anti-trafficking statutes criminalizing the sale of humans, child labour, forced labour and various sexual offences, while in Zanzibar, traffickers can be prosecuted under the Penal Act, which outlaws slavery, abduction and kidnapping (Bureau of International Labour Affairs, 2017). Although Tanzania does not fully meet the minimum standards for the elimination of trafficking, which are monitored by the United Nations Office on Drugs and Crime, it is making significant efforts to do so (USDOS, 2019). It has adopted a new National Action Plan and is putting a lot of effort into prosecuting offenders. In partnership with international organizations, the government has facilitated several training sessions for law enforcement officials, including police officers and magistrates (Mbalamwezi., 2016). However, according to USDOS, 2019, Tanzania has neither effectively implemented its policy of identifying victims nor the provisions in the 2008 anti-trafficking law for protecting or repatriating them. It has not reported investigating any trafficking offences, it has convicted fewer traffickers than before, and offered convicted traffickers the option of a fine in lieu of imprisonment, which led to Tanzania being downgraded to Tier 2 on the Watch List (USDOS, 2019).

With regard to preventative measures, Tanzania has been making an effort to prevent trafficking by providing the Anti-Trafficking Secretariat (ATS) and anti-trafficking body with sufficient funds (USDOS, 2019). The Anti-Trafficking Committee, which oversees and directs the ATS, met twice during the reporting period. Although the new national action plan was to be put into effect from 2018-2021, this did not happen due to lack of funding. As regards protection measures, some notable efforts have been made to protect victims of trafficking in Tanzania, but more resources are needed to keep up the good work (Bureau of International Labour Affairs, 2018).The government mostly relies on NGOs to provide counselling, rehabilitation and shelter for victims of trafficking (Mbalamwezi, 2016). The Anti-Human Trafficking Unit changed the policy of requiring victims of trafficking to go to a police station to make a statement. Instead, a female police officer in casual clothes visits shelters to obtain the statements of victims of sex trafficking in a private setting (Musinguzi, 2017).The Unit has also recruited a female police sergeant to establish good relationships with female victims. In addition, the government has been facilitating the repatriation of Tanzanian victims of trafficking from Thailand, Nepal and India (USDOS, 2019).

With regard to prosecution, Tanzania's Anti-Trafficking in Persons Act criminalizes human trafficking for labour and sex, stipulating punishment of two to 10 years' imprisonment, a fine of five million to one hundred and fifty million shillings, equivalent of 2, 180 to $43, 570, or both, for offences involving adult victims. It also stipulates a sentence of 10 to 20 years' imprisonment, a fine equivalent to $2, 180 to $65, 360, or both, for offences involving child victims (USDOS, 2019).Although the penalties are stringent enough, stipulating a fine in lieu of imprisonment for sex trafficking does not match the penalty imposed for the serious crime of rape. Tanzania has been asked to consider eliminating the alternative sentence of a fine, but so far no progress has been made in amending this provision (USDOS, 2019).Furthermore, the anti-trafficking law contains a separate procedural provision that requires the police to obtain a warrant before arresting anyone for trafficking offences (Tonahet al., 2017). This provision hinders prosecution efforts as it takes much more time to enforce the law, but it does not apply to other serious offences.

Tanzania has not provided are port on the number of suspects that have been investigated, prosecuted and convicted of human trafficking offences. Officials complicity in trafficking offences have never being reported, while corruption within the judicial system is reported to be anon going challenge, impeding enforcement of the law (USDOS, 2019). With the support of an international organisation, Tanzania was able to devise a national centralized anti-trafficking data collection and reporting system, through which the government can upload information on traffickers' profiles and cases of victims, but the data entered are limited and are not shared (USDOS, 2019). The government has continued to include human trafficking components in standard police academy training, but did not report how many new recruits received this training during the reporting period (Musinguzi, 2017).

Tanzania is also reluctant to fund and facilitate the repatriation of foreign victims of trafficking, although required to do so by its anti-trafficking law (USDOS, 2019), which mandates the government to provide them with legal alternatives to their repatriation, if their safety or that of their families is endangered, but most of the time the government does not give them a temporary residence permit (USDOS, 2019). Although the Tanzania Protection Act of 2015 and Anti-Trafficking Act give victims of crime and trafficking the choice of whether or not to participate in prosecution efforts, trafficked victims have been expected to testify in trafficking cases without being given any protection as witnesses, which has deterred some victims from testifying in court, although trials are held in camera (USDOS, 2019).

Although the 2008 Anti-Trafficking Act stipulates that the police and immigration authorities must follow standard procedures for investigating cases of human trafficking and identifying victims, these have not been widely used due to the lack of funds for disseminating them (USDOS, 2019). This Act states that the government must provide victims with a temporary shelter and psycho-social counselling, and help them to be reunified with their family, but not every victim is given shelter (Musinguzi, 2017). Child victims are usually placed in special shelters and the government enrols them in government schools or vocational centres. Female adult victims are usually accommodated in a shelter dedicated to young girls, but no shelters are provided for adult men, and it is still unclear which ministry is responsible for assisting adult victims of trafficking (USDOS, 2019). Some embassies in Tanzania, such as the Oman embassy, provide temporary shelter for a number of migrant workers, as well as those who may have been trafficked. However, because Tanzania's immigration officials do not have a procedure for identifying and screening vulnerable people, they may detain or deport many victims of trafficking, charging them for immigrating illegally. For instance, in February 2019, it was reported that the government initiated the return of more than 2, 000 Ethiopians held in Tanzanian detention centres without having screened any of them to determine whether they were victims of trafficking (TIPR, 2019).

Uganda

Uganda is located at the middle of the African Great Lakes region and shares a border with Tanzania, Kenya, the Democratic Republic of Congo, Rwanda, Uganda and South Sudan. Uganda is a major destination for trade and tourism due to its centralized position in Africa (The Human Trafficking Institute, 2019), but is considered to be the largest refugee-receiving country in Africa (UNHCR, 2020), although it is making every effort not to be the source, transit and destination country of the vicious crime of trafficking in persons (Offia, 2020b).With a population of about 45 million people with an average age of 15.9, Uganda is regarded as having the lowest population globally (Offia, 2020b), but the lack of quality education, adequate employment opportunities and social welfare structures to adequately meet their needs leaves citizens, particularly those living in villages and settlement areas, vulnerable to trafficking (Kagumire, 2018: Atim, 2018). Refugees living in camps in northern Uganda and in settlements around Kampala are also a sitting target of trafficking networks (Women's Link Worldwide, 2018).

Ugandans are trafficked mostly to Oman, UAE, Saudi Arabia and Jordan, mainly for labour and sexual exploitation, while Uganda is a known route for the trafficking of East Africans, as well as Indians and Bangladeshis, who are trafficked to South Africa (The Human Trafficking Institute, 2019). Trafficked victims from East African counties are taken to Uganda for labour and sexual exploitation (Kagumire, 2018), while in Uganda, women, men and children are trafficked from the country side to towns like Kampala (USDOS, 2019).Children, both girls and boys, are largely trafficked from Karamoja in the north to large towns and exploited as peddlers, prostitutes and beggars (Kagumire, 2018: ECPAT International, 2013).

The growing economic disparity and lack of employment opportunities has also resulted in making the population vulnerable to the crime of human trafficking (Offia, 2020b). Youths seeking greener pastures migrate to the Gulf States to work as labourers, receptionists, security officers, construction workers, domestic staff and nannies (MISR, 2007), which puts them at risk of being exploited by traffickers. To protect its citizens, the Ugandan government introduced the Labour Externalization Programme to help Ugandans access safe, formal and regular pathways to employment abroad (Atim, 2018).Trafficking syndicates in Uganda frequently use intimidation and violence to constrain victims to work in their businesses or as commercial sex workers (New Vision, 2017). Apart from that, the indigence of people makes them vulnerable, a situation in which exploitation thrives (Daily Monitor, 2018).

In 2009, Uganda passed the Prevention of Trafficking in Persons (PTIP)Act, No. 7 prohibiting all forms of human trafficking (Igoye, 2019), and provides for the prosecution of offenders and protection of the rights of victims and survivors of trafficking. The USDOS Report indicates that, since the PTIP became law, the prosecution of offenders has noticeably improved from three prosecutions with only one conviction in 2009 to 50 prosecutions and 24 convictions in 2017 (USDOS, 2018). Nevertheless, the criminal justice system in Uganda has not been sufficiently prepared to deal with human trafficking, and so, because traffickers believe they are not at risk of going to jail, this encourages them to target victims (Offia, 2020b).

Numerous reports have indicated that Ugandans have been compelled to work as slaves on arrival at their destination, which at times leads to death (Uganda Police, Annual Crime Report, 2017: African Development Bank 2017: USDOS, 2019: International Labour Organisation). The Uganda Association of External Recruitment Agencies (UAERA) reported that there are over 150, 000 workers from Uganda in the Middle East, generating over $500 million per annum, which is remitted to their families back home (IOM, 2014).

Uganda has adopted comprehensive policies for refugees such as the Self-Reliance Strategy (SRS) and the subsequent Development Assistance to Refugee-Housing Areas (DAR) embodied in the 2006 Refugees Act and 2010 Refugees Regulations. The policies have many impressive aspects including, opening Uganda's door to all asylum seekers irrespective of their nationality or ethnic affiliation; granting refugees relative freedom of movement and the right to seek employment; providing prima facie asylum for refugees of certain nationalities, an giving a piece of land to each refugee family for their exclusive (agricultural) use. Nevertheless, the policies do not help reduce vulnerability to trafficking to Uganda Refugee (The World Bank, 2016). This is due to the underlying poverty and vulnerabilities exacerbated by weak basic social services delivery, poor infrastructure, and limited market opportunities in the refugee hosting settlement areas that impact refugees and host communities alike (The World Bank, 2016).

With the number of human trafficking cases continuing to increase, the government realised that prosecutors need to be enabled to see that justice is done, that traffickers are convicted and victims protected. It therefore embarked on training and building the capacity of government officials in the criminal justice system, sensitising the public, licensing and registering labour recruitment agencies, and entering bilateral agreements concerning labour with destination countries (Offia, 2020b). Although this was vitally important, little consideration was given to attending to the root causes of trafficking (Offia, 2020b), or providing victims with educational support, shelter, psycho-social care, or legal aid (The Human Trafficking Institute, 2019). Section 21 of the PTIP established the Coordination Office for the Prevention of Trafficking in Persons (COPTIP) to coordinate the counter-trafficking efforts of civil society organisations and the government. Since its establishment, the COPTIP has made considerable progress in combating trafficking, through creating and implementing a National Action Plan for the Prevention of Trafficking in Persons.

Notwithstanding the progress made in the development of ant-trafficking measures in Uganda, their implementation is limited, and the risk of people being trafficked still persists (Kagumire, 2018). Because a substantial number of government workers are not familiar with the PTIP law, children are still trafficked to work on the streets and Ugandans continue to leave the country to work in the Middle East (USDOS, 2019). This suggests that, although Uganda is making progress in combating human trafficking, more still needs to be done to eliminate trafficking in the country (Kagumire, 2018). Officials' involvement inhuman trafficking syndicates and corruption persists, constraining law enforcement. Security officers and ground-handling companies at Entebbe Airport, officers at Malaba border, and officials of the Civil Aviation Authority have been reported to be complicity in the trafficking of persons, but the government has remained silent on whether the officers involved have been held accountable (USDOS, 2019). In 2015, a Ugandan diplomat and his wife were reported to have committed labour trafficking and related crimes while in the US, but they could not be prosecuted or charged there due to diplomatic immunity. To date, the Ugandan government has not taken any action to hold the diplomat and his wife accountable (USDDOS, 2019).

Furthermore, the media alleged that police officers have been involved in trafficking children and women refugees. High-level officials, alleged to be involved with/or partially own some labour-recruiting companies suspected of trafficking persons, have in hibited law enforcement agencies from carrying out their operations. NGOs maintain that immigration officers at border crossings have facilitated the passage of trafficked victims, and several senior police officials in Kampala shielded traffickers from being arrested and prosecuted. In 2014, the Commissioner from the Ministry of Finance was charged with child trafficking and to date the government has not provided an update on the progress of his prosecution, as it is suspected that he has used various tactics to delay the trial, including intimidating witnesses.

It would appear that counter-trafficking measures in many African countries have been ineffective because most have focused on arresting, convicting and punishing offenders, which is a worthy cause (Offia, 2020a), but these measures do not address the root causes of the crime, and so proactive measures are needed to find a durable solution (IOM, 2018).

Recommendations

Based on the above observations and findings, the following recommendations are made.

Address Root Causes (Poverty and Unemployment)

Essentially, Kenya, Tanzania and Uganda need to improve their economy, as poverty is the major factor pushing human trafficking in these countries. Although the current worldwide Covid–19 pandemic will have an extensive impact on the global economy and even worse on developing counties like those in East Africa, this could be the perfect time for them to make a coordinated effort to clamp down on the trafficking of persons. The East African Bill needs to be revisited to consider the effects of Covid-19 on forced migration and migration for work, and its relationship with human trafficking, by adding provisions aimed at the eradication of human trafficking in the region.

It is estimated that Covid-19 will cause the loss of up to 195 million jobs globally, particularly in the informal sector in developing countries (Offia., 2020b).This will aggravate the already high level of poverty, unemployment and inequality in Kenya Uganda and Tanzania, leading to more people migrating looking for work. However, since borders have been closed and travel greatly restricted due to the pandemic, this may result in more irregular and clandestine migration routes being used, which could increase people's vulnerability to trafficking. Therefore, greater efforts need to be made now to reduce the level of poverty and unemployment to curb trafficking in persons, which should be aimed at building the capacity of the public, particularly those in low income areas, who are semi-literate and unemployed.

Since Kenya and Tanzania are home to several refugees like Uganda, the progressive approach to refugee management adopted by Uganda is recommended to Kenya and Tanzania to reduce refugees' vulnerability to trafficking. Polices, which promote free movement and right-to-work arrangements for refugees, enable refugees to contribute to local economies' social incorporation and development. With the underprivileged social-economic situation in African countries, a shift in refugee assistance philosophy is also crucial. Refugees should be viewed as economic actors in charge of their destiny, a development approach rather than as beneficiaries of aid a humanitarian approach. To ensure impact, the focus should be on trans formative investments that will address refugees and host communities' pressing needs, and that will jumpstart local economies. This will reduce poverty and mitigate the risk of human trafficking for vulnerable refugees and their host communities.

The idea of a Universal Basic Income (UBI), which has gained more attention in European countries, could have been an ideal solution to address poverty and unemployment as the primary root causes of trafficking in African countries. With a UBI, the government would give every adult the same fixed, monthly payment regardless of work status, health, or wealth (Minogue, 2018). However, economists have raised many weighty reasons to be cautious about UBI already (Minogue, 2018: Francese, M &Prady D, 2018). Among UBI's challenges is that it is offered as a solution to technological unemployment, but jobs are not disappearing; instead, work is changing (Francese, M & Prady D, 2018). Viewed by some as an alternative to work, UBI would shrink the labour force. By definition, a smaller labor force would mean lower economic output and lower tax revenues to invest in the future (Brooks, 2020). While UBI's motivation is admirable, it is not the right solution to the countries' core economic problem because of opportunity concentration (Francese, M & Prady D, 2018). Given the current economic circumstances of African counties, the governments may be even less willing to fund such a massive project in the face of overstretched budgets.

Enhance the internal and international coordination of stakeholders

Efforts to tackle human trafficking in East Africa must move out of conference rooms and focus directly on how to end this terrible crime. The EAU must prioritise multilateral anti-trafficking approaches. It must view trafficking in person as an urgent matter needing a region-wide approach to ensure that it is precluded, those at risk are protected, and offenders are prosecuted and convicted, which it could do by enabling collaboration and joint efforts, setting targets for member states, and encouraging mutual assistance. For this to happen, it is essential that a centralized regional and national anti-trafficking system is established for the collection and sharing of data that could be used by local and international agencies investigating, detecting and tracking those involved in trafficking.

Monitor and ensure proper enforcement of laws

East African countries have approached trafficking in persons mainly as a human rights concern rather than a criminal offence, diverting their efforts and attention from the criminal dimension (Daghar, 2020). More efforts need to be made to investigate, prosecute and convict trafficking offenders, including complicity public officials, and impose the appropriate penalty. The anti-trafficking laws should be amended to remove the sentencing provisions that allow fines in lieu of imprisonment, and the procedures pertaining to trafficking-related arrests should be aligned with those pertaining to other serious crimes.

Anti-trafficking legislation should also recognise trafficked persons as victims, who are entitled to the protection of their basic human rights. Laws on immigration, labour, health and child protection must be reviewed and amended to cover all aspects of trafficking, so as to provide a comprehensive framework for addressing this wickedness, which must then be enforced and their implementation monitored. Detection and investigation need to be improved through networking and collaboration among stakeholders, as corruption is rampant, hampering these efforts. Law enforcement officials need to be able to recognize trafficking when they see it because, if they do not, they may ignore a case or take inappropriate measures. Additional training needs to be provided at all levels of the government, particularly law enforcement officials, thereby enabling them to identify and respond to human trafficking issues. The remuneration of officials handling human trafficking issues should be improved so that they have no need to be corrupt.

Improvevictim protection

The protection provisions in the anti-trafficking legislation should be fully implemented by allocating resources to a fund for assisting victims. Training should focus on the proactive identification of potential victims, and the policies and procedures for referring victims to protective services should be made available to them. The establishment of an official process is needed, whereby law enforcers can refer trafficked victims to those in higher authority for assistance, which means that they need to be trained in how victims of trafficking can be best assisted. To achieve this, the governments would need to allocate a budget for anti-trafficking activities, and build a comprehensive framework aimed at preventing victimisation and re-victimisation, protecting those who have suffered, and prosecuting the criminals.

Increase oversight of local and overseas recruitment agencies

Governments should increase their oversight of local and overseas recruitment agencies and prosecute those involved in fraudulent labour recruitment. They also need to protect migrant workers more by raising employers' security deposits and removing recruitment fees charged to migrant workers. Before departure, it should be explained to migrant workers that they must obtain the approval of the embassy and a residence permit, which will help to minimize the risk of being exploited. A mutually enforceable standard contract should be established, a formal complaints mechanism for returning workers and a blacklist of abusive employers publicised. States must combat the factors contributing to migration, striving to provide for their citizens in ways that diminish vulnerability to trafficking, and to develop alternatives to the exploitation that at times is inherent in the demand for cheap labour and services. Governments must be vigilant in enforcing laws and monitoring activities so as to minimise the profits made from trafficking in persons.

The Protocol to the Forced Labour Convention, 1930, and the Forced Labour (Supplementary Measures) Recommendation, No 203 of 2014, confers governments and employers' responsibilities to protect workers from fraudulent and abusive practices. More specifically, the Protocol and Recommendation contain provisions aimed at "protecting persons, particularly migrant workers, from possible abusive and fraudulent practices during the recruitment and placement process" (Protocol, Article 2:d) and on the "promotion of coordinated efforts by relevant government agencies with those of other states to facilitate regular and safe migration and to prevent trafficking in persons, including coordinated efforts to regulate, license and monitor labour recruiters and employment agencies and eliminate the charging of recruitment fees to workers to prevent debt bondage and other forms of economic coercion" (Recommendation, Para 4:i). In line with these international laws, States should ensure that migrant workers who have experienced abusive and fraudulent recruitment practices or subsequent exploitation have access to justice and effective remedies such as compensations.

Sensitize the community and stakeholders on human trafficking

As a matter of urgency, the existing knowledge about human trafficking should be extended to making the public aware of this issue, as the extent to which they are aware that organized criminal groups are involved in trafficking and the dire fate of the victims is unclear. Many aspects of human trafficking remain poorly understood even though it is now a priority issue in many states. Information on the magnitude of this problem is still limited (Msuya, 2019). Knowledge about the intersection of migration and trafficking has not yet brought about a consensus on the underlying forces and their implications for the well-being of citizens. It so distressing that some victims probably do not press charges against the culprits because they do not know that they are in fact victims of human trafficking. Evidently, there is still not enough information to support a comprehensive action plan for addressing the different dimensions of the problem of human trafficking but educating the public about human trafficking should be the number one priority.

Conclusion

Human trafficking is a dynamic phenomenon with a range of interlocking forces, factors and processes. It would be erroneous to describe human trafficking essentially as an economic-cum-security issue, perhaps due to the factors that entrap people. It is one of the world's most serious transnational crimes and one of the most complex human rights challenges of our time. The prevalent forms of trafficking in Kenya, Uganda and Tanzania are labour exploitation, sexual exploitation, forced marriage and child trafficking. In East Africa, employment in countries for residents of other countries, and employment in other countries for residents, are amongst the most significant factors that push and pull people to enter in to situations where they are at great risk of being trafficked. Kenya Tanzania and Uganda have adopted numerous international legal instruments and guidelines aimed at ending human trafficking and protecting victims, but the challenge oft ran slating these instruments into national laws and ensuring their implementation remains. Several regulations and guidelines, including systems and procedures for a national referral mechanism, have been developed to strengthen the capacity of law enforcement agencies and the judiciary to protect victims and prosecute offenders.

Although the governments of Kenya, Tanzania and Uganda are committed to combating human trafficking, and have taken several steps to ensure that preventive and protective measures are in place, a number of challenges exist, particularly in relation to the economic situation in these countries. For example, their anti-trafficking legislation acknowledges only certain forms of exploitation or certain categories of victims, and it has also failed to be comprehensive in its approach, to address all aspects of trafficking, and to ensure the rights and protection of victims, particularly when prosecuting offenders is the main objective. Trafficking in persons will not be eliminated merely by establishing a penal and law enforcement regime. Criminalisation is imperative, but has not yet been achieved. A multi-pronged approach is needed, such as taking appropriate social and economic measures, which will address the root causes of migration and trafficking, such as poverty, economic disparity and unemployment.

REFERENCES

Adepoju, A. (2005). Review of research and data on human trafficking in Sub-Saharan Africa", in Laczko, F. and E. Gozdziak (eds), *Data and Research on Human Trafficking: A Global Survey,* Geneva: International Organization for Migration (IOM).

Africa Economic Development Institute, (2020) Human Trafficking in Africa, Retrieved from http://www.africaecon.org/index.php/africa_business_reports/read/77.

Atim, S. (2018). Human trafficking and sexual exploitation: Experiences of Ugandan male and female diasporic returnees in Kampala, Master Thesis, Makerere University.

Awareness Against Human Trafficking (HAART), (2015). *Human Trafficking in Kenya: Analysis of data obtained from victims,* Nairobi: HAART.

Bello, P.O. & Olutola A.A. (2020). The Conundrum of Human Trafficking in Africa *IntechOpen*, Retrieved from: https://www.intechopen.com/online-first/the-conundrum-of-human-trafficking-in-africa.

Brooks, J. (2020) "The Universal Income Grant: An old idea that may have a new impetus in South Africa." Daily Maverick : Retrieved form https://www.dailymaverick.co.za/article/2020-07-27-the-universal-income-grant-an-old-idea-that-may-have-a-new-impetus-in-south-africa/.

Concern Worldwide, (2020). The 10 Refugee Crises To Follow in 2020, *Concern Worldwide.* Retrieved from https://www.concernusa.org/story/largest-refugee-crises/

Conduct Science, (2020) Global Data on Human Trafficking Conduct Science. Retrieved from

https://conductscience.com/global-data-on-human-trafficking/.

Crisp, J. (2000) A State of Insecurity: The Political Economy of Violence in Kenya's Refugee Camps Vol. 99 (397) 601-632.

Daghar, M. (2020). Kenya's reforms are not protecting its people from trafficking Gaps in laws and their enforcement expose trafficking victims to a well organised criminal market. Institute for security studies (ISS) Retrieved from. https://issafrica.org/iss-today/kenyas-reforms-arent-protecting-its-people-from-trafficking.

ECPAT International, (2013). Global Monitoring: Status of action against commercial sexual exploitation of children-Uganda. 2nd Edition Retrieved from http://www.refworld.org/docid/53aab9e214.html.

Emser, M. (2015). Factors inhibiting the identification and investigation of human trafficking cases, *AfricLaw.* https://africlaw.com/2015/02/20/factors-inhibiting-the-identification-and-investigation-of-human-trafficking-cases/

Fitzgibbon, K. (2003). Modern-day slavery?The scope of trafficking in persons in Africa, African Security Review, 12 (1) 12 (1), 81-89.

Fong, J. (2004). *Review on trafficking in West and East Africa*, Global Alliance Against Traffic in Women, Bangkok.

Francese, M and Prady D (2018) "Universal Basic Income: Debate and Impact Assessment" International Monetary Fund, Working Paper No. 18/273 Retrieved from https://www.imf.org/en/Publications/WP/Issues/2018/12/10/Universal-Basic-Income-Debate-and-Impact-Assessment-46441.

Government of Tanzania, (2001). Tanzania National Plan of Action for Orphans and Other Vulnerable Children, Dar re salaam: The United Republic of Tanzania Prime Minister's office.

HAART, 'Human Trafficking in Kenya: Analysis of data obtained from victims', August 2015.

http://reporting.unhcr.org/sites/default/files/Uganda%20Country%20RRP%202019-20%20%28January%202019%29.pdf

Human Rights Watch, (2003).*Abducted and abused: Renewed conflict in Northern Uganda*, New York. Human Rights Watch.

Igoye, A. (2019). Fighting human trafficking, *The independent* Retrieved fromhttps://www.independent.co.ug/fighting-human-trafficking/.

International Organization for Migration (IMO) (2008), *Human Trafficking in East Africa: Research Assessment and Baseline Information in Tanzania, Kenya, Uganda and Burundi*. Geneva: IMO.

International Organization for Migration (IOM) (2018). Assessment report on the human trafficking situation in the coastal region of Kenya. Retrieved from

International Organization for Migration (IOM), (2014).*Labour Migration Management Assessment*.Uganda: IOM. Retrieved form https://publications.iom.int/books/labour-migration-management-assessment-uganda.

International Labour organisation (ILO), (2017) ILOactivities in Africa 2004–2006

Eleventh African Regional Meeting Addis Ababa, April 2007. Report of the Director-General.

Kamala, E. E., Lusinde, J., Millinga, J., Mwaitula, M.J., Gonza, M.G. Juma, et al. (2001). *Tanzania Children in Prostitution: A Rapid Assessment*, ILO-IPEC, Geneva.

Kagumire, R., (2018). Stranded in the Middle East: Uganda Must Do More to Prevent Trafficking.Heinrich-Böll-Stiftung. Retried form https://za.boell.org/en/2018/10/10/stranded-middle-east-uganda-must-do-more-prevent-trafficking.

Kamazima, R. S., Kazaura, M.R., Ezekiel M. J. & Kamazima A. C. (2018) Internal Trafficking in Persons in Tanzania: Qualitative Evidence from the Tanzania-Uganda Borderlands, Kagera Region. *BAOJ HIV*.4 (1).1-11.

Kaunga, J., (2008): *International Labour Organization;* Review of Existing Child Labour/ Initiatives. Experiences and Lessons Learned and Strategies for Further Interventions in Selected Pastoralists communities in Kenya. Kenya: Laikipia.1-35.

Labor Bureau of International Labor Affairs, (2018). Tanzania: Findings on the Worst Forms Of Child. US Department of Labor. Retrieved from https://www.dol.gov/agencies/ilab/resources/reports/child-labor/tanzania

Makerere Institute of Social Research, (2007). The magnitude of human trafficking in Uganda: a case study of major cities and towns in Uganda, Retrieved form https://opendocs.ids.ac.uk/opendocs/bitstream/handle/20.500.12413/5558/Makerere%20Institute%20of%20Social%20Research-MAK-res.pdf?sequence=1&isAllowed=y .

Mbalamwezi, T., (2016). International Obligation in Preventing Trafficking in Person: An Examination of the Anti- Trafficking Law In Tanzania. Masters Thesis, Mzumbe University.

Migiro, K., (2016). Human trafficking rife among displaced Kenyans, charity researchers say, Retrieved from http://af.reuters.com/article/topNews/idAFKCN0WO22I.

Minogue, R. (2018) "Five Problems with Universal Basic Income."*Thirdway.*Retrieved from https://www.thirdway.org/memo/five-problems-with-universal-basic-income.

Msuya, Norah Hashim (2017) Tradition and Culture in Africa: Practices that Facilitate Trafficking of Women and Children, *Dignity: A Journal on Sexual Exploitation and Violence:* 2 (1) 1-36.

Musinguzi, B. (2013). Human trafficking: The modern form of slavery eating up East Africa *Daily Monitor.* Retrieved from https://www.monitor.co.ug/Magazines/PeoplePower/Human-trafficking--The-modern-form-of-slavery-/-/689844/1974562/-/rj8l5s/-/index.html.

Musinguzi, B. (2017). Human trafficking: The modern form of slavery eating up East Africa, Retrieved from http://www.monitor.co.ug/Magazines/PeoplePower/Human-trafficking--The-modern-form- of-slavery-/-/689844/1974562/-/rj8l5s/-/index.html.

National Crime Research Centre (NCRC), (2015). *Human Trafficking In Kenya 4th DRAFT REPORT,* Nairobi: NCRC. Retrieved from http://crimeresearch.go.ke/wp-content/uploads/2018/05/Human-Trafficking-in-Kenya.pdf.

National Crime Research Centre 2015 Human Trafficking In Kenya 4th Draft Report. Retrieved form http://crimeresearch.go.ke/wp-content/uploads/2018/05/Human-Trafficking-in-Kenya.pdf.

Odhiambo, A.T., (2017). A Critique of the role of the Government in Combatting Human Trafficking in Kenya.Thesis, Strathmore University Law School.

Offia, F. (2020b). 20 Years After Palermo Protocol: Towards a stronger East African regional anti-trafficking framework. *Oxford Human Rights Hub*. Retrieve form http://ohrh.law.ox.ac.uk//20-years-after-palermo-protocol-towards-a-stronger-east-african-regional-anti-trafficking-framework/

Ofia, f. (2020a). How Uganda has dealt with human trafficking. *Oxford Human Rights https://www.rte.ie/*

brainstorm/2020/0220/1116471-how-uganda-has-dealt-with-human-trafficking/.

Pearson, A. (2004). Getting the evidence into practice, *International Journal in Nursing practise*. 10 (5) 197–198.

Pearson, E. (2003). *Study on trafficking in women in East Africa, a situational analysis including current NGO and governmental activities, as well as future opportunities, to address trafficking in women and girls in Ethiopia, Kenya, Tanzania, Uganda and Nigeria,* Germany: Eschborn: Deutsche Gesellschaft für Technische Zusammenarbeit (GTZ).

Prefworld, (2018).2018 Trafficking in Persons Report – Tanzania. Retrieve form https://www.refworld.org/docid/5b3e0a624.html.

Rickard C. (2019). Human Trafficking Reports Show Sub-Saharan Africa A Global Player *AFRICANLII*. Retrieved from https://africanlii.org/article/20190718/human-trafficking-reports-show-sub-saharan-africa-global-player.

Rickert, M. (2009). Wilberforce's work is not done: Ending Human Trafficking and Modern Day slavery *Forum police* 89 1-49. http://digitalcommons.liberty.edu/gov_fac_pubs/89

Ruto. S., Kameri-Mbote, P. & Muteshi-Strachan, J. (2009) Promises And Realities Taking Stock Of The 3rd UN International Women's Conference.

SADC Secretariat, (2017). Preventing and Combating Trafficking in Persons: Lessons from the SADC Region Southern African Development Community (SADC). Retrieved from https://www.sadc.int/files/1115/0953/7902/EN_TIP_Lessons.pdf.

Stop the Traffik, (2016) Coalition of Anti-Human Trafficking CSOs for UPR: Kenya. Stop the Traffik, 1-18.

The Human Trafficking Institute, (2019) Snapshot of Uganda, Retrieved from https://www.traffickinginstitute.org/uganda/.

The International Labour Organization (ILO), (2006).*Emerging good practices on actions to combat child domestic labour in Kenya, Tanzania, Uganda, and Zambia,* Tanzania: ILO.

The Regional Mixed Migration Secretariat (RMMS) (2013).Mixed Migration in Kenya: The scale of movement and associated protection risks. Nairobi: RMMS. Retrieved form http://www.mixedmigration.org/wp-content/uploads/2018/05/005_mixed-migration-kenya.pdf .

The Regional Mixed Migration Secretariat (RMMS) Mixed Migration in Kenya: The scale of movement and associated protection risks 2013http://www.regionalmms.org/fileadmin/content/rmms_publications/series_booklettwo.pdf.

The World Bank (2016) "Uganda's Progressive Approach to Refugee Management" The World Bank Retrieved fromhttps://www.worldbank.org/en/topic/fragilityconflictviolence/ brief/ugandas-progressive-approach-refugee-management.

Thipanyane, T., (2015). Human Trafficking: African Perspective, *Jurist* Retrieved from http://www.jurist.org/forum/2015/03/tseliso-thipanyane-trafficking-africa.php.

Tonah, S., Setrana, M.B., & John A. (2018).*Migration and Development in Africa: Trends, Challenges, and Policy Implications.* London: Lexington Books.

UNHCR Uganda, (2019) *Country Refugee Response Plan :The integrated response plan for refugees from South Sudan, Burundi and the Democratic Republic of the Congo, January 2019 – December 2020*. Kampala: UNHCR.

UNICEF, (2005).*Innocent Insight: Trafficking in Human Beings Especially Women and Children in Africa,* 2nded, Florence: Innocenti Research Centre. Retrieved from https://www.unicef-irc.org/publications/pdf/trafficking-gb2ed-2005.pdf

United States Department of state (USDOS), (2014). Trafficking in Persons Report United 2014, Office to Monitor and Combat Trafficking in Persons. Retrieved from https://2009-2017.state.gov/documents/organization/226847.pdf.

United States Department of State (USDOS), (2006). Trafficking in Persons Report 2019, Office to Monitor and Combat Trafficking in Persons. Retrieved from https://2009-2017.state.gov/j/tip/rls/tiprpt/2006/index.htm.

United States Department of State (USDOS), (2019). Trafficking in Persons Report 2019, Office to Monitor and Combat Trafficking in Persons. Retrieved from https://www.state.gov/wp-content/uploads/2019/06/2019-Trafficking-in-Persons-Report.pdf.

United States Department of State, 2014 Trafficking in Persons Report 2019 - Kenya, Retrieved from http://www.refworld.org/docid/53aab9e214.html.

USAID, (2007).*Anti-Trafficking in Persons Program in Africa: A Review.* Washington DC: USAID.

Zimmerman, C. (2006). *Stolen smiles: a summary report on the physical and psychological health consequences of women and adolescents trafficked in Europe*. London: London School of Hygiene and Tropical Medicine.

Zimmerman, C., Hossain, M. & Watts C. (2011). Human trafficking and health: A conceptual model to inform policy, *intervention and research, Social Science & Medicine* 73 (2) 327-335.

CHAPTER IV

Vulnerability of Women at Work Place: Legality and Loyalty

Hrushikesh Meher[1]

Introduction

Women are expected to play divergent roles in India. Their potentialities have been given prime concern in respect of Indian family structure and function. Apart from playing major role in shaping society, they devote valuable times to earn bread and butter for the family members and dependents, thereby contribute more in developing quality of life. Our culture pays more importance to them. Indian history has witnessed notable women whose contributions towards various fields are remarkable. We have also long history of neglect, torture, brutality, socio-cultural and religious deprivation because of male dominated society. Indian laws are found to be more conscious about rights of women to save them from prejudice and discrimination. The gravity of vulnerability has been realised. Social and cultural value are carefully preserved. Still there are gender biased dealings in work place where women fall prey. Though the existing laws have given enormous opportunity to protect them from different violations, they have suffered a lot due to social stigma. Gender bias exists in every aspect of society—from the workplace to the political arena (Morris, 2019). Women are found to be helpless and compelled to remain silent before the power abuse and

1. Biju Patnaik State Police Academy, Ranasinghpur, Bhubaneswar-751019

legal defuse. Law have become weapons of stronger who owns power and authority, a matter of time taking exercises with investigation and trial, but not paved the way towards the innocent women who time and again become victim of vulnerability. Now, time has come to realise and analyse how far the existing law has protected the rights of women and able to punish the offenders. If the rights of women are looked into, the dignity of society can be properly preserved. Therefore, Hillary Clinton rightly says, "Human rights are women's right and women's rights are human right, once and for all".

Objectives

1. To examine the constitutional provisions, local and special laws, central laws applicable for protection of rights and dignity of women.
2. To analyse different dimensions of violation of legal provisions as well as rights of women in India.
3. To have a quest for protection of legal rights and social obligation with regard to vulnerability of women at work place.

Offences relating to Women

Though Indian women are considered to be the mother Goddess and treated heavenly, they are not free from exploitation and affected with criminal acts by others. They are subjected to various forms of violation and exploitation. The major forms of criminal acts which they have ever experienced in Indian context are as follows:-

- Traditional practice – Sati Practice, Dowry, Child Marriage, Dogma of Widow remarriage
- Gender discrimination –
    - Rape & sexual assault
    - Eve teasing (Article- 14, 15 & 21) – dealt under IPC 294, 509

  - ♦ Stalking
  - ♦ Acid attack
  - ♦ Sexual harassment at Workplace
- ➢ Trafficking of women and children
- ➢ Child sexual abuse
- ➢ Honor killing
- ➢ Cyber Offences

Protection of Rights of women under Constitutions of India

Life is most precious for everyone among all the pecuniary goods of the world. It has been seen that, even if a person is suffering from intolerable pain and pathos never wants to give up his loving life. But human life cannot be sustained without having certain requisite conditions. Dignity plays a most important role here. Life without dignity is meaningless. Therefore, dignity must be preserved when we think of human life. To upheld dignity, liberty is a pre-condition which creates a congenial environment to realise that, a person is able to lead life in society having human consciousness. In this context, Article 21 of Indian Constitution is taken into consideration. It is a Fundamental Right and guaranteed to all. It speaks about right to life and personal liberty. No one can be deprived of his life and personal liberty except according to the procedure established by law. It means, women are included and protected.

If we analyse the Indian social structure and the role of family, the place of women is something far behind. They are neither treated as protector nor producer. Rather, they are assigned with the task of giving birth, rearing and caring of children. The task of collection of wood and preparation of food was entrusted to the women folk in ancient India. Their lives were protected by male members of the family and dignity was sacredly taken care of. Today also in modern era, people are found to be very callous towards the life and dignity of women folk. Many of them are subjected to brutality. Some are publicly hurt and assaulted. Some are burnt by the husband and relatives on demand of dowry. Some fall prey to molestation, rape, trafficking, prostitution and neglected like any kind. Finding no other way, some also resorted to end their lives by following the path of self demolition and suicide.

Let us analyse about the right to Equality enshrined in the Constitution of India under Article 15 (1). This prohibits discrimination on the grounds of religion, race, caste, sex or place of birth. This sounds well in constitutional arena and judicial phenomena. Women are thought to be 2nd option and never preferred in lucrative job, business hub, social status or religious functions. If we look forward to 'Sabarimala Issue' in Kerala, the discrimination in worship in sacred place is also under the domination of male. Implication of Constitutional provisions with regard to right to equality is something discriminatory in practical field. Rather women are found to be more vulnerable when there is question of demand of right to equality.

Article 19 provides Right to Freedom for all, which includes both women, men and also third gender. It guarantees freedom of speech and expression, movement, practising trade and profession. All these are myths in Indian social and cultural traditions. Monopoly of men prevails everywhere. Say for example in Indian family structure, it is more patriarchal though there exists some matriarchal family structures also. Male person always heads the family having dominant role. From the process of decision making to safety and security, responsibility lies in the hands of men. In agrarian and rural society, even women used to take their meals after men are properly fed. In a family where there is question of scarcity of food, women have to spend days with empty stomach.

This is because of the traditional belief that, men are protector and producer. They should enjoy the lion share and women have the bare necessity of life support. We have not created a congenial environment so far, where women can move freely without any hindrance. The dream of Mahatma Gandhi-"When women of this country will feel free to move in the street at midnight, we can say that India has got actual freedom " has just remain in day dream. The incidences in Indian society in last decades have created turmoil in the country like 'Nirbhaya case of Saket-New Delhi, Gummy case of Rajashtan, Anjana Mishra case of Bhubaneswar, Chhabirani case of Biluakhai River Bank, Biridi, Jagtsingpur, Bebina Behera case of Pipli in the State of Odisha have created a long list of vulnerability of women. We have also witnessed brutal attacks including rape, murder and trafficking of innocent girl children for varieties of illegal purpose every now and then. These incidences have jeopardized the fundamental and constitutional rights of women. Likewise, practising trade and profession freely has left no scope to women in the competition market where male citizens have reign over it. A lot of debate has come up pertaining to equal distribution of employment among male and female. Engagement of women in household activities has made them some way unfit to compete with the employment market in different fields. Nobody cares to make use of the inherent potentialities of women, rather make them weak. We are not confident regarding their performance and strength. Participation of women in rural political activities and governance is a mockery. Local self-governance has given certain reservation of seats to women aiming at women's empowerment. In reality, in many instances, the husband or other relatives of women representatives play vital role in practice. They act only as rubber stamp. In trade and commerce, also there is dominance of male. No women freely prefer to enter into trade and commerce because of feeling of male dominance. Except in some tinny industries, all the mega industries are run by male members as we believe that women are weak and innocent. Therefore, the legal obligation towards profession has acted upon some other direction.

Article 15's Clause (3), empowers the State (lawmakers) from making special provisions in favour of women (and children). Equality does not identify who and how we are. The provision itself says that there is some sort of discrimination of women with regard to equality and this is to make up for social, domestic and cultural injustice ever women have suffered all over India. This has been enumerated as positive discrimination where women are required to participate and empowered. But the question who are the lawmakers and for whom? The drafting committee of Constitution of India who made the provision of emancipation of women led by Dr. Ambedkar consisted of seven member team and all are males. No woman member was chosen. It is a great irony that male members make law for women and again execute law by them. Participation of women and problem they confronted are not presented by them while making law.

Commoditization of women through Trafficking

It is disheartening to note that, women folks are made commoditisation and a wide market has been created all over the country. From trading to smuggling women are cheaply dealt with to meet the demand of men. Here the provision under Article 23 (1) which prohibits the practice of human trafficking in India has become mere mockery while we come across the wide network. Trafficking has become a criminal practice and process of recruiting, contracting, procuring or hiring a person for exploitation. It is a crime of crimes being organized in nature. Here, women are treated as commodity. They are being taken from one place to another, sexually exploited, sold in different places for different purpose. Thus, trafficking has been viewed as a basket of crimes. In this basket one can find out the elements of abduction, kidnapping, illegal detention, illegal confinement, criminal intimidation, hurt, grievous hurt, sexual assault outraging modesty, rape, un natural offence, selling & buying of human beings, servitude, criminal conspiracy, sale of human limbs, abetment etc. Exploitation of the trafficked persons are seen in all forms i.e. Physical, Mental and Sexual which take place in Brothel, Dance Bar, Massage Parlour, Industry, Domestic House, etc. Women are commercialised for revenue generation. This works are done through a demand and supply chain and so many people those who are stake holder like recruiter, transporter, transferer, harbourer and receiver are taking share of huge benefit. They are sold for the purpose of prostitution, sexual exploitation, forced labours, housekeeping, agriculture work, begging, removal of organs, etc. They are also used in criminal activities. The actors in this crime are those who are mainly known to the victims (relatives, friends, colleagues, neighbours) who coerce or force the victims into trafficking through their organised channels, sometimes the victims passing through various intermediaries, and finally reach the destination where they are forced into sexual activity (prostitution) or economic activity (forced labour) or both. Traffickers primarily target women because they are disproportionately affected by poverty and discrimination. The global sex trade is the fastest growing form of commerce, worth $32 billion annually. In fact, human trafficking is the fastest growing area of organized crime and the third largest income revenue for organized crime after narcotics and arms sales (Obstel Gyneocol, 2013).

International laws and laws framed in India direct that the government is obliged to protect their citizens from trafficking through different programmes and steps being taken for prevention as well as protection. In this regard, several laws have come into force in India to protect the women from different forms of violation in general and trafficking in particular. A glimpse of certain measures has been discussed below:

- Trafficking in Human Beings or Persons is prohibited under the Constitution of India under Article 23 (1)
- Sections 366 (A) and 372 IPC, prohibits kidnapping and selling minors into prostitution respectively. Penalties under these provisions are a maximum of 10 years' imprisonment and a fine.
- Protection of Children from Sexual offences (POCSO) Act, 2012, which has come into effect from 14th November, 2012 is a special law to protect children from sexual abuse and exploitation.
- The Immoral Traffic (Prevention) Act, 1956 (ITPA) is the premier legislation for prevention of trafficking for commercial sexual exploitation.
- Criminal Law (amendment) Act 2018 has come into force wherein Section 370 of the Indian Penal Code has been substituted with Section 370 and 370A IPC which provide for comprehensive measures to counter the menace of human trafficking.
- There are other specific legislations enacted relating to trafficking in women and children:
    - Prohibition of Child Marriage Act, 2006,
    - Bonded Labour System (Abolition) Act, 1976,
    - Child Labour (Prohibition and Regulation) Act, 1986,
    - Transplantation of Human Organs Act, 1994,
    - Juvenile Justice (Care and Protection of Children) Act, 2000
    - Information Technology Act, 2000

Apart from specific Sections in the IPC, State Governments have also enacted specific legislations to deal with the issue.

(e.g. The Goa Children's Act, 2003, The Punjab Prevention of Human Smuggling Act, 2012).

Tragedy of women at workplace

The impact of globalisation and urbanisation has acted upon a great social change. Influence of western countries has changed the mindset of Indian citizens. Gender sensitisation and women empowerment have come up. Traditional belief system has lost its value and modified characteristics have gained its importance. Indian women have come up to the open market instead of meeting family demands inside the four walls of dwelling house. They have learnt to compete with their counterparts. The presence of women folks are now days seen in varied fields. To realise the constitutional goal and enhance the international standard, special provisions and reservations are made for women's emancipation. But, several hurdles have come up in their personal life and social life for having active participation in the work place. Their life has stake into danger. Dignity has sacredly damaged. They are subjected to vulnerability and affected with severe mentally and physically exploitations. They have not been spared by their fellow colleague, boss and others in sexual exploitation and harassment. Unwelcome behaviour and sexual gesture posed by other male members humiliate them. Some of the glaring examples which the women come across in work place are as follows:-

1. Physical Contact and advances
2. A demand or request for sexual favours
3. Making sexually colored remarks
4. Showing pornography
5. Any other unwelcome physical, verbal, nonverbal conduct of sexual nature
6. Telling dirty jokes, making sexual remarks about a person's body, etc.

7. Demand or request for sexual favours in lieu of office promotion
8. Spreading rumors about a woman's sexual relationship with anybody

1. Physical Contact

Women have their physical boundaries that is beyond intruded upon. No one will feel comfortable being touched by others. It deteriorates one's respect and self-esteem. But there are instances of so many subtle interactions followed with physical contacts in work place, though non actionable are discomfortable. Most of the people in work place try to touch the body of co-worker and if it is a woman, their intention is towards sexual pleasure. They know the rules about inappropriate or offensive touching. Physical contact with co-worker like shaking hands, pats on back is a common form (Rachel Zupek, 2010). However, women during their career in work place are exposed to misogyny, sexism, work place bullying or even subjected to sexually harassment by male superiors (Yasmeen Hossain, July 4, 2017). While they attend office putting attractive dress, sometimes their counterparts are found to ogling at her and blame making unnecessary responsible for attractive weariness. Of course, various male co-workers seem to be very positive.

2. A demand or request for sexual favors

October 2017 in the US and October 2018 in India, the "Me Too Movement" is a sparkling and glaring example of demand of sex in work place to solicit sex by co-workers. In October, 2018 a string of women journalists and actors shared their harrowing accounts of experience on social media for showing misconduct of prominent media professionals, supervisors, colleagues or people they met in the course of earning their livelihood. A lot of debate and discussion regarding effect of law on sexual harassment of women at work place in India took place. Many women front staged on the street raising complaints and reassuring them of support.

3. Making sexually colored remarks

Some people while working with women are in a habit to use metaphor, phrase in an imaginative way to describe something having some other meaning. To make the powerful description they use words having same qualities aiming at sexual connotations and sexual innuendos. This types of using words having double meaning and the inner sense have sexual remarks fall within the definition of sexual harassment. In this connection the case of *Jishu Sengupta & Others vs. The State of West Bengal & Anr.*, decided by the High Court of Calcutta on 4th November, 2016 is taken into accounts. The Court held that statements with sexual connotations and sexual innuendos are *"sexually coloured remarks"* and fall within the definition of sexual harassment under Section 354 A of the Indian Penal Code. It observed that speaking in metaphors, means the use of words and phrases in an imaginative way to describe something else in order to show that the two things have the same qualities and to make the description more powerful. In another Calcutta High Court case, *Albert David Limited vs. Anuradha Chowdhary and Ors.*, (2004) 2 Cal LT 421 (HC), with respect to a cold environment being created due to an air conditioner, the comment *"…come close to me, you will start feeling hot,"* was held to be a sexually coloured remark.

4. Showing pornography

Viewing porn is one of the behavioural addictions of some persons those who satisfy their impulsion towards sexual urge. Now a days various tools and technologies are available to create pornographic videos, audios, etc. Various magazines and photos are available plenty in the market. In order to fulfill sexual desire some persons resort to the path of viewing porn pictures by storing in their smart phone or computer. Showing such porn to the women colleagues are evident in many cases. This arouses the sexual demand. This attracts the sexual assault and damage of work environment.

5. Any other unwelcome physical, verbal, nonverbal conduct of sexual nature

Inappropriate nature with regards to sexual advances, requests for sexual favours and other verbal or physical conduct of a sexual intention finds place under this definition. The common forms of verbal sexual conducts are:

- Offensive jokes of a sexual nature or sexist nature
- Repeated and unwelcomed requests for sexual favors
- Repeated and unwelcomed requests for dates
- Excessive and unwelcomed flirting
- Threats regarding adverse employment action if sexual favors are not granted
- Unwelcome compliments of a sexual nature

The non-verbal sexual communication includes lewd or suggestive gesturing, winking and luring, etc. Women are subjected to exploit of all these types of sexual demands from their superiors, colleagues and sometime subordinates also.

6. Telling dirty jokes, making sexual remarks about a person's body

Having a beautiful look and fair body built for women working in office bears unfair advantage in some occupations. Here, beauty makes certain aspects of life much more difficult with others. The common response at work place for many women found to be fuelled by implicit sexist prejudices. To make the working environment more pleasant and for amusement of fellow workers some play dirty jokes making sexual remarks at work place. They enjoy lot if their counterparts happen to be female and participate in the jokes. If the body of such women is found to be fair or sexist look, it becomes more exited of amusement.

7. Demand or request for sexual favors in lieu of office promotion

Every organisation has certain norms for promotion. It is especially based on merit, hard work and skill. But some executives utilise inappropriate suggestions asking for sexual favours or work-related advancement to the working women. In certain cases to make the character role sound some also seek sexual favour. The specific types of sexual harassment for favouring promotion is termed as "guid pro quo". It is a legal phrase which means an employer usually favours or date, in exchange of a pay raise, a promotion or special opportunities at work. The intention behind this act is sexual advancement and implied overtly that, if women do something to the boss, she will get something in return. This makes extremely difficult challenge for many women to meet the demand.

8. Spreading rumours about a woman's sexual relationship with anybody

It is a way of blaming women for her perceived sexual promiscuity. This act also known as "Slut-shaming". When male colleagues failed to satiate their need demanding of sex or sexual favour, they go on rumour like sexual promiscuity of the women worker. It insults women in work place. It is considered that a woman who engages herself with sexual act with other persons except her husband is said to have lost her chastity. Some people spread rumours against women co-workers in work place as a way of intimidation and get pleasure. In Indian context, women feel shame and anxiety which compels them to end their lives by resorting to suicide also.

Causes of Sexual Harassment

Notions of Masculinity

There are several reasons that lead to Sexual harassment at workplace. The principal cause being psychological issues faced by men. Their unwelcome and undesirable behavior is a result of their notions of masculinity and dominance over women. Majority of men who though superficially support the idea of gender equality believe that they have the right to sex regardless of consent.

Depression and Anxiety

High level of depression and anxiety, drug addiction and personal problems also invoke men to harass their female colleagues for fun and temporary pleasure.

Power Relation

Sexual harassment is, above all, a manifestation of power relations. Women are much more likely to be victims of sexual harassment precisely because they more often than men lack power. They are in more vulnerable and unsecured positions, lack self confidence, or have been socialized to suffer in silence. Some times sexual harassment is also seen as a power game, where man insists on sexual favors in exchange of benefits he can dispense with due to his privileged position. The 'Casting Couch' is probably the best-known example of such power game.

Patriarchal Structure

The basic reason behind almost all types of harassment or violence against women lies in our ***society's patriarchal***

structure where a male always thinks himself superior than the woman in every aspect of life. This superiority complex manifests itself in various kinds of discriminatory practices against women in general and working women in particular. Thus, a male colleague would not like his female co-employee to work with him equally or he would not like her to reach at a higher position in the office; and to make her feel inferior or to make her uncomfortable or in order to harass her, different kinds of techniques are used by male colleagues and prominent among these are sexually colored techniques such as indecent remarks, unwelcome conduct, showing of vulgar images or videos or any other similar behavior.

Sexual Perversion

Apart from this, sexual perversion of mind among certain individuals is also one of the major reasons of sexual harassment of women at workplace. While more and more female employees are being recruited by both public and private sectors, such men have got an easy access to indulge in sexually perverted behaviors.

Jealousy at Workplace

Jealousy at workplace is also a reason for such crimes against women employees; a male employee would not like to see his female colleague to get success, promotion or incentives by the employer and in jealousy, he would harass her through sexually perverted behavior. It is also linked to perceived superiority feeling among men that a woman could never become better than her male counterpart could.

Feeling of Contempt and Disrespect

Apart from the above reasons, a general feeling of contempt and disrespect for women among male colleagues is also a prominent reason whereby women are considered only as an object to fulfill sexual desires of men. We might respect women in our homes but other women in the society are not treated as such. Women at workplace is no different; male colleagues consider them as their object of play, vulgar comments and jokes, obscene gestures, gossips of sexual nature etc are the norms of any workplace. Though, in our society we claim to respect and worship women but in reality various types of crimes committed against women show that our claim in nothing but a falsity.

Professional Impact of Sexual Harassment of Women

Sexual harassment of women in work place leads to diminish dignity of women and hence has great bearing on professional sphere. Several negative outcome a working women has to confront with like decrease work performance, absenteeism, loss of pay, less promotional opportunities, criticism from friends, colleagues, subjected to gossip, scrutiny at work, publicly sexualized, being ostracized, tension for career, weak support network, withdrawal and isolation, etc. have to be encountered.

Impact in Personal Life

When a working women come across various forms of sexual harassment, she feels insecure and her personal life also affected in so many ways like depression, anxiety, panic, traumatic stress, shame, self blame, fatigue, weak, time mismanagement, feeling betrayed, feeling powerless, loss of confidence, esteem, lack of trust on people, etc.

Provisions of Law to Safeguard Women from Sexual Harasshment at Workplace

The Sexual Harassment of Women at Workplace (Prevention, Prohibition and Redressal) Act, 2013 defines the places which are to be taken into consideration as work place and the redressal mechanism in case of vulnerability of women at work place. It includes all women whether engaged directly or through an agent including a contractor, with or without the knowledge of the principal employer. They may be working for remuneration, on a voluntary basis or otherwise. Their terms of employment can be expressed or implied. Further, she could be a co-worker, a contract worker, probationer, trainee, apprentice, or called by any other such name. The Act also covers a woman, who is working in a dwelling place or house. It also includes all workplaces whether owned by Indian or foreign company having a place of work in India. As per the Act, workplace includes: - Government organizations, including Government company, corporations and co-operative societies; - Private sector organisations, venture, society, trust, NGO or service providers etc. providing services which are commercial, vocational, educational, sports, professional, entertainment, industrial, health related or financial activities, including production, supply, sale, distribution or service; Hospitals/Nursing Homes; Sports Institutes/Facilities; places visited by the employee (including while on travel) including transportation provided by employer; a dwelling place or house. The Act defines the Unorganised Sector such as any enterprise owned by an individual or self-employed workers engaged in the production or sale of goods or providing services of any kind; any enterprise which employs less than 10 workers.

Prevention of Sexual Harassment Complain Mechanism

The Sexual Harassment of Women at Workplace (Prevention, Prohibition and Redressal) Act, 2013 has made certain provision for combating sexual harassment of women at work place. These are provisions of three tier complain committee to redress the grievances of sexual harassment. Such as :-

- Internal Complain Committee
- Local Complain Committee
- State level Complain Committee

Internal Complain Committee at Institutional level:-

1. Every employer of a workplace shall, by an order in writing, constitute a Committee to be known as the "Internal Complaints Committee shall be constituted at all administrative units or offices.
2. The Internal Committee shall consist of the following members to be nominated by the employer, namely
   - A Presiding Officer who shall be a woman employed at a senior level
   - At least two Members from amongst employees preferably committed to the cause of women or who have had experience in social work or have legal knowledge
   - One member from amongst non-governmental organizations or associations
3. Every member nominated for three years
4. SHAW Report presentation of ICC within 90 days

Local Complain Committee at District level

1. Every district should form local complaint committee which receive SH cases where the ICC has not constituted

due to having less than 10 workers or the complaint is against employer

2. The district magistrate or the collector has the power to exercise the Act and act as district officer.
3. The district officer shall be designated as nodal officer for tehsil or municipality to receive the complain and forward it to LCC within 7 days.
4. Chairperson nominate the eminent woman from social work field who is committed to the cause of women
5. One member from women working in block, tahsil or municipality
6. Two members from non govt. organizations working on women issues
7. The concerned officer dealing with social welfare or W&CD in the district
8. ICC shall in a year submit a brief report to the district complain committee

State level Complain Committee

1. A state level complain committee should form to address the issue at state level with Chairmanship of Secretary W& CD department with members from different departments.
2. Every district level Complain Committee should yearly provide a brief report to the State level Complain Committee

Complaints Mechanisms

1. All workplaces should have an appropriate complaints committee.
2. A woman should head the complaints committee and no less than half of its members should be women.

3. There should a third party member, preferably a woman who has experience working with women /social issues.
4. Complaints procedure must be time bound.
5. Confidentiality must be maintained.
6. Witness must not be victimized.

Short Comings of the Law

Constitutional Provisions, Provisions of Law in Central Act and State Legislations are sound enough aiming at protection of women from different forms of violations and at different places of their occupations. There is lots of hue and cry for protecting women from different types of violence. Some recent amendments in terms of punishment of grave sexual offence recommend stringent punishment. In spite of that, the vulnerability of women in India is a serious concern. Crime against women is considerably rising. The graph never comes down. Offenders are found to be in upper hand than the victims in terms of societal acceptance. Here, stigma over rides the laws. The women victims are looked down, criticized and questioned against their chastity. If the victim of crime happens to be un-married or a young girl, arranging customary marriage becomes herculean task. Laws sacredly protect the social stigma and care for follow up action. Furthermore, crime against women are coming under various central and special laws. There is no conclusive law enacted so far to use as shield and sword for women. The Sexual Harassment of Women at Workplace (Prevention, Prohibition and Redressal) Act, 2013 is found to be toothless. All the penal provisions thereof are non-cognizable in nature where an assailant can get more scope to reoffend. The provisions thereof are found to be more directives and guidelines. It focuses grossly on redressal mechanism and lenient on penal provisions. When the perpetrators are in upper hierarchical position, the provisions do not penetrate with a complete length and strength.

In terms of laws relating to Human Trafficking, the definitions of perpetrators are varied and place of occurrences extends up to territorial horizon. The actions are somewhere licit and somewhere illicit. Hence, it is very difficult on the part of law enforcement agency to identify the invisible gap between illicit trade and licit business. On the other hand, protection to the aggrieved persons is not clear for which many cases ended with compromise. Delay in trial is another drawback which victims of crime do not rely on justice delivery system.

Indian society being culturally operates with a patriarchal family structure and male dominated social system, women folk fall prey on many social injustices. They become soft target of the male offenders. Although Indian laws are in favor of womanhood, the practice and obligations are something different. This threatens the women safety and sole reason of vulnerability. It is a high time to think and re-think about vulnerability of women in India with bunches of robust laws in hand.

Conclusions

Women are not commodities. They are considered to be the breeding grounds for social, cultural, educational and moral development. While dealing with women in work place, all decency has to be maintained. Dignity is prime consideration which everybody should realise and show the behaviour by which an women in work place feel confident and secured. Laws with regard to protection of women to be strictly adhered to. Moral and ethical values are to be preserved aiming at a balanced society. Hence, it can be said that, a loyal individual having regards to law is contributing a lot towards peaceful development of society.

REFERENCES

- Morris S. (2019) : A Look at Gender Bias in Society; available at https://www.thoughtco.com/gender-bias-4140418).
- Despande N. and Obstel G.N. (2013) : Sex Trafficking of Women and Girls; available in https://www.ncbi.nlm.nih.gov/pmc/articles/PMC3651545/).
- Rachel Z. (2010) : Physical contact at work -- what are the boundaries? available at http://edition.cnn.com/2010/LIVING/worklife/02/08/cb.getting.physical.at.work/index.html
- Yasmeen H. (2017) : Workplace harassment problems of women in India and how to deal with them; available at http://www.careerizma.com/blog/workplace-harassment-problems-women-india/)
- Constitution of India 1950
- The Sexual Harassment of Women at Workplace (Prevention, Prohibition and Redressal) Act, 2013

CHAPTER V

Challenges and Prospects of an absent Methodology: A Brazilian Perspective on International Drug Trafficking, Women Mules and Human Trafficking

Izabela Zonato Villas Boas[1]
Ana Cláudia Ruy Cardia Atchabahian[2]

Introduction

The facilitation of international migrations around the world generates benefits for both migrants and reception States. However, there is a counterproductive facet represented by the possibility of transnationalization of certain crimes,

1. Master student in Political and Economic Law at from Mackenzie Presbyterian University. Master by the International Institute of Legal Sociology in Oñati (Spain). *Lato Sensu* Graduate Student in Constitutional and Administrative Law at Escola Paulista de Direito. Graduated in Law from Mackenzie Presbyterian University. Member of the Research Group "Invisible People: Prevention and Combat of Internal and International Trafficking in Persons", from Mackenzie Presbyterian University. Member of the Research Committee on Sociology of Law. Academic assistant of Prof. Dr. Ana Cláudia Ruy Cardia Atchabahian at the Faculty of Law of Mackenzie Presbyterian University.
2. PhD and Master of Laws from the Pontifical Catholic University of São Paulo. Professor of Private International Law at Mackenzie Presbyterian University. Advisor to the Latin American Branch of the Global Business and Human Rights Scholars Association. Member of the Working Group in Supply Chains and Human Trafficking of the Uniform Law Commission. Member of the Human Rights Commission of the Brazilian BAR Association (São Paulo branch). Coordinator of the Study Group "Mack DH&E: Human Rights and business" and Coordinator of the Research Group "Invisible People: Prevention and Combat of Internal and International Trafficking in Persons", both from Mackenzie Presbyterian University. Lawyer and human rights and business consultant in São Paulo, Brazil.

such as drug trafficking and human trafficking. Both crimes, together with weapons trafficking, constitute the most profitable criminal activities in the world, with a revenue of approximately 150 billion dollars (ILO).

International human trafficking and international drug trafficking are crimes that have the power to affect humanity regardless of their racial, national, socioeconomic and gender characteristics. It is known that the exploitation of human vulnerabilities based on the realization of efforts to improve socioeconomic conditions and even to escape degrading situations enhances the submission of victims of drug trafficking and human trafficking, especially in view of the promise of rapid capital gains made by recruiters.

For the purpose of this research, the work will focus on the perspective of the female gender related to both crimes, as well as with the eventual connection between them. The justification for the above mentioned cut, that is, the possibility that women victims of drug trafficking are also victims of human trafficking is mainly due to the fact that, at the international level, most of the trafficked persons belong to the group formed by women (UNODC, 2018, p. 10). In addition to this factor, the growth of female incarceration due to international drug trafficking reaches 60% in Latin American countries, such as Brazil and Argentina (Wola, 2016, p. 03).

In light of this, this research will consider the assumptions arising from the study carried out by Howard Campbell, on drug trafficking (Campbell, 2008, p. 233-267), as well as the document presented to the Instituto Terra, Trabalho e Cidadania (ITTC) by Luísa Luz de Souza (Souza, 2013), regarding the consequences of the punitive discourse against female mules of international drug trafficking in Brazil. Although the sources might not represent the actual state of this matter, it is known that there is a deficiency of materials that connect both crimes. With that in mind, this paper will also focus on a research by GERRY QC, HARRÉ, NAIBAHO, MURASZKIEWICZ and BOISTER (2018, p. 187), named "Is the Law an Ass When It Comes to Mules? How Indonesia Can Lead a New Global Approach to Treating Drug Traffickers as Human Trafficked Victims", that brings an approach to the theme under the Indonesian perspective, highlighting that the absence of application of the non-prosecution of victims of trafficking undermines the effort to combat transnational human trafficking.

It will thus be verified how the crimes of drug and human trafficking take advantage of the female vulnerability, turning them into objects not only for the purpose of exploiting their bodies, but also using them as means of transporting drugs between world borders. Moreover, this study is also based on the paper co-authored by, Felipe Chiarello de Souza Pinto, Ana Cláudia Ruy Cardia Atchabahian and Caroline Lopes Placca on the obstacles in the definition of a global methodology for collecting data on the crime of human trafficking from the study of the Global Reports prepared by the United Nations Office on Drugs and Crime (UNODC) (Pinto, Atchabahian, Placca, 2018).

For the purposes of this article, it is worth noting, therefore, that although the central focus of the analysis is female participation in both crimes simultaneously, this cut does not prevent the victimization of men and children (UNODC, 2018, p. 10) but rather guarantees importance to the highest level of vulnerability and consequent criminalization of women before the selected cut.

In addition to the previous analysis, it is questioned in the present study whether it is possible to demonstrate the existence of an eventual correlation between discrimination against women, drug trafficking and human trafficking. In addition, this paper seeks to verify whether, faced with this possibility, there are difficulties in organizing and collecting this data in order to correlate the two crimes and to measure how trafficked women can also be used as drug trafficking mules.

The inductive method will be used to reach the main conclusions and the methodology will start from the analysis of primary sources (such as United Nations reports on drug trafficking and trafficking in persons and related documents) and secondary bibliographic sources on the above mentioned matters.

Object of study: Violation of rights, objectification and commercialization of women victims of human trafficking and drug trafficking

This item will contextualize the issue of the historical violation of women's rights, its consideration as an object and its consequent treatment as goods. The analysis is performed by taking into consideration that the current globalization process exposes a scenario in which consumption overlaps human relationships and vulnerabilities, as well as that trafficking in women for the purpose of sexual exploitation constitutes the most frequent modality of this crime, in accordance with the 2018 UNODC Global Report on Trafficking in Persons (UNODC, 2018, p. 10).

According to Martha Fineman, although the human vulnerability is universal, constant and complex, it is also particular; in other words, even though vulnerability is inherent to the human condition, each person is individually positioned differently in the networks of economic and institutional relations. The author understands that the individual experience of vulnerability will depend on the quality and quantity of resources that each person has or can command (Fineman, 2010, p. 269).

Even though the author believes that vulnerability cannot be eradicated, Fineman says that society can compensate and reduce vulnerability through programs, institutions and structures. To this end, States should be more active and responsive, guaranteeing and improving equal opportunities among individuals in society (Fineman, 2010, p. 260).However, it is important to note that there are socio-cultural particularities that must be observed as they aggravate the victim status of women.

The UNODC (2013, p. 13) understands that, in the context of human trafficking, vulnerability usually refers to inherent, environmental or contextual factors, usually combined with causes such as poverty, social inequality, discrimination and gender violence. In addition to these factors, other intrinsic issues are relevant, such as unemployment, precarious work and low wages.Added to this is discrimination against women, understood by the Convention on the Elimination of All Forms of Discrimination against Women (CEDAW) as distinctions, exclusions or restrictions based on sex, with the aim or result of harming or nullifying women (UN, 1979).

It appears then that social contexts of economic deprivation are responsible for increasing the possibility of the individual being subjected to human rights violations: they increase human vulnerability and facilitate the operation of traffickers and exploiters of drug and human trafficking. Therefore, it is noted that the oppressive character is intrinsic to the crime, which is marked by the devaluation and inequality of the female gender, turning women who are in search of better living conditions into victims of crime and reduced to the aspect of objects – being victims of trafficking in persons for the purpose of sexual exploitation.

For these reasons, there is a greater degree of vulnerability for women, being it physical, psychological, socioeconomic and / or cultural, which makes them more susceptible to being abused by criminals who seek profit from the development of criminal activities. This exploitation is the result of the overvaluation of consumption and the devaluation of human qualities, as the trafficked victim starts to be considered as an object for consumption and to be sold as a commodity. Thus, it appears that the factors that strengthen vulnerability make women more likely to be victims of trafficking are a consequence of proportionately degrading factors resultant from exploitation.

In this context, it is emphasized that not only the social context of origin of the victim of trafficking - both drugs and people - is relevant to the analysis; a reflection on the State where they live is also imperative. According to Souza (2013, p. 03), international drug trafficking presents a differentiation between producer and intermediate States on the one hand, and recipient and consumer States on the other; according to the author, there is an international division of labor with implications for the category of anti-drug policies applied.

Consequently, Souza states that even though drug trafficking is a global reality, Latin American women are more affected. As a result, the author suggests that public policies in these regions should prioritize alternatives that seek to reduce female victimization (Souza, 2013, p. 07).

It is also possible to consider a parallel with what Boaventura de Sousa Santos distinguishes between northern and southern states. The author considers metropolitan countries as those of the North, and colonial countries as those of the South, clarifying that the latter are peripheral and semiperipheral regions colonized by them, as well as highlighting the existence of abyssal lines between metropolitan and colonial states (Santos, 2016, p. 26, 33), especially in relation to its socioeconomic character.

As for human trafficking, the reality presented is no different from that of drug trafficking. According to the 2018 UNODC Global Report, the Latin American region is also characterized as a place with high potential for this criminal modality (UNODC, 2018, p.29). as well as States of the African continent (Santos, Gomes, Duarte, Baganha, 2008, p. 30) - two regions marked by profound inequalities and which fit the theory of Boaventura de Sousa Santos on the States of the global north and south.

With regard to the reduction of vulnerabilities, it is important to mention the United Nations (UN) 2030 Agenda for Sustainable Development and its 17 Sustainable Development Goals (SDGs) (UN, 2015). This is a universal agenda that, through the SDGs and its 169 goals, seeks the effectiveness of everyone's human rights and, for the central aspect of the present work, the achievement of gender equality and women's empowerment (SDG 5). It is remarkable that the SDGs are integrated and indivisible, and hence, among them, those that are most directly linked to the reduction of female vulnerability are: (i) providing opportunities for inclusive and quality learning and education for all (SDG 4); (ii) seek gender equality and empower all women and girls (SDG 5); and (iii) and reducing inequality in and between States (SDG 10). Thus, it appears that the crimes of drug and human trafficking, in addition to worsening human vulnerability, are contrary to the principles of social and sustainable development worldwide.

It is possible to conclude that to commercialize women as an object is, in fact, the same as to dehumanize them and to withdraw their rights to have rights (Arendt, 1998, p.330).In this scenario resulting from the female vulnerabilities exposed to the crimes of drug trafficking and human trafficking, victims are exploited and have their fundamental rights violated, as will be examined in the following item.

Drug trafficking and its possible correlation with human trafficking: analysis of crimes at the international and domestic levels

This item previously seeks to trace peculiarities of the crimes of drug trafficking and human trafficking to demonstrate possible similarities and connections between them.

Such crimes have reached an increasing number of women, and it is sometimes possible that both occur in the same context, leading to the arrest of avictim of trafficking in persons for being also recruited as a mule for the drug trafficking.

Drug trafficking

The term "mule" is used to refer to persons who carry out the task of transporting small amounts of drugs, especially quantities around one or two kilos of cocaine (Wola, 2016, p. 21). In face of the international drug trafficking, there is an increase in the number of foreign female mules without previous passage through the prison system (Wola, 2016, p. 21), which is justified since women are recruited to act as mules based on false promises of rapid and easy enrichment or by threaten made by their recruiters.

According to Souza (2013, p. 9), although women have achieved greater autonomy over time, they have been one of the groups most affected by anti-drug policies. The author argues that this occurs since the change in social relations did not necessarily bring them a better condition of life, access to education and equal working conditions. In this sense, women responsible for supporting the family are in a greater position of vulnerability, and therefore, among the few alternatives to achieve some financial security or even independence, they end up being associated to drug-related crimes.

Therefore, in 2009, the UNODC, through its Narcotics Commission, published Resolution No. 52/1, with the purpose to promote international cooperation and address the involvement of women and girls in drug trafficking, especially as mules (UNODC, 2011, p. 1).The above mentioned document presents exclusively gender issues in the elaboration of international policies on drug trafficking, noting that the involvement of women and girls with this crime represents a risk to the well-being and development of children, families and communities.

Furthermore, it recognizes that women tend to be among the most vulnerable groups, with less access to education, work and financial resources (UNODC, 2011, p.1).In a survey conducted by Howard Campbell (2008), on the border between the United States and Mexico, it was identified that the involvement of women in drug trafficking can be demonstrated in four ways. The first one is represented by the minority of women in a position of command in criminal organizations. This position is reached, for example, by high-level traffickers attracted by power and the possibility of relative independence from the male domain (Campbell, 2008, p. 250). The second position is held by few women in criminal organizations, representing middle-level arrangements, which provide less freedom than men (however, they still manage to manipulate gender stereotypes to their advantage in the world of drug trafficking (Campbell, 2008, p. 253)).

The third position, with a low level of influence, is occupied by the mules, representing most of the women involved - especially single mothers -, responsible for performing traditional trafficking strategy roles. In this scenario, they receive significantly less economic benefits and power. Nevertheless, they are more vulnerable to gender oppression, although in sporadic cases there is independence from male domestic control (Campbell, 2008, p.256).

The fourth and last position is occupied by women who do not traffic drugs but are negatively affected by the male traffickers with whom they relate, which Campbell presents as a "gender entrapment". Hence, a large number of women are indirectly involved in trafficking as they have relationships with traffickers (Campbell, 2008, p. 256 and 257). It is important to note, however, that the socioeconomic need can turn these women directly involved with the referred crime.

In view of the four positions presented, Campbell argues that drug trafficking often leads to female victimization, especially when they are inserted at the lowest levels of the drug trafficking hierarchy. On the other hand, in the case of high-level traffickers, although in a lower proportion than other positions, drug trafficking ends up being a kind of medium for female empowerment (Campbell, 2008, p. 260).

Moreover, as seen, although it is possible for women to occupy a leading position in drug trafficking, it is common for this central role to be played by men, which causes women to exercise more subordinate positions and demonstrates an involvement with a greater degree of vulnerability and exposure for them. This is also represented by the expressive increase in female incarceration for committing crimes of this nature (Campbell, 2008).

Souza (2013, p. 5) believes that the massive incarceration, especially of the lowest levels of drug trafficking - hardly accessing the highest levels of drug trafficking -, is a reflection of the "war on drugs" and the consequent adoption of prohibitionists and criminalizing policies.

In Brazil, the policy of combating drug trafficking is portrayed by Law No. 11.343 of 2006, which defines the abovementioned crime, as well as establishes its punishment, which is equivalent to the heinous (extremely serious) crimes provided for in the Brazilian Penal Code.Article 33 of Law No.

11.343 of 2006 provides for a prison sentence of at least five and a maximum of fifteen years for different conducts, such as importing and exporting drugs, among other verbs related to practices related to the main crime.Paragraph fourth of this article brings the possibility of reducing the punish from one sixth to two thirds, if the person who commits the crime is a primary agent, has a good record and does not engage in or join a criminal organization.

Given this, the subordinate and vulnerable involvement of women in drug trafficking causes them to be exploited as "mules", making them more exposed to the crime and, consequently, favoring and facilitating their incarceration. This possibility is particularly serious when women in this category are placed in situations of drug transport between different jurisdictions. For this reason, foreign women imprisoned as mules overcrowd the prison system, not only in Brazil, but in other Latin American states, such as Argentina and Costa Rica, which means that female mules represent more than 60% of the incarcerated women (Wola, 2016, p. 03).

Furthermore, as presented by Souza (2013, p. 08), the abuse of their vulnerability or the existence of coercion and / or deception in the recruitment of the woman mules can mean that they were also victims of human trafficking. Given this reality, it is necessary the reflection regarding women that occupy low levels of drug trafficking and are victims of international human trafficking organizations for the most diverse forms of exploitation.

Trafficking in persons

Previously known due to slavery and serfdom, practices that had their base abolished by legislations around the world and were no longer acceptable for many years, human trafficking in its current form is also criminal conduct, composing the so-called modern slavery (Pinto, Atchabahian, Placca, 2018, p. 38).

Trafficking in persons presupposes the exploitation of human beings. Unlike its characteristics of the past, today physical force is not necessarily used to detain and subject victims to inhuman conditions, with fraud and abuse of the psychosocial vulnerability of people seeking better living conditions being more frequent. (Pinto, Atchabahian, Placca, 2018, p. 37).

Human trafficking is a crime that can have national and international effects, where the ability to operate across borders is typical of transnational criminal organizations, which uses to operate with a high degree of impunity (UNODC, 2018, p. 8 and 30). The International Labor Organization (ILO) office in Brazil expresses that, especially in relation to women, human trafficking presupposes the naturalization of inequalities and human rights violations, which reduces the "humanity of the other", transforming victims in non-humans, non-rights holders and consequently not materially equal (ILO, 2012, p. 7).

Although trafficking can originate victims of all social classes, ages, gender, population out of conflict or in conflicting environments, the ILO expresses that women represent 99% of the victims of forced labor in the commercial sex industry (ILO). In addition, there are secondary factors that contribute to the increased vulnerability of the victim, such as internal conflicts in his State of origin, family dysfunction, socioeconomic situation and even previous work with prostitution (2008, p. 28). It appears, therefore, that female victims are the main target of this forced labor market and consequent exploitation - especially sexual -, which is aggravated when fragile socioeconomic conditions are met by such groups.

Internationally defined in 2000 by the "Protocol to Prevent, Suppress and Punish Trafficking in Persons Especially Women and Children, supplementing the United Nations Convention against Transnational Organized Crime", also known as the Palermo Protocol[1] - which came into force in Brazil in 2004 (Brazil, 2004) -, the treaty brings aspects about crime prevention, protection of victims and punishment of criminal agents. Its gravity is clarified in the Rome Statute of the International Criminal Court, which since 1998, in its art. 7, 2, "c", brings the understanding that human trafficking is a crime against humanity[2].

According to the UNODC 2018 Global Report on Trafficking in Persons, in accordance with art.3 of the Palermo Protocol (Brazil, 2004) and also with art. 149-A of the Brazilian Penal Code (Brazil, 2016) - included in the Brazilian legislation through Law No.13, 344, of 2016, which concerns the protection and repression of human trafficking in Brazil - this crime can be carried out by criminals through the use of physical violence and coercion, as can also occur within the abuse of vulnerabilities[3], power and deception.

---

1. "Recruitment, transportation, transfer, harbouring or receipt of persons, by means of the threat or use of force or other forms of coercion, of abduction, of fraud, of deception, of the abuse of power or of a position of vulnerability or of the giving or receiving of payments or benefits to achieve the consent of a person having control over another person, for the purpose of exploitation. Exploitation shall include, at a minimum, the exploitation of the prostitution of others or other forms of sexual exploitation, forced labour or services, slavery or practices similar to slavery, servitude or the removal of organs".
2. "Article 7. Crimes against humanity 1. For the purpose of this Statute, "crime against humanity" means any of the following acts when committed as part of a widespread or systematic attack directed against any civilian population, with knowledge of the attack: (...) 2. For the purpose of paragraph 1: c) "Enslavement" means the exercise of any or all of the powers attaching to the right of ownership over a person and includes the exercise of such power in the course of trafficking in persons, in particular women and children". International Criminal Court. (1998) *Rome Statute.*
3. Abuse of a position of vulnerability is generally understood to mean that the victim has no real other choice than to be exploited. (UNODC, 2013, p. 45)

The measures presented by the Palermo Protocol, as clarified in its article 14, must be interpreted and applied in such a way that victims of trafficking in persons do not suffer any type of discrimination.

Given that, the UNODC (2008, p. 253) recommends the principle of protection and assistance, whereby it understands that the involvement in illegal activities is a direct consequence of the condition in which the trafficked person is found[1]. Thus, criminal prosecution, imprisonment or other punishments can represent barriers beyond the already existing exploitation. In this regard, in order to avoid increasing the vulnerability of people in situations of trafficking, States should not propose measures to criminalize migration.

The UNODC 2018 Global Report clarifies that the data presented on the detected victims refer only to the visible part of human trafficking, even though UNODC has participated in other studies that explore the hidden part of this crime (UNODC 2018, p. 33). The referred document indicates that trafficking in persons for the purpose of sexual exploitation is the most frequent form of trafficking, and that women are the most identified victims. In addition, the number of girls detected is increasing, which means that, together, in the last 15 years, women and girls represent more than 70% of its victims (UNODC, 2018, p. 10, 25, 33).

Different types of human trafficking prevail on each continent, with no uniformity in all regions. The document under analysis, therefore, emphasizes that trafficking for sexual exploitation is most frequently identified in the Americas, Europe, East Asia and the Pacific. In addition, it warns that

1. According to the document, "Trafficked persons shall not be detained, charged or prosecuted for the illegality of their entry into or residence in countries of transit and destination, or for their involvement in unlawful activities to the extent that such involvement is a direct consequence of their situation as trafficked persons".

in Central America and the Caribbean girls are more often detected as victims of this type of trafficking, while women are more identified in other sub-regions (UNODC, 2018, p. 12).

Finally, despite the general information presented by that report, it is necessary to go through a more in-depth analysis with regard to the connection between the crimes under study. Therefore, it is necessary to analyze the effectiveness of the UNODC data collection methodology.

The UNODC data collection methodology: inaccuracies in the concomitant recognition of human trafficking and drug trafficking crimes

This topic is based on the study conducted byFelipe Chiarello de Souza Pinto, Ana Cláudia Ruy Cardia Atchabahian and Caroline Lopes Placca in which the UNODC Global Reports on human trafficking were analyzed in order to verify - in the methodology adopted in each of the reports published between 2009 and 2016 - the main developments and difficulties encountered by that UN agency in collecting data for the production of its reports.

The authors note that the evaluation of data obtained by the UNODC is done through an analytical interpretation of the number of detected cases of human trafficking worldwide, in which the patterns and flows of human trafficking at the national, regional and international levels are acknowledged based on the number of cases identified and the characteristics and profiles of the victims, offenders and the circumstances of the cases (Pinto, Atchabahian, Placca, 2018, p. 49 and 50).

The analysis shows that the Global Report of 2016, as well as that of 2018, still resembles the previous ones, recognizing that there are imprecisions due to the difficulties in obtaining uniform data, as well as the inexistence of a pre-established standard by the States themselves with regard to organization and data collection, as well as the domestic implementation of the Palermo Protocol. Situations like these directly influence the UNODC's ability to reliably express the true extent of the crime of human trafficking. (Pinto, Atchabahian, Placca, 2018, p. 50).

Due to the time lapse since the publication of the first report in 2009, the 2016 Global Report brings innovations in relation to the previous ones, namely: it presents an evolutionary panorama of the internal ways of combating the crime of human trafficking and demonstrates the evolution of legislation States seeking to criminalize traffickers and protect victims as provided for in the Palermo Protocol. (Pinto, Atchabahian, Placca, 2018, p. 52).

Improvements were also verified in the UNODC methodology, such as the elaboration and distribution of a questionnaire to the States. Even so, there are obstacles in the standardization of the methodology, considering how different jurisdictions fight the crime, the difficulties inherent in the organization of the internal organs of the States or even the absence of a methodology capable of carrying out internal data collection, way that the information obtained only express a reality received from the collaborating States (Pinto, Atchabahian, Placca, 2018, p. 52).

Considering that the research carried out by Atchabahian, Placca and Pinto analyzes the Global Reports until 2016, a brief mention of the methodology used in the 2018 report is necessary. Moreover, the information that comprises the most recent report represents 142 States - ten more than in previous editions -, which the UNODC understands that represents 94% of the world population (UNODC, 2018, p. 15).

In addition, the report recognizes that, although there have been improvements in the availability of data and information on human trafficking, there are still significant gaps in the recognition of this crime that affect large parts of the globe, such as Africa, the Middle East and Asia, also due to the lack of systematization of data collection (UNODC, 2018, p. 15).

It is also necessary to further investigate the connection between human trafficking and drug trafficking and how this link is handled by the UNODC reports.Despite mentioning the various forms of exploitation provided for in the Palermo Protocol (sexual exploitation, forced labor, begging and forced marriage, among others), the Reports fails to address the exploitation related to the illicit drug trade.However, notwithstanding this omission, when describing statistics on convictions of criminals, it informs that in some locations it is possible that the low number of convictions may be a reflection of low levels of trafficking activity, or even of limited capacity to detect the crime (UNODC, 2018, p. 23).

On the other hand, the UNODC Thematic Document on Combating Trafficking in Persons in Situations of Conflict brings the possibility of human trafficking in cases where people are forced to commit crimes, such as theft and drug sales (UNODC, 2018-b, p.16).

Therefore, it can be said that the UNODC assumes a limited capacity to measure data on human trafficking at a global level. In addition, there are also imperfections in the measurement of data, given that in the Global Report there is no express mention of the exploitation of people through the forced consent of crimes - information that is brought in its Thematic Document.

The World Drug Report (2020, p. 58), mentions the subject superficially, pointing to research carried out in 2012 by Shelley. In a global analysis of the connection between both crimes, Shelley (2012, p. 250) verifies that there is no universal relationship between drugs and human trafficking, in this perspective, she understand that "drugs increase the submission and passivity of the human trafficking", and more than that, "ensures that they are less likely to free themselves from this abusive relationship".

Once the reality of global data collection is seen in accordance with the correlation and concomitance of crimes of human trafficking and drug trafficking, it will be assessed how Brazil deals with this issue in light of the gender issue considered in the previous items.

The possible correlation between drug trafficking and human trafficking crimes in Brazil: preliminary reflections

The Palermo Protocol and the Brazilian criminal law do not expressly recognize human trafficking for the purpose of committing crimes, and, in addition, drug trafficking in Brazil is considered as similar to a heinous crime.

However, as seen in the previous item, the UNODC recognizes the possibility of the commitment of human trafficking for the execution of drug-related crimes, despite not having data that portrays this situation in a way that is consistent to reality.

Conversely, in 2011, the European Parliament and the Council of the European Union, through Directive No. 2011/36 / EU, came to understand that, in addition to the modalities provided for in the Palermo Protocol, the expression "exploitation of criminal activities" should be considered as the exploitation of people for crimes such as petty, theft and drug trafficking or other similar activities subject to penalties and which imply financial gains (European Parliament, 2011).

In Brazil, related to the Ministry of Justice and Public Security, the National Committee to Combat Trafficking in Persons (CONATRAP), currently governed by Decree No, 9.833, of 2019 (Brazil, 2019), is responsible for coordinating the activities of public bodies and private entities in combating human trafficking and also for coordinating the National Plan to Combat Trafficking in Persons (PNETP).

Between 2018 and 2022, the III PNETP (Brazil, 2018) is in force, which does not yet have data on the connection of both crimes, but foresees in its goal 2.5 the elaboration of studies on the link between human trafficking and the recruitment of drug trafficking mules, as well as foresees in its goal 4.2 the development and support of initiatives to articulate public security and intelligence actions to combat both types of trafficking in the country (Brazil, 2018).

Regarding the production of data on human trafficking by the Ministry of Justice and the Ministry of Women, Family and Human Rights, research carried out by Dias Filho (2020, p. 183) finds that there are difficulties in interinstitutional data sharing that result in the absence of concrete information that could help more effectively combating this crime.

Considering the Brazilian reality, the research "Diagnosis of Trafficking in Persons in Border Areas in Brazil" (Brazil, 2013, p. 158, 221), demonstrates that border regions are marked by poverty, which makes people more susceptible to being exploited for crimes like trafficking in persons.

From the perceptions of the work carried out by the Brazilian Association for the Defense of Women of Childhood and Youth (ASBRAD) -still in the context of borders -, it is noted that, even though the cases are underreported, drug trafficking and human trafficking are crimes that are possibly directly related (ASBRAD, 2018, p. 56).In addition to these perceptions ASBRAD (2020) organized a webinar to address the relationship between female mules and human trafficking, calling attention to the difficulty of the relationship between these crimes, however, recognizing the existence – even though there is almost a total absence of documents that prove this connection.

Moreover, it is known that in addition to foreign women arrested for drug trafficking, there was an increase in the number of Brazilian women who are arrested when trying to leave the country carrying drugs. Souza believes that this rise is a consequence of the coercion exercised by criminal networks that traffic these women to be exploited in other continents, such as Europe (2013, p. 14).

In this point, rule 66 of "The United Nations Rules for the Treatment of Women Prisoners and Non-custodial Measures for Women Offenders", also known as Bangkok Rules, expressly mentions the need to implement the Palermo Protocol, seeking to protect victims of trafficking and avoid the secondary victimization of these women; otherwise, the "Criminalization limits the trafficking victims' access to justice and protection and decreases the likelihood that they will report their victimization to the authorities" (UNGA, 2011, p. 47). In fact, one of the conclusions that can be drawn from the study of these crimes and the Indonesian legislation, is that failure to observe the principle of non-persecution undermines combat transnational human trafficking (Gerry QC, Harré, Naibaho, Muraszkiewicz and Boister, 2018, p. 187).

In view of these circumstances, it is important to note that, even if the consent for exploitation exists, this does not alter the crime of human trafficking. Hence, it is verified that the implicit vulnerability to gender - added to socioeconomic conditions - makes women to be seen as an object, commodity or product, which represents "a natural consequence of a society that tends to value consumer goods at the expense of human qualities (Pinto, Atchabahian, Placca, 2018, p. 39).

Conclusion

This paper sought to analyze whether there is a relationship between drug trafficking and human trafficking crimes, as well as to demonstrate the difficulties in measuring how women victims of human trafficking can also be used as drug trafficking mules.

The first part of the research was dedicated to the understanding of the vulnerability, which, according to Fineman, is inherent to human beings. However, there are factors that can further emphasize it, such as the social context, violence and discrimination against women. In this situation, in the face of the abuse of human vulnerabilities, women become victims of human trafficking, are induced to be mules of drug trafficking and even become victims of both crimes. It was also noted that the trafficked women are converted to objects, being commercialized as a merchandise by criminal networks.

In the second part of this paper, the study by Campbell on female mules and the paper written by Souza on the imprisonment of female mules in international drug trafficking as possible victims of human trafficking were analyzed and used as a basis for the research. In this regard, particularities were drawn about both crimes, demonstrating that, as seen, the vulnerability of women can result in their use as objects without the incidence of rights.

Lastly, given this reality, through the analysis of its documents and reports, it was found that the UNODC is aware of the modality that involves both crimes, such as trafficking in persons for the purpose of committing acts related to drug trafficking. Nonetheless, there is no measurement of this connection - although there is knowledge -, especially in relation to the absence of a single methodology for data collection by States and the differences between jurisdictions regarding the understanding of the crime of trafficking in persons.

It was found that, in the dynamics of drug trafficking, women occupy positions at lower levels, which makes them more exploited and more easily imprisoned and replaced. The arrest of these women not only hinders the decrease of the activity of trafficking, but also has negative effects, such as the mass incarceration and has negative consequences for the imprisoned women and those who depend on their incomes. Circumstances like these lead to the observation of the continuousness of a cycle of poverty, marginality and recurrence, further aggravating the vulnerability of these women.

Moreover, as seen in international norms such as the Palermo Protocol and the Bangkok Rules, the ideal now sought is the non-criminalization of victims of human trafficking. In this sense, it is necessary to distinguish women who are unjustly imprisoned - who have been victims of human trafficking due to deception or abuse of their vulnerable situation - and women who decide to be mules. This distinction is important since the victim of trafficking in persons should not be punished, even if is being used as a mule for drug trafficking without having any real knowledge of his/her condition.

In this respect, from the opinion of Souza, the studies of Campbell and Pinto, Atchabahian and Placca, as well as the analysis of documents from UNODC, it was found that there is a difficulty in conducting an accurate survey of data – situation that can be proved through the absence of official documents and researches that establish this connection. However, the understanding of the European Parliament and the European Union was presented, in which the exploitation resulting from trafficking in persons relies on other forms of exploitation, such as the abuse of persons for criminal activities such as drug trafficking.

Hence, it appears that the correlation between crimes is possible, but that, to date, no materials have been developed to accurately apprehend this connection. It was possible to verify that it is usually the reports related to human trafficking that mention the possibility of drug trafficking, but that the opposite does not occur, even though many times human trafficking is the precondition for the commission of that crime.

Indicators that consider together the three main points of this research, namely, human trafficking, drug trafficking and the vulnerability of women are needed, in order to result in data that are more reliable. With those standards, States like Brazil can also consider the concomitant existence of these crimes in their reports, documents and legislation, facilitating the elaboration of public policies that consider the metrics of this nature. As seen, UNODC's efforts to implement and improve the data collection and systematization methodology are not enough; it is mainly necessary for States to be responsive in making this measurement.

Another measure that could bring greater commitment and represent better responses from States would be that, when analyzing the information obtained in the Global Reports, readjust their policies and methodology, seeking to collaborate more effectively with the coming reports - although there is no international norm that seeks standardization and greater effectiveness in data collection with regard to this matter.

Consequently, with respect specifically to the focus of this research, States may - although not required by UNODC -, investigate and report the internal occurrence of human trafficking for the exploitation of crimes related to drug trafficking, eventually establishing their data collection methodologies on the concomitance of those crimes, but without criminalizing the victim of trafficking in persons who may eventually be used as a mule for drug trafficking.

In Brazil, although reports and data showing this connection between crimes have not been found, in the III PNETP there is a provision for the development of studies related to the topic of this paper, as well as preliminary materials produced by ITTC and ASBRAD.

As long as there are no understandings that, in the context of this research, the crime of human trafficking precedes forced exploitation to commit acts related to drug trafficking, women will be victims twice: first of the recruiters and, later, of the laws.

REFERENCES

Arendt, H. (1989). *As origens do totalitarismo.* Companhia das letras.

ASBRAD. (2018). *Percepções Sobre o Tráfico de Pessoas e Outras Formas de Violência Contra a Mulher Nas Fronteiras Brasileiras.* Guarulhos.

ASBRAD. (2020). Ep. 7 "Mulas" do Narcotráfico. https://www.youtube.com/watch?v=HnKrS8o0dcU

Brazil. (2004). *Decree No. 5, 017, of 12 March 2004.* Promulgates the Additional Protocol to the United Nations Convention against Transnational Organized Crime Relating to the Prevention, Repression and Punishment of Trafficking in Persons, Especially Women and Children.

Brazil. (2019) *Decree No. 9, 833, of June 12, 2019.*Provides for the National Committee to Combat Trafficking in Persons.

Brazil. (2013). *Enafron Research.*Diagnosis of Trafficking in Persons in Border Areas.National Secretary of Justice.

Brazil. (2006).*Law No. 11, 343, of 2006.* Institutes the National System of Public Policies on Drugs - Sisnad; prescribes measures to prevent the misuse, attention and social reintegration of drug users and addicts; establishes rules to suppress unauthorized production and illicit drug trafficking; defines crimes and takes other measures.

Brazil. (2016). *Law No. 13, 344, of October 6, 2016.* Provides for the prevention and repression of internal and international human trafficking and measures for the care of victims; amends Law No. 6, 815, of August 19, 1980, Decree-Law No. 3, 689, of October 3, 1941 (Penal Procedure Code), and

Decree-Law No. 2, 848, of December 7, 1940 (Penal Code); and repeals provisions of Decree-Law No. 2, 848, of December 7, 1940 (Penal Code).

Brazil. (2018).*III National Plan to Combat Trafficking in Persons*. Ministry of Justice and Public Security.

Campbell, H. (2008). Female Drug Smugglers on the U.S.-Mexico Border: Gender, Crime, and Empowerment. *Anthropological Quarterly, 81* (1), 233-267.

Dias Filho, A. J. (2020). Rede de dados e informações sobre o tráfico de pessoas no brasil: o desafio da produção, da integração e do compartilhamento interinstitucional. In: Smanio, G. P., Pinto, F.C.S., Atchabahian, A.C.R.C., Andreucci, A. C. P. T. Junqueira, M. A. (Eds).*Pessoas invisíveis:* prevenção e combate ao tráfico interno e internacional de seres humanos

European Parliament. (2011). *Directive 2011/36/EU of the European Parliament and of the Council of 5 April 2011 on preventing and combating trafficking in human beings and protecting its victims and replacing Council Framework Decision 2002/629/JHA*. https://eur-lex.europa.eu/legal-content/en/TXT/?uri=CELEX%3A32011L0036

Gerry QC, F. Harré, T.Naibaho, N. Muraszkiewicz, J. Boister, N. (2018). Is the Law an Ass When It Comes to Mules? How Indonesia Can Lead a New Global Approach to Treating Drug Traffickers as Human Trafficked Victims. *Asian Journal of International Law*, 8 (2018), pp. 166–188.

Fineman, M. A. (2010). The Vulnerable Subject and the Responsive State.*Emory Law Journal*, Vol. 60; Emory Public Law Research Paper No. 10-130.https://ssrn.com/abstract=1694740

International Criminal Court. (1998). *Rome Statute*.https://www.icc-cpi.int/resource-library/documents/rs-eng.pdf

International Labour Organization.*Forced labour, modern slavery and human trafficking*.<http://www.ilo.org/global/ topics/forced-labour/lang--ja/index.htm>.

International Labour Organization. (2012).*Cidadania, direitos humanos e tráfico de pessoas: manual para promotoras legais populares.* https://unesdoc.unesco.org/ark:/48223/pf0000219464.

Pinto, F. C. S., Atchabahian, A. C. R. C., Placca, C. Lopes. Estatísticas relacionadas ao tráfico de pessoas: dos relatórios do UNODC à busca de uma metodologia compreensiva sobre o tema. In: Smanio, G. P., Pinto, F.C.S., Atchabahian, A.C.R.C., Junqueira, M. A., Andreucci, A. C. P. T. (Eds). (2018). *Mulheres invisíveis*: panorama internacional e realidade brasileira do tráfico

Santos, B. S. (2016). Para uma nova visão da Europa: aprender com o Sul. *Sociologias*, Porto Alegre, ano 18, n. 43, set/dez, p. 24-56

Santos, B.S. Gomes, C., Duarte, M., Baganha, I. (2008). *Tráfico de mulheres em Portugal para fins de exploração sexual.* Colecção estudos de género.https://eg.uc.pt/bitstream/10316/86955/1/Trafico%20de%20mulheres%20em%20Portugal%20para%20fins%20de%20exploracao%20sexual.pdf.

Shelley, L. (2012). The relationship of drug and human trafficking: a global perspective.*European Journal on Criminal Policy and Research*, vol. 18, 241–253.

Souza, L.L. (2013). *As consequências do discurso punitivo contra as mulheres "mulas" do tráfico internacional de drogas: idéias para a reformulação da política de enfrentamento às drogas no Brasil.* Instituto Terra, Trabalho e Cidadania.

United Nations. (1979) *Convention on the Elimination of All Forms of Discrimination against Women* (CEDAW).

United Nations. (2000). *Palermo Protocol.*Protocol to Prevent, Suppress and Punish Trafficking in Persons Especially Women and Children, supplementing the United Nations Convention against Transnational Organized Crime.

United Nations. (2015). *Sustainable Development Goals.*https://sustainabledevelopment.un.org/?menu=1300.

United Nations General Assembly. (2011)*United Nations Rules for the Treatment of Women Prisoners and Non-custodial Measures for Women Offenders* (the Bangkok Rules).https://www.unodc.org/documents/justice-and-prison-reform/Bangkok_Rules_ENG_22032015.pdf

UNODC. (2008). *Toolkit to Combat Trafficking in Persons.* https://www.unodc.org/res/cld/bibliography/toolkit-to-combat-trafficking-in-

UNODC. (2009). *Resolution No. 52/1.*Promoting international cooperation in addressing the involvement of women and girls in drug trafficking, especially as couriers.

UNODC. (2013). *Issue Paper - Abuse of a position of vulnerability and other "means" within the definition of trafficking in persons.* United Nations publication.

UNODC. (2018)*Global Report on Trafficking in Persons.*United Nations publication, Sales No. E.19.IV.2.

UNODC. (2018-b).*Countering Trafficking in Persons in Conflict Situations* - Thematic Paper.United Nations publication.

UNODC. (2020). *World Drug Report 2020.*United Nations publication, Sales No. E.20.XI.6

Wola. (2018). *Women, Drug Policies, and Incarceration*: A Guide to Policy Reform in Latin America and the Caribbean. EUA, Washington. https://www.wola.org/wp-content/uploads/2016/10/Portuguese-Report-WEB-Version.pdf

CHAPTER VI

Southeast Asia Regional Integration and Cooperation: The Nexus Between Human Rights and Trafficking in Persons

Destin Nurafiati Ristanti[1]

Introduction

The issue of human trafficking has gained attention on a global scale. It is not only a form of modern-day slavery and a gross violation of human rights, but human trafficking is also the fastest growing form transnational organized crime (Reilly, 2006), the most profitable illicit business and the third-highest source of income for the criminal organization after drugs and arms trafficking (Mahmoud & Trebesch, 2010). Human trafficking is as old as slavery and continues to the present world as modern-day slavery (Wheaton, Schauer, & Galli, 2010) due to the adaptability and resilience of transnational organized crime. As a complex issue, the exact definition of human trafficking considerably varied among scholars and institutions (Laczko, 2005), and there was no universal definition agreed upon trafficking in person until the United Nations Convention against Transnational Organized Crime and its supplementing protocols was signed in Palermo.

Article 3 of the Protocol to Prevent, Suppress and Punish Trafficking in Persons, Especially Women and Children defined human trafficking as (UNODC, 2004):

1. Graduate School of Asia-Pacific Studies, Waseda University, Japan

> The recruitment, transportation, transfer, harbouring or receipt of persons, by means of the threat or use of force or other forms of coercion, of abduction, of fraud, of deception, of the abuse of power or of a position of vulnerability or of the giving or receiving of payments or benefits to achieve the consent of a person having control over another person, for the purpose of exploitation. Exploitation shall include, at a minimum, the exploitation of the prostitution of others or other forms of sexual exploitation, forced labour or services, slavery or practices similar to slavery, servitude or the removal of organs.

While there are still debates over the definition and specific aspects of trafficking in this convention, it is the first instrument with the underlying assumption that trafficking is a severe violation of human rights (van Liempt, 2006), and it is the first UN legal instrument with a standard definition of trafficking for its signatory parties (Aronowitz, 2003). Despite the debate over the definition, the shared understanding of trafficking in person offered by the protocol has become a consensus among the scholars, and a broadened definition will cover a larger concept of exploitation (Dinh, Hughes, Hughes, & Maurer-Fazio, 2019).

There are no countries immune to the broad implication of human trafficking, and estimating the number of trafficking in person is a challenging task. Nonetheless, a study conducted by the International Labour Organization (ILO, 2005)estimated that at least 12 million people are the victims of forced labor, and as many as more than 2 million of the total number are being exploited as the result of human trafficking. As the most profitable in the illicit industry, the estimated total profit derived from the use of forced labor reached to US$150 billion per year (ILO, 2014). The majority of the profit is generated in Asia, with two-thirds in this region coming from forced sexual exploitation (ILO, 2014).This estimation can provide an idea of the extent of human trafficking. However, the challenge in assessing the extent of trafficking in person in Southeast Asia happened due to several reasons: many easily penetrable border which resulted in trafficking goes undetected; difficulty in identification of trafficked person due to citizenship and birth record administration; and, the fear of deportation once trafficked person make a report to law enforcement (Blackburn, Taylor, & Davis, 2010).Other drivers and causes—for instance, economics and globalization—are also contributing to the complexity and the scope of human trafficking in Southeast Asia; and make trafficking issues becoming arduous.

In this chapter, I analyze regional integration and cooperation concerning human trafficking and human right by focusing on the Southeast Asia region. Trafficking in persons happened across the globe, and Southeast Asia becomes the greatest hub of this illicit business (Perry & McEwing, 2013). Association of Southeast Asia Nation (ASEAN) is the regional institution which provides a framework for the regional integration and cooperation in the Southeast Asia region, and a significant counter-trafficking instrument. This institution established the ASEAN Economic Community (AEC), which aims to contribute to the region's development and economic growth. It has created an opportunity for people to have a better life by having decent works, whilst it makes them vulnerable to exploitation and posing a higher risk of becoming trafficked people.

Globalization and Economic Integration as the Drivers in Human Trafficking in Southeast Asia

Human trafficking is a longstanding phenomenon. In the contemporary world, this phenomenon is arising and sticking out as one of the complicated issues driven by globalization. Trafficking in persons benefits through a global condition that creates a supply and demand chain supporting human trafficking (Nagle, 2008). The idea of globalization and human can be drawn through the argument about the link between globalization and the illicit economy. It comes from the idea that globalization offered opportunities for transnational commerce to grow, deregulation of the international market and the construction of economic and trading bloc—ASEAN, EU—which resulted in weakened or abolished border control and provided opportunities for illicit transnational commerce (Edwards & Gill, 2004). As the consequences of globalization, border deregulation, and regional integration—along with the privatization of industry and focus on profit—have fueled human trafficking (Sanders, 2012), particularly in terms of the sex market in Southeast Asia.

Globalization blurred boundaries and created openness. Then, the openness to the movement of goods and services can be an indication of economic integration and represent the movement of people (Danailova-Trainor & Belser, 2006) and the countries that can cope with this economic openness may gain more than those were not (Asra, Estrada, & Pernia, 2005). Globalization builds a borderless world where the economy becomes integrates, and the movement of people, goods, and services can be easily done, while the gap between the rich and the poor is expanding because globalization also facilitates capital transfers and transnational economic transactions. Contrary to the idea that economic integration and free trade promoted by globalization can be utilized to improve the economic state of affairs, economically stable countries exploit less developed countries for cheaper labor and goods. Developing countries appear to be forced to agree to provide cheap, exploitable, and disposable labor and goods for the markets (Sanders, 2012). As a result, globalization seems to provide hope that developed countries can provide opportunities to get decent jobs that are difficult for countries of origin to provide, thus people are vulnerable to the risk of exploitation and human trafficking.

ASEAN Economic Community (AEC) - Development and Poverty in Southeast Asia

The Association of Southeast Asian Nations (ASEAN) is a regional institution in the Southeast Asia region. It was established by Indonesia, Malaysia, Philippines, Singapore, and Thailand in 1967 through the ASEAN Declaration (ASEAN, 2020). In the following years, other countries in the region then joined ASEAN so that the membership of this institution as it is known today. This institution, in principle, provides a framework for its members in the economic, socio-cultural, and political-security fields. The firm commitments from its members have accelerated the formation of the ASEAN community to be established in 2015. ASEAN Community consists of three pillars, namely the ASEAN Economic Community (AEC), ASEAN Political-Security Community (APSC), and ASEAN Socio-Cultural Community (ASC). From these three pillars, it appears that AEC is the pillar that is in harmony with one of the ASEAN objectives stated in the ASEAN Declaration, namely accelerating the economic growth in the Southeast Asia region. Moreover, it is in aligned with the ASEAN Vision 2020 that view a shared mutual agreement of Southeast Asia Nations as outward-looking, living in peace, stability and prosperity, bonded together in partnership in dynamic development and a community of caring societies (ASEAN, 2020).

The establishment of the ASEAN Economic Community is a significant milestone in the Southeast Asia region. It brings opportunities in the form of a massive market of US$2.6 trillion and over 622 million people; thus, it became the third-largest economy in Asia and the seventh-largest in the world (ASEAN, 2020).This community is also expected to create an environment in the region that can foster a more robust intra-regional trade and enhance the development of its member countries (Asra et al., 2005)so that the less-developed members can eventually catch up with other members that already have developed in the region.

Globalization and the ASEAN Economic Community have created a condition where free trade is becoming easier. It is not only carried out among ASEAN member countries but also with other developing or developed countries. The free trade agreements between developed and developing may raise people's standard of living. However, on the other hand, those agreements may create a wider socioeconomic gap between developed and developing countries (Chastain, 2006). Thus, poverty, unemployment, the lack of equal opportunity, and people are becoming susceptible to exploitation. In addition, human trafficking is considered not only a result of globalization but also a part of the process where it involves a functional integration of dispersed economic activities. Simultaneously, the increasingly integrated economy enables human trafficking to thrive (Brewer, 2009). Globalization is marked by the free trade, free flow of capital, and the cheaper labor that transcends the nation-state boundaries. Globalization has created a comparative advantage in goods and cheap labor, resulting in human objectification and exploitation for economic ends (Brewer, 2009). Furthermore, the high demand for cheap labor resulted in labor trafficking exploited in a slave-like condition.

Human Rights and Human Trafficking within the Framework of ASEAN

Every individual has the right to decent work, and it cannot be resisted if the economic integration in the Southeast Asia region is considered creating opportunities in the labor market. However, this situation may also result in vulnerable groups of people being trapped in human trafficking, either in forced labor or sexual exploitation. As the form of modern-day slavery, human trafficking is a gross violation of human rights under the norms of international law, and it is criminalized by many nations (Nagle, 2008). In the Southeast Asia region, there are three international regimes considered to address the human trafficking issue (Renshaw, 2015), which are: The United Nations Trafficking Protocol (Palermo Protocol), Trafficking Victims Protection Acts (TVPA), and ASEAN Convention against Trafficking in Person (ACTIP).

The first regime is a global level instrument set by the United Nations to establish a standard of trafficking in persons and institute the cooperation parameter among the signatory parties. Although the UN Convention and its supplementing protocols are considered more likely as law enforcement rather than a human rights instrument (Gallagher, 2002). The Trafficking in Person Protocol created a global consensus in defining trafficking; internationally disseminating the prohibition of human trafficking and slavery; and, promoting human rights protection and assistance to the trafficked people. However, it appears that the Protocol lacks policing power; hence many countries allocated the resources and stipulated new laws to combat human trafficking (Obuah, 2006).The second regime is TVPA, which implemented by the United States. This instrument categorized countries into tiers based on the countries' compliance and efforts to combat trafficking in persons as specified in the TVPA and imposed sanctions on the countries that failed to meet the minimum standard. The third regime is ASEAN Convention Against Trafficking in Persons, Particularly Women and Children (ACTIP), which functioned as a regional instrument to combat trafficking in the Southeast Asia region.

The ACTIP was signed in 2015 and came into force in the six ASEAN member countries that have ratified the

Convention. Although ACTIP is considered as a non-binding instrument, the signing and ratification of this Convention showed that the countries in the Southeast Asia region had taken a significant step to combat trafficking in person and the stronger legalization of the anti-trafficking instrument in Southeast Asia (Yusran, 2018).In this Convention, ASEAN members recognized trafficking as a violation of human rights and an offense to human dignity (ASEAN, 2015a). The basic principles of ACTIP adhere to the global consensus regarding human rights and trafficking—namely the Universal Declaration of Human Rights, ASEAN Charter, the ASEAN Human Rights Declaration, the UN Convention against Transnational Organized Crime and its anti-trafficking protocol—in order to combat trafficking in person concurring the protection of human rights of the trafficked people, and promoting cooperation among the member states to fight against the issue.

The discussion about human trafficking entails human rights (Obokata, 2006) because trafficking in persons is a gross violation of human rights. In the Southeast Asia region, the ASEAN Intergovernmental Commission on Human Rights (AICHR) was established in 2009. This institution is designed to be an integral part of ASEAN and acts as an overarching institution responsible for promoting and protecting human rights in the region (AICHR, 2020). The Southeast Asia region has the institution, the instrument, and the framework to combat human trafficking; moreover, some ASEAN member countries have enacted anti-trafficking laws and mechanisms against trafficking. However, the Trafficking in Persons Report issued by the U.S Department of State (2019) has placed most ASEAN member countries—exceptthe Philippines—onthe Tier 2 or Tier 2 watch list. It shows that most member countries are considered not providing sufficient domestic human rights laws and mechanisms against trafficking in persons due to a lack of shared and efficient anti-human trafficking standards (Kranrattanasuit, 2014).

Although ASEAN already has AICHR as its human rights regional institution and ACTIP as an anti-trafficking legal framework, dealing with human trafficking as a human rights violation issue in Southeast Asia can be arduous due to the ASEAN way. Non-intervention—a principle in the ASEAN way—is viewed as a hindrance to human rights development in the region (Kranrattanasuit, 2014). This principle may be significant for stability in the region, but it may not be applicable in terms of human rights violation issues. In addition to the non-intervention principle, respect to sovereignty and consensus in decision making has affected the establishment of AICHR, which then resulted in a weak authority in implementing human rights (Hara, 2019). It means that the principles upheld by the ASEAN member countries appear to create a state that prevented AICHR from functioning adequately and taking firm action when human rights violations occur; thus, there are calls to make a stronger AICHR.

Human Trafficking in Southeast Asia: Between Cross-border and Domestic Trafficking

It is a challenging task to measure the prevalence of human trafficking. Along with a different pattern of trafficking that emerged in different places (UNODC, 2018), the difficulty to assess the size of human trafficking is because trafficking in person takes place underground, unidentified or misidentified; and, unreported (Parreñas, 2011).Nonetheless, there has been a study conducted by some institutions to estimate the prevalence of human trafficking in global, regional, and state level. The Global Report on Trafficking in Person stated that most of the victims detected globally are trafficked for sexual exploitation, albeit it must not be consistent across the regions (UNODC, 2018). The Global Slavery Index 2018 estimated that

Asia and the Pacific region has the second-highest prevalence—after Africa—of human trafficking as modern slavery; with the details are forced labor became the highest prevalence while forced marriage is the second-highest (Walk Free Foundation, 2018).Many studies show that the estimation of human trafficking prevalence in Southeast Asia focused on women and children. In this region, women are mainly trafficked for prostitution or sexual exploitation, forced labor, forced marriage, and domestic workers; meanwhile, children are trafficked into forced begging, domestic workers, child brides, and baby trafficking (Yusran, 2018).Women and children are vulnerable to human trafficking, but this group also appears to be more perceptible to observe; hence, most studies and reports estimate the prevalence of human trafficking focused on women and children.

As previously explained about the effect of globalization on human trafficking in Southeast Asia, it can be seen that the economic disparities in the Greater Mekong Subregion have become the driver of the trafficking of women and children from Myanmar, the Lao People's Democratic Republic, and Cambodia to Thailand; meanwhile, women and children from Vietnam have been trafficked to Cambodia for sexual exploitation, and to China for forced marriage and domestic work (ILO, 2005). Also, human trafficking from this subregion is related to the pressure to migrate from the rural area, start to a new life, and escape from poverty, which makes people become vulnerable and falling into trafficking. The form of human trafficking in this subregion varies from exploitation in industries, forced begging, domestic worker, prostitution, forced labor in fishing boats sailing in Thailand, Malaysian, and Indonesian water (World Vision International, 2013). Regional integration has created a more borderless region, facilitating people's movement and opportunities to get a decent job. However, the malleable border created a tourist boom that prevailed in Southeast Asia, which then resulted in sex tourism.

As one of the transnational crimes in Southeast Asia, human trafficking is becoming more serious because organized crime groups have exploited the opportunities as globalization created an integrated economy and free trade. Thus, this can result in competition to get the maximum profit at the least cost. In this case, the fisheries have recently been known to put pressure on production costs to get the most significant profit (Tickler et al., 2018). Cutting production cost lead to cheap labor; therefore, the global fishing industry becomes the hot spot of forced labor. Overfishing also worsened the situation in which the fishing industry turned to vulnerable migrant workers to maintain its profit (The ASEAN Post, 2019), and Southeast Asia are the major sources for such labor.

The increasing number of detected trafficked people has been more pronounced in the U.S and Asia. It indicates the result of states' capacity to detect, record, and report data of trafficking victims, and it reflects how countries have committed to criminalizing different forms of exploitation (UNODC, 2018). Trafficking in person is not limited to cross-border, but it is plausible to occur domestically within the state's national border. The ILO estimated that traffickers exploited 77 percent of all trafficked people in their country of residence. Aside from cross-border trafficking in person, human trafficking within the national borders of ASEAN member countries is also prevalent, particularly in coastal states, namely Indonesia, Myanmar, the Philippines, Thailand, Malaysia, and Vietnam. However, the extent of domestic trafficking is difficult to assess than cross-border trafficking (Blackburn et al., 2010).To combat trafficking in Southeast Asia, ACTIP is signed by ASEAN member countries, and its implementation is based on the ASEAN Plan of Action Against Trafficking in Persons, Especially Women and Children. Both

ACTIP and Plan of Action are the regional instrument in Southeast Asia to fight against trafficking in person. However, it appears that regional and international cooperation under this Plan of Action focused on strengthening the rule of law and border control among ASEAN member countries; and, enhance cross-border cooperation and sharing intelligence to disrupt trafficking operation (ASEAN, 2015b), hence it prone to cross-border trafficking than domestic trafficking.

Conclusion

Human trafficking has existed for a long, and it has been a complicated issue for any part of the world. In the contemporary world, globalization has brought convenience and create a world where national borders no longer limit people. Globalization also benefited regional integration, such as ASEAN, to support its member countries' development. On the other hand, globalization has also become a driver for trafficking in persons because people are prone to go to the more developed countries, and these people are vulnerable to exploitation and trafficking in person. To combat human trafficking, ASEAN has set its regional instrument and Plan of Action to accommodate its member countries to cooperate; nonetheless, the regional cooperation within this framework appears to focus on cross-border trafficking and less focus on within-border trafficking. There are still shortcomings faced within the Southeast Asia region to protect trafficked people's human rights; thus, a more robust human rights institution may be necessary to protect human rights in the region adequately.

REFERENCES

AICHR. (2020). About AICHR: Structure, works and history of the AICHR. Retrieved from https://aichr.org/about-aichr-2/#

Aronowitz, A. A. (2003). Trafficking in human beings: An international perspective. In D. Siegel (Ed.), *Global organized crime* (pp. 85-95). Netherland: Kluwer Academic Publishers.

ASEAN. (2015a). *ASEAN Convention against Trafficking in Persons*

ASEAN. (2015b). *ASEAN Plan of Action against trafficking in persons, especially women and children*. Retrieved from http://www.asean.org/wp-content/uploads/2015/12/APA-FINAL.pdf

ASEAN. (2020). Association of Southeast Asia Nations. Retrieved from https://asean.org/

Asra, A., Estrada, G. E., & Pernia, E. M. (2005). ASEAN Economic Community: Implications for poverty reduction in Southeast Asia. *Roadmap to an ASEAN Economic Community.Singapore: Institute of Southeast Asian Studies,* 218-245.

Blackburn, A. G., Taylor, R. W., & Davis, J. E. (2010).Understanding the complexities of human trafficking and child sexual exploitation: The case of Southeast Asia. *Women & Criminal Justice, 20* (1-2), 105-126.

Brewer, D. (2009). Globalization and human trafficking. *Topical Research Digest: Human Rights and Human Trafficking, 2009,* 46-56.

Chastain, C. (2006). The nexus between free trade agreements and the trafficking of human beings. *Wash.U.Global Stud.L.Rev., 5,* 587.

Danailova-Trainor, G., & Belser, P. (2006).*Globalization and the illicit market for human trafficking: An empirical analysis of supply and demand.*

Dinh, N., Hughes, C., Hughes, J., & Maurer-Fazio, M. (2019). Human trafficking in Southeast Asia: Results from a household survey in Vietnam. *Journal of Human Trafficking,* 1-21.

Edwards, A., & Gill, P. (2004). After transnational organised crime?: The politics of public safety. *Transnational organised crime* (pp. 278-295) Routledge.

Gallagher, A. (2002). Trafficking, smuggling and human rights: Tricks and treaties. *Forced Migration Review, 12* (25), 8-36.

Hara, A. E. (2019). The struggle to uphold a regional human rights regime: The winding role of ASEAN Intergovernmental Commission on Human Rights (AICHR).*Revista Brasileira De Política Internacional, 62* (1).

ILO. (2005). *A global alliance against forced labour*. Geneva: International Labour Office.

ILO. (2014). *Profit and proverty: The economics of forced labour.* Geneva: International Labour Organization.

Kranrattanasuit, N. (2014). *ASEAN and human trafficking: Case studies of Cambodia, Thailand, and Vietnam.*Martinus Nijhoff Publishers.

Laczko, F. (2005).Data and research on human trafficking. *International Migration, 43 (1-2)*, 5-16.

Mahmoud, T. O., & Trebesch, C. (2010). The economics of human trafficking and labour migration: Micro-evidence from Eastern Europe. *Journal of Comparative Economics, 38* (2), 173-188.

Nagle, L. E. (2008). Selling souls: The effect of globalization on human trafficking and forced servitude.*Wis.Int'L LJ, 26*, 131.

Obokata, T. (2006).*Trafficking of human beings from a human rights perspective: Towards a more holistic approach.*Martinus Nijhoff Publishers.

Obuah, E. (2006). Combating global trafficking in persons: The role of the United States Post-September 2001. *International Politics, 43* (2), 241-265.

Parreñas, R. (2011). *Illicit flirtations: Labor, migration, and sex trafficking in Tokyo* Stanford University Press.

Perry, K. M., & McEwing, L. (2013). How do social determinants affect human trafficking in Southeast Asia, and what can we do about it? A systematic review. *Health and Human Rights, 15* (2), 138-159.

Reilly, A. A. (2006). Slavery legislation vs. trafficking legislation in prosecuting the crime of female sexual slavery: An international perspective. In C. v. d. Anker, & J. Doomernik (Eds.), *Trafficking and women's rights*. Basingstoke England: Palgrave Macmillan.

Renshaw, C. (2015). Human trafficking in Southeast Asia: Uncovering the dynamics of state commitment and compliance.*Mich.J.Int'L L., 37*, 611.

Sanders, A. (2012). Sex trafficking in Southeast Asia: How neo-liberalism has bolstered the global sex trade. *On Politics, 6* (1)

The ASEAN Post. (2019). Is the fish you eat caught by 'slaves'? Retrieved from https://theaseanpost.com/article/fish-you-eat-caught-slaves

Tickler, D., Meeuwig, J. J., Bryant, K., David, F., Forrest, J. A., Gordon, E., Sumaila, U. R. (2018).Modern slavery and the race to fish. *Nature Communications, 9* (1), 1-9.

U.S Department of State. (2019). *Trafficking in person report June 2019.*U.S Department of State Publication Office of the Under Secretary for Civilian Security, Democracy, and Human Rights. Retrieved from https://www.state.gov/wp-content/uploads/2019/06/2019-Trafficking-in-Persons-Report.pdf

UNODC. (2004). *United Nations convention against transnational organized crime and the protocol thereto*. New York: United Nations.

UNODC. (2018). *Global report on trafficking in person.*United Nations. Retrieved from https://www.google.com/url?sa=t&rct=j&q=&esrc=s&source=web&cd=&cad=rja&uact=8&ved=2ahUKEwj0zZqjioPqAhURE6YKHRqiCQsQFjAAegQIBhAB&url=https%3A%2F%2Fwww.unodc.org%2Fdocuments%2Fdata-and-analysis%2Fglotip%2F2018%2FGLOTiP_2018_BOOK_web_small.pdf&usg=AOvVaw1iSCLawc-1PasK0Za7fuNj

Van Liempt, I. (2006). Trafficking in human beings: Conceptual dilemmas. In Cristien L. van den Anker, & J. Doomernik (Eds.), *Trafficking and women's rights* (pp. 27-42)

Walk Free Foundation. (2018). *The global slavery index.* Retrieved from https://www.globalslaveryindex.org/2018/findings/regional-analysis/asia-and-the-pacific/

Wheaton, E. M., Schauer, E. J., & Galli, T. V. (2010). Economics of human trafficking. *International Migration, 48* (4), 114-141.

World Vision International. (2013). *Tackling human trafficking in the Greater Mekong Sub-region*. Bangkok: World Vision East Asia Regional Office.

Yusran, R. (2018). The ASEAN Convention against trafficking in persons: A preliminary assessment. *Asian Journal of International Law, 8* (1), 258-292.

CHAPTER VII

The Role of Women as Traffickers of Human Beings for the Purposes of Sexual Exploitation: Empowerment or Subordination?

Carmen Meneses Falcon[1]

Introduction

The trafficking of people and the trade in human beings has become a problem of great concern for the countries of the European Union. The causes of these phenomena are many, but two in particular appear to be fundamental. On the one hand, low economic development, high levels of social inequality and the lack of safety in many countries inside and outside the borders of Europe, which mean that many families live in conditions of significant poverty and have the desire to prosper beyond the borders of their country. On the other hand, the considerable flows of migrants that have in recent decades been streaming toward Europe, and the border restrictions that Europe has set up against those that are outside its borders (Ellis and Akpala, 2011). These limitations on border crossing increase the dependence of sub-Saharan women on traffickers' networks to get them across the borders (Modupe-Oluwa and Heumann, 2014).

Trafficking in human beings, according to the Protocol to Prevent, Suppress and Punish Trafficking in Persons[2],

1. Universidad P. Comillas, Spain, Correspondence should be addressed to Carmen Meneses-Falcón. Department Sociology and Social Work. c/ Universidad Comillas 3, 28049 Madrid

2. Palermo Protocol 2000

involves three elements (Molland, 2011): a) an *action*, the recruitment of a person to whom a job or activity in another place is offered, and who is transported, crossing borders or not; b) a *method*, deception as what is promised is not real, or the person does not receive all the necessary information for their decision, coercion, threats or violence will be present at some moment in the process, if not from the start; and c) a *purpose*, once at the destination, the purpose is the exploitation of that person for profit. The particular variety we are focusing on here is sexual exploitation, but it can also be for labour, for the human organ trade, the commissioning of crimes, or forced marriages. Frequently, the levels of coercion or violence can be psychological, with people from their most immediate environment involved. The harm produced in the victim is not always physical in this process, which is why it is very difficult to identify the crime appropriately. Trafficking can also take place within borders or countries themselves, although the reality in Spain is that most victims come from other countries with worse socioeconomic situations than those existing in western Europe. Among these countries, it is worth highlighting Latin American countries, sub-Saharan African countries, particularly Nigeria, and eastern Europe, mainly Romania (Memoria Fiscalía General del Estado [Public Prosecutor's Office Report], 2017).

The gender inequalities in the process of trafficking for the purpose of sexual exploitation are multiple. The first is the difference between men and women regarding who is the trafficker and who is being trafficked. The situation of trafficked women with regard to violence, family vulnerability and lack of protection or inequality in the legal sphere, due to the positions that they occupy in the trafficking networks, is a key theme for gender studies and has received little attention.

In the 2015 Eurostat report, it was highlighted that over three years, from 2010 to 2012, 30, 146 victims were registered in the 28 Member States: 80% of these victims were female, and 69% of the victims were trafficked for the purpose of sexual exploitation. However, 70% of suspected traffickers were male. These data therefore show that 30% of the traffickers are women, but little attention has been paid to this fact, bearing in mind that in other crimes there is less female presence. If women are accessing this criminal structure, understanding who they are, how they are organized and how they exploit their victims can help in reducing the crime. In general, few studies have looked at gathering information directly from the traffickers, but doing so can offer valuable information for a better understanding of the trafficking and smuggling phenomenon. A study with actors who are outside the law presents considerable challenges for criminology and for research methodology (Becker 1963).

In this paper, the roles acquired by women as traffickers in the trafficking of human beings for the purpose of sexual exploitation are analysed; and we attempt to understand the meaning and perceptions the traffickers have of this crime.

Methods

This study is descriptive and exploratory and uses a qualitative methodological design, by means of interviews, participant observation and case studies.For the preparation of this work, different sources of information have been utilized: first, court judgments on the trafficking of human beings for the purpose of sexual exploitation have been compiled; 82 sentences were obtained from 2012 to May 2017, from which we selected those that satisfied the objectives of this study; second, participant observation, carried out in contexts of prostitution, and interviews of police officers from different Spanish police forces that were conducted in another study (Meneses et al., 2019); third, six interviews of people convicted of trafficking human beings, currently serving their sentences, have been carried out. The Spanish Prison Service granted us the interviews in a prison where seven people were serving sentences for trafficking. Having been asked and given the informed consent for the interview, six agreed to participate. All six were convicted of trafficking for the purpose of sexual exploitation (five women, three Nigerians and two Romanians, and one man, of Paraguayan nationality). In July 2017 there were sixty-one people serving sentences in Spanish prisons for human trafficking, of whom 40% were women. Interviewing traffickers can present considerable difficulties in terms limitations of access and methodology (Troshynski and Blank, 2008), and this study was no exception. In order to ensure confidentiality, the prison was requested to deliver a letter of invitation to interview to those persons condemned for the crime of trafficking for sexual exploitation. The prison's social worker was given the task of proposing the idea of the interview to the prisoners, and if they agreed, to collect their signed agreement. The interviews were conducted in the prison where the six people convicted of sex trafficking were serving their sentence.

The interviews were carried out by two people (one of them the lead author of this paper). The interviewees were guaranteed confidentiality and that the information they provided would neither benefit nor be detrimental to their penitentiary situation. The interviews could not be recorded as voice recorders were not permitted inside the prison. Notes were taken, according to which the interview developed, and upon completion, they were reproduced, almost literally, by each researcher separately, and the two resulting versions were subsequently checked against each other. The interviews each lasted one hour, approximately. The interview outline was structured with questions that would account for the interviewee's history from leaving their country of origin until the present day – all of their migration process. Thus a narrative was obtained from all of the interviewees. The interviews took place in November 2017.

One of the Nigerian women was interviewed twice due to her excellent contribution in terms of the information she provided. Of the six people interviewed, four (two Nigerian women, a Romanian woman and a Paraguayan man) provided highly useful information. The other two did not admit the facts and therefore the interviews only yielded secondary information, more on smuggling than on trafficking.

Of the 82 judgments on trafficking obtained, once read and reviewed, 31 were selected that belonged to victims coming from Romania (18 sentences) and Nigeria (12 sentences), although one originating from Russia was included due to its particular relevance. We managed to obtain the judgments of all of the women we interviewed, which enabled us to triangulate their narratives in the details that overlapped. But the triangulation of the narratives was otherwise impossible for obvious reasons. Nevertheless, that the people themselves admitted the facts for which they were convicted was valued as an element of veracity. Even so, key questions were asked several times in each interview in order to pursue the rigour required.

Content analysis, both of the interviews and the selected judgments, was then undertaken, driven by the study objectives. The *proven facts* were extracted from the judgments, once selected, given that this was a social analysis and not a legal one. The judgments and interviews were divided into segments according to the key categories that facilitated the research (roles, contact, exploitation, meanings…). The content segments of each analysis category were then compared, after which the next step was the interpretation of the results.

Results

The typical image of a trafficker has been laid out as a man who is unknown and far removed from the victim, a man who always employs hard violence and deceit, and who constantly abuses his victims; but this image is not always borne out (Surtees, 2008). Since the year 2000, when the crime of trafficking was defined in the Palermo convention, the modus operandi of traffickers has varied considerably as the police have come to understand the crime better and to disband trafficking groups. Our data show that the characteristics of traffickers have varied substantially, and there has always been female participation in the crime, albeit it small. Women have been present, assuming different roles, depending on the origin of the victim and of the traffickers. The roles most undertaken by women have been those of recruiters in their communities, neighbourhoods or countries of origin, and those of exploiters or controllers in prostitution. In many cases, these women were previously victims themselves, and whether voluntarily as a way to earn money – generally the Nigerian women – or under coercion – for many Romanians – they have participated with or become traffickers, and this process has been different depending on nationality. Below we set forth these aspects in greater detail, the result of the analysis of the conducted interviews and the court judgments.

Analysis of court judgments on trafficking for sexual exploitation

The analysis of the 31selected judgments leads us to set forth the following results (see final appendix):

- In the Nigerian trafficking groups, we found broad networks with a distribution of functions. Smaller networks composed of two or three people also exist, in which a woman is always involved. This situation did not occur among the Romanian convicts in the court judgments studied, which showed that they acted on a smaller level.

Raquel (*name given*) undertakes a wide range of roles within the network (of various accused with different functions). She is involved in tasks of controlling, overseeing and money collection from the victims who work as prostitutes on the street, she houses the victims in her residence, of which she is the tenant. She has authority and command over the female bosses of controllers. She also takes responsibility for contacting organization members to ensure the arrival of women to Spain, she manages the debt balances of the victims and carries out an important role in the reception and sending of money between Spain and abroad that is generated by the organization. (Judgment 109/2016)

Pura, from Uromi, Nigeria, with legal residence in Spain, by mutual agreement with her husband, Cecilio (who has not addressed this proceeding at any time), born and resident in Nigeria, decides on the transportation to Spain of Nigerian citizen XXX, for the purpose of gaining profit from her work in the activity of prostitution. (Judgment, 733/2014)

- Recruitment occurred mainly in areas and in families known by the traffickers in all of the cases examined; and in almost all, the female recruiter was a woman known to the victim, of the same nationality, who took on this activity alone or with the assistance of her partner (Judgment 733/2014, female trafficker with role of recruiter and exploiter, and her husband responsible for the journey through Africa and not convicted). In the cases in which the recruiter was a man, he was also known by the family of the victim, or she had a romantic relationship with him (loverboys), mainly in the case of the Romanian women (Judgment 4/2015). The recruiters and exploiters had legal residence in Spain.

In May, 2013, Ms Adela, who had met the accused, Amador, in Giurgiu (Romania), the home city of both of them, when she was fourteen years old and with whom she had a short romantic relationship, travelled to Madrid by bus from Romania to meet said Amador. Six years after their breakup they had regained contact through Facebook and the accused, from Spain, convinced her to restart a romantic relationship with him and to work and live together in Spain. He took charge of organizing her journey to Madrid, and went to collect her from the bus, going together to the locality of XXX. Once there, the accused tells her that she has to prostitute herself, where and how, as well as the prices she has to charge and the hours she has to do it, or else the life of her two-year-old son and her family, who remained in Romania, would be in danger. (Judgment 4/2015)

The accused, Adolfina and Consuelo, acted in mutual agreement to bring citizens of their country to Spain for the purpose of sexual exploitation, in which activity the mother of both, resident in Benin City (Nigeria), collaborated, as well as other people who have not been identified. In the year 2012, a relative of victim A made contact with the mother of Adolfina and Consuelo to facilitate her journey to Spain, to which the mother agreed after speaking with her daughters, making the victim believe that she was going to work as a hairdresser. Likewise, Victim B also went to the mother of the accused with the same aim of coming to Spain, although this victim knew that she was going to work as a prostitute, an activity she had decided to pursue in order to help her family, who were in a precarious financial situation, as her father was unemployed, her brothers were students and they had lost their home. To both of the victims the mother of the accused, after speaking with her daughters, she said that they would organize the journey, and that this would create a debt of 50, 000 euros, a sum the witnesses did not understand. (Judgment 177/2015)

- In those court judgments involving the conviction of several people, men and women, mostly regarding Nigerian networks, differentiated roles between both sexes were discerned. The men were mainly responsible for the journey from Nigeria to Spain; the women for the control and exploitation of the victims in Spain (Judgment 109/2016).
- While the debts of the Nigerian victims were between 30, 000 and 50, 000€, in the case of the Romanian victims the sums were not detailed in the court records, partly because the debt would be the sexual exploitation itself until the trafficker saw that he/she could not attain any more money out of the victim, whom he/she would then leave.
- The exploitation stage was mainly developed by the female Nigerian traffickers, who might be helped by other women or traffickers, the latter being their husbands. The Romanian victims were controlled by other women with the help of the male trafficker, who was usually in the prostitution zone, also controlling. The female traffickers take on the controlling of the victims, overseeing the number of clients they had, the time spent with them, and the money they earned, and informed the male trafficker, who collected the money. In this case, as we have mentioned, women controlled other women, themselves having been through the first role of victim already, and in both cases with a romantic relationship with the trafficker, which often made filing a complaint very difficult.
- The description of physical aggression toward the victims in the exploitation phase, generally when they refused to continue, was more prevalent when the aggressors were men rather than women, and to a greater extent of Romanian nationality.

"...where she was assaulted by the accused, Eugenio, who whipped her repeatedly with a cable folded in two all over her body, delivering punches to her face and lightly stabbing her with the point of a knife in various parts of her body, such as the neck, legs and hands, and also beating her with an iron bar on both arms. Furthermore, he forcefully gave her a tattoo on the inside of her right wrist, consisting of a barcode and below the number 2000, using the same needle tattooing machine that he used to tattoo the victim. With an electric razor he shaved off the hair from her head and her eyebrows, and blew flour in her face with a hairdryer, while he laughed. Later, he stuck a red wig that he had acquired on her head." (Judgment 34/2015)

Case Analysis. Female traffickers for sexual exploitation

The analysed interviews show us that women were introduced into the structure of the trafficking of persons for the purpose of sexual exploitation as recruiters or exploiters of other women, as has been described in other studies (Kwan, 2010; Mancuso, 2014). Of the five women interviewed in prison, three of them had previously been victims. For the other two, this could not be discovered because they did not recognize the trafficking crime. All of them were mothers, aged between 31 and 46 years old, and all were serving a sentence of eight years or longer.

TABLE: VII (A)

Convicted of trafficking victims

Interviews	Provide information	Penalty	Nº victim
Geranea, 40 years old, Nigerian	No	8 years	1
Janet, 38 years old, Nigerian	Yes	12 years	2
Javier, 37 years old, Paraguayan	Yes	18 years	2

Rosa, 46 years old, Romanian	No	16 years	1 minor
Yoly, 31 years old, Romanian	Yes	38 years	3
Clarisa, 36 years old, Nigerian	Yes	8 years	1

The table above shows the people convicted of trafficking who were interviewed. For the analysis of the roles they carried out, we will focus on three interviews as a study of different cases.

Women as Recruiters/Traffickers

The cases we have collected show that the inclusion of women in trafficking structures is conditioned by intersectional variables that condition the role that they can carry out.

Among the Nigerian women interviewed, it was common to take on the role of recruiter, in general voluntarily. Sometimes they may have taken it on with the intention of improving their situation with regard to the traffickers, when they were victims. More specifically, they were able to be recruiters with a series of prior circumstances:

a) They recruited other women without the intention of exploiting them, trafficking networks simply acted to help them get established in the target country, where these women were already settled and possessed legal Spanish documentation.

b) On other occasions, they had been victims of other traffickers (female or male) who sent them to their communities to recruit other women. In exchange, they could reduce or eliminate their debt.

c) Sometimes, they themselves were victims and at the same time from Spain, where they were being exploited, they recruited other women from their neighbourhoods of origin, helping them to come to Spain to exploit them in prostitution and with that money they paid their traffickers. In other words, they held the role of victim and trafficker at the same time, but without being coerced by their traffickers to undertake the second role.

d) Alternatively, they were victims themselves and once they had settled their debts with their traffickers, they repeated the scheme and recruited other women close to their family or neighbourhood to bring them to the target country and exploit them, earning the money that others earned off them.

e) Other women, who were victims and paid off their debt, resort to the exploitation of other female peasants for economic reasons. They do not see trafficking for sexual exploitation as a crime but as a form of migration and helping other women in their community in exchange for earning money. They reproduce what they experienced before, because the meaning of trafficking is different for women of sub-Saharan origin, especially Nigerians, than for Europe.

In the case of the Nigerian women, they displayed themselves to the women from their places of origin as models of success in Europe to be emulated. These were Nigerians with Spanish documentation, with work, and settled in Spain. Their situation was very attractive to other women. Their families, neighbours and even the women they aimed to recruit, were not aware, in most cases, totally or partially, of the reality that they had been through. It did not prove particularly complicated to recruit other women who saw them as having purchasing power and living in Europe, the main dream of many women.

These cases reveal that the women who performed this recruiting role were more successful than when the men did so, for various reasons (Kwan, 2010). First, they were women, and women had more trust in women, as there was felt to be greater symmetry for being the same sex. Second, when the fate was to work in prostitution – for in some cases it was known that this was the activity they were going to have to undertake, although without knowing the conditions in detail – the transmission of information was more fluid and with greater confidence between women. Third, they tended to recruit other women who were known to them, whether through the neighbourhood, belonging to a family network, or friendship. In all of our interviewees' cases and in almost all of the court judgments analysed, the female victims recruited were known to the traffickers – that is, there was a direct or indirect relationship of trust through their families or neighbours. These women were called "*madam*", and had a very considerable support network in Nigeria and Africa – lawyers, for the documentation, transporters for the journey to Europe, and so on (Ellis and Akpala, 2011; Mancuso, 2014).

In the case of the Nigerian women, a significant number of them had not worked in prostitution before arriving in Spain. But in the case of the Romanian women, the recruitment was able to take place in a female population that already practised prostitution (Surtees, 2008). Whatever the case, three of the interviewees were victims before becoming traffickers. We detail the case of Clarisa:

Clarisa arrived in Spain in 1999 when she was eighteen years old. At the time of the interview she had been in Spain for nineteen years. In Nigeria she had been attending secondary school but was unable to continue her education, and she asked a friend to bring her to Spain, since she had residency here, with a job. The friend requested 10, 000 euros, which she had to pay when she arrived, little by little. Her friend prepared everything, including passport and documentation. She travelled by plane to Morocco, and from there to Ceuta by boat. From Ceuta to Algeciras she was assisted by the Red Cross. She stayed in Ceuta for a year and she was given a residence permit. When she reached Algeciras she travelled to Madrid by bus, where she had a contact for a place to stay. She paid off her debt in two years by practising prostitution. She worked in a brothel, which according to her was safer, because those working on the street had greater problems. Then she had different jobs. She was sentenced to eight years in prison for bringing a compatriot over from Nigeria. She says that it was the girl's family that asked her own family to persuade her to help the bring the girl to Spain. She paid a *Boss/Jefe* in Nigeria to bring her to Spain and they then had to pay her 20, 000 euros. This Boss took charge of bringing the girl. She arrived in 2012 and had been in Spain for three months when she filed a complaint against Clarisa, given legal advice by an NGO. Clarisa said: "*She hasn't paid me anything, I don't why she has filed a complaint against me and they have convicted me.*" The victim who reported her went to Alicante to work because Clarisa did not want her in her house. She believes that she lodged a complaint against her in order to obtain residency papers in Spain. According to Clarisa, she brought her to Spain by plane so that she would not have to go through the difficult experience of travelling through Africa.

Clariseparated the recruitment and facilitation pattern of coming to Spain that was employed in her case, and she did so once she was legally settled in Spain. In this case, it appears that the recruitment arose through a request from her family, who had in turn been asked by the family of the victim, a young woman of the same nationality and ethnicity.

In the Nigerian examples, the difference in coming by plane or crossing Africa to Spain or Italy, which were the main European destinations, depended on the support of the network of connections that facilitated the journey (Ellis and Akpala, 2011). By plane was more expensive and riskier because their documentation tended to be false, but no intermediaries were needed. In contrast, the journey overland requires a considerable network of support and connections to facilitate border crossings and confront the dangers that can arise, and for this the presence of a man was indispensable. In this case, the profits would be shared. However, such a difference did not occur for the victims coming from Romania. The victims could travel accompanied or not, but there were no difficulties to face on the journey, whether by plane or by road, because it was within Europe.

Women as Exploiters/Traffickers

The second role carried out by women was that of exploiter, once their compatriots had arrived in Spain. After the victims had crossed the Strait of Gibraltar, the exploiter had to get in touch with them, provide them with lodging and order and instruct them into prostitution, collecting the earnings gained and thus paying their debt. Let us look at the case of Janet, who had first been a victim before becoming an exploiter.

Janet, 38 years old.Nigerian. One day her friends spoke to her of the possibility of going to Europe, and they introduced her to a man who told her he was a lawyer, and he organized her documentation to go to Italy. Before leaving Nigeria, she made a pact using Voodoo in which she committed to a contract to pay a significant sum, in liras (the pre-euro Italian currency), but she was not aware how large a sum it was until she reached Italy. They told her that she had to return the money working as a prostitute. On the journey she was accompanied by a man she called Boss, along with two other women. The initial idea was to go to Ghana, from Ghana to Guinea, and then to a third country to take a plane. But the plans changed and they came overland across the desert. The documentation was false and taking a flight meant a greater risk of detention. They travelled in several lorries filled with men and women, crossing the desert towards Algeria and then on to Morocco. The lorry Janet travelled in broke down and they were stranded in the desert for two days until it was fixed. They reached Algeria and the lorry driver paid the border police to let them cross. Once in Morocco, they went to a camp with a large population of sub-Saharan Africans. Her Boss died there and she spent a few months in the camp. She made contact with a woman from the network who provided her with the means to cross the strait and gave her instructions on what to do on arrival in Spain. The sea crossing took place at night and lasted several hours. She did not know how to swim, similar to most women who cross the strait by open boat. Men, women and children were aboard. The boat broke down, and they found themselves adrift in the middle of the straits until a Guardia Civil Maritime Service helicopter came to their aid. In Spain, they were looked after by the Red Cross, and after 24 hours, having said that she had a contact in Madrid, she was given the money for the bus journey. There she met her female Boss, the one who had organized her passage across the strait and to whom she had to pay her debt, along with three other Nigerian women. After a few months she moved to Belgium to practise prostitution, because there one earned more money, and in almost two years she paid off the debt she had with the Boss. When she returned from Belgium she went to Barcelona, where she worked at a printer's for two years, and then returned to Madrid. She now had her residency and work permits, and thus was available as a contact to bring other women over from Nigeria. Along with her brother she brought two women to Spain, she contacted them and paid the money to bring them over. Her brother was responsible for undertaking the journey with them up to putting them in the boat to cross the Strait of Gibraltar. Janet met them in Madrid and instructed them that they had to work for her, to pay off a debt of 30, 000 euros each. However, these two women lodged a complaint against her, on advice from an NGO.

Janet embodies two roles: first, that of the victim, although in her account there is no mention of threats or coercion, neither at the time of recruitment nor when she was exploited.

She signed a contract under a Voodoo ritual in which she committed to paying a debt for going to Europe and she knew that it would be paid through prostitution. She knew that she had to fulfil her commitment. This could be designated trafficking or smuggling – the dividing lines are not so clear (Ellis and Akpala, 2011; Modupe-Oluwa and Heumann, 2014).

The second role, that of exploiter, once she was settled and living legally in Spain, reprised the experience she had with her own female *Boss*. In her account, she does not mention the details of the recruitment of the two women. It is understood that the recruitment and the overland journey, from Nigeria through the desert and African countries until the Strait of Gibraltar, was taken on by a man, in this case her brother, with a cost of 10, 000 euros for each woman he accompanied. Other studies have stated that this journey across Africa could not be done by one or several women alone but that a man was needed, whom they called Boss or *Husband* (Alomar and Plasencia, 2014; García de Diego, 2015). The risks and dangers that the described roles entailed were very different and were gendered. The danger faced by the female traffickers working in sexual exploitation was of being reported, detained and imprisoned. The punishment for the crime of trafficking is quite severe, at eight years imprisonment for each victim. The danger for other members of the trafficking network, generally men and who worked on the journeys and border crossings through Africa, was less in terms of detention and conviction. However, they had to face the dangers that could arise during the journey from Nigeria to Morocco. In fact, Janet was serving an eighteen-year term whereas her brother remained free, and she did not understand how charges had been brought against her.

> Janet does not understand why they lodged a complaint against her and why she is in prison, if she made an agreement with the women as she herself had

> done with her own Boss. *"This is how it is in Nigeria. They have not honoured the contract. Everyone knows that sooner or later we will see each other in Nigeria because they live in the same neighbourhood as I do."* She consented to the interview with us because she needs to tell her side of the story somehow. She is indignant, she feels betrayed because she fulfilled her side of the bargain and they have not. (Interview notes, 31/11/2017)

Another method of participation by women was with their partner, although each one took on different roles. This is the case of Yoly, Romanian, 31 years old.

Yoly arrived in Spain in 2007 at the age of 21, with her boyfriend of the time, to practise prostitution – a Loverboy method. After two months she did not want to continue working as a prostitute and her partner forced her to do so. She fell in love with another Romanian man who resolved the matter with her former partner. Yoly went to live in her new boyfriend's apartment, which he shared with other Romanian men and three Romanian women who practised prostitution on Montera Street in Madrid. It is not clear which of the Romanian men whom she lived with, including her partner, worked in sexual exploitation, but from her statement it seems that they all were, herself included, given that she and her partner were those convicted. One of them, her partner, paid 500 euros to bring each of these women from Romania in order to work in prostitution, although the cost of the bus ticket was some 100 euros; and each of them had to pay him 800 euros a week. The victims were 19 and 20 years old and knew that they were coming to work in prostitution, according to Yoly. She did not understand that without having killed anyone she had received such a heavy sentence. She thought that the women wanted to change procurers and that is why they reported them. Yoly found it difficult to recognize that she took charge of the women, that she controlled them so that they did not keep the money they earned from prostitution. That was why they charged her and her partner. She did not mention that the other two Romanian men who lived with them were also convicted and that they also trafficked women for the purpose of sexual exploitation.

In this case, the main role of recruiting, controlling and exploiting was taken by the Romanian men, aided by a woman, of the same nationality. The use of manipulation and psychological coercion, in the guise of a boyfriend, was the method used to break and deceive the victims, all Romanians. This is known as the Loverboy method, and it featured in many of the court judgments analysed. Physical violence was used with regularity by the male traffickers, but appeared more frequently in the older court judgments compared to later sentences and the current day, a characteristic that has also been confirmed in the interviews conducted with the Spanish police. The role of women was secondary and in coalition with a male trafficker, who was almost always their partner. Although Yoly did not mention it, she was also recruited as a victim through the lover boy method.

Discussion and Conclusions

Looking from the perspective of gender enables a different approach to the world of trafficking of human beings for sexual purposes, making women visible not only as the objects of trafficking but as participants of it at different levels of its structure. Women's participation as traffickers is found in both organized crime as crimes that are organized (Finckenauer, 2019).

When women enter into criminalized structures, they acquire subordinate roles that correspond to the dependent roles they occupied in their countries of origin, but they also start to acquire other more active roles that enable them to participate in the structure of the network's activity, in those that are more effective due to their female role. Our data show a diversity of positions depending on geographical and cultural contexts. The roles practised in trafficking for sexual exploitation are influenced by the nationality of the women, being different for the female Nigerian traffickers compared to the Romanian women.

Far from the traditional image of traffickers as men, and even though there is a diversity of characteristics, we can posit that a not insignificant sector of traffickers are women, who recruit other women of the same nationality, ethnicity and language as themselves. The women who were recruited to bring them to Europe for sexual exploitation belonged to their local communities, within their family, friend or neighbourhood network. Even in the example of the Paraguayan interviewee, whom we have not included as a case, the recruiter in his country of origin was his mother, and the two women he brought to Spain were known to his family. Therefore, prior knowledge of the victims in the recruitment area is the norm in most of the cases analysed. However, we do not know the positions of women within the network structure: from the data obtained it is likely that their activity is placed at a low or middle level where they can attain a position of empowerment and are important figures for other women. According to Spanish police data, the most dangerous and powerful roles remain male. While in the case of female Nigerian traffickers, there can be certain positions of power in the recruitment and sexual exploitation network, our data do not show these same roles for female Romanian traffickers. The traditional roles subordinate to men, generally their partners, were predominant both in the interviews and in the court judgments analysed of Romanian cases.

One aspect that it is necessary to examine is the impact that the participation of women in trafficking and trafficking networks produces in their families. In other criminal areas such as drug trafficking, the inclusion of women in dependent positions in criminal structures has caused a social and penitentiary crisis due to the family de-structuring it causes by giving rise to abandonment of children (Penal Reform International and Thailand Institute of Justice, 2018).

Other aspects explored in this paper should be studied in detail. From the information gathered in the interviews and other work done (Meneses, 2017), the crime of trafficking has different meanings depending on the culture. For female traffickers coming from countries such as Nigeria, trafficking was not perceived as a crime but as a contract-commitment between fellow countrywomen, which is sealed with a Voodoo ritual, used in many other important events in the lives of Nigerians and other sub-Saharan people (Dols, 2012). Given that the meaning of the crime of trafficking of human beings was very different, it was not understood, first, that the women who were recruited might not honour the agreement like the rest of the women who had gone through the same circumstances; and, second, that they should be punished with such heavy sentences when it formed part of an agreement or contract that was very common in their place of origin. For certain sectors of poor women, it was the only way they had of getting to Spain or Europe, because they could not fulfil the requirements imposed by European migration laws (Modupe-Oluwa and Heumann, 2014). Moreover, the dichotomy between consent and coercion or pressure to honour the agreement reveals a very blurred line. This was the case for the Nigerian women, or that of satisfying the request of a romantic partner in the case of the Romanian women. This leads us to think about the divergence between the expert discourse and that of the women themselves who understand the trafficking of people as a form of beginning the migration process that will lead them to a better life.

Our data are in agreement with those from other studies carried out in Spain, which allows us to state that a significant proportion of Nigerian and Romanian women have undergone a double process of victimization in the crime of trafficking for sexual exploitation (Villacampa and Torres, 2015). On the one hand, they suffered the situation of being a trafficking victim without being identified and given aid – that is to say, that nothing happened in their first process of victimization that might have led to their situation being recognized. And on the other hand, they suffered a second, institutional victimization due to the consequences of being traffickers, which they understood as a way of facilitating their compatriots' process of migration to Europe, not as a crime with such heavy punishments.

The results of this exploratory study also show that, in the case of Nigerian female traffickers, the women take on the leading role in the recruitment and exploitation of victims, whereas the Romanian women are in a secondary role, undertaken in coalition with their partners. In the two cases, the risks are shared between men and women in a different way. Carrying out their roles in Spain, when they are accused and tried, the women suffer the sentences that are established in the penal code, which are heavy sentences because it is a highly penalised crime. Yet the Nigerian men who are in charge of the journey and transport from Nigeria to the crossing of the Spanish border, commit their crime outside of Spanish and European territory, and therefore it is in many cases impossible to convict them, as can be observed in the court judgments. Perhaps the risks they run have other characteristics, those that can arise when accompanying the victims on the overland journey through African countries up to Morocco.

Another of the aspects that has emerged from our fieldwork and which we believe needs specific research is the victims' formal complaints against the female traffickers. In the cases analysed in the interviews and in some court judgments, in these complaints there was significant involvement of NGOs in advising the victims. This matter requires an examination of the role of NGOs in the reporting of the crime, which is very difficult to identify and to prove. The victims are ignorant of their rights, but making a formal complaint entails a series of rights such as a work permit and residency. There are two routes to being identified and aided as victims, the social and the judicial (Modupe-Oluwa and Heumann, 2014): while the former is taken by social services and NGOs, the latter is used by the public prosecutor and the police, which tends to be quicker in giving protection and rights, preliminary to lodging a complaint against the traffickers for their detention and trial. There are many studies that have shown that the victims tend not to report because they put their lives and those of their families in danger. However, in the judgments of the Nigerian victims we have analysed, along with the interviews of the female traffickers, these complaints are indeed brought about. There are different ways to interpret this: first, as these are trafficking networks that are not particularly organized or are very family-based, there is greater confidence that the threats made for reporting are not carried out; second, because it is women who have a more predominant role, there is a perception that there is less danger of the threats being carried out than if it were a man. Therefore, a formal complaint by the victims of trafficking may only occur when their traffickers belong to less structured or more informal and closer networks and with a significant presence of women in the roles or recruitment and exploitation. Hence the following questions emerge: is it possible that the reporting of the crime is more likely to come about when the recruiter and exploiter is a woman than when the trafficking network is run or controlled by men? Is it possible, as Modupe-Oluwa and Heumann (2014) postulate, that the only victims who can be identified, protected and helped are those who inform on their traffickers, although the price is to report a family member, a friend or a neighbour? These questions require greater information and examination.

This study has limitations due to it being an exploratory investigation of the roles of traffickers and the influence of being a man or a woman in this crime. The expansion of new cases and interviews of traffickers would document and improve the hypotheses expounded and upheld in this study and it is hoped that this work will continue. Nevertheless, this is a pioneering study in Spain, given that studies on traffickers are scarce in the international literature and almost non-existent in Spain. We can conclude that it is necessary to look into the meanings of the crime of human trafficking from all sociocultural perspectives, with the aim of understanding from a non-ethnocentric view. If the victims, from their cultural and symbolic system, understand the crime of trafficking as a form of migration process, it is possible that the NGOs are indirectly supplying the meaning, from a European perspective, that it is a crime that threatens human rights, whereas for some women it is merely paying a debt through a contract made in their countries of origin. We should lay out prevention strategies, among which is a better understanding of the meanings of the crime, in which western culture clashes with other cultural systems. It is a serious crime for Europeans, but it is not perceived in the same way by citizens from other countries, where the violation of human rights and violence against women are not a priority.

Funding: This Project is part of the National RDI Project, "VISIBILITY FOR THE VICTIMS OF HUMAN TRAFFICKING: acting against the trafficking of women for sexual exploitation", subsidized by the Ministry of Science and Innovation of Spain, Reference: CSO2014-5520907732.

This research project was approved by the Ethical Committee of the Comillas University de Madrid on 15th September 2014.

Declaration of Conflicting Interests: The authors declared no potential conflicts of interest with respect to the research, authorship, and/or publication of this article.

Acknowledgements. Our sincere thanks to everyone who has provided information for the completion of this report. At people interviewed in prison who collaborated, providing us with highly valuable information and to the professionals of Madrid Prison Centre VII, *Estremera*

REFERENCES

Alomar M, Plasencia X. (20149. Historias de tráfico, trata y prostitución. Proceso migratorio de mujeres nigerianas a Mallorca. Mallorca. Casal Petit.https://casalpetit.files.wordpress.com/2014/03/historias-de-trefbfbdfico-trata-y-prostituciefbfbdn-web.pdf

Becker H. (1963). Outsiders: studies in the sociology of desviance. New York: Free Press.

Dols, A. (2012). El vudú como elemento de coacción en el delito de trata. Revista General de Derecho Penal, 18:1-27.

Ellis T, Akpala J. (2011). Making sense of the relationship between trafficking in persons, human smuggling and organised crime: the case of Nigeria. The Polisce Journal, 84:13-34.

Finckenauer, J.O. (2019). Human trafficking, modern day slavery and organized Crime, in Clark J.B and Poucki S. Human trafficking and Modern day slavery.Los Angeles: Sage. Pp215-231.

Fiscalia General del Estado. (2017). Memoria 2017. Madrid: Fiscalia General del Estado. Ministeria de Justicia.

Kwan, Ch. (2010). Human trafficking for sexual exploitation in the UK: Case study of Eastern Europe and the Baltic States´Women. International Area Review, 13 (1):105-126.

Mancuso M. (2014). Not all madams have a central role: analysis of a nigerian sex traffiking network. Trends Organ Crim 17:66-88.

Meneses-Falcón, C. (2017). "Sueños rotos": La trata de mujeres y niñas con fines de explotación sexual, en Blanco A, Chueca A y López-Ruiz JA. (coord.). Informe España 2017. Madrid: Universidad Pontificia Comillas, Catedra J.M. Martin Patino

Meneses-Falcón, C., Urío, S., &Uroz-Olivares, J. (2019). Financing of Traffickingin Human Beings in Spain. In Shentov, O., Rusev, A. & Antonopoulos, G.

(eds.), *Finanancing of Organised Crime: Human Trafficking in Focus.* Sofia: CSD, on line

Modupe-Oluwa E and Heumann S. (2014). Migration, sex work and exploitative labor conditions: experiences of Nigerian Women in the sex industry en Turin, Italy, and Counter-Trafficking Measures. Gender, Technology and development. 18 (1):77-105.

Molland S. (2011). I am helping them: traffickers, anti-traffickers and economies of bad faith. The Australian Journal of Anthropology, 22:236-254.

Penal Reform International and Thailand Institute of Justice, (2018).Global Prison Trends 2018. London: Penal Reform International.

Troshynski E, Blank J. (2008). Sex trafficking: an exploratory study interviewing traffickers. Trends Organ Crim. 11:30-41

Villacampa C, Torres N. (2015). Trafficked women in prision: the problem of double victimisation. Eur. J. Crim. Policy Res. 21:99-115.

Wijkman, M., Kleemans, E. Female offenders of human trafficking and sexual exploitation. *Crime Law Soc Change* 72, 53–72 (2019).

https://doi.org/10.1007/s10611-019-09840-x

APPENDIX VII (A)

Analysis of sexual trafficking sentences in Spain

Nº	Sentence City	Origin	Handling victim	Profit from victim	Traffickers	
J2.01	**9/2013** Barcelona	Romania	Under-age (under 18)	Benefits from prostitution	Her cousin with her couple	Physical aggressions
J3.02	**153/2013** Madrid	Romania	Kidnapped woman. She was sold someone else for 3000 euros. She was released with a client´s help.	3.000, 00	Romanian couple	Physical aggressions
J5.04	**269/2014** Castellón	Romania	The victim is under age.	No data	4 accused 1 man, his wife, his sister and her mother.	Exploitation in brothel. Control and surveillance by the women.
J8.05	**186/2014** Valencia	Nigeria	3 woman victims, one of them was under age	50.000	6 accused 5 woman captured in Nigeria and exploited in Spain	

J9.06	**261/2014** Madrid	Romania	*The A victim was seduced by her captor (boy lover).* B victim was required to control A victim, who was captured as the same way as A victim.She was threatened with hurting her daughter and was subdued to a high control of her services and her incomes. She was also force to have sexual relations until she was pregnant of twins for one of her clients and having them. She was forced into prostitution when she was not recover from birth.	controller, victim and condemned	1 male trafficker, fake boyfriends Female trafficker, controller, victim and condemned	A client help to fill a complaint
J10.07	**733/2014** Madrid	Nigeria	A victim was contacted by the accused´s husband in Nigeria, but both acquaintances of the family.	No data	Female trafficker with husband from Nigeria	Use the asylum service

J11.08	**217/2014** Vigo	Romania	At least less than 3 accused. The eighteen victims were cheated by her *Lover Boy,* for going to Spain, the boyfriend´s parents had a club where she was forced into prostitution.		3 accused 1 man, couple´s mother	Victim was sold to another accused for 1000 euros. Exploitation in brothel
J12.09	**3/2014** Madrid	Romania	*The victim* was under age that was living in a center of minors in Italy because of practice prostitution for induction of her cousin.		2 accused, female cousin´s victim, and her couple, a man.	Physical aggressions and maltreatment
J13.10	**333/2015** Madrid	Romania	The victim is under age, who was sexually exploited by her mother. She was helped by her sons who controlled and surveillance the victim.		4 accused. 1 woman, mother´s victim. 3 brothers' victim.	
J14.11	**33/2015** Pontevedra	Nigeria	Three victims. *A Victim, B Victim was moved to London with the aim to obtain benefit from the debt of her move.* C Victim was threatened with vudu and was moved to Paris.	45.000	5 accused. A couple, a captured woman. Another woman and 2 men.	

J15.12	**1/2015** Madrid	Russia	At least 61 victims.Recruit to young women with economic needs from marginal contexts. They are recruited by agencies from local advertisements and newspapers. They come Spain as tourists to be exploited in brothels. The flights to Spain are not direct to the country to avoid suspicions and they also make fake bookings in hotels. The victims are introduced in Schengen space through Hungry, Finland or Poland by the traffickers. .	From 4000 to 6000 €	16 accused. Several women.	
J16.13	**57/2015** Palmas de Gran Canarias	Nigeria	2 victims	30.000 euros	4 accused: A recruiter woman. Her male couple and another women and her brother.	

J17.14	**80/2015** Valladolid-	Romania	2 accused. The victim's mother is deceived to authorize her under-age daughter to travel, in order to look after a little boy in Madrid. However, the victim is sexually exploited to practice prostitution by another female trafficker, that also practice prostitution. In addition, her male couple controls the victim's money.	Exploitation in Brothel	Two trafficker, couple	Fake documentation because of her minor age.
J18.15	**379/2015** Madrid	Romania	Three victim, one of them the traffickers was friend of her parents. The victim were accommodated with other woman that they practice prostitution		1 male traffickers	
J19.16	**947/2015** Barcelona	Romania	1 victim, exploitation in two apartments,	35.000	1 accused men	Threat to tell her family that she was a prostitute. Physical aggression.

J20.17	**451/2015** Lleida	Nigeria	2 Nigerian, under-aged victims weretraveling in a flight from London. They were rejected in Barcelona's borderbecause of fake documentation. They were taught how to travel to Madrid by bus and they meet the traffickers in bus station Mendez Alvaro, in Madrid.		2 men accused, in charge of the move to Spain.	
J21.18	**4/2015** Madrid	Romania	A victim, a love of her childhood contact her by internet and ask her to go to Spain. When she arrives she is force to prostitution in Torrejon with the help of another peasant. She did not receive any money for prostitution. She was attacked and abused in several occasions.		2 men accused	Threat to hurt her family
J22.19	**34/2015** Madrid	Romania	4 victims, one of them was underage with a barcode tattoo. Continuous aggressions		5 accused, a woman	

J23.20	**8/2015** Ávila	Romania	2 victims were recruited by known traffickers from childhood. One of the victims has an emotional relationship with one of the traffickers. The victims were exploited in the brothel.		2 accused men	The victim is threatened to be attacked her and her son in her original country. Sexual abused. She is also threatened with acid and weapons.
J24.21	**809/2015** Madrid	Romania	2 victims	Weekly 1000€	2 accused, a couple	She had help from a client.
J25.22	**177/2015** Madrid	Nigeria	two victims living in Benin City, for a job as a hairdresser, previous vudu ritual.	50.000	2 accused women	
J26.23	**420/2016** Madrid	Nigeria	5 victims	35.000	3 men and 2 women	Baby maltreatment
J27.24	**109/2016** Barcelona	Nigeria	5 victims	From 30.000 to 55.000	8 accused 3 female traffickers	Some physical aggression

J30.25	**157/2016** Valencia	Nigeria	*2 victims*	70.000 and 40.000	2 accused. Sister and brother	Aggressions and violations
J31.26	**6/2016** Zaragoza	Romania	In the victim's birthday she met someone who she fell in love and he force herself to practice prostitution.		2 men, one of them acts as fake boyfriends.	They threat her family.
J32.27	**538/2016** Madrid	Nigeria	*2 victims* Transfer to Tenerife	4000 euros	Nigerian couple	Fake documentation and introducing the victims in a CIE.
J33.28	**786/2016** Madrid	Romania	2 victims. One of them was released by one of the clients	minimum of weekly 400€.	Romanian man and woman.	She was threatened to tell her family that she was practicing prostitution.
J34.29	**1002/2016** Madrid	Romania	*Victim'sneighbor from her original country is encouraged to travel to Spain for working.*		A female trafficker (neighbor in Romania)	Domestic service= prostitution

J35.30	**97/2017** Albacete	Romania	*Three victims*		A woman that knew them and a man.	Exploitation in a brothel.
J36.31	**67/2017** Madrid	Nigeria	*The victim* was trick for studying in Spain.	50.000	3 women	Sexual exploitation in France and Spain. The trafficker uses the asylum service
J37.32	**166/2017** Madrid	Nigeria	The victim was taken to Morocco with her 3 years old daughter. She was intercepted by the police when crossing the strait. Finally, she was hosting by Red Cross. Her daughter was trapped during 4 to be able to practice prostitution.	50.000	2 women 2 men	Naked photos. She was threatened to send those pictures to Nigeria. Physical aggressions.

CHAPTER VIII

The Space Frames of Human Trafficking with Sexual Exploitation Purposes in Argentina: A Geographic Analysis of Court Rulings

Magdalena Moreno[1]

Introduction

In the following chapter a spatial analysis of 120 federal court ruling cases of human trafficking with sexual exploitation purposes, dictated between 2008 and 2014[2] in Argentina will be presented. In other words, this work seeks to inquire about the manners in which the State, by means of judicial interpretations, presents the spatial dimension of the phenomenon of human trafficking with sexual exploitation purposes. The paper is organized in four parts. The international definition of human trafficking, as well as a reflection about the possibility of the existence of multiple interpretations of it, is presented in the first part. The second one features a brief introduction of the theoretical framework from which the problematic is approached: Geographies of sexualities. Subsequently comes a description of global dynamics in which the phenomenon of human trafficking is framed, to present afterwards the

---

1. Center for Geographical Research at the National University of the Center of the Province of Buenos Aires (CIG/IGEHCS/UNCPBA), Argentina.
2. This time period responds to the fact that in Argentina, the Act on the Prevention and Punishment of Human Trafficking and Assistance to its Victims (Act No. 26, 364) was adopted and promulgated in 2008; and was valid when the investigation took place.

national court rulings of this crime, in order to analyze the space frames that are configured in Argentinian territory. After the geographic examination of court rulings and to conclude, some questions produced by the legal discourse in Argentina, arise around the space frames of human trafficking with sexual exploitation purposes.

Human trafficking as a spatial heterogeneous phenomenon

Human trafficking with sexual exploitation purposes is an issue that displays various edges for its study. Even if in the Argentine state, the legal regulations of human trafficking[1] exist since the late nineteenth century, it is since the United Nations Convention against Transnational Organized Crime and its protocols, that an international scale definition of the matter was agreed. Held in the year 2000 in Palermo (Italy) and ratified by the National state by the Act No. 25.632 in 2002, in its article No. 3 is determined that:

> (...) "Trafficking in persons" shall mean the recruitment, transportation, transfer, harbouring or receipt of persons, by means of the threat or use of force or other forms of coercion, of abduction, of fraud, of deception, of the abuse of power or of a position of vulnerability or of the giving or receiving of payments or benefits to achieve the consent of a person having control over another person, for the purpose of exploitation. Exploitation shall include, at a minimum, the exploitation of the prostitution of others or other forms of sexual exploitation, forced labour or services, slavery or practices similar to slavery, servitude or the removal of organs. (Palermo Protocol, 2003: 2)

1. From this point on, when human trafficking is mentioned, reference is made to trafficking for the purpose of sexual exploitation.

Despite of the establishment of a universal definition about human trafficking throughout this international agreement, there are various interpretations of it, since it has been used for the analysis of the phenomenon by diverse organizations, whether political institutions or civil society organizations, as well as academic and journalistic literature. In this manner, those who take part of different organizations and institutions often describe special space frames revealing that human trafficking for sexual exploitation purposes is not a universal and homogeneous phenomenon, but that the subjectivity of the people working in each institution plays a fundamental role in its definition. For example, each federal judge applies a personal understanding in situations regarding prostitution of others, identifying them or not as cases concerning human trafficking, in accordance to their interpretations. Considering that the concrete situations that englobe human trafficking as a phenomenon are diverse, the space frames with respect to this are presented in this chapter under the interpretation of the Argentine Federal Justice.

The mentioned complexity of the matter adds to the fact that human trafficking is constituted as a criminal offence and in consequence, it is practiced in clandestine ways. This represents an important difficulty in order to acquaint its development in material terms. In that sense and according to the information about the issue available for Argentina, different official documents which take up statistics and reports of the United Nations Organization (UNO) and the United States Department of State, were revealed, even though they do not clarify the sources of that information or the methodology for producing the data.

For their part, the geographic studies undertaken by international organisms or government agencies of the dominant states about human trafficking, are centered in mapping the statistics produced, but in general, they do not question the strictness of the sources. However, it is after the files the UNO developed and its reproduction by various social organisms, that human trafficking was installed as a public agenda concern, generating public policies driven by the political society as well as public pressure from civil society so as to eradicate it. Facing the various interpretations, the different parties grant to the matter, it becomes difficult to rigorously characterize the tangibility of human trafficking with sexual exploitation proposes at a national scale. On this account, the data retrieval each social actor, in this case the federal justice, presents about the spatial framework of the phenomenon, becomes more relevant.

Therefore, investigating human trafficking with sexual exploitation purposes from a geographic perspective, requires reconstructing the space frames of the phenomenon. To do so, it is necessary to survey the discourses about the problematic in addition to the preconceptions about those spaces, in other words, how they were conceived. Nevertheless, these statements about human trafficking must be reproduced with a critical perspective, thinking of them as not necessarily reflecting what effectively and in a material sense occurs in human trafficking, but as a specific exposure of the matter.

Geographies of Sexualities

Geography seeks to study space, understood as one more instance of social totality. Until the 1970s, space was considered as a homogenous category in terms of gender and the spatial experience of a certain hegemonic subject (man, cisgender, white, heterosexual, occidental, homeowner, among other characteristics) was presented as representative of the entire society. With the contributions added first by Geography of women, and then by Gender geography, it started to become visible that not all subjects relate to space in the same way. Subsequently, the Geographies of Sexualities were developed after incorporating queer theory.

Geographies of Gender and Sexualities study problem areas related to space, taking the sex-gender structure in which societies are organized into account. In other words, they examine the ways in which social processes create, reproduce and transform space; while also being modified by it, depending on the organization of society in regards to gender. This area of study incorporates theoretical contributions of feminism and queer theory into Geography, enabling reflection on gender matters in connection with the production of space. It is from this perspective that a gender and geographic analysis of human trafficking for sexual exploitation is proposed.

Studying the geographical framework trafficking in persons, space is considered to be relational, modifiable which reports to social relations. In agreement with Massey (2011) space is proposed to be thought as a product of social interrelations, as a possibility of existence of multiplicity, heterogeneity and plurality. Space, as understood as constituted by social relations, is always a work in progress, it is not a finished product.

These heterogeneous socio-spatial relations are also gender relations. Just as space and society are dialectically produced from each other, gender also holds this characteristic. Following Butler (1990) and the idea that gender is created and maintained through discourse and daily acts, it is understood as a discursive construction and a relational fiction. With this, daily spatial and gender exercises are the ones that construct space and identities. It is on the basis of this framework that gender violence practices[1] are inserted, as it occurs with

1. " (...) violence against women shall be understood as any act or conduct, based on gender, which causes death or physical, sexual or psychological harm or suffering to women, whether in the public or the private sphere." (Inter-American Convention on the Prevention, Punishment and Eradication of Violence against Women, 1994: 1). In addition, it can be argued that gender-based violence also includes violence against sexual dissidents, i.e. LGBTTQI (Lesbian, Gay, Bisexual, Transgender, Transsexual, Queer, Intersex).

human trafficking with sexual exploitation purposes which is conceived as one of the most extremes forms: in Argentina more than 99% of the people being forced to human trafficking with sexual exploitation purposes are women.

Global dynamics associated to human trafficking

A brief contextualization of the current dynamics of globalization linked to the subject will be made in order to understand the conditions of possibility of human trafficking.

Global scale of economic activities carried out through the growth of financial markets and expansion of international service trades characterize the current scenario. According to Sassen (2003), the current concentration of control functions generates the development of advanced production services, which are carried out by people facing labor precariousness, working outsourced and for minimum wages. On the other hand, the expansion of informal economy sets the stage for flexibilization and deregulation of workforce, provoking a deepening of inequalities. Thus, this situation presents a gender bias: it has been proven that feminization of workforce as a phenomenon carries women to covering vacancies in the most precarious labors while receiving the lowest payments.

The current moment of feminization of survival added to the feminization of workforce explained before, can be understood by the historical role in which women have been assigned tasks in housekeeping, support and reproduction of everyday life. So as to fulfill with these (unpaid) labors, women seek in migration for possible solutions and therefore, migration itself suffers feminization processes. Thereby, the ongoing dynamics of globalization reveal the systemic connection between the growth of illegal circuits and the feminization of cross-border circuits. In other words it is women who are exploited in illegal circuits[1] who seek in migration and prostitution, other ways for survival.

Consequently, alternative cross-border survival circuits, which are linked to illegal networks intended for human exploitation (generally women), of those how are disadvantaged and are part of the strategies deployed in the current stage of capitalism. At the same time, in this historical period and simultaneously to the free movement of capital, more and more restrictions are placed on the mobility of people such as border controls, increasing the problem instead of eradicating human trafficking. For example, in the absence of immigration permits women turn to traffickers to carry out their migration process. Furthermore, women that have been trafficked are often considered in the destinations countries as "illegal immigrants" and consequently governments proceed to repatriation or imprisonment. Undoubtedly this creates an even more vulnerable situation and revictimization for women. It is in this context that human trafficking with sexual exploitation purposes constitutes a global scale problem with local peculiarities.

The problematization of human trafficking as a matter of criminal justice

As previously mentioned the Prevention Law of Trafficking in Persons and Assistance to its Victims (Act No. 26.364) was passed in Argentina in 2008. From then on, Human trafficking was configured as a problem to be addressed by the federal criminal justice, playing down the importance or influence to

1. Saskia Sassen (2003: 41) conceptualizes these illegal circuits as "counter geographies of globalization. These counter geographies are deeply intertwined with some of the main constitutive dynamics of globalization: the formation of global markets, the intensification of transnational and trans local networks and the development of communication technologies (...)".

other possible ways of approaching the issue, as the economic or social-space perspective. In this sense, Pitch (2003) proposes the following thought:

> Demanding the criminalization of an act implies problematizing it in a particular way: if the solution to a problem is part of the problem, the criminalizing response is part of the characterization of the issue to which it is applied. And it is because of the criminalizing response, in its nature a strict answer, which does not allow gradations, continuous scales of assessment nor flexible and elaborated cognitive approaches; that these characteristics to the problem are transferred, constricting it within these terms. (Pitch, 2003: 130)

In order to study spatial patterns of human trafficking and since it constitutes a federal crime, judicial sentences dictated by the Argentine Criminal Justice on the above mentioned crime were surveyed and systematized. These sentences represent the way in which the Judiciary, strictly speaking, the judges of the sixteen Federal Courts of Argentina, express themselves about human trafficking. The fact that it is a federal matter means that the scale on which investigations will be carried out and sentences handed down (whether condemnatory or acquittals) is of national order. Thus, courts of provincial jurisdiction are not proficient to conduct the course of an investigation about human trafficking and cannot dictate sentences. This particularity is justified by the justice operators themselves under the argument that those who administer justice must not be linked with individuals involved in the felony. That means, when it comes to federal justice, close relationships between judges and people being judged are not created, since they may live in different provinces or not share daily activities.

Another argument for the federal justice system to deal with complaints of human trafficking is that, since this is a crime that takes place at an interprovincial, national or even international level, it requires from the justice system, a treatment with territorial jurisdiction throughout the Argentine Republic. This means that, the case will be opened in one of the federal jurisdictions, depending on where the legal complaint is filed. For these reasons, human trafficking with sexual exploitation purposes is a federal crime, to be judged in criminal jurisdiction.

Space frames of an (in)visible phenomenon

The following is a spatial analysis of 120 cases of court sentences for human trafficking with sexual exploitation purposes[1]. Table VIII (A) below shows the distribution of the total number of sentences dictated in Argentina by year.

TABLE VIII (A)

Amount of sentences dictated between the years 2008 and 2018.

Years	2008	2009	2010	2011	2012	2013	2014	2015	2016	2017	2018
Amount	1	6	17	30	23	31	28	18	9	17	17

Source: own elaboration based on court rulings

Considering the long time judicial investigations usually take to reach a verdict in Argentina, a question arises as to why there was a certain promptness in sentencing once the Human Trafficking Act was passed.

Of the 120 court sentences analyzed, 95 resulted in a prison sentence and 25 in acquittal. The latter will remain outside the universe of analysis because, according to the legal perspective, the criminal conduct was not proven, that is, the crime of human trafficking was not configured.

1. The court rulings in Argentina for human trafficking with sexual exploitation purposes handed down between 2008 and 2018 make up a total of 197. The investigation analyses 120 because of the current state of the ongoing investigation.

Beginning with the analysis of these sentences, Figure VIII(a) provides information about the gender identity of the persons who were convicted of the crime of human trafficking. Although the sentences are usually written in a language that shows only male subjects, the gender identity of these persons has been determined from other data provided by judicial documents. On this point, it is necessary to introduce a clarification under the assumption of cisexuality that takes place on a daily basis:

In a world where people are seen either as men or as women, and where it is taken for granted that we all are cisgendered and cisexual, those of us who are transgendered and also transsexual are in effect erased from public consciousness. (Serano, 2007: 4)

Considering this assumption and according to the information provided by the justice system, it is believed that in the sentences all convicted individuals are considered to be cisgender, that is, they identify themselves with the gender they were assigned at birth:

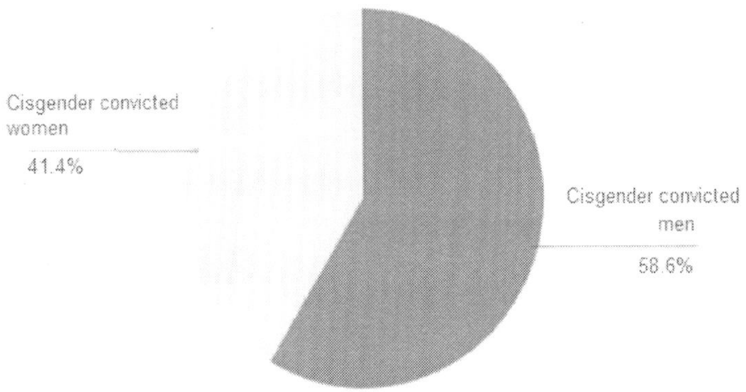

Figure VIII (a): *data on the gender identity of convicted persons.*

Source: own elaboration based on court rulings

As can be seen in Figure VIII (a), there is a majority of males who committed the crime of human trafficking (116 cisgender males versus 82 cisgender females). Although this crime is conceived as one of the most extreme forms of gender-based violence and it is assumed that the perpetrator is the generically dominant group (heterosexual men and cisgender), in Argentina's judgements this is called into question. Gender violence, in these cases, would be exercised by both women and men towards women (in all these judgements, according to the judicial discourse, the victims are cisgender women). In relation to this, a new question of investigation can be introduced: did the cisgender women who are found guilty by the Criminal Justice actually commit the crime or did they perform functions within brothels, for example, without other possibilities of choice and the judiciary system, for not having incorporated the gender perspective, sentenced them to prison anyway?

With reference to the spatial network, the following is a geographical analysis of the judicial discourse according to the following spatial aspects revealed: the modality of the transfer of the exploited persons; means of transport used for the transfer; characteristics of places of exploitation (public or private); freedom of movement of trafficked persons; places of recruitment of women who were later sexually exploited; and places where the sexual exploitation took place.

Regarding the modality of the spatial displacement of those who were later sexually exploited, it can be stated that, although a significant number of sentences do not provide further details about the stage of the transfer, those that do provide information that the transfer took place, reveal the following options: a) the person was accompanied by the traffickers; b) trafficked women were transferred without company; or c) part of the relocation was accompanied and another was not (combined modality). This distinction is important because it shows whether the women were also being controlled during the transfer or whether they were able to ask for help. As Figure VIII(b) shows, the majority of transportations (59.5%) were carried out in the company of the convicted persons and in only 31% of the cases women travel unaccompanied to the place where the sexual exploitation took place.

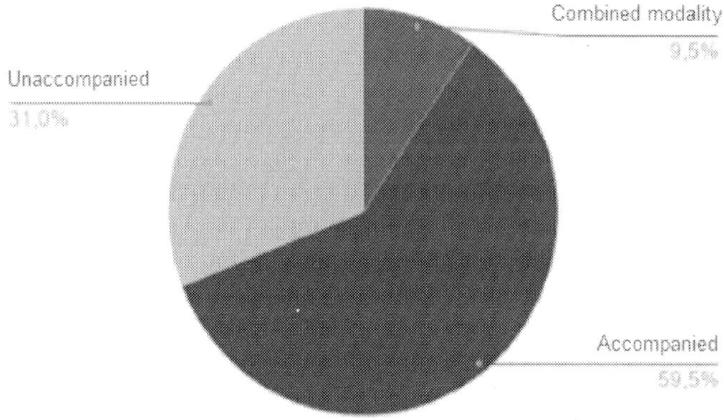

Figure VIII (b): *transfer modality of trafficked persons*

Source: own elaboration based on court rulings

By way of example, two cases of the combined transfer mode can be read below:

> They traveled unaccompanied, but with the ticket from Caaguazú (Paraguay) to Retiro (Argentina) obtained by those who had operated in the capture. From there they were transferred, after a four-hour wait, by a couple [defendant] in a car to Tandil (Argentina). (Case No. 2267. Judgment of November 12, de 2010);

> RJM and GAB [defendants] traveled to Paraguay to capture the victims and arrange their transfer to Argentina. In January 2008, MLRR [trafficked woman] entered Argentina by walking through the border crossing point [from Paraguay] with ten other women.

> On the Argentinean side a van was waiting for them, there was GAB, who left the place once saw them get into the van that took them to Miramar (Argentina). (Case No. 2306. Judgment of March 11, 2011).

In this way, the accompanied displacement (entirely or in some part) limits the possibilities of interrupting the crime of trafficking at the stage of transfer, since the exploiters will intervene directly if they are detained by the institutions that seek to control these situations.

With regard to the means of transport used to transfer women from the catchment area to the place where the sexual exploitation takes place, Figure VIII(c) shows that there are four modalities: a) use of public inland transport (bus, taxi); b) use of private inland transport (private car or motorbike); c) combination of public inland transport together with private transport (bus and car, for example); and d) combination of public air transport together with private land transport (plane and car, for example). This last modality presents the lowest percentage of cases (3.9%) and refers to cases in which women moved from the Dominican Republic to Argentina by plane.

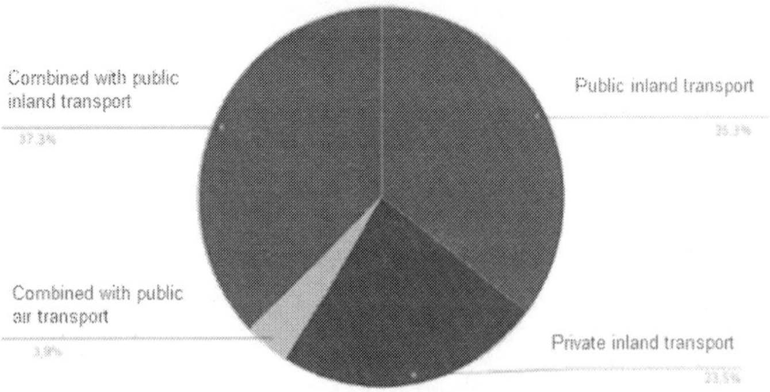

Figure VIII (c): *means of transport used for the transfer.*

Source: own elaboration based on court rulings

Figure VIII(c) shows that in a large number of cases public inland transport is used, i.e. no new routes are designed or specific transport is used but the existing infrastructure in the country to commit the crime of human trafficking. Consequently, it could be thought that a large part of these movements could be prevented or interrupted by a strong public policy aimed at raising awareness among those who drive public transport or those who inspect this sector.

Once the relocation is completed, women are sexually exploited in places that may be public (bars, brothels, nightclubs, etc.) or private (apartments or private homes). The data presented in Figure VIII(d) was found in the sentences analyzed:

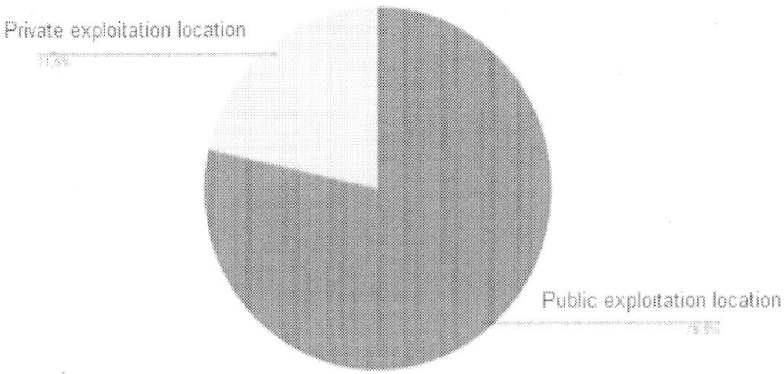

***Figure VIII (d):** characteristics of the exploitation site.*

Source: own elaboration based on court rulings

As can be seen, the vast majority (78.5%) of sexual exploitation took place in public places, despite the fact that in Argentina this type of commercial premises is prohibited. This could show some connivance between those who are in charge of these places of sexual exploitation and those who must control they do not function. By way of illustration of these situations, there is a statement from a woman who was trafficked: "she stated that when referring to the people who went to the premise, the witness answered that all kinds of people went, including police or investigators, and they never had security. (Case No. 2853-C. Judgment of August 2013).

In connection to the movements allowed to trafficked persons, it is interesting to show the different situations presented by the sentences. While some of the women were allowed to go out almost freely, others were locked up. An example of the first situation can be read in the following sentence, in which the trafficked girl (minor) went to school every day: "She got up at 6 in the morning, went to school, came back and laid down in bed. She was not allowed to sleep because if a client came she had to serve him." (Case No. 999. Judgment of March, 2010).

In other cases, trafficked women traveled to visit family members for holidays: "I would go out for a walk with the other women and to the house of one of the women's boyfriends. The victim traveled for Mother's Day to Formosa." (Case No. 1.864/09. Judgment of July 26, 2010).

In contrast, other sentences show situations of clear confinement: "L [the accused] put a lock on the gate and smeared it with black oil so that they would not climb it." (Case No. 91/2009. Judgment of April 29, 2010); "She had tried to escape but they always guarded her and followed her everywhere. There was a permanent control over them. They could not leave or had to be accompanied. Every night they were controlled and checked, even in the bathroom" (Case No. 2267. Judgment of November 12, 2010).

Within situations where trafficked women were restricted in their movements, there are certain shades. For example, in some cases they were locked up, as referred to above, and in others the women were controlled but to a lesser extent, as the following quotes show: "During the week I did not leave the house, only on Sundays with the defendant. (Case No. 2271. Judgment of February 8, 2010). "They could leave, they had a key to the place, but they had to ask the owner's permission." (Judgment of November 12, 2010).

On the other hand, the following maps {Figure VIII (e)} present the locations shown in the judicial sentences about the places women were captured for sexual exploitation in Argentina. As it can be seen, in the north and centre of the country the greatest number of recruitment sites are registered. This may correspond to the unmet economic needs of these areas which is directly related to the feminization of survival. In a large number of cases, the women who are recruited are responsible for supporting the household. In relation to the places where sexual exploitation is consumed, the mapping shows a predominance in the centre of the country, which contrasts with a certain social imaginary that exists about the area of sexual exploitation in Argentina being in Patagonia (southern part of the country) linked to extractive activities with high profitability rates. However, the cases of human trafficking reaching the justice system show that the phenomenon presents a spatial heterogeneity and the location of the places of exploitation is not necessarily related to the areas of the country where the greatest purchasing power is registered.

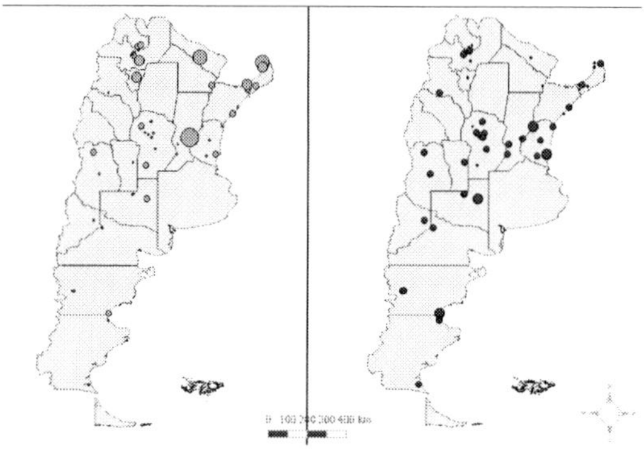

***Figure VIII (e):** captivation sites (left) and sexual exploitation (right) in Argentina*

Source: own elaboration based on court rulings

While there are places of sexual exploitation that are located in urban areas, a similar number of these places are in rural areas, far from commercial and service areas, making it even more difficult for women who are being exploited to escape these places. This can be seen in the following satellite images where the exploitation sites have been located. As example, Figure VIII (f) shows the "Whiskería: el deseo de las Vampiras" located on National Route No. 19, kilometer 302 in the small town of Piquillín. There are agricultural land lots around the place of exploitation.

***Figure VIII (f)**: positioning of a sexual exploitation site*

Source: own elaboration based on a satellite image from *Google Maps*

A similar situation is reflected in figure VIII (g), which indicates that the place where the sexual exploitation took place was operating on Route No. 12, kilometer 1252. As can be seen, the place is located on a route, far from a population centre and close to farming areas, with a small population. This makes it difficult to communicate with other persons not linked to sexual exploitation to get out of that situation.

Figure VIII (g): *positioning of a sexual exploitation site*

Source: own elaboration based on a satellite image from *Google Maps*

The following images (figures VIII (h) and VIII (i) also show these characteristics of the exploitation sites: open areas, without urban agglomerations around them:

Figures VIII (h) and VIII (i): *sexual exploitation permises*

Source: National Rescue and Accompaniment of Persons Affected by the Crime of Trafficking Program (2012: 22 y 34)

At the same time, the precariousness of many of the places of exploitation and the lack of communication between them suggest that, at least according to the Argentine federal justice system, there is no complex spatial network of human trafficking for sexual exploitation in this country. Nor would this problem have an organizational deployment in the form of territorial networks, as is often the case when dealing with the phenomenon.

Conclusion

To conclude, it is interesting to take up the topics raised above. Firstly, a question is raised regarding the judicial effectiveness of the investigations and sentences for the crime of human trafficking with sexual exploitation purposes, just one year after the incorporation of Act No. 26, 364. It would be interesting to inquire about the political effects of the sanctioning of the law and whether there was a political decision of a State intervention (through the Judiciary) to prosecute the crime of human trafficking. This can be thought of within the framework of the anti-trafficking campaign that has been developed in recent years, initiated by the United States Department of State, and now has expanded to a global scale (Varela, 2013). This campaign consists of a series of legal and institutional instruments that seek to sanction and eradicate human trafficking, through humanitarian policies that regulate the existence of human beings. Various actors, such as non-profit organizations, States or international organizations, develop a series of practices that aim, at least in terms of discourse, to help those human beings who are unprotected or in a disadvantaged situation. In this way, instead of giving them a place of agency, they create subjects who need to be helped: " *(...) inequalities are erased in favour of exclusion, domination is transformed into discomfort, injustice is named in the words of suffering, violence is expressed in terms of trauma*". (Fassin, 2016: 17)

Thereby, a clear reality that justifies intervention is built: action is needed to help subjects who are obviously in a disadvantaged situation. When displaying moral feelings in the governmental policies, a rhetoric that can be thought as "politics of compassion" is generated and, governmental practices legitimizing this compassion are carried out. This does not lead to the equalization of rights, but, on the contrary, increase the inequality: *"politics of compassion are politics of inequality"* (Fassin, 2016:12). One can find, within these state policies, those referring to human trafficking and, in particular, judicial sentences referring to it. It is worth asking then if the sentences analysed here, and the resulting space frames of human trafficking that are identified, would not be part of the anti-trafficking discourse of the aforementioned campaign and contribute to the construction of that reality; which makes state intervention evident, generally by the repressive state apparatus.

Regarding the gender perspective, it is important to note that the judgments show the lack of the perspective itself. This can be seen through several aspects. The first is linked to the failure to use inclusive language to better represent the gender identities of the subjects involved in the crime. At the same time, there is a cisexual assumption that underlies all the rulings since it is assumed that all the subjects involved are cisgender. Although Act No. 26, 743, known as the "gender identity law" was passed in 2012, that is, after the sentences analyzed here, only some of them show transgender identities. At the same time, this allows us to highlight, that prosecutions of human trafficking are not representative nor do they investigate what happens in relation to this problem and to transgender women.

In addition, it should be noted that on several occasions cisgender women were sentenced to prison for having committed the crime of human trafficking, without taking into consideration that they themselves had been trafficked or that they were in situations of gender violence that prevented them from withdrawing from the criminal situation that was taking shape.

Lastly, with respect to the geographical variables, it is important to note that, according to the federal criminal justice system, in Argentina, human trafficking with sexual exploitation purposes is not spatially configured in the form of a network, but would appear to have a linear behaviour. In other words, each human trafficking case is not linked to the others forming connections throughout the national territory, but rather are presented as isolated situations. This shows an important difference from what the social opinion believes about the omnipresence and complex geographical network of the criminal organization of human trafficking with sexual exploitation purposes.

REFERENCES

Acharya, A. K. and Salas Stevanato, A. (2008) Algunas consideraciones teóricas acerca del tráfico de mujeres en el contexto de la globalización. Revista de Ciencias Sociales, vol. XIV, núm. 2; pp. 220-239

Borinsky, M. (August 9, 2016) La Justicia Federal Argentina: organización y funcionamiento. Infobae. Available in: https://www.infobae.com/opinion/2016/08/09/la-justicia-federal-argentina-organizacion-y-funcionamiento/

Butler, J. (1990). El género en disputa. El feminismo y la subversión de la identidad. Barcelona, España: Paidós.

Constitution of the Argentine Nation, Fourth Section, Article 120.Legislative information. Argentina, December 15, 1994. Available in: http://servicios.infoleg.gob.ar/infolegInternet/anexos/0-4999/804/norma.htm

Inter-American Convention on the Prevention, Punishment and Eradication of Violence against Women (1994) "Convention of Belém do Pará". Available in: https://www.oas.org/juridico/spanish/tratados/a-61.html

Daich, D. y C. Varela (2014) Entre el combate a la trata y la criminalización del trabajo sexual: las formas de gobierno de la prostitución. Delito y Sociedad 38 año 23 2º semestre: pp 63-83.

Fassin, D. (2016) La razón humanitaria. Una historia moral del tiempo presente. Buenos Aires: Prometeo.

Ibarra García, M. V. e I. Escamilla Herrera (Coords.) (2016) Geografías feministas de diversas latitudes. Orígenes, desarrollo y temáticas contemporáneas. México: Universidad Autónoma Metropolitana.

Iglesias Skulj, A. (2014) La trata de mujeres con fines de explotación sexual. Ciudad Autónoma de Buenos Aires, Argentina: Didot.

INECIP and UFASE (2012) La trata sexual en Argentina. Aproximaciones para un análisis de la dinámica del delito. Obtained from: https://www.mpf.gob.ar/protex/files/2013/10/Informe_INECIP_Ufase_2012.pdf

INECIP (2013) ¿Qué hicimos con la trata? Un recorrido por las principales políticas públicas de trata sexual en Argentina. La Plata, Argentina.

Act No. 24.050 Competencia Penal. Legislative information. Argentina, December 30, 1991. Available in: http://servicios.infoleg.gob.ar/infolegInternet/anexos/0-4999/449/norma.htm

Act No. 25.632 Agreement of the Human Trafficking Convention. Legislative information. Argentina, August 1, 2002. Available in: ttp://servicios.infoleg.gob.ar/infolegInternet/verNorma.do?id=77329

Act No. 26.364 Prevention and Punishment of Human Trafficking and Assistance to its Victims. Legislative information. Argentina, April 9, 2008. Available in: http://servicios.infoleg.gob.ar/infolegInternet/anexos/140000-144999/140100/norma.htm

Act No. 26.842 Prevention and Punishment of Human Trafficking and Assistance to its Victims. Legislative information. Argentina, May 9, 2012. Available in: servicios.infoleg.gob.ar/infolegInternet/anexos/205000-209999/206554/norma.htm

Act No. 26.743 Gender Identity. Argentina, April 9, 2008. Available in: http://servicios.infoleg.gob.ar/infolegInternet/anexos/195000-199999/197860/norma.htm

Massey, D. (2011) For Space. Los Angeles: SAGE.

Public Prosecution Ministry of Argentina (2015).Human Trafficking and Exploitation Office. Report on the first 100 convictions for trafficking in persons.

________________ (2014).Prosecution Unit for Assistance in Extortion Kidnapping and Human Trafficking. Report on Human Trafficking with sexual exploitation purposes in Argentina. Approaches for an analysis of the dynamics of the crime.

Office to Monitor and Combat Trafficking in Persons of the United States Department of State (2012) Report on Human Trafficking.

United Nations Office on Drugs and Crimes (2009) Global report on trafficking in persons. Obtained from http://www.unodc.org/documents/human-trafficking/Global_Report_on_TIP.pdf

________________ (2016) Global report on trafficking in persons. Obtained from https://www.unodc.org/documents/data-and-analysis/glotip/2016_Global_Report_on_Trafficking_in_Persons.pdf

Osóio Machado, L. (1997) Movimento de dinheiro e tráfico de drogas na Amazônia. En M. Ribeiro de Melo; S. D. Seidel. (org). Drogas, hegemonia do cinismo. São Paulo-SP: Memorial da América Latina, v. 1, pp. 217-252.

Pitch, T. (2003) ¿Mejor los jinetes que los caballos? El uso del potencial simbólico de la justicia penal por parte de los actores en conflicto. En: Responsabilidades Limitadas. Actores, Conflictos y Justicia Penal (pp. 123-159) Buenos Aires: Ad-hoc.

National Judicial Branch, Federal Criminal Court of Comodoro Rivadavia.Case No. 999. Judgment of March, 2010.

National Judicial Branch, Federal Criminal Court of Paraná."S – INFRACC. Act No. 26.364". Case No. 1.864/09. Judgment of July 26, 2010.

National Judicial Branch, Federal Criminal Court of Posadas."s/ trata de personas". Case No. 91/2009. Judgment of April 29, 2010.

National Judicial Branch, Federal Criminal Court of Mar del Plata. Case No. 2271. Judgment of February 8, 2010.

National Judicial Branch, Federal Criminal Court of Córdoba."GMS & FNB w/inf. arts.145 bis, 145 ter & 125 bis, Criminal Code". Judgment of November 12, 2010.

National Judicial Branch, Federal Criminal Court of Mar del Plata. Case No. 2267. Judgment of November 12, 2010.

National Judicial Branch, Federal Criminal Court of Mar del Plata. Case No. 2306. Judgment of March 11, 2011.

National Judicial Branch, Federal Criminal Court of Catamarca. Case No. 111. Judgment of May 11, 2011.

National Judicial Branch, Federal Criminal Court of Paraná. "JAE w/ inf. Act No. 26.364". Case N° 2044/1. Judgment of August 4, 2011.

National Judicial Branch, Federal Criminal Court No. 1, Mendoza. "C. P. C. G. w/Inf. Art.145, Criminal Code". Case No. 2853-C. Judgment of August, 2013.

Programa Nacional de Rescate y Acompañamiento a las Personas Damnificadas por el Delito de Trata (2012) Retratada. Un recorrido en imágenes sobre la trata de personas en la República Argentina. Ministerio de Justicia y Derechos Humanos de la Nación. Argentina.

Protocol to Prevent, Suppress and Punish Trafficking in Persons (2000) Palermo, Italy. Obtained from: http://www.ohchr.org/Documents/ProfessionalInterest/ProtocolTraffickingInPersons_sp.pdf

Sassen, S. (2003) Contrageografías de la globalización Género y ciudadanía en los circuitos transfronterizos. Editorial traficantes de sueños.

Serano, Julia (2007) Desmontando el privilegio cisexual. Traducción libre de Akntiendz Chik, en Excluded. Making Feminisn and Queer Movements More Inclusive. Available in: http://akntiendz.com/?p=6315

Unidad de Asistencia en Secuestros Extorsivos y Trata de Personas e Instituto de Estudios Comparados en Ciencias Penales y Sociales (2012) La trata sexual en Argentina. Obtained from: https://www.mpf.gob.ar/protex/tipo_de_recurso/informe-estadistico/

Unidos por la justicia Asociación Civil (2010) Manual de intervención de casos de trata de personas en Argentina. Obtained from http://www.fundacionmariadelosangeles.org/images/pdf/manual-de-intervencion-de-casos-de-trata-de-personas-en-argentina.pdf

Varela, C. (2013). De la "letra de la ley" a la labor interpretante: la "vulnerabilidad" femenina en los procesos de judicialización de la ley de trata de personas (2008-2011). Cadernos Pagu, (41), 265-302. Obtained from https://periodicos.sbu.unicamp.br/ojs/index.php/cadpagu/article/view/8645102

________ (2015) en La campaña anti-trata en Argentina y la agenda supranacional. En Género y violencia en el mercado del sexo. Política, policía y prostitución. Buenos Aires, Argentina: Editorial Biblos.

CHAPTER IX

Domestic Forced Labor in Mexico: The Hidden Reality of Some Indigenous Women Domestic Workers

Diego Lopez Naranjo[1]

Introduction

Over the past two decades, the term modern slavery has been coined in the world to refer to a series of criminal acts. In Mexico; according to the Global Slavery Index (2016) 376, 800 people are victims of modern slavery. Most of them are known to be victims of trafficking in persons for the means of sexual exploitation, but some of them have been identified as victims of forced labor; up to 70% of these victims, regardless the type of modern slavery they experience, are exploited by organized crime groups (Walk Free Foundation, 2016b). While most victims of modern slavery and trafficking in persons in Mexico are being exploited sexually, forced labor and involuntary servitude are also a considerable problem in the country. Such crimes are highly punished by international organizations, such as the International Labor Organization (ILO). Since the ILO Convention on Forced Labor, it is argued that "forced or compulsory labor designates all work or service required of an individual under threat of any penalty and for which the individual does not volunteer" (ILO, 1930) and therefore violates the human rights of victims. Subsequently to this agreement, ILO came with the Convention on the Abolition of Forced Labor 1957 and the Protocol of 2014 on the Convention on Forced Labor, 1930.

1. Applies to sex trafficking only

Forced labor is considered one of the most common forms of modern slavery. According to the International Labor Organization (ILO), 21 million people are victims of forced labor, of which 11.4 million women and girls (ILO, 2017). In the year 2000, just at the beginning of 21st century, the United Nations created the Protocol to Prevent, Suppress And Sanctioning the Trafficking in Persons, in order to fight against trafficking in persons. One of the most relevant aspects of this protocol is that they established a global definition of human trafficking. The following definition of human trafficking can be found in Article 3, section a) of the protocol:

> *"By the treatment of persons - shall mean the recruitment, transportation, transfer, reception or reception of persons, using the threat or use of force or other forms of coercion, abduction, fraud, deception, Abuse of power or a situation of vulnerability or the granting or receipt of payments or benefits to obtain the consent of a person having authority over another, for the purpose of exploitation.*
>
> *Such exploitation shall include at least the exploitation of the prostitution of others or other forms of sexual exploitation, forced labor or services, slavery or practices similar to slavery, servitude or the removal of organs " (United Nations, 2000).*

Even though the terms forced labor, slavery and servitude are included in the definition of Human Trafficking they are not equivalent. Each form of modern slavery has its own characteristics. Still "the common element of these three figures refers to the fact that all three are forms of human exploitation" (De la Torre Martínez, 2013). Among other definitions on trafficking and forced labor, specifically of women, Acharya (2009) presents the definition of Herzfeld (2002), who "states that trafficking in women can be defined as a form of slavery, whose main characteristics are : Forcing victims to work under threats or using violence; Controlling, usually through threats, mental and physical abuse; Victims are dehumanized, treated as commodities, they can be sold and bought as if they belong to someone, they are deprived of their freedom of movement and any possibility to choose their own work " (Herzfeld in Acharya, 2009). Here, Herzfeld mentions the threats to the victims and their deprivation of liberty to choose their own work, that is to say that they work of forced way. Also, De la Torre Martínez differentiates between forced labor and servitude "In forced labor the person is imposed against their will and, therefore, violating their autonomy, the performance of a specific job. In servitude, working conditions are so extreme, the relationship of subordination is so marked up and the relationship of dependence is so strong that the person also loses his autonomy, but also being de facto "trapped" in relation to exploitation" (De la Torre Martínez, 2013).

Forced Labor and Trafficking Laws in Mexico

Besides the international conventions, a number of legal changes have been adopted in Mexico to combat trafficking in persons, forced labor and servitude. First of all, since its creation The Political Constitution of the United Mexican States of 1917, recognizes in its 1st Article that slavery is prohibited in the country. As a result of the latest amendments to the Constitution, specific actions are being taken against the crime of trafficking in persons. Article 19 of the Constitution establishes "preventive detention, in cases of organized crime, willful homicide, rape, abduction, trafficking in persons, crimes committed with violent means such as weapons and explosives, as well as serious crimes determined by law Against the security of the nation, the free development of personality and health " (Mexico, DOF January 27, 2016).

In addition, the Federal Labor Law of 1970 in its Article 2 establishes that labor standards should promote decent work, meaning decent work as "the one in which the human dignity of the worker is fully respected; There is no discrimination by ethnic or national origin, gender, age, disability, social status, health conditions, religion, immigration status, opinions, sexual preferences or marital status; There is access to social security and a salary is paid; Continuous training is provided to increase productivity with shared benefits, and there are optimal conditions of safety and hygiene to prevent work risks " (Mexico, DOF June 12, 2015). These conditions do not exist in forced labor, although they do not occur in many cases of non-forces labor, such as paid domestic work, in which the majority of domestic workers do not have the legal benefits required by the law. Although, there are some issues regarding domestic work, because there is a special chapter that address domestic work as a specific form of work that doesn't require the same benefits as other jobs. This has been discussed and criticized by political activist and union leader Marcelina Bautista: "The law discriminates against domestic workers. From the 13 articles regarding domestic work (of the Federal Labor Law) there is no mention to social security benefits, to the need of an employment contract nor the need of a stablished work schedule is discussed, therefore it is the opposite of what we should have, said Marcelina Bautista." (Soto, 2015). This is a complicated issue because labor laws don't protect domestic workers against unacceptable working conditions as they should.

Subsequently, as mentioned by Acharya (2012), in 2007 two laws were created to protect women against violence and human trafficking: The General Law on Women's Access to a Life Free of Violence and the Law to Prevent and Punish Trafficking in Women People. The first law "In its article 4, it clarifies that in the elaboration and execution of the federal and local public policies four points have to be taken into account regarding the protection of women: The legal equality between the woman and the man; respect for the human dignity of women;

nondiscrimination; and the freedom of women " (Acharya, 2012). The second law was replaced in 2012 by the General Law to Prevent, Punish and Eradicate Crimes in the Area of Trafficking in Persons and for the Protection and Assistance of Victims of these Crimes 2012, which is the strongest and most specific instrument to combat human trafficking and similar forms of exploitation. It specifically recognizes the crime of forced labor in its Article 22, sanctioning it with a penalty of 10 to 20 years in prison, and from 5, 000 to 50, 000 days of minimum wage of fine, it also emphasizes in which situations the crime of forced labor is committed, the following points describe these situations:

> *"I. Use of force, threat of force, physical coercion, threats of physical coercion to that person or to another person, using force or threat of force from a criminal organization; II. Serious harm or threat of serious harm to the person who puts him or her in vulnerable condition; III. The abuse or threat of denunciation to the authorities of their irregular immigration status in the country or any other abuse in the use of the law or legal process, which causes the taxpayer to submit to unfair conditions or that undermine their dignity" (Mexico, DOF March 19, 2014).*

However, practical efforts in enforcing the law have focused on the problem of trafficking in persons for the purpose of sexual exploitation, which has been widely identified in Mexico by the authorities but there are little efforts to identify forced labor or servitude cases and to enforce the law in these matters, is a problem that in Mexico is barely surveyed.

In México, identified cases of forced labor have been mainly revealed in the agricultural sector, mostly in the corn and tomato fields, as well as in the coal and silver mining industry (Walk Free Foundation, 2016b). Such is the case of day laborers in San Quintín, Baja California where on 16 March of 2015 they mutinied in a great strike because of the poor working conditions in which they were held. "We all saw as normal, that people were suspended for three or four days or that they were dismissed without compensation, just for demanding that our rights (as workers) shall be respected, or for trying to force the bosses to pay for overtime in the days that we had to rest, " said Jose Ignacio García, 19 years old and who has been working since he was 12 years old in the fields of the valley of San Quentin" (Animal Politico, 2015). The general public hardly knows about these cases and the reality of this form of exploitation remains hidden in Mexico, as it has been said before authorities have not make enough efforts to recognize this problem in Mexico and are more focused on trafficking in persons for the means of sexual exploitation.

Besides all the efforts to elaborate new laws regarding human trafficking and forced labor, the enforcement of these laws to effectively combat these problems has been very lax. Acharya, Suarez and Ontiveros (2016) found that in Mexico the official information on the crime of trafficking in persons is incomplete and contradictory, which helps to conceal the true scope of the problem. On the other hand, the authors mention that corruption within the security forces prevents the investigation of cases of trafficking in persons (Acharya et al., 2016). This is an issue that is not only present in the prosecution of human trafficking and forced labor crimes, but a complex problem in the whole judicial system in the country. Still, things become more complicated when addressing issues like forced domestic labor because domestic work is already being discriminated by labor laws and lacks the same grade of protection than other forms of work. Thus, while Mexico is making efforts to combat the crimes of human trafficking and forced labor in general, implementation of these laws hasn't been as efficient as expected.

Working Environment of Domestic Workers in Mexico

Working conditions for domestic workers have been one of the main points of discussion of academic research and is today, one of the main demands of trade unions and associations of domestic workers in Mexico. Most of these employees work under a scheme of informality where they lack labor rights; that is, they do not receive the benefits of the law, they work longer hours than those stipulated by law, they do not have social security and in some cases, they even lack sufficient holidays and rest days. As it was already mentioned Marcelina Bautista has criticized the lack of protection that domestic workers receive from The Federal Labor Law. The labor protection is left to the will of the people that hire these domestic workers and, in some cases, working conditions in the household are totally unacceptable. It's been recognized that female domestic workers in Mexico suffer various forms of physical, verbal and symbolic violence, with the most affected employees being the ones of indigenous origin (CONAPRED, 2014).

Domestic workers are sometimes referred as "servant, maid, or domestic worker which are terms used to define this salaried person who is responsible for a series of reproductive tasks within a home that is foreign to him" (Chaney and García Castro (1993) in Chavarría, 2008). According to Durin (2013), many domestic workers are young indigenous migrants who are called being referred in many of these ways, some even derogatory, and are particularly vulnerable to violence and mistreat:

> *"Because they are mainly indigenous, when they start their work, they do not handle the codes of conduct of the employing families; they were socialized in different value systems, even some do not dominate the use of the national language. The living conditions in the communities of origin where they grew are very different from those of*

the homes where they are employed. The ways of cooking, cleaning, and organizing spaces are different, so these young people who arrive to the city, are immediately placed through a process of resocialization and job training. [...] For this same reason, in their first work experience, it is common for young women to experience humiliations due to the fact that they do not know how to do cleaning tasks properly" (Durin, 2013).

On the other hand, Chavarría (2008) indicates that one of the first forms of vulnerability to which young indigenous people who immigrate are exposed to (and that is sometimes not considered) is the urban space by itself, in one of the testimonies of a young woman named Fernanda in the interviews carried out by the author, this situation is clearly observed: "at the beginning I suffered a lot, because I did not know anything, but afterwards I got used to the city and the work [...] when leaving the bus station I was scared of the size of things, everything was huge, I thought there was a lot of traffic and a lot of people. I did not know where to look, even in my dreams I had never imagined something like that" (Fernanda in Chavarría, 2008).

A study carried out by the National Council for Preventing Discrimination (CONAPRED) entitled *Conditions of employment of domestic workers (2014)* shows the conditions of exploitation in which many domestic employees live in Mexico. This study was conducted in October 2014, surveying 1243 domestic workers and 1240 employers. The surveys were conducted in the cities: Mexico City, Guadalajara, Monterrey and its metropolitan area, Puebla, Tijuana and Tuxtla Gutierrez. From the respondents, 23% were women of indigenous origin, being particularly greater in the city of Monterrey with 40% and in the city of Tuxtla Gutiérrez with 49% of the total of the people surveyed (CONAPRED, 2014).

The results of the study reveal several forms of abuse executed to these workers, in the first instance 36% of respondents stated tha they started working when they were under age and 21% did when they were not working age. That mean, that a fifth of the respondents were victims of child exploitation in some point of their lives. On the other hand, a large part of the surveyed domestic workers lack of labor rights: 96% of the respondents stated that they had not signed a labor contract, 75% had never received a salary increase, 66% had no vacation, 46% worked more than 8 hours a day and up to 6% of those surveyed do not have any resting days. Also, most the surveyed domestic workers declare that in case of any labor dispute with their employees they don't use any formal authority to solve it, (only 10% of the respondents used formal authorities to resolve their disputes). Among the most common labor disputes there is a number of abuses that have been reported by the surveyed domestic workers, particularly in the case of indigenous women workers: 33% of the respondents stated that they have perceived or know of someone who has perceived a treatment with contempt because of its indigenous origin and 25% stated that they have been banned or know of someone who has been banned from speaking in their native language.

In general, being treated with contempt is one of the most recurrent statements mentioned by domestic servants surveyed, which means that they are constantly humiliated. Up to 29% of stated that the most common issue at their job is being humiliated, either because of their status as domestic worker, by her physical appearance and even by the fact of being a woman. Among other types of more serious abuses: 12% of women workers reported sexual harassment and 7% reported physical violence (CONAPRED, 2014). These statements and the abuses received by these women show a series of problems that denote how vulnerable domestic workers can be especially those of indigenous origin.

Cases of Domestic Forced Labor in Mexico

Even though the problem of forced labor in domestic work hasn't been addressed as it should, some cases are beginning to draw attention to this problem, confirming the existence of some situations in which forced labor is present in Mexico not only in the agricultural and mining sector, but also in domestic work. For example, in the year 2015, the Zunduri case came to light, where exploitation and violation of human rights are clearly visible. This is the case of a young woman who spent two years chained involuntarily ironing clothes at a dry cleaner in Mexico City (Naják and Paullier, 2015). During this time, she suffered severe physical torture, where she was found in deplorable health conditions, presenting the overall health of an 81-year-old despite being only 23 years old at the time of rescue.

Confinement was one, but not the only way of violence carried over Zunduri, she was also being subjected to extreme work, and when she occasionally made mistakes and burned clothes, she was exerted physical violence as punishment (being burned with the iron) and also her employer charged her excessive amounts of money for her mistakes, entering in an endless cycle of debt with the employer. (Naják and Paullier, 2015). This case shows a specific form of forced labor known as debt bondage, this "is a practice similar to slavery because it involves a debt that cannot be paid in a reasonable time. The employer/executor who engages in this criminal practice inflates artificially the amount of the debt, often adding exorbitant interests, deducting little or nothing from the debt and increasing the amount of time that the called debtor should work" (Jordan, 2011). This is a case of trafficking in persons for the means work exploitation, is a serious offense that violates the labor rights of individuals, their physical integrity and their freedom. Juana Camila Bautista, prosecutor for trafficking in persons in Mexico City, considers the Zunduri case as the first case of labor slavery in Mexico City (Jiménez, 2015, Najár and Paullier, 2015). We could hardly say that this is the first case of this kind documented in Mexico City, although it is possible that it is the first case to be prosecuted in this manner.

There are also other cases that can be accounted for some form of human trafficking or forced labor in the domestic work. For example, there is also the case of Adelina, who did not suffer the torture suffered by Zunduri, but was a victim of physical abuse and threats from her employers. Adelina is a domestic worker in Mexico City, who after 40 years of being a domestic worker she had suffered a series of abuses and violence. She explains he first experience as a domestic worker back in 1975 when she migrated from Puebla, and when was only 16 years old: "The first lady I worked with grabbed me from the shoulders and threw me against the wall, threatening me that I should not complain with my parents because she had money and could put me in jail by falsely accusing me of robbery. I was very afraid" (Toribio, 2015). Without being chained in the same way as Zunduri was, Adelina felt chained by working against her will for one person, because she was afraid of her threats.

Despite the case of Adelina and the case of Zunduri, it seems to be very few known cases of forced labor or involuntary servitude in the domestic sector in Mexico. Even the Global Slavery Index (2016) does not mention such cases, that is to say that in Mexico the problem has not been recognized. However, there is at least one case where there has been prosecution for Forced Labor crimes against an employer, the case of Guadalupe Pérez Castillo who was a victim of forced labor for 30 years and escaped 4 years ago. When she was 10 years old, a woman came to her house at Las Agujas, a rural poor indigenous community in Veracruz, with a translator (because

Guadalupe and her family didn't speak Spanish) asking for a baby-sitter for one of her children, in exchange for her services she will pay her, send her to a good school in the city, and was willing to send a monthly fee to her poor family (Romo, 2017). Her mother sent Guadalupe to work with the woman. "At first I was excited because I was going to be able to help my family without having to sell fruit, I wanted to study, my dream was to have a career one day" (Perez in Romo, 2017). Once she arrived at her new working place, she realized that things were different than promised. She was obliged to do all the domestic work in the house and to take care of all the children in the family (not only one), with no payment at all.

As a forced domestic worker, Guadalupe only received the leftovers of the food and she didn't have a bed to sleep on. "She said that we, the indigenous people, were used to sleep on the ground, like animals. She had a sofa, but she would not let me use it because she said that I was going to wrecked it" (Perez in Romo, 2017). She managed to escape when she was almost 40 years old and her captor was older and unable to retain her. With the help of her lawyer, Guadalupe managed to press charges against her captor and she was convicted for forced labor and slavery offenses (Romo, 2017). This case is the most illustrative for addressing the problem of domestic forced labor. Like this one, there should be more known cases that can help us understand the severity of the problem, and to make it more visible to society and policy makers.

Final Considerations

Trafficking in persons, forced labor and servitude are serious offenses against the dignified life, liberty and physical integrity of persons. Investigating this type of crimes is of great importance, because these practices continue to affect millions of people around the world, being held against their will in jobs. The efforts of international organizations such as the International Labor Organization and the United Nations, mentioned in the previous section, have been essential to make this problem visible in the world. In Mexico, the legal and public policy instruments that have been developed, such as the General Law to Prevent, Punish, and Eradicate Crimes in the Area of Trafficking in Persons and for the Protection and Assistance of Victims of these Crimes have been the product of these efforts, and have raises awareness and recognition of certain problems regarding modern slavery, however, much remains to be done to combat the problem of forced labor in domestic work. Although the problem of trafficking in persons for the purpose of sexual exploitation is widely identified in Mexico; trafficking in persons for the purpose of forced labor or servitude is a problem that is hardly seen in Mexico. In the domestic sector these practices are not even recognized as an issue by the authorities in the country, even though there are a few known cases that show the reality of this problem.

On the other hand, it is important to mention that trafficking in persons and forced labor can have serious consequences on their victims, especially in terms of their health. Acharya and Clark indicate that women victims of trafficking experience a greater degree of violence on the part of the people around them, and that this type of abuse is reflected in the great majority of victims who suffer serious consequences in their Health (Acharya & Clark, 2014). This is clearly seen in the case of Zunduri who, as mentioned earlier, presented severe damage to his organs due to malnutrition and physical abuse. Although, the consequences of physical health are not the only ones that are being observed, Acharya and Clark also mention that women treated suffer from other types of abuse, including forced or coerced drug and alcohol use, social restrictions and economic exploitation. These have not only physical but also psychological impacts that affect the mental health of the victims (Acharya & Clark, 2014).

Taking into account the above, it is essential to conceive within this hidden reality, what is the extent of the cases of forced labor in the domestic sector in Mexico and what are their characteristics. Particularly if they affect vulnerable groups such as indigenous women, who by their social status tend not to be recognized by the authority and in many cases, as mentioned in the first section of this work, do not even denounce. It should be noted that the relevance of this work prevails in understanding the conditions in which the victims live and knowing their consequences; in order to conceive the reality of this problem and thus, have a better panorama on how to protect the victims and help them to have a better and decent life.

REFERENCES

Acharya, A. (2009). Un Análisis Conceptual Del Tráfico De Mujeres Y Su Tipología De Origen. Andamios: vol.6, no.12. México. Recuperado el 25 de enero, 2017 de http://www.scielo.org.mx/pdf/anda/ v6n12/v6n12a14.pdf

Acharya, A. (2012). Tráfico de mujeres en México: El caso del estado de Nuevo León. Marco legal para combatirlo. Espacio Abierto, vol. 21, núm. 4, octubre-diciembre, 2012, pp. 629-652

Acharya, A. (2016). Trafficking of women for sexual exploitation in Mexico and their identity crisis. International Review of Sociology, 26:2, pp. 322-336

Acharya, A. & Clark, J. (2014).Trafficking of women and vulnerability to HIV/STI infection in urban Mexico. Genus, 70 (2-3).

Acharya, A., Suárez, A.; & Ontiveros, F. (2016).Trafficking Of Women And Children In Mexico: An Assessment Of Anti-

Trafficking Laws. Revista de cercetare si interventie sociala, 2016, vol. 53, pp. 5-21

Animal Político. (2015). ¿Qué provocó el desalojo de jornaleros en Baja California?. Recuperado el 25 de enero, 2017 de http://www.animalpolitico.com/2015/03/que-provoco-el-desalojo-dejornaleros-en-baja-california/

Consejo Nacional Para Prevenir La Discriminación. (2014). Condiciones laborales de las trabajadoras domésticas. Secretaría de Gobernación, Gobierno Federal. México. Recuperado el 25 de enero, 2017 de http://www.conapred.org.mx/userfiles/files/ TH_completo_FINAL_INACCSS.pdf

De la Torre Martínez, C. (2013). Trabajo forzoso, formas modernas de esclavitud y trata de seres humanos. Instituto de Investigaciones Jurídicas, UNAM. Recuperado el 25 de enero, 2017 de https://archivos.juridicas.unam.mx/www/bjv/libros/ 8/3567/15.pdf

Durin, S. (2013). Servicio doméstico de planta y discriminación en el área metropolitana de Monterrey. Relaciones 134, primavera 2013, pp. 93-129. México.

Gutiérrez Chong, N. (2013). Capítulo 9. Tipos de violencia contra las poblaciones indígenas. Etnicidad Y Conflicto En Las Américas, Vol. II, pp. 17-45. México: UNAM, Instituto de Investigaciones Sociales.

Instituto Nacional de Estadística y Geografía. (2015). Estadísticas A Propósito Del Día Internacional Del Trabajador Doméstico (22 De Julio). Aguascalientes. Recuperado El 25 de enero, 2015 De http://www.inegi.org.mx/saladeprensa/aproposito/2015/domestico0.p df

Jiménez, G. (2015). Encadenada fue obligada a planchar ropa por 2 años. Excélsior, Ciudad de México. Recuperado el 25 de enero, 2017 de http://www.excelsior.com.mx/comunidad/2015/04/26/1020859

Jordan, A. (2011, February). Slavery, Forced Labor, Debt Bondage, And Human Trafficking: From Conceptional Confusion To

Targeted Solutions. Program On Human Trafficking And Forced Labor (2). Center For Human Rights & Humanitarian Law

Matías, P. (2017). Oaxaca: mujer indígena es "castigada" a latigazos en su intento por formar parte del cabildo. Proceso. Recuperado el 25 de enero, 2017 de http://www.proceso.com.mx/471506/oaxaca-mujerindigena-castigada-a-latigazos-en-intento-formar-parte-del-cabildo

México. Constitución Política De Los Estados Unidos Mexicanos, Diario Oficial de la Federación, 5 de febrero de 1917. Última reforma, 27 de enero de 2016

México. Ley Federal del Trabajo, Diario Oficial de la Federación, 1 de abril de 1970. Última reforma, 12 de junio de 2015

México. Ley General Para Prevenir, Sancionar Y Erradicar Los Delitos En

Materia De Trata De Personas Y Para La Protección Y Asistencia A Las Víctimas De Estos Delitos, Diario Oficial de la Federación, 14 de junio de 2012. Última reforma, 19 de marzo de 2014

Naciones Unidas. (2000). Protocolo Para Prevenir, Reprimir Y Sancionar La Trata De Personas, Especialmente Mujeres Y Niños, Que Complementa La Convención De Las Naciones Unidas Contra La Delincuencia Organizada Transnacional. Palermo, Italia. Recuperado el 25 de enero, 2017 de http://www.senado.gob.mx/comisiones/trata_personas/docs/protocolo_PRSTP.pdf

Nájar, A. & Paullier, J. (2015). El escalofriante relato de Zunduri, la esclava de la tintorería de Ciudad de México. BBC Mundo, Ciudad de México. Recuperado el 25 de enero, 2017 de http://www.bbc.com/mundo/noticias/2015/04/150428_mexico_esclav itud_tintoreria_relato_zunduri_jp

Organización Internacional del Trabajo. (1930). Convenio sobre el trabajo forzoso, 1930. Ginebra. Recuperado el 25 de enero, 2017 de http://www.ilo.org/dyn/normlex/es/f?p=NORMLEXPUB:12100:0::NO:: P12100_ILO_CODE:C029

Organización Internacional del Trabajo. (1957). Convenio sobre la abolición del trabajo forzoso, 1957. Ginebra. Recuperado el 25 de enero, 2017 de http://www.ilo.org/dyn/normlex/es/f?p=NORMLEXPUB:12100:0::NO::P12100_INSTRUMENT_ID:312250

Organización Internacional del Trabajo. (2011). Convenio sobre las trabajadoras y los trabajadores domésticos, 2011. Ginebra. Recuperado el 25 de enero, 2017 de http://www.ilo.org/ dyn/normlex/es/f?p=1000:12100:0::NO::P12100_INSTRUMENT_ID: 2551460

Organización Internacional del Trabajo. (2014). Protocolo de 2014 relativo al Convenio sobre el trabajo forzoso, 1930. Ginebra. Recuperado el 25 de enero, 2017 de http://www.ilo.org/dyn/normlex/es/ f?p=NORMLEXPUB:12100:0::NO::P12100_INSTRUMENT_ID:3174 672

Organización Internacional del Trabajo. (2017). Trabajo forzoso, formas modernas de esclavitud y trata de seres humanos. Recuperado el 25 de enero, 2017 de http://ilo.org/global/topics/forced-labour/lang-es/index.htm

Romo, R. (2017, 1 de Mayo). Una mujer, originaria de Veracruz, fue esclavizada durante 30 años. Expansión (CNN). Recuperado el 2 de agosto, 2017 de https://expansion.mx/nacional/2017/04/30/unamujer-originaria-de-veracruz-fue-esclavizada-durante-30anos?internal_source=PLAYLIST

Soto, G. (2015). La intrincada ruta para formalizar el trabajo doméstico en México. Opinión y Análisis, El Economista. Recuperado el 25 de enero, 2017 de http://eleconomista.com.mx/economicon/2015/10/12/intrincada-ruta-formalizar-trabajo-domestico-mexico

Toribio, L. (2015). Empleo doméstico "casi es esclavitud". Excélsior, Ciudad de México. Recuperado el 25 de enero, 2017 de http://www.excelsior.com.mx/nacional/2015/03/30/1016257#view-4

Walk Free Foundation. (2016a). Global Slavery Index 2016. Retreived January 25, 2017 from http://www.globalslaveryindex.org/

Walk Free Foundation. (2016b). Global Slavery Index 2016, Country Studies: Mexico. Retreived January 25, 2017 from http://www.globalslaveryindex.org/country/mexico/

Watson, K. (2015). Maids in Mexico: Defending the rights of domestic workers. BBC Mexico and Central America. Retrieved January 25, 2017 from http://www.bbc.com/news/business-35113707

CHAPTER X

"Push-Pull" Factors Influencing the Demand and Supply of Human Trafficking: A Theoretical Framework for Identifying and Assessing Human Trafficking

Carmen Monico
Rachel E. Williams Faller
Haley Cole
Jennifer Toller Erausquin

Introduction

Human trafficking or trafficking in persons is a modern form of slavery. The International Labour Organization (2017) estimates that there are 40.3 million victims of human trafficking globally, including 25 million people in forced labor and 15 million people in forced marriage. Although many types of human trafficking are identified around the globe, in the United States, human trafficking is characterized as forced labor and sex trafficking, as explained later. Because victims of human trafficking are often coerced into silence, assessing its occurrence, prevalence, and incidence, can be extremely difficult. However, human trafficking can be analyzed using social science theoretical principles while considering the needs, beliefs, and interests of victims. This is why a simple framework for identifying and assessing victims is likely to miss the multidimensional nature of human trafficking. The study reported in this chapter aims to offer a multilevel, interdisciplinary framework for identifying and assessing human trafficking.

In this chapter, the authors summarize the first phase of an ongoing project, a literature review conducted for the development of a theoretical framework explaining the "push" factors (those enabling the supply side) and the "pull" factors (those driving the demand) influencing human trafficking. This first phase examines a wide range of its forms in the literature. The second phase of the research project will focus specifically on sex trafficking in North Carolina since only service providers of survivors in that state will be interviewed.

The chapter is organized into four parts. The first section introduces the definition and scope of human trafficking in the United States, and the second section explains the method used in this research project. The third section introduces the push and pull factors from the perspective of how they affect vulnerable populations or those at greater risk of human trafficking. Finally, the fourth section focuses on the implications for future research.

Human Trafficking Definition

Human trafficking is a global and local issue, increasingly present but hidden, that influences societies, communities, and individuals around the world. The 2000 United Nations Protocol to Prevent, Suppress, and Punish Trafficking in Persons stresses that human trafficking involves the "threat or use of force or other forms of coercion, of abduction, of fraud, of deception, of the abuse of power or of a position of vulnerability or of the giving or receiving of payments or benefits to achieve the consent of a person having control over another person, for the purpose of exploitation" (p. 2). Thus, traffickers use force, fraud, or coercion, creating a pervasive cycle of bondage that keeps victims subjected to exploitation.

The United States enacted international conventions through the 2000 Trafficking Victims Protection Act (TVPA) with the implementation of a three-pronged approach:

prevention, protection, and prosecution. The TVPA reauthorization of appropriations was possible through the Trafficking Victims Protection Reauthorization Act (TVPRA) in 2003, 2005, 2008, and 2013. The two most prevalent types of human trafficking recognized in the United States are sex trafficking, which includes the actions of "recruitment, harboring, transportation, provision, obtaining, patronizing, or soliciting of a person for the purpose of a commercial sex act [defined as a purpose]" and labor trafficking that involves "involuntary servitude, peonage, debt bondage and slavery [the other purposes]" (U.S. Department of Health and Human Services, 2018, p. 1). The means of human trafficking are well-defined:

> Force includes physical restraint, physical harm, sexual assault, and beatings. Monitoring and confinement is often used to control victims, especially during early stages of victimization to break down the victim's resistance. Fraud includes false promises regarding employment, wages, working conditions, love, marriage, or better life. Over time, there may be unexpected changes in work conditions, compensation or debt agreements, or nature of relationship. Coercion includes threats of serious harm to or physical restraint against any person, psychological manipulation, document confiscation, and shame and fear-inducing threats to share information or pictures with others or report to authorities. (U.S. Department of Health and Human Services, 2018, p. 1)

Human trafficking is a hidden phenomenon, meaning it can be difficult to locate, identify, and support victims because of traveling patterns of victims and traffickers, victims' reluctance to recognize the danger of their situation or protection under the law, and various other concerns (Newton, Mulcahy, & Martin, 2008, p. vi). The lack of a comprehensive framework makes it difficult to obtain accurate statistics on the scope of human trafficking or characteristics of victims. Furthermore, people involved with the issue are often unwilling to cooperate or provide information, because it is an illegal activity (Hepburn & Simon, 2010). Complications emerge in the monitoring, assessment, and reporting of human trafficking, given the differences registered in the prevalence and incidence at the international and national levels, as well as in key states, main cities, and even in small counties. The section on sex trafficking presented next is important as the frame of reference for understanding how the factors inferred from the literature review influence the population most affected by this type of human trafficking. This is in part because sex trafficking has been more studied, particularly in the United States.

Sex Trafficking

Each year, an estimated 100, 000 to 300, 00 Americans are at risk of becoming victims of sex trafficking (Bounds, Delaney, Julion, & Breitenstein, 2017). Yet, despite the extent of this issue, there is a lack of consensus in the literature on sex trafficking about how it should be defined. Some literature cites gender as a defining factor of sex trafficking. Castro's (2014) report on gender-based civil rights violations asserts that sex trafficking is "rooted in gender-based discrimination" (para. 2). Yen (2008) views sex trafficking from an economic standpoint, as it is based on a business model that sells someone repeatedly to supply sexual services to meet a demand (Yen, 2008). Jayson (2013) expands upon this concept of sex trafficking as a certain kind of market.

Drug dealers have found lucrative opportunities in sex trafficking. Jayson (2013) refers to sex trafficking victims as a product; the author cites that unlike drugs, humans are reusable products, and because of this they are more profitable. Hampton and Lieggi (2017) describe who is implicated in the illicit act of sex trafficking, rather than what the act of sex trafficking is. They cite that perpetrators can be pimps, police, other sex workers, and former or current customers (Hampton & Lieggi, 2017). Human trafficking has multiple effects on "vulnerable populations, " or those at greater risk of becoming a prey of exploitation by perpetrators, as explained next.

Populations More Vulnerable to Human Trafficking

Three populations most vulnerable to becoming human trafficking victims are geographically located throughout the 50 states and Washington, D.C. and include "children under the age of 18 induced into commercial sex; adults (age 18 or over) induced into commercial sex through force, fraud, or coercion, and children and adults induced to perform labor or services through force, fraud, or coercion" (National Human Trafficking Hotline, n.d., p. 1). The same source confirms that "While human trafficking spans all demographics, there are some circumstances or vulnerabilities that lead to a higher susceptibility to victimization and human trafficking" (p. 1) such as runaway and homeless youth, victims of violence and trauma, and foreign nationals.

Thus, populations at greater risk of human trafficking are expected to display poorer health and worse social outcomes compared with those of the population as a whole. The literature review conducted as part of the first stage of the study confirms that human trafficking affects the most vulnerable populations. Next, the study method will be presented, in particular, how the literature review was implemented and the framework developed.

Method and Literature Review

The authors' ongoing research project examines the multiple factors contributing to human trafficking globally and nationally, and based on an examination of the experience of service providers to victims of human trafficking in North

Carolina, to ultimately propose a comprehensive, multi-sector intervention strategy for replication in other states and countries. The research project is organized in two phases: the first focused on identifying the "push-pull" factors influencing human trafficking based on an extensive literature review, and the second will define a framework for intervention for North Carolina through the development of interviews with providers of servicers to human trafficking victims and survivors. This chapter reports findings from the first phase; the second phase will be reported in a future publication, once the informant interviews are conducted.

The literature review was conducted using the databases PubMed, EMBASE, CINAHL, Psyc INFO, Soc Index, Directory of Published Proceedings (Inter Dok), Open Grey, Eldis, Popline, DFID Research for Development, SciDevNet, World Bank Documents and Reports, WHO, Catalog of US Government Publications, Science Direct, Web of Science, Google Scholar, Pro Quest, Public Health Topic Pages, HSRIC, and Grey Literature Report (greylit. org). Publications were limited to those in English; those focused on North America (U.S., Canada, and Mexico) were prioritized. Search terms included "human trafficking, " "sex trafficking, " "slavery, " or "sex work/sex trade, " and poverty, environment, politic*, education, family, conflict, war, abuse, rape, culture, econom*, government, policy, armed conflicts, literacy, SES, drug trafficking, drug abuse, demand, supply, prostitution, pornography, transportation, service industry, farms, entertainment, business, industry, agriculture, sports, recreation, anniversaries, and special events.

The literature review covered best practices to prevent and address human trafficking within North America, as indicated above. A database of 73 references was created and administered in Zotero, a free, online tool used to collect, organize, cite, and share research. In addition, reports from various victim services and anti-trafficking organizations within the region were studied. The analysis of the literature review produced a theoretical framework on the push-pull factors of human trafficking, which is systematically outlined below and depicted for easy reference in a set of four figures explained in subsequent sections.

Inferred Theoretical Framework on Push and Pull Factors

Using the factors identified during our literature review, the authors developed a conceptual framework considering the supply and demand for human trafficking presented in Figure X(a). Factors were categorized as either "push" factors (those that supply sex trafficking) or "pull" factors (those that contribute to demand of sex trafficking). These effects are demonstrated by the arrows to and from human trafficking for push and pull factors. A bidirectional arrow between push and pull factors shows their interaction through these mechanisms, not a causal relationship. The factors are not listed in hierarchical order, and do not all apply to all types of human trafficking, all countries, or all situations. Thus, the framework cannot be used as a blueprint but rather as a guide for assessing human trafficking.

During the literature review, mechanisms through which the factors interact were also identified, as outlined in the center of Figure X(a). The framework also includes barriers trafficking victims experience in seeking help and barriers providers, communities, and governments face in providing help to trafficking victims. These barriers are shown as outside forces that block victims' pathways out of trafficking that will end the pervasive cycle of bondage for exploitation.

Push Factors Affecting Vulnerable Populations

The authors found that different push factors put certain populations at a disproportionately higher risk of being trafficked. Push factors depicted in Figure X(b) are characterized as those that enable the supply side of sex trafficking, or more simply those that push people toward or into sex trafficking. This approach does not deny the strength and resilience sex trafficking survivors have displayed. In fact, populations subjected to racism, sexism, ableism, and other forms of oppression are more vulnerable to becoming prey of human trafficking. As discussed below, poverty, drug use, lack of social support, limited education, and other influential factors can all make people less likely to anticipate, cope with, resist, and recover from negative life events.

Poverty: The most commonly stated push factor in sex trafficking research is poverty (Barner, Okech, & Camp, 2018; Gajic-Veljanoski & Stewart, 2007; Logan, Walker, & Hunt, 2009). Research indicates young females from low socioeconomic backgrounds are at a high risk of victimization. Poverty negatively affects one's educational access and attainment, access to social services, environment (social and physical), and general mental health outcomes. Reid (2014) found that receiving at least a high school education acts as a protective factor for sexual victimization, substance abuse, and intimate partner violence. Trafficking victims often remain entrapped due to fear, lack of knowledge of alternative outcomes, enforced isolation by traffickers, and shame (Logan et al., 2009).

Adverse socioeconomic conditions: Unemployment, country economic and/or political instability, and government corruption are all push factors related to poverty (Gajic-Veljanoski & Stewart, 2007). Another risk factor intertwined with poverty is being homeless or being a runaway or a throwaway. Specifically, women and girls sleeping rough are more prone to seek out affection or protection from male companions (Pierce, 2012). Many homeless women and girls have little or no education, which fuels the desire for jobs among this population (Pierce, 2012).

Social conditions: Social inequality and social dysfunction are also heavily cited as leading to a plethora of prominent push factors. Konstantopoulos et al. (2013) identified determinants of sex trafficking, including child sexual abuse, family dysfunction, early exposure to violence, financial insecurity, lack of formal education, and lack of alternative economic opportunities. Hampton and Lieggi (2017) found that in past studies on American trafficking victims, the majority of victims reported experiencing multiple types of trauma, including mental, emotional, verbal, and physical child abuse and neglect. In their study, Hampton and Lieggi (2017) observed victims reporting that they experienced abuse from single or multiple perpetrators, which could include biological, step, or adoptive father; mothers; a romantic partner; sisters; uncles, grandfathers; and neighbors.

Reports of abuse are further described in medical records of sexually exploited children, which can provide insight into a patient's social, physical, and mental well-being. In Moore, Houck, Hirway, Barron, and Goldberg's (2017) study of 25 child victim's medical records, they found that 88% of patients were subject to maltreatment or sexual assault, potentially correlated with the 60% of the group who reported a history of runaway behavior. Constant exposure to abuse, exploitation, and violence within families and peer networks can alone be the catalyst for increased risk of being trafficked. These factors can also be precursors of other conditions such as addiction and mental health disorders. Fetal alcohol syndrome, substance abuse, and mental illness are all additional risk factors for trafficking likelihood (Pierce, 2012).

Family context: Familial dysfunction, mental illness, and abuse all act as stressors and have detrimental effects on mental and emotional health. Reid (2011) applied Agnew's general strain theory to observe the detrimental effects of caregiver strains on their children in relation to trafficking risks. This research found that girls in the United States who experienced abuse or maltreatment also experienced higher rates of substance abuse at a young age, higher rates of running away, and higher rates of sexual degradation. Sexual degradation of self/others was the most statistically significantly factor related to child maltreatment, as well as the likelihood of being prostituted as a minor (Reid, 2011).

It is important to understand the interaction of these multiple pull factors (e.g., various socioeconomic conditions and family dynamics) in the context of sex trafficking. The combination of seeking male companionship and having a desire to work becomes a gateway for exploitation. Traffickers extort profit from this population by creating false narratives where the trafficker plays the role of savior and protector whom a trafficking victim may be coerced by or indebted to. Poverty results in lags in education and can also lead to a lack of awareness of exploitation and domestic abuse behavior. Consequently, those who cannot appropriately identify markers of abuse within their home or social lives are less likely to perceive signs of coercion and social deviance often employed by sex traffickers to subject victims into bondage for exploitation.

Pull Factors Affecting Vulnerable Populations

While push factors "drive people away from certain environments" (Barner et al., 2018, p. 140), provoking or predetermining affiliation with sex trafficking, pull factors are those driving the demand for sex trafficking. Pull factors depicted in Figure X(c) ensure the perpetuation of the business. Pull factors are found to berooted on economic reasoning. For instance, human trafficking grows with an increased demand for commercial sex, and traffickers use the promise of increased opportunities to prey victims into human trafficking (e.g., people living in poor environments seeking better livelihood) (Barner et al., 2018; Gajic-Veljanoski & Stewart, 2007).

Sexism and victimization: Pull factors are also often connected to social factors. Sexual objectification of women/ gender inequality, high demand for commercial sex among men, profitability of commercial sex trade, social discrimination, and complicit law enforcement all drive demand for sex trafficking (Konstantopoulos et al., 2013). Sociological theory is commonly used to analyze cycles of victimization in human trafficking. In Lopez and Minassians' (2018) study on adolescent sex trafficking models, the authors apply Parsonian functionalism, Bronfenbrenner's social ecology, and adolescent psychology to their claims. the authors' model emphasizes environmental factors in conjunction with social factors that make human trafficking more likely, as a form of "trafficking susceptibility." This model uses environmental constructs that include a sociological view concerned with inequality, which surmises to limited life chances (Lopez & Minassians, 2018).

Environmental context: A sociological view is concerned with one's physical environment (i.e., neighborhood) and the legal system of the environment (Lopez & Minassians, 2018), andthe environment in connection to traffickers, meaning the prevalence of traffickers and psychopathic characteristics seen in traffickers (Lopez & Minassians, 2018). Psychopathic tendencies along with the impressionable adolescent brain can lead to Stockholm syndrome, which perpetuates entrapment (Lopez & Minassians, 2018). Lopez and Minassians' (2018) research conclude that these constructs of environmental and social factors prohibit positive opportunities and options for victims. Additional sociological aspects of human trafficking cited in the literature include race, ethnicity, culture, and gender.

Cultural dimensions: Cultural factors can interact with racial and ethnic factors as well as social turmoil to lead to ideal conditions for trafficking. Moloney (2015) explains how culture encompasses religion, forges patriarchy in a society, promotes either individualism or communalism in a society, and shapes attitudes towards sex, gender, and family roles. For example, in a developing country where women have limited rights and violence in the nation is present, that environment could provide the best circumstances for trafficking to continue.

Bondage for exploitation through coercion: Coercion of a trafficker on a victim is a pervasive pull factor driving sex trafficking, which leads to the creation of a bondage for exploitation. Carpenter and Gates (2016) studied gang involvement among prisoners in San Diego. Eighty percent of those interviewed indicated being affiliated to a gang and having played the role of "facilitators" of sex trafficking. Gang members involved in sex trafficking reported that the most prevalent forms of coercion were created througheconomic bondage, by exerting psychological exploitation, and by using chemical substances among victims (e.g. drugs). They also used physical and sexual violence as forms of coercion for exploitation.

Mechanisms of Interaction Between Push and Pull Factors

Push and pull factors work simultaneously, even synergistically, are facilitated by structural factors, including the intersectionality of multiple marginalized identities and social locations; patriarchal systems of education, employment, family, and law enforcement; gender-based violence; and forced displacement and migration. Intersectionality is a theoretical framework that describes how an individual's social identities (e.g., race, socioeconomic status, gender, etc.) interact "to reflect interlocking systems of privilege and oppression" (e.g., racism, classism, sexism, etc.) at a larger social level (Bowleg, 2012). In this framework, intersectionality is one mechanism of how push and pull factors interact to contribute to human trafficking. For example, women and girls from poor neighborhoods (push factors) may experience sexism and a lack of economic opportunities (pull factors). The intersection of these identities and social locations creates a unique, oppressive situation that places these women at higher risk of being trafficked (Busch-Armendariz, Nsonwu, & Heffron, 2017).

Patriarchal systems are the result of social ideologies and system structures that create and reinforce men's power over women (Hunnicutt, 2009). These systems are important in the context of sex trafficking because a majority of victims are women. Patriarchal systems can occur at both the micro (e.g., family structures) and macro (e.g., policy, culture) levels (Hunnicutt, 2009). They contribute to sex trafficking through decreasing women's independence and increasing their hardships (Moloney, 2015; Seyhan, 2009). In this framework, patriarchal systems interact with push and pull factors, resulting in varying levels of this lack of independence and increase in hardships. For example, patriarchal systems may influence laws forbidding women from various forms of employment. Women living in poverty in an area with a law against female employment are more likely to become victims of trafficking than poor women in areas without this law, since poverty (a push factor) and lack of employment opportunity (a push factor influenced by patriarchal systems) make them more vulnerable to coercion into trafficking (a pull factor).

Related to patriarchal systems is gender-based violence. This is characterized as any act "that results in, or is likely to result in, physical, sexual or psychological harm or suffering to women, including threats of such acts, coercion or arbitrary deprivation of liberty, whether occurring in public or in private life" (United Nations, 1993). Hunnicutt (2009) argues that "male violence against women [which is mostly most prevalent] serves a dual function: It is a tool to exploit men's position of advantage and to maintain the patriarchal order... [; individual] violent behavior is linked to pathological social arrangements... [thus,] violence against women is more a consequence of patriarchies than the cause of them" (pp. 559–561). Masculine gender norms within a patriarchal system are determined by multiple factors beyond gender, such as socioeconomic status—a higher socioeconomic status places a maleat a higher level in the patriarchy (Hunnicutt, 2009).

The framework includes gender-based violence as a mechanism in which push and pull factors interact and intensify. For example, women with male partners who try to verbally coerce them into sex trafficking to make money for the family are at risk of being trafficked. However, women with male spouses who engage in gender-based violence may be at higher risk of being trafficked, since the threat of violence is likely a stronger coercion tool.

Finally, forced displacement and migration also affect how push and pull factors interact and contribute to human trafficking. Forced displacement and migration occur when individuals or groups are forced from their homes or areas of habituation due to conflict or war, natural disaster, or violations of human rights (United Nations High Commissioner for Refugees, 2017). Forced displacement and migration is a mechanism that increases the effects of push and pull factors, causing those that are displaced to be more vulnerable to becoming victims of trafficking. For instance, many routes used for trafficking are also used for migration, putting those affected by forced displacement in direct contact with traffickers (UnitedNations Office on Drugs and Crime, 2016). Individuals affected by push and pull factors, such as poverty and cultural factors, coming into direct contact with traffickers are more likely to become victims of trafficking than individuals affected by similar push/pull factors who have not been displaced.

Barriers to Victims' Help-Seeking Behavior and Access

Barriers to seeking help include stigma, fear, perception of service quality, isolation, and Stockholm syndrome. These barriers, depicted in Figure X(d), prevent victims of trafficking from seeking help to escape. Stigma may prevent victims from seeking help because they are afraid they will be judged or mistreated because of their situation (Ijadi-Maghsoodi, Bath, Cook, Textor, & Barnert, 2018; Konstantopoulos et al., 2013). Fear of being treated like a victim, retaliation, being prosecuted for other crimes, and lack of confidentiality may also prevent victims from seeking assistance (Caliber Associates, 2007; Ijadi-Maghsoodi et al., 2018; Konstantopoulos et al., 2013; Logan, 2007; Logan, Walker, & Hunt, 2009).

Victims may also feel that available services are inadequate to help them (Ijadi-Maghsoodi et al., 2018). Isolation may prevent a victim from seeking assistance because they do not have the ability to access services or ask for help (Logan, 2007; Loganet al., 2009). Finally, Stockholm syndrome may prevent victims from asking for help because they do not feel they are victims and have a special attachment to the people trafficking them (Lopez & Minassians, 2018).

Barriers to Service Provision for Victims and Survivors

Barriers to service provision include lack of resources, lack of provider expertise, working with law enforcement, and lack of collaboration with stakeholders. These barriers, depicted in Figure X(d), prevent services for trafficking victims from offering adequate assistance, if any assistance at all.

Literature on victims has found that personal barriers victims face may deter them from seeking services. Ijadi-Maghsoodi et al.'s (2018) survey among commercially exploited youths found that participants had concerns of confidentiality, shame, fear, self-reliance, and low-quality health services that created barriers for victims contemplating seeking help. Ijadi-Maghsoodi et al.'s (2018) survey, along with Konstantopoulos et al.'s (2013) public health analysis of trafficking, reported it is common that victims do not want to be associated with the stigma of being a sex trafficking victim and are skeptical of the healthcare system and its ability to address issues of sex trafficking. Furthermore, Logan (2007) reported many victims remained entrapped in sexual slavery as a result of isolation, confinement, threats and violence, sexual degradation, and false promises. These tactics also fuel the shame, anxiety, and fear experienced by victims that create a barrier to seeking help.

Lack of resources, such as money and infrastructure, is the largest barrier to service provision (Conyers & Scott, 2018; Sullivan, 2010). Without these resources, services cannot be available to victims. Lack of provider expertise on human trafficking can cause them to miss identifying victims when they come into contact with them (Caliber Associates, 2007; Konstantopoulos et al., 2013; Young, 2012). Furthermore, providers may not have expertise in the areas where victims need assistance (e.g., social services, providing emotional support, etc.; Caliber Associates, 2007).

Working with law enforcement can become a barrier due to conflicting obligations. Although providers are concerned with the well-being of the victim, law enforcement is concerned with upholding laws and reducing criminal activity (Alagbala, 2013; Caliber Associates, 2007). This conflict is especially evident in the case of human trafficking because of its nature: criminal activity is combined with victimization throughout perpetuation, rescue and restoration. Finally, the lack of collaboration between stakeholders also creates barriers to providing services to victims (Henderson, 2017; Konstantopoulos et al., 2013; Sullivan, 2010).

Victims of human trafficking often have multiple needs to address, such as financial security, physical health, education, housing, and mental health (Leahy, 2010). Many of the social systems in place to address these needs function independently or as specialized units. Without collaboration between the multiple stakeholders involved in anti-trafficking work, victims and survivors may not have their needs met, putting them at risk of remaining or becoming victims of trafficking again.

Implications for Human Trafficking Research

Emerging from the literature review is the need to further investigate the work of victim service programs and anti-trafficking agencies supporting survivors, the approaches they use to train the personnel involved in the identification and assessment of human trafficking, and how they coordinate service delivery. Cannon, Arcara, Graham, and Macy (2018) reviewed research methods in human trafficking and called for research recruitment strategies in investigations of human trafficking in relation to health. The authors predicted that more investigation into methods of identifying victims would inform health needs and service delivery among that population (Cannon et al., 2018). This source also found few peer-reviewed research surrounding human trafficking and health or studies on prevention work and intervention programs with victims and survivors.

Conclusion

Human trafficking is an issue affecting people and societies around the globe, transcending national borders, and affecting disproportionally populations most vulnerable to becoming prey. Traffickers use force, fraud, or coercion, enabling the creation of a pervasive cycle of bondage that keeps victims subjected to exploitation. Although human trafficking is increasingly prevalent, it manages to remain elusively concealed, largely because it is an illegal activity often involving organized crime networks. Furthermore, victims tend to remain silent to survive, or are unable to recognize their victimization. These conditions contribute to the difficulty of the prevention, protection of victims, and prosecution of traffickers. Complications also come from the different approaches used for measuring, monitoring, and assessing the prevalence and incidence of human trafficking at the international and national levels, including at the state, city, and county levels. Although useful, standardized measures can easily miss the complexity in which human trafficking occurs from the onset through the lifetime of its victims and survivors.

In this chapter, the theoretical framework inferred from secondary research identifies "push" factors (those that supply sex trafficking) or "pull" factors (those that contribute to demand of sex trafficking). Mechanisms of interaction between push and pull factors are identified, and how each of these factors affects vulnerable populations, defined as those at greater risk of human trafficking. Barriers to victims' help-seeking behavior and access are also flagged, as well as barriers to service provision of victims and survivors. The push-pull factor framework is offered not as a blueprint but as a guide for a more comprehensive identification and assessment of human trafficking locally and among vulnerable populations in order to better implement the three-pronged approach outlined in the 2000 Trafficking Victims Protection Act (TVPA).

This first phase of the study also suggests that empirical research from professional practice in combating human trafficking is needed in order to improve services to human trafficking victims. The second phase of the study will investigate the specific approaches service providers use in North Carolina to prepare their personnel for the better identification and assessment of human trafficking and the improved coordination of service delivery.

REFERENCES

Alagbala, L. A. (2013). *Power, law, and culture: Service providers' perspectives of the contributing factors to the perpetuation of the human sex trafficking industry within the United States* (Ph.D. dissertation). The Chicago School of Professional Psychology, Illinois. Retrieved from https://search.proquest.com/central/docview/1346230416/abstract/59BD7F10D8D14AA4PQ/5

Barner, J. R., Okech, D., & Camp, M. A. (2018). "One size does not fit all": A proposed ecological model for human trafficking intervention. *Journal of Evidence-Informed Social Work, 15* (2), 136–149. https://doi.org/10.1080/23761407.2017.1420514

Bounds, D., Delaney, K. R., Julion, W., & Breitenstein, S. (2017). Uncovering indicators of commercial sexual exploitation. *Journal of Interpersonal Violence*, 886260517723141. https://doi.org/10.1177/0886260517723141

Bowleg, L. (2012). The problem with the phrase women and minorities: Intersectionality—an important theoretical framework for public health. *American Journal of Public Health, 102* (7), 1267–1273.

Busch-Armendariz, N. B., Nsonwu, M., & Heffron, L. C. (2017). *Human trafficking: Applying research, theory, and case studies.* Thousand Oaks, CA: Sage.

Caliber Associates. (2007). Evaluation of comprehensive services for victims of human trafficking: Key findings and lessons learned. (No. 218777). Fairfax, VA: Author. Retrieved from https://www.ncjrs.gov/pdffiles1/nij/grants/218777.pdf

Cannon, A. C., Arcara, J., Graham, L. M., & Macy, R. J. (2018). Trafficking and health: A systematic review of research methods. *Trauma, Violence, & Abuse, 19* (2), 159–175. https://doi.org/10.1177/1524838016650187

Carpenter, A., & Gates, J. (2016).*The nature and extent of gang involvement in sex trafficking in San Diego County.* (No. 249857). California: University of San Diego and Pt. Loma Nazarene University. Retrieved from https://permanent.access.gpo.gov/gpo83674/249857.pdf

Castro, M. R. (2014). *Sex trafficking: A gender-based civil rights violation*. Washington, DC: US Commission on Civil Rights. Retrieved fromhttps://permanent.access.gpo.gov/gpo73529/SexTrafficking_9-30-14.pdf

Conyers, J., & Scott, R. C. (2018).*Domestic minor sex trafficking*.Pub.L. No. 111–146, § Committee on the Judiciary. Washington, DC: US Government Publishing Office. Retrieved from https://www.gpo.gov/fdsys/pkg/CHRG-111hhrg58250/pdf/CHRG-111hhrg58250.pdf

Gajic-Veljanoski, O., & Stewart, D. E. (2007). Women trafficked into prostitution: Determinants, human rights and health needs. *Transcultural Psychiatry, 44* (3), 338–358. https://doi.org/10.1177/1363461507081635

Hampton,M.D.,&Lieggi,M.(2017).Commercialsexualexploitation of youth in the United States: A qualitative systematic review. *Trauma, Violence & Abuse*, 1524838017742168. Retrieved from https://doi.org/10.1177/1524838017742168

Henderson, M. F. (2017, October). *Human trafficking in North Carolina: Strategies for local government officials*. UNC School of Government Public Management Bulletin. Retrieved from https://www.sog.unc.edu/file/72806/download?token=FX9LR-J4

Hepburn, S., & Simon, R. (2010).Hidden in plain sight: Human trafficking in the United States. *Gender Issues, 27* (1/2), 1–26. https://doi.org.ezproxy.elon.edu/10.1007/s12147-010-9087-7

Hunnicutt, G. (2009). Varieties of patriarchy and violence against women: Resurrecting "patriarchy" as a theoretical tool. *Violence Against Women, 15* (5), 553–573.

Ijadi-Maghsoodi, R., Bath, E., Cook, M., Textor, L., & Barnert, E. (2018).Commercially sexually exploited youths' health care experiences, barriers, and recommendations: A qualitative analysis.*Child Abuse & Neglect, 76*, 334–341. https://doi.org/10.1016/j.chiabu.2017.11.002

International Labour Organization. (2017). *Global estimates of modern slavery: Forced labour and forced marriage*. Retrieved from http://www.ilo.org/global/publications/books/WCMS_575479/lang--en/index.htm

Jayson, K. G. (2013). *Human trafficking in North Carolina: Human beings as a commodity*. North Carolina Governor's Crime Commission. Retrieved from https://ncdps.s3.amazonaws.com/s3fs-public/div/GCC/pubs/Human_Trafficking_North_Carolina_2013.pdf

Konstantopoulos, W. M., Ahn, R., Alpert, E. J., Cafferty, E., McGahan, A., Williams, T. P., ... Burke, T. F. (2013). An international comparative public health analysis of sex trafficking of women and girls in eight cities: Achieving a more effective health sector response. *Journal of Urban Health: Bulletin of the New York Academy of Medicine, 90* (6), 1194–1204. https://doi.org/10.1007/s11524-013-9837-4

Leahy, P. J. (2010). *In our own backyard: Child prostitution and sex trafficking in the United States*.Pub. L. No. J-111-74, § Committee on the Judiciary. Washington, DC: US Government Publishing Office. Retrieved from https://www.gpo.gov/fdsys/pkg/CHRG-111shrg58003/pdf/CHRG-111shrg58003.pdf

Logan, T. (2007).*Human trafficking in Kentucky*. Lexington: University of Kentucky. Retrieved fromhttp://www.cdar.uky.edu/CoerciveControl/docs/Human%20Trafficking%20in%20Kentucky.pdf

Logan, T. K., Walker, R., & Hunt, G. (2009).Understanding human trafficking in the United States.*Trauma, Violence, & Abuse, 10* (1), 3–30. https://doi.org/10.1177/1524838008327262

Lopez, D. A., & Minassians, H. (2018). The sexual trafficking of juveniles: A theoretical model. *Victims & Offenders, 13* (2), 257–276. https://doi.org/10.1080/15564886.2017.1329173

Moloney, C. J. (2015). Sociology of human trafficking. In M. J. Palmiotto (Ed.), *Combating human trafficking: A multidisciplinary approach* (pp. 27–45). Boca Raton, FL: CRC Press.

Moore, J. L., Houck, C., Hirway, P., Barron, C. E., & Goldberg, A. P. (2017).Trafficking experiences and psychosocial features of domestic minor sex trafficking victims.*Journal of Interpersonal Violence,* 886260517703373. https://doi.org/10.1177/0886260517703373

National Human Trafficking Hotline. (n.d.).*The victims.* Retrieved from https://humantraffickinghotline.org/what-human-trafficking/human-trafficking/victims

https://www.ohchr.org/en/professionalinterest/pages/protocoltraffickinginpersons.aspx

Newton, P. J., Mulcahy, T. M., & Martin, S. E. (2008).Finding victims of human trafficking. Illinois: University of Chicago, National Opinion Research Center (NORC). Retrieved from https://www.ncjrs.gov/pdffiles1/nij/grants/224393.pdf

Pierce, A. S. (2012). American Indian adolescent girls: Vulnerability to sex trafficking, intervention strategies. *American Indian and Alaska Native Mental Health Research* (online), *19* (1), 37–56.

Reid, J. A. (2011). An exploratory model of girl's vulnerability to commercial sexual exploitation in prostitution. *Child Maltreatment, 16* (2), 146–157. https://doi.org/10.1177/1077559511404700

Reid, J. A. (2014). Risk and resiliency factors influencing onset and adolescence-limited commercial sexual exploitation of disadvantaged girls.*Criminal Behaviour and Mental Health, 24* (5), 332–344. https://doi.org/10.1002/cbm.1903

Seyhan, O. (2009). *Identifying social and political correlates of national human trafficking scores: An extension of Bales's theory of modern slavery.* (Ph.D. dissertation.). The University of Texas at Dallas. Retrieved from https://search.proquest.com/central/docview/305058740/abstract/59BD7F10D8D14AA4PQ/2

Sullivan, T. (2010, August). The human trafficking training and services provision survey for North Carolina. *SystemStats, 27* (4). Retrieved from https://files.nc.gov/ncdps/documents/files/SystemStats_2010vol27no4_Human Trafficking Train Services Prov Survey.pdf

Trafficking Victims Protection Act (TVPA) of 2000. U.S. Government Publishing Office. Retrieved from https://www.govinfo.gov/content/pkg/BILLS-106hr3244enr/pdf/BILLS-106hr3244enr.pdf

United Nations. (2000). *Protocol to prevent, suppress, and punish trafficking in persons especially women and children, supplementing the United Nations Convention against Transnational Organized Crime.* Human Rights Office of the High Commissioner. Retrieved from https://www.ohchr.org/en/professionalinterest/pages/protocoltraffickinginpersons.aspx

United Nations General Assembly. (1993). *Declaration on the elimination of violence against women.* (UN Publication No.A/RES/48/104). Retrieved from http://www.un.org/documents/ga/res/48/a48r104.htm

United Nations High Commissioner for Refugees (UNHCR). (2017). *Global trends: Forced displacement in 2016.* Geneva, Switzerland: Author. Retrieved from https://www.unhcr.org/5943e8a34.pdf

United Nations Office on Drugs and Crime. (2016). *Global report on trafficking in persons 2016.* (No. E.16.IV.6). United Nations. Retrieved from https://www.unodc.org/documents/data-and-analysis/glotip/2016_Global_Report_on_Trafficking_in_Persons.pdf

U.S. Department of Health and Human Services. (2018). *Fact sheet: Human trafficking OTIP-FS-18-01.* Office on Trafficking in Persons. Retrieved from https://www.acf.hhs.gov/otip/resource/fshumantrafficking

Yen, I. (2008). Of vice and men: A new approach to eradicating sex trafficking by reducing male demand through educational programs and abolitionist legislation. *Journal of Criminal Law & Criminology, 98* (2), 653–686. Retrieved fromhttps://search.proquest.com/central/docview/218397954/abstract/59BD7F10D8D14AA4PQ/31

Young, S. E. (2012). *A qualitative analysis of aftercare service provision for survivors of sex trafficking in North Carolina.* (Ph.D. dissertation). The University of North Carolina at Chapel Hill. Retrieved from https://search.proquest.com/central/docview/1240661187/abstract/59BD7F10D8D14AA4PQ/58

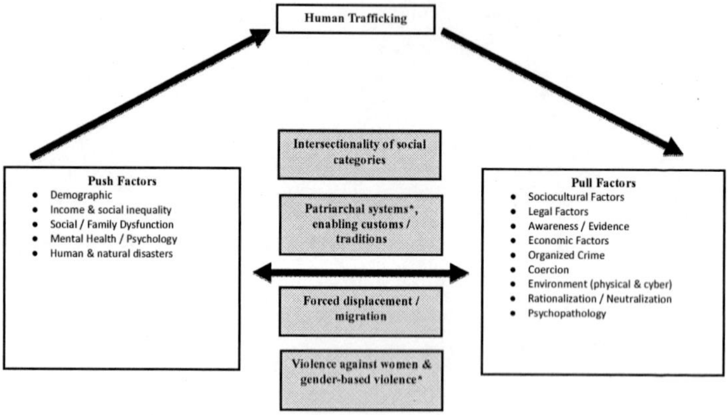

Figure X (a): *"Push-Pull" Factors Influencing the Demand and Supply of Human Trafficking*

*Applies to sex trafficking only

Push Factors

- **Poverty**
  - Socioeconomic status
  - Financial instability
  - Feminization of poverty*
- **Demographics**
  - Age
  - Lack of education
- **Social inequality**
  - Job opportunities
  - Access to social services
  - Civil & political liberties
  - Oppression
- **Social / Family dysfunction**
  - Neglect / Abuse (caregiver strain)
  - Foster care
  - Lack of support systems
  - Isolation
  - Running away
  - Homelessness
  - Early exposure to drugs or violence
- **Psychology / Mental health**
  - Adolescent decision-making*
  - Mental illness
  - Need to feel loved*
  - Addiction
  - Lack of coping ability*
  - Relationship with trafficker
  - Sexual denigration*
  - Intellectual disabilities
- **Human disaster**
  - Civil wars
  - Ethnic conflicts
- **Natural disaster**
  - Local communities
  - Regional, within countries
  - Regional, across countries

Figure X (b): *Push Factors Affecting Vulnerable Populations*

*Applies to sex trafficking only

Pull Factors

- **Sociocultural Factors**
  - Globalization
    - *Structural-functionalism / conflict perspective*
    - *Cultural tolerance*
  - Gender inequality / sexism*
  - Culture values around youth & promiscuity*
  - Cultural "moral crusade"*
  - Normalization of violence
  - Pimp culture*
  - Social apathy
  - Lack of awareness
  - Discrimination (religion, race / ethnicity, social class)
  - Toxic masculinity*
- **Legal Factors**
  - Government apathy
  - Inadequate legislation
  - Uncoordinated law enforcement efforts
  - War on Drugs
  - Lack of prosecution
- **Awareness / Evidence**
  - Lack of definition
  - Inconsistent measures
- **Economic Factors**
  - Profitability
  - Client demand
- **Organized Crime / Gangs**
  - Trafficking / migration routes
- **Coercion turned into bondage**
  - Emotional, financial, physical, chemical
  - Other forms of violence
- **Environment (physical & cyber)**
  - Geography (major transport routes land / sea / air, agricultural economy, military bases)
  - Internet
    - *Anonymity of buyers & sellers*
    - *Ease of access*
- **Rationalization / Neutralization**
  - Justifications by johns*, traffickers, & victims
  - Blaming the victims
  - Excusing perpetrators
- **Psychopathology**
  - Tolerance for violence
  - Power & control

Figure X (c): *Pull Factors Affecting Vulnerable Populations*

*Applies to sex trafficking only

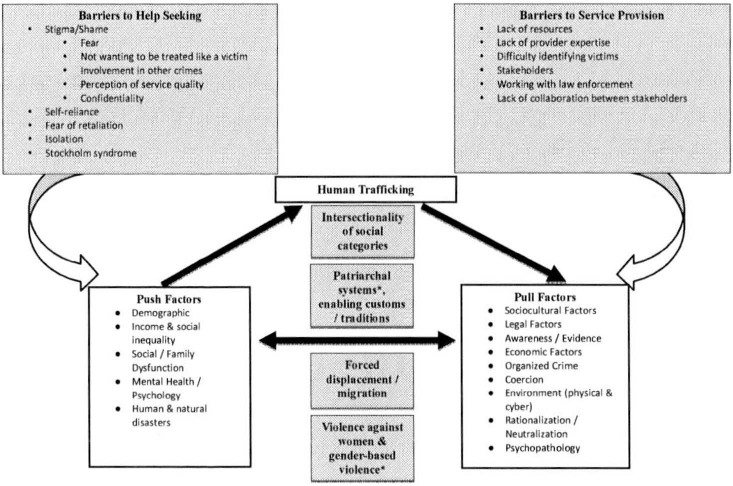

Figure X (d): *Barriers to Victims' Help Seeking and Access, and to Service Provision of Victims and Survivors*

*Applies to sex trafficking only

CHAPTER XI

Characteristics and Health of Indigenous Men Victims of Human Trafficking in Mexico

Arun Kumar Acharya[1]
Mannel R. Barragan Codina

Introduction

Trafficking of men, women and children is a serious violation of human rights that often involves extreme forms of abuses, violence and exploitation (Pocock, et al, 2016, ILO, 2012, Bales, 2012). The United Nations defines human trafficking as *"the recruitment, transportation, transfer, harboring or receipt of people, by means of the threat or use of force or other forms of coercion or abduction, fraud, deception, through the abuse of power or of a position of vulnerability or by giving or receiving payments or benefits to achieve the consent of a person having control over another person for the purpose of exploitation. Exploitation shall include at a minimum the exploitation of the prostitution of others or other forms of exploitation, forced labour or services, slavery or practices similar to slavery, servitude or the removal of organs"* (United Nations, 2000).

International Labour Organization (ILO) estimates suggest that men comprised 60% of total forced labour in sectors including fishing, agriculture and factory work in 2012. Experts generally agree that victims of human trafficking experience extreme levels of exploitation, violence, and

1. *Sambalpur University, India and Autonomous University of Nuevo Leon, Mexico*
2. *Autonomous University of Nuevo Leon, Mexico*

suffer a wide range of physical health problems and injuries (Stoakes, 2015, Zimmerman et.al 2011, Zimmerman et al., 2008, IOM, 2008, Falb et.al, 2011, Pocock et.al, 2016). For people who are trafficked, violence and risk of injuries are a continuous process throughout the period of coercion and exploitation and it persists even after the individual leaves the trafficking situation. Thus, unlike most other victims of crime, human trafficking victims have a prolonged and repeated trauma that may result in short and long-term physical injuries and disabilities (WHO, 2012, UNODC, 2014).

In the case of Mexico, attention on the human trafficking problem has increased in the last decade. The document published by the United Nations Office on Drugs and Crime (UNODC) on Diagnóstico Nacional sobre la Situación de Trata de Personas en México (National Diagnosis on the Situation of Trafficking in Persons in Mexico) indicates that Mexican men trafficked with false promises with high wages for the purpose exploitation in agriculture, industry, bars and construction sectors (UNODC, 2014). In a recent study on *"Human Trafficking and Sex Industry: Does Ethnicity and Race Matter?"* Gutierrez Chong (2014), stated that indigenous women in Mexico are highly exposed to trafficking due to structural poverty, marginalization, social exclusion and a traditional patriarchal culture. Although, there is an increasing literature on human trafficking especially of women and girls in the Mexican context, no systematic study has been carried out in the country to understand the trafficking of men and their health issues, particularly among the indigenous population. Thus, presenting an example from Monterrey city, Mexico, this paper explores the dynamic and characteristics indigenous men victims of human trafficking and their health status. Furthermore, this analysis will contribute to the design of effective intervention programs at national and international levels to address the unmet health needs, and especially the mental and physical care, required for victims of trafficking.

Background

The 2019 Trafficking in Persons Report provided by the U.S. Department of State indicates that Mexico is a source, transit and destination country for sex trafficking and forced labour. Mexican men, women and children are exploited in forced labour in agriculture, domestic service, food processing factories, construction, the informal economy, begging, and vending in both the United States and Mexico. The groups most vulnerable to human trafficking in Mexico include indigenous people, women, children, individuals with mental or physical disabilities, migrants, and LGBTI Mexicans (USDOS, 2017).

The Global Slavery Index ranked Mexico 114 out of 167 countries on slavery index and estimated that currently 341, 000 numbers of people living in modern slavery (Walk Free Foundation, 2018). The study conducted by Polaris on Diagnostic on Labour Trafficking in Mexico in 2017 indicates that in Mexico nearly 380 thousands men are victims of labour trafficking (Polaris, 2019). The trafficking of men for the purpose of forced labour and exploitation has become a public concern, especially young and adult indigenous men from economically marginalized areas, lured through false promises and exploited in different commercial sectors, agriculture, bars and in industry (UNODC, 2014).This rapid increase in the number of men victims lies in general increment of migration flow from rural areas. Many studies have identified that the volume male dominated indigenous migration has increased because; the proportion of income and agricultural products in the rural economy has decreased; the extension of agrarian property has decreased and there are more young people without land; and the rural world has become impoverished (Arias, 2013, Lastra Pimienta and Bolaños Vera, 2005).

In the last few years, some significant effort has been made to understand both the domestic and international trafficking in persons in Mexico (USDOS, 2015, Montalvo, 2014,

CNDH, 2012), however, none of the research have studied the dynamic of men trafficking in Mexico. Some of the media documentation affirmed that trafficking of young indigenous men for the purpose of forced labour has increased particularly to northern states of Mexico (Godoy, 2019, Martinez, 2016). The study of Polaris describe that Mexican men are predominantly trafficked to work in agriculture, construction sector, maquila sector, textile industry, mining, hotel/bars and other informal sectors (Polaris, 2019).

In addition, along the U.S.-Mexico border the trafficking of men has become a lucrative business (Ugarte et.al, 2003). Young boys and men are lured through false promises of employment and a better life in the United States, most of them are suffer different types of physical violence and they also suffer a higher grade of mental and physical health degradation (Ugarte et.al, 2003, Polaris, 2019). Men who are trafficked for the purpose labour exploitation often experience high rates of physical violence and have had serious physical injuries at work, victims who experience extremely excessive overtime at work, limited freedom, poor living conditions, threats, or severe violence were more likely to report symptoms of depression and anxiety (Kiss et.al, 2015, Zimmerman et.al, 2011, Zimmerman et al., 2008, Zimmerman and Watts, 2003, Pocock et.al, 2016, Krug, 2002, Shandro, et.al, 2016). Thus, it is important to consider that violence and exploitation of human trafficking victims by their perpetrator have long term physical health consequences on the victims, which we have analyzed in this study taking the example of Monterrey, Mexico.

Methods

Data collection

This study attempts to analyze the health consequences of both men victims of human trafficking. Human trafficking victims are treated as a hidden population, and it is extremely difficult to establish a reliable sampling frame. This tends to make randomized sampling strategies unsuitable. Therefore, a snowball sampling technique was utilized during our fieldwork. Interviews of trafficked men were carried out in two steps: The first step involved establishing contact with key informants to identify trafficked men, and the second step was to interview men victims of human trafficking.

Step 1 Identification of Key Informant

To identify labour trafficking victims in Monterrey, Mexico, we first reached out to an undergraduate student named "Norberto" who works in a dance bar as a waiter. We approached him seeking collaboration with this project, because he had good knowledge of the area and businesses in downtown Monterrey. Once we discussed the project with Norberto, he said she would try to help, but because it is difficult for her to move from one place to another, he was unsure about whether he would be able to locate many indigenous men victims of trafficking. After few days, Norberto contacted us over telephone and shared information of one man and the name of the bar where he was working.

Similarly, for men victims of other types of labour trafficking, we contacted "Noe" working as a supervisor in a construction company in the municipality of Juarez[1]. Noe a young boy originated from the state of Veracruz and belong to Otomígroup, also work as a community leader for their indigenous group, and therefore has good knowledge of people who might be victims of trafficking.

1. The Monterrey city comprises 12 municipalities; Apodaca, Cadereyta Jiménez, Escobedo, García, Guadalupe, Juárez, Monterrey, Salinas Victoria, San Nicolás de los Garza, San Pedro Garza García, Santa Catarina and Santiago.

Step 2: Interview with trafficking victims

After receiving the information on victims of trafficking, Francisco Ontiveros, a postgraduate student at the Instituto de Investigaciones Sociales [Social Science Research Institute], Universidad Autónoma de Nuevo León [Autonomous University of Nuevo Leon] and myself, visited the designated place and contacted the victims and described the objective of the study. After concluding the interview, we asked victims to help us find more indigenous men who are victims of trafficking, we also offered to pay her $100 pesos per person in return. Using the snowball technique, we were able to interview indigenous men victims of human trafficking in Monterrey city.

All interviews lasted for around 40 to 50 minutes, and using the snowball sampling technique, we interviewed a total of 32 men labour trafficking victims (N=32) during February 2016 to March 2017 with the help one research assistant. Interviews were conducted in Spanish and audio taped and followed an open-ended guide that was pilot tested.

Ethical consideration

In this study, before and during the interviews, we followed the World Health Organization (WHO) ethical and safety recommendations for interviewing men victims of trafficking written by Zimmerman and Watts (2003), including the relevant ethical and methodology procedures such as safeguarding participants' confidentiality, anonymity, and safety. It is also necessary to mention that, although they agreed to the interview through their friend, we still obtained their consent and always explained to them the sole purpose of our study, the subject to be discussed, its risks as well as its benefits. Moreover, we never asked any questions that could cause a discriminatory reaction, nor did we question their sentiments or judge their decision or character. There were men who became very emotional and preferred not to continue the interview, so we respected their decision and stopped at that point. In addition, we have used pseudonyms in the paper to protect the men's identity.

Data analysis

In this study we have analyzed the fieldwork information in two ways. The first was by using SPSS version 17 software, which systemized the socio demographic data of men victims of trafficking. In each interview, we obtained information on their current age, marital status, educational level, indigenous language, sector of exploitation, date since the trafficking took place, violence, injuries and disabilities they suffered. Secondly, using Critical Discourse Analysis (CDA), we analyzed the words (discourses) of the victims of trafficking, which revealed how traffickers or owner of establishment used their power to maintain an exploitive situation. From the discourses of victims, we analyzed how establishment owner treat or control victims, how they coerced into trafficking situations, what kind of violence persists against the victims and different types of health problems suffered by victims. This qualitative information was analyzed together with the quantitative information to understand the magnitude and seriousness of the trafficking problem in Mexico and its future implications.

Results

Socio-demographic characteristics

The socio-demographic characteristics of indigenous men victims of trafficking indicate important determining factors of human trafficking as well as the profile of this illegal market. Out of 32 interviewed indigenous men victims of trafficking, 20 men (62%) are younger than 20 years old and including

4 victims of ages of 12 years, who are working as waiters in a night club and the eldest victims of 38 years (Table XI (A) mainly engage in a construction company as a labourer. According to a young boy Javi, 16 years old: *"traffickers feels that young boys are very good for night club and massage parlors, as they are very easy to control emotionally and physically, also they are highly productive and complete work quickly, never complain of over work, however, adult (men) are very good for manual labour, as they have experience, so they can work easily and adapt in a different environment"* (Javi, 16 years old, Puebla state).

On the marital status of victims of trafficking in Monterrey city, we observed that 20 men (62.5%) are unmarried, 8 men are (25%) living with their partners and 4 men (12.5%) are currently married. The bivariate analysis on marital status and the sector of exploitation indicates that 28 out of 32 unmarried men are currently exploited in various sectors, which explains higher recruitment of young and unmarried boys. A trafficker described: *"Young and unmarried men are like new engine; they have stamina and energy to work for more time. They are eager and hungry to get a job and earn money, which help us to manipulate their vulnerability to control them in our hand"* (Trafficker "2", 43 years, 2017).

In Table XI (A), we present the educational status of indigenous men victims of trafficking, which indicates that 7 men (nearly 22%) never attended school, 13 victims (nearly 41%)have received an elementary education, and 12 (37.5%) have studied until junior high school. In this study we did not ask victims about their ethnic group, however, we did ask which indigenous language they and their relatives speak. Analysis indicates that out of 32 interviewed men, 9 speak (28%) Náhuatl, majority 14 men (43.7%) speak Otomí, 3 men (9.3%) speak Mixteco, only one man said he speak Mazahua language, however, 5 men (15.6%) did not want to mention their language.

TABLE XI (A)

Characteristics of indigenous trafficked men in Mexico (N=32), 2016-17

Variables	Number	Percent
Current Age		
Less than 15 years	2	6.2
16 to 20 years	18	56.2
21 to 25 years	6	18.8
More than 25 years	6	18.8
Marital Status		
Unmarried	20	62.5
Living relationship	8	25.0
Married	4	12.5
Education level		
Never attend school	7	21.8
Upto primary	13	40.6
Junior high school	12	37.5
Indigenous language		
Náhuatl	9	28.1
Otomí	14	43.7
Mixteco	3	9.3
Others	1	3.1
Do not mention	5	15.6

Source: Based on fieldwork, 2016-17

On our interviewed sample trafficked men are mostly originated from the central part of Mexico, 12 out of 32 victims comes from the state of Veracruz, followed by Oaxaca (7), San Luis Potosí (7) and Puebla (5) and rest are from other states such as Guerrero andHidalgo.

Causes of trafficking

The reason behind trafficking of indigenous men is a combination of various factors. To understand the causes of human trafficking among indigenous men, we asked victims during the interviews: *What are the main reasons that resulted in falling into a trafficking network?* Most of the boys and men responded with more than one cause, which can highlight that trafficking is a *multi-factorial* phenomenon. The factors cited by the victims have been categorized into three parts: Economic factors, Family factors and Personal Factors. 31 of 32 men (nearly 97%) victims of trafficking cited poverty, unemployment and household economic problems as their main reason to fall into trafficking network and 24 victims (75%) said family problems such as domestic violence and dysfunctional families[1], However, 12 (37.5%) of victims of trafficking have identified personal factors such as: marrying their girlfriend, searching to earn more money and migrating to the U.S. as their principal causes to enter into the trafficking network in Mexico.

Although, trafficking is a multi factorial phenomenon, the economic factor plays an instrumental role to push many young boys and men into trafficking network, as it can be understand in the case of Javi a 16-year-old boy victim of trafficking from the State of Puebla, he said: "*my family is a big one; we are five brothers and sisters, I am elder one. My father is a farmer, used to cultivate beans and nopal (Cactus), however, the production is not self sufficient, thus my mother used sell "dulce" (Candies) in market and sometime in front of village school. Because of poverty and money problem none of us brother and sister could studied. In 2011, my father had severe heart attacked and when we took him to hospital in Puebla city they asked us to deposit 50, 000 pesos ($2, 500 usd) for the immediate operation and as could not find money my father died after one day. One year later my mother also died because of some disease and thereafter I am taking responsibility of my siblings.....*

1. A dysfunctional family is a family in which conflict, misbehavior, and often child neglect or abuses on the part of individual parents occur continuously and regularly, leading other members to accommodate such actions (Senthil, 2016).

Few years ago when Don Mauro (name of trafficker) offer me a job in Monterrey with a salary of 30, 000 pesos ($1500 USD) per month, I accepted it, although after reaching I came to know that is very less what he promised me..." (Javi, 16 years old, Puebla).

TABLE XI (B)

Sectors of exploitation of indigenous trafficked men in Mexico (N=32), 2016-17

Variables	Number	Percent
Sex worker	3	9.3
Begging	3	9.3
Waiter in Bar/night club	10	31.2
Construction	6	18.7
Street seller	8	25.0
Worker in maquiladora	2	6.2

Source: Based on fieldwork, 2016-17

Sectors of exploitation

In the collected 32 sample, we have identified the sectors where indigenous men are primarily exploited in the city. Men are mainly exploited (n=10, 31%) as waiter in bar and in night club, whereas, some men are exploited as bagger (n=3, 9.3%), construction labourer (n=6, 18.7%), street vendors (n=8, 25%) and worker *maquiladora* (n=2, 6.2%), (Table XI (B)).

The analysis on their time spent in a trafficking situation, in the studied sample we found that 6 out 32 (18.7%) of indigenous boys and men have spent less than one year, whereas the majority of victims (n=18, 56%) have spent one to three years and 7 victims (21.8%) have spent 3 to 5 years in trafficking and only one victim (3.1%) said he has spent 5 to 7 years in exploitive situation (Table XI (C)). From the narrative of victims, it is assume that trafficker or the owners of the establishment they do not prefer to keep victims more time, as Efrain, an 18 years old boy from the state of Guerrero said: *"el patron no quiere chavos que sean grande de edad.... dice que son muy cabrones, no tiene miedo al patrón, por eso es difícil de someter a trabajar múltiples.... Pero los chicos pequeñitos son fáciles de someter y meter a trabajar cualquier cosa y no dicen nada, porque saben que si no obedecen puede sufrir violencia o maltrato........ (boss does not want people who are elder in age... He says, they are very bad and not obedient, as they do not have fear to boss, that is why it is difficult to put them in multiple workers... But little boys are easy to subdue and put them anything to work as they don't say anything, because they know that if they don't obey, they can suffer violence or mistreatment ....)"* (Efrain, 18 years, Guerrero).

TABLE XI (C)

Time in trafficking of indigenous men in Mexico (N=32), 2016-17

Variables	Number	Percent
Time in trafficking		
Less than one year	6	18.7
1-3 years	18	56.2
3-5 years	7	21.8
5-7 years	1	3.1

Source: Based on fieldwork, 2016-17

When it asked the victims on their living condition, all participants (n=32, 100%) reported poor hygienic condition of their living place and do not have ventilations facility, 18 (56%) victims said they do not have water facility, 27 victims (84%) said their place is overcrowded and 31 victims (nearly 97%) reported they are not getting adequate food to eat (Table XI (D)).

TABLE XI (D)

Living conditions of trafficking victims men in Mexico (N=32), 2016-17

Variables	Number	Percent
Poor hygienic condition	32	100.0
No water facilities	18	56.2
No ventilation	32	100.0
Overcrowded	27	84.3
Insufficient food	31	96.8

Source: Based on fieldwork, 2016-17

The results indicate that trafficking victims are living in an inhumane condition. In this regards, Jose a 16 years trafficking victims originated from the Oaxaca state and presently working in a construction site narrate: "*I am working in this place since last three years. Before, I left my village community, Patron promised me a well paid job in Texas (USA), however, instead of taking there, he brought me Monterrey and obligates me to work here. He said after one year he will find out a suitable time to send me Texas and till now he has said nothing. He paid me 800 pesos ($40 usd) per week which is very less and forced me to work more than 12 hours everyday. Hardly I get a rest day for me. Like me there are another 20 chavos (boys) are here. We are living in a small room without bathroom and sanitary. In breakfast he gives us bread and eggs and in lunch tortilla (bread), rice and beans and in dinner only tortilla and beans. Once in a week he provides us meat. In summer our life becomes very complicated as we do not have proper ventilation facility. We cannot complain or demand any things to him, in case any guy demand any things he just put fine on our salary. We are leading a barbaric life and in my village our domestic animal leads better life than us*". (Jose, 16 years, Oaxaca)

Reports of Violence and exploitation

The trafficked men once they get trapped by the trafficker, it is almost difficult for them to escape; victims are subject to violence and exploitation in different forms including verbal abuse, threatening including physical and sexual violence. In the collected 32 sample of male victims of human trafficking in Monterrey city, the findings show that the majority of victims (n=26, 81%) worked every day of the week with no breaks, while nearly 3 men (9.3%) of victims said they worked 5 to 6 days a week (Table XI (E)). Similarly, on our question on how many hours worked per day, the findings indicate that 28 of 32 men victims (87.5%) said they worked more than 10 hours per day and the majority of these work as sex worker, waiter in bar or night club, bagger and street seller. However, some men responded that they work fewer than 8 hours, most of them worked in construction sector. Guillermo a 13-year-old boy who is working as a street seller said: "*I do not have liberty to decide how many hours I can work... as every day I have to sell a fixed amount of products (fruits and nuts), often it terminate after 10 pm in the night. I also do not get off day... sometimes, once a month they allow me to visit my friends at the "Alameda"*[1]*and that also only for few hours...*" (Guillermo, 13-year-old, Veracruz).

Victims of trafficking, especially men and boys experience high levels of psychological, physical, economic, sexual, verbal and symbolic violence. All 32 respondents have indicated that they frequently suffer verbal abuses and threatening of violence, nearly one third victims (n=23, 71.8%) reported experienced of physical violence such as slapped, kicked, dragged, beaten up and 7 victims (21.8%) have indicated that they have suffered sexual violence by the owner or by other persons. Among the interviewed participants 10 men (31%) also said they have experienced economic violence such as not getting paid by their employer or being fined at the job (Table XI (E)).

1. Alameda is a central park, located in the downtown area of Monterrey.

In the bivariate analysis on the sector of exploitation and violence we observed that men and boys who worked as waiter in bar or night club, sex worker, street seller have reported higher levels of sexual and physical violence, while victims who work as bagger or in construction sector reported higher percentage of verbal violence and threatening violence and no payment (Table XI (E)). For example; Guillermo a 13-year-old from the state of Veracruz said: "*almost all boys here suffer violence everyday in their life. El Patron do not tolerate any mistake, in case a boy by mistake change the glass or sitting arrangement then patron scold him. In case we break a bottle or any object of the bar, then the consequence is severe..... Violence is common in this life and we have habituated to it....*" (Guillermo, 13-year-old, Veracruz).

On the other hand, Pedro a 13 years boy from San Luis Potosi who exploited as sex worker narrates: "*one day I was not feeling good as suffering from cold and fever, however it was a weekend and the Patron insisted me have sex with a client. Although, I was not interested, he forced me have sex, later the same client complained to Patron that he was not satisfied with (my) service and asked to return paid money. Parton returned his money, and later in the evening Patron took me to downstairs of the bar and asked his other employers to accompanied him. In the downstairshe asked his employers (there were three employers) to have oral and anal sex with me. Few minutes later I vomited and had severe pain and bleeding for the sexual intercourse, however they didn't respect my pain and request and they continued......*" (Pedro, 13 years, San Luis Potosi)

TABLE XI (E)

Exploitation and violence against indigenous trafficked men in Mexico (N=32), 2016-17

Variables	Number	Percent
Days worked/week		
Everyday	26	81.2
Five to Six days	3	9.3
Two to Four days	2	6.2
No fixed days	1	3.1
Hours worked per day		
8 to 10 hrs	4	12.5
More than 10 hours	28	87.5
Violence type		
Physical violence	23	71.8
Sexual violence	07	21.8
Verbal abuses and threatening of violence	32	100
No payment and fine	10	31.2
Violence perpetrator		
Owners	26	81.2
Clients	4	12.5
Others	2	6.5

Source: Based on fieldwork, 2016-17

Health problems

Trafficking victims often experience various health problems due to the violence and exploitation and thus, we asked victims: "*Have you experienced any kind of health problems after entering into the trafficking network*?" and table XI (F), presents the descriptive analysis of this question. Our findings indicate that victims reported numerous types of health problems and most of them lead to severe physical and internal body damage to the victims. The most commonly reported health issue is different type of injuries such as head injury (n=27,

84%) followed by skin damage (n=26, 81%), mouth and teeth injuries (n=31, 96.8%) and eye injury (n=16, 50%). Some victims also reported broken bones (n=7, 21.8%), back pain (n=11, 34%), dizziness (n=17, 53%) and weight loss (n=28, 87.5%), however, in self reporting health problem, some male victims also cited mental health issues such as frequent feeling of depression (n=23, 71.8%) and poor emotional condition (n=11, 34%). On the contrary, a high proportion of victims also reported internal health problems such as frequent urine infection (n=17, 53%), chest pain (n=13, 40.6%) and frequent headache (n=21, 65.6%).

TABLE XI (F)

Self Reported health problems by the indigenous trafficked men in Mexico (N=32), 2016-17

Variables	Number	Percent
Head injuries	27	84.3
Broken bone	7	21.8
Skin damage	26	81.2
Mouth and teeth injuries	31	96.8
Eye injury	16	50.0
Back pain	11	34.3
Dizziness	17	53.1
Weight loss	28	87.5
Depression	23	71.8
Poor emotional condition	11	34.3
Urine infection	17	53.1
Chest pain	13	40.6
Frequent headache	21	65.6

Source: Based on fieldwork, 2016-17

Discussion and Conclusions

In this study we can highlight that human trafficking highly associated with serious health problems of victims. Men trafficked for the purpose of forced labour and labour exploitation and this phenomenon involves social, cultural and economic factors that create vulnerable situations for many young boys and men in Mexico. The findings of our research indicate that men victims of trafficking are very young, unmarried and have very little education, and the majority of them are from the States of Veracruz, followed by Guerrero, Oaxaca, San Luis Potosí and Puebla. There are numerous studies, for example Granados Alcantar (2005), Juárez-Sánchez (2015) on the indigenous migration that indicates these States are known as "*expulsion zones*" of indigenous population to different parts of Mexico and United States.

Our finding shows that there are few push factors, such as poverty, lack of employment opportunities in the community and domestic violence, are some of the principal reasons that young indigenous boys become victim of human trafficking. Previous studies have addressed the particularities that changes in the economic, social and family spheres such as domestic violence, physical and sexual abuse in the family, alcoholism and disintegration of families, either through death (leaving orphans and widows) or separation, are viewed to increase the risk of trafficking (Russell, 2014; Poucki, 2012; Huda, 2006; IOM, 2008; Adepoju, 2005; ILO, 2006).

Our results also confirm that there are certain pull factors that attract young indigenous boys into trafficking network, for example better quality of life in Monterrey city, higher salary and its proximity to the United States which may provide an opportunity to migrate in the long term. Nevertheless, once they reached the city they were exploited in different sectors and forced to live in hazardous environments without proper payment and sufficient days to rest.

The findings of our study report that trafficking victims suffered wide range of violence in the hands of their Patron (employer), which has severe long-lasting health consequences. Employers use the vulnerability condition of victims and execute different types of harassment and violence, such as sexual, physical verbal and psychological (Montiel, 2009; Scarone Adarga, 2014) and it continues until the wishes of the perpetrators are met, and as a result victims are particularly susceptible to various kinds of health problems due to this violence (Zimmerman et.al, 2014, Acharya and Bryson, 2014, Oram, et.al, 2016). Our obtained information from the field indicates that trafficking victims suffer different types of abuses and violence, which lead to multiple physical and internal body health problems. However, it is important to observe prevalence health problems is very high among the victims and this shows how their bodies are treated as "*objects*" and they are used and reused for economic benefits by the employers.

Finally, despite the limitations in this study such as a sample representation, our research provides urgently needed information of a sub-population that is completely invisible in Mexican society. As previously documented, victims of human trafficking face many health issues which reduce their chances to live a good post-trafficking life. Similarly, many of them become permanently disabled, which pushes victims into precarious situations. It is important that policy makers as well as practitioners become aware of these issues and include them in anti-trafficking programs. In 2014, the Mexican Government implemented the National program to prevent, punish and eradicate crimes in matters of trafficking in persons and for the protection and assistance of those victims 2014-2018. Objective 2 of the program specifies that the *States must provide comprehensive care, protection and assistance to victims of trafficking in persons*. The model of care, protection and assistance composed with an institutional framework that includes health, education and employment sectors. Although the national program specifies the comprehensive care for victims of human trafficking, it does not mention the mental and physical care for these categories of people. It is therefore necessary for government to create instruments in the national program to address the unmet health needs of victims of human trafficking.

REFERENCES

Acharya, A. K. and Bryson, C. J. (2014).Trafficking of women and vulnerability to HIV/STI infection in urban Mexico.*Genus: Journal of Population Sciences*, Vol. LXX, No. 2-3.

Acharya, A. K. and Cervantes, J. J. (2009).Female Migration and Urban Informal Sector in Monterrey Metropolitan Region. *Journal of Social Science*, 21.

Acharya, A. K. and Sanchez-Martinez, M. L. (2018). Trafficking of Women in US-Mexican Border Cities: An Analysis on the Physical and Mental Health Condition of Victims, *Journal of Trafficking and Human Exploitation*, 2 (1), June, https://doi.org/10.7590/245227718X15260460483715

Acharya, A. K. (2016). Trafficking of women for sexual exploitation in Mexico and their identity crisis. *International Review of Sociology*, 26 (2), 322-336. http://dx.doi.org/10.1080/03906701.2016.1155357

Adepoju A. (2005). Review of research and data on human trafficking in Sub-Saharan Africa. *International Migration*, 43 (1/2): 75-98.

Arias, Patricia (2013). Migración, economía campesina y ciclo de desarrollo doméstico. Discusiones y estudios recientes. *Estudios demográficos y urbanos*. México, El Colegio de México, 2013, vol. 28, núm. 1, pp. 96-98.

Azaola, E. and Estes, J. R. (eds.). (2003). *La Infancia como Mercancía Sexual: Mexico, Canada y Estados Unidos*. Mexico: Siglo XXI.

Bales, K. (2012).*Disposable People: New Slavery in the Global Economy*. University of California Press, 3rd Edition.

Beyer, C. and Stachowiak J. (2003).Health Consequences of Trafficking of Women and Girls in Southeast Asia.*The Brown Journal of World Affairs*, X (1): 105-117.

Cacho, L. (2010). *Esclavas del poder: Un viaje al corazón de la trata sexual de mujeres y niñas en el mundo*. México: Grijalbo.

CNDH (Comisión Nacional de los Derechos Humanos). (2012). *La trata de personas*. Retrieved from http://www.cndh.org.mx/sites/all/doc/cartillas/8_Cartilla_Trata.pdf.

COHA (Council on Hemispheric Affairs). (2009). *Modern Day Slavery in Mexico and the United States*, December 21, 1250 Connecticut Ave, N.W., Suite 1C Washington, D.C. Retrieved from http://www.coha.org/modern-day-slavery-in-mexico-and-the-united-states/

Dalla, R.L. (2000). Exposing the Pretty Woman Myth: A qualitative Examination of the Lives of Female streetwalking Prostitutes. *Journal of Sex Research*, 37:344-353.

Deshpande, N. A., and Nour, N. M. (2013).Sex Trafficking of Women and Girls.*Reviews in Obstetrics and Gynecology*, 6 (1), e22–e27.

Durin, S. (2008).*Entre luces y sombras. Miradas sobre los indígenas en el área metropolitana de Monterrey, México*, Publicaciones de la Casa Chata, CIESAS, Mexico.

Esteinou, R. (2011). Selling bodies and Sexual exploitation: Prostitution in Mexico. In Dalla, R.L, Baker, L. M., Defrain, J., Williamson, C. (Eds.), *Global Perspectives on prostitution and sex trafficking: Europe, Latin America, North America and Global*, Lexington Books, USA.

Falb, K. L., McCauley, H. L., Decker, M. R., Sabarwal, S., Gupta, J. and Silverman, J. G. (2011).Trafficking mechanisms and HIV status among sex-trafficking survivors in Calcutta, India. *International Journal of Gynecology & Obstetrics*, 113: 86–87. doi:10.1016/j.ijgo.2010.11.009

Farley, M., Cotton, A., Lynne, J., Zumbeck, S., Spiwak, F., Reyes, M.E., Alvarez, D., and Sezgin, U. (2003). Prostitution and trafficking in 9 countries: Update on violence and posttraumatic stress disorder. *Journal of Trauma Practice*, 2 (3/4), 33-74.

Global Alliance Against Traffic in Women (GAATW). (2000). *Human Rights and Trafficking in Persons: A Handbook*, GAATW, Bangkok, Thailand, December.

Godoy, Emilio (2019). Los jornaleros, las mayores víctimas del trabajo esclavo en México, Inter Press Service, 29th March, 2019. http://www.ipsnoticias.net/2019/03/los-jornaleros-las-mayores-victimas-del-trabajo-esclavo-mexico/

González, R. (2003). *Violencia contra las mujeres deja un millón de víctimas anuales en México*, CIMAC, Mexico.

Granados Alcantar, J. A. (2005). Las nuevas zonas de atracción de migrantes indígenas en México. *Investigaciones Geográficas*, 58, 140-147.

Gutiérrez Chong, N. (2014).Human Trafficking and Sex Industry: Does Ethnicity and Race Matter?, *Journal of Intercultural Studies*, 35 (2), http://dx.doi.org/10.1080/07256868.2014.885413

Huda, S. (2006). Sex trafficking in South Asia.*International Journal of Gynecology and Obstetrics*, 94, Elsevier Ireland.

Instituto Nacional de Estadística y Geografía (INEGI). (2011). *Perspectiva Estadística de México*, December, INEGI, Mexico.

International Labour Organization (ILO). (2012). *ILO global estimate of forced labour: results and methodology*, Special Action Program to Combat Forced Labour (SAP-FL), Geneva.

International Labour Organization (ILO). (2006).*Emerging good practices on actions to combat child domestic labour in Kenya, Tanzania, Uganda, and Zambia*, International Labour Office, Tanzania, 93 p.

International Organization for Migration (IOM). (2008). *In Eastern Africa. Research assessment and baseline information in Tanzania, Kenya, Uganda, and Burundi*. Geneva: International Organization for Migration.

International Organization for Migration (IOM). (2008).*Human Trafficking in Eastern Africa: Research Assessment and Baseline Information in Tanzania, Kenya, Uganda, and Burundi*,

International Organization for Migration, 17 route des Morillons, 1211 Geneva 19, Switzerland, 79 p.

Jiménez-Naranjo, Yolanda and Mendoza-Zuany, Rosa Guadalupe (2016).La educación indígena en México: una evaluación de política pública integral, cualitativa y participativa. *LiminaR: Estudios Sociales y Humanísticos,* XIV (1), Centro de Estudios Superiores de México y Centro América, San Cristóbal de las Casas, México.

Juárez-Sánchez, J. P. (2015). Migración indígena hacia espacios agrícolas marginados de México: Un caso para contar. *Agricultura, sociedad y desarrollo,* 12 (1), 87-105.

Kara, S. (2010). *Sex Trafficking Inside the Business of Modern Slavery,* Columbia University Press.

Kiss, L, Pocock, N.S, Naisanguansri, V., Suos, S., Dickson, B., Thuy, D., ... Zimmerman, C. (2015). Health of men, women, and children in post-trafficking services in Cambodia, Thailand, and Vietnam: an observational cross-sectional study. *Lancet Glob Health;* 3: e154–61, http://doi.org/10.1016/S2214-109X (15)70016-1

Kramer, L. (2003). Emotional Experience of Performing Prostitution.In Farley, M. (Eds.) *Prostitution, Trafficking and Traumatic Stress.* Binghamton, New York: Haworth.

Krug, E. G. (2002).*World Report on Violence and Health*. Geneva: World Health Organisation.

Lastra, Pimienta Rodrigo and Bolaños, Vera Martha (2005). *Dinámica migratoria interestatal en la República Mexicana.* Estado de México: El Colegio Mexiquense, 2005, p. 29.

Martínez León A. (2016). Para entender el trabajo forzoso o esclavitud moderna, *El Economista,* 22 de noviembre de 2016. https://www.eleconomista.com.mx/arteseideas/Para-entender-el-trabajo-forzoso-o-esclavitud-moderna-20161122-0134.html

Monroy, P. (2010). México: pasividad ante explotación sexual infantil. *Contralínea,* September, México DF, http://contralinea.info/archivo-revista/index.php/2010/09/05/mexico-pasividad-ante-explotacion-sexual-infantil/

Montalvo, T. L. (2014). Víctimas de trata en México se duplican en el último año: la mayoría son mujeres y niñas. *Animal Politico,* Noviembre 26. Retrieved from http://www.animalpolitico.com/2014/11/victimas-de-trata-en-mexico-se-duplican-en-el-ultimo-ano-la-mayoria-son-mujeres-y-ninas/

Montiel-Torres, O. (2009).*Trata de Personas: Padrotes, iniciación y Modus operandi,* Instituto Nacional de Mujeres, Mexico City, Mexico.

Moreira, I. C. C. C. and Monteiro, C. F. (2012).La violencia en el contidiano de la prostitución: invisibilidades y ambigüedades. *Revista Latino-Americana de Enfermagem,* 26 (5), September-October.

Oram, S., Abas, M., Bick, D., Boyle, A., French, R., Jakobowitz, S., …. Zimmerman, C. (2016). Human trafficking and health: A survey of male and female survivors in England. *American Journal of Public Health,* 106 (6), 1073-1078. http://dx.doi.org/10.2105/AJPH.2016.303095

Pedroza Flores, R, Villalobos Monroy, G and Reyes Fabela, A. M. (2015).Compensatory Policies Attending Equality and Inequality in Mexico Educational Practice among Vulnerable Groups in Higher Education. *Journal of Education and Learning;* 4 (4), Published by Canadian Center of Science and Education.

Pocock, N. S, Kiss L., Oram, S., and Zimmerman, C. (2016). Labour Trafficking among Men and Boys in the Greater Mekong Subregion: Exploitation, Violence, Occupational Health Risks and Injuries. *PLoS ONE* 11 (12): e0168500. https://doi.org/10.1371/journal.pone.0168500

Polaris (2019). Diagnóstico – trata de personas con fines laborales en México, Polaris and Fundación Walmart, May, 2019. https://polarisproject.org/wp-content/uploads/2019/09/Diagno%CC%81stico-Trata-De-Personas-Con-Fines-Laborales-En-Me%CC%81xico.pdf

Pouki, S. (2012).*The quest for root causes of human trafficking: a study on the experience of marginalized groups, with a focus on the republic of Serbia* (Doctoral dissertation), Graduate Program in Global Affairs, The State University of New Jersey. Retrieved fromhttp://dga.rutgers.edu/sites/default/files/uploads/2012/10/The-Quest-for-Root-Causes-of-Human-Trafficking-A-Study-on-the-Experience-of-Marginalized-Groups-with-a-Focus-on-the-Republic-of-Serbia.pdf

Raphael, J. and Shapiro, D.L. (2004).Violence in Indoor and Outdoor Prostitution Venues.*Violence Against Women*, 10 (2): 126-39.

Raymond, J. (2004). Prostitution on demand: Legalizing the buyers as sexual consumers. *Violence Against Women*, 10 (10): 1156-86.

Ruíz Torres, M. A. (2003). La Explotación sexual de Niños en Dos Ciudades Turísticas: Cancún y Acapulco. In Azaola, E. & Estes, J. R. (Eds), *La Infancia como Mercancía Sexual: Mexico, Canada Estados Unidos*, Siglo XXI, Mexico.

Russell, A. M. (2014). Victims of Trafficking: The Feminization of Poverty and Migration in the Gendered Narratives of Human Trafficking. *Societies*, 4, 532–548; doi:10.3390/soc4040532

Scarone Adarga, M. (2014).Violencia laboral intramuros. Hostigamiento sexual y otras formas de violencia contra la mujer en las maquiladoras de Sonora y Baja California. *Revista: Región y Sociedad*, (4).

Senthil, M. (2016).Impact of Family Dysfunctions on Child and Adolescents Mental Health.*The International Journal of Indian Psychology*, 4 (1), No. 76, DIP: DIP: 18.01.028/20160476

Servan-Mori, E., Torres-Pereda, P., Orozco, E., and Sosa-Rubí, S. G. (2014).An explanatory analysis of economic and health inequality changes among Mexican indigenous people, 2000-2010. *International Journal for Equity in Health*, 13 (21). http://doi.org/10.1186/1475-9276-13-21

Shandro, J., Chisolm-Straker, M., Duber, H. C., Findlay, S. L., Munoz, J., Schmitz, G., ...Wingkun, N. (2016). Human Trafficking: A Guide to Identification and Approach for the

Emergency Physician.*Annals of Emergency Medicine*, 68 (4) DOI: 10.1016/j.annemergmed.2016.03.049

Silverman, J. G., Raj, A., Cheng, D. M., Decker, M. R., Coleman, S., Bridden, C., ..., Samet, J. H. (2011). Sex Trafficking and Initiation-Related Violence, Alcohol Use, and HIV Risk Among HIV-Infected Female Sex Workers in Mumbai, India. *The Journal of Infectious Diseases*, 204 (Suppl 5), S1229–S1234. http://doi.org/10.1093/infdis/jir540

Stoakes, E., Kelly, C. and Kelly, A. (2015). Revealed: how the Thai fishing industry traffick, imprisons and enslaves. *The Guardian*. Retrieved from http://www.theguardian.com/global-development/2015/jul/20/thai-fishing-industry-implicated-enslavement-deaths-rohingya

Ugarte M. B, Zarate L, and Farley M. (2003).Prostitution and trafficking of women and children from Mexico to the United States.*Journal of Trauma Practice*. 2 (3):37–41. doi:10.1300/J189v02n03.

United Nations Office on Drugs and Crime (UNODC). (2014). *Global report on trafficking in persons*. Retrieved from https://www.unodc.org/documents/data-and-analysis/glotip/GLOTIP_2014_full_report.pdf

United Nations. (2000). *Protocol against the smuggling of migrants by land, sea and air, supplementing the United Nations convention against transnational organized crime*, United Nations, New York,

United States Department of State (USDOS). (2016). *The Trafficking in Persons Report-2016*.Retrieved from http://www.state.gov/g/tip/rls/tiprpt/2016/.

United States Department of State (USDOS). (2017). *The Trafficking in Persons Report-2016*. Retrieved from https://www.state.gov/j/tip/rls/tiprpt/2017/

World Health Organization. (2012). *Human trafficking: Understanding and addressing violence against women*. Retrieved from http://apps.who.int/iris/bitstream/10665/77394/1/WHO_RHR_12.42_eng.pdf

POPULAR RESISTANCE MOVEMENTS AGAINST THE BRITISH RULE

SURVEY OF MODERN INDIA SERIES

POPULAR RESISTANCE MOVEMENTS AGAINST THE BRITISH RULE

Edited by
RAJ KUMAR

ANMOL PUBLICATIONS PVT. LTD.
NEW DELHI-110002 (INDIA)

ANMOL PUBLICATIONS PVT. LTD.
4374/4B, Ansari Road, Daryaganj
New Delhi-110 002

Popular Resistance Movements Against the British Rule

First Edition 1999

ISBN 81-261-0233-0

PRINTED IN INDIA

Published by J. L. Kumar for Anmol Publications Pvt. Ltd., New Delhi-110 002 and Printed at Mehra Offset Press, Delhi.

Contents

Preface

There is vast literature on the history of Modern India. We have been mainly influenced by Stanley Lane-Poole, J. N. Sarkar; R. S. Tripathi, Beni Prasad, P. Saren, A.L. Srivastava and S.B.P. Nigam. These writers have left a great legacy in the form of documents translated, articles and books written. Dr. Sita Ram Sharma has supervised this compilation, Archana Chaturvedi, S.S. Abidi and many other friends have helped in various ways and we are grateful to them.

Readers must be thankful to Mr. J. L. Kumar whose brain child this work is and who has most expeditiously published it in present form.

—Raj Kumar

CHAPTER 1

Bhonsla Resistance

After winning the make-believe battle of Plassey, Clive wrote: "I am fully persuaded that after the Battle of Placis, I could have appropriated the whole country to the Company and preserved it afterwards with as much case as Mir Jaffeir, the present Subah now does, through the fear of the English arms and their influence." Clive and his tribe were at least honest about their actions and did not clothe them in sanctimonious phrases. They called loot and forgery by their genuine names and were content. It was another generation of rulers that gilded their aggrandizement by high-sounding terms, such as Subsidiary Alliance and Doctrine of Lapse. A century later other terms were coined, often reduced to alphabets in the form of various Treaty Organisations.

But subjugation has its odour by whatever name it may be called. The name that was beloved of Wellesley was Subsidiary Alliance. He pointed out how it had the advantage of keeping "the evils of war at a distance from the sources of our wealth and our power"—a process of bleeding white without shedding blood. But what the Empire Builders did not learn was that they built their edifices on a volcano of suppressed feelings and bitter humiliation. The fires may be driven underground, but they smoulder and burn silently and wait only for an opportunity to erupt. Resistance to oppression is a law of Nature. Therefore, the origins of resistance in Madhya Pradesh have to be traced to the period when the bonds of foreign rule were fastened on it with the signing of the Subsidiary Alliance in 1816. Strangely enough it was Appa Saheb Bhonsle who had signed away the freedom of these territories that took the lead in the resistance.

A significant and impressive ceremony took place at the Court of the Raja of Nagpur on 25th November 1817. Appa Saheb Bhonsle, who had ascended the *Gadi* in February 1817 at the sudden and mysterious death of Parsoji, drove in state to his army camp, and in the presence of his ministers, army chiefs and nobles of the kingdom he was invested with the *Khilat,* the robes of honour presented to him by the Peshwa. He was also decorated with the emblem of Imperial Command, the *Jari Patka* and the title of Senapati. These marks of recognition by which the new Bhonsla King proclaimed himself a member of the Maratha Confederacy under the Peshwa's leadership would at any time have had considerable political significant: but in November 1817, it was a provincial prevent for on the 5th November 1817, the Peshwa, Baji Rao II, had made a sudden and dramatic attack on the British Residency at Poona and captured it with little difficulty. The Peshwa and the British were, thus, at open war. In this context the ceremonial acceptance of the honours and titles from the Peshwa by Appa Saheb could have only one political meaning—a meaning that was not lost on Mr. Jenkins, the Nagpur Resident. When Ramachandra Wagh, the trusted minister of Appa Saheb, personally delivered to Mr. Jenkins an invitation to be present and assist at the investiture ceremony, his reply was a firm remonstrance against "the acceptance of the Khilat or of any titles from a power now at open war with the British", and a flat refusal to give the sanction of his presence to such an act.

The protests of the Resident, however, proved of no avail. Appa Saheb's answer to it was to post his troops immediately in a strong position to attack the Residency, if necessary. The investiture did, in fact, set the seal on a concerted plan between the Peshwa and Appa Saheb to join in an effort to overthrow the British power and establish their independence. Ever since Appa Saheb came in full possession of the kingdom of Nagpur he had been contemplating the removal of the lengthening shadows of British influence and "the restoration of the Maratha empire to its pristine splendour and powers". This mean, indeed, to continue the policy of his uncle, Raghoji II, whose correspondence with Peshwa. Sindhia and Holkar had the object of promoting a spirit of concert and union amongst all Marathas, directed against the British ascendancy (Prinsep's *Transactions,* Vol. I, p. 358). In pursuance of this object he had been in correspondence with Baji Rao II. He had been kept informed of the gathering of forces at Poona since the latter part of October. Their plan was to strike simultaneously at the seats of British power at Poona and Nagpur, to surprise the forces at both these capitals, and sweep them from their territories, so that their independence which, by their Subsidiary Alliance they had forfeited may be won back again.

The Peshwa and Appa Saheb had both made their way to power through the expediency of the Subsidiary Alliance. This Alliance was an ingenious method of enslavement, which owed its origin to Lord Wellesley and had successfully destroyed the independence of all the powerful States of India. It was a curious system of double-government under which real power was in the hands of the British Resident, while the responsibility for good or had government lay with the ruler. Henry Laynson writing in observed way.

> "If there was a device for ensuring male government, it is that of a native ruler and minister both relying on foreign bayonets, and directed by a British Resident."

Another able administrator of the period, Sir Thomas Munro, was also equally critical of this arrangement. Writing to the Governor-General in 1817, he said:

> "There are many weighty objections to the employment of a subsidiary force. It has a natural tendency to render the government of every country in which it exists weak and oppressive, to extinguish all honourable spirit among the higher class of society, and to degrade and impoverish the people."

Most of the British Residents or Agents, barring some rare exceptions, exercised "the harlot's privilege of having power with-out responsibility" (Nehru: *Discovery of India*).

The Subsidiary Alliance was negotiated on behalf of Appa Saheb by his two trusted ministers, Nago Pant and Narayan

Pandit, who met Jenkins on the night of 24th April 1816. After some prolonged negotiations regarding the terms of the Alliance an agreement was finally reached on all points, including the size and composition of the subsidiary force which was fixed at six battalions and one regiment of Horse of which two battalions were to be stationed at Nagpur. The Raja was to pay annually Rs. 7½ laks for maintaining the subsidiary force, it being stipulated that in the event of any irregularity in the payment of this subsidy, the British Government would be entitled to demand the cession of territory within the Bhonsla kingdom yielding an equivalent annual revenue. In addition, the Raja was to maintain at his own cost a force of 3,000 Horse and 2,000 Foot, in the discipline and management of which the British Resident would have the right of giving advice. One interesting stipulation which, the minister of Appa Saheb insisted on including in the treaty, has a curious historical interest. They were keen that it should be specified that cows and bullocks should not be killed within the Nagpur territory. This was, however, refused. The Resident only gave a verbal assurance that no cows or bullocks would be killed on any account within the city itself, but the troops, when in the field, were not to be restricted in this particular (Prinsep's *Transactions*, Vol. I. p. 364).

Having settled all the terms of the treaty satisfactorily, a meeting was arranged in great secrecy in dead of night on the 27th May 1816 in the house of Nago Pant at Nagpur. Here Appa Saheb put his signature to this historic document in the presence of the Resident. In view of the strong opposition to a Subsidiary Alliance which a group in the palace had steadily maintained, it was agreed not to make this document public until the subsidiary force provided in the treaty had actually reached within a day's march of the city. This it did on the 8th of June 1816, and on the following day the treaty was made public.*

---

* Sir John Malcolm referring to the Subsidiary Alliance with Nagpur says "in the actual condition of India, no event could be more fortunate than the Subsidiary Alliance with Nagpur."

Such was the manner in which this great Kingdom of the Bhonslas, situated in a strategic position in the centre of the Peninsula, striding across the Narmada valley and the Satpura range down to the borders of the Nizam's Dominion, fell into the clutches of the British power. Henry Prinsep, the contemporary historian, describes it as—

> "the most important extension of the system of our relations with the native powers of India that had taken place since the general settlement of them 10 years before".†

It had been the anxious desire of the British to bring this area within their sphere of influence so that the gap between the territories in the north and the south, which had already submitted to them, could be bridged. Appa Saheb, like his colleague, Baji Rao II, accepted this humiliating agreement under the well-known principle of expediency than "the end justifies the means". To both of them the Subsidiary Alliance was only a means to the achievement of political power. Once they had been firmly established in their kingdoms they dust little time in concerting a plan to oust the British and restore the glory and independence of their Confederacy.

---

† "The arrangement enables me to leave unguarded about three hundred miles of frontier, for which I had difficulty to allot defence; it totally over-sets the plan at which Scindiah has been secretly working for inducing the Peshwa to re-establish the Mahratta confederacy, it deprives Scindiah of troops and treasure, on which he calculated in all his hostile speculations; it gives me, by the junction of Colonel Doveton's Corps with the Nagpur forces, an efficient army on the open flank of Scindiah's country, and it renders the interception of the Pindaries, should they venture another inroad into our southern territories, almost certain. I regard this event as giving me the fairest ground of confidence that I shall be able to achieve all I wish to effect for the Company's interest without any war, this rests on our presumption of the Peshwa's fidelity: If he be treacherous (and there is no answering for a Mahratta) we might have a struggle, but the consequences of such a contest could not now be doubtful, and it would only make the ultimate arrangement more beneficial to the Company". (Private Journal of Lord Hastings, entry on June 1, 1816.)

Commenting on what transpired later, Prinsep says:

"Judging from subsequent events, it would seem to have been regarded by the contracting party as a mere stepping stone to absolute authority in internal affairs, a necessary expedient at the moment for breaking a formidable faction backed by a still more formidable soldiery."

He adds further on:

"Indeed, from the time that Appa Saheb felt himself secure in the full possession of the honours and authority of the Raj, he ceased to regard British alliance as a necessary prop to his rule and began to be sensible of the humiliation of appearing to the Maratha nation as the first of the Bhonsla dynasty who had made a voluntary sacrifice of political independence."

It is, therefore, not surprising that no sooner was he well established in power than he got into secret contact with the other Maratha Powers with the object of uniting with them to shake off the British connection. He particularly exchanged correspondence with Bajirao in the months of April and May 1817, when the latter was himself making preparations in poona for attacking the Residency. They exchanged assurances of mutual support and concerted action when the time came to strike. Their plan was to strike suddenly with overwhelming forces at the Residencies of Poona and Nagpur when the major part of the British force were engaged in a desultory action against the Pindaris and their armies scattered in different parts of Central India. The leaders of the Pindaris could be trusted to engage the British in a never-ending chase in the meanwhile. If the plan succeeded the British would disappear from the Deccan as swiftly as they had appeared there.

But the best-laid schemes of mice and men do often go awry. The first to strike was the Peshwa. On the 5th November a large army of infantry, cavalry and mounted guns, which had gathered on the Paravati Hill, with Baji Rao at its head, swooped down on the Residency at Poona. The Resident, Mr. Elphinstone, and his men managed to retreat across the river Moola, and join the brigade at Kirkee. The Residency and the houses and valuable property with large quantities of records fell into the hands of the Peshwa. He then advanced on the British brigade at Kirkee. The battle was fought fiercely, the heavy guns of the Peshwa opening a steady cannonade, while Bapu Gokhale, the Peshwa's General, made a spirited charge on the left flank of the Resident's forces and succeeded in surrounding a detachment. In the desperate fight that ensued one of the gallant soldiers of the Marathas, Moro Dikshit, who was entrusted with the honour of guarding the *Jari Patka,* the Maratha standard, was killed. Next day the British army was heavily reinforced by the battalions that joined them from the south and from the east. They returned to the charge with added vigour, and were able to recapture Poona. The battle of Kirkee proved a grave defeat to the Peshwa's forces and they had to fly southwards, hotly pursued by General Smith.

It is probable that the attack on Nagpur Residency was meant to synchronise with the Peshwa's attack on Poona. But Appa Saheb was still biding his time. As if to defy the overbearing Resident, who was attempting to strengthen his position by calling for reinforcement from Col. Adam's division south of the Narmada, Appa Saheb chose the 24th November as the date for the ceremonial investiture of *Khilat* and *Jari Pataka,* as described earlier, That he chose to challenge the Resident by this patently defiant gesture at a time when the Peshwa was himself in flight, gave to his act a sharper edge. He answered Jenkins' refusal to attend the Court ceremony by posting his men in an attacking position, and on 26th November at about sunset, his Arab infantry fired upon the Residency pickets.

Thus began the historic Battle of Sitabuldi which, during about twenty hours of fierce fighting, came very near to ousting the British from these parts. Of the two hills of Sitabuldi, connected by a ridge, the northern hill was manned by Captain Sadler and three hundred men under him. On the 27th, the Arab infantry of Appa Saheb, which had kept up an artillery fire all the morning, succeeded in killing Captain Sadler and seriously wounding his Second-in-Command, besides inflicting severe loss in men and equipment. Seeing the confused state to which the British troops on this hill had been reduced, the Raja's infantry rushed up the hill and captured the position including the 6-pounder gun which they now turned upon the other hill, where the rest of the British forces were stationed. It proved immediately successful, killing three of the officers, including the Resident's First Assistant, George Southeby. It appeared that the capture of the second hill would also be effected immediately, after which the Residency could not resist.

But at this moment, reinforcements came to the rescue of the British forces. Captain Fitzgerald led a column of his reserves from the Residency grounds, and in a desperate charge succeeded in reaching the smaller hill, while his cavalry took possession of the guns set up by the Arab infantry. By about the afternoon of the 27th, the Raja's forces were dispersed from the surrounding houses and villages, and the battle of Sitabuldi was lost. British troops poured into Nagpur from every quarter, for they knew that it was of the greatest importance that "the Bhonsla should be crushed as early as possible in order that the other potentates might be deterred from following in the same career". Appa Saheb, seeing that discretion was the better part of valour, sent his vakils to the Resident expressing his sorrow at what had happened, and regretting the attack which be wholly disavowed. He knew that it was more conducive to his interest, with the prospect of making a more successful attempt later, if he now temporised with the British and retained his power over his dominions, rather than be forced to an ineffectual flight like Baji Rao. He, therefore, mounted his horse, and accompanied by his two ministers, Nago Pant and Ramachandra Wagh, rode to the Residency and surrendered himself to Jenkins. Assurances were given to the Resident that the army would be disbanded. The conditions offered by the Resident stated, among other things, that Appa Saheb should reside within the Residency. The resistance shown by some of his troops, especially those led by the Sirdars Mun Bhut and Ganpat Rao, was gradually broken by the superior forces under General Doveton, and the Bhonsla palace was captured and the British flag flew over it. It was the intention of the Resident to leave the Raja shorn of all powers for future resistance. As Prinsep says with engaging frankness;

> "Mr. Jenkins was resolved to assume and act upon the principle of reducing the head of the Bhonsla State to the

condition of a mere pageant, and giving the British Government a control over every branch of internal as well as of external administration, to the extent of imposing a ministry of its own selection."

To make the subordination complete and tangible, the Sitabuldi hills were to be fortified by the British, and the whole country to have practically a military occupation. In addition, the Raja was required to cede in perpetuity territories equal to the full charge of the subsidiary force. The districts demanded were those to the north of the Narmada, besides Surguja. Jashpur, Sohagpur and Sambalpur to the east, all the valley to the south of the river and as far as Chhapara, together with Multai, Betul, Gwaligarh and all the remaining possessions of the Raja in Berar.

These terms were agreed to by Appa Saheb, and he returned to his own palace on 9th January 1818. But it was not to be expected that he would accept meekly conditions so galling and suicidal. The desperate pass to which he had been reduced forced him to concede the terms at the time. But as soon as he entered his own palace once again, on which he saw the hated British flag fly, he began to meditate the means to retrieve his lost fortunes and rehabilitate his independence. He issued secret instructions to the Qiledars of his fortresses in Mandla and Chauragarh not to surrender them to the British if they attempted to occupy them. He ordered the captain of the Chanda fort to recruit forces, especially Arabs. He held secret consultations with his trusted advisers, Nago Pant and Ramachandra Wagh. He also took the precaution of sending his treasure to Chanda and other forts, so that it may not be within easy grasp of the Resident. At the same time he sent messengers to Baji Rao, who had all this while been evading the British pursuit, to come to his aid. On 14th March, one of the messengers sent by Appa Saheb was seized by the Resident's agents but fortunately they could not get hold of the letter which the messenger was carrying to Baji Rao.

The person to whom this appeal for aid was made was, in the meanwhile, advancing to the east, having successfully outmanoeuvred the British who were pursuing him from three directions. At a village called Koregaon, on the last day of the year 1817, a bitter fight ensued between the Peshwa's forces and a detachment under Captain Staunton. The Arab regiment under the Peshwa made a determined attack, killing three of the British officers and wounding two, besides causing a large number of casualties among the men. But in a desperate countercharge the British forced the Peshwa's army to retreat, and move towards south-east. Another fierce clash between the Peshwa and the British pursuers took place on 20th February at Ashti which was noted for the brilliant general-ship and heroic death of Bapu Gokhale, the Peshwa's distinguished general. Bapu was among those patriots who were fired by a passion to restore the Maratha empire to its ancient splendour. 'He was the genius behind all the military plans of the Peshwa.' He was always to be found at the post of the greatest danger. After his death there was none to take his place, so that from now on Baji Rao himself had to direct the operations.

It was at Ashti that the Peshwa received the messengers sent to him by Appa Saheb soliciting his aid. They brought a letter in the handwriting of Appa Saheb, containing a brief despatch reading, "Sumana Meer to Gangana Dobeeya", *i.e.*, "assist me in any way you can". The names contained in the letter were those of two saints well-known in Marathi legend for their timely help to each other in the hour of danger. The Peshwa sent back the Nagpur messengers with a written reply promising all help. He had also received information that at Chanda preparations for war were being made, and that a force under Chandoji Bhonsla had gathered at Bhandara. The fortresses of Mandla and Chauragarh were reported to be put in a condition to stand a siege, and the hill people were up in arms.

Thus encouraged, Baji Rao marched in the direction of Chanda hoping to effect a junction with Appa Saheb's forces. The advance division of the Maratha army reached the banks of the Wardha early in April at a point near Wani where the Wardha joins the Painganga. The British, who had received information that Chanda was to be the rallying point of resistance, had in the meanwhile ordered several detachments in this direction to intercept such a move, and, so, Colonel Scott with the greater part of the Nagpur forces reached Warora almost at the same time that Baji Rao reached Wani. Another British force went through Hinganghat towards the Wardha, and a third advanced up to Pandharkawada.

The battle was fought at a place called Seonee, about 12 miles north of Pandharkawada. It was a desperate engagement. Baji Rao was surrounded by the forces of the British marching towards him from three directions. At no time was the loss of the leadership and courage of Bapu Gokhale felt so bitterly as on this occasion. Against the heavy firing from horse-artillery from all directions, the Peshwa's army could not make a determined stand, They, therefore, adopted the only course open to them, namely, to break up into small groups and escape through the surrounding jungles.

The British army then advanced on Chanda where Bhujangrao, Zamindar of Ahiri, and his brother Kondu Bapu, had fortified themselves and had undertaken a large-scale recruitment to their army, especially Arabs and Pindaris. The British troops laid siege to the strong fort of Chanda, which, however, could not hope to hold out for long. The Qiledar of the fort, Ganga Singh, distinguished himself by his valour and put up stout resistance. The British troops were able to effect a breach and enter the fortress. Ganga Singh died a hero's death, fighting to the last, and it is recorded that even the English Captain who captured the fort openly expressed his admiration for the heroism of the Qiledar.

For two months the scattered forces of Baji Rao faught desultorily in different parts of the Bhonsla dominions, some expousing the cause of Appa Saheb, some as mere adventurers and some joining isolated groups of Pindaris. Baji Rao himself, with a small remanent of his army went towards Asirgarh, and later finding himself bereft of men and means, surrendered himself to Sir John Malcolm on 18th June 1818. He had to pass the rest of his life on the banks of the Ganges at a place called Bithur, near Cawnpur, where he, no doubt, filled the young mind of his adopted son, later known as Nana Saheb, with that passionate zeal to drive away the foreign power from his motherland, which was to burst into action in 1857.

The cause of Appa Saheb found another champion in Lanji, further east of Nagpur, where a powerful Zamindar, Chimna Patel, raised the standard of revolt. Chimna Patel had reason to be grateful to Appa Saheb not only because of the long association of his family with the Bhonslas, but because Appa Saheb had always treated him with friendliness and trust. He attacked the Kamavisdar of Lanji, seized his person and killed and captured many of his men. On hearing this, the Resident of Nagpur sent a large force under Captain Gordon who, however, found it not easy to reach the place owing to the difficulty in crossing the Kanhan and Vainganga rivers. Chimna Patel had in the meanwhile fortified himself at Kamtha which commanded a strong defensive position. The two forces met at a village called Navargaon where a fierce engagement was faught. The forces of Chimna patel, finding their position precarious, withdrew inside the fort of Kamtha which was soon surrounded by Captain Gordon. The whole day they held out in the fort against heavy bombardment by the British forces. Ultimately the gate of the fort was forced open with the aid of elephants and Kamtha was captured at a considerable cost. The British forces followed up this success with the capture of the remaining fortresses in this region, especially Ambagad and Warad. The revolt was suppressed and Chimna Patel was confined a prisoner in his own fort of Kamtha.

To return to Nagpur where events had rapidly moved to a climax. The British Resident had watched with growing uneasiness the frequent messages that were passing between Appa Saheb and the Peshwa. Intercepted papers seemed to indicate a deep plan between them to join their forces in another effort to attack the British forces. It was rumoured that the Raja was about to fly to Chanda to join Baji Rao. Jenkins, therefore, decided to act immediately without waiting for instructions from the Governor-General. On the 15th March, he sent a picket party of soldiers under Captain Browne to the Bhonsla palace where they broke into the apartments of Appa Saheb and arrested him along with his two ministers Nago Pant and Ramachandra Wagh. The whole thing was done so suddenly, that no resistance was possible. The prisoners were brought to the Residency and placed in close confinement under separate guards. To lend a Colour of justification for this high-handed act Appa Saheb was now accused, for the first time, of the murder of Parsoji.

Nothing further was, however, done at the moment because the British were then preoccupied with stopping the advance of the Peshwa. After the battle of Seonee had succeeded in scattering Baji Rao's forces, Jenkins turned his attention to Appa Saheb. Meanwhile the Governor-General also had informed the resident that Appa Saheb should be escorted in safe custody to Allahabad where an old palace of the Mughals had been selected as a place suitable for his confinement. On the 3rd May 1818, Appa Saheb with his two ministers was marched off from Nagpur, under a strong escort led by the same Captain Browne, who had violated the privacy of the Raja and arrested him in his own apartments.

The road that lay in front of them was the historic Nagpur-Jabalpur road, which through centuries had been a vital highway across the Bhonsla territory connecting the south with the north. On 3rd May 1818, the compact and colourful troop escorting the prisoners and consisting of four companies of sepoys and a squadron of horse marched northwards along this road. The route lay through mountainous and thickly wooded country largely occupied by Gonds, with the hordes of Pindaris ensconced safely in their hilly fastnesses. Captain Browne and his men were anxious to cover the ground as quickly as possible, halting only when darkness or sickness forced them to do so. In fact when Appa Saheb desired to stop for a day at Ramtek so that he might worship at the historic temple built there by his ancestors, Captain Browne would not hear of it.

Meanwhile, it would seem that the senior Rani of Appa Saheb, Umabai, had secretly despatched a trusted man named Ganga Singh with a few others, who had been tested for their unquestionable loyalty, and furnished them with adequate money to effect the deliverance of her husband. While Captain Browne and the escort halted for the night at Puzdar on the 5th May, a small party of sixteen Hindustani soldiers joined them. At first Captain Browne was suspicious and when, on being questioned, they could not give him a satisfactory account of themselves, he ordered them to be disarmed. But later the leader of the batch produced a note, apparently signed by Captain Dunsmure, establishing the *bona fides* of these men. Thereupon their arms were restored to them, and they followed the escort on their onward journey.

On 12th May, Captain Browne and his men reached Rachur, a place about 30 miles from Jabalpur, and they decided to camp there for the night. The tent where Appa Saheb was lodged was strongly guarded by batches of six sentries, each doing duty in shifts throughout the night. It would appear that the platoon that joined the escort *en route* at Puzdar managed to take on guard-duty in the night, and had their plans ready for the rescue of Appa Saheb. This guard was due to be relieved at 3 a.m. on the night of the 12/13th May. A little before that hour one of them went into the tent, made Appa Saheb put on a sepoy's uniform, shuffled up the bed-clothes to resemble the form of a sleeping person, and then walked back to his tent and thence into the night. Appa Saheb dressed in the sepoy's uniform, joined the other sentries, mounted guard for the few minutes that still remained before the next sentries relieved them at 3 a.m. Thereafter it was easy enough for him to walk away quite unsuspected with his rescuers in the darkness. The wild countryside and the night rendered their escape safe.

The flight was undetected till daybreak. A non-commissioned officer of the guard that assumed duty at 3 a.m., perhaps anxious to win his commission by his zeal, peeped into the tent to make sure that the prisoner was there. He saw in the dim light the rounded form on the mattress and was satisfied. It was only in the morning when the escort struck tent and made ready to resume the march that the escape of Appa Saheb was detected. A hue and cry was raised immediately. A muster of all men was ordered at once, which revealed that the six men who had mounted guard at the tent before his escape, were also missing. Their names were Ramdin Singh, Umed Singh Chhatri, Andan Singh Chhatri, Sital Misra, Bentar Singh and Nida Upadhyay—all members of the party of Hindustani sepoys who joined the escort at Puzdar.

Confusion and alarm possessed the escort camp. Search parties were sent in all directions. Wild reports reached the camp, many of them mutually contradictory, regarding the movements of the fugitives. Some said that they had been sighted at Pathalghuttee, about 12 *kos* north of Dhuma. Others said that they had seen them going in the direction of Hurrai. Captain Browne sent a party of horse to Lanji, two squadrons under Major Cumming who commanded the 7th Cavalry Regiment were despatched towards Hurrai. But pursuit proved of no avail. The impregnable forests and friendly chieftains in the neighbourhood effectively concealed the flight of Appa Saheb. The common people in the villages in whose minds the person of the former King was clothed with the sanctity of royalty, welcomed him to their abodes. The result was that after a few days of futile search Captain Browne had to report to Nagpur that all his search parties had come back without any success. Captain C. Browne himself, who had to bear the main responsibility for the escape of Appa Saheb was court-martialled on a charge of negligence of duty. It would, however, appear that no convincing evidence of his neglect was available, and he was, therefore, acquitted and posted back to his regiment.*

It would be interesting to speculate what sort of man was Appa Saheb, who at a comparatively young age assumed the leadership of resistance to the British power in this territory. At the time that he was deposed and arrested, Appa Saheb could not have been more than 21 or 22 years of age. For his age he undoubtedly appears to have been a man of extraordinary shrewdness and political insight. Impetuous he obviously was, and also inordinately ambitious. Even during the time of his uncle, Raghuji II, he had proved himself a leader of ability. In

* The trial by court martial of Capt. Browne took place at Hoshangabad on 25th July. The Judgment said:

"The court having maturely weighed and considered the whole of the evidence for and against the prisoner, together with what he has urged in his defence, and the summing up of the Deputy Judge Advocate, are of the opinion that Capt. Browne is not guilty of the charge alleged against him, and they do fully and honourably acquit him of the whole and every part thereof."

fact the initial antipathy which Raghuji II exhibited towards him was due to his awareness that Appa Saheb was bound to cost his own imbecile son, Parsoji, from the throne sooner or later. And yet, in his dying moments, Raghuji II had wisely summoned Appa Saheb to his bedside and entrusted to him the care of Parsoji. It is, therefore, no wonder that his escape from the escort of Captain Browne was the beginning of a desperate attempt to organise a large-scale resistance against the British. The story of Appa Saheb from this moment onwards is a story of undaunted and persistent endeavour to gather a striking force, win friendly support and to build up a sufficiently strong opposition against the British with the aid of kings and chieftains from all over the country, from the Gond chieftains of Pachmarhi up to Ranjit Singh of Lahore.

THE WANDERINGS OF APPA SAHEB

After Appa Saheb and his companions had made good their escape, they appear to have proceeded towards the Mahadeo Hills in the Satpuras where Thakur Mohan Singh of Pachmarhi, Chain Shah, Raja of Hurrai and several Gond chieftains could be depended upon to support him. With the help of these leaders Appa Saheb planned to organise a strong enough force before he openly attacked the British. It is a tribute to the loyalty and honour of these chieftains and zamindars that the tabulous prize of two lakhs of rupees and a jagir worth Rs. 10,000 a year which the British authorities had offered as a reward for the apprehension of Appa Saheb, did not tempt anyone of them to betray him. Not, for that matter, were even the common villagers of Betual, Mandla, and Hoshangabad where Appa Saheb freely wandered, tempted by such a rich award to play false to him. On the contrary, thousands of men in every part of this area eagerly offered themselves for recruitment into Appa Saheb's forces, and within a short time after his escape it was estimated that he had under him an army of about 20,000 men. They consisted mainly of Gonds, Arabs and Sikhs, and included some disbanded soldiers of Baji Rao and a large number of Pindaries.

An indication of the gathering strength of Appa Saheb is seen in a letter of the Jabalpur Commandant addressed to Jenkins. Resident at Nagpur, dated 24th July 1818. He says:

"By daily reports from Seoni, Chhapara and Addagaon, it would appear that the Gonds and followers of Appa Saheb are daily gaining strength and committing excessive depredations in all the districts south of Deogarh hills. They write to me from Chhindwara and Chaurai that all the village there are desolate and some in Seoni have also suffered. If this mischief increases, I must take some of the troops from this town and try if we cannot drive them back into their mountains."

So widespread appeared to be the support that the cause was receiving, that Capt, Adams who commanded the subsidiary force says in one of his letters to Jenkins:

"I certainly am of the opinion that our attention should be principally directed to the confinement, if possible, of Appa Saheb to his present circumscribed situation and to the prevention of considerable bodies from effecting a junction, an object which, it appears to me can only be properly effected by having strong detachments in healthy and commanding positions."

Yet, in spite of all these efforts the number of those who came to the support of Appa Saheb increased from day to day. We are told that one of the influential Gonds, a Jagirdar of Sagar, was in correspondence with him. On 31st August 1818, J.H. Maddock, Assistant to the Governor-General, writing to Brigadier-General Watson, commanding a Division in Sagar, says:

"I have already been given to understand that one of the gond chiefs who is a Jagirdar of Sagar has been in treasonable communication with Appa Saheb. It seems more likely that the arrival of an emissary of his to sound the minds of the late Government of Sagar and of other Jagirdars has given rise to the conversations which were overheard by the two persons whose depositions were taken down, so that any night an attack for the object of plunder has been meditated on the town of Sagar."

About a month later, in September 1818, we have again a reference which indicates the support which the cause was gaining. In a letter from C.A. Mallony, Commissioner of Narmada, it is states:

> "Raja Keerut Singh has been in intrigue with Appa Saheb. He lives at Patna and Bullaha. I have summoned him. If he attends, I shall be able to prevent him continuing his aid to Appa Saheb, but if he refuses to attend, I shall take measures against him."

One of the earliest successes which Appa Saheb's army had was near Betul where a large body of his men, estimated to number about 15,000 had gathered. Captain Sparke, who was at Betul, heard of this concentration and, with a strong force of about 3,000 soldiers, fell upon them on 20th July. In the skirmish Captain Sparke and all his men were killed and only a few servants of the Captain returned to Betul to tell the story. The army of Appa Saheb took possession of Melghat, Bhainsdehi, Satner and Amla. Meanwhile, a strong regiment of the British marched on Multai which had, by that time, been evacuated by Appa Saheb. Chagrined at the failure to capture him, the British arrested three leading zamindars of Multai who had been known to have helped Appa Saheb, summarily tried them by court-martial, and hanged them.

By the end of the year, however, it became clear that a strong resistance against the British was not possible if Appa Saheb kept himself confined to the Mahadeo Hills region. In fact, detachments of the British army marching from different directions had practically surrounded this area. It was, therefore, decided that he should leave the Mahadeo Hills. But it was no easy matter to penetrate the ring of the British army especially because of the heavy prize that had been proclaimed on Appa Saheb's head. However, accompanied by Chittu Pindari and a troop of 500 men, Appa Saheb left Mahadeo Hills on 1st February 1819. Captain Jones was at Borda when he received this news, but in order to put him off by a wrong scent, it was given out that Appa Saheb was proceeding by way of Shahpur. Thus while Captain Jones and his regiment hastened in the direction of Shahpur to cut him off, Appa Saheb was safely on his way towards Sawligarh. Captain Jones soon realised his discomfiture, and having learned the correct

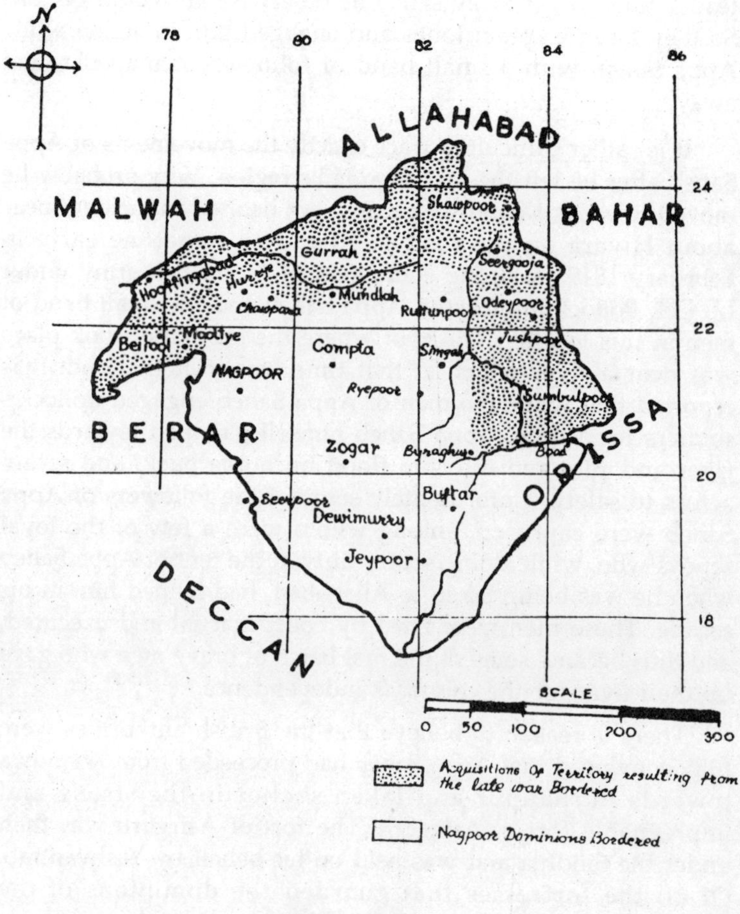

MAP OF

BHOSLA KINGDOM

(1818)

whereabouts of the fugitives, he quickly turned round, and by forced marches came up against the troop that was accompanying Appa Saheb. Seeing the superior strength against them, the men realised that it was important to allow their leader time to get away safely as otherwise all would be lost. So they faced Captain Jones and engaged him in action while Appa Saheb with a small band of followers managed to get away.

It is rather difficult to trace exactly the movements of Appa Saheb after he left the Mahadeo Hills region. Very probably he moved towards Khandwa, because we hear of an incident near about Hivara on the road to Khandwa sometime early in February 1819. A strong contingent of the British army under Lt.-Col. Pollock intercepted Appa Saheb and his small band of men in this locality. The spot where the encounter took place was near a river which at that time was in high flood. It is reported that while the men of Appa Saheb engaged Pollock's soldiers for a time, Appa Saheb himself galloped towards the river and plunged into the flood on horse back, and swam across to safety. Unfortunately some of the followers of Appa Saheb were captured, among whom were a few of the loyal sepoys who, while doing sentry duty at the tent of Appa Saheb when he was being taken to Allahabad, had helped him in his escape. These men were tried by court martial and executed, and thus became some of the first batch of brave men who gave up their lives for the country's independence.

There is reason to believe that the British authorities were fully convinced that Appa Saheb had proceeded from Khandwa towards Burhanpur and taken shelter in the strong and impregnable fort of Asirgarh. The fort of Asirgarh was then under the Sindhia and was held on his behalf by Yashvantrao. Of all the fortresses that guarded the dominions of the Mughals, the fort of Asirgarh was perhaps the most impregnable. Malleson describes it as:

> "a very famous fort lying 290 miles north-east of Bombay. It is built on an isolated hill, detached from the Satpura range dividing the valley of the Tapti from that of the Nerbudda. It has a history which has sent its name through the length and breadth of India. Alike in the times of the

Hindu, of the Mohammedan, and of the British overlordship, it has been considered a place worth fighting for."

A large contingent of the British army, surrounded the fort and demanded its surrender. This they did in spite of the fact that Sindhia was at that time on friendly terms with the British authorities. It would appear that they were trying to find an excuse for capturing this important fortress, since it would give them a commanding position over the Deccan. The British army kept up the siege from the 16th of February till the 9th April 1819. During this time, the Qiledar of the fort, Yeshvantrao, had sent an emissary to them saying that Appa Saheb was not in the fort. When ultimately the fort was surrendered to the British, they realised that the person they were after was not there.

What had actually happened was that on 15th February 1819, Appa Saheb had gone from Dhulkot to Burhanpur where he secretly stayed in a private house. It was dangerous for him to move about in this area since the British army, in full strength, were stationed all round Asirgarh fort. Therefore, Appa Saheb left Burhanpur for Hundia in the disguise of a gosain. Crossing the river Narmada, he then entered the territory of Bhopal. It appears he tried to induce the Nawab to join him, but in this he was not successful. It was, however, generous of the Nawab not to have apprehended him and handed him over to the British authorities. His movement from here onwards appear to be confusing, but it seems clear that he approached the rulers Sindhia, Holkar and Jaipur for their support. There is also evidence that he was in communication with the Raja of Rewa. For a few days he took shelter with the Raja of Mundi. We learn from a letter from Calcutta to the Resident as Nagpur, which is dated 9th July 1824, that Appa Saheb was then in Lahore. The powerful ruler of Lahore at that time, Ranjit Singh, gave him shelter for a few days while he was attempting to gain strength among the rulers in that part of the country. The letter from Calcutta mentioned above also says that he was being financed from Nagpur and was carrying on recruitment in the Lahore territory.

It would appear that the efforts of Appa Saheb to form a confederated force to oppose the British did not prove successful. He ultimately proceeded to Jodhpur where he seems to have decided to live in seclusion. The Maharajah of Jodhpur received him with kindness, and strongly resisted the British inducements to hand the prisoner over to them. Appa Saheb took up his residence at Manmandir and seems to have devoted himself to religious studies. The popular esteem and respect which even then he enjoyed is evidenced by numerous writings of the period. One poem which was very popular at the time gives us an idea of the warm welcome which the Jodhpur Maharajah gave to this intrepid leader, who during all these years of trials and misfortune. Undaunted by failures, passionately cherished the hope of regaining the independent Kingdom.

But the exile was not destined to fulfil his patriotic mission. On 15th July 1840, while still living under the hospitality of Jodhpur, Appa Saheb died there at the young age of 44 years.

NAGPUR UNDER TUTELAGE

The affairs in Nagpur following the deposition of Appa Saheb revealed the growing ascendency of British influence in all spheres of administration. An infant prince, the grandson of Raghuji II, was placed on the throne to give to this policy of encroachment an appearance of justice and propriety. The Governor-General's Secretary wrote to the Resident on 18th June 1818, saying:

> "You are apprised that the Governor-General contemplated elevating to the *masnad* of Nagpur the infant son of Nana Gujar by a daughter of the late Raja Raghoji Bhonsle. You will, therefore, proclaim the young prince Raja of Nagpur, and invite Baka Bai to exercise the office of guardian of the young Raja as a Regent of the State."

The prince was at that time about ten years of age. Baka Bai was the senior widow of the late Raghoji II and had been, in the time of Appa Saheb, strongly opposed to him. All those who had been on the side of Appa Saheb in the palace were eliminated, and Gujaba Dada whom he had forced to retire to Banaras, was called back and appointed to the office of Diwan.

But the Resident was convinced that all real power should be exercised by the British. Every department in the capital as well as in the interior was placed under the direct control of British officers. "It is now imperative", says Jenkins "that we should no longer rest on the merits of any native minister for the preservation of the State: and that the establishment of the new government on the principle of combining our own interests and reputation with the welfare of the minor prince and his subjects, could only be effected by taking into our hands for a time at least, the direct administration of affairs" (Jenkins's *Supplementary Report,* p. 30). Since, in the opinion of the British the so-called "welfare of the minor prince" was indistinguishable from the interest and reputation of the British themselves, there was no difficulty in setting up an administration for the single purpose of entrenching the British rule and preventing the possibility of another anti-British movement rising in the State. British officers were posted in charge of every department, including even the mint and the treasury. The army was placed exclusively under the British Government, the Raja being permitted to keep only a small retinue as an ornament "for the maintenance of his personal respectability."

At the time these changes were introduced they were represented as merely temporary arrangements. But it was obvious that positions of power once conferred cannot be easily withdrawn, especially when self-interest was better served by their retention. Thus, writing in 1825, Prinsep confesses that: "the difficulty of withdrawing has led to a continuance (of British administration) even to the present time. In fact, the entire administration has been, and is still conducted by the Resident and persons of his selection." (Prinsep's *Transactions,* Vol. II p. 391).

The history of colonial expansion all the world over is full of instances in which the imperial power first captures positions of advantage, and then justifies its continuance on altruistic grounds. It is sometimes facetiously remarked that the British won their Empire in India in a fit of absent-mindedness. The fact, however, is that at the crucial moments of history, the British Empire-builders in India were anything but absent-minded. The Report submitted by the Resident, Mr. Jenkins, soon after the deposition of Appa Saheb, reveals a studied and carefully worked-out plan to bring the territories of Nagpur under British control. A gloomy picture is presented of the State as it stood under the deposed king, and the imperative need to impose British officers and other selected by the Resident is urged as the only way to establish peace and prosperity in the territories. It was considered expedient to introduce a new system of revenue assessment and collection, a British-controlled civil administration and a complete control of the army. Having thus occupied all key positions, the next step is to justify the continuance of this control. The public benevolence that is supposed to flow from this arrangement is the strongest reason why the control should not be withdrawn. In fact, it is argued that the people themselves would be averse to a return to the former state of affairs. And so, in the interest and for the lasting blessing of India's teeming millions, the British reluctantly have to remain, much against their wishes! Such is the logic of imperial rule. As Henry Prinsep puts it, with truly evangelical zeal:

> "A population that has once been accustomed to an administration conducted on principle by British officers of integrity. Acting for the public good, will never yield a ready obedience to the rapacious agents of a native despot; and it is the height of tyranny to deliver them over, bound hand and foot, to become the victims of any vicious system that chance or caprice may substitute for that to which they have been accustomed." (Prinsep's *Transactions,* Vol. II, p. 393).

That was how the "White Man's Burden" accumulated: the idea of the foreign ruler as a saviour and redeemer, who found himself called upon to assume the burden of ruling over a nation so that they may be saved from the tyranny of their own independence! This process continued through several decades, deceiving none but the credulous, until the burden refused any longer to be borne upon the White Man's shoulders.

But that was much later. Meanwhile it would be interesting to examine the kind of administration which was introduced in the Nagpur territories, and which was supposed to possess excellent virtues. The basis of the administration was the treaty which the Resident had prepared for the acceptance of the Raja after it was approved by the Governor-General. Under this treaty all the powers of the Raja, both in internal and external affairs, were taken over by the British, who would nominally exercise them in the Raja's name in that part of his territory reserved for him. It was clearly provided that the Raja "shall pay at all times the utmost attention to the advice of the British Government on all subjects connected with His Highness's interests, the happiness of the people and the mutual welfare of both states, and shall conduct the affairs of his government by the hands of ministers and other officers in the confidence of the British Government". The army was to be always under the direct control of the British officers. The treaty also provided for the eventual resumption of the management of the country in the event of bad government on the Raja's part. It was on terms such as these that the Resident proposed the transfer of the administration to the Raja after the expiry of his minority. But the transfer would be only of such portion of the territory as they considered within the ability of the Raja to govern. The rest would continue to be governed by the British, in the manner in which the whole territory was administered by them during the minority.

For the purpose of management, the Resident divided the territory into three divisions, Deogarh, Chanda and Chhattisgarh, and appointed, in each of them, a British officer with the designation of Collector, which was subsequently changed to Superintendent. Later on, Deogarh above the ghats was formed into a separate jurisdiction under a Superintendent, and Deogarh below the ghats was further divided into two divisions, namely, Nagpur and Wainganga districts.

The collection of revenue was to be made by petty Indian officers appointed by the Superintendents, on a fixed salary. Fresh assessments were made in terms of money, and the existing cultivators were allowed to plough their lands on payment of the newly-assessed revenue. It will be pointed out later how the village administration introduced by the British had the effect of uprooting the ancient village institutions and destroying the village economy. For the present it is enough to say that the cumulative effect of all the changes that were introduced by the British was to impoverish the people, and create disaffection in their minds. This is borne out by the views of some of the outstanding Englishmen who administered these areas, and had intimate knowledge of the people and their minds. Sir John Malcolm who held high office in Central India and U.P., and to whom the Peshwa had surrendered in 1818, says:

> "The change to a colder system of policy, and the introduction of our laws and regulations into countries immediately dependent upon us, naturally excite agitation and alarm. Disgust and discontent succeed to terror and admiration: and the princes, the chiefs and all who had enjoyed rank or influence, see nothing but a system dooming them to immediate decline and ultimate annihilation." (Sir John Malcolm: *A Memoir of Central India*, Vol. II).

The effect of the large-scale incursion of British influence and British personnel in all positions of control in the administration, was to create among the people, particularly among those who had formerly wielded power in these territories, a sense of sullen frustration which demoralised them. The superior conquerors displaced the local people all along the line and consigned them to the meanest jobs. The famous Minute that Sir Thomas Munro sent to Lord Hastings in 1817, though immediately based on his experience in Madras State, applies with equal force to the condition of the people in all parts of the country where British men displaced local dignitaries. "Foreign conquerors have treated the natives with violence, and often with great cruelty but none has treated them with so much scorn as we; none has stigmatised the whole people as unworthy of trust, as incapable of honesty, and as fit to be employed only where we cannot do without them. It seems to be not only ungenerous but impolitic to debase the character of a people fallen under out dominion." Sir Thomas Munro was one of those rare British administrators who came to this country with a broad and liberal background, and succeeded in not losing it amidst the selfishness and greed that were rank in the British community in India. He could therefore, frankly confess that "there is perhaps no example of any conquest in which the natives have been so completely excluded from all share of the government of their country as in British India." (Thompson and Garrett, p. 658).

Wherever British influence spread and settled, it ate into the fabric of public life, and stifled the human spirit. Among the foreign personnel who manned all the important posts in the country, there were many who were mere adventurers, whose only interest was to amass a private fortune, heedless of the people's welfare as well as of the professed policy of the British Government. What is said of the neighbouring State of Hyderabad under the British, was equally true of the Nagpur Territory when the British began ruling it. "Nothing seemed to flourish there except corruption ... the wretched people were dragooned into submission, and the required payment extorted from them, at the bayonet's point or the sabre's edge." (Kaye's *Life of Metcalfe,* Vol. II).

In soil such as this, the seeds of revolt readily germinate. Not unlike this was the general state of the Bhonsla Territory during the years that the minor king served as a figure-head and excuse for the spread and consolidation of foreign power in all parts of it. When in 1830 Raghoji III attained his majority, the situation had become almost irretrievable, and the Resident's administration had been too deeply entrenched for any change to be introduced, granting that the young king had the will and the ability to do it—which was by no means the case. Of this we shall see more later.

SAGAR-NARMADA TERRITORIES

One of the obvious historical facts which most of the English historians could not, or would not take notice of, is that India, prior to the arrival of the British, was in a flourishing and prosperous condition. It is customary ror books on Indian history. Written mostly by foreigners, to describe the condition that existed in India when the English merchants arrived, as one of confusion distress and poverty, from which, it is made to appear, the benevolence of English interference redeemed them. Among the few contemporary writers who did see the facts more clearly and record them fearlessly, is Major Evans

Bell, who was for some time Assistant Agent to the Governor-General in Nagpur Territory after the British had taken possession of it. In his "Memoirs of General Briggs", he refers to the false and fantastic notions which were prevalent concerning the condition of the country under its native princes. The English rulers of India conceive of that condition as one of such extreme misery and oppression that any change could hardly fail to be a change for the better, while a change which substituted British rule for what they summarily describe as oriental despotisms must be equivalent to a translation from darkness to light. "This condition of wretchedness is never demonstrated. It is assumed to be like a mathematical axtom which requires only to be stated in order to command acquiescence. And yet even upon the surface of things, there is much which would seem to render this assertion, so confidently and constantly made, a highly questionable one. It was not the wretchedness and poverty of India which first attracted European adventurers thither. It was on the contrary, as they themselves describe, its wealth, the magnificence of its princes, the high level of civilisation and prosperity to which its people had attained. And even in these days it is impossible for the least observant traveller to journey through India without meeting in all parts of the country the indications of a grandeur and an opulence that have only recently decayed. The most convincing proof of the general order and security prevailing in India under the native princes is to be seen in the irrigation tanks, the mango groves, the wells, caravanserais, mosques and temples—now too often in ruins—which meet the eye so frequently in almost every province. These—and they must formerly have been more numerous—were nearly all the creation of private liberality. They demonstrate also the wealth and public spirit of the people, and are not less important in passing judgement upon the safety with which the evidence of wealth could be openly displayed.

"In 1829, Colonel Sleeman caused an estimate to be made of the public works of ornament and utility which in a single district of Jabalpur—now included in the Central Provinces—were due to the munificence of private persons anterior to the British rule. 'The population of the district amounted to about half a million, and there were, in various parts of town and country, created by individuals for the public good, and with no view to personal return or profits, 2,286 tanks, 209 large wells with flights of steps extending from the top down to the water in its lowest stages, 1,560 wells lined with masonry but without stairs, 369 Hindu temples and 92 mosques. The estimated cost of these works amounted to £ 866,640. In addition to these, two-thirds of the towns and villages were embedded in groves of mango and tamarind trees mixed with the banyan and peepal, all planted at the cost of private citizens at an estimated cost of £ 12,000.'

"Extracts of a similar purport might be multiplied indefinitely, and show beyond all possibility of dispute that India under the native princes was possessed of wealth and abundance of goods, that her upper classes were remarkable for their liberality and public spirit, and that the industrial and lower classes were in a thriving condition. What is the explanation of all this—so contrary to the common legend, officially propagated, of disorder and misery from which we were divinely commissioned to rescue the wretched Hindu? It would be absurd to ascribe the prosperity of India to the character of her kings and princes, reigning at Delhi or elsewhere. Great kings, it is true, are to be found among them, but extremely bad ones in far greater numbers. But, after all —

"Of all the ills that human hearts endure,
How small the part that kings can cause or cure.'

"It is not in the character of the kings and princes of India, but in that of the constitutional order at the head of which they were placed, that we must look for the explanation." The events that occurred in the Sagar-Narmada territories, after the British took possession of, is a fair illustration of this fact.

The districts of Sagar and Damoh had been bequeathed by Raja Chhatrasal of Bundelkhand to the Peshwa, and after the deposition of the Peshwa by Lord Hastings, these districts were ceded to the British in 1817 under the Treaty of Poona. But it was not till March 1818 that this part of the country was actually occupied by the British, and even then only after they had overcome the resistance offered by Vinayak Rao who administered the Sagar kingdom on behalf of the widow of its occupant under the Peshwa. General Marshall took possession of Sagar and its dependencies, and proceeded to occupy the districts ceded by Appa Saheb after his defeat in the Battle of Sitabaldi. These were the districts of Mandla, Betul, Seoni and the Narmada valley. Resistance was offered by the Qiledar of Mandla who had received private orders of Appa Saheb not to deliver up the place. But General Marshall, reinforced by forces from Jabalpur, besieged the fortress and battered the walls, so that the next morning the fort surrendered.

These territories, partly obtained from the Peshwa and partly from the Nagpur kingdom, were formed into what was called the Sagar-Narmada Territory in 1820, and placed under an Agent to the Governor-General. The country was interspersed by hills and valleys, largely covered by jungles, except in the uplands of Sagar and in the valleys of Narsimhapur, Hoshangabad and Jabalpur. The tract possessed natural fertility and great productive capabilities which, under proper management, could be made to yield rich results. But under British administration the result, perhaps inevitably, was to impoverish the land and create a large and influential class of dispossessed persons who bore a grudge against the foreign rulers and would, therefore, willingly lend their ears to any scheme calculated to subvert authority.

It would be useful to examine briefly the consequences that generally flowed from the establishment of British control over Indian territories. The conquest of our country by the British differed from that by the previous invaders in one vital feature. The military adventurer and warlord, whether from Afghanistan or Persia, invaded the country, established his supremacy in certain parts of it, brought with him his court and culture, but he refrained from any attempt to upset or modify the immemorial institutions in the country which he governed the social and economic life of the people. The structure and constitution of society remained, by and large, unaffected by the dynastic changes that took place in the country. Like the supple trees in their vast jungles, the people bowed before the raging storm and Jet it pass, and still remained unbroken.

Not so the conquest by the British. In province after province the same story of complete disruption of economy and social structure followed in the wake of their occupation. "A number of English officers, charged to overflowing with self-complacent philanthropy and natural confidence, are let loose upon the devoted region. They set to work under the impression, excited and slightly justified by recent revolution or war, that the material to be operated on is a population quite without social or political form, and void of anything like order, and upon which, consequently, they can impress any shape that is most pleasing to themselves. They are the potter and the people are to be as clay in their hands." (Major Bell: *"Memoirs of General Briggs."*)

One of the first casualties in this process is the old village economy, and its revenue, and its revenue. From ancient times the economy was based on the produce of the land. For all purposes of Government record, every village was embodied in its harvest for the year. This was the chief source of revenue. Government's share was calculated on a ratio of this harvest, and was collected in kind, not in cash. The grain was the medium of exchange in the village, the currency with which payments were made to the village priest, or *chamar or lohar*. The system of village self-government gave to the whole social structure a firms foundation based on mutual obligation and trust. As long as the State got its share of the produce from the village, it was content to leave the allocation of each villager's share to the Village Panchayat themselves. One of the consequences of this system was that the people rarely fell into arrears of revenue, and the State was saved from all the protracted legal processes of collection and the intricacies of land tenures.

But when the foreign power took possession of a province, all this was at once changed. "Our first act in a newly acquired district was to decree that the land revenue should henceforth be paid in coin, without having previously ascertained if there was sufficient coin in circulation to allow of such a sudden and drastic change. ... A pressing demand for specie glutted the markets with an immense quantity of produce which had to be sold for whatever it would bring." *(Ibid.)* One can well imagine the impact of this change on the cultivators. The value of their produce in terms of money at once fell.* It was not possible for them to pay their full revenue and meet their own requirements. They invariably fell into arrears—which formerly was unheard of--and the result was that they were proceeded against in a weary process of civil suit. It became necessary to keep elaborate records of tenures and rights which were made transferable. All these records had to be kept in charge of a servant who invariably became a petty official of the Government. Thus, instead of conferring any right on the cultivator, the British administration had the effect of making the cultivator a helpless victim of a miserably paid village official the keeper of the records, who generally made up for his poor salary by all kinds of corruption and imposture. The revenue assessment in the Sagar-Narmada Territory had been particularly heavy. R.M. Bird, Member of the Sadar Board of Revenue, North-Western Provinces, who toured the Sagar-Narmada Territory in 1834 has recorded that "the nominal demand is too high for the present condition of the territory.... The reduction of the present high nominal *jamma to* an amount which can, on an average of years, be collected is an indispensable preliminary to the introduction of a successful system of administration" ("Note of Sagar-Narmada Territory" by R.M. Bird). It was, therefore, obvious that the owners of land would be forced into distress, and if the course of law were relentlessly pursued, must be dispossessed. Indeed this was what happened to numerous Taluqdars, Thakurs and Zamindars in this area during the first decade and more of British rule.

Along with the uprooting of the economy of the village, the social and political set-up of the village was also destroyed. The Indian village had always formed a kind of petty republic, self-contained and self-governed by the Panchayat and the headman, most of whom, though hereditary, could be set aside

---

* "The ryot was forced to dispose of part of his produce to meet a cash demand and had only one channel through which to sell. He had to think of wealth in terms of money instead of as cattle or grain; money was a medium of which he knew little".

(Thompson and Garrat: *British Rule in India*, p. 428).

NARSINGPUR REGION (1842)

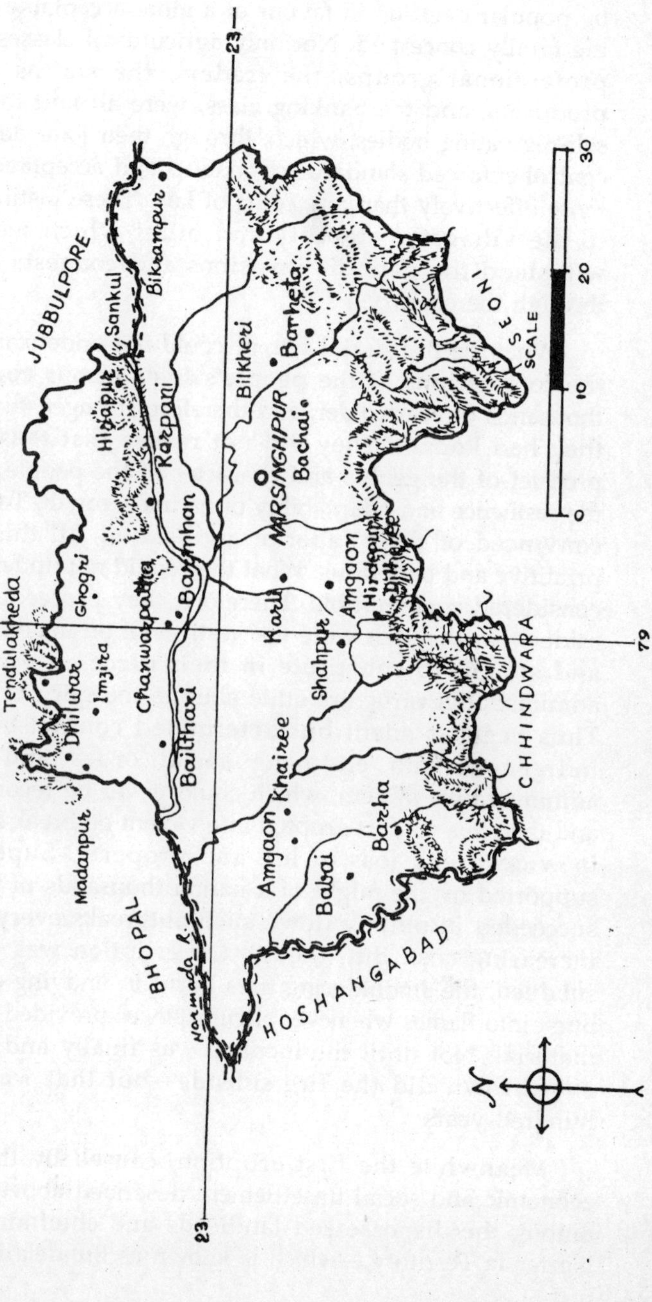

by popular decision in favour of a more acceptable member of the family concerned. Not only agricultural classes, but other professional groups, the traders, the smiths and other producers, and the banking class, were all knit together into self-regulating bodies, which, through their joint decisions and control enforced standards of conduct and acceptance of justice more effectively than any court of law. These institutions gave to the villages a stability and order which were able to withstand the periodic invasions and conqests that swept through the country.

What the British did not, or could not understand was that the foundations of the people's lives in our country were thousands of years older, and therefore stronger, than anything they had known. They did not realise that these were the product of the genius and character of the people, possessing the resilience and adaptability of natural growth. To the British, convinced of their superior civilisation, all this appeared primitive and barbarous. What they could not understand, they considered contemptible. Therefore, they proceeded to sweep aside what they felt were the vestiges of an uncivilised world, and sought to substitute in their place an economy and administrative structure quite alien to the spirit of the people. Thus began a silent but determined conflict between the indigenous and enduring social order and the alien administrative system, which could never be reconciled. Now and then this conflict erupted into violent outbreak and resulted in widespread loss of life and property. Superior force, supported by the might of a nation thousands of miles away, succeeded in putting down such outbreaks every time at an increasing cost. But, though the eruption was, for a time, subdued, the smouldering fires burnt in undying embers, and burst into flames whenever circumstances provided combustible material. Not until the incubus was finally and completely overthrown did the fire subside—but that was to take a hundred years.

Meanwhile the first eruption, caused by the political, economic and social unsettlement described above, took place among the dispossessed landlords and chieftains of Sagar-Narmada Territory,—which is known as Bundela Rising.

BUNDELA RISING, 1842

The owners of land in the Sagar-Narmada Territories belonged mainly to the Gond, Lodhi and Bundela Rajput clans. They were petty Chiefs, Thakurs and Zamindars who had been accustomed to a considerable amount of freedom under the Peshwas, provided they paid the annual revenues assessed on them. The cession of these territories to the British by the Peshwa and the Raja of Nagpur led to a period of military action by the British army before they could occupy them. Resistance was kept up at several important fortresses such as Damoh, Sagar and Mandla. But by 1819, most of the districts had been subjugated, and in 1820, as stated earlier, the Sagar-Narmada Territories were formed and placed under the control of an Agent to the Governor-General. The process of settlement of these districts was accompanied by large-scale dispossession of long-standing malguzars, some of whom were suspected of hostile intent while some others had defaulted in their payments. Against those who had fallen in arrears legal action was taken and, after much harassment, were deprived of their lands and property.

Two influential Bundela Thakurs in the north Sagar, Jawahar Singh Bundela of Chandrapur and Madhukar Shah of Narhut were served with decrees of the Civil Courts of Sagar early in 1842, and were threatened with attachment of property. Their answer to it was to defy the order. Attack the police, some of whom they killed, and rise in open rebellion against the Government. They were joined by a large number of discontented landlords and Gond leaders in the region north of the Narmada. The seething elements of opposition and revolt which had so far remained suppressed were set free by this open resistance which served as a rallying point. The uprising was most successful in Narshimhapur district. Practically every landlord of the Chawarpatha pargana joined the rebels, either openly or covertly. The leader of the revolt in this district was Rajah Dilhan Shah, the Gond Chief of Madanpur. He was joined by several malguzars, and they captured Deori and the entire Chawarpatha tract.

The timing of this revolt was admirably chosen. The British army had only recently suffered from a most disastrous campaign in Afghanistan. "Of the 16,500 men that had started from Kabul a week before, all were destroyed excepting 120 prisoners under Akbar Khan, and only one, Dr. Brydon, reached Jalalabad to narrate the painful story of the tragic retreat." (Muzumdar and Ray Chaudhary: *An Advanced History of India*, p. 757). It was this depleted state of the British army that led the Bundela leaders to believe that the time was opportune for a rising. "They were impressed with a conviction that it was in their power to assert independence, and the exaggerated accounts of our Kabul disasters and the extremely reduced state of the military forces in the Division led them to think that the Government could not coerce them." (Captain Boland's letter to the Agent to the Lieutenant-Governor, Sagar and Narmada Territory, dated 5th January 1843.)

Captain W.H. Boland who was the Principal Assistant at Hoshangabad, in his report to the Agent at Sagar, quotes the statement of one Chunilal of Chawarpatha who was a witness to the capture of the Chawarpatha fort. The insurgents then proceeded to Brahman where they fired on the Naib-Tahsildar who was on the opposite bank of the river. They took possession of this place, and offered presents and prayers to the fort deities, and fed the Brahmins. They appointed one of the local leaders. Trimbak Rao, the Amil of Chawarpatha and Berhman, and then proceeded to Sooathulla where the Bundela Chief, Thakur Ranjit Singh, joined them. From there the insurgents made their way through Jherra Ghat towards Maharajpur which they took.

It was remarkable how the revolt spread like a forest fire enveloping the entire region. This simultaneous outbreak at a number of places spread over a vast area made it impossible for the British, with their much reduced strength, to meet the insurgents with adequate force. The Bundelas in the meanwhile decided to consolidate their position. They posted their men at all the important ghats of the Narmada that gave access to their territory. "Beltharee Ghat was consigned to Chiman's protection, Baria Ghat to Brijbhukan Jamadar, Sagore Ghat to Khet Singh, malguzar of Sooatulla, Kirpani Ghat to Rao Mahukam Singh. The Jheera Ghat was made over to the Sooatulla men. They were to prevent the passage of any servants of Government, and the boats were all swamped." (Captain Boland's letter). They also proceeded to appoint their own patwari, nazir, serishtadar in the captured area, who were all allowed their villages free of rent on condition that they faught faithfully against the British.

For a time the British were unable to understand the real cause of this widespread and successful revolt. Writing in April 1842, the Secretary to the Governor-General says:

> "It is probable, they (the Bundelas) have been excited by the arrest, during the past and preceding year, of a number of their relatives for acts of rebellion committed in Scindia's Territory."

The truth is that the malady was far more deep-seated. The rugged and independent chieftains of this area had never really got reconciled to the British rule. As already pointed out, the land and legal administration which came with the British rule further roused the people. It is significant that this area was precisely the portion of Central Provinces that played a prominent part later during the 1857 movement.

The spirit of revolt spread rapidly. With Narshimhapur and Sagar up in arms, the next to rise was Jabalpur. The Junior Assistant at this town writes in April 1842; "the consternation to be naturally expected as the result of this successful inroad (by the insurgents) is spreading throughout these territories on account of the eruption reaching the ears of the people: and the alarm at Jabalpur has been so great as to render it necessary to postpone the departure to Sagar, until confidence in the public of Jabalpur is restored . . . Instructions have been sent to District Officers at Hoshangabad, Seoni, Betul and Damoh to increase their police, and I propose to superintend the execution of the orders, as far as possible, in person." The leading spirit of the Jabalpur revolt was Raja Hirde Shah of Heerapur who had been in correspondence for some time with the other Thakurs, sounding them about a joint rising against the British. Captain Brown writing to Major Sleeman explains how from the intercepted letters he had come to know that the time fixed for the outbreak was the Dussera festival: "As in former times it was usual for all persons of rank to assemble at this season at the residence of the chief local authority, advantage was taken of the custom to invite the suspected parties to visit me at Jabalpur. Some came, others did not: and amongst the latter was Raja Hirde Shah". (Letter from Captain C. Brown to Major Sleeman dated 20th November 1842).

It was soon after this that the followers of the Raja led by Gajraj Singh attacked the police post of Gujpura. The Jabalpur detachment thereupon advanced towards Hirapur, but were delayed owing to the difficulty in crossing the Narmada. When they ultimately reached Heerapur, they found that the Raja had fallen back on Tejgarh. His intention appeared to be to march towards Chawarpatha so as to effect a junction with the forces under the Thakur of Madanpur. The British officers found it extremely difficult to track down and tackle these insurgent leaders, because they could not get any reliable information about them. Captain Boland, rather ruefully admits "I have been disappointed in my expectation that the malguzars who attended me would cause the surrender of the rebels still in arms against us; and I regret to state that some of them while professing the strongest fidelity to Government were affording supplies and protection to the insurgents." He mentions how one Thakur Mardan Singh who was asked to act as a guide to the British forces in their attack on the rebels at Peeparwani, deliberately misled the police, and secretly sent word to the insurgents to keep out of the way. Another landlord, Sukhlal Tiwari of Pendra, gave shelter and protection to the rebels while on their way from Madanpur to Heerapur, while all the time acting as an adviser to the British. It is obvious that the success of the Bundela insurgents was largely due to the support which they received from the people of the area. "The progress of the insurgents was open. They moved in a mass in broad day light and were unmolested by the large and powerful Taluqdars through whose lands they passed, and in the vicinity of whose towns they encamped... They have plundered little or nothing and must consequently have been supplied by the Rajas." (Captain Boland's letter.) It is because of the people's support that Raja Hirde Shah when attacked by Captain C. Brown was able to make his way across the river, encamp at Budhgaon and Bachia. He then passed through the territory of the Raja of Dilheri to Chaugaon, a place near the fort of Chauragarh.

Observing the movements of Raja Hirde Shah, General Tombs ordered Colonel Watson to Tejgarh. Hirde Shah had, in the meanwhile, doubled back with the intention of getting into Bundelkhand, and on his way a British detachment fell upon him, not far from Tejgarh. Although Raja Hirde Shah escaped, several of his party were captured or killed, and some property was also seized. Hirde Shah made his way to Jaitpur where he effected a junction with the ex-Raja of that place. The successes achieved by the chieftains, both in capturing important forts and villages and in effectively escaping the pursuing British who appeared to be checkmated every time, resulted in the temporary elimination of foreign power from a large part of the trans-Narmada portion of Narsimhapur, Sagar and Jabalpur. The ranks of the insurgents increased. The audacity and quickness of their movements which were reminiscent of the army of Shivaji, rendered the British almost helpless. Hirde Shah and his men successfully evaded Colonel Watson, and went back to Heerapur which they recaptured, driving away the police, who had been left there for its protection, with much loss of life. (File No. 783/1842).

The capture of Tendukhera by the Thakur of Madanpur was even more encouraging. This village in Hoshangabad district occupied a strategic position. It had been used by Captain Wakeman only a few weeks before for camping his detachment. Dilhan Shah, Thakur of Madanpur, who, as we have already seen, had fortified Chawarpatha, now advanced with a large body of men towards this village. The Tahsildar at Narsimhapur was instructed to check this advance and protect the village by meeting them with all the available force. But when the Tahsildar saw the number and strength of the insurgents, he precipitately fled from there, and the force at his command followed his gallant example! Thus Tendukhera was captured without a shot being fired.

Till practically the end of 1842 the desultory fighting between the insurgent chieftains and the British forces was kept up at a number of places. None of these engagements was of a decisive nature, because the Bundelas kept up a guerilla warfare in the mountains and jungles of their country. They could never be effectively wiped out, nor could they be captured. The wild countryside of Bundelkhand and the Narmada valley provided them with excellent places of refuge whenever they were overpowered by superior force.

Partly for this reason, and partly from an awareness of their own depleted position after the disasters of the retreat from Kabul, the British were inclined to come to terms with the insurgents. Captain Boland writing from Hoshangabad to the Agent at Sagar suggests a prudent way of settling the trouble: "As it would be impossible and impolitic to punish so large a body of influential people, I would suggest that the principal Jagirdars, Taluqdars and Gond Rajas be summoned in and promised forgiveness for the past, if they take an active part against the insurgents. Until some such measure be adopted, I anticipate no decided results and an indefinite prolongation of the existing state of disturbance." (Letter, dated 5th January 1843).

Some success had, in the meanwhile, come to the British, though nor wholly by their own valour. On 17th November 1842, they had issued a proclamation calling upon all the chieftains to lay down arms. The Proclamation read:

> "Whereas the Raja Hirde Shah had been foolish enough to follow the example of the insurgents and plunderers, and whereas the said Raja having opposed the Government troops has fled, the Agent to the Lieutenant-Governor is desirous of his apprehension.
>
> "But in order to comfort and assure all land-holders, possessors of estates and property, this proclamation is issued to impress upon all, that the British Government is not desirous of punishing any but the leaders of the insurgents. Therefore, all those who may have been induced to do so through intimidation or ignorance, or inability to resist them are called upon to dismiss their fears, and are invited to wait upon either the District Officer or the Agent and explain their reasons for having joined the insurgents.

The Agent may himself enquire minutely into their cases and guarantee their lives. All persons who may have any plundered property in their possession are requested to bring it to the Agent as the best proof of their innocence. The Agent is bent on the apprehension and punishment of the ring-leaders only."

One of the results of this proclamation was that Colonel Ely who was pursuing the Raja of Heerapur towards Pathan was able to report that "with the help of the Raja of Shahgarh they had been able to capture Raja Hirde Shah of Heerapur and his whole family on the 22nd December 1842". The capture of Hirde Shah and his party was a major set-back for the insurgents. The prisoners were sent to Chunar *via* Damoh under a strong police escort, and were then sent to the Jabalpur jail. Some indication of the anxiety which the British authorities had regarding the influence which Raja Hirde Shah exercised over the minds of the people in these territories, is provided by the fact that while they were conducting him and his family under a strong police guard from Tejgarh to Jabalpur, Major Sleeman, Agent to Governor-General in Bundelkhand, wrote to Captain Brown, informing him that while Hirde Shah and the other persons were being taken through the town of Damoh, the people of the town, who knew him, should be asked to confront him, so that there may be no doubt among the people about the capture of their leaders. It was their hope that, following on the arrest of Hirde Shah and his men, the other leaders of the rebels would surrender, one by one.

Captain Boland had suggested, "should they after this warning still persist in their present course of aiding the rebels, I would strongly suggest a severe example being made of some influential man". Perhaps it was with this motive that when Captain Wakeman captured Madhukar Shah of Narhut, he was publicly executed, and his body burnt behind the Sagar jail. Madhukar Shah, however, became a popular hero, and the subject of folk-songs and folk-lore which are widely current in this area. At the place where his body was cremated a *chabutra* has been raised and the people who live in Gopalganj still look upon this monument with great reverence.

By April 1843 the disturbance was practically suppressed. No doubt, when the Gwalior Durbar commenced their hostilities in this year against the British, some of the chiefs of Sagar-Narmada Territory, who had long historic ties with Sindhia, also broke out in sympathetic rebellion. But this was soon suppressed.

Thus this remarkable attempt to overthrow the British power in the Sagar-Narmada Territory, which at one time appeared almost within reach of a successful conclusion, collapsed after a period of 18 months. The reasons for the failure of this movement are obvious. The different Bundela chieftains who rose up against the British chose to act independently and in isolation. Although it is obvious that these leaders had at least the passive support of the people, and they chose for their attack only the seats of foreign power, like the Government offices and the police thanas, the movement failed to gather any momentum because there was no coordinated plan and an over-all leadership among the insurgents. If, in 1842, the Bundelas had been able to find a leader of dominating influence and genius, such as Raja Chhatrasal, it would have been possible for this movement to have developed into a major offensive, and served as a spear-head for a liberation campaign. But as it turned out, they were acting in separate groups with no pre-arranged design of a campaign, and were opposed by the well equipped and ably-led British army who, when the first shock of surprise was overcome, were able to round them up in isolated groups, and thus suppress the revolt effectively. Yet, in the story of India's attempts to throw off the foreign rule, this episode of resistance by the Bundela chieftains occupies an important place.

CHAPTER 2

Traditional India's Struggle

The Revolt of 1857 was the most dramatic instance of traditional India's struggle against foreign rule. But it was no sudden occurrence. It was the culmination of a century long tradition of fierce popular resistance to British domination.

The establishment of British power in India was a prolonged process of piecemeal conquest and consolidation and the colonisation of the economy and society. This process produced discontent, resentment and resistance at every state.

This popular resistance took three broad forms: civil rebellions tribal uprisings and peasant movements. We will discuss the first two in this chapter.

The series of civil rebellions, which run like a thread through the first 100 years of British rule, were often led by deposed *rajas* and *nawabs* or their descendants, uprooted and impoverished *zamindars, landlords* and *poligars* (landed military magnates in South India), and ex-retainers and officials of the conquered Indian states. The backbone of the rebellions, their mass base and striking power came from the rack-rented peasants, ruined artisans and demobilised soldiers.

These sudden, localised revolts often took place because of local grievances although for short periods they acquired a broad sweep, involving armed bands of a few hundreds to several thousands.

The major cause of all these civil rebellions taken as a whole was the rapid changes the British introduced in the economy, administration and land revenue system. These changes led to the disruption of the agrarian society, causing prolonged and widespread suffering among its constituents. Above all, the colonial policy of intensifying demands for land revenue and extracting as large an amount as possible produced a veritable upheaval in Indian villages. In Bengal, for example, in less than thirty years land revenue collection was raised to nearly double the amount collected under the *Mughals*. The pattern was repeated in other parts of the country as British rule spread. And aggravating the unhappiness of the farmers was the fact that not even a part of the enhanced revenue was spent on the development of agriculture or the welfare of the cultivator.

Thousands of *zamindars* and *poligars* lost control over their land and its revenues either due to the extinction of their rights by the colonial state or by the forced sale of their rights over land because of their inability to meet the exorbitant land revenue demanded. The proud *zamindars* and *poligars* resented this loss even more when they were displaced by rank outsiders—government officials and the new men of money-merchants and moneylenders. Thus they, as also the old chiefs, who had lost their principalities, had personal scores to settle with the new rulers.

Peasants and artisans, as we have seen earlier, had their own reasons to rise up in arms and side with the traditional elite. Increasing demands for land revenue were forcing large numbers of peasants into growing indebtedness or into selling their lands. The new landlords, bereft of any traditional paternalism towards their tenants, pushed up rents to ruinous heights and evicted them in the case of non-payment. The economic decline of the peasantry was reflected in twelve major and numerous minor famines from 1770 to 1857.

The new courts and legal system gave a further fillip to the dispossessors of land and encouraged the rich to oppress the poor. Flogging, torture and jailing of the cultivators for arrears of rent or land revenue or interest on debt were quite common. The ordinary people were also hard hit by the prevalence of corruption at the lower levels of the police, judiciary and general administration. The petty officials enriched themselves freely at the cost of the poor. The police looted oppressed and tortured the common people at will. William Edwards, a British official, wrote in 1859 that the police were 'a scourge to the people' and that their oppression and exactions form one of the chief grounds of dissatisfaction with our government.'

The ruin of Indian handicraft industries, as a result of the imposition of free trade in India and levy of discriminatory tariffs against Indian goods in Britain, pauperised millions of artisans. The misery of the artisans was further compounded by the disappearance of their traditional patrons and buyers, the princes, chieftains, and *zamindars*.

The scholarly and priestly classes were also active in inciting hatred and rebellion against foreign rule. The traditional rulers and ruling elite had financially supported scholars, religious preachers, priests, *pandits and maulvis* and men of arts and literature. With the coming of the British and the ruin of the traditional landed and bureaucratic elite, this patronage came to an end, and all those who had depended on it were impoverished.

Another major cause of the rebellions was the very foreign character of British rule. Like any other people, the Indian people too felt humiliated at being under a foreigner's heel. This feeling of hurt pride inspired efforts to expel the foreigner from their lands.

The civil rebellions began as British rule was established in Bengal and Bihar, and they occurred in area after area as it was incorporated into colonial rule. There was hardly a year without armed opposition or a decade without a major armed rebellion in one part of the country or the other. From 1763 to 1856, there were more than forty major rebellions apart from hundreds of minor ones.

Displaced peasants and demobilised soldiers of Bengal led by religious monks and dispossessed *zamindars* were the first to rise up in the Sanyasi rebellion, made famous by Bankim Chandra Chatterjee in his novel *Anand Math,* that lasted from 1763 to 1800. It was followed by the Chuar uprising which covered five districts of Bengal and Bihar from 1766 to 1772 and then, again, from 1795 to 1816. Other major rebellions in Eastern India were those of Rangpur and Dinajpur, 1783; Bishnupur and Birbhum, 1799; Orissa *zamindars*, 1804-17; and Sambalpur, 1827-40.

In South India the Raja of Vizianagram revolted in 1794, the *poligars* of Tamil Nadu during the 1790's, of Malabar and coastal Andhra during the first decade of the 19th century, of Parlekamedi during 1813-14. Dewan Velu Thampi of Travancore organised a heroic revolt in 1805. The Mysore peasants too revolted in 1830-31. There were major uprisings in Vizagapatam from 1830-34, Ganjam in 1835 and Kurnool in 1846-47.

In Western India, the chiefs of Saurashtra rebelled repeatedly from 1816 to 1832. The Kolis of Gujarat did the same during 1824-28, 1839 and 1849. Maharashtra was in a perpetual state of revolt after the final defeat of the Peshwa. Prominent were the Bhil uprisings, 1818-31; the Kittur uprising, led by Chinnava, 1824; the Satara uprising, 1841; and the revolt of the Gadkaris, 1844.

Northern India was no less turbulent. The present states of Western U.P. and Haryana rose up in arms in 1824. Other major rebellions were those of Bilaspur, 1805; the *taluqdars* of Aligarh, 1814-17; the Bundelas of Jabalpur, 1842; and Khandesh, 1852. The second Punjab War in 1848-49 was also in the nature of a popular revolt by the people and the army.

These almost continuous rebellions were massive in their totality, but were wholly local in their spread and isolated from each other. They were the result of local causes and grievances, and were also localised in their effects. They often bore the same character not because they represented national or common efforts but because they represented common conditions though separated in time and space.

Socially, economically and politically, the semi-feudal leaders of these rebellions were backward looking and traditional in outlook. They still lived in the old world, blissfully unaware and oblivious of the modern world which had knocked down the defences of their society. Their resistance represented no societal alternative. It was centuries-old in form and ideological and cultural content. Its basic objective was to restore earlier forms of rule and social relations. Such backward looking and scattered, sporadic and disunited uprisings were incapable of fending off or overthrowing foreign rule. The British succeeded in pacifying the rebel areas one by one. They also gave concessions to the less fiery rebel chiefs and *zamindars* in the form of reinstatement, the restoration of their estates and reduction in revenue assessments so long as they agreed to live peacefully under alien authority. The more recalcitrant ones were physically wiped out. Velu Thampi was, for example, publicly hanged even after he was dead.

The suppression of the civil rebellions was a major reason why the Revolt of 1857 did not spread to South India and most of Eastern and Western India. The historical significance of these civil uprisings lies in that they established strong and valuable local traditions of resistance to British rule. The Indian people were to draw inspiration from these traditions in the later nationalist struggle for freedom.

The tribal people, spread over a large part of India, organised hundreds of militant outbreaks and insurrections during the 19th century. These uprisings were marked by immense courage and sacrifice on their part and brutal suppression and veritable butchery on the part of the rulers. The tribals had cause to be upset for a variety of reasons. The colonial administration ended their relative isolation and brought them fully within the ambit of colonialism. It recognised the tribal chiefs as *zamindars* and introduced a new system of land revenue and taxation of tribal products. It encouraged the influx of Christian missionaries into the tribal areas. Above all, it introduced a large number of moneylenders, traders and revenue farmers as middlemen among the tribals. These middlemen were the chief instruments for bringing the tribal people within the vortex of the colonial economy and exploitation. The middlemen were outsiders who increasingly took possession of tribal lands and ensnared the tribals in a web of debt. In time, the tribal people increasingly lost their lands and were reduced to the position of agricultural labourers, share-croppers and rack-rented tenants on the land they had earlier brought under cultivation and held on a communal basis.

Colonialism also transformed their relationship with the forest. They had depended on the forest for food, fuel and cattle-feed. They practised shifting cultivation (*jhum, podu,* etc.) taking recourse to fresh forest lands when their existing lands showed signs of exhaustion. The colonial government changed all this. It usurped the forest lands and placed restrictions on access to forest products, forest lands and village common lands. It refused to let cultivation shift to new areas.

Oppression and extortion by policemen and other petty officials further aggravated distress among the tribals. The revenue farmers and government agents also intensified and expanded the system of *begar*—making the tribals perform unpaid labour.

All this differed in intensity from region to region, but the complete disruption of the old agrarian order of the tribal communities provided the common factor for all the tribal uprisings. These uprisings were broad-based, involving thousands of tribals, often the entire population of a region.

The colonial intrusion and the triumvirate of trader, money tender and revenue farmer in sum disrupted the tribal identity to a lesser or greater degree. In fact, ethnic ties were a basic feature of the tribal rebellions. The rebels saw themselves not as a discreet class but as having a tribal identity. At this level the solidarity shown was of a very high order. Fellow tribals were never attacked unless they had collaborated with the enemy.

At the same time, not all outsiders were attacked as enemies. Often there was no violence against the non-tribal poor, who worked in tribal villages in supportive economic roles, or who had social relations with the tribals, such as *telis, gwalas, lohars,* carpenters, potters, weavers, washermen, barbers, drummers, and bonded labourers and domestic servants of the outsiders. They were not only spared, but were seen as allies. In many cases, the rural poor formed a part of the rebellious tribal bands.

The rebellions normally began at the point where the tribals felt so oppressed that they felt they had no alternative but to fight. This often took the form of spontaneous attacks on outsiders, looting their property and expelling them from their villages. This led to clashes with the colonial authorities. When this happened, the tribals began to move towards armed resistance and elementary organisation.

Often, religious and charismatic leaders—messiahs—emerged at this stage and promised divine intervention and an end to their suffering at the hands of the outsiders, and asked their fellow tribals to rise and rebel against foreign authority. Most of these leaders claimed to derive their authority from God. They also often claimed that they possessed magical powers, for example, the power to make the enemies' bullets ineffective. Filled with hope and confidence, the tribal masses tended to follow these leaders to the very end.

The warfare between the tribal rebels and the British armed forces was totally unequal. On one side were drilled regiments armed with the latest weapons and on the other were men and women fighting in roving bands armed with primitive weapons such as stones, axes, spears and bows and arrows, believing in the magical powers of their commanders. The tribals died in lakhs in this unequal warfare.

Among the numerous tribal revolts, the Santhal *hool* or uprising was the most massive. The Santhals, who live in the area between Bhagalpur and Rajmahal, known as Daman-i-koh, rose in revolt; made a determined attempt to expel the outsiders—the *dikus*—and proclaimed the complete 'annihilation' of the alien regime. The social conditions which drove them to insurrection were described by a contemporary in the Calcutta Review as follows: 'Zamindars, the police, the revenue and courts alas have exercised a combined system of extortions, oppressive exactions, forcible dispossession of property, abuse and personal violence and a variety of petty tyrannies upon the timid and yielding Santhals. Usurious interest on loans of money ranging from 50 to 500 per cent; false measures at the *haut* and the market, wilful and uncharitable trespass by the rich by means of their untethered cattle, *tattoos,* ponies and even elephants, on the growing crops of the poorer race; and such like illegalities have been prevalent.'

The Santhals considered the *dikus* and government servants morally corrupt being given to beggary, stealing, lying and drunkenness.

By 1854, the tribal heads, the *majhis* and *parganites,* had begun to meet and discuss the possibility of revolting. Stray cases of the robbing of *zamindars* and moneylenders began to occur. The tribal leaders called an assembly of nearly 6000 Santhals, representing 400 villages, at Bhaganidihi on 30 June 1855. It was decided to raise the banner of revolt, get rid of the outsiders and their colonial masters once and for all, and usher in *Satyug*. "The Reign of Truth,' and 'True Justice.'

The Santhals believed that their actions had the blessings of God. Sido and Kanhu, the principal rebel leaders, claimed that Thakur (God) had communicated with them and told them to take up arms and fight for independence. Sido told the authorities in a proclamation: 'The Thacoor has ordered me saying that the country is not *Sahibs*. . . . The Thacoor himself will fight. Therefore, you *Sahibs* and Soldiers (will) fight the Thacoor himself.'

The leaders mobilised the Santhal men and women by organising huge processions through the villages accompanied by drummers and other musicians. The leaders rode at the head on horses and elephants and in *palkis*. Soon nearly 60,000 Santhals had been mobilised. Forming bands of 1,500 to 2,000, but rallying in many thousands at the call of drums on particular occasions, they attacked the *mahajans* and *zamindars* and their houses, police stations, railway construction sites, the *dak* (post) carriers—in fact all the 'symbols of *diku* exploitation and colonial power'.

The Santhal insurrection was helped by a large number of non-tribal and poor *dikus*. *Gwalas* (milkmen) and others helped the rebels with provisions and services; *lohars* (blacksmiths) accompanied the rebel bands, keeping their weapons in good shape.

Once the government realised the scale of the rebellion, it organised a major military campaign against the rebels. It mobilised tens of regiments under the command of a major-general, declared Martial Law in the affected areas and offered rewards of upto Rs. 10,000 for the capture of various leaders.

The rebellion was crushed ruthlessly. More than 15,000 Santhals were killed while tens of villages were destroyed. Sido was betrayed and captured and killed in August 1855 while Kanhu was arrested by accident at the tail-end of the rebellion in February 1866. And 'the Rajmahal Hills were drenched with the blood of the fighting Santhal peasantry.' One typical instance of the heroism of Santhal rebels has been narrated by L.S.S. O'Malley! 'They showed the most reckless courage, never knowing when they were beaten and refusing to surrender. On one occasion, forty-five Santhals took refuge in a mud hut which they held against the Sepoys. Volley after volley was fired into it. . . . Each time the Santhals replied with a discharge of arrows. At last, when their fire ceased, the Sepoys entered the hut and found only one old man was left alive. A Sepoy called on him to surrender, whereupon the old man rushed upon him and cut him down with his battle axe.'

I shall describe briefly three other major tribal rebellions. The *Kols* of Chhotanagpur rebelled from 1820 to 1837. Thousands of them were massacred before British authority could be re-imposed. The hill tribesmen of Rampa in coastal Andhra revolted in March 1879 against the depredations of the government-supported *mansabdar* and the new restrictive forest regulations. The authorities had to mobilise regiments of infantry, a squadron of cavalry and two companies of sappers and miners before the rebels, numbering several thousands, could be defeated by the end of 1880.

The rebellion (*ulgulan*) of the Munda tribesmen, led by Birsa Munda, occurred during 1899-1900. For over thirty years the Munda *sardars* had been struggling against the destruction of their system of common land holdings by the intrusion of *jagirdars, thikadars* (revenue farmers) and merchant money-lenders.

Birsa, born in a poor share-cropper household in 1874, had a vision of God in 1895. He declared himself to be a divine messenger, possessing miraculous healing powers. Thousands gathered around him seeing in him a Messiah with a new religious message. Under the influence of the *sardars*, the religious movement soon acquired an agrarian and political content, Birsa began to move from village to village, organising rallies and mobilising his followers on religious and political grounds. On Christmas Eve, 1899, Birsa proclaimed a rebellion to establish Munda rule in the land and encouraged 'the killing of thikadars and *jagirdars* and Rajas and *Hakims* (rulers) and Christians.' *Satyug* would be established in place of the present-day *Kalyug*. He declared that 'there was going to be a fight with the dikus, the ground would be as red as the red flag with their blood.' The non-tribal poor were not to be attacked.

To bring about liberation, Birsa gathered a force of 6,000 Mundas armed with swords, spears, battle-axes, and bows and arrows. He was, however, captured in the beginning of February 1900 and he died in jail in June. The rebellion had failed. But Birsa entered the realms of legend.

CHAPTER 3

The Extremist Challenge in Maharashtra

Militant nationalism, more commonly known as extremism, had its birth in Maharashtra, although it lasted far longer in Bengal, spread much farther there and assumed a more intense form. The historical tradition of Maharashtra had much to do with this birth; the tradition was one of resistance to foreign rule to preserve independence. Maratha achievements under Shivàji and the first two Peshwas were fondly cherished in local memory; Maratha decay and destruction caused by the British hostility was remembered, Extremism in Maharashtra received its impulse from this twofold spirit: determination to oust the foreign rule, and yearning for *swaraj*.

Almost exclusive Brahmanical leadership was typical of radical nationalism in Maharashtra; but then, also typical was its deep influence on the Masses. And that because the *raison d' etre* of the movement lay in its projection of the contemporary social and economic grievances of the people. Phadke, the Chapekar brothers, Tilak, Savarkar, Khaparde, Munje and other top leaders were all Brahmins, the elite in Maharashtrian society, the most exposed to western influences, the greatest beneficiaries of the British rule as forming the lower echelons of the British administration—and yet potentially its bitterest enemies. For it was the British who had frustrated the Maratha ambition of an Indian empire under the Brahmin Peshwas. Poona was witness to the triumph and tragedy of the Peshwa rule; the city was the political storm centre and cultural hub of resurgent Maharashtra. The government was aware of all this, it kept an anxious, watchful eye on the Brahmins, particularly the Chitpawans.

Hindu religion and culture formed the bedrock of Maharashtrian nationalism, its abiding source of inspiration. The lost soul of India under foreign rulers could be retrieved only by the restoration of the Hindu value system. *Swadharma* and *swaraj* were synonymous, not merely complementary. Viewed in this light, nationalism was more than a mere political ideology; it was a religious creed. Fighting an alien rule was not just an article of political faith; it was a religious obligation of the people at large. Deep seated religious sentiment had to be used as a means of unifying the Hindus for a common political objective. The Maharashtrain extremist leaders, like their Bengali counterparts, thus found a moral and spiritual foundation for their militant political programme. As Tilak pointed out, "God and our country are not different. In short, the country is one form of God." Deification of the nation would cleanse, politics.

To the militant nationalists, love for the country was a consuming passion, and hatred towards foreign rule a spur to determined activity. To them freedom was not a concession mercifully given by a foreign power but a right to be wrung from its unwilling hands by relentless pressure on it. The extremists differed from the moderates in regard to both their ideals and the way to realise them. Self rule was their ideal; self-sacrifice, their way. Overt opposition to the British rule, an unmitigated evil, was their mood of self-assertion.

Religion, deep rooted in tradition, influenced the political temper of the common people while western political thought had a perceptible bearing on the political activities of the Maharashtrain intelligentsia. Religious romanticism apart, militant nationalisms had another element in it: it reflected the current socioeconomic problems, and therein lay its mass appeal. This practical approach to politics, and not just hoary idealism, was the distinctive feature of Maharashtrian extremist leaders.

As in Bengal, national education was an integral part of radical nationalism in Maharashtra. It was a means of reclaiming self-confidence and self-purification to tone up the national character. National schools and colleges became the nurseries of vibrant patriotism.

The extremists demanded the end of British economic exploitation, industrial development in the country, boycott of foreign goods and the use of Indian products. *Swadeshi* was both a means of safeguarding the national economic interests and a means of salvaging the national self-respect.

A vigorous press typified the changing temper of the times. The *Kesari, Maratha, Kalpataru, Kal* and *Maharashtra Mitra,* to name only a few papers, all carried a message: nationalism was not a political programme only; it demanded complete consecration of self to the motherland. Suffering for the country was the constant refrain of the radical press.

II

The 1870s portended trouble for the government in the Bombay Presidency. The festering agrarian discontent over the Government's land administration sparked off the Deccan riot which was brutally suppressed. This was grist to the mill of the leaders of new Maharashtra. Justice Ranade's Poona Sarvajanik Sabha focused public attention on contemporary issues while the powerful writings of V.K. Chiplunkar, were both scathing commentaries on the misdeeds of the Government and an attempt at buoying up the sagging national spirit. Chiplunkar's was a mission of strengthening the moral fibre of the nation by instilling in it the cult of service and suffering for the country. He lampooned the pre-Government element in society and made "the sycophants and place hunters squirm under the lash of his words."

Then there was V.B. Phadke who planned an armed peasant revolt to end the British rule; and to this end he sought the support of the Nizam's Ruhella troops. He raided the landlords and usurers fleecing the peasants whose misery had been aggravated by the famine of 1876-77. Phadke warned the

Government against its continued exploitation of the country, asking it to reduce the taxes and salaries of European officers. He demanded that the Government undertake extensive public works and provide employment to people. Calling himself Shivaji II, he conjured up the memory of assertive Hindu nationalism under the Marathas. Organised terrorism and mass mobilisation were his *modus operandi*. He would establish a Hindu republic and restore the pristine purity of the Hindu religion.

Rightly called "the father of militant nationalism in India, Phadke's political career ended with his death in 1883 as a prisoner. But his spirit of dauntless courage and sacrifice passed into an enduring legend. The *Deccan Star* struck the national mood: "in the eyes of his country men, Vasudev did no wrong." For the government and the Anglo-Indian press, Phadke's ideas were "insane," but they were worried over this fresh instance of "Brahmin conspiracy in Maharashtra." Even Ranade with all his moderate views on political events, could not escape the Government's suspicion.

Radical nationalism was till now a growing feeling. Bal Gangadhar Tilak turned it into a conclusive force. For Tilak, freedom of the country was not just a romantic ideal; it was an attainable goal which called for unity in the country men to make their consistent and continuous pressure on the Government effective. With Tilak agitational politics in India came of age. He ushered in an era of direct action; militancy, not mendicancy, was the new note. Tilak fell out with the moderate Ranade, Telang and Gokhale on both political and social issues, ultimately wresting from them the control over the Poona Sarvajanik Sabha and the Deccan Education Society.

Tilak made common cause with the simmering discontent of the people, and this gave his political programme the intended thrust. He handled the current socioeconomic issues in such a way as to serve a threefold purpose: to inflame the public opinion against the Government, to brighten his own public image, and to justify his course of action as against that of the moderates. No Maharashtrian leader then, could claim as much mass support as Tilak; none could sway the public temper as much either. Indeed, his *Kesari* and *Maratha* marked a new breakthrough in Indian journalism.

For Tilak, India's sacred literature was as useful a means of instilling self-confidence in his country men as contemporary international events were for them model to emulate. Through frequent references to the *Gita* and the *Mahabharata* in his speeches and writings, Tilak emphasised that if the cause was just, triumph in the struggle was certain. Alongside, he exhorted the people to adopt Russian methods of agitation and appreciate the daring of the nihilists. Tilak broadened the public mind by familiarising it with events in Japan, Persia and Turkey—all suggesting Asian resurgence.

In 1882, Tilak and his close associate, Agarkar, were tried in the Bombay High Court for defamatory comments on a Kolhapur political case and he was sentenced to three months imprisonment. This was followed by his trenchant criticism of the Ilbert Bill agitation in 1883. Then he led a strong attack on the Age of Consent Bill, 1891, mere to protest against an alien Government's interference with Hindu social institutions than as an opponent to any social change whatever.

Radicalism in Maharashtra was viewed by the Government as a Hindu revivalist movement with an unsettling effect on the Muslim mind. It found a clear link between the anti-cow killing agitation and Hindu-Muslim riots in the Bombay Presidency in the 1890s. Tilak was not the founder of the anti-cow killing societies in Maharashtra, but he made cow protection as "one of his most potent tools" to organise his correligionists. In the 1891 session of the Congress at Nagpur, several Congress leaders spoke on the need for cow protection, which led Lord Lansdowne, the Viceroy, to warn the Secretary of State for India that the anti-cow killing movement had transformed the Congress from "a foolish debating society into a real political power, backed by the most dangerous elements in native society."

Tilak popularised the Ganapati and Shivaji festivals throughout Maharashtra and later outside it. Both were symbols of resurgent Hindu nationalism with a distinct socio-religious purpose. Their object was to forge unity in the Hindu community and energise it with spiritual values and a sense of pride in part glories. On these festive occasions he spread political education through villages by means of dramas and songs on political themes.

In fact, the Shivaji festival was a "national hero worship," and around Shivaji's name "rallied all the newly aroused national pride and enthusiasm of the Maharashtrian people." The Shivaji legend was resurrected to retrieve for the people of Maharashtra their historic pride in *Swarajya.* During the Ganapati festival leaflets were circulated, calling the Hindus to arms, urging the Marathas to rebel as Shivaji had done against foreign rule, and emphasising that religious outbreak should be made the first step towards the overthrew of the alien power. Not only low caste Hindus, even Muslims participated in the festival which was looked upon as a "joint national duty." With this began in Tilak's career the "period of pronounced hostility to the Government."

"The poison of anarchy" churned by the Shivaji cult took its first toll in 1897 when the Plague Commissioners, Rand and Ayerst, were killed by Chapekar brothers at Poona. This view of the government was further reinforced by the bitter condemnation of the Plague Commissioners' activities in the nationalist Press. The *Kesari* and *Kalpataru* reminded the Government that the revolt of 1857 was caused by the British disregard of socio-religious susceptibilities of the Indian people. The *Maharashtra Mitra and the Sudharak* urged the Hindus and Muslims to resist the *zulm* of the soldiers who enforced the plague regulations. Tilak set up Hindu plague hospitals and collected public donations for their support. What he objected to was not the suppression of the epidemic by the Government, but its use of soldiers to break into the privacy of homes for flushing out the plague victims. He wrote in the *Maratha:*

> Plague is more merciful to us than its human prototypes now reigning in the city.

Tilak toured the countryside his agents urging the famine stricken farmers to withhold land tax until the Government had mitigated their plight. He not only lamented the distress of the peasantry but roused them to articulate their grievances.

Reports came thick and fast that Tilak was bent on "systematically opposing and misrepresenting measures of Government." Charged with sedition, Tilak was condemned to eighteen months imprisonment. This proved to be his political baptism. Hereafter his stock in public esteem would rise in proportion to his denigration in the moderate-dominated Indian National Congress.

For this Congress with no mass following nor effective policy, Tilak as other extremists, had an unconcealed contempt. The Congress an elitish body:

> met once a year and repeated the same speeches, like the frogs of variegated colours, appearing every rainy season and croaking, some like bulls, others like goats.

He outlined a new line of action for the Congress:

> Let us now try to force our grievances into their ears by strong constitutional means. We must give the best political education possible to the ignorant villagers. We must meet them in terms of equality teach them their rights and show how to fight constitutionally. Then only will the Government realise that to despise the Congress is to despise the Indian nation.

The Congress was little impressed. At its Amravati session in 1897, the President, Sir Sankaran Nair, expressed his conviction that the decline of the British rule would lead to anarchy, war and rapine in India. The moderates even opposed the resolution condemning Tilak's imprisonment, and that when Surendranath Banerjee himself testified that "the nation was in tears" for Tilak. Indeed, as the *Times of India* noted, Tilak's activities "marked a sharp and sudden breaking asunder in the native political society."

Its most apparent manifestation was the quickened pace of extremism in Bengal and the Punjab. The partition of Bengal reinforced the relations between the militant nationalists of Bengal with their counterparts in Maharashtra, both having the common programme of *Swadeshi, Swaraj,* National Education and passive resistance to foreign rule. Swaraj was declared the goal of the Congress in 1906, it being the "foundation and not the height" of India's future prosperity, as Tilak put it.

In the Congress split at Surat in 1907, Tilak had a big hand, However, later in all the provincial and district political conferences which Tilak organised in Maharashtra he dwelt on the need for unity in the Congress ranks.

Tilak visited Calcutta in 1906. There he gave a call to the people to organise resistance to the Government and to boycott the administration. Non-cooperation in revenue collection, judicial administration and military service was to be followed by the non-payment of taxes. He urged the people to be prepared to fight if their demands were rejected by the Government, for

> mere protests backed by self-reliance will not help the people. . . . Three Ps—Prayer, Pleas and Protest—will not do unless backed by solid force.

Aurobindo, Bipin Pal and Lajpat Rai shared Tilak's views and worked in close concert to form a pressure group in the Congress. Aurobindo saw in Tilak "the one possible leader for a revolutionary party." To Bipin Pal, Tilak was the "great Hindu nation builder . . . the only reincarnation, so to say, of the civil ideas and possibilities of the great Hindu race."

The Shivaji festival in Bengal became a popular form of political demonstration, Tagore's soul-stirring poem on Shivaji made the Maratha leader a household name in Bengal. Members of revolutionary societies in Bengal practised the Maratha war cry "Hara Hara Mahadeo." Revolutionary literature in Bengal had much in common with that in Maharashtra, Sakharam Ganesh Deuskar, a Marathi Brahmin in Calcutta, became widely known in revolutionary societies in Bengal by his translation of Marathi political literature into Bengali.

Maharashtra, like Bengal, had many votaries of the Cult of the Bomb, who appeared to the government as having the blessing, if not active support, of Tilak and his associates. Tilak's visit to Calcutta, the Bengal C.I.D. reported, gave a strong impetus to the "revolutionary crime" in the province. At Poona a great deal of experimenting with explosives was reported; also at Bassein. At Benaras, Baroda, Gwalior, Nagpur and other places in C.P. and Berar. Tilak's ideas swayed the public mind, especially among the local Maharashtrian people. P.S. Kankhoje's Arya Bandhav Samaj, a revolutionary association with which Tilak had close links, made attempts at sowing disaffection in the army and the tribal population of the Central Provinces.

The Government came upon the extremists with a heavy hand. Lajpat Rai and Aurobindo were imprisoned, followed by Tilak in 1908, in whose newspaper articles and editorials the Government found his support for terrorism with assassination of European officers as its declared motto. Charged with subversive activities and incitement to violence, Tilak was deported to Mandalay for six years. The rigorous Press Act that followed sought to muzzle the extremist press in Maharashtra as elsewhere. Public annoyance at Tilak's deportation burst forth in riots in Bombay and Pandharpur, leading to police firing.

The deportation was a great event in Tilak's life. It invested him with the aura of a martyr his image magnified from being the leader of a party to a popular hero. He was now "the real symbol of the new age," "the Guru, the idol, the fetish of the Maratha masses."

Extremists in Maharashtra found a direct correlation between national education and national regeneration, as was evident in the functioning of the Deccan Education Society under Tilak's stewardship. In the district political conferences in 1908-09 at Poona, Dhulia and other places resolutions were passed in favour of national education. The course structure in the national schools of Maharashtra and C.P. and Berar was based on the syllabus of the National Council of Education in Calcutta which received financial support from some institutions in Maharashtra.

III

Tilak's deportation only scotched the fire of extremism in Maharashtra, not killed it. By then a younger and a more determined generation of radical nationalists had been reared by him; of these men, V.D. Savarkar was the most prominent. As a student of the Fergusson College, Poona, Savarkar organised a patriotic society. An ardent supporter of *Swadeshi* and boycott of foreign goods, he, in 1905, arranged a bonfire of foreign cloth before a cheering crowd which his political mentor, Tilak, addressed.

For Savarkar, Joseph Mazzini of Italy held an irresistible appeal, after whose party, The Young Italy, he modelled his *Mitra Mela* at Nasik. It developed into a more well-knit association under a new name, *Abhinav Bharat* with its programme of achieving national independence by armed revolt. The *Abhinav Bharat* had a profound influence on the youth of Maharashtra, convincing it of the incompatibility of foreign rule and national development. It claimed membership even among government employees.

Expelled from College, Savarkar went to London on a "Shivaji Fellowship," which Tilak arranged for him. He quickly assumed the leadership of the India House, the rendezvous of Indian political activists abroad. In 1907 he and his associates celebrated the Golden Jubilee of the Revolt of 1857 as the First War of Indian Independence. He published a book on the Revolt which the Government lost no time in proscribing. To Indian revolutionaries he sought to supply arms surreptitiously; to him terrorism was the first stage of revolution. In 1909, the British police arrested him on a charge of complicity in the murder of Sir Curzon Wylie by Madanlal Dhingra.

Savarkar was in Paris when he was implicated in the Nasik conspiracy which claimed the life of Jackson, the District Magistrate. While being brought to India from London for trial, he jumped from the ship near Marseilles, hoping to escape into the safety of the French territory. The attempt failed, the French authorities delivering him up to the British Government. For thirteen years he languished in the Andaman prison, his spirit unsubdued, his faith in vigorous militant Hinduism as aglow as ever.

Savarkar's was a familiar name in Bombay, Kolhapur, Aund, Gwalior, Baroda, Satara, Nagpur, Amravati, Yeotmal and many other places where secret revolutionary societies functioned. Blowing up railway tracts and bridges, assassinating European officers, using and manufacturing arms and ammunition and spreading disaffection in the army and police constituted the programme of these associations which had close links with secret societies in Bengal. In 1910 the police reported about deep laid conspiracies in east Khandesh, Sholapur and Aundh, and in July 1913, there was an attempt to create disturbances in the Deccan by distributing among the local people incendiary leaflets in Marathi which were believed to have been written by some conspirators in Poona.

IV

Tilak returned to India in 1914; nationalism in India now received a fresh spurt with the new message Tilak gave it, Indians must agitate for Home Rule, Ireland being their model. Tilak's "responsive cooperation" with the government enmeshed in the World War was contingent on its grant of self-rule to India. Acting in close cooperation with Annie Besant, Tilak spread the message of Home Rule to villages by undertaking extensive tours through them.

The Home Rule movement made the Tilakites a great force in the Congress where their influence increased after the death of Gokhale and Pherozshah Mehta in 1915. At the Lucknow Congress in 1916, Tilak played an important role in bringing about unity between the moderates and extremists, and a rapprochement between the Congress and the League.

The increasing popularity of the Home Rule movement both worried and angered the Government, whose keenness to suppress it, was however, balanced by the fear of the risk involved in the step. For Home Rule was not just a fond project of the Tilakites; it had now become the demand of the Congress itself as was clear from its resolution in 1917. Edwin Montagu, the Secretary of State for India, found that the,

> capture of the Congress organisation by Mrs. Besant and Tilak is complete. . . . The Congress is completely identified with the Home Rule.

Montagu, after his meeting with Tilak, was convinced that he was "the most important leader in India at the moment."

In India the Home Rule movement had caught on; the next step was to mobilise world opinion in its favour; such an opinion, so it was believed, the British could hardly ignore. With this expectation Tilak sent Lajpat Rai, N.S. Hardikar and K.D. Shastri to the USA where President Wilson was an avowed champion of nationalism and self-determination. Tilak also wrote to Clemenceau, the French Premier, to support the cause of Indian Home Rule. In 1918 he went to London himself and sought the help of the British Labour Party for the cause.

Tilak accepted the Montford reforms, but did not give up his demand for self-rule. For the Khilafat movement he had sympathy, since he saw in it a means to forge unity between the Hindus and Muslims. In 1920 Tilak formed the Congress Democratic Party only to die a few months later as, indeed, "the uncrowned king of nationalist India."

Tilak was the apostle and high priest of extremism in Maharashtra, a force which grew and found fulfilment in his policies and programmes. In fact, the impact of extremism as a political ideology could be best studied by charting the course of Tilak's political life itself.

CHAPTER 4

The Indian Movement of 1857-59: A Case of Bihar

BACKGROUND, GENESIS AND NATURE

Bihar's role in the history of India's successful struggle for freedom has been highly significant and inspiring. No doubt the verdict of Plassey (23rd June, 1757) was in favour of the English East India Company. But their rising supremacy was challenged in the course of a few years, first by Mir Qasim alone (1762-63) and again in 1764 by a confederacy of three allies, Mir Qasim, Shuja-up-daulah, the Nawab of Oudh, and Shah Alam II, Emperor of Delhi. A British military officer, with experience of Indian affairs, remarked in 1857: "From the days of Mir Kasim Ally, Patna had always been a rebellious city." Conjunction of some favourable circumstances helped the English to overpower the allied powers at Buxar on the 23rd October, 1764, and Buxar supplemented the work of Plassey in "riveting the shackles of the Company's rule upon Bengal and Bihar."

For a century after this the expansion of the British dominion in India, and the growth of an Indo-British administrative system, naturally conducted India through manifold processes of transition political, economic, social and cultural. This for various reasons, generated fumes of discontent of which there were occasionally open manifestations in anti-British out-break, in different parts of this vast country including Bihar.

The insurrection of Raja Chait Singh of Banaras had repercussions on the contiguous province of Bihar. Some of the Bihar Zamindars, discontented with the English Company , rose against it and espoused the cause of Chait Singh. On the 29th August, 1781, Mr. Grome, the Collector of Saran, wrote to Mr. Ross:—"Reza Cooly Cawn, formerly the Aumil of Sasaram, is at this time with Raja Chait Singh. Many of the inhabitants of that district, and probably Oojains, a tribe of Rajpoots, are sincerely attached to him. Petambar Singh, of the family of the Ticcari Raja, is most intimately connected with Chait Singh, and his dependants are remarkable good soldiers. He has also a number of horsemen in his pay." It is stated in a letter of Mr. Ross to Major Hardy, commanding the Patna Militia, dated the 6th October, 1781, that "One Fatteh Shah was giving trouble in Saran at this period, while several Zamindars and others in the jurisdiction of the Revenue Chief of Patna armed and clothed their dependants in the military accountrements of the Company." Narain Singh, Zamindar of Seres and Kutumbah (in the Gaya district), also then resisted the march of the Company's troops near foot of the Sasaram hills. For this he was arrested and sent as a state prisoner to Dacca on the 5th March, 1786. Raja Akbar Ali Khan of Narhat and Samai (in the Gaya district) also rose against the Company at this time.

After the treaty of 21st January, 1798, between the English East India Company and Saadat Ali of Oudh, by which the latter was recognised as the Nawab of Oudh, Wazir Ali, another claimant to the *masnad* of Oudh, was sent to Banaras to live there as a pensioner. Discontented with this lot, Wazir Ali planned an all-India conspiracy against the English and had some confederates in Bihar, including Raja Mitrajit Singh of Tikari in the old Bihar district of the Patna Division.

In fact, there was a strong undercurrent of discontent in Bihar against the English East India Company for various reasons, even before 1857. In 1845-46, when in the course of the First Anglo-Sikh War the English were faced with a grave situation due to stubborn and formidable resistance of the Sikh Army, and "all the resources of the (Company's) Government" were being drawn to the North-Western Frontier there was a plan at Patna to assail and uproot their authority. About it, the

British military officer, already referred to, wrote in 1857: "Even so lately as 1846, its (Patna's) Mahomedan nobility had endeavoured to take advantage of our balanced fortunes on the banks of the Sutlej. They had then succeeded in corrupting some of the native officers and sepoys stationed at Dinapore."

William Tayler, Commissioner of the Patna Division, till the month of August 1857, thus referred to it: "For some years past, this city (Patna) has been considered a very sink of disaffection and intrigue. In 1846, a dangerous plot was detected, in which many of the Mahomedans of Patna, and the neighbouring districts were concerned and in which attempts had been made to tamper with the Sepoys. . . . That the conspiracy of 1846, was but a branch of a more general plot is the opinion of many who are well acquainted with the country, and that the object of that conspiracy was the destruction of the English, the overthrow of the British Government and the re-establishment of a Mahomadan dynasty, is, I imagine beyond all doubt."

It is significant to note, on the authority of recently discovered evidence, that Kunwar Singh of Jagdishpur, the Bihar hero of the Movement of 1857-59, was also suspected by the English of being involved in this anti-British riot of 1845-46.

The Magistrate of Patna, while giving an account of it to the Secretary to the Government of Bengal in his letter, dated the 27th, December, 1845, noted: "I have received information that Baboo Koomar Singh one of the most influential Zemindars in the neighbourhood and a resident in the Shahabad district is supposed to be also implicated in this conspiracy—it is a well known fact that this baboo during the late excitements, on account of the prisoners, came to this city (Patna) and was in communication with Rahut Alee." "I have received letters," communicated Mr. Elphinstone Jackson, officiating Magistrate of Shahabad, to the Secretary to the Government of Bengal, on the 23rd, January, 1846, "containing the information that Baboo Koomar Singh, a most influential Zemindar in this district, and a man most highly popular with all the inhabitants of Arrah and other towns of Shahabad is suspected of being leagued with the Patna conspirators and that letters bearing his seal have been discovered clearly proving his guilt." The Bengal

Government did not approve of Koomar Singh's arrest apprehending that it "may have the effect of exciting the people to opposition."

Ishree Prasad, a Deputy Magistrate at Patna, wrote to the Commissioner of Patna, on the 27th, August, 1870: "In 1845 many Rajahs and Zamindars of Bihar Province having conspired had tried to tamper with Regiment No. 1 (under Major Rowcroft). . . . Monshee Rahut Alee was the principal person who managed through Sheikh Peer Bux, a Monshee of the Regiment and the Pundit (Durga Pershud, Dugra Prasad) of it, whose name I do not know, to plant Mutiny in the Regiment. The Regiment was promised six months' pay in advance and a day was fixed for the rising. A Havildar of the Regiment gave information to the Commanding Officer of the same. The Monshee and the Pandit of the Regiment were arrested and many letters from several Zamindars and influential men showing their connection with the conspiracy were found in their possession. The Pundit and the Monshee confessed. Monshee Rahut Ally and Khaja Hasan Ali Khan, an influential man.... were arrested. The letters criminating Monshee Rahut Ali found then, still exist in the Patna Foujdaree records. The letters bearing the seal of Babu Kunwar Singh of Jagdeespore are available in the said records. The investigation went on for a long time and it ended thus in 1846. That the Monshee and the Pandit, notwithstanding their confession, did not identify Rahut Ally and Khaja Hasan Ali Khan and consequently they were released. Only the Monshee and the Pundit of the Regiment were imprisoned, and Maulvi Neaz Alee, the Law officer of Patna, Burkut Ullah, the Government pleader of the Civil Court, Patna, and Meer Bakar, Daroga of Kolguat, Patna, were dismissed. . . . From a Robkaree existing in Foujdari records of Patna it appears that Khaja Hasan Ali Khan was released by the order of the Superintendent of Police contained in a letter, dated the 27th October, 1846. It is worth notice that several Zamindars and influential persons were exposed in 1846. Though by their influence they carried off their days and succeeded to screen themselves then, yet in 1857 all became known. For instance, Moulvie Alee Kureem was suspected in 1846, in 1857 he was declared an open rebel, though escaped under the amnesty. Baboo Kunwar Singh of Jagdeespore was accused in 1846. It is useless to say what happened of him in 1857. One Hasan Ali Khan, a police Jamadar in Tirhut, was suspected in 1846, and he was hanged in 1857."

There were discontent and open risings also among some of the Adivasis of Chotanagpur and among the Santals. Thus in 1831-32 smouldering discontent found expression in a rising of the Coles in Chotanagpur. More formidable than this was the movement organised by the Santals in 1855-57 in a wide area extending from the vicinity of Burdwan to Bhagalpur, under the leadership of four brothers, Sidhu, Kanhu, Chand and Bhoirab, who were inhabitants of village Bhagnadihi near Barhait in the heart of the *Damin* area of the Rajmahal subdivision of the district of Santal Paraganas. Its causes were deeply rooted in the changing conditions of that period and its suppression caused enormous strain to the Company's Government.

The prevailing feeling of discontent against the Company's Government in India among certain sections of its population were noticed by some important British officers. Writing in the *Calcutta Review* of 1851, Sir Henry Durand, who became later on the Foreign Secretary to the Government of India, gave the following warning to his countrymen: "Retribution follows misgovernment with an iron step and crushes with inevitable ruin the children and the children's children of an oppressing nation. Strange as it may seem to some of our readers, this idea is present amongst the millions of India." William Tayler, officiating Commissioner of Patna, communicated to W. Grey, Secretary to the Government of Bengal, on the 27th June, 1855, as follows: "The minds of the people in these districts are at present in a very restless and disaffected state and they have generally conceived the idea that there is an intention on the part of Government to commence and carry through a systematic interference with their religion, caste, and their social customs."

In view of all these it would not be correct to regard the Revolt of 1855-59 as an isolated and sudden outbreak. Rather, it was the culmination of accumulated discontent in various quarters due to different factors for which the new alien masters of the country were thought to be responsible.

There is no doubt that during the period of one century preceding 1857, marked by the rapid stride of British imperialism in India, which brought in its wake changes in different spheres of life, there were several elements of discontent against British rule, all of which being focussed into one produced the fierce flame of 1857-59. E. A. Samuells, successor of Tayler as Commissioner of Patna, recorded in his letter to Bengal Government, dated 25th Septemebr 1858: "From all the information which has reached me, I believe the mutiny to have been the result of causes long in operation." Hedayet Ali Khan, a Subedar and Sirdar Bahadur in the Bengal Sikh Police Battalion, commanded by Captain T. Rattray, writes in a contemporary account of the movement, dated August 1858: "All the above mentioned fact, *viz,* the carrying of the Army into Cabeel (Kabul), the erection of the hospital at Saharanpore, the issue of the order that all the sick men or women, whether high or low caste, should resort for treatment to this hospital, the swearing of recruits to go wherever they were ordered, the messing together in jails, cutting of beards of prisoners, and also of the Sepoys in a prescribed fashion, the annexation of Oudh, the observations of the missionaries, the introduction of the Rifle, and further the confiscation of the Jageers that had been granted for perpetuity by the Emperor of Delhi, the introduction of house tax, and the Sepoys being required to pay postage for their letters which they were not required to pay, all these facts combined together and set the whole army and the country mad."

Opinions have long been sharply divided on the nature of this movement,—whether it was in meaning and origin mere military revolt or was the outburst of an organised conspiracy aiming at the overthrow of the British Empire. Even persons directly connected with this movement have expressed diametrically opposite views regarding it. In the opinion of Sir John Lawrence it was nothing more than a military rising of which the cartridge incident was the proximate cause. But Sir James Outram expressed the view that it was the result of a Muhammadan conspiracy which utilised Hindu grievances to its own advantage. The cartridge incident, according to the latter view, "precipitated the Mutiny before it had been thoroughly organised and before adequate arrangement had been made for making Mutiny a first step to popular insurrection." Taking a mean between these two views, a later writer, Mr. Innes, has observed that "the panic was engineered by political intriguers; but the insurrection was not organised. None of the Native rulers had made up their minds to rise. There is every indication that the Sepoys took their leap blindly in the dark, not knowing whither they were going. But there is also every indication that Nana Saheb on one side and a Mogul faction on the other had a great deal to do with working them up to take the leap, and that the Mogul faction at least had a tolerably definite idea of the use which was to be made of the leap when taken." Holmes holds much the same view and writes that "before the story of the greased cartridges was circulated there was no definite plot for a general rising of the Bengal army, and it is improbable that such a plot was formed even after the first mutinies . . . civil disturbances, except in a few isolated regions and on the part of a few embittered or fanatical groups, never amounted to rebellion. . . . These rebellions (in Jhansi and Oudh) arose in consequence of the Mutiny, and there is no evidence that any of the rebels, except the Nana, conspired before it began." Sir Charles Aitchison, who wrote a biography of Lord Lawrence in 1892, observes that Lord Lawrence's "view does not account for the phenomena . . . the Mutiny of the army assumed in places the character of a partial rebellion of the people already made uneasy by military revolt, innovation and change." Prof. P. E. Roberts contradicts this opinion by stating that "on the whole in spite of the fact that in some districts the people seem to have risen before the sepoys, Lawrence's view seems most nearly approximate to the truth. We may assume, therefore, that the rising was mainly military in origin but it occurred at a time when, for various reasons, there was much social and political discontent, and that the mutineers were promptly joined by interested adventurers, who tried to give it a particular direction to suit their own scheme."

In the days of early revolutionary nationalism in India during the present century, appeared Shri V. D. Savarkar's book on this movement which he described as the "*Indian War of*

Independence, 1857." Several others have in recent time subscribed to his view.

The first manifestation of the movement of 1857-59 was naturally in the more inflammable quarters of the Sepoy Army of the English. But it is not correct to regard it as a mere military rising. In part two of the *Narrative* of the British Military Officer, referred to already.

CHAPTER 5

Agrarian Revolts

The Kisan Movement has had a history of at least 120 years since the British regime came to be established in India. To those of us who are used to peasant agitations organised and led by some conscious leaders having a political ideology and struggling for the collective and progressive welfare of peasants, the earlier agitations of peasants may seem to be rather unorganised and spasmodic groupings of the semi-conscious masses in the dark. Yet a brief review of such groupings will be of great interest to us who are anxious to develop a conscious, organised and militant kisan movement bent upon the achievement of Kisan and Muzdoor Raj.

Mass Emigration

The Districts of Cuddapah, Kurnool, Anantapur and Bellary were ceded to the British by the Nizam about the beginning of the 19th Century. The local peasants were made to pay in full the excessive land revenue and other innumerable ceases and imposts previously imposed by the Nizam, where as in the past the Nizam's Collections were not so regular: the burden of such taxes became too heavy. But all the complaints made by peasants were of no avail and the British administrators were anxious only to increase their collections year after year. In their unholy anxiety to increase their collections, the Collectors insisted upon every ryot taking a particular portion of waste land, whose event was increasing into cultivation and paying tax on it in proportion to the land cultivated by him whether such land is cultivated or not and desired or not by the peasant.

In despair large numbers of peasants of these districts, now known as Rayalasima had begun to emigrate to the neighbouring forests and Mysore only to escape from these increasing burdens of taxes. They had abandoned their lands and homes and beloved surroundings since at that time, the possession of land became more a burden than an asset. This naturally opened the eyes of the Government. Hundreds of deserted villages and lakhs of acres of abandoned land smote the rulers in the face and threatened the solvency of the Provincial Government. In a hurry, Sir Thomas Munro was sent to settle the land revenue payable by peasants and the Government agreed to his proposals and carried out in 1820-30 the drastic reduction of land revenue and he systematised the survey and settlement and land records. This was the first triumph of our peasants during the nineteenth century.

Famines and Peasants

Between 1770-1897 there were several disastrous famines all over India: those of Rayalasima were the worst, resulting in the death of lakhs of workers and peasants. Special mention has to be made of the famine years 1770, 1896 and 1897 when millions of poor people died for want of food and water. The advent of railways had only slowly enabled the State to import cereals and pulses to the famine stricken areas and so in most places the prices of food grains had gone up and even the higher and lower middle classes were being hopelessly impoverished by their attempts to purchase food and raiment and maintain themselves during times of unemployment. It is a sad commentary on the political capacity of our people that despite such terrible sufferings of the masses and the mass-deaths of workers and peasants and the outbreaks of cholera and other epidemics, in the wake of starvation and consumption of horrible things (ending in cannibalism also) no real and effective mass protest was organised by anyone or any organisation against such inhuman state of things.

Yet some dare-devils preferred dacoity to degrading death as a result of starvation and a large number of bandits began to infest the towns and countryside, striking terror into the hearts of not only the townsmen and rich people but also the big landlords and even the local officials. Coupled with the new spirit of philanthropy and public spirit that was slowly manifesting itself in the towns and through the newspapers, this growing danger to the property and safety of the propertied classes was responsible for forcing Government to appoint successive Famine Commissions and to devise and enforce the Famine Relief System. That this system was devised not so much with any laudable philanthropic sentiments as by the anxiety of Government to protect the institution of property and stave off the growing threat to the established order is indicated by the content of this Famine Relief System.

To ascertain whether there is any famine at all in any area. Test Works have to be run for 15 days to employ workers on the hardest and most cruel task of breaking stones for 8 to 10 hours a day in burning sun and blinding winds, on a payment of ¾ anna per day *i.e.* a wage which is not enough to give even half of a full meal a day. If the suffering workers flock to such test works in ever growing numbers for those 15 days, then alone is a famine considered to exist. Even after a state of famine is declared to exist and famine relief works are opened, workers are paid only 1½ annas per head per a day of ten to twelve hours for work that breaks anyone's strengths and spirit. Thus the most meanminded and cruel relief has been provided for our famished masses with a view just to prevent them from defying the society as a whole because of gnawing hunger and also to tie them down to work, which succeeds in weakening them. Thus the very potential revolutionary capacity of peasants and workers was met first by some relief and next by a process which weakens them every moment.

Famines occurred in 1868 in Northern India.
1876-8 in South India.
1888-9 in Madras.
Again there were famines in 1891, 1896, 1899, 1906, 1907.
1877 famine:—area affected 200.000 square miles.
Population affected:—360 lakhs.
1878 N.W.F.P. and Punjab—220 lakhs of people were affected. Mortality 55 lakhs.

Expenditure Rs. 8 crores and loss of revenue Rs. 3 crores.
1874 Bengal Famine. Cost Rs. 6.75 crores.
1875-8, South Indian famine. Cost Rs. 9.25 crores.

Estimate of annual cost of famine in loss of revenue and actual expenditure made in 1878—150 lakhs of pounds (sterling).

There Famine Commissions were appointed in 1880, 1898, 1901.

Recommendations of Famine Commissions

1. Extension of irrigation at a total cost of Rs. 44 crores.
2. Granting loans and advances to cultivators to enable them is execute private agricultural improvements.
3. Emigration.
4. Promotion of agriculture.

Action taken by Government

1. Famine Code.
2. Agricultural Loans Act.

   Land Improvement Act.
3. Deputation of Sir Frederick Nicholson and his report on Continental Cooperative Movement.
4. Passing of the Indian Co-operative Act 1911.
5. Development of Minor Irrigation and unproductive Irrigation Works.

Bengal Tenants Outburst

The Bengali Zamindars prospered under the aegis of Permanent Settlement at the expense of the industry and of the hard working peasants. The special gift of nature to Bengal, the culture of jute which came to be in great demand in the world has only enriched these zamindars and served only as another level with which rents can be forced upon them. Legal and illegal imposts were multiplied and Nazaranas or premiums were heaped upon peasants. Owing to the tightened alliance between the British and zamindars during and after the Indian Mutiny, even the Courts had begun to decree that the land itself had also belonged to Zamindars and peasants were only tenants-at-will. There seemed to be no limit to the capacity of zamindars and their persecution of the peasants. Just about

1870-80, the economic depression had also contributed its share towards the growth of poverty of peasants. Naturally peasants—the various grades of them began first to fall into arrears of rent, then to be threatened with the loss of lands and eviction from their homesteads. It thus so happened that thousands of peasants came to consciously refuse the rents, disobey the dictates of Courts, obstruct their eviction and finally to fight with whatever weapons were available, (the agents of Courts and Zamindars). A regular state of anarchy came to prevail in a large part of Bengal and Santal countryside and a reign of terror was set afoot. The state rushed to the rescue of its allies, the Zamindars, mowed down thousands of peasants and established a counter and more cruel and organised state of official terrorism. Thus in blood and fire was the great uprising of suffering tenants of Bengal and Santhal Parganas suppressed.

But it only served as a warning to the British Government and so an enquiry Committee was appointed and the first statute the Bengal Tenancy Act was passed, conferring permanency of tenure upon some classes of tenants and thus staying off the immediate danger.

The next agitation came from Mahratta in 1875. The Mahratta peasants to their horror, learnt that according to the British Civil Law, they could be imprisoned for their failure to pay off their debts, whenever demanded by their creditors. They were hard hit by the slump in cotton prices after the cessation of Civil War in America and so the burden of their debts became too unbearable. Just at that time, the moneylenders began to take advantage of the Civil Laws and purchase the lands of peasants, evict their debtors from their ancestral houses and consign those of them who became unable to pay in time to Civil Debtors Jails. This was the limit for the patience of the warlike Mahratta Peasants. So they rose in their thousands against these money-lenders. They raided the houses of money-lenders, tore away almost in a frenzy the promissory notes and other papers, pertaining to their debts to them. In many places, they were obstructed by some money-lenders and so resorted to violence. Several money-lenders and their supporters were killed or beaten badly. Even a large number of police were severely dealt with, whenever they had tried to save money-lenders or whenever they attempted to harass peaceful peasants. For a time, it looked as if the whole Mahratta country-side was up in arms against the British Raj itself. When the British Government took its cue from this fury of the masses and hurriedly passed the Deccan Agriculturists Relief Act, whereby no peasant of Mahratta could be sent to the Civil Debtors jail for failure to repay debts.

Protection of Punjab Peasants

A similar uprising took place in the Punjab in 1890-1900 against the growing alienation of peasants' lands to the money-lenders of towns. The Sikh, Muhammaden and Hindu peasants who had till recent past enjoyed an independent Sikh state could not brook the superiority of the money-lenders, conferred upon them by the British Civil Laws. No wonder the murders or assaults on money-lenders began to increase rather alarmingly. The British Government quickly passed the Punjab Land Alienation Act in 1902-03 prohibiting the transferring of land from Kisan tribes or other classes and prohibiting the usufruct mortgages for more than twenty years.

Similarly because the Punjab peasants began to protest against the oppressive incidence of land revenue, the Government passed the Shaharanpur Rules, according to which the Land Revenue should never exceed 50 per cent of net-income from land, either at the original settlement or at any resettlement.

Thus it can be seen that the four major fights apart from the war of Independence put up by our peasants in their crude and primitive fashion have resulted in considerable concessions from government. The British Government had also shown itself quite capable of meeting mass movements more than half way, lest the masses should either through their struggles develop their political consciousness or fall into the hands of politicians. There were neither political organisations nor class organisations at that time either to stimulate, engineer and develop peasants, risings, or to exploit the spontaneous uprising of peasants with a view to strengthen any-political movement for freedom.

Hence the extraordinary vigilance displayed by Lord Curzon to examine the complaints made by Ramesh Chandra Dutt, C.I.E. that the land Revenue Assessment was too heavy, that British Government did wrong in undermining the strength and influence of Zamindars and that government should not have refused to extend Permanent Settlement of land revenue to all parts of India. He obtained fairly detailed reports of land revenue practices from all provincial Governments and in the resolution of the Governor-General in Council, he laid down general principles, to guide, the settlement officers and Provincial Governments in making settlements and resettlements. It was through that resolution that Lord Curzon insisted that in no case the resettlements ought to exceed 18 per cent of the original assessment. At the same time, he laid it down as the policy of Government to protect peasants as against the rapacity of Zamindar. The Resolution of Government of India on 'Land Revenue Policy'. This he did, in 1905 in order to prevent the Indian National Congress, of which R.C. Dutt was the economist, to capture the heart of the peasants. He wanted to make the Government pass for the real champion of peasants. But unfortunately the Indian National Congress did not follow up its advantage by adopting a bold and forward policy in regard to the protection of peasants.

There was, however, one great struggle engineered by our nationalists under the leadership of the Congress on behalf of our voiceless peasants. It was aimed at the abolition of the *Indenture System.* According to this system, lakhs of our peasants and workers used to be somehow or other induced to sign some indenture bonds, agreeing to work for a specified number of years for some specified employer on his estate and in his province or country and consenting to all the penalties that the employer might inflict upon them for any breach of the bonds. Under this system our rural folk used to be recruited for work in South Africa, Malaya, Ceylon and other overseas countries and also for plantation work in Assam, Bengal, Madras and U.P. For years, lakhs of these unfortunate people who had agreed to go and work on the estates of employers, most of whom were Europeans, were persecuted in an unspeakable manner. There was not an indignity that could not be hurled at them and not a punishment that could not be procured by their influential employers from the too willing courts for even petty offences. The criminal law of our country and the legal systems of other countries were so criminal in their conception and effect that in actual practice, our indentured labourers were converted into virtual slaves of their employers. Against this inhuman system, our Indian National Congress waged a relentless war and the great Bankim Chandra Chaterjee brandished his powerful pen for espousing the cause of these sufferers. At last the Congress had triumphed and the indenture system was abolished by Government which had agreed to shoulder the responsibility for the safety, economic well-being and cultural uplift of all immigrant and emigrant labour. Today Government of India has its agents in Ceylon, Malaya, Burma and South Africa to look after the interests of our emigrants and Protectors in Assam to watch the interests of our plantation labourers. Thus Government of India also seeks to secure a minimum wage for our workers in ceylon and Malaya, in addition to fighting for their political status.

1905-19: It is however true to say that the Indian National Congress did not lay as much stress on the need for relief for our peasants, during 1905-19 as it did on the needs of our industrialists. There were many causes for this but the most important of them was the predominant voice our industrialists and disciples of Justice Ranade led by Ferozshah Mehta, and Gokhale, were then having in the counsels of the Congress. Our nationalists continued to press for the establishment of permanent settlement of land revenue, the abolition of salt-tax and excise revenue; but since they were preoccupied with their fight for protection for our industries and state assistance to our industrialists, they could not do anything more than formally reiterating these demands on behalf of our agriculturists. Even in this regard, for some reason, not easily explicable, they kept themselves scrupulously silent about the fate of our crores of zamindari tenants of U.P., C.P., Orissa, Bihar, Bengali Assam and Madras. Lord Curzon's challenge to Ramesh Chandra Dutt, an ex-President of the Congress that it was the Government which had done more to protect tenants from the rapacity of Zamindars, remained unanswered probably because the then leadership of the Congress was so over-whelmingly zamindari and capitalistic in its class content.

Champaran Struggle 1917-8

The next phase in the awakening of our Kisan owed its development and success to the leadership of Mahatma Gandhi and Rajendra Prasad in the famous Champaran struggle against the indigo planters, many of whom were Europeans, who were persecuting the local Bihari peasants to grow Indigo against their will on (Tinkathia) pain of paying higher taxes and collecting several illegal exactions. Mahatma Gandhi initiated the method for that time extremely novel and original, of conducting a systematic and authoritative enquiry into the real nature and degree of the sufferings of the peasants at the hands of the planters. Thousands of suffering peasants flocked round the Mahatma and Rajendra Prasad and detailed their woes. But the Provincial Government took fright and prohibited them from pursuing their enquiries. On their refusal to obey this prohibitory order, there arose a crisis, in which the arrest of Mahatma Gandhi and subsequent release were followed by the appointment of an enquiry Committee with Mahatmajee as one of its members. Eventually the Bihar Government accepted the recommendations of the Committee whose report bears the imprint of Mahatma's personality. An enactment based on the Report relieved peasants from their most immediate and pressing troubles and freed them from the special impost laid on them by the Indigo planters. But just as the earlier Congress agitation led by Ramesh Chunder Dutt against temporary settlements did not embrace the exploitation of our peasants by Zamindars, so also this agitation led by the Mahatma in Champaran did not lead up to any fight against the main causes for the terrible poverty and sufferings of Champaran peasants, namely the excessive rents and exorbitant incidence of debts. It may be because of Mahatmaji's growing habit which later on came to be considered as one of his political virtues of concentrating upon one thing at a time. But it does strike one as rather significant that both he and Rajendra Prasad should have remained scrupulously silent upon the ravages of the zamindari system and the extreme need for liberating peasants from its cluches. Anyhow, this Champaran Satyagraha movement of 1917 i.e. during the Great War had the excellent result of awakening not only of the Bihar peasantry but also the general public of India to the tremendous revolutionary potentialities latent in the bosom of our peasants.

Kaira Satyagraha

Soon the Kaira and Bardoli drought and the consequent failure of crops claimed the attention of Mahatama Gandhi. The half blind Bombay Government insisted upon its pound of flesh by demanding the payment of land revenue despite the inability of peasants to pay. Gandhiji's Satyagraha came to the rescue of these much harassed kisans and Bombay Government had also to eat the humble pie in the face of this rising peasant revolt led by such an implacable fighter. It suspended the kist collection. It was during this campaign that Com. Indulal Yagnik, now the Joint Secretary of the All India Kisan Committee received his first lessons in field work for our kisans. Even here Mahatmaji did not complicate his campaign by trying to tackle the other troubles of our kisans such as their indebtedness, alienations of lands.

These two campaigns succeeded in establishing Mahatmaji as a magic man of peasant satyagraha and to some extent awakening our peasants to the use of satyagraha for achieving their purposes. It is true that the great majority of our peasantry was still unaware of politics, and was therefore not politically affected by these triumphs. But they did open the eyes of a growing number of the educated kisans, like myself, to the political possibilities of our peasants' mass-action.

Non-Co-operation Movement

But it was left to the great nation-wide Non-co-operation movement, which succeeded in drawing in one effort millions of peasants with its magical slogan of 'Swaraj in one year,' into its orbit. It shook our peasants free from their age old political slumber and dragged them, almost against their traditions into the whirlpool of our national political life. For the first time they were told, to their great satisfaction and wonder, that it was quite legitimate for them to refuse to pay land revenue, the payment of which, they had come to look upon almost as a religious duty. To them, in those early days of our national movement of direct action and in that first flush of their political awakening, Swaraj meant freedom from all tax burdens and especially the abolition of land revenue. Naturally they hugged to their hearts both Mahatmaji's name and the slogan of 'Non-payment of Taxes.' When therefore Gandhiji commenced his preparations for his open conspiracy of 'Non-payment of taxes' campaign in Bardoli, the whole Kisan India opened its eyes and began to spontaneously refuse or delay the payment of land revenue or rent. Throughout India millions of peasants, believing that the end of the British Raj was within sight, abstained from paying their rents or revenue and began to watch political developments with bated breath. If only Mahatmajee had given the much wanted command to our Kisans not to pay their taxes, as was feared by the British and anticipated by our kisans, who knows if Lord Lloyd's fear of the destruction of British power in India might not have actually materialised. As it was, instead of that command, Mahatmaji suddenly withdrew the whole non-co-operation movement and thus left millions of our peasants as well as the country in mid-air.

With what consequences? Those lakhs of peasants alone know to their bitter cost. They came to be penalised in thousand and one ways by their zamindars, who not so long ago had been so terror-stricken and who were only too glad to wreak vengeance upon their kisans who had the temerity to hope for a better future; those millions of peasants and workers alone can tell what terrible disappointment they suffered when their very first hope of a bright life was frustrated and their aspiration of winning Swaraj was dashed to the ground. With the imprisonment of thousands of active Congressmen whose association with the peasantry was very intimate and with the return to quasi-normal life of the other disappointed and dazed Congressmen, our peasants found so few to fend for them and almost none to lead them in their struggles against the enraged British Government and its more cruel allies, the Zamindars.

Pedanandipad Campaign

The real revolutionary significance of this first mass upsurge of our peasantry can be guessed from the phenomenal and dramatic success of the following uprisings in particular. One took place in Pedanandipad area of Guntur District. There for a good few weeks, there was virtually Kisan Raj. In that area event the British mounted police and regular Military forces could not make peasants give them even information regarding the direction to any village pond or well, not to speak of giving any supplies of food or water or payment of taxes.

Oudh Kisan Rising

Laljee made an eloquent mention of this in his autobiography. There lakhs of peasants rose spontaneously against the oppressive zamindars and demanded not only Swaraj but also the removal of their suffering. It did not subside, even after the Bardoli debacle until the Government hurriedly passed the Oudh Rent Act of 1921 which conferred the permanency of tenure upon the tenants. Luckily for the Government, its ruse, played once before in Maharashtra soon after the Deccan riots of 1897, negotiating with a peasant rising by offering something to appease it, succeeded in Oudh also, with the result that the Agra tenants of the same Province have had to go without the benefit of permanency of tenure until in 1938 the Congress Government has introduced its bill to that effect.

Two other struggles need a mention in this connection, the No-tax campaign of Karnatak and the Moppla Rebellion of Malabar. The former bode fair to become as frighful an affair as that of Pedanandipad but the withdrawal of non-cooperation movement sabotaged it at its very early stage.

Moppla Rebellion

The latter proved to be disastrous to all concerned, except the British. In Malabar, Mopplas who are Moslems by religion are mostly either agricultural workers, or tenants or the most depressed section of intermediary landholders with or without personal cultivation. They were then being exploited mercilessly by the Nambudris who were the virtual owners of the land and who had the absolute right of electing any intermediary peasant, known as Kanamdar or any of the actual cultivators. In fact these Nambudris, who were Brahmins were often aided by Kanamdars, most of whom were Nairs and they were freely exercising their right to evict peasants from their homesteads and raising the rents at their will and pleasure. No wonder an agitation sprang up in the wake of the Religious Revivalist movement which later on was prostituted by the Justice Party. Its leaders were the late Sir M. Krishnan Nair and Mr. M.P. Narayana Menon. One joined the Justice Party and rose to be an executive Councillor of the Madras Government and the other entered the Congress and came to be condemned for transportation for life for the alleged crime of having incited Mopplas to wage war against His Majesty's Government to be released only in 1936.

This rent reduction and permanency of tenure agitation, awakened the peasants, both Hindus and Moslems to the need for political action. It helped Krishnan Nair to be returned to the Madras Legislative Council. It gave a tremendous initial significance to the Non-cooperation Movement of Malabar. But soon a communal turn was given by some very responsible Moslem leaders and all the pent up enemity and disgust of peasants in general and Moppllas in particular burst up like a volcano and resulted in blood-shed. The frightened Nambudris had in the meanwhile made common cause with the leaders of Kanamdars agreed with the Justice Party, of which the earstwhile leader of tenants M. Krishnan Nair was an important pillar, over a compromise tenancy legislation and rallied all the Hindus to aid them and thus helped to make the whole thing a communal fight. The poor peasants who were thus mislead by their religious leaders and intrigued by their landlords and deceived by their colleagues. The Hindu tenants who were in their turn humbugged by the Justice Party, rushed headlong with their false religious slogans of hostility and war against Hindus in general and their suicidal means of blood and fire. Thus in a few months the heroic peasants of Malabar were either mowed down by British fire or consigned to Andamans in all their thousands. This fight has become notorious for the train-tragedy in which nearly 80 Mopplas died of suffocation in a closed railway wagon and also for the treachery perpetrated upon our innocent peasants by religious leaders, reformist tenant agitators and the withdrawal of all Congress advice, leadership and support from the sufferers just at the right nick of time.

Sitarama Raju's Fight

In the wake of the failure of the Non-cooperation Movement and the six year sentence upon Mahatma Gandhi a dreadful gloom had set in all over the Country, except in a tiny quarter, it lies on one of the broad backs of the Eastern Ghats, in the Jeypore Zamindari and on the Borders of the Narsipatam Taluk. There was enacted one of the most romantic dramas of revolutionary life of modern India. Alluri Sitarama Raju a Kshatriya of west Godavari District, went there and befriended with the Koyas and other hill-people of that tract. He became a Sadhu, and an expert healer both by spiritual powers and herbs. He saw the sufferings of those ignorant but militant people helpless at the hands of forest and excise officials. His appeals to officials for mercy were in vain. Those hill-tribes were not allowed to carry on their 'Podu' or 'Jungle' cultivation. They were made to pay too many dues upon so many of their activities such as gathering fuel, grazing their cattle in forests, felling fuel, grass, fruit, or gum, gathered in the forest to any outsiders. Thus their very traditional mode of life was threatened by government. Raju saw no way out of it except through rebellion. When all his appeals for justice were in vain, he welcomed the spontaneous rising of those proud, martial and brave Koyas against the Government. That rising soon became a violent revolution and it was suppressed at great cost to human life on both sides and to the Indian finances, by a merciless and ruthless use of fire and iron by the British Government.

Thanks to the post-autonomy and Congress Governments, M.P. Narayan Menon and hundreds of other Malabar victims, and the few survivors of the Sitarama Raju's 'Pituri' were released recently.

Kamagatamaru

After the war another epoch of our peasant struggle began.

Just after the war the magic word went abroad that the British Prime Minister's plighted promise to India that Swaraj would be granted soon after the war was over was broken and that the word came for all patriots to strike their last blow at British Imperialism to wrest from it India's Swaraj. Mahatma Gandhi's weapon of Satyagraha evoked tremendous hopes in the hearts of our nationalists. It was in that atmosphere that hundreds of Punjab peasants flocked to the banner of revolution. Their brethren who had emigrated to Canada, U.S.A., and South America not only sent large sums of money but also despatched a shipload of men, money and ammunition to aid their revolutionary work. Hopes were raised all over the Punjab countryside of the impending struggle and advent of Swaraj. But alas, the British got scent of it, captured those famous Kamagatamaru heroes, clapped many more peasants of Punjab villages into jails and persecuted in an unspeakable fashion many thousands of the brave Sikh peasants for their share in that adventurous scheme.

The Aka movement of Hardoi in U.P. stirred up the peasantry of Sitapur, Raibarelli, Faizabad and several other Districts in 1922-23 *i.e.* just after the Bardoli withdrawal of Satyagraha and at the time of the Mopplla and Sitarama-Raju's 'Pituri'. It was led by Nadari Pari, an actual peasant and the whole countryside responded to him to a man. Government found it so hard to tackle it since actual peasants were at its head and the leaders were not specially wedded to the Gandhian ideas of non-violence in regard to every detail. Eventually it was suppressed as all other peasant struggles by the blood and fire of Government.

But all these great and spontaneous risings of our peasants from one end of the country to the other succeeded as nothing else had during the previous sixty years since the great Indian war of Independence, to bestir our peasants bring them into the whirlpool of our national politics, evoked in their hearts great and even extravagant hopes and encouraged them to dream glorious dreams of peace, plenty and prosperity on the advent of Swaraj. If not for anything else, atleast for having opened the eyes of crores of our peasants who would otherwise have continued to vegetate with their Curzonian contentment and sense of atrophy, and brought them once for all into our political area, the great Non-Cooperation Movement and Mahatmaji's slogan of 'Swaraj within one year' were more than justified. But how one wishes that the Congress had provided some defence forces to protect our peasants on their retreat. How one deplores the failure of our leaders to take a more realistic view of things and prevented such a sudden and almost heartless (one is almost tempted to say, irresponsible) withdrawal of Congress support from our peasants. Three conclusions force themselves upon our minds as a result of this cursory survey of the effect of introduction national politics into the life of our peasants, since 1917, by Mahatma Gandhi and his followers, working through the Indian National Congress. That our peasants were taken by surprise, they had either to absorb the political thought of the day even if there were one or were not provided with any political machinery in the shape of a self-confident, self-conscious and local autonomous Congress or Kisan organisation to stand up for them through thick and thin and to constantly guide them. Instead as soon as Mahatmaji withdrew his Non co-operation movement and abandoned all aggressive political action, the local Congress Committees went limp and Congressmen became devoid of any initiative or leadership. Indeed Congress had fought shy of having anything more to do with Moppllas of Koyas or U.P. or Punjab Kisans or others and Congressmen instantly dropped all Kisan work. Need one wonder then if all over India, our peasantry quickly relapsed into their traditional political somnombulence, nursing an awful bitterness against our politicians and their own miserable fate.

The second conclusion is that in too many cases were our peasants struggles exploited either by communalists or religious maniacs who had little respect to the creed of non-violence, that our peasants were defenceless against their bad leadership, denied as they had been of any political training, organisational ability or knowledge of the effects and consequences of agitational work, which could be gained only through their active participation in their class or political organisations. Naturally there was too much exhibition of violence at the fag end of our kisan struggles of those hectic days of 1920-23 and it frightened away our Congressmen and thus denied them of any active sympathetic, day to day support and guidance of the Congress, which they then needed much more than at any other time.

The third conclusion is that owing to their abandonment by the Congress once their revolutionary temper went beyond the mild expectations of the Congress leaders and thus upset the calculations of the reformist leaders of the Congress of different provinces of these days by threatening to shake to their roots the very economic foundation of society, our peasants came in for the cruel intentions of Government and zamindars and were persecuted hopelessly for years in many a way.

It was in 1923 July-December, just when the members of Moppla rebellion were dying out and the Sitarama Raju's fight was going on that I had begun to organise Ryots Associations (or Kisan Sabhas as they had later on come to be known all over India) Agricultural and Labour Unions in the Andhra on my return from England. I met with instantaneous success in Guntur District with the ryots since they were all disillusioned about the Government and the Justice Party which persuaded them into the belief that no reprisals would be taken against them for their support to the Pedanandipadu No-tax campaign and later on, inflicted heavy penal-rates of assessment for their having dared to support the Congress to bring 'Swaraj within one year' also helped them to rally to my call to organize themselves into Ryots Associations.

It was just at that time that a very bitter controversy was going on between the pro-changers headed by the late Moti Lal Nehru and C.R. Das and No-changers led by Srijit C. Rajagopalachari as to whether Congress should enter the legislatures or not. Though in several provinces, Swaraj parties were organised the Congressmen went into legislatures under their auspices, in the Andhra and in Guntur District in particular, orthodox Congress leaders succeeded in preventing any great development of the Swaraj Party. Naturally this gave an opportunity to our Ryots Association to formulate its Election Manifesto, set up a selection committee and nominate its candidates and make them sign the peasants pledge and conduct the electioneering on purely peasants lines. At all the stages, even orthodox Congress leaders cooperated with our Ryots Association. While the Non-Brahmin Party eschewed all Brahmin candidates, our Ryots Association selected a Brahmin candidate, thus demonstrating at its very inception, its non-communal character and politics. Three out of its four candidates were successful. One was sent to the Central Assembly and two to the local council and two of them eventually joined the Congress and distinguished themselves in the country's cause. This unexpected success of the Ryots Association and the splendid response given by peasants to its call excited the fear of Government and jealously of some Congressmen and most of the justicites. So from all sides we were attacked about the further need for such associations. We could have gone on developing Ryots Associations all over the province if only we had a sufficient number of workers to carry on propaganda. Unfortunately we had none and we did not then think of organising a Kisan school to train youths for this work and to develop a selfrelient and independent cadre or comrades for this extra congress work. Since neither the local congress workers who were themselves few in number and hardpressed for time and resources nor peasants themselves were forthcoming to aid us. Our Ryots Associations marked very little progress between 1924-1926, beyond spreading themselves to West Godavari and Krishna Districts also and spreading and popularising the idea of independent class organisations for peasants and workers.

Bihar and U.P. Kisan Sabhas of 1926-27

In 1926—some comrades began to organise Kisan Sabhas in Bengal, Punjab and U.P. on more or less idealistic lines with a revolutionary programme. As they were too often mistaken for communist organisations by the local Governments which were only too anxious to nip in the bud everything that savoured of revolutionary temper, they were banned before they could take deep roots.

CHAPTER 6

The Peasant Revolt

Recent researches amply refute a fairly widespread assumption that unlike in China and some other countries peasant revolts in India, even during British Rule, were a rare and insignificant phenomenon. Indian peasants did not understandably behave in quite the same way as the peasants in other countries did. (Indeed, even in India, the peasant revolts scarcely conformed to any particular pattern.) The assumption about the meekness and submissiveness of the Indian peasantry (which is sometimes explained in terms of the role of certain institutions such as the caste system) is, however, largely unfounded, and particularly in the Presidency of Bengal, the number of peasant revolts during British rule, was far from negligible. The revolt of the Pabna peasants (1873) can be taken as an illustration of a significant type of such revolts.

1. Two notable Things about Ishafshahi, the Main Centre of the Revolt

The centre of the revolt was the Ishafshahi pargana belonging to the Sirajganj sub-division of the district of Pabna. Though the revolt eventually spread beyond it, it was here that 'the movement . . . has chiefly prevailed" during 1873 and continued for long afterwards. The origin of the revolt in this pargana was not coincidental, and two particular things about it are notable in this connection. The pargana, a large tract containing 272 separate estates with 695 villages, was the most populous and flourishing of the Serajgunge sub-districts', as the Inspector General of Police once described it in 1872. Its agricultural resources had, as noted later, considerably increased over the years. A growing population necessitated much new cultivation and also a more intensive land use in considerable areas, a process to which the improving quality of the land there contributed not a little. The increase since the Crimean war (1854-55) in the cultivation of jute, a highly remunerative cash crop for the cultivators, had introduced a fresh element of dynamism in the economy. This encouraged reclamation of waste lands, and the migration of the peasant population from the western parganas of the district suffering from the endemic outbreaks of malaria, a movement considerably induced by the growing jute cultivation in the eastern paraganas, further stimulated the process. These developments inevitably increased the market value of the land, and encouraged the zamindars to increase rent, and increased rent, often enforced by dubious devices, was undoubtedly one of the greatest solvents of established relations in rural Bengal. The second notable thing about the pargana was the particular nature of estate—management by the leading zamindars. The 'principal' and presumably the largest estates of the pargana (not the entire pargana, as is sometimes thought) were owned by five zamindari families: the Tagores of Calcutta, the Sannyals of Shalop, the Banerjis of Dacca, the Bhaduris of Porjana and the Pakrassis of Thul. A marked feature of estate-management by such zamindars, except perhaps the Tagores of Calcutta, was a heavy reliance on extra-legal or illegal coercions, including physical violence, for the purpose of increasing rent and for other related purposes. Such practices were scarcely recent innovations, and seem to have been more or less systematically adopted from the very beginning of the purchases of such estates. Not that such practices were rare elsewhere. In these big estates, however, they had two striking features. A far larger peasant community was simultaneously affected by them. Secondly, the owners of these estates also happened to be markedly rich persons, and the command over enormous resources undoubtedly largely accounted for their determination, (particularly in the cases of the Banerjis, the Sannyals, and the Pakrasis) to go to any length to achieve their purposes. They abhorred the idea of compromises with the peasantry, and the latter's attitude naturally stiffened as a result. Peasants thus deciding to rebel had a reassuring thing to count upon: the bitterness of a large peasant group against the zamindars and the possibility of drawing it into the movement when it actually occurred.

1.a The Story of the Revolt

The organised revolt which the contemporaries called *Proja Vidroha* and which visibly alarmed Government and prompted them to quick actions for coping with the so-called 'law and order' situation first occurred in May 1873 and continued in this form for two or three months. This was, however, far from an abrupt and unexpected explosion. The earlier phase of the movement had only casually been mentioned in the official reports, mainly because it was too feeble to survive the zamindars, counter—offensive and also because, despite occasional breaches of 'peace', it did not create a serious law and order problem.

The resistance of the peasants prior to 1873 is evident from the earlier cases of violence with which the zamindars had reacted. Such violence was presumably necessitated by the peasants' opposition to what the zamindars had asked for. Such cases were very many. The Sub-divisional Officer of Ishafshahi while identifying the rent question as the main source of the intensifying bitterness between the zamindars and the peasants of the region thus wrote of the former's methods in this:

> 'The zemindar wishing to raise rents commences by gaining over for a consideration a few headmen, who carry with them a small party, generally composed of the more idle and violent villagers, who look for employment and pay as long as the quarrel lasts. The ryots are called to the agent's office, and when there, give way and promise anything. On their return home, they refuse to hold by the compact, and then they are considered to be at open feud with the zamindars and the minority who stand by him. This is the state of things, in a great number of villages, and I *know many in which it has continued for years.'*

Nolan, Assistant Magistrate of Sirajganj, had similar experiences:

> 'Judging only from the cases which have come before me judicially, and being regularly proved, it is clear that the zemindars of Eshafshahi are a turbulent set of men, without any respect for law and very little for life, in their dealings with their ryots and with one another. This compels those who have to deal with them to be firm, and if weak to unite.

This was scarcely a recent phenomenon. In the estates of the Sannyals 'who reside in the centre of the pergunnah, and are the largest landowners, so that their demeanour has given a character to the whole', such practices were about thirty years old. Nolan punished a member of the family 'for encouraging by his presence in the village the plunder of the house of a headman of considerable wealth, because he refused to consent to an enhancement. Some other families were no less notorious: The Bhadurys once sent a band of up-country men with swords to make the ryots pay income-tax. Their *burkundazes* looted Tearbond village three years ago (1870), and killed a ryot with a spear in the right. . . . The agents of Bandopadhya family kidnapped a ryot this year on his return from the moonsilt's court, and kept him ten days in confinement.

That such violence continued to recur suggests that this eventually paid, despite the prices which the zemindars had occasionally to pay for this. The sporadic resistance by the peasantry was evidently not enough to daunt them. It seems the peasants could not hold out for long, and gave in. This is evident from the success of the zemindars in collecting numerous *abwabs* and also in increasing the rate of rent, mainly by means of altering the standard of measurement and also of converting the *abwabs* into a kind of 'legal' rent. As a consequence,

> 'in time the total amount collected per *bigah* in Eshafshahi came to be much larger than in the neighbouring lands of other pergunnahs, perhaps treble the rate of Barabazar, where the land is at least equally portable, and which not only adjoins, but interlace with Esafshahi'.

That coercion and violence had a major role in such success of the zamindars is evident from the fact that the peasants had seldom formally consented to such rent increases, and that they questioned their legality on suitable occasions. However, whatever the reasons, the peasants, except in 'very few cases', preferred not to contest zamindars' claims, in courts, and even in such cases 'the decisions of the courts were contradictory'. Not that such legal fights were entirely futile. The zamindars themselves admitted the illegality of certain cesses. The area of disagreement was still very large, and the peasants' discontent had been simmering.

The zamindars, however, continued to ignore it, and certain developments, which will be explained later, made them more determined in this. Till then they had been content with collecting the *abwabs* as far as possible, without asking for any alteration in the *asal* rate. They now decided to consolidate the *abwabs* with the *asal*, fearing that unless this was quickly done a considerable part of their rental income would be in danger. This involved a large increase in the *asal* rate of the peasants. The Tagore family, for instance, 'demanded an increase, first of eight annas, them of 4 annas per rupee, upon a rent already high'. The question, however, was to enforce the demand. The existing law did provide for an increase of rent. However, the grounds on which this was permissible did not quite suit the zamindars at the moment. Rent could be increased where cultivation had increased, or the value of the agricultural products had risen, or where the rent was lower than the one in the neighbourhood, in spite of a similarity in the quality of the lands in the two places. Since what the zamindars wanted was a consolidation of the *awabs* with the *asal*, such legal provisions did not help them much. The existing law, however, provided a way out. The legal constraints on the increase of rent were not binding where contractual agreements empowered a zamindar to do it. Some zamindars sought to take advantage of this big loophole in the law, and the Banerji family took the lead. The family succeeded in getting some peasants to consent to agreements, the deeds of which were eventually registered, giving it enormous powers in regard to matters concerning rent. The peasants were made to agree to pay not only the high rent rates of the time, but also the cesses which the zamindars would impose from time to time in future.

A new standard of measurement with a pole of 14 cubits 14 fingers, each cubit being 18 inches and not 23.75 inches as before was now introduced. The zamindars did feel that such acts of their would provoke opposition. The new agreements were therefore also designed to provide against this eventuality. The zamindars claimed powers 'to eject the ryots whenever they might quarrel'.

Despite the intital successes of the Benerji family in this, as the registration of a large number of such deeds of agreements showed, the opposition which the zamindars sensed did not take long to come. The village Urkandi took the lead in this. Some peasants there questioned the validity of such aggreements, ostensibly by repudiating the authority of the agent, who had been previously asked to receive those deeds on behalf of the peasantry. The Banerjis, knowing as they did what was happening, refused to give in, and feeling that a retreat at this stage would utterly ruin their cause decided to strike back. They had evidently miscalculated the strength of the rebels' feelings, and believed the peasants could still be cowed by terror and by threats of legal actions. Forty-three peasants were thus sued in the Munsiff's court at Shazadpur, the ostensible allegation being that they had stopped paying rent though they had been paying it for the last few years. The Munsiff, assuming the genuineness of the measurement papers produced by the Banerjis, decided the case against the peasants. (April, 1872). The peasants were, however, far from demoralised, and decided not to give up the legal fight. Their petition to a superior court asking for a review of the case particularly emphasised the untrustworthiness of the zamindar's evidence, and the Civil Judge of Rajshahi did find that the measurement papers were all forged, and reversed the decision of the lower court, (December, 1872).

This victory proved a decisive turn in the development of the resistance movement. The hazards of a defeat in this encounter were evidently enormous, and in view of the big difference between the rent rate claimed by the Banerjis and the one which the Civil Judge had decreed, as the following table shows, the peasants had every reason to have been jubilant.

Isu Sirdar of Village Urkandi

(1) Type of land	(2) The rate claimed by the zamindar	(3) The rate decreed by the Judge	(4) % of the difference (approx.)
Homestead	Rs. 5-10	Rs. 2-8	-55
Fasali	Rs. 1-14	Rs. 0-10	-66
	Shonai Paramanik of Village Doolabari		
Homestead	Rs. 3-12	Rs. 2-8	-33
Fasali	Rs. 1-11	Rs. 0-10	-63

The peasants, morale was understandably high. Their jubilation was only partly due to the immediate economic gains which this victory had ensured. The judgement in this case was reassuring to the peasants for a far more important reason: it was an official action which has exposed the misdeeds of the zamindars, and the peasants felt they could consequently rely in future on the official machinery in their fight against such misdeeds. This conviction gave them immense moral strength. Other incidents which had happened in the meantime added to it. During the course of the case one of the peasants involved therein was kidnapped by an agent of the Banerjis. The local administration quickly intervened, punishing the offender and setting the peasant free.

There is no doubt that the case and some of its aftermaths decisively influenced the subsequent plans of the rebel peasants. Nolan, Assistant Magistrate of Sirajganj, was not sure 'whether these and some other successes in the courts turned the scale, or the movement was the natural result of the reaction against exorbitant demands after the first surprise was over. Taylor, Magistrate of Pabna, was more emphatic:

> 'The rest of the ryots, encouraged by the result of these suits, refused to execute *caboonuts* and even those who had executed them and presented them for registry refused to deliver them to the zamindars when returned by the registry court; they repudiated certain payments, whether rent or illegal cesses which had been, from time to time, added to their dues, and united for the purpose of mutual aid and support.'

The Commissioner of Rajshahy explained how this helped the movement: It is quite clear to me that the effect of such a number of decisions in favour of the villagers which had successfully held out would be to facilitate the spread of discontent in neighbouring villages.

The effects were particularly visible in those regions where big pockets of resistance had already emerged. For instance, the peasants of Thul Chur resisted the recent income tax cess and captured those who came to compel them to pay. Jugtollah in the Sannyal's estate has never yielded to any recent demand. And there were other villages similarly situated. Such resistance necessitated a formal organisation, and the particular devices of the zamindars, that is, the reliance on 'the usual weapons of force and fraud, false accusation of riot and attacks by clubmen, eventually resulted in strengthening it, since the ryots had thereby acquired a certain familiarity with criminal courts, and with the organisation necessary for the conduct of a dispute with unscrupulous zamindars'. The story of the peasants' victory in the Banerji's estates now immensely reassured them, and they joined the wider movement without the slightest hesitation.

February to July 1873 were crucial months for the growth of the movement. 'In the spring the ryots commenced to organise themselves for systematic resistance. . . . In May the League spread'. By the beginning of June, nearly the whole of the Banerjis' estates, 'with the most trifling exceptions', were engulfed. By the end of June two hundred and sixty nine villages out of the total of six hundred and ninety five in Ishafshahi had joined the movement, and at the time Nolan was reporting (1 July 1873), he found that 'ten or twelve more come in daily'. The movement soon spread to the estates of the Tagores, who unlike the Banerjis and the Sannyals had seldom had recourse to violent methods for increasing rent, and were ready for compromises. Dwijendra Nath Tagore, a member of the family, thus wrote to the Government of Bengal on 1 July, 1873: 'the feeling of insecurity pervading the villages is so great that danger is apprehended at any place and every moment, and unless vigorous and prompt measures be adopted . . . the mischief will spread far and wide'. It was also during July that the movement spread beyond the Sirajganj sub-division to the

Sadar. The preventive measures of the Government undoubtedly resulted in weakening the rebel organisation, mainly by disrupting the links between its different units. During the last few. days of July the ryots evidently failed, in some places at least. To strike back as effectively as before when the zamindars retaliated. The momentum of the movement, however, does not seem to have been lost. The movement further spread, and there were indications that the zamindars had begun to relent, except in the cases of determined zamindars like the Banerjis.

The two contrasting developments—the increasing evidence on the one hand, of a certain flexibility in the attitude of the zamindars, and the growth of the movement despite it on the other—have been thus reviewed in the official reports on the situation as it prevailed at about the end of August:

> There have been compromises in many villages, the zamindars giving up a small portion of their demand. Seven or eight villages have received leases at reduced rates. In one a principal sharer let out the land for ever at fixed rates. Other zamindars are getting ryots to pay by promising that whatever terms are in the end gained by the unionists will be extended in them.
>
> But on the other hand the movement is extending itself very rapidly to new grounds. Many estates which were formerly supposed to be settled, are joining the union. This is the case particularly in the north, towards Bograh, and I have authentic information that ryots of that district are giving in their adherence. In fact the progress which was arrested by the terror caused by the punishment of those who took part in them, is now going on as rapidly as ever. Even villagers who appear to be on good terms with their zemindars refuse to pay cesses which they regard as illegal, but the zamindars consider a part of their rent'.
>
> There is hardly any portion of the district from which ryots have not come in and filed petitions praying for protection against zemindars, which is the mode whereby they declare their adhesion to the rent union. ...'

A perceptible change seemed to have occurred by October and November. The revolt in its old form had almost disappeared. Such was at least the general impression of the local officers who had been touring the affected areas. The Pabna Magistrate's version that 'the disturbances had been suppressed' provides a clue to an understanding of the change. As we have noted later, the firm 'law and order' measures of the Government crippled the movement more than anything else, and the elaborate organisation which the rebels had built up over these months evidently crumbled.

However, the spirit of the revolt survived. The virtual breakdown of communication between the different units of operations scarcely amounted to a formal dissolution of the united movement, in the sense that different villages were now left to themselves, taking decisions on fundamental issues independent of what the rebels in the neighbourhood or elsewhere felt about it. Within a village the peasants seem to have been still bound by a kind of oath not to deal with the zamindars individually. The usual strategy of the zamindars during such clashes, that is, to win over some leading the unity in the movement, seldom worked now. The failure of the zamindars in this, particularly when all the peasants were not firmly committed to the rebel cause (the Pabna Magistrate found that even in the estates of the Tagores who were far less obdurate than some other leading zamindars 'about half the ryots were not *bedrohee* (rebellious'), is a measure of the strength of the peasants' convictions.

The obstinacy of most of the principal zamindars had of course a role to play in sustaining the militancy of the rebels. Except the Tagores and a number of 'petty landholders' who were understandably scared by the prospects of losing their rental income for an indefinite length of time, the zamindars firmly resolved not to yield, and this reinforced the inflexibility of the peasants' attitudes, since they felt the zamindars would construe any vacillation as a sign of weakness, and strike back hard.

A certain organisation for taking collective decisions seems to have still survived, though the appropriate machinery for enforcing such decisions was lacking. Taylor during his tour came across a number of instances where individual peasants or isolated groups of peasants arguing with him were reluctant to commit themselves to a decision, and even where they arrived at one, sometimes they retracted soon after returning from their villages. This happened presumably because the hard core of the rebels did not approve of this decision. The failure of the compromise talk in the estates of the Tagores can be taken as an illustration. The Tagores agreed to go to quite a length towards conceding the ryots' demands, and at one point Taylor felt almost sure of finalising an agreement. The talk eventually broke down with the ryots failing to reach an agreed decision. This also happened in the estates of some minor zamindars like Banwarilal. He went farther than the Tagores and offered to accept the rent rates which, according to the peasants themselves, were admitted in the court. 'But the ryots, nevertheless, will not give in, the fact being that so long as nothing is done in the Banerjees' estates no compromise would be effected anywhere'.

Such an attitude remained unchanged even by about the middle of November, 1873. The Magistrate's Diary of 17 November reads: Conferred with the ryots and talookdars, and found that, as a rule, the ryots had nothing really to complain of, but were simply determined to refuse rents so long as the majority of ryots did so. . . . Some ryots boldly admitted that they would not pay rents so long as others refused'. Taylor thus explains this:

> 'The fact is that they are members of a combination and cannot and will not arrange their disputes unless associates and neighbours also agree to the compromise. It is to be remembered also that all these estates are so interlaced and the ryots living on them so connected by family or marriage ties that it is most difficult to deal with one at a time'.

No signs of change were visible even by the end of the year 'We then remain', Taylor despairingly wrote in his letter of 20 December, 1873, 'faced with the fact that a large body of ryots are at open feud with their zamindars and are either paying the rent they acknowledge to be due into court, or are preparing to do so'.

2. Origins of the Movement

The narrative of the growth of the resistance has occasionally referred to the crucial role of the rent question in this. The rent question in this case (and also in general) was essentially related to the attempts of the zamindars at increasing rent, and the rural tensions of the time were more or less universally explained in such terms. 'Enhancement', as a Collector of Midnapur once observed, 'is the principal disturbing cause in the harmony of rural life throughout Bengal. Whenever a pergunnah is in a restless, disturbed, troublesome state, the Magistrate need not ask what the cause is. He knows that beforehand'.

What were the specific features and distinctiveness of the rent question in Pabna at the time ? What led the zamindars to increase rent? Why did they increase rent in some particular ways rather than the others? Why did the peasantry unitedly resist it? Such questions need to be examined. Such an examination is particularly worthwhile in view of the fact that the essence of the rent question is apt to be obscured because of the excessive emphasis on the alleged despotism or high-handedness of the zamindars. The zamindar did behave despotically. The pertinent question, however, is to account for it. In fact a number of estates where such highhandedness of the zamindars was largely non-existent were also eventually convulsed by the revolt.

Those who tend to blame the revolt primarily on such despotism seem to question the justifiability of any kind of rent increase. This is, however, a questionable position to take. The existing law did provide for an increase of rent, and peasants themselves admitted it. They seldom questioned its permissibility where cultivation had increased and where despite an essential similarity in the quality of the lands rent rates for some had for long been lower than those for the others. The point of dispute was the size of the increase the zamindars asked for from time to time.

In explaining the increase of rent by the zamindars stress has sometimes been laid on the so-called elements of 'speculative investment' in the purchases of landed estates. The presence of such speculative elements is, however, a point to be established and not one to be just assumed. 'Speculative investment' is a valid concept in the context of the presence of other viable alternatives for a prontable employment of the liquid cash of such persons concerned, and the purchase of landed estates was preferred because of a comparatively higher rate of return from these. It is, however, doubtful if the number of such cases was significant. Moneyed persons seem to have been persuaded to transfer part of their fortunes to the purchase of landed estates mainly by the prospects of a secure income from land over a fairly long period rather than by the prospects of a larger return on their capital in the short period compared to the rate of return on other kinds of investments. Indeed, with the increasing evidence of the hazards to which such moneyed persons were exposed where they decided to continue the level of their investment in the non-agrarian sectors the scope for a rational calculation of the comparative rates of return from different sources was rapidly diminishing, (this occurred, for instance, during the period between 1826 and 1848), and the concept of 'speculative investment' was therefore largely irrelevant under the circumstances.

Purchasers of estates were normally more energetic than the old established local families in the matter of increasing rent, and the leading new zamindars of Eshafshahi were not any exceptions. The movement of rent in the pargana and its phases are impertectly known. Official reports suggest that the new zamindars sought to increase rent and thus antagonised the peasantry from the very beginning. What led the zamindars to this is, however, inadequately explained. We have some-what better information about some of the later increases, and there is scarcely any doubt that the agricultural resources of the region had considerably increased in the meantime. Kailash Chandra Mukherji, who was a practising lawyer at a law-court in Shazadpur, and was asked by the Government to examine some aspects of the rent question, 'consulted' for the purpose all my experienced pleaders, who have acted both on the part of the zamindars and ryots', and thus commented on this phenomenon:

> 'It is known to all the people that the lands of this district were marshy and very sandy before, which hardly yielded one crop before: and some lands yielded only *chinwa* and other coarse crops; but by degrees the lands have naturally improved, and have yielded sometimes three crops'.

Indeed, by the time of the revolt Eshafshahi had become the 'most populous and flourishing' region in the district. (Some of the factors in this have been noted earlier.) The increasing resources 'naturally excited the jealously of the Zamindars', and they readily claimed a share. They were, however, prudent not to after the existing rate of rent as far as possible, and followed the more or less general custom of asking for a few more *abwabs*. However, as Mukherji noted, 'they demanded gradually an increase, and when for some years the ryots paid their demand, they added the amount increased in the ryots' jummas and treated the entire sum as their lawful rent'. The real rent rates and the *abwabs* were thus eventually so much mixed up that it became nearly impossible in very many places to identify such rates, and also the composition of the *abwabs*.

Rent Act X of 1859 sought to clarify the grounds on which rent increases were permissible, but this scarcely helped matters. Zamindars found them largely impracticable. Two old grounds were retained. Increase of rent was permissible where ryots had added to their original holdings. This, obviously, did not affect the *rate* of rent. Secondly, where the rent rate on a particular class of land was lower than the *pargana nirikh* i.e. the 'prevailing rate', on similar lands in 'adjacent places' zamindars could raise the lower rate to the level of the 'prevailing rate'. Act X of 1859 added a new ground: the legality of raising the rent rate where the value of the produce had increased, and the main factor in this that was emphasised at the time was the phenomenon of rising prices.

Enforcement of such grounds was most often a frustrating job for the zamindars. The 'prevailing rate' was mostly a myth. Nolan thus commented on it:

> What is a prevalent rent rate? . . . I have not seen a case in which evidence was laid before the court which would have enabled a reasonable man to come to decision on this point Rates vary so much from village to village that it is impossible to say that one rate is prevalent. Then there is no means of ascertaining what places are to be considered adjacent'.

It was a meaningful concept only where the rent rates were based on the classification of soils, which was rare in Bengal.

Typically, a peasant paid rent for his entire holding composed of the homestead and the arable land containing oils of different qualities. Zamindars intending to enhance rent on the basis of this rule had not only to prove the similarity of specific plots, but also the general similarity of holdings'. This was often an impossible task. Even where the rent rates were once based on the classification of soils, other circumstances obscured and, in some places, obliterated their traces. Zamindars, with their notoriously illkept accounts, seldom succeeded in identifying whatever traces had survived.

The rule relating to the increase in the value of the produce was not any more helpful to the zamindars. In the beginning they were only rarely keen on making use of it, and it was the European indigo planters who took the lead in this. (With the revolt of the indigo peasants in 1859 the planters decided to use a quick increase of rent on its basis as an instrument of coercion. The peasants were asked to choose between the continuation of indigo cultivation and the liability to pay a considerably increased rent). Zamindars thereafter followed the example and partially succeeded. However, such successes were becoming increasingly rare, particularly after the transference of the rent cases from the revenue officers to the civil courts by the Bengal Act VIII of 1869. The Bengal Board of Revenue thus accounted for this. Zamindars had numerous formalities to fulfil for winning the rent suits in the civil courts, and the onus of establishing their case by full legal proof lay entirely on them. Suits were often rejected because of the inadequacy of the evidence which zamindars provided on the past history of prices and rent. As long as the revenue officers tried them, the zamindars won very many suits despite their failure to provide all the necessary evidence.

> The Revenue officers seem to have entered upon the cases . . . with the knowledge that, as a rule, prices of produce had risen very much . . ., and that, where rents had not been recently revised, they were in general far below the normal competitive rates; hence they were satisfied with such evidence as was adducible.

Things changed with the transference of the rent suits to the civil courts. The courts, unlike the revenue officers, did not assume the fact of the price rise, but relied exclusively on the ordinary rules of evidence. Zamindars found it extremely difficult to prove when rent was previously fixed and what was at that time the gross value of the produce.

> The zamindars soon found that a large proportion of their suits were defeated by preliminary objections, and even when they did reach a trial on the merits, so difficult was it to supply such evidence as would satisfy the courts, that almost without exception the cases broke down.

The rapid growth off jute cultivation and the belief of the zamindars that jute had enriched its growers tempted the zamindars to increase their rent. Act X was not much use to them either in this. A higher differential rent on jute lands on the ground that jute was a more remunerative crop than rice was not legally permissible. They could have made out a case for increase of rent where jute had permanently replaced rice, (so that the entire holdings of the jute peasants had been devoted to jute) and where the prices of jute tended to rise over the years. In fact, however, jute seldom occupied more than one-third to one-fourth of the holdings of a peasant. Rent in Bengal was mostly assessed on the entire holdings of individual peasants. So even assuming that the zamindar could prove that the prices of raw jute had risen, how could he establish his cases for an increase of rent on the entire holdings of the peasants merely on the basis of the increased value of the produce of a small part of such holdings? Moreover, zamindars scarcely knew how much of their holdings the individual jute peasants cultivated with jute. Again, the area under jute cultivation largely depended on the movement of jute prices, and such prices widely fluctuated.

Not that the zamindars invariably failed in increasing rent in such cases. In Shazadpur, for instance, as Kailash Chandra Mukherji found, 'land which yields three kinds of crops per annum has the larger share of rent, especially the land which yields jute plants'. Such successes were however limited.

Since the existing law did not help the zamindars much in regard to an increase of rent, they tended to rely on extra-legal measures for this, particularly where they were convinced of a recent improvement in the agricultural resources, and consequently of the propriety of their claim for a share in these. However, partly because the peasants strongly felt over an alteration in the rate of rent and partly because the zamindars did not bother much about the composition of the total rent payment as long as the system assured them of an increase from time to time the zamindars usually preferred to add a few more *abwabs* to the existing rent demand.

The system served the zamindars well, and it would perhaps have been continued for sometime more but for some other developments, which led the zamindars to feel that it was not any longer safe to continue it. Two recent measures of the Government particularly frightened the zamindars. Campbell, Lieutenant Governor of the time, was determined to suppress the *abwabs* and ordered an investigation into their nature in the different districts. The second measure of Campbell, which appeared equally ominous to the zamindars, was to ask from them details of their rental income from various sources, since it was on such estimates of income in different zamindar is that the distribution of the recently introduced road cess would be based, and zamindars were threatened with severe penalties in cases of false returns. The zamindars feared that the numerous *abwabs* from which a sizable part of their rental income was derived would soon be brought to light. Indeed, they seem to have been frightened as much by such measures as by the particular change in the attitude of the Government towards them which had prompted such measures. The zamidars were aware of the pro-ryot sympathies of Campbell and also that he meant business. Moreover, though the Government intended to keep secret the investigation into the *abwabs*, the peasants somehow came to know of this, and construed it into a kind of disapproval of such *abwabs* on the part of Government. This had perhaps much to do with the opposition of the peasants at the time to such *abwabs* in various parts of eastern Bengal districts.

The zamindars decided to act quickly and wanted the existing *abwabs* consolidated with the rent. Their stakes were great, and they risked losing a sizable part of their income by any delay. They intended to make up also for part of the loss which the liability to pay the road cess would eventually involve. How much they feared they would lose without this consolidation is inferable from the quantum of increase in the rent that they asked for. The Tagore family demanded an increase, first of eight annas, then of four annas per rupee, upon a rent already high'. The Banerjis asked for a larger increase—an increase of more than 100%. At the same time they were cautious not to leave anything to chances, and in order to prevent the ryots from backing out of their verbal promises they sought to bind them by formal legal documents.

The high-handedness of the zamindars was thus only partially attributable to their alleged proneness to violence, (Some zamindars were undoubtedly capable of a greater violence than the others). It had a complex background. The right of a zamindar to increase rent was admitted by the country's law. The difficulties of the zamindars in this were, however, very many. No doubt they were themselves to blame for some of these. The estates were poorly managed, the accounts were ill-kept, and their understanding of the economic situation was imperfect. However, the existing law relating to increase of rent was also inadequate and ambiguous, and made the zamindars' difficulties insuperable at times, particularly where an alternation in the rate of rent was involved. This led the zamindars to adopt devices which, though not legal, assured them of a certain increase in the rent. The peasants occasionally protested, without endangering in most cases the normal income of the zamindars. Such a danger appeared imminent as a result of certain measures during Campbell's administration, and the only means of averting it, which was conceivable to them at the time, was to consolidate the existing rent rate with the *abwabs,* supporting their claim as far as possible by formal legal agreements. The apparatus of violence which the zamindars had devised and refined over the years perhaps came into existence independently of such developments, or was only partially related to these (the recurring inter-zamindari quarrels being a more decisive factor in this), but this could be readily used on such occasions as these.

The consolidation of the *asal* with the *abwabs* was an exceptional demand for the peasants to meet. The zamindars probably asked for more than what the admissible *abwabs* were worth, fearing that such a source of income would be soon gone for ever. The peasants would lose even where the consolidation did not include any additional *abwabs*. They did accept certain *abwabs*, but questioned the legality of many more. They, however, continued to pay them, hoping that they would repudiate them when suitable occasions came. The consolidation would preclude this.

The increased rent quantum would bear hard upon the peasants even in normal times. The agricultural depression of the time aggravated the situation in very many regions. The depression assumed the form of a sharp fall in the prices of agricultural commodities, particularly jute and rice.

The cultivation of jute as a commercial crop rapidly increased, particularly since the 1850's . The Crimean war (1854-55) had a decisive role to play in this. The war cut off the supply of flax, the main source of which was Russia. The Dundee mills looked for a substitute and Bengal jute provided it. The war ended soon, but the position of jute in the international market remained unshakable. The cultivation of jute was stimulated by the increasing consumption of raw jute in the new jute mills around Calcutta, a development made possible by the coming of the railway age and the exploitation of the coal mines, which provided an easy source of power for such mills. Judging by the exports the jute market continued to expand since then. A minor crisis intervened in the years between 1866 and 1868, but the recovery was quick. In 1872-73 came the first major setback, and the first big fall in jute prices, after a long period of continuous expansion of jute cultivation since the Crimean war, occurred during this period. The recovery from the crisis of 1866-68 was followed by a boom, and, according to the Jute Commission of 1873, an enormous increase in the jute cultivation occurred during 1872-73. However, to great disappointment of the growers prices soon slumped. We do not know what exactly was the demand position in that year. Contemporary reports suggest that the poor quality of jute of the year had a big role to play in depressing the demand, though we are not told if this alone had caused the entire fall in the demand. The inferior quality of jute–a well-founded complaint according to the Jute

Commission, was due partly to the wrong choice of lands by the peasants in their haste to produce as much as possible. The Jute Commission emphasised the role of inadequate labour in this, particularly in the western districts of Bengal. Jute cultivation required more labour than rice cultivation, but while the cultivation of jute suddenly increased to an unprecedented extent, the labour supply position remained unchanged. In fact the supply was depleted by the malaria epidemic of 1871-72. The coincidence of jute harvest with early rice harvest and with *aman* sowing further added to the difficulty of the jute growers in employing additional labour, even where they could afford it. The peasants in Sirajganj had not such a problem to face. However, the general crisis of confidence caused by the poor quality of the jute in very many parts of Bengal, and thus contributing to the price slump also inevitably affected them, though perhaps not as much as it did the peasants elsewhere.

Price per maund of jute in 1872 and 1873

(1) Varieties of jute	(2) Price in 1872	(3) Price in 1873	(4) % of the difference: Lowest prices compared	(5) % of the difference: highest prices compared
	Rs. As. Rs. As	Rs. As. Rs. As		
Uttariya	4-0 to 6-4	2-8 to 4-0	—31.2	—36.0
Deshwal	2-8 to 4.0	1-14 to 3-0	—25.0	—25.0
Desee	3-0 to 3-12	2-0 to 2-8	—33.3	—33.3
Deora	2-0 to 3-0	1-2 to 1-8	—43.7	—50.0
Dacca-Narainganj	3-0 to 4-8	2-0 to 3-8	—33.3	—22.2
Backrabadi	3-0 to 3-8	1-14 to 2-10	—37.5	—25.0
Janoporey	2-12 to 3-4	2-0 to 2-8	—17.2	—23.0

(*Source* Hem Chandra Kar, *Report on the cultivation of and jute in trade*, Appendix B. Statement No. 5, Statement of Srihari Saha, 12 March, 1873)

In view of the price fall the peasants did not even consider it worthwhile to harvest the entire jute crop. In Dacca and Mymensingh, two major jute districts, 'everywhere.... quantities of the jute grown last season had been left abandoned on the fields. The falling market in Calcutta seems to have created a

Movement of prices of 'common rice' in the Sirajganj Sub-division between 1869 and 1873: Quantities (in seers) sold per rupee

Year	Jan.	Feb.	March	Apr.	May	June	July	Aug.	Sept.	Oct.	Nov.	Dec.
1869	N.A.	N.A.	N.A.	N.A.	22.8	20.8	20.2	20.13	21.0	19.6	21.7	22.2
1870	22.8	23.8	23.15	23.15	21.12	19.14	22.5	22.8	24.12	28.15	25.10	24.8
1871	24.8	22.10	27.00	24.6	25.0	23.6	32.6	28.8	28.8	27.8	27.8	27.8
1872	27.8	29.00	27.8	27.00	26.3	29.0	27.0	28.0	27.0	28.4	27.0	27.12
1873	28	26.00	25.00	28.4	25.12	26.0	28.0	22.4	24.8	17.0	15.3	14.8

(*Source*: A.P. Mac Donnell, *Report on the food-grain supply and famine relief in Bengal and Bihar, Calcutta*, 1876, Statistical Appendix, p. 38).

N.A. = Not Available

panic amongst the cultivators, so much so that in some instances, even the jute which had been cut and put in the water to steep, was abandoned entirely'. In the context of this setback for the peasants, indeed the most severe one since they took to jute cultivation as a cash crop, the recent increase in the rent quantum naturally appeared to them as an intolerable burden.

The peasants suffered all the worse because of the simultaneous fall in the prices of rice, though the fall in the jute prices was far steeper.

The depression seemed to have set in from about July 1871, and continued till July 1873. The recovery thereafter was entirely due to the acute harvest failure in very many parts of Bihar and Bengal, which created a ready market for the surplus stock in Sirajganj. The depression was not anything particular to the region, and its fairly long spell was largely due to its pervasiveness. (It is notable that the downward trend was particularly visible in the usually surplus zones of the eastern and northern Bengal districts, and as a source of supply to the metropolis and other regions Sirajganj now could, scarcely compete with these zones).

3. The crucial issue in the revolt of the Eshafshahi peasants: increase of rent or violations of the occupancy status of the peasantry?

The crucial role of the rent question in the revolt which has thus been stressed in the preceding sections has recently been questioned. The crucial issue, it is argued, relates to the question of the peasants' status, the main determinant of which was the existence or non-existence of what was known as 'occupancy right'. (The concept of occupancy right became part of the *written* law of the country since the passing of Act X of 1859. A peasant acquired the occupancy status by 'holding', which did not necessarily mean directly cultivating, land continuously for twelve years. An occupancy peasant had a superior status in the legal system primarily because a zamindar could not indiscriminately increase his rent, but had to do it under certain constraints). 'The fundamental cause of the friction', the root of agrarian discontent', it is concluded, 'was the tendency of the landlords to tamper with the tenants right of occupancy . . . more enhancement of rent was not the primary objective of the Pabna landlords. Their principal concern was to take away all the right which Act X of 1859 had conferred on the occupancy ryots in order to clear the way for the future ejectment of the latter and the subsequent re-allotment of their holdings at competitive rental based on the current market value of land'.

The author seems to have assumed that but for this the peasants would have continued, 'without any serious protest', to meet the increased rent demand of the zamindars.

The view is of questionable validity. Occupancy right was admittedly a constraint on the zamindars' attempts at increasing rent, and zamindars were naturally keen on finding devices for undermining it. The pertinent question, however, is whether the Pabna zamindars in general were guilty of this, and whether such actions alone caused the revolt. In other words, what was the context of such actions of the zamindars? Were they unrelated to the immediate question of increasing rent?

The evidence that has been adduced in support of the case that the Eshafshahi zamindars in general had systematically violated the occupancy rights of the peasants (the largeness of their scale is also perhaps presumed) 'in order to clear the way for their future ejectment and the subsequent re-allotment of their holdings at competitive rental based on the current market value of land' is inadequate and unsatisfactory. The only piece of evidence that is cited is the extortion by the Banerjis of a certain kind of *kabuliats* from the peasants. The phrasing of such documents, to which we have referred earlier, clearly shows that they were not primarily designed for the destruction of the peasants' occupancy right. Their scope was far wider, and it is surprising that other aspects of their contents have been ignored. Nolan thus summarised these contents: by such agreements 'the ryots were to render permanent in the form of rent a disputed cess, to accept the zamindar's measurements, and to agree to pay all taxes which might hereafter be imposed. There was also a clause in most of the *kabulayats* empowering the zamindars to eject the ryots whenever they might quarrel'.

It would be misleading to isolate the provision for 'ouster', and to stress it as the most essential part of the *kabuliats*. The 'quarrels' for which the peasants would be penalised by such ousters specifically related to the question of rent, and the context in which the zamindars decided to adopt such devices has been noted earlier. In this the zamindars took advantage of a loophole in the law. Act X or 1859 while imposing constraints on the increase of rent by zamindars where the occupancy status of peasants was admitted also, curiously enough, provided for the suspension of this particular statutory provision where zamindars and peasants had entered into contracts by which peasants had signed off their rights. Private contracts were thus allowed to supersede public statutes.

The peasants' reactions to the *kabuliats*, first in village Urkandi and then in several others, also show how they felt concerned about these. They wanted the local courts to intervene and quash such contracts, arguing chiefly that the evidence on the basis of which the zamindars sought to make out a case for an increase of rent was all sham. They presumably felt that if this position was upheld the case for 'ousters' would also fall through. Of the illegality of such ousters they were convinced, but this does not seem to have much bothered them at the time.

The emphasis on the alleged violations of the peasants' occupancy status as having the decisive role in the revolt in Eshafshahi is apt to mislead also because of another reason. While such *kabuliats* were more or less confined to the estates of the Banerjis, the revolt was more or less pervasive, though it had first occurred in these estates. The non-existence or partial existence of such *kabuliats* in other estates was attributed by Taylor, Magistrate of Pabna, to the failure of the Banerjis in establishing their case in the civil court, which convinced the peasants also elsewhere of the illegality of such agreement. 'But for this discovery [on the part of the peasants] I have no doubt that the other zamindars would have followed the example of the Banerjees.

The view which locates the 'root' of the agrarian discontent in Pabna in the violations of peasants' occupancy status by the zamindars seems to have assumed the emergence since 1859 of a large and district community of occupancy ryots, with a superior status in the land, compared with the rest of the peasantry. Whether a considerable group of such peasants existed or not in Eshafshahi is only partially relevant to an understanding of the revolt there. (Judging by the available evidence it appears that the zamindars were scarcely interested in degrading an occupancy ryot to a so-called tenant-at-will unless this also involved the question of a rent increase. Even the provision for ouster in the *kabuliats* did not necessarily specifically apply to the occupancy ryots alone. The Banerjis asked for an increase of rent, forewarning the ryots that opposition to this would be met by their ejection from their holdings. Ejections from land for non-payment of rent were also permissible under the existing law. The grounds for ejections in the *Kabuliats* in the Banerjis' estates were not arrears of rent, but quarrels with the zamindars. However, such quarrels mostly related to the question of rent. It would be wrong to assume that only the occupancy peasants were capable of such quarrels, and it is therefore inferable that the *kabuliats* were not designed for undermining their position alone). It is, however, arguable whether the mere incorporation in Act X of 1859 of the provision in regard to occupancy right had automatically led to the emergence of such a group. The kind of social development which such an emergence would indicate does not seem to have occurred in very many places of Bengal. This is evident from the non-existence in such places of any real distinction between the so-called occupancy ryots and non-occupancy ryots. Herschel, a civilian with a wide knowledge of the agrarian customs of different parts of Bengal, thus confidently asserted in 1876: 'I do not know an instance at present of any village in Bengal in which the landlord can show which of his tenants have rights of occupancy and which have not *i.e.* where both exist or may be supposed to exist'. In some government estates attempts were made to distinguish between the two groups, but, as Herschel says, 'It is simply to fill up forms that the figures are obtained'. He has 'never known a *thesildar* [collector of revenue] in *khas mahals* [government estates] suggest that he could settle the question of rent by turning out a few tenants-at-will and introducing others who are ready to come.' He concludes:

> 'If it [the distinction between occupancy ryots and non-occupancy ryots] has penetrated here and there, it has only led to speculations as to the meaning of the distinction. I take it that in the rural mind the meaning is this: that of the two men one has and the other has not a right to hold at the rate which is fair to both of them'.

In Bakarganj, as the district collector once remarked, the concept of occupancy right became relevant only in times of disputes between zamindars and peasants. 'There is no term in general use among the peasantry which corresponds with an occupancy ryot. When they come into court their *muktear* [legal adviser] will explain to them the necessity of providing the twelve years' occupancy, but the virtue lying in the number twelve is absolutely unknown to the people at large'.

The view that the zamindars sought to destroy the occupancy rights of peasants in order to clear the way for their future ejectment and the subsequent re-allotment of their holdings at competitive rental based on the market value of land' is also of doubtful validity. With the rising value of land and the increasing demand for it resulting from population growth, rising agricultural prices, particularly since the Mutiny, and other related developments the zamindars had admittedly acquired, in several places, a superior bargaining position in relation to their peasantry, and succeeded in appropriating as rent part of the increased land value. This, however, scarcely amounted to the existence of a so-called competitive rental based on the current market value of land. The findings of a detailed official investigation into the question during Temple's administration amply refute such an assumption.

In fact, Temple himself believed that such 'competitive rates of rent' prevailed and suggested that a system of rent based on this concept would be a rational one, gradually replacing the archaic system of rent payment of the time, consisting of a nominal rate and of a number of ill-defined cesses. A distinctive feature of Temple's approach to the rent question was his assumption of the inevitability of a rise in rent. Like some contemporary political economies Temple believed:

> 'If the value of land is to increase with the rise in prices and the improvement of produce it follows that their must be moderate and gradual augmentation of rent throughout the country from time to time. . . . If the material resources of the country are to grow and expand, if the culture of new staples is to flourish . . . if in short agriculture is to advance, them concurrently some augmentation of rent is to be expected.

Temple, however, had to reconcile this concept of rising rate of rent with the accepted legal notion that the so-called occupancy ryots, unlike the non-occupancy ryots, had a special claim to legal protection against an increase of rent. In Temple's new scheme the rent of non-occupancy ryots was 'left to mutual arrangement between landlord and tenant, and to adjust itself just as prices and market rates adjust themselves'. Temple took 'competitive rates of rent' as the basis for the determination of the rent rates of occupancy ryots.

His scheme was, however, judged entirely unrealistic by almost all the local officers. The so-called competitive rate of rent turned out to be a myth. The Commissioner of the Presidency Division expressed a more or less representative opinion:

> The notion of competitive rent has even yet obtained to footing in the rural economy of Bengal . . . near the Presidency there is perhaps some little competition for land, but even this is local rather than general .... It is not in fact what we understand by free competition at all: that is, it is not a competition of capital and skill determined by profits .... rent in such cases is merely the result of the relation of the numbers who want the land on the one side to the quantity of land on the other, and the numbers who want the land are not determined by the considerations of the profits it gives to capital, but by the necessary of subsistence'.

4. Composition of the Rebel Peasants

A pertinent question in this connection is the composition of the rebel peasants. It is safe to assume that the entire peasant community was not committed to the rebel cause. In fact, as we have noted later, a great deal of coercion on the part of the rebel leaders was necessary for winning over some unenthusiastic, hesitant, and, in come cases, positively hostile sections of the peasantry. It would be futile to try to understand the behaviour of the rebels in terms of the notion of an all-encompassing peasantry, and it would be worthwhile to note the differences in the situations of its various sections, since such differences largely determined their particular attitudes to the revolt. 'There are differences', as a recent study in the peasant rebellions of the 20th century says,

> 'in behaviour and outlook between tenants and proprietors, between poor and rich peasants, between cultivators who are also craftsmen and those who only plough and harvest, between men who are responsible for all agricultural operations on a holding they rent or own and wage labourers who do their work under supervision of others in return for money. One must distinguish between peasants who live close to towns and are involved in town markets and urban affairs and those living in more remote villages.'

The composition of the rebel peasants of Eshafshahi is however difficult to analyse in view of the inadequacy of the available contemporary data. Contemporary reports rarely distinguished between different sections of the peasantry, and the word peasant or ryot was seldom used to indicate or describe a particular kind of production organisation: it merely denoted a broad spectrum of rent-paying community. Such a community did include persons who cannot properly be called peasants. The criterion by which to define a peasant necessarily relates to the particular kind of production organisation in this particular case, and peasants are definable as 'populations that are existentially involved in cultivation and make autonomous decisions regarding the process of cultivation'. The category thus covers 'tenants and sharecroppers as well as owner-operators, as long as they are in a position to make the relevant decisions on how their crops are grown'.

This category excludes a certain section of the big holders who had a prominent role to play in the peasant economy, particularly in the eastern and northern Bengal districts. Temple called such a holder 'a small agricultural capitalist', who took the initiative in founding new agricultural settlements, providing the necessary capital for the first work of reclamation and taking proper measures for ensuring its continuity. This initial involvement in the production eventually ceased, and from an entrepreneur he changed into a mere rent-receiver, the largest part of his income being derived from the difference between the rent which he received from his 'under-tenants' and the one that he paid to his immediate landlord. He resisted any intrusion into this preserve. Baffled in having a share in the growing agricultural resources of the regions, zamindars occasionally sought to eliminate such holders altogether. Their difficulties in these were very many, as the peasant revolt in the Tushkhali estate of Bakarganj (1855-58), which such big holders actively encouraged, showed, and sometimes they gave up. Temple's government had also a bitter encounter with such holders in some *khas* estates and prudently retreated.

Such holders probably also existed in Sirajganj. However, they do not seem to have had much to do with the organisation of the revolt in Eshafshahi. Nolan and other local officers who investigated the origins of the revolt and met in this connection zamindars and numerous representatives of their seldom came across the point of view that the rent increase that the zamindars had asked for was justifiable in terms of the particular question of 'tenancy'. The zamindars scarcely argued that their ryots should pay them more mainly because the ryots have been receiving for long a great deal still more from their undertenants. Such demands on the part of zamindars were quite usual in very many parts of eastern Bengal and also elsewhere, and here was no reason why the Eshafshahi zamindars would have been particularly forbearing to the privileged group of big holders.

On the other hand, the revolt does not seem to have been made by a group of destitute peasants either. The point needs to be stressed in view of the usual explanations of the peasant revolts in Bengal in terms of the allegedly increasing pauperizaion of the peasantry, the implicit assumption being that the destitute peasants rebelled in a mood of desperation. Some recent studies in the peasant rebellions in different parts of the world, particularly in the 20th century, have also sought to relate these to some fundamental structural changes in the agrarian economy resulting primarily from the fast disintegration of the 'self-sufficient village economy' with the growth of a market economy. E.H. Jacoby has particularly noted how the dissolution of the old village economy and 'foreign trade and foreign ideas disturbed the established equilibria within the indigenous society'. E.R. Wolf has also stressed the idea: 'The peasant rebellions of the 20th century are no longer simple responses to local problem. They are but the parochial reactions to major social change. The spread of the market has torn men up by their roots, and shaken them loose from the social relationships into which they were born'. The resultant tension has been aggravated what Wolf called 'the three crises: the demographic crisis, the ecological crisis and the crisis in power and authority'.

Some revolts in Bengal did result from widespread dislocations in society and economy: for instance, the ones in Rangpur (1783), Midnapur (roughly between 1780 and 1810) and the Santal Parganas (1855-82). The Eshafshahi revolt, however, belonged to a different type. Occasional fluctuations in the rice and jute markets (as, for instance, in 1872-73) caused much hardships to the peasantry, but the effects of the spread a money economy to which the peasants were thus exposed were quite different from the ones which Jacoby and Wolf have described. The peasants could adjust to such short-term fluctuations, primarily because of the predominance of the subsistence sector in the peasant economy, and when baffled by the erratic behaviour of the market for their cash crops they could quickly retreat into the more or less stable and secure zone of the subsistence economy, though they suffered a great deal during the transition. The peasants under the circumstances preferred minimising risks to maximising their 'profits'. At least at the time the revolt took place such a transition was not a very difficult process.

It is still an unsettled question whether the Bengal peasants tended to become poorer over the years during British rule, and where the fact of such impoverishment is indisputable it is difficult to be sure about the exact role of the operation of the zamindari system in this. However, the theme of increasing impoverishment' of the peasantry does not seem to apply to a number of regions in the eastern and the northern Bengal districts during a period of about two decades before the occurrence of the Pabna revolt, and there are indications that certain elements of dynamism had been introduced into the peasant economy. Local officers particularly noted the recent growth of the agricultural resources of Eshatshahi. An important factor in this was the rising agricultural prices during this period. The trend was visible since the early 1850's, and a marked spurt in the prices took place between 1855 and 1859. 1860 and 1861 were years of low prices, but the upward trend reasserted itself, as the following table shows.

Average prices of common rice in 'Eastern' and 'Northern' Bengal between 1861 and 1873 (Quantities in Seers)

(1) Years	(2) Quantities 'Eastern'	(3) sold per rupee 'Northern'	(1) Years	(2) Quantities 'Eastern'	(3) sold per rupee 'Northern'
1861	34.18	33.67	1868	23.71	29.14
1862	32.49	33.77	1869	19.80	24.37
1863	29.46	30.74	1970	22.85	26.46
1864	25.95	28.77	1871	22.59	28.33
1865	17.50	15.06	1872	26.78	27.69
1866	16.47	19.22	1873	24.25	22.99
1867	22.30	19.48			

(*Source: Prices and Wages in India,* Govt. of India) 9th Issue, Calcutta, 1892.

The phenomenon was not confined to the eastern and northern Bengal districts. It was nearly universal. These was, however a difference, particularly as far as the rising prices of certain periods were concerned. In considerable parts of western Bengal and Bihar the sudden rise in the prices during 1865 and 1866, as is evident from the following table, resulted from an acute scarcity of food-grains, caused by a shortfall in the production, and were scarcely beneficial to the peasantry in general.

Quantities per rupee: in seers

Districts	1864	1865	1866
Midnapur	27.3	16.5	9.88
Hugli	23.57	12.86	17.4
Nadia	19.00	12.00	13.99
Bankura	29.92	27.36	11.68
Birhum	29.37	23.06	12.00
Burdwan	28.00	26.12	9.79
Patna	35.26	23.24	17.35
Sahabad	25.49	16.99	13.99
Muzaffarpur	21.69	14.8	10.2

(*Source*: same as in the preceding Table)

Plenty prevailed in most parts of Eastern and northern Bengal which largely escaped the natural disaster, and the contemporary rise in the prices in the region was entirely caused by a boom in the exports to the afflicted areas, which enriched considerable sections of the peasantry. The fall in the prices in 1872 and 1873 was admittedly a setback. However, a certain stability in the grain market by then prevented a further fall, which abundant harvests such as the ones of these years would normally have caused several years ago. The Commissioner of Dacca found how despite the slump the peasants in very many places held back part of their supplies instead of rushing to an overstocked market. The collector of Bakarganj thus remarked:

> 'Now-a-days a larger harvest is followed by an increased exportation, and prices remain much the same. Traders now go to the remotest parts of the district, in quest of cheap grain; and boats go to Dacca with paddy which they had bought in the distant wave-beaten island of Manpura.

What exactly happened in the little world of Eshafshahi is unknown. A densely populated and a fairly prosperous region like Eshaishahi probably experienced a similar phenomenon.

It has sometimes been argued that the peasants seldom benefited from the rising prices, since most of them were obliged, because of their chronic indebtedness, to hypothecate their crops to their creditors, so that it was such creditors who mostly appropriated the normal gains from the rising prices. Such a view is only partially valid. Innumerable contemporary reports suggest that cases of 'free' sales were very many, grain-traders including affluent peasants constituting only one of the several groups of creditors and it would be wrong to assume that the available surplus stock was eventually marketed principally through this mechanism. Even where the pre-existing credit relations resulted in restricting such freedom, the rising prices, by eventually reducing the real debt obligations of the peasants, strengthened their bargaining position in relation to their moneylenders, Moreover, a sizable part of the marketed rice was provided by the relatively substantial holders (very many of the small holders having not much to spare), and though a number of them were also not free from debt, this did not necessarily in solve a lien of the creditors over their crops.

The increasing cultivation of jute introduced a further element of were particularly fond of jute. This is understandable. Where, as in Pabna and several other parts of northern and eastern Bengal, jute had only recently replaced indigo, which was admittedly an unremunerative crop the change—over was a distinct economic gain. Where jute was an additional crop and not just an alternative one to rice, jute provided an additional source of income. However, it was only in the highly fertile lands that the peasants could grow both rice and jute in the same season. Such lands were limited. Where jute was an additional crop, or grown on a part of the peasants' holdings and they cultivated with advances, it was these advances which made jute attractive, since they came at the time when the peasants had nearly run out of their stock of grain. Jute had also other attractions. Jute was 'for all practical purposes the only money crop for the Bengal peasant', and in point of remunerativeness jute, other things being equal, was superior crop to rice.

The revolt does not therefore seem to have been made by a group of destitute peasants undergoing a process of 'steady impoverishment'. Their protracted legal battle against the zamindars, both before and after the revolt, which was admittedly an expensive affair, also confirms this impression.

Very little is known about the participation of the 'analytically marginal groups' such as landless agricultural labourers including a section of poor sharecroppers. It is not improbable that the rebel peasants succeeded in rallying a section of them, particularly where they were casually employed by such peasants. Such a participation could not perhaps be sustained for long, and, so far as we know, the programme of the rebels did not hold out any promise for improving their conditions of work.

5. Organisation of the Revolt

The quick growth of the revolt from a small nucleus has been noted in an earlier section. How did the first rebels draw into the movement peasants from other regions?

Available evidence suggests that the growth was far from a spontaneous one, in the sense that other peasants simply joined the movement once it had started somewhere, without any efforts on the part of the rebel leaders. Certain elements of spontaneity did exist, since the central issues in the revolt had some common features, and the regional differences scarcely overshadowed them. The revolt, however, did not just erupt; it was largely made and organised.

Organisation of such a revolt had intrinsic difficulties. In fact, that peasants 'are slow to rise' and are 'especially handicapped in passing from passive recognition of wrongs to political participation as a means of setting them right' have been more or less universally recognised. The sources of the difficulties in the way of organising a peasant revolt (particularly where a small peasant economy prevailed, with the numerous units of production, mostly individual peasant households, being only superficially integrated) are not difficult to identify. These relate to the relative isolation of different villages, which was largely a function of a small peasant economy, to the heterogeneity of the various groups composing the peasantry, to the usual absence of a uniform system of relationship in different regions between peasants and landlords or other forms of authority exercising political and economic control and appropriating in the process part of the peasants' surplus, and in certain cases to the habitual submissiveness of the peasantry. That is why peasants in very many places are 'often merely passive spectators of political struggles or long for the sudden advent of a millennium, without specifying for themselves and their neighbours the many rungs on the staircase to heaven.

The rebel leaders of Eshafshahi, who had all such difficulties to face (and that on a considerable scale because of the vastness of the area which the revolt had gradually engulfed, with about three hundred villages having joined it by June, 1873) were initially helped by a number of circumstances. The religious composition of the peasantry was undoubtedly one. The peasants were mostly Muslims, and the Joint Magistrate of Dacca once explained how this strengthened a resistance of this kind. 'Combination is much more easy among a sect whose faith enjoins absolute social equality than among Hindus who are divided into endless varieties of caste, jealous and distrustful of each other'. It is, however, remarkable that the rebel leaders seldom played up the existing communal differences, and the revolt did not anywhere degenerate into a confrontation between the predominantly Hindu zamindars and the predominantly Muslim peasants, and unlike in the cases of a number of peasant revolts in Dacca, Mymensingh and some other districts of eastern Bengal between 1905 and 1929, the Eshafshahi revolt had scarcely any communal dimension. Secondly, the rebel leaders had not necessarily to start from the scratch. The sustained legal battles which preceded the actual revolt necessitated a certain kind of organisation, and this provided a base for the leaders to build upon. Thirdly an aspect of the existing law relating to increase of rent tended to create a feeling of unity among the peasants of a certain area, particularly where the estates to which they belonged happened to be interlinked. The law, as noted earlier, encouraged equalisation of rent rates for lands of similar quality and location. Nolan thus explained how this helped the spread of the revolt:

> 'It becomes the interest of every ryot to prevent enhancement in any land near his own, although at first sight he might seem to have nothing to do with the matter. If he lets his neighbours be rackrented without assisting

them in the legal, and often in the physical, resistance they might have to offer, he himself will be rackrented. Every rise in rents is in law a good precedent, and it may be applied far and wide, each new enhancement being in itself a sufficient reason for extending the area of the highly taxed range of country. For instance, the Bandopadhya estates are interlaced with land belonging to the Tagores and Sandyals, which again are connected with Bunwari Lal's property. We may be sure that if the Bandopadhya's got their kabulyats, the Tagore's would ask for similar ones next year; and if the ryots refused, might be able to get them through the courts. Then would come Babu Bunwari Lals' turn and so on through the sub-division and the district. Thus, our law in a manner invites and compels our ryots to combine into leagues and unions which are elsewhere only known in manual trades....'

Fourthly, the pre-existing pockets of resistance, not directly connected with the main stream of the Eshafshahi revolt, (such as the Thul Char and Jagtallah, to which we have referred earlier) could be more easily drawn into the movement and be transformed into spearheads of offensive than certain other regions where the idea of resistance had only recently penetrated. The infrastructure of resistance in such pockets was presumably more refined and efficient, since the peasants there were used to resisting violence by violence, which under the circumstances required greater tact and courage than the usual legal battles in the civil courts.

When the revolt had actually started the initial official reaction to it greatly reassured the peasants and consequently helped its growth. A government 'Proclamation' issued sometime in June 1873, thus read:

'Whereas in the district of Pubna, owing to attempts of zamindars to enhance rents and combinations of ryots to resist the same, large bodies of men have assembled at several places in a riotous and tumultuous manner, and serious breaches of the peace have occurred. This is very gravelly to warn all concerned that while on the one hand the Government will protect the people from all force and extortion, and the zamindars must asserts any claims they may have by legal means only, on the other hand the Government will firmly repress all violent and illegal action on the part of the ryots, and will strictly bring to justice all who offend against the law, to whatever class they belong .... It is perfectly lawful to unite in a peaceable manner to resist any excessive demands of the zamindars, but it is nor lawful to unite to use violence and intimidation'.

The peasants seem to have imperfectly understood it contents, and in a mood of excitement they read more into it than what it actually said. Government were strongly critical of the zamindars' actions, and approved of a 'peaceful' resistance to them. They also unambiguously said that any wrong steps on the part of the peasants would not be condoned. From the phrasing of the proclamation it is inferable that Government have found them guilty of these and have therefore admonished them to mend their ways. The peasants apparently ignored this part of the proclamation, and construed it as an unqualified endorsement by Government of their stand. This reassurance enabled them to plan their strategy of resistance, since they knew it for certain that with the Government firmly committed against them they did not have any chances of victory. Indeed, the very first measure of the peasants, as soon as they decided to join the revolt, was to inform the local police of this decision, with a request that the police should 'keep the peace', evidently implying that the zamindars were the potential threat to peace and that they should therefore be forestalled in this.

After the revolt had started at some key centres the rebel leaders had a two-fold strategy to follow: to win converts through preaching their ideals and to devise means for maintaining the unity in the movement and also for meeting a possible counter-offensive of the zamindars.

The formulation of the slogans suggest that the revolt had a short radical phase. Though the available evidence is inconclusive, the rebels seem sometime to have thought in terms of elimination of the zamindars altogether, and of holding land directly under the Queen. This was not perhaps a causal talk, and it undoubtedly animated a considerable section of the rebel peasants. The promptness with which Government intervened and clarified their stand on the issue suggests that the idea became at one time quite a popular one. The 'Proclamation' of June 1873 explicitly said:

> 'It is asserted by the people who have combined to resist the demands of the zamindars that they are to be the ryots of Her Majesty the Queen, and of Her only. These people, and all who listen to them, are warned that the Government cannot and will not interfere with the rights of property as secured by law: that they must pay what is legally due from them to those to whom it is legally due.'

It is surprising how the peasants' vision of a new order was associated with the Queen. Indeed, this did not happen in Eshafshahi alone: it was a common slogan of the rebel peasants also elsewhere. (The peasants were presumably ignorant of the harsh dealings of Government with the ryots in the *khas* estates. A taste of this would perhaps have made them far less enthusiastic about the idea). This is however explicable. The peasants wanted only the power and authority of the zamindars abolished, and not all kinds of power and authority. The rebel peasants in Eshafshahi were scarcely anarchists. At the same time they also could not think in terms of replacing the authority of the zamindars by the one of the peasant community itself. On the other hand, the authority of the state did not appear to them as a residual one; it enveloped their existence. Where they had nothing to choose between this authority and any other, both equally oppressive to them, they looked upon the state as a 'cold monster'. The Eshafshasi peasants under the circumstances tended to look upon it as the only benign authority after elimination of the zamindars.

The radical phase was soon over. A short 'no-rent phase of the movement might give an impression that this resulted from a repudiation by the peasants of the authority of the zamindars. This is unfounded. The no-rent movement had everywhere outlived the radical phase. The Government of Bengal once described at as a shrewd device on the part of the peasants for forcing their zamindars to come to terms: 'The combinations to resist the payment of all rent . . . are merely attempts to bring the zamindars to terms by keeping them out of all rent till they settle the questions in dispute'. This looks plausible, and was perhaps true of certain regions. In general, however, the plans to stop rent inevitably resulted from the fundamental disagreement between the peasants and the zamindars over the quantum of rent, particularly when the two sides were openly at war and when a numerous peasant community was involved in it. The peasants did not naturally think it worthwhile to continue paying rent till a solution was found for it. 'All combinations on rent questions in Bengal', the Government of Bengal concluded, 'are apt to result in withholding all rents; for in fact in the very nature of things a dispute about the rate of rent must stop all payment except through the court. The zamindars would not acknowledge a payment on the terms desired by the ryot and the ryot would not pay it without a receipt which will support his side of the question'.

An agreement on the complex rent question which could remove the tangle was difficult to reach even during normal times. With the beginning of the revolt attitudes of both sides inevitably hardened, leading them further apart and to a complete breakdown of the dialogue at times, so that a solution was out of the question. Most zamindars were unwilling to relent, and even by the middle of September, 1873, as the Magistrate of Pabna found, 'The principal zamindars of Eshafshahye, except the Tagore family, appear to have . . . no intention of making any concessions'. The Banerjis were particularly obdurate, and the Magistrate was pretty confident that but for this a thaw would have come. They were ready for compromised in the beginning, but their attitude increasingly stiffened with time. 'Rich and strong-handed landowners like Ishan Chandra Banerjee', the Magistrate judged, 'are in no hurry, and are content to wait for a year or two and see what may happen. They have hopes of being able to coerce the ryots in many ways, and eventually to bring them to better terms than they could obtain by a compromise'. The Magistrate sought to revive the lost dialogue between them and their ryots, but failed. 'The Banerjees seemed determined to push matters to extremities. None of the shareholders cared to be present at the time the talks for a compromise were to start. Their representatives 'appeared to look on their tenants as rebels, who were to be punished and not conciliated, and to care little for the opinion of any officer of government'. Institution by them of fresh suits against the ryots during the two-week stay of the Magistrate at Shahzadpur indicated their temper. The Pakrassies were no less adamant. 'In answer to my notice only one junior member of the family attended at my camp'. The Sannyals, the Bhaduries and the Bhattacharyyas did not flinch either: It is pretty well-known that they have no intention of compromising with the ryots as a body'.

At the same time the peasants too 'seem to be quite determined to abate nothing of their demands'. They wanted a 'final' settlement, and resolved not to yield as long as the zamindars did not promise one. Such an 'obstinate stand the ryots are determined to make against the zamindars in order to get their supposed rights' was largely due to their fear that the zamindars would soon start misbehaving unless they were bound by such a settlement.

The no-rent movement inevitably resulted from such irreconcilable attitudes. The rebel leaders, however, scarcely deluded the peasants in the neighbourhood by saying that joining the revolt would set them free from the obligations of rent payment for ever. They had a positive and apparently pragmatic) programme to offer. The programme, which evidently reflected the wishes of considerable sections of the peasantry, included (a) restoration of the rates of rent prevalent under the Nator Raj—10 annas a *bigah;* (b) abolition of all illegal cesses; (c) introduction of a new standard of measurement and (d) formalisation of such changes by the distribution of *pattahs* incorporating the terms, so that the zamindars might not easily retract as soon as the revolt ended.

What mattered more at the time was not just promises, but immediate action, and the rebel leaders soon got down to business. At a certain stage of the revolt the ryots apparently succeeded, though temporarily, in replacing the authority of the zamindars. Decisions on he rates of rent which would be payable from now on necessitated a measurement of the lands. The peasants did not wait till the zamindars did it, and hastened to do it themselves. Measurements alone did not lead to a solution, and in very many places the rent question seemed to be an intractable one. What did the rates of rent of the Nator days exactly mean? How in view of the changed circumstances was it possible to revive such rates? Such questions were apparently imperfectly understood by the peasants themselves. Investigations by Kailash Chandra Mukherjee and others revealed that the rent rates of the Nator times had scarcely survived. In some rent-suits which Mr. Mukherjee judged the rate of rent decreed for the usual cultivable land (*matan*) was Rs. 1 and 8 annas. The prevalent rates widely varied, ranging from 10 annas to Rs. 2 and 8 annas; but the 'average rate' was Rs. 1 and 4 annas.

From a strictly legal point of view the ryots were at a disadvantage. They had been paying a certain quantum of rent for quite sometime. The revolt intervened, and they abruptly disowned their obligations. The Commissioner of Rajhshahi repeatedly asked the rebel leaders to take a more flexible attitude in this:

> 'I have endeavoured to impress upon them that they should render the rent previously paid by them, and in the event of its being refused, they should deposit it in the civil court .... People should understand that they cannot set themselves up as judges of what is fair and equitable rent, which by law is presumed to be rent paid in the previous years unless shown by a suit in court to be the reverse'.

Did the ryots actually believe that it was practicable to restore the rent rates of the good old days? Nolan doubted it:

> 'I have heard and believe that they [rent programmes of the ryots] are put forward on the principle of asking for a great deal that you get enough. The ryots would, I believe, be satisfied if the Tagores would withdraw their recent demands for 4-anna increase, and if the Bandopadhyas and the Pakrassies would give up an old illegal cess to the same amount and if similar concessions were made elsewhere'.

It is difficult to conclude if Nolan had misjudged the real mood of the peasants. It could be that they had considerably retreated from their original position by the time Nolan was reporting (July, 1873). However, the talk of restoring the rent rates of the Nator days does not seem to have been entirely motivated by the kind of shrewd calculations which Nolan attributed. The peasants' real temper at the time is understandable. True that they had been for long paying a rent rate which was far higher than the one that they were now asking for, and whatever the peasants' feelings about the propriety of the zamindars' demands, the system had come to stay. The revolt made all the difference. They questioned now all legal and customary precedents, and it removed at once the backwaters of ages. The revolt was inseparable from the dream of a happy order. This, however, could not be built on makeshitts and patchworks. The system had to be built anew, and the Nator system seemed to have provided an enduring base to build upon.

Not much is known about how the rebel leaders preached their ideals, and established and maintained contacts with the new recruits. The First contacts were evidently made through the messengers which the leaders sent from the original base of operations. Apparently, after the initial impulse was given, the local leaders seem to have taken over. Evidence is inconclusive about whether the different regional movements that thus grew up could be vertically controlled. It seems that such contracts were becoming increasingly difficult to maintain in view of the administrative measures for the purpose of preventing 'breaches of the peace'. The Assistant Magistrate of Sirajgunj, for instance, 'ordered proclamations to be made at all *thannahas* and outposts forbidding the ryots to visit villages other than their own in parties of more than ten, and forbidding the use of musical instruments (such as buffalo horn), for the purpose of invoking assemblies, intimating union, or causing terror'. 'All assemblies' were similarly 'dispersed' by the police, so that even within the boundary of a village the rebels found it difficult to meet together in a big group.

Just 'preaching' through messengers did not, however, do when it came to the question of devising means for maintaining the unity in the movement and for frustrating a possible counter-offensive from the zamindars. All villages did not respond with equal enthusiasm, and some apparently hesitated. It was suicidal for the rebel leaders to allow such hesitations to undermine the unity in the movement, particularly in view of the well-known vidictiveness of the zamindars and of their firmness not to let things drift.

The movement passed to a distinctly new phase when the rebels had such questions to face. Persuasions did not suffice, and certain coercive methods, which did not necessarily invariably involve violence to person and property, became unavoidable. Though such methods were mostly aimed against the zamindars and their representatives, vacillating sections of the peasantry and unwilling villages as a whole do not also seem to have been spared in certain cases. The Magistrate of Pabna thus summarised his findings:

> 'The original intention of the League was simply to pay no rents; but finding, it seems, that all villages did not join the combination, and without such that only a partial success would accrue, messengers were despatched to those who kept aloof to hold out threats of armed bands being sent to plunder them, unless they at once declared themselves to be the ryots only of the Queen, whose Mofussil representative was Raja Ishan Chunder Roy. These messengers, were not, it seems, confined to the Sirajganj sub-division, but were sent over also to the Sudder side. Either dissatisfied with the effect of such messages, or to make sure that the effect obtained should not die out, the unionists formed large bands of men, visited all villages along the line of the route over which they travelled, at some places being content with threats alone, at others making the ryots join the procession .... It may be fairly presumed that they [leaders like Ishan Roy and Shambhu Nath Pal] advised at least a show of force to make the combination complete. They were too wise to direct any act of violence, and such acts in every case were brought about by other than the original intention of the assembly.'

Such groups which moved from village to village, and also the local ones inevitably included some 'unattached' elements, and certain actions of theirs occasionally tended to obscure the basic issue, that is, consolidation of the unity in the movement through a certain coercion. 'Among these large assemblages', the Pabna Magistrate noted,

> 'there were, of course, many bad characters and men who had wrongs to avenge. Such men, I believe, taking advantage of their large numbers, the feat that they created wherever they went, and the opportunity in general, plundered for sake of booty or created mischief for revenge. In some places the very same bands have simply abused men of one village, taken a *nuzzur* [perquisite] of Rs. 2 from men of another, committed mischief to the walls of houses in a third, and plundered in a fourth'.

Such cases, when too many in a locality, were undoubtedly damaging to the rebel cause, and it is unknown how the hard core of the rebels tackled such elements.

It was the particular attitude of the zamindars which necessitated such coercions in a far larger number of cases. The zamindars painted the rebels black, and the local officers, knowing as they did that some coercions and violence did occur, could not be sure under the circumstances of their exact extent.

The zamindars sought to convince the Government that the movement was from the very beginning based on violence. A long petition to the Government from a group of Shazadpur lawyers was presumably arguing their case. "The rebellious ryots . . . furnished with deadly weapons', it alleged, committed riot and attacked and beat zamindars' men wherever opportunity allowed them to do so'. It mentioned some specific cases of violence affecting some leading zamindars, some members of the zamindari bureaucracy and a pleader of a local court. The lawyers, however, seem to have been concerned with describing what they believed was a general situation, and sought to create an impression that a climate of violence had been fast spreading. The rebels were accused of 'threatening, attacking, and even plundering, the houses of those who were unwilling to accompany them'. They became

> 'so powerful that no one-nay, a stranger, can walk safely in his way or go from one place to another without making himself known that he is also one of the rebellious

> creatures. . . . They have taken the reins of Government into their own hands, inasmuch as the aggrieved among them is not allowed to complain before any civil or criminal court . . . but is bound to bring his grievances into the knowledge of their head.... ·

The local officers who investigated such complaints did not prejudge the issue. They were of course aware of the possible elements of subjectivism in the zamindars' judgment. 'It is their interest to represent the other party as a band of madmen headed by desperates', observed Nolan. He also found that the employees of the zamindars had occasionally deliberately misinformed them: 'it is the interest of their *tehsildars* [collectors of rent] who have generally gone with the ryots to pretend to their masters that they have acted under compulsion'. At the same time he admitted the difficulties of the zamindars under the circumstances to substantiate their allegations: 'the whole country being on the popular side, it is no doubt difficult to get witnesses to the occurrence of riots'. He was apparently convinced by the explanation of one of the affected *tahasildars* for the delay in lodging his complaint: 'he did not complain because he thought he would have no witnesses. This is a real reason for the absence of substantial charges'. This was partly confirmed by a report from a Police-Inspector Krishna Sundar who was asked to investigate the fact of an 'illegal assembly' at Sallop.

> 'He found that a number of unionist ryots did meet and go in a threatening manner to some villages which had not hitherto joined. But as the villages visited subsequently went over to the union, no member of the mob can now be identified'.

It would therefore be a legitimate inference that cases of coercion and violence did occur, though their exact extent is unknown. Such cases, as Nolan thought, were not unnatural under the circumstances: 'The ryots commenced in a good spirit, as was shown by their sending in deputations from each village to my court and requesting that the police might be ordered to keep the peace. But when large masses of men are excited against persons who have never shown any moderation in dealing with them, they may be carried into excess of which they would never have thought themselves capable'. The immediate programme of the rebels that is, the one relating to the rent question, did not necessitate such coercions. They questioned the zamindars' rent demands, and the combined opposition to these resulted in a deadlock—a virtual no-rent movement. By this the ryots went quite far, and as long as they accepted the institution of zamindari and also the institution of rent which was necessitated by this there was no point in going further. The peasants did go beyond it when they feared a counter-offensive from the zamindars, or where this actually came. 'An authentic account of an illegal assembly' at Sallop which Nolan heard and reported may be cited as an evidence of this. 'The ryots no doubt wished to send messengers to the villages, and it would not have been safe to go in small numbers or unarmed, as the unscrupulous Sandyal zamindars reside at Sallop, and their followers would probably have kidnapped any envoy sent to their ryots'. Initially (at least till about the end of June, 1873) the zamindars, apparently caught unawares by the revolt and overwhelmed by the sheer number of their enemies, discreetly refrained from suppressing the movement by violence, and the ryots also could largely do without it. In fact, the increasing evidence of the strength of the League frightened some zamindars into moving to safer zones even where 'outrages' were not committed. The rebels during this period were therefore particularly careful that the uncommitted local groups, not necessarily peasants, whom the zamindars could try to win over, could be immobilised, by threats or a use of force, thus completing the relative isolation into which the zamindars had been forced. It is revealing that of the thirteen 'accusations' which were brought against the ryots between 15 June and 3 July, 1873 and which the Joint-Magistrate of Sirajganj tried, eight related to 'illegal assemblies accompanied by trespass on the houses of absent persons obnoxious to the unionists'. (Of these five were proved).

With the 'law and order' measures of Government considerably reducing the strength and effectiveness of the League the number of such cases probably diminished. Government once permitted 'peaceful combinations', but under the circumstances the exact borderline between a 'peaceful combination' and an 'illegal assembly' tended to be obscured, and sometimes government did not take enough care to be sure that this was non-existent. The revival during this time of confusion of inter-zamindari quarrels and the recurring clashes between different village groups, largely unconnected with such quarrels but resulting from a desire to settle old scores, undoubtedly created a difficult situation for the local officers. With the League consequently being reduced to fragmented and isolated units of operations, it lost its old confidence to enforce its will. The official reports on the revolt sent after about the end of August only casually described the activities of the League as a distinct organisation, with only scanty information on the 'law and order' situation, and it is difficult to conclude whether such cases of coercion completely disappeared.

This particular phase of the movement (when some coercions on the part of the rebels were unavoidable for the purpose of maintaining the unity in the movement and of frustrating a possible counter-offensive from the zamindars) has sometimes been completely ignored. The Pabna revolt has been called 'an agrarian revolution by due course of law'. The movement, it is argued, had throughout a 'legalistic-passive' character and never 'degenerated into a *jacquerie*'.

'Agrarian revolution' in this particular context seems to be a misleading phrase. The revolt scarcely appreciably affected the rural power structure, let alone the structure of political power in general. 'Due course of law'? The peasants rebelled precisely because the usual course of law could not provide a real solution for their problems. The revolt was of course preceded by a sustained legal battle, but the effective phase of such a struggle seems to have come to an end with the legal victory of the peasants of Urkandi. The total defiance of the authority of the zamindars, which the revolt actually amounted to, was at least an extra-legal phenomenon. Why the revolt has been called a 'passive' one has not been properly explained. This anyway seems curious. The revolt was not just a mere wish, a mere protest: it was the expression of a collective will, with an elaborate organisation, involving about, three hundred villages, for its realisation. The league was essentially based on a confidence that only the activity of such a kind would enable them to cope with the oppressors. Legalistic? The local officers found that the zamindars had exaggerated the cases of collective coercions. However, they did not doubt that such cases did occur, though they failed to know under the circumstances how widespread and how frequent they actually were. Moreover, such cases of coercions and violence scarcely indicated a state of 'degeneration' of the movement, if this is intended to mean a fall from its original qualities, a reversion to a lower type. It merely indicated a change in the strategy of the battle when the circumstances had changed, and the rebels did feel that such a change would strengthen their movement. This involves a question of understanding the different phases of a movement, and it is instructive to explain why such phases emerged. It is pointless to argue that one particular phase belongs to a superior type and the one or ones that followed to an inferior type. After all, what would be the criterion of judging it?

5a. Leadership of the organisation and the question of the participation of other social and economic groups

Who provided the leadership of the movement? Were the peasants capable of an independent initiative? Was their action spontaneous? Numerous studies in peasant movements in different parts of the world have stressed the incapacity of the peasantry for an independent action. According to Engels, 'the peasants alone could never make a revolution as long as they were confronted by the organised power of the princes, nobility and the cities. Only by allying themselves with other classes could they have a chance of victory'. Ronald Mousnier analysed the peasant uprisings in 17th century France, Russia and China and thus concluded: 'In none of these three countries can it be said that the peasants took the initiative in these revolts. They were always begun by other elements'. Barrington Moore also inclines to such a view. While explaining how 'a revolutionary potential arises among the peasantry' he finds:

> 'Whether or not this potential becomes politically effective depends on the possibility of a fusion between peasant grievances and those of other strata. By themselves the peasants have never been able to accomplish a revolution.... The peasants have to have leaders from other classes'.

What exactly happened in Pabna? The revolt there presumably called into existence a number of local leaders. The contemporary reports however, provide information about only one or two. Though their representativeness remains an open question, the present study is confined to them.

Ishan Chandra Ray was probably the most outstanding of the leaders. The Shazadpur lawyers in their petition to the government called him the 'instigator' of the 'rebellion':

> 'Ishan Chunder Rae has become a king of the rebellious creatures. He decides their disputes and awards punishments to those whom he finds guilty in any offence. When the ryots of any village become anxious to rebel, they go to the said Rae and write their agreements in his presence, and by paying him a large amount as *nuzer* are then reckoned among the rebellious men'.

The Rajshahi Commissioner referred to him as 'the first promoter of resistance in the villages in the Banerjee' estates.... There is no doubt that he was generally looked up to as the inaugurator of a new regime in which zamindars were to be superseded'. The Magistrate of Pabna also concluded that he 'has been chiefly instrumental in bringing about this combination .... Wherever I have travelled I have found the name of Rajah Ishan Chunder Roy in the mouth of every one'. The rebels 'declared themselves to be the ryots only of the Queen, whose Mofussil representative was Raja Ishan Chunder Roy'. His name had such an irresistible appeal that peasants from Faridpur and Rajshahi came with presents to meet him in Sirajganj and asked for *hukumnamas* (order) authorising them to rebel in their districts. Even Ray's refusal did not daunt them, and they left saying: 'The leader (*karta*) has ignored our appeal; but we shall rebel with his name'.

Who was Ishan Chandra Ray? How was he drawn into the movement? Nolan who claims to have 'known him of old' thus describes him: he is 'a small landholder and possesses considerable means besides his property'. His landed status was presumably not a high one. He was known as a *talukdar*, and he was also a leaseholder of a certain portion of an estate included in the villages of Daulatpur and Gopalpur. Nolan's description of him also as a 'local capitalist' indicates other sources of his income and other spheres of his activities. We wish Nolan could elaborate on this appellation. The only relevant piece of information is that he was a trader.

His involvement in the revolt was related by the local officers entirely to his bitterness against some of the leading zamindars. According to the Rajshahi Commissioner, he 'personally suffered indignity at the hands of the Banerjees'. The Pabna Magistrate found out that he 'has been greatly oppressed by some of the leading zamindars, and is consequently too ready to do anything to injure them in return. How this came about has not, however, been properly explained. The rift tended to widen, and even developments, with which such zamindars were not directly involved, contributed to it. Nolan thus described one of these. This was connected with a dispute over the proprietary title to a certain estate included in the villages of Daulatpur and Gopalpur. The claim of two widows was contested by another group of four widows. The dispute notwithstanding, 'these ladies have leased their rights to the two most powerful men in the neighbourhood'—the first group to Braja Sundar Bhaduri, 'a leading *mooktear* [pleader]', and the second group to Ishan Ray. This quarrel of Ishan Ray's with a local pleader became linked up with his hostilities against the zamindars mainly because Bhaduri was 'an agent for several zamindars and a man of influence among them'. The dispute had continued for long involving a considerable amount of litigation in the civil court with no definite result' and leading 'from time to time to breaches of the peace'.

Such episodes understandably heightened Ray's bitterness against the zamindars, but this scarcely explains his commitment to the peasants' cause. Such a commitment and the acceptance of him as a trustworthy leader by the peasants presupposed a long association with the peasantry. Nolan's report provides a clue to the question. He 'has for years given countenance to a few ryots who were at feud with their landlord or their landlord's lessees'. He helped the ryots in prosecuting criminal and probably civil cases with money and advice'. How this association began and developed is unknown.

A common enmity towards the zamindars had perhaps a role in drawing them together, and it is also likely that some kind of credit relations cemented the bond. When the revolt started help from such a resourceful person like Ray was supremely reassuring to the rebels.

Did Ray's participation develop eventually into a participation of a wider group, to which economically and socially he belonged. A conclusive answer is difficult to offer. Ray was perhaps not a lone outsider in the rebel camp. The frequent clashes of the kind in which Ray was involved and the persistent inter-zamindari quarrels had presumably alienated a number of such influential local personalities, who though not sharing the rebels' convictions sided with them out of a motive of settling old scores.

The contemporary reports refer to Shambhu Nath Pal as another significant leader. However, we know much less about him. Pal, according to Nolan, was a Kayastha, and 'formerly a servant of the Bandhopadhay's. The Magistrate's diary of 27 October, 1873 describes him as a 'headman'. We are not told why he left his job under the Banerjis or what his specific responsibilities as a village headman were. The old kind of *mandals* who had a decisive role to play in the Rangpur uprising (1783) seem to have nearly completely disappeared by the time of the revolt, as a detailed enquiry during the time of Campbell revealed. The post had ceased to be confined to an established family of *mandals,* and could be acquired now by any successful local men, who included quite a number of substantial peasants, but were not necessarily exclusively peasants. Moreover, the power and prestige which the post once gave its holder had also remarkably diminished over the years. Some of the old responsibilities perhaps still remained. The Pabna Magistrate's description of Pal shows that he had a thorough understanding of the rural problems of the time, particularly the ones relating to the intriguing rent question. It Wam Pal who argued the peasants' case before the magistrate, particularly trying to refute the point of view of the zamindars that the increased rent demand was based on a recent measurement of the lands.

Without a more detailed knowledge of the social and economic background of many other leaders who presumably emerged during the revolt it is difficult to answer the question that has been asked at the beginning of this section. Judging by the *recorded evidence,* it seems that the participation of non-peasant groups having a crucial role to play in the revolt was limited. (And its scale was much smaller than in some well-known cases of peasant revolts in Europe, such as the revolt of 1381 in England led by John Ball and Wat Tyler, the peasants' war of 1525 in Germany and a number of uprisings in 17th century France which Ronald Mousnier has described). The Eshafshahi peasants seem to have been an extraordinarily confident group, and though the first impulse probably came from Ishan Ray and few other charismatic personalities, the revolt derived its main strength from the sense of purpose and the moral fervour of the rebel peasants.

6. The Attitude of the Government towards the Revolt

While deciding to strike the rebel peasants seem to have implicitly assumed that the government would not come out openly against them. Indeed, as Nolan puts it, 'the ryots are eager to carry Government officials with them in their resistance to what they consider illegal oppression'. How far were such hopes of the peasants fulfilled?

Government were far from hostile to the revolt while it first broke out. Such permissiveness was largely due to their particular assessment of its causes. The local officers more or less agreed in blaming the revolt on the wrong methods of the zamindars in regard to increase of rent. Campbell later recalled how it all came about: 'The Lieutenant Governor believes every one is agreed that the first fault was that of the zamindars or some of them'. Illegal cesses had been imposed from time to time, and all on a sudden the zamindars sought to formalise them. 'Some of them certainly proceeded in an extortionate manner. The result was the union and violent outbreak of the ryots'. Moreover, unlike in some previous cases of peasant revolts (such as the Rangpur uprising, the Ferazi movement and the tribal revolts) the plans of actions of the rebels in Pabna had scarcely any anti-Government stance. Popular slogans and sayings of the time, such as 'We shall be the ryots of the Queen and Queen alone', and '*Māhārānir Hāoā Baichey*' (A new wind is blowing—the wind of the Queen) reflect a faith of the peasants in the capacity of the existing institutions of the Government for doing good to them. They did not share the later radical notions that such institutions were designed primarily for promoting the class interests of the zamindars. Since they did not think in terms of any revolutionary redistribution of landed property, and wanted only minor adjustments within the existing framework, which was not logically incompatible with the existence of small properties such as theirs', it was self-defeating for them to defy such institutions. The 'anti-colonial' content which is sometimes called one of the essential aspects of 'the radicalism in the peasant revolts in India' was markedly absent here and Government could consequently afford to be more generous to the rebels.

Government in the beginning even went to the extent of approving of 'peaceful combinations'. However, they also candidly stated their views about the limits of their permissibility. Such 'combinations' would be tolerated merely as a means of opposing the illegal rent demands of the zamindars. If the framework of the existing institution of zamindari was thereby questioned they ceased to be permissible, and Government reaffirmed their commitment to the defence of the existing property rights. Sometimes, the rebels seem to have been animated by the ideas of eliminating the zamindars altogether. Such thoughts, however, scarcely crystallised into a systematic social philosophy, and Government had not to bother about it later.

What really worried the Government was the so-called 'law and order' problem. The local officers were feeling increasingly sceptical about the possibility of keeping the movement within 'the bounds of law'. In fact, as we have noted earlier, the 'law and order' question was throughout an intriguing one, and Government found it not an easy matter to decide where 'the order' had broken down and also whether the rebels alone were to be blamed for this. The Government measures were therefore largely preventive in character. Whatever the origins, such measures eroded more than anything else the vitality of the movement.

The local officers seem to have prejudged the issue in some cases. Nolan, for instance, was undoubtedly guilty of a hasty actions when he was handling the situation in the area included in the Ulapara police station, and his action was based on an assumption (which he did not care to test) that the peasants with a distinct tribal descent were more prone to violence than others. 'As long as their league'. Nolan argued,

> 'was confined to the comparatively civilized ryots of Shazadpure, I did not think special measures necessary for the preservation of the peace. It has now spread to Qolaparh, where the cultivators are much more rough and ignorant; many of them *Bonyas* [tribals], and the majority of them unaccustomed to united action'.

Even the 'civilised ryots' were soon to be penalised, and it all inevitably ended up with the decision 'to break up the combination', as Nolan put it. The initial warning of the Government to the rebels has an ominous undertone;

> 'The movement must be met with firmness, and the leaders should be informed that, though the zamindars will not be allowed in any way to oppress them, they will be severely dealt with for any overt act which may endanger the public peace, or for any unlawful demonstrations to the danger and annoyance of peaceable inhabitants'.

The measures that followed show that Government did mean it. Intervillage movement of the rebels 'in parties of more than ten' was forbidden. The contacts between the different groups were thus largely disrupted, and a movement like the one in Pabna, which comprehended about three hundred villages would simply wither away without such contacts. Even within the bounds of a village the rebels found it increasingly difficult to meet together for the purpose of taking vital decisions. Blowing of buffalo horns or 'other musical instrument' for 'invoking assemblies' or for 'intimating union' was prohibited. Where the rebels did manage to meet despite such difficulties, the police was ordered to 'disperse such assemblies'. A particular strategy of the rebels proved eventually self-defeating. The peasants invariably informed the local police of their decision to join the movement, and the local officers, thus forewarned, could concentrate their efforts in appropriate places. Where a 'breach' of the peace was feared, the officers sought to prevent it by 'binding' some local leaders to 'keep the peace', and when they judged that such breaches had occurred the leaders were immediately arrested. The Pabna Magistrate felt that the removal of Ishan Ray from the scene would soon demoralise the rebels and

> 'for the sake of preserving the peace and showing the uneducated ryots that he has none of the powers which they believe him to possess. I have taken bail from him to remain with me till further orders'

— a step he judged 'a most necessary act of policy'.

It remains an open question whether such measures were exclusively or primarily aimed at protecting the class interests of the zamindars. A conclusive answer is difficult to suggest without a more detailed knowledge of the composition of the groups which the rebels peasants sought to coerce or actually coerced into falling into line. However, there is hardly any doubt that the rebels, who during the whole course of the active revolt were in a superior strategic position in relation to the zamindars, were hit far harder than the zamindars. A grave threat to the authority of the zamindars was thus removed.

However, once the revolt had been 'suppressed', Government were not guilty of a decisively partisan attitude. Campbell was reluctant 'to precipitate too much direct Government action', and felt a 'there is much to be said for a policy of masterly inactivity'. This did not mean that Government had entirely kept aloof, leaving the battle to be fought out by the two warring groups. They only sought to avoid siding with either group. The local officers were throughout on the move trying, by means of their moral influence and authority, to persuade the two groups to a compromise, and in fact whatever, successes were achieved towards this were largely due to their initiative.

Beyond this they were unwilling to go. The zamindars sent up a howl that their rental income has been endangered, and they wanted the Government immediately to intervene. The appointment of a special Commission with extra-ordinary powers in regard to settlement of rent disputes and the restoration of the jurisdiction of the revenue authorities over such disputes would, they argued, go a long way towards solving their difficulties. Government straightaway rejected such pleas. 'The Lieutenant Governor must confess to have had some feeling of repugnance to concede the special machinery and extra-ordinary powers sought by the zamindars'. As regards the second suggestion, Campbell agreed with the Dacca Commissioner's view that 'the zamindars now get more law and less rent', and that they occasionally suffered because of the usual tardiness of the legal process. This, however, he argued, did not justify a complete reversal of the process: 'it would be unjust to hand the ryots back to any courts less scrupulous regarding the provisions of the law in their favour'.

Campbell's argument in this regard rested on two broad assumptions: the zamindars had misrepresented their present 'rent difficulties', and such difficulties, even where they were real, had not much to do with the existing legal machinery. The difficulties of the zamindars did not result, as the local officers informed Campbell, from any denial by the peasants of their obligations to pay rent. 'They ryots have not generally shown a disposition to refuse all rents, but on the contrary offer rents which the zamindar consider inadequate and have in many cases deposited rents in court. While the zamindars ask too much the ryots offer too little'. This, again, happened not because of the particular nature of the legal machinery, but because of the tactlessness of the zamindars in asking for too much at a time.

An intervention in favour of the ryots, Campbell argued, was not justifiable either. His main assumption in this was that the peasants, particularly in the eastern Bengal districts, could quite do without this. Their capacity for 'litigations' against the zamindars and their 'strong power of union' have time and again been demonstrated.

> 'There is no doubt that the general tendency of the increasing knowledge and independence of the ryots, and the general march of affairs, is to render less and less possible the old undefined and unsatisfactory relations between the landlords and ryots'.

This reluctance directly to side with either group was based on a more fundamental assumption that the present turmoil would soon die down of itself. This at least was the lesson to Government of the agrarian movements in the past. 'From time immemorial there have been serious rent disputes in different parts of Bengal, and not infrequently they have settled themselves to a degree which one might hardly have expected when things were at their worst'.

Surprisingly enough, Campbell was reluctant to commit himself to a firm policy towards a solution of the rent question, which admittedly was at the bottom of the recent agrarian tension in Pabna and also elsewhere, and he did not have a consistent policy to follow. Sometimes he felt such a solution was badly needed, but he seemed to have been moving between two extremes: either a total solution, or no attempt at the solution at all at the time. 'If the settlement is to be effective, it must not only get the zamindars out of their present difficulties; it must bind them for the future. It must settle all questions of possession, measurement and rates. . . . The Lieutenant Governor would not advocate interference unless it is carried to the point'. Sometimes he felt it would not be worthwhile at the moment to attempt such a solution, since it seemed to him unnecessary. 'Such disputes must inevitably occur in so vast a country with so complicated tenures under so loose and unsettled system, with so little record and definition of rights'. In other words, he did not think that 'the evils are so undoubt that we can interfere thoroughly and effectually'. Government could therefore afford to wait: 'the defects of the existing law were not yet fully developed, and I thought that in Bengal at any rate the ryots were sufficiently holding their own'. Campbell seems to have also felt that he might find it difficult to persuade the Viceroy to his point of view. This was what he presumably meant when he said that he did not think 'the political circumstances of the time sufficiently favourable'. He was aware that Northbrooke held views 'which were much more conservative, than those on which I had been acting with the support of previous viceroys'. He found him 'very much indisposed to any interference between landlord and tenant', and he was cautious to move fearing that any action on my part might bring into prominence a divergence of views'. In fact with increasing popular discontent over what the *Friend of India* called 'over-Government or Stracheyism', over excessive legislation, enhancement of land revenue, increased local cesses and imposts and, above all, income tax, Northbrooke was wary of further interference. The Duke of Argyll, Secretary of State, too was not quite in sympathy with Campbell's reform measures. 'Reports' of Campbell's 'intentions' touched the 'susceptibilities of the Duke of Argyll in regard to the position of landlords', and Argyll 'cautioned me against any undue interference with the rights which had been given by the fundamental laws of the Bengal system'.

7. The Results of the Movement

The actual results of the movement still largely remain an area of darkness'. We know very little about it from the official reports. This is explicable. First, most of the leading zamindars rejected the compromise formula that the local officers had suggested. As a result, such officers gradually lost contact with what happened later. Secondly, the revolt concerned Government mainly as an administrative issue—as a problem of 'law and order'. Once the immediate problem had been largely solved, Government did not care to know what happened to the warring groups, at least as long as the local courts could be trusted to look after them. The statistics that the courts provided from time to time suggest a state of a protracted legal fight, but its results were mostly ignored.

That 'agrarian revolution' as a description of the broad results of the revolt is a misleading phrase has been noted earlier. The revolt seems to have only marginally affected the power and authority of the zamindars. It was the petty zamindars who were mostly keen on a compromise, and they did concede some of the peasants' demands. Even this did not lead to any crisis in their authority. In fact, to the extent that this pacified the peasants their authority was stabilised.

Two kinds of development seem to have occurred. Some zamindars preferred to get rid of the rent problem for a long time to come by fixing the rent rates of the peasants, though they asked for a big initial payment as compensation for the subsequent loss in their income which this inevitably involved (An earlier section refers to this). The offer was presumably acceptable only to a small group of substantial peasants. The second and the more typical development was the continuity of the old bitterness, though the arena had now shifted to the law courts. The leading zamindars, except perhaps the Tagores, scarcely flinched from their firm decision not to yield, and uncompromising were the rebels too.

According to an official report of 1875 the Eshafshahi pargana was 'still divided into two hostile camps', with the 'rent unions as strong as ever'. A 'genuine' understanding was reached in only one estate. By the next year signs of exhaustion were visible in the camp of the rebels. Despite the defeat of the zamindars in 93 typical rent suits the peasants were more eager for a compromise, and 'the ryots have given up a great deal and the zamindars something'. The rebels lost more ground by 1882. In that year the district Collector explained the reluctance of the peasants to take up a fresh fight by their memory of 'defeat and loss' with which such a 'course . . . since the time of the Pubna riots, has been associated in their minds'.

The peasants bent under extra-ordinary pressure—the relentless legal battle fought by the zamindars at an enormous cost supplemented by all possible sorts of coercion. The Pubna Magistrate's description in 1873 of the attitude of the leading zamindars that the rich and strong-minded landowners like Ishan Banerjee are in no hurry and are content to wait for a year or two, and see what happens' also applied to the later years. They sought to wear out the rebels primarily by means of perpetual legal suits, despite their failure in a number of them. The Banerjee family lost 300,000 rupees in the contest, but still fought on. Holding out against such determined foes for long required a command over immense resources which the rebels understandably lacked.

8. Summary and Conclusions

Here ends the story of the 'agrarian protest' of 1873 in Pabna. Unlike in some earlier cases of such protests, the group that was most articulate in this was the peasantry. Other groups did participate, but their interests were scarcely reflected in the protest, and the various other antagonistic relations which the operation of the zamindary system had produced over the years could not determine the general strategy of the movement.

The particular methodological question that has been stressed in this study is that it would be wrong to explain the revolt in some universal terms, such as the working of the zamindary system, the rent problem in general and the general behaviour of the peasant economy. It has to be related to the particular local variations of such universals. The particular did follow from the universal. However, the particular need not necessarily have happened at that particular moment of history. The universal issues, including the ideological ones, appeared 'only in very prosaic guise in the villages'.

In Pabna the decisive particular moment came when the zamindars had abruptly increased the rent demand and sought to enforce it by dubious methods. This is explicable. 'Economic deterioration by slow degrees can become accepted by its victims as part of the normal situation. Especially where no alternative is clearly visible, more and more privation can gradually find acceptance in the peasants' standards of what is right and proper. What infuriates peasants (and not just peasant) is a new and sudden imposition or demand that strikes many people at once and that is a break with accepted rules and customs'. The timing of such an abrupt increase in the rent demand was also a crucial factor. This coincided with an agricultural depression—a sharp fall in the prices of jute and also a considerable fall in the prices of rice. The sudden and large increase in the rent demand affected most of the peasants, and the question of status, *i.e.* the question whether a ryot was an occupancy ryot or not, was only marginally relevant.

The revolt need not be related to the so-called 'disintegration of the peasantry'. Increased rent demands of the zamindars and the occasional fluctuations in the economy did adversely affect the peasants, but seldom resulted in any such 'disintegration'. Agricultural resources tended to increase during the past two decades, and the peasants as a group of small property holders had also a share in this and by the time of the revolt they seem to have acquired a certain status in the existing landed society.

This partly was the reason why the rebel peasants did not think in terms of a radical redistribution of property. Their primary concern was to stem any encroachment on their small properties, and they looked for certain guarantees in this. The existing legal machinery did help them to some extent, but this was found wanting at a certain stage. Even when the peasants rebelled, they scarcely rejected this machinery, and the suppression of the revolt only resulted in reinforcing their dependence on this machinery.

CHAPTER 7

Muslims and Indian Freedom Movement

In his *Modern Trends in Islam,* Sir Hamilton Gibb has thus advised scholars who investigate themes involving divergent and delicate interpretations:

> In these days when we are enveloped in an atmosphere charged with propaganda, it is the duty of every investigator to define precisely to himself and his audience the principles which determine his point of view. (pp. x-xi)

Instead of defining my point of view, I would like to lay down certain parameters within which an objective review of the nature and extent of Muslim contribution to freedom movement may be attempted. A realistic approach to the situation is possible only if the following facts are kept in mind:

(1) The fall of the Mughal Empire was not merely the collapse of a political system; it was the end of a civilisation which had derived its hue and colour from different cultural traditions of India, and was basically *Indian* in character. It was not without significance that when Bahadur Shah Zafar stood up against the British Government, all Indian groups—even those which were till then opposing the Mughals—gathered under his banner. The reaction to the fall of the Mughal Empire was therefore registered in the value-systems governing the life of the people in different spheres. The British occupation of the country was followed by liquidation of the old social order, an order which was knit together by deep rooted feelings of co-

existence. The indigenous arts and crafts were replaced by an economy which looked to the interest of the British industries more than the plight of the Indian worker. A whole class of aristocracy, *mansabdārs* and Government servants, which had flourished under the aegis of the Mughal Empire, was thrown out of employment. The famous Urdu poet Mir said:

(Those who were proud of their crown and throne till yesterday, are deprived of alms today.)

All the institutions and trusts which state patronage had kept alive, were starved and pulled down. The Christian missionary propaganda to bring about a change in religious demography added another dimension to the situation. It was a battle to be fought on all fronts—political, religious, social and economic. No real history of the freedom movement can be written if any of these fronts is ignored.

(2) Shah Wali-Allah of Delhi (ob. 1762) had read portents of decline in the disturbed economic equilibrium of the country, decrease in production and increase in parasites. In his opinion the fall of the political system was preceded by the fall of the economic system.

In the eighteenth century Bengal was the economic prop of the Mughal Empire. The revenues received from Bengal supplied life blood to the Mughal Empire, "During the time of Mohammad Shah," writes Shah Wali-Allah "one *crore* came (to Delhi) from Bengal. This amount was sent by the *subahdar* without delay. Notwithstanding the payment of this (huge) amount, the *suabdar* of Bengal was the richest among the nobles of Hindustan." Thus the economic arteries of the Mughal Empire were in Bengal. Its fall was tantamount to the fall of India.

(3) Geo-political developments had changed the areas of conflict and confrontation. In the past invaders had come through the north-western frontiers, but now the oceans had

become vulnerable. Even in the heyday of Mughal power, no serious attention was given to the danger coming from the seas. Akbar ignored the overtures of the Ottomans to form an alliance against the Portuguese influence on the seas. The insecurity of the Mughal commercial ships was deplorable. The shifting of the centre of political gravity from the north-western frontier to the Indian Coastal areas was a development for which the Mughal Government was not prepared, but which deeply coloured the Indian freedom struggle and determined its dimensions.

(4) The foreign companies—Portuguese, French, Dutch, English-initially masquerading as trading companies, developed political ambitions and threw out their tentacles in all directions. The British East India company succeeded in obtaining concessions from the Mughal Emperors and stabilised its economic hold. The process of foreign control was thus through apparently legal but really exploitative methods. As a result of the economic control of its resources by the East India Company, the Mughal Government at Delhi became rickety and invertebrate.

(5) Industrial Revolution and scientific development in the West had brought about a total change in the methods of warfare, means of communication and the sources of economic viability. In all the battles fought by the freedom fighters they displayed extraordinary valour and matchless spirit of sacrifice but, as Mawlana Nadhir Ahmad Dehlavi once remarked, medieval acrobatic art of warfare could not stand the new tests of military organisation and tactics. From Narkul Birya to 1857, all battles were lost on account of outmoded methods of warfare.

(6) When the futility of military operations for the overthrow of foreign domination came to be realised, other methods of resistance were explored.' Non-cooperation was deemed to be an effective instrument to paralyse a foreign Government but public opinion had to be mobilised for it. It was a change of avenue from the battle-field to the platform. It was realised that under the changed circumstances an intelligent, well-informed bourgeoisie was a *sine qua non* to

carry forward the freedom struggle. The Hindus created this bourgeoisie earlier than the Muslims. The Muslims needed concentration on Western education if they wanted to participate in the new type of political struggle that began in the last quarter of the 19th century. Sir Sayyid played the most important role in creating a Muslim bourgeoisie.

(7) Interest in movements of the Muslim world had tremendous impact to the Indian freedom struggle. It awakened the Indian masses. The view that Muslim involvement in movements pertaining to Tripoli, Balkan, Khilafat, *etc.* was a deviation, is absolutely baseless. It was through these movements that Indian masses were taught to agitate.

Main Phases of the Freedom Struggle

The story of the rise and fall of British power in India covers a span of 190 years—in 1757 the Battle of Plassey brought them to power, in 1947 they left the country after partitioning it. We may follow the march of events to have a full and fair view of the political developments during this period.

The main stages in this freedom struggle may be identified as follows:

(i) 1757 to 1799: From the Battle of Plassey to the Fall of Seringapatam and the death of Tipu Sultan.

(ii) 1799 to 1831: The period between two disasters: death of Tipu Sultan and the defeat at Balakot. In the Vellore Mutiny of 1806 the descendants of Tipu played a part and suffered expulsion. The Liberation Movement, organised by Sayyid Ahmad Shahid with great zeal and dedication, met a serious disaster at Balakot in the north-western region in 1831. In the same year Mir Nithar Ali alias Titu, fell fighting at Narkul Birya in Bengal.

(iii) 1831 to 1857: after Balakot to the upheaval of 1857. The Moplah outbreaks of 1849-1855 and the Sadiqpuri agitations reflect Muslim feeling of resentment during this period. 1857 was the culmination of a long process of resentment and bitterness at foreign domination.

(iv) 1857 to 1908: the aftermath of 1857 and the British repression of Muslims. Emergence of three different approaches to the situation: (a) Tendency to migrate to Hijaz; (b) determination to pursue freedom struggle by developing the spirit of non-cooperation and resolute rejection of service and social contact with the British; and (c) concentration on Western education in order to bring Muslims on par with other communities and turn them into an effective bourgeoisie.

The British Army Commission evolved during the period the formula of 'counterpoise of Indians against Indians.' The Partition of Bengal was intended to create bitterness between the Hindus and the Muslims. There were Muslims, like Mawlana Abul Kalam Azad, who joined the revolutionaries of Bengal, opposed the Partition of Bengal and worked for creating revolutionary centres in different regions.

(v) 1908 to 1924: During this period developments in Muslim countries attracted the attention and agitational polities began. But these agitations had direct impact on the Indian freedom movement. Through support of liberation and resistance movements in Muslim countries Indian feelings were aroused against foreign rule.

Muslim journalistic activity during this period played a very important role in arousing public feelings against the British. *Comrade, al-Hilal, at-Balagh, Hamdard and Zamindar* were in the forefront of national struggle and their contribution to the freedom movement cannot be under-estimated.

British repression touched its highest watermark in the Jallianwalah Bagh massacre on April 13, 1919. Large number of Muslims were also shot dead.

The Non-Cooperation movement was made possible by the ground prepared by the agitations organised in connection with developments in Muslim lands. The slogan of panIslamism was raised by the imperial powers to sabotage collaboration between the Muslims and the non-Muslims. Not-withstanding British efforts to the contrary, Hindu-Muslim collaboration and cooperation during the period was remarkable.

(vi) 1925 to 1936: Constitutional struggle began during this period. The Simon commission (1927), the Nehru Report (1928), the Irwin-Gandhi Pact (1931), the Round Table Conferences had deep and far-reaching impact on Muslim attitudes. The Muslims played an important role in the Civil Disobedience Movement of 1930. But fears began to loom large on Muslim mind about their future as a minority.

There was complete identity of views and approach between the Hindus and the Muslims so long as the militant or the non-cooperative phase of the freedom struggle continued. Parting of ways came when constitutional struggle began and safeguards and reservations were claimed by the Muslims. Mawlana Azad combated from the very beginning all concepts of minority and advised the Muslims to have faith in God rather than in their numerical strength. But the feeling of protection once aroused in a minority could be allayed only by large-hearted treatment of the majority. The Nehru Report conceded 25% of seats in the Central Assembly while the Muslims demanded 33%. After a good deal of bargaining 27% were conceded. A difference of 6% of seats estranged Muslims in 1928. In 1935-37 the inclusion of two, rather than one, Muslim leader in U.P. Cabinet dashed all hopes of united political struggle to the ground. Separatist politics raised its head and Muslim leadership began to cut itself off from the mainstream of freedom movement. An in-depth study of forces and factors which led Mawlana Muhammad 'Ali, Mawlana Shawkat 'Ali, Mr. Jinnah, Mawlana Hasrat Mohani, Mawlana Zafar 'Ali Khan and others, who were initially ardent supporters of the Congress, to sever their relations with the Congress, is a great desideratum.

(vii) 1937-1947: Provincial Autonomy to Freedom. This was the last and the final phase of struggle for liberation of the country, which was characterised by deepening suspicions, lack of trust and goodwill and failure to allay fears. The Muslim participation in freedom struggle was unabated. The Muslims joined the Indian National Army, participated in demonstrations in Bombay, and sacrificed lives in the Quit India Movement of 1942. Negotiations and parleys conducted at the official and the non-official levels, instead of bridging the gulf, hardened the attitudes and accentuated the difference. The story told by Mawlana Azad in his *India Wins Freedom* needs an objective and dispassionate appraisal.

The Battle of Plassey

The Battle of Plassey was the first Indian confrontation with the British forces. The English army comprised 950 infantry and 150 artillery men, supported by 2100 Indian mercenaries, Seldom had an army with such a limited number achieved such a remarkable success. Siraj al-Dawlah offered resolute resistance but was betrayed by Mir Ja'far (c-in-c), Nand Kumar (*Fawjdar* of Hugli) and Amin Chand. He was defeated, caught and killed. The Battle of Plassey sounded the death knell of the Mughal Empire and paved way for the consolidation of British power. Siraj al-Dawlah's tragic end dashed to the ground all hopes of saving the country from foreign domination. Raja Ram Narain Mawzun wrote in deep anguish

(O denizens of the wild, you are well aware. Tell (me) details of Majnun's death. The mad man has expired but what has at last happened to the wilderness.)

Iqbal has given expression to the revulsion of Muslim feelings at the betrayal of Mir ja'far which brought about the fall of Siraj al-Dawlah and the end of Mughal hegemony. His poem in which hell refuses to accept the obnoxious bodies of traitors—ja'far and Sadiq—shows how deeply Muslim conscience was shocked at the result of the Battle.

Tipu Sultan an The Battle of Seringapatam

The first well planned and determined resistance to British domination of the country after the Battle of Plassey came from Tipu Sultan who, according to Iqbal, was the last arrow in our armoury.

Tipu Sultan (1750-1799) pursued with determination and vigour the anti-British policy of his father, Hydar Ali, He sought an alliance with the Ottomans and the French against the British, and sent his ambassadors to France, Turkey and Iran. Fully conscious of the nature of the struggle, he undertook naval reorganisation and acquired twenty frigates and 40 war ships. Kirpatrick says that his was a very 'alarming plan of a marine establishment.' Apart from reorganisation of army, Tipu turned his attention to economic and commercial development. He appreciated the dimensions of the Industrial Revolution and was keen to develop industries. Like the great trading companies of European nations, he established his factories and trading agencies in coastal towns. He employed French artisans sent to him by Louis XVI. silk, sugar, arms, paper and textile industries were developed by him with remarkable speed. Cottage industries were also encouraged. Vigorous armament plans, involvement in international trade and establishment of factories, indicated the first response of India to scientific and industrial developments in the West. This policy was based on the realisation that industrial and scientific development alone could provide the necessary strength to fight the Western powers.

Tipu refused to join Wellesley's system of Subsidiary Alliances as other princes had done and mobilised all his resources to challenge the British power. In 1799 Tipu fell fighting for the freedom of the country. In the same year the Turkish fleet suffered a serious defeat at the Battle of Navarino. Fall of Seringapatam and Navarino marked the beginning of the decline of Muslim power and prestige. But at the same time their appeared, as Iqbal has noticed, new movements for political revival and intellectual reorientation of the Muslim peoples.

The fall of Seringapatam was a great calamity. No other anti-British movement in subsequent years was military so well organised as that of Tipu Sultan. The members of Tipu's family persisted in their anti-British activities and participated in the Sepoy Mutiny of Vellore (1806). They were deported to Calcutta.

Stir in Bengal

In 1776-77 Majnun Shah, a religious leader of Bengal,

known by his designation of *Faqir*, rose against the British control of Bengal. He established two centres of opposition to British authority in the Nepal *taai*-one in Makwanpur and the other at Kathmandu. In Bengal Madar Ganj and Mahasthan (in Bogra district) were his strongholds. Majnun Shah particularly attracted the villagers to his movement. They provided food and shelter to his followers in the rural area. For about ten years he organised his resistance movement with great zeal and determination. Its military potential was limited but he succeeded in creating that fervour in which every man instinctively lays his hand on the sword hilt. His work was taken up by his son Chiragh 'Ali Shah who attracted Hindus to his fold. Bhawami Pathak and Devi Chaudharani were important Hindu supporters of his movement. His followers attacked the factories of the British and seized their goods, cash and weapons. When the British entered into alliance with the Maharaja of Nepal, the training and recruiting centres of Chiragh Ali Shah were ruthlessly liquidated. Resolute opposition of Majnun Shah's followers and their effective organisation made Lord Minto confess that the Government had not the strength to deal with them.

Another movement with an identical programme was launched in 1775 by Karam Shah from Susang *parganah*. Both Hindus and Muslims joined him. On his death in 1813 his son Tipu assumed charge of the movement. He attacked the *zamindars* of Shirpur who were obstructing freedom plans. Within a short time he established his own courts. These courts performed their functions for some years (1831-33) but were eventually rooted out by the British.

The movements of Majnun Shah and Karam Shah were initiated without any military resources needed to combat a power like the British but they registered deep resentment of the Muslim masses to foreign dominating of the country.

Fatwa of Shah Abd al-Aziz

After the entry of Lord Lake's forces in Delhi (1803). Shah 'Abd al-Aziz, the son and successor of Shah Wali-Allah of Delhi issued a fatwa declaring all land under British occupation as *dar al-harb*. It was the first attempt to buttress the freedom struggle through recourse to religion. The concept of *jihãd* articulated such strong feelings of resistance in Muslim people that the British government appeared more concerned about this idea floating in the atmosphere than sporadic expressions of armed resistance. They realized that the spirit thus generated could not be met by bullets alone. A reorientation of religious outlook was necessary to root out feelings of jihãd from Muslim mind. Some of the literature produced under the inspiration of British to explain or explain away the meaning of *jihãd* in Muslim religious parlance brings to focus the nature of the problem. But the concept of *jihãd* went on supplying motive power to Muslim struggle for freedom. We find Theodore Beck, Principal of the M.A.O. College Aligarh writing to Badr al-Din Tyabji on 7 May 1880:

> The older people of Delhi remember the last Emperor of the House of Timur. Add to this that religious fanaticism is not dead. The cry of *jihãd* is heard now and then. And add moreover that the people are easily excitable and love a fight—as they did at Delhi and Etawah—and we have we think the gravest reasons for fearing that if this kind of agitation spreads, the whole of Upper India may one day be aflame.

In the Non-Cooperation Movement it was again invoked.

The Fara 'IDI Movement

The Farã 'idi Movement, started by Haji Shari 'at-Allãh (A.D. 1781-1840) played a very important role in the freedom struggle. Shari 'at-Allãh had lived in Hijaz for twenty years (1799-1818) and had nursed his freedom aspirations there. He appeared on the stage at a crucial moment in the history of Bengal. According to James Wise, from 1765 when the East India Company established its control over the *dïwãnï* of Bengal, Bihar and Orissa to the day that Haji Shari 'at-Allãh appeared in the field, Muslims were disorganised like a herd without a shepherd. He gave them that unity of purpose and motive power which transformed them into a determined resistance movement. He particularly worked among the lower sections of the people, labourers and peasants, and infused in them restless spirit of opposition to an alien system.

In 1840 Hãjĩ Shari 'at-Allãh died and his son Mawlavi Muhammad Muhsin alias Düdü Miyãn succeeded him. It was under him that the Farã 'idi Movement became a force to be reckoned with. Unfortunately the nature and significance of the Farã 'idi Movement has not been properly assessed so far. In fact no historian, like Mawlana Ghulãm Rasül Mehr who brought to light forgeries in documents peltaining to the Mujahidin Movement, has been able to discover forgeries in Fara 'idi documents. The Fara'idi Movement had a definite political orientation and a political objective. Dumpier, Commissioner of Police in Bengal, said in his statement before the court trying Dudu Miyan that the aim of his movement was to turn out the British from India.

Dudu Miyan's movement was a comprehensive one—it combined religious economic and political objectives. He raised the slogan *al-Ard li-Allah*-'the land belongs to Allah.' It was a revolutionary declaration, and *inter alia,* meant the liquidation of *zamindari* which enjoyed British support. He further declared that India was a *dar al-harb*. It was an echo of the *fatwa* issued by Shah 'Abd al-'Aziz in Delhi. They stopped Friday and *'Id* prayers and applied the laws of *Shari'at* as laid down for organisation of life in *daral-harb*. The main centres of Fara'idi activity were the rural areas of Bengal. The cities were strongly garrisoned by foreign contingents and the British factories were so thoroughly protected that it was difficult to organise any anti-British movement in urban areas.

The Fara'idis had an elaborate programme of resistance against the British. They formed a parallel Government in rural areas—organised the peasants, and established *panchayats*. Faridpur and Bari Sal saw the functioning of Fara'idi authority at its peak. Dudu Miyan appointed his deputies in these areas and assigned specific territorial responsibilities to them. The administration of Dudu Miyan tackled with courage and vision all problems created by the *zamindars,* the indigo planters and others. Perhaps they had clear realisation of the fact that a readjustment in economic relationship was absolutely necessary for the success of the liberation movement.

Jihad Movement of Sayyid Ahmad Shahid

Sayyid Ahmad Shahid (ob.1831) belonged to the school of Shah Wali-Allah and gave practical shape to Shah 'Abd al-'Aziz's *fatwa* of *Jihad*. The nature and programme of his movement was destroyed by the English historians and those who wrote under their inspiration. Mawlana Sayyid Abul Hasan Ali Nadwi, himself a descendant of a great *mujahid* leader, has brought to light a letter which Sayyid Ahmad Shahid had addressed to Raja Hindu Rao in order to enlist his support for his struggle against the British. It runs as follows:

> You know well that foreigners from across the Seas... who (do business and) deal with merchandise, have become rulers of the country. They have destroyed the honour and position of big nobles and princes. The ruling class and those who worked in the political field are sitting (inert) in secluded corners. So a group of humble and poor people has made up its mind to (enter the field). These people have no material aims. They have taken up the challenge to meet the situation in a spirit of devotion and service of God. They are not inspired by any desire to gain worldly goods or gather material benefits. When the country is cleared of foreigners and enemies and their objective (of liberating the country from foreign domination) is achieved, they will not be interested in Government, office or honour. They would leave the work of administration for those who are men of political experience and desire to involve themselves in it.

This letter throws light on the aims and objectives of Sayyid Ahmad Shahid in organising his *Jihād* movement. He and his devoted band of followers infused a revolutionary ardour in every sensitive soul throughout the length and breadth of the country. During his stay in Calcutta he made deep impact on the lives of the people who gave up all material comforts and became determined revolutionaries. According to Sir Sayyid Ahmad Khān, all wineshops in Calcutta were closed and there was a remarkable, almost dramatic, change in the life-pattern of people when Sayyid Ahmad started his preachings there. Thousands of people from different parts of Bengal made a becline to Calcutta and joined his movement.

Sayyid Ahmad Shahid's movement attracted to its fold all those groups and individuals who were struggling to liberate the country from foreign yoke. In fact it appears that all resistance movements merged in the movement of Sayyid Ahmad Shahid. The Fara'idi, the Wahhabi, and the Mujahidin movements combined to pursue common ideals. Even the descendants of Tipü Sultãn associated themselves with Sayyid Ahmad Shahïd.

Sayyid Ahmad Shahïd generated a revolutionary spirit of sacrifice in the people by preaching *Jihãd* as a religious obligation. People began to pray to God:

(O God! Grant me also martyrdom—the finest of religious devotions)

It came to be popularly believed that.

(Whoever enters the army of God and prepares himself for sacrifice in the way of God, he is the beloved of the beloved of God [the Prophet] and God is happy with him. [O People] support the Imam of the Age and sacrifice your lives in the way of God.)

Resistance at Narkui Birya

Mir Nithar Ali *alias* Titu came under the influence of Sayyid Ahmad Shahïd in Hijaz. On his return to Calcutta in 1829, he worked ceaselessly to prepare people for resistance against the British domination. In October 1831 he erected, a strong defence line of bamboos at Narkul Birya and declared that the rule of the East India Company had ended. He claimed to have wrested from the British all the power that they had usurped. According to hunter his followers comprised three or four thousand people. Ghulãm Ma'süm was their Commander. On November 14, 1831, Alexander attacked Narkul Birya but was repulsed and it was with difficulty that he could save his life. An English indigo planter then attacked Narkul Birya but he was also defeated. An English contingent with heavy artillery was then rushed from Calcutta. Titu Miyan resisted this force with 6000 people and fell fighting. Ghulãm Ma'süm and 350 *mujãhidïn* were taken prisoner and put in Alipore jail. People saw them being taken to the jail but never heard about them again. Perhaps they were ruthlessly put to death. Some 90 years later when Mawlana Āzād was imprisoned in the same Alipore jail, a world of historic visions and memories flashed across his mind. He was treading the path of the *Mujāhidīn,* he felt.

Strangely enough the defeat of Balakot and Narkul Birya took place in the same year (1831). Simultaneous collapse of resistance movements in the north-western frontier and in Bengal gave a serious jolt to freedom struggle but the spirit which Sayyid Ahmad Shahīd had generated continued to work for decades. Sir Sayyid saw groups of people marching to Balakot long after the death of Sayyid Ahmad Shahīd and the collapse of the movement.

After Balakot

In Delhi the descendants of Shāh 'Abd al-'Azīz kept the revolutionary spirit alive. The efforts of Mawlavī Nasīr al-Din Dehlawī (ob. 1839). Mawlavi Walāyat 'Ali 'Azimbādi (ob. 1852), Mawlavī 'Ināyat 'Ali Ghāzī (ob. 1858), Mawlana 'Abd-Allāh 'Azīmbādī (ob. 1902) and others kept the torch burning in extremely difficult circumstances. Five conspiracy cases were filed against the *Mujāhidīn* and terrible punishments were inflicted upon them. These cases were:

Ambala Conspiracy Case	1864
First Patna Conspiracy Case	1865
Malda Conspiracy Case	1870
Raj Mahal Conspiracy Case	1870
Second Patna Conspiracy Case	1871

Mawlana 'Ināyat 'Ali Sādiqpūrī provoked the rebellion of Regiment' 55 of Mardan and was condemned to death on that account.

In the Ambala Conspiracy Case, 11 persons were given life imprisonment and were deported to the Andamans. One of them was Mawlana Walāyat 'Ali 'Azimbādī. His nephew Mawlana 'Abd al-Rahīm (ob. 1923) wrote *al-Durr al-Manthūr* about the horrible fate of the Sadiqpur family at the hands of British officers. The entire locality where these freedom fighters had their houses was razed to the ground and the land was given over to the Municipal Board (1865). This whole tragedy of demolition and destruction was enacted on an *'ïd day*. 'Abd al-Hamïd has given in *amathnavï* pathetic details of the ruthless destruction of houses and property wrought by the police. Even educational institutions in the complex, where instructional work was carried on night and day, were reduced to rubble. When Mawlana Yahyã Ali heared in the Andamans about this destruction, he wrote to his wife: "Thank God that He has considered you fit for this ordeal."

Mawlana 'Abd al-Jalïl Shahïd of Aligarh, also a follower of the *Jihãd* movement, laid down his life fighting the British. After the tragedy of Balakot, the *Mujãhidïn,* particularly the Sadiqpuri group, carried on the struggle for sometime and suffered at the hands of the British. In fact Balakot had generated a spirit of sacrifice which took time to be subdued. The Mujãhidin, designated as Wahhãbis by the British, rose up again in 1857, and had to bear the brunt of the revengeful fury of the British. Dr. Majumdar's view that the Wahhãbis had not played any part in the freedom struggle is wrong and unfounded. No reader of Hunter's *Indian Mussalmans* would be left in any doubt about their role.

Early Muslim Non-Cooperation and Resistance

The Muslim religious classes decided in the early decades of the 19th century to non-cooperate with the British by rejecting their services and by abjuring social contact with them. They resisted their aggressive imperialistic designs in their own way. Two examples may be cited here. Shãh Muhammad Sulaymãn of Tawnsa (ob. 1850), a great Chishti saint in the line of Shaykh Nizãm al-Din Awiyã, and Shãh Ghulãm 'Ali (ob. 1824), a great Naqshbandi saint in the line of Shaykh Ahmad Sirhindi Mujaddid-i Alf-i Thãni, discouraged people from entering the Government service or establishing any sort of contact with the British. Shãh Muhammad Sulaymãn considered the Britishers "tyrant usurpers." He told his followers that remaining hungry and naked was better than serving the enemies of faith. Even dying of hunger, he said, was better than service of the British. One day on hearing about the activities of the British officers in Multan, he asked one of his disciples: 'Why don't you throw arrows at the Farangis?"

Shãh Ghulãm Ali also considered the service of the British illegal and forbidden. When at the persistent request of certain persons, Shãh 'Abd al-'Azïd permitted Mawlana 'Abd al-Hayy to do the job of giving religious opinion in Calcutta, Shãh Ghulãm Ali resented it and wrote to Shãh 'Abd al-'Aziz disagreeing with this relaxation of the policy of non-cooperation. Sir Sayyid's family had close spiritual links with Shãh Ghulãm 'Ali, but when he joined the service of the British, the descendants of Shãh Ghulãm 'Ali refused to accept his offerings.

Quietly but in a very determined way this approach of non-cooperation and resentment influenced the Muslim attitude towards British Government. The Christian missionary activities further embittered the attitude of the Muslim religious classes. Mu'min (ob. 1851), the famous Urdu poet, wrote a spirited *Mathnavï Jihãdïya* in which he exhorted people to rise against the British and organise a *Jihãd* campaign for their overthrow. Travelyan has pointed out how bitter and non-cooperative feelings had spread to every section of the people after the annexation of Awadh: the water-carriers stopped supplying water, the maid servants left their services and the cooks and servants defied their officers.

Upheaval of 1857

The Upheaval of 1857 was an outburst of feelings against the British and had its roots deep in the anger and anguish which had been accumulating in the hearts of the Muslims. The Vellore Mutiny and the Moplah uprisings in the South, and insurgencies in some towns and *quashes* of U.P. were unmistakable expressions of growing discontent. Since most of the accounts of the movement of 1857 were written by foreign historians, the real dimensions of the upheaval could not be assessed for long. Recent studies have, however, thrown valuable light on the nature of the movement and the extent of Muslim involvement in it.

The so-called "Mutiny" was a joint Hindu-Muslim venture. If among the princes and the governing classes, figures like Rani Laxmi Bai, Nana Sahib, Nahar Singh, Hadrat Mehal, Nawab 'Ali Bahãdur, Nawab Tafaddul Hussain, Bahãdur Khãn, Nawab

Mahmūd Khān and others, played an important role in the struggle, public figures like Tatiya Topi 'Azīm-Allāh Khān, Bakht Khān, Vazir Khān and others fought the British with courage and determination. Among the *'Ulamā'* there were men like

1. Mawlana Ahmad-Allāh Khān
2. Hāji Imdād-Allāh
3. Mawlana Qāsim Nānawtavi
4. Mawlana Rashid Ahmad Gangohi
5. Mawlana Fayd Ahmad Badā'ūni
6. Mawlana Liyāqat 'Ali
7. Mawlana Fadl-i Haq Khayrābādi
8. Mawlana 'Abd al-Qādir Ludhyānavi

who stirred public sentiments and challenged British authority on religious grounds. Hāji Imdad-Allah's Shamli encounter was a historic episode which continued to inspire generation after generation of the *'Ulama'* of Deoband.

Mawlana Ahmad-Allāh's wounds, received in several encounters with the British, became malignant but his rebellious spirit could not be suppressed. When he laid down his life, people mourned his death as a national loss.

The most effective weapon in the armoury of the *'Ulmā'* was religious decree (*fatwā*) legalising rebellion against the usurper. Mawlana Ismā'il Shahid had declared early in the 19th century.

(Obeying every usurper of power is not a law of the *Shari'at*).

In 1857 several *'Ulamā'* issued *fatwās* permitting rebellion against the British. Mawlana Fadl-i Haqq Khayrābādi has referred to such *fatwās* in his al-Thawrat *al-Hindiyah*. The spirit of revolution and rebellion that permeates the pages of his work gives an insight into the feelings of the contemporary *'Ulamā'*.

The Muslims were in the forefront of freedom struggle in 1857 and so they had to bear the main brunt of British fury. One has to patiently collect the material suppressed or kept in guarded secrecy pertaining to Muslim participation in the struggle and the tortures they had to suffer. Thousands of Muslim families were cut out root and branch, thousands of Muslims were hanged on slightest suspicion and their bodies were kept hanging for crows and kites. Wells were filled with corpses and terror was struck in the hearts of the people. A poet thus refers to the horrible scenes of massacre:

(They—the British—have dragged people out of their houses and have piled dead bodies, one over the other. There is neither grave, nor coffin, nor the mourners.)

Mufti Sadr al-Dïn Äzurda, a distinguished figure in the academic circles of Delhi, gave expression of his poignant feelings of horror and distress in the following verses:

(Every day horror and sadness drives me to the wilderness. There is demented head, stone and [beating of the] breast. The heart gets splintered into pieces when I think of [my] association with Mustafã Khãn. Why should Äzurda not run into wilderness and turn a mourner, when innocent Sahbã'ï is thus executed.)

Mughal Delhi, the most vibrant symbol of Mughal civilisation, disappeared somewhere in the dust raised by the turmoil of 1857. Earlier poets had written *Shahr Äshübs* of Delhi, now they started writing *Marãthï-i Delhī.* (Elegies of Delhi). They shed tears of blood, not only at the loss of political power and prestige but at the end of a civilisation under whose aegis they had built their social and cultural institutions. The *divãn khãnahs* of Delhi in particular were great centres of culture and learning. Sir Sayyid and Mawlana Äzãd's father shed tears at their disappearance in 1857 and Hãli wrote:

(Do not talk about the late Delhi, O Friend. We have not the heart to hear this [woeful] tale.)

This emotional shock at the loss of Delhi-culture created pessimism and inertia in some, but emboldened others to pursue with greater vigour their anti-British activities.

Aftermath of 1857

The British officers who had let loose forces of terrible repression after the turmoil of 1857, considered "Wahhabi a by-word for a rebel. They took stern action against 'Ulamã' of that provenance and other Muslim leaders involved in freedom struggle in different towns and villages of India. Many of the 'Ulama' were condemned to life imprisonment and transported to the Andamans. Sayyid Isma'il Husayn, Munir Shikohãbãdi, Mufti 'Inãyat Ahmad Kãkorvi. Mufti Mazhar Karim Daryãbadi. Mawlana Fadl-i Haqq Khayrãbãdi and others reached Andamans in heavy chains and fetters, facing all sorts of tortures on the way. Munir has described in pathetic verses the privation and hardships that he had to face while on his way to Andamans. It is significant that almost all those banished to the Andamans were Muslims.

Three distinct reactions to this situation emerged: (1) some *'Ulamã'* decided to leave India and migrated to Hijaz to refurbish their spiritual life and prepare for a prolonged struggle against British rule. (2) Some of the *'Ulamã'* of Delhi and Deoband persisted in their anti-British attitude and Mawlana Rashid Ahmad Gangohi, Mawlana Muhammad Qãsim Nanawtavi and some other disciples of Haji Imdãd-Allãh Muhãjir Makki adopted an attitude of rejection and refutation of British rule. The foundations of the Deoband *Madrasah* were laid on anti-British feelings. (3) Sir Sayyid viewed the situation from a different angle and reacted to it differently. It is most unfortunate that the basis of his approach has been entirely wrongly presented. It is time that we look at the whole problem objectively.

Role of Sir Sayyid

Sir Sayyid had seen the disastrous end of the two most determined Muslim efforts to overthrow foreign rule—Balakot and 1857. He realised that armed struggle with the British—who were trained in the new methods of warfare and had the potentials of Industrial Revolution at their command—was bound to prove futile. It could lead to loss of life and property without carrying the freedom struggle an inch forward. Pragmatic considerations demanded an entirely different type of mobilisation and preparation to achieve tangible results. Addressing a meeting at Lucknow he said.

> (These days thousands of Irish men are prepared to sacrifice their lives. High placed people who support the (Irish] movement are afraid neither of imprisonment nor the bayonets of police. Kindly find out for me ten persons in India who would like to face the bayonets.)

His grim political realism saw clearly the next stage of political struggle which was bound to be constitutional rather than militant. And the Muslims were least prepared for it because there was no education in them and they were ignorant of the dynamics of constitutional battles. He, therefore, concentrated on Western education and said that only education could be the means of achieving their political rights and objectives. Addressing a gathering in Amritsar on 29 January 1884, he said.

(If the Government had not given us our right for which we are complaining, high education is so effective that it would force them to give those rights to us willy-nilly).

Those who have presented Sir Sayyid as an opponent of freedom movement have done scant justice to history and historical truth. No one who did not aspire for freedom could make the following forthright and forceful declaration:

> (I am a Muslim and a native of India and an Arab by race. These two facts that I am from an Arab family and am a Muslim will help you to appreciate that both from the religious and racial points of view I am a true radical. The Arabs do not like that instead of themselves some one else should rule over them... [Islam] does not like the concentration of wealth at one place... People who think that instead of constitutional Government there should be despotic rule in India are mistaken.)

In another speech he said that Indians should understand the new economic challenges of the time and strive to establish their own trading companies and establishments in different parts of the world. Once he said:

> Remember this forecast of mine that the day is not far off when a man from each district will enter the legislature.

The day will come when you will yourself legislate and act upon it.

When in 1907 Mawlana Muhammad 'Ali thus paid tribute to Sir Sayyid' memory he demonstrated in unmistakable terms that Sir Sayyid was responsible for preparing the generation for freedom struggle.

(You taught us to strive and agitate. If we are the end, you are the beginning of this struggle.)

The efforts of Nawwāb 'Abd al-Latif (1828-1893) and Sayyid Ameer 'Ali (1849-1928) were also directed towards the same objective; creation of an educated Muslim class well versed in methods of constitutional struggle, Sir Sayyid went to Calcutta on 6 October, 1863, and addressed a gathering in Persian at the residence of Nawwāb 'Abd al-Latif and passionately appealed to him to arrange 'Western education for Muslims for their future lay in it. As a result, the Muhammadan Literary Society came into being in Calcutta and Sir Sayyid included the nawwāb among the members of his Scientific Society established at Aligarh.

Sir Sayyid and his movement for Western education prepared the Muslims for participation in the freedom struggle with confidence and courage. The only Indian leader who could appreciate this dimension of Sir Sayyid's role was Pandit Jawaharlal Nehru. He wrote:

> Sir Syed's decision to concentrate on western education for Muslims was undoubtedly a right one. Without that they could not have played any effective part in the building up of Indian nationalism of the new type and they would have been doomed to play second fiddle to the Hindus with their better education and far stronger economic position. The Muslims were not historically or ideologically ready then for the bourgeoisi nationalist movement as they had developed no bourgeoisie, as the Hindus had gone. Sir Syed's activities therefore, although seemingly very moderate, were in the right revolutionary direction.

The generation created by Sir Sayyid's educational movement—Mawlana Muhmmad 'Ali, Mawlana Shawkat 'Ali,

Mawlana Hasrat Mohãni, Mawlana Zafar 'Ali Khan and others played an important role in the freedom struggle. And who can deny that political stage in the decades that followed was not dominated by those figures.

Battle of The Press

Change in circumstances and the nature of political struggle demanded brisk journalistic activity both to broadcast Muslim discontent and to prepare the people for mass struggle and resurgence.

Sir Sayyid was the first Indian to fight for freedom of the press as a right of the people. His, *Aligarh Institute Gazette* had the following inscription on the front page:

> Liberty of the press is a prominent duty of the Government and natural right of the subjects.

It was the first declaration of its kind in India and Lala Lajpat Rai and his father looked upon him at one stage as "no less than a prophet of the nineteenth century." Cognizant of the role of press in constitutional struggle, Sir Sayyid launched his movement for the freedom of the press. He got Mill's book *On Liberty* translated into Urdu in order to broadcast ideas of freedom. In 1876-78 the Government thought of suppressing the native newspapers. Sir Sayyid fought against such a move "to throttle the freedom of the vernacular newspapers," and wrote:

> Lord Lytton is not so ignorant as to be a party to any such disgraceful behaviour. It will not only harm Indians but would annoy Englishmen.

His efforts in this direction had far-reaching effect on the liberation movement. The journalistic activities and achievements of Mawlana Muhammad Ali, Mawlana Äzãd, Mawlana Zafar 'Ali Khan and Hasrat Mohãni were in facts inspired by Sir Sayyid and shall always remain an important landmark in India's freedom struggle. Mawlana Äzãd's articles in *at-Hilãl* and *at-Balãgh* were written in characters of fire: Muhammad 'Ali's *Comrade* and *Hamdard* supplied fire and fervour to the freedom movement and awakened the masses from their slumber and prepared them for sacrifice in the cause of freedom. Zafar Ali Khãn's *Zamindar* was another powerful vehicle for mobilising public sympathies for the political struggle. Securities of these journals and papers were forfeited again and again, but they carried on freedom propaganda with indomitable courage and force of conviction. If ever a realistic and objective assessment is made of the contribution of press to freedom struggle, the role of Muslim journalists would top the list. It inspired people to lay down their lives in the cause of freedom. When Mawlana Muhammad 'Ali wrote.

The spirit of humility and self-sacrifice which Thou had bestowed on Husain bin 'Ali through their ancestor Ibrãhim and Ismã'il . . . and the determination with which they had faced all tortures and hardships in the desert [of Kerbala], I seek the same steadfastness and patience from Thee.)

He created a sensation in Muslim intelligentsia. He taught them to detest life which was hesitant to surrender itself to the noble cause of freedom. His verses inspired a whole generation with revolutionary ideas.

(How can one who is afraid of death, survive. If the desire to live is such, it is as fatal as death. O Jawhar! What do you think of? This is the real job to perform and you have to do this. Lay down your life.)

Again,

(Perhaps today the wish for Jawhar has been fulfilled. There was a corpse lying uncared for, without wrapping sheet and grave.)

> Punishments had no effect on him. He was prepared for supreme sacrifices at the altar of freedom:
>
> (One who deserved to be hanged has been sentenced to imprisonment. How sad that I was prevented from permanent release.)

Similarly Äzãd breathed fire in the hearts of the people through his journals, *al-Hilãl, al-Balãgh and Payãm*. When he expressed the restless ambition of his own heart in the following words, he carried the revolutionary spirit to a point of fever heat:

> This is a situation which a Tradition of the Prophet, as recorded by Bukhari, applies: "I swear by God who holds my life that I want to be slaughtered in the way of God, revived again and slaughtered again, then again revived and slaughtered." There is such a pleasure in getting injured and killed in this way that I long for resurrection after being killed again and again.

Instead of defending himself in sedition cases, he pleaded guilty and said:

> The Prophet of Islam has said: The best death is of that person who speaks the truth before a tyrant Government and is executed in punishment.

His articles and statements in law courts are valuable literature of our freedom struggle. No voice was raised in India for freedom which was louder and pierced the hearts of the people more than the voice of Muslims.

Äzãd and Muhammad 'Ali were taller trees in a forest; there were others who fought for freedom through the columns of their journals and papers.

Role of Poets in National Awakening

Similarly the poetic literature of the period which breathes feelings of bitter anguish at foreign domination throws valuable light on Muslim struggle for freedom. Kroeber says in his *Configuration of Culture Growth* that poetry reflects better than prose the aspirations of a people Hālï. Shibli, Iqbal, Akbar Allahabadi, Zafar 'Ali Khān, Jawhar, Hasrat and others appealed to the innermost sentiments of the people. It was Sir Sayyid who had for the first time rejected the concept of act for the sake of art and had used poetry for national revival and regeneration. Hāli's *musaddas* is a living monument to Sir Sayyid's efforts in this direction. In Iqhal this purposeful poetry touched its pinnacle on glory. Hasrat Mohāni and Zafar 'Ali Khān used their poetic talent to work up public sentiments against the British. It is time that comprehensive collections of Muslim writings—both in prose and verse—hearing on freedom struggle are prepared and published. This would bring to focus the Muslim role in freedom struggle. So long as this literature survives, there can be no doubt about the revolutionary role of the Muslims in Indian polities.

Role of Women

Very often the role of Muslim women in freedom struggle is either totally ignored or lightly treated. Within the limitations imposed by society on their activities, they played an important role in the awakening of freedom feelings. Mawlana Muhammad 'Ali's mother travelled throughout the country with his message of *Khilāfat* agitation. The wives of Mawlana Hasrat Mohani, Dr. M. A. Ansari, Mawlana Muhmmad 'Ali and Mawlana Äzād had to bear the brunt of freedom struggle but they boldly faced all the hardships and provided moral support to their husbands. The Presidential Address that Mawlana Muhammad Ali's mother gave at the All India ladies Conference at Ahmadabad, on 30 December 1921, and exhorted women to create their volunteer corps for freedom struggle, shall remain a landmark in Indian freedom movement. Amongst those killed at the Jallianwala Bagh was a Muslim woman also.

Impact of Pan-Islamic Movements on Indian Freedom Struggle

A number of developments in the Iṣlamic world—Tripoli, Balkan, Turkey, Khilafat etc.—attracted the attention of the

Muslims in India and they organised mass protests for them. Some writers have expressed the opinion that these movements were deviations and distracted the Muslim attention from the Indian Freedom Movement. Nothing can be farther from the truth. In fact these movements created that stir in Indian feelings which made the Indian freedom struggle a really mass movement. It is undeniable that the Turkish and Khilafat movements prepared the Indian mind for mass struggle. Never before mass resentment was expressed in this way. Further, Indian sympathy for freedom movements in the Islamic world created a favourable opinion for India in the Islamic world. When the first Prime Minister of independent India, Pandit Jawaharlal Nehru, launched his policy of Non-Alignment, the Arab response was instant and sincere. The Khilafat Movement might appear irrelevant in the Indian context only to those who lack political vision. The fact, however remains that it was the Khilafat Movement which taught public agitations, mass movements and developed a spirit of non-cooperation. Mahatma Gandhi's political insight appreciated the impact of Khilafat Movement in Indian freedom struggle and he remarked in *Young India* (April 1924) that he would not allow the spirit generated by the Khilafat Movement to die. The nature of pan-Islamism at this time was essentially anti-colonial. Pandit Jawaharlal Nehru has correctly observed:

> Pan-Islamism in 1914 and later was an anti-imperialistic force. It weakened the British people in their war effort and it coloured the background of the Khilafat movement in India.

No student of historical literature would be left in any doubt about the nature and impact of these movements if he carefully goes through the contemporary records—speeches articles resolutions—which discuss Indian freedom aspirations side by side with discussions about freedom struggle in Muslim lands. The programme of non-cooperation was announced by Mahatma Gandhi for the first time from the Khilafat platform.

Revolutions through Religion

The *'Ulmā'* spared no efforts to prepare public mind to liberate the country from foreign domination. From Shāh 'Abd al-'Azïz onwards there is an unbroken tradition of the *'Ulama* participating in freedom struggles and providing religious prop to the movement. The activities and sacrifices of Hãji Imdãd-Allãh Muhãjir Makki. Shaykh al-Hind Mawlana Mahmüd Hasan, Mawlana Husayn Ahmad Madani and Mawlana 'Uhyd-Allãh Sindhi deserve full and fair appraisal in any history of the Indian freedom movement. They faced imprisonment and exile, torture and tribulation in their relentless struggle for emancipation of the country.

In their endeavour to awaken freedom sentiments, the *'Ulamã* made full use of religious concepts and terminology. Many of the religious terms which found currency during the period have greater political relevance and significance than hitherto appreciated *Dãr al-Harb, Hijrat, al-Ard li-Allãh, Hizb-Allãh, Dãr al-Irshãd, Jihãd, and Amir-i Shari'at* were not hollow concepts. They breathed religious fervour in Muslim liberation struggle and gave a religious dimension to it. The concept of dãr *al-harb* changed the entire basis of Muslim religious life in a land so declared; *hijrat* was a practice whose efficacy was demonstrated by the Prophet himself and was indication of determination to retire to a safe place and consolidate position for confrontation; *al-ard li-Allãh* was a revolutionary concept which, as Iqbal has said, meant:

> (What greater revolution can be visualised in the realm of thought than the concept: "This land belongs to Allãh and not to Kings.")

Dãr al-Irshãd was religious training centre, while the concept of *Amir* was propounded by Ibn Taymiyah as a means of struggle against hostile powers. This whole terminology prepared Muslim mind for freedom struggle. In January 1922 Mawlana Äzãd said in a statement:

> The spirit that Mahatma Gandhi is infusing today in the religious life of the Hindus, *at-Hilãl* finished this job in 1914. This is a strange coincidence that new life and energy was generated in Muslims and Hindus when both of them

turned to movements of religious education in place of Western culture.

Reference may be made here to two very significant efforts made by the *'Ulamā'* for the overthrow of British power. The Silk Letter Conspiracy (1915-16) was an effort to enlist foreign support for revolutionary programmes and establish a Provisional Government in Afghanistan. Shaykh al-Hind Mawlana Mahmüd Hasan of Deoband, Mawlana Äzād, Mawlana Husayn Ahmad Madani, Mawlana Ubayd-Allāh Sindhi and Raja Mahendra Pratap were involved in it. C.R. Cleveland, Director, Central Intelligence, wrote to Sir William Vincent, Member, Home Department, that the Silk Letter Conspirators had decided "to throw in their lot with the Afghans and Turks against the British Government" and that Mawlana Äzād and Mawlana Ubayd-Allāh Sindhi had worked for it.

The Hizb-Allāh founded by Mawlana Äzād in 1913 was a revolutionary organisation for the overthrow of the British power. The pledge signed by its members shows that a deep spirit of sacrifice has inspired the organisation. Its branches were established at several places and like the Italian Carbonari it carried on its work in a clandestine manner. Mawlana Äzād had arranged even supply of arms to those who joined the organisation and pledged to lay down their lives in the way of God.

The Non-Cooperation Movement

When Mahatma Gandhi launched the Non-Cooperation movement, the Muslims fully responded to it. Mawlana Äzād, Shaykh al-Hind Mahmüd Hasan, Mawlana Husayn Ahmed Dr. M.A. Ansari, Hakim Ajmal Khān, Dr. Saifuddin Kichlew. Mawlana Muhammad Ali, Mawlana Shawkat 'Ali, Mufti Kifāyat-Allāh. Mawlana Zafar Ali Khān and Mawlana Hasrat Mohāni pushed forward the movement. The following facts may be noted in this connection:

(a) It was at a Khilafat Conference held at Meerut that Gandhiji "preached for the first time the non-cooperation programme from a public platform."

(b) On 28 February 1920, the Khilafat Conference met at Calcutta under the Chairmanship of Mawlana Äzãd and passed resolutions for the boycott of British goods. It appealed to the Muslim legislators and other to resign. A few months later (in June 1920) the Central Khilafat (Committee met at Allahabad and resolved:

> That the Swadesi movement should be undertaken in right earnest.

It is undeniable that the Khilafat platform was used for preparing people for the Non-cooperation Movement.

(c) A *fatwã* was issued declaring all Government services as *harüm*(forbidden). Meeting held to explain and broadest this *fatwã* criticized the British Government so bitterly that C.A. Borrow, Chief Commissioner of Delhi, wrote to H.D. Craik, Secretary to the Government of India, on 2 September 1921:

> A few more such meetings may any day result in an outrage of explosion of an anti-European character.

(d) Mawlana Äzãd's article "On Boycott" was an open incitement to non-cooperation and rebellion. He put forward religious arguments to justify his demand of the boycott of goods manufactured by the British. His eloquent exhortations touched many hearts when he said:

> Where can I get the bugle whose strident blare may awaken forty crore hearts from their deep slumber ?

(e) In the literature pertaining to freedom struggle the statements of Shaykh al-Hind Mawlana Mahmüd Hasan, Mawlana Husayn Ahmad Madanï, Mawlana Muhammad Ali, Mawlana Äzãd and other *'Ulamã'* shall remain a landmark. These statements provided *élan* and ideological strength to the freedom movement.

(f) To enlist public support for the Non-cooperation Movement, Muslim leaders like Mawlana Muhmmad 'Ali, Mawlana Shawkat 'Ali and Mawlana Äzãd made extensive tours of the country and mobilised public opinion in favour of the Non-cooperation Movement.

(g) The role of Aligarh in the non-cooperation struggle is often misrepresented. It is true that the Aligarh administration of those days stood by the Government, but Aligarh Old Boys and the Aligarh Students came out in full support of the Non-cooperation Movement.

In fact the response to Gandhiji's call to leave Government institutions was greater in Aligarh than in Benaras. A section of Aligarh teachers and Old Boys broke off from M.A.O. College and established the Jamia Millia Islamia—a National University. The College was closed for a month and it was reported:

> A strong undercurrent of unrest amongst the student population was swaying their college life.

On the contrary, the response in Benaras was very poor. The *Pioneer* wrote (December 1920):

> Mahatma Gandhi's visit to Banaras and his mischievous attempt to wreck the Hindu University have been a total failure .... The members of staff criticised in unmistakable language several aspects of Gandhi's programme of non-cooperation.

While fully cooperating with the Hindus in the struggle for freedom, efforts were made by Muslim leaders to create a feeling of national consciousness and retain the unity of the Indian nation. There was complete Hindu-Muslim cooperation in all the movements, even those of Tripoli, Khilafat, etc. Munshi Danayak Prasad Tãlib's "Äh-i Mazlümãn-i Tarãblus" is full of pathos and anguish at the tortures suffered by the people of Tripoli.

Similarly great tolerance and cordiality prevailed in the celebration of Hindu-Muslim festivals. *Independent* of Allahabad reported (Oct. 1920) about Ramlila and Muharram processions being taken out in a spirit of cordiality and goodwill and both communities participated in the religious festivals of the other community. "If the practice," wrote the *Independent*, "is encouraged there will be no occasion for Hindu-Muslim quarrels and the bureaucracy will have one argument less for its continuance."

In his anxiety to maintain Hindu-Muslim unity Mawlana Äzãd remarked that he would not accept freedom if it was at the cost of Hindu-Muslim unity. Loss of freedom was India's loss, of Hindu-Muslim unity was the loss of humanity, he declared again and again. He rejected all ideas of majority and minority as British instruments to create a wedge between the Hindus and the Muslims. Mawlana Husayn Ahmad Madanï's views about the unity of the Indian nation were bold and were inspired by the highest ideals of national consciousness.

Mawlana Äzãd began his political career by opposing the partition of Bengal and ended it by opposing the partition of the country.

After 1857 the British left no stone unturned in creating bitterness between the Hindus and the Muslims in order to destroy the unity of the Indian nation. In 1857 Sir Henry Elliot's *History of India* was published in eight volumes. In a memorandum submitted to the Home Government Sir Henry Elliot spelled out his motives in undertaking that literary project. His idea was that if this material was placed before the people it would make Hindus look with competent and horror at the Muslim rule and all patriotic movements would loose their appeal. "It will make our native subjects more sensible of the immense advantages occurring to them under the mildness and equity of our rule." He thus blackened the Indian past to glorify the British present and injected the virus of communal tension in our national life. When Elliot was busy driving a wedge between the Hindus and the Muslims, Sir Sayyid was declaring:

(Look upon your country as a temple—at the top of which is God and at the foot of which are the people who are one and equal).

Perhaps inspired by this approach. Iqbal had said:

(For long the world of heart is lying forlorn. Come, we should build a new temple in our land.)

During the Non-cooperation period the Muslim-Hindu unity reached its highest watermark. Mawlana Äzãd declared Hindus as resembling *Ahl-i Kitãb* and permitted their entry in mosques. The entire Muslim leadership came under the banner of Mahatma Gandhi.

Constitutional Struggle and the Parting of Ways

When constitutional struggle began and questions of safeguards for minorities, separate electorates, reservations of seats etc. came up, the parting of ways began. The Nehru Report did not satisfy Muslim demands. The introduction of Provincial Autonomy, linguistic chauvinism, differences over seats in U.P. Cabinet, created a fear complex in the mind of the Muslims.

How did men like Mawlana Muhamad Ali, Mawlana Zafar 'Ali Khan, Mawlana Hasrat Mohani, Mr. Jinnah and others who were always spousing the national cause fell apart and left the Congress? No objective history of the Indian freedom struggle can ignore to investigate the reasons.

If on one side Sirãj al-Dawlah and Tipü Sultãn laid down their lives fighting for the cause of freedom, the movements of Narkul Birya and Balakot, which were entirely managed by the Muslims, accentuated feelings of hatred against the foreign rule; the sacrifices made by the Muslims in 1857 constitute a glorious chapter in the history of India's freedom struggle. In the years that followed, Muslims threw themselves headlong in the freedom struggle. There was hardly any turn in the freedom movement at which Muslims did not collaborate and cooperate with other Indian communicates in their anti-British programmes. In protests against the Rowlatt Act (1919), the visit of the Prince of Wales (1921), boycott of the Simon Commission (1927) etc., the Muslims were active in protests against the imperial authority. There appear 55 Muslim names among the martyrs of the Jallianwala Bagh. Even a Muslim woman, 'Umar Bibi, was among those who were gunned down by the British soldiers. In the Civil Disobedience Movement of 1930 large number of Muslims participated and the number of those killed was not small. In the Indian Army and Navy Revolts, the Muslims were involved at all levels. In the agitations staged in Bombay in connection with the revolt of the Navy many Muslims were killed. Muslims were killed in the Quit India Movement of 1942 also. In fact there was hardly any torture or ordeal which the Muslims did not face in their struggle for freedom. Hasrat's condition in the prison during the month of Ramadãn was pitiable. He had to grind fixed quantity of grain while fasting. One has to drink water at short intervals while grinding, but due to Ramadãn Hasrat could not take water and had to go on grinding, thirsty, exhausted and tortured. When he offered his prayers in shorts given to prisoners, his heart bled. He could bear tortures but did not like to be before his Lord in a half-naked condition. Many leaders lost to their wives and children when in prison for the sake of the liberation of the country. Mawlana Äzãd refused to apply for parole when his wife was on death bed and was crying to see her husband's face before departing to the world beyond. Mawlana Muhammad 'Ali's only daughter, Ämina, died when he was in jail.

Viewed as a whole, Muslim participation in the freedom struggle was resolute, determined and relentless from the very beginning. The militant resistance programmes were largely organised by them—Seringapatam, Narkul Birya, Balakot were Muslim responses to the British challenge. In 1857 the Muslims and the Hindus fought shoulder to shoulder but the brunt of the struggle was borne by the Muslims as they had a past of resistance and rebellion. In the Civil Disobedience movement also Muslim participation was second to none. In fact the Khilafat Movement had prepared the ground for mass struggle. No student of the political history of India can deny the fact that during the 190 years of British rule, the freedom struggle passed through many phases—militant, non-cooperative and constitutional—but at no stage did the Muslims hestitate to lay down their lives for the cause of freedom.

CHAPTER 8

Popular Movements and the Coming of Freedom with Partition, 1945-47

The years nineteen forty five and forty seven at British rule have been both well and ill-served by historians. Thanks to the *Transfer of Power* series edited by Mansergh, certain types of official documents are more easily available for the 1940s now than for any other period of Indian history, and a mass of historical literature exists on the tortuous negotiations between British Congress and League politicians which culminated in a freedom which was also a tragic Partition. In very sharp contrast, there is hardly any systematic historical research so far, except for a few useful accounts by participants, on the sporadic, localised, but often extremely militant and united mass actions which constitute the second major strand of these years: the movement for release of INA prisoners, the RIN Mutiny of 1945-46, the massive post-war strike wave which was at its height in 1946, and, in 1946-47, the Tebhaga upsurge in Bengal, Punnapra-Vayalar in Travancore, and the Telengana peasant armed revolt in Hyderabad. The tendency has been to consider the first theme in isolation from the second, and indeed it is fatally easy, given the abundance of materials, to get engrossed in the world of the Simla Conference, Cabinet Mission, Interim Government; and Mountbatten Award and tacitly assume it to have been more-or-less self-contained. Professor Gopal's *Jawharlal Nehru* (Volume I) contains many details about the UP agrarian movements in the 1920s and early 1930s, but very little about the popular upsurges of 1945-47—a shift of interest which may appear not unjustifiable, for Nehru and other top Congress leaders had now little direct connection with grassroot movements.

It is the central argument of this paper, however, that in this as well as in other periods of modern Indian history, the decisions and actions of leaders, British or Indian, cannot really be understood without the counterpoint provided by pressures from below. Certain obvious world developments apart, it was popular action, above all, which made continuance of British rule impossible. Fear of popular 'excesses' made Congress leaders cling to the path of negotiation and compromise, and eventually even accept Partition as a necessary price—while the limits of popular anti-imperialist movements made the truncated settlement of August 1947 unavoidable. Detailed studies of the popular movements demand much more research, yet it is the contention that even the easily-available sources (like the Mansergh volumes, or Wavell's *Journal*) really contain abundant evidence to substantiate this thesis, and can be used to throw some new light on vital decision-making processes.

To radical-minded contemporaries in the late 1940s, this argument—together with its concomitant, a somewhat unflattering picture of the national leadership—would have appeared acceptable and even rather obvious. Today, owing to a variety of reasons, it is in contrast a bit unfashionable in many quarters. What had been the standard left critique of 'bourgeois betrayal' has become discredited, and in part rightly so, by its own crudities as well as by the disasters brought about by bouts of ultra-left sectarianism'. The reaction against the debunking of the Indian political leadership by the 'Cambridge school' has also encouraged some of our top-left historians to take up a position at times rather difficult to distinguish from a conventionally nationalist standpoint. Yet even an initially healthy reaction can go too far, and perhaps a closer look at the events of 1945-47 can provide something like a corrective.

II

The framework for post-war developments was set by the aftermath of the 1942 revolt, together with the socio-economic impact of the last three years of the War.

The total confrontation of August 1942 paradoxically enough, ultimately strengthened forces preferring a compromise on both sides. The British had required no less than 57 army battalions to suppress what Linlithgow privately described as 'by far the most serious rebellion since that of 1857, the gravity and extent of which we have so far concealed from the world for reasons of military security". British policy during the early years of the War had often been deliberately provocative. From 1940 onwards, the bureaucracy had been planning a wholesale crackdown on the Congress on the pattern of 1942, compromise efforts had been repeatedly spurned, and Linlithgow Wavell, and Churchill had successfully torpedoed the Cripps initiative at the last moment. After Quit India, the British would never again risk such a confrontation, and that the decision in 1945-46 to try for a negotiated settlement was not just a gift of the new Labour Government is indicated by the attitude of Wavell, the army commander who succeeded Linlithgow in October 1943, who was by no means an ultra-liberal. In a letter to Churchill dated 24 October 1944, Wavell pointed out that it would be impossible to hold India by force after the War, given the likely state of world opinion and British popular or even army attitudes (as well as the economic exhaustion of Britain he might have added). "We have had to negotiate with similar rebels before, *e.g.* De Valera and Zaghlul", and it would be wise to start negotiations before the end of the War brought prisoners' release, demobilisation, and unemployment, creating "a fertile field for agitation, unless we have previously diverted their [Congress] energies into some more profitable channel, *i.e.* into dealing with the administrative problems of India and into trying to solve the constitutional problem". Churchill's pig-headedness (Amery once commented in an aside during a Cabinet meeting that the Prime Minister knew "as much of the Indian problem as George III did of the American colonies") delayed the process somewhat, but this was precisely what the British were able to persuade the Congress leadership to do after 1945.

From the point of view of the Congress leaders, as D.D. Kosambi noted in a brilliant piece of contemporary history writing in 1946, " . . . the glamour of jail and concentration camp served to wipe out the so-so record of the Congress ministries in office, thereby restoring the full popularity of the organisation among the masses". Rightist Congress leaders, who throughout the late-1930s had urged more and more cooperation with the British and pursued increasingly conservative policies as ministers, and for whom 1942 had been something like an aberration (probably dictated in part by a belief that Japan and Germany were winning), could now bask in the glory of patriotic self-sacrifice even while concentrating all their energies on a compromise settlement. 1942 became their electoral trump card, as well as a very convenient stick with which to heat the Communists—though in private Patel would comment on 30 May 1946: "The Bombay atmosphere has been terribly spoiled by the underground and the Satara crowd." Though the Socialists—who had done most of the actual fighting in 1942—emerged with greatly enhanced prestige, the Left alternative as a whole had been weakened in two ways. The Left was now divided as never before, for the searing memory of charges and counter-charges, of 'treachery' and 'fifth-columnist' activity, erected a wall between the Socialists and the followers of Bose on the one side, and the Communists on the other. Brutal repression mustal so have exhausted many peasant bases, built up through years of Gandhian constructive work or radical Kisan Sabha activity. It is significant that the principal centres of rural rebellion in 1942—Bihar and eastern U.P., Midnapur, Orissa, and the Maharashtra-Karnataka countryside—played relatively little part in he anti-imperialist upsurge of 1945-47.

The economic impact of the last three years of the War on the whole aggravated this exhaustion of popular forces, even though it also led to acute discontent and occasional and sporadic near-revolutionary out-bursts in 1945-47. Though India was spared actual military devastation (apart from the Kohima-Imphal border, and some air-raids), mass suffering was none the less acute, for war meant rampant inflation (notes in circulation shot up from Rs. 2300 million in 1939 to Rs. 12,100 million in 1945), corruption and black-markets, and above all the terrible famine of 1943 in Bengal. As Amartya Sen has emphasised in a recent article, mortality figures remained higher than normal in Bengal for five or six years after 1943, for malnutrition left its population particularly susceptible to epidemics. It may not be irrelevant to note, also, that excess mortality (taking 1941-42 as 'normal') in 1943 was the highest among all West Bengal districts in Midnapur (+137.6%), the politically most militant region during Quit India. The consequent breakdown of social mores must have greatly strengthened the 'lumpen' elements in big cities who would provide ample combustible material for communal riots on a totally unprecedented scale from August 1946 onwards. Certainly in contemporary Bengali literature famine, riots, and Partition often merge into a continuum, all producing acute social dislocation and breakdown of norms.

Yet War and famine also meant super-profits for some, and, as in 1914-18, a major step forward for the Indian bourgeoisie. War demand and enforced import-substitution led to advances in textiles, iron and steel, cement and paper, and some Indian entry into engineering and chemicals—though the British still obstructed the development of indigenous shipping, automobile and aircraft production. Industrial growth, however, remained fairly slow, gross production rising only to 120 in 1945 if 1937 is taken as base-year (thought steel rose to 142.9, chemicals to 134.1, and cement to 196.5). The really fantastic increase was not in production but in profits, particularly speculative gains through profiteering in food, share-market operations, War contracts, and the black-market in general. The bourgeoisie was coming of age in India, Kosambi pointed out in 1946, but it was a specific kind of bourgeoisie, characterised by "ravening greed" and mania for speculation rather than initiative or efficiency in developing production. Technological backwardness made it look for foreign collaboration, now that the changed economic and political situation promised to give it additional leverage in conducting negotiations. Birla and Tata led an Indian Business delegation to the West in the summer of 1945, and concluded agreements with Nuffield and Imperial Chemicals. The same bourgeois leaders were quite willing to accept or even urge state investments in sectors like heavy industries, power, or irrigation where initial profits were bound to be low, even while haggling over specific types of state intervention and complaining about too many controls. Even the 'Bombay Plan' drawn up by India's leading capitalists was prepared to accept a "temporary eclipse" in "freedom of enterprise" in the interest of development, and included a number of surprisingly warm references to the "Russian experiment. A clear-cut split between a collaborationist or 'compradore' and a 'national' bourgeoisie is not too easy to establish even in China; it is certainly untenable for India. To quote Kosambi's contemporary analysis again, the bourgeoisie "needs Nehru's leadership," just as in previous periods of mass struggles it had been intelligent enough "to exploit for tits own purposes whatever is profitable in the Mahatma's teachings and to reduce all dangerous ennunciations to negative philosophical points".

As a class which had never had it so good amidst unprecedented mass misery, the bourgeoisie was naturally averse to any further round of popular struggle which could have unmanageably radical consequences, and its formidable influence was cast firmly on the side of a negotiated compromise settlement after 1945. Fear of popular 'excesses' has often been a recurrent element in bourgeois behaviour in many other countries and times, and can be readily explained in terms of a rational calculation of class interest. Indian business groups, however, fell short of the 'national bourgeois' ideal-types also in their frequent preference of sectional over country-wide class interests. This became very important indeed during the last years of British rule, for, as the events of 1945-47 tragically proved, the price of a negotiated 'transfer of power' was an encouragement of divisive forces culminating in Partition.

The rapid advance of the Muslim League, which took full advantage of the suppression of the Congress, in the closing years of the War certainly owed something to British encouragement. The League Ministries in Assam (August 1942) and NWFP (May 1943) became possible only because most Congress MLAs were in jail. The pro-Congress Muslim Premier of Sind was dismissed by the Governor (October 1942), and European MLAs in Bengal propped up the Nazimuddin Ministry from March 1943'. But much more was involved in the League advance than assembly intrigues and official patronage.

Pakistan was being presented to the Muslim peasants of Bengal and Punjab as the end of Hindu zamindar and *bania* exploitation: Abul Hashem, for instance, the dynamic secretary of the Bengal Muslim League from November 1943, did his best to cultivate a radical image for his party. Pakistan at the same time promised "the hedging off of a part of India from competition by the established Hindu business groups or professional classes so that the small Muslim business class could thrive and the nascent Muslim intelligentsia could find employment". The economic muscle behind Muslim separatism thus no longer came only from old-fashioned talukdars and zamindars as in the days of the Aligarh Movement or of Nawab Salimullah of Dacca. The Ispahanis, a Calcutta-based Muslim business family with all-India connections, helped Jinnah in asserting his control over Bengal Muslim politics by outsting Fazul Huq. Ispahani and Adamjee financed League papers (like the *Calcutta Star of India* and the Delhi *Dawn*), a Federation of Muslim Chambers of Commerce and Industry was started in April 1945 with Jinnah's blessings, and Muslim banks and an airways company were planned soon after the War. Hindu business groups, on their part, had been often extremely orthodox, with strong revivalist, cow-protectionist, and Mahasabha links, and the two forms of communalism as usual fed each other. Hindu communalist opinion after 1946 came increasingly to accept Pakistan, provided Bengal and Punjab were also partitioned; this was felt to be a lesser evil, as compared to the inevitable 'subordination' of Hindus to Muslim majorities in these two provinces in any democratic and regionally autonomous set-up. It is interesting, and little-known, that G.D. Birla, the business magnate closest of all to the Congress, seems to have visualised something similar as early as July 1942; "You know my views about Pakistan. I am in favour of separation, and I do not think it is impracticable or against the interest of Hindus or of India."

III

The complex interactions between British policies, Congress attitudes, and popular outbursts during 1945-47 can best be grasped through a firm chronological framework. Four phases can be distinguished here: (i) from the surrender of Germany and Japan (in May and August 1945) to February 1946 (the RIN revolt, coinciding with the announcement of the Cabinet Mission); (ii) February-August 1946 (from Cabinet Mission to the Calcutta riots); (iii) August 1946-February-1947 (when Wavell was replaced by Mountbatten an Attlee fixed a deadline for British withdrawal); and (iv) February-August 1947, the working out of the Mountbatten Plan.

Till the autumn and winter of 1945-46, British policy on the whole was marked by continuity rather than change. Though in June 1945 (with Germany defeated and British elections just a month ahead) Churchill at last permitted Wavell to release Congress leaders and start negotiations, the Simla Conference (25 June-14 July) was allowed to be shipwrecked on the rock of Jinnah's insistence that only the League had the right to choose the Muslim members of the proposed new Executive Council (which would be entirely Indian but for the Viceroy and the Commander-in-Chief, but would still be within the 1935 structure of a central executive not responsible to the Assembly). This, it needs to be emphasised, was a fantastic demand in mid-1945, for the League then ruled (and that largely on Congress sufferance) only in Sind and Assam. The Punjab Unionist Ministry under Khizar Hyat Khan had openly broken with Jinnah in mid-1944. The NWFP once again had a Congress Government once its MLAs had been released, and even the Nazimuddin Ministry in Bengal had fallen in March 1945. So far (till August 1946, in fact) there was little evidence that the League would be able to organise real mass sanctions behind its Pakistan demand. Yet by dissolying the Conference Wavell in effect gave Jinnah the veto he was asking for—in sharp contrast to British attitudes a year later, when the Congress would be invited, however reluctantly, to form an Interim Government on its own.

The massive Labour victory of July 1945 initially did not bring about any major change, even though the new Prime Minister (along with Cripps) had been party to the informal Filkins agreement with Nehru in June 1938 by which Labour leaders had promised a complete transfer of power to a constituent assembly based on universal suffrage when they came to power. Wavell's private fears that with "too big" a majority, Labour might try to hand over "India to their Congress friends as soon as possible" were soon revealed as exaggerated. By December 1946, he would realise that most Labour leaders—like Foreign Secretary Bevin, for instance–were "in reality imperialists" who "like everyone else hate(s) the idea of our leaving India but like everyone else . . . (have) . . . no alternative to suggest". The announcement of new central and provincial elections (last held in 1934 and 1937) made on 21 August 1945 was inevitable now that war had ended. It was welcomed by bureaucrats like the UP Governor Hallet as the "first step" towards providing "constitutional activities for the agitators". After consultations with the new Labour Government, Wavell on 19 September merely reiterated the promise of "early realisation of full self-government" (the term 'independence' was still being avoided). Post-election talks were promised with MLAs and Indian states for setting-up a "constitution-making body" (a step back, this, from the Filkins acceptance of a constituent assembly based on universal franchise), and efforts would be made again to set up an Executive Council "which will have the support of the main Indian Parties". How little British policies had changed as yet was indicated by the initial decision to put on trial no less than 600 of the 20,000 INA prisoners, while another 7000 would be dismissed from service and detained without trial. Indian troops were sent out to help restore French and Dutch colonial rule in Vietnam and Indonesia, though about this Wavell did express some nervousness.

The decisive shift in British policies during the ensuing months obviously had an international dimension in the world-wide weakening of imperialist forces. Fascism had been routed, socially-radical regimes with Communist leadership or participation were emerging throughout Eastern Europe and seemed on the point of doing so even in France and Italy, the Chinese Revolution was forging ahead, and a tremendous anti-imperialist wave was sweeping through South-East Asia, with Vietnam and Indonesia in the vanguard. A war-weary, economically ravaged, Britain no longer had the resources to hold on to an entire sub-continent by force. That the British came to realise this, however, at this specific moment was above all due to mass pressure—and not anything done by the top national leadership, Congress or League.

The autumn and winter months of 1945-46 have been perceptively described by Penderel Moon editing Wavell's *Journal* as 'The Edge of a Volcano'. The very foolish decision to put the INA men on trial, and that too in the Red Fort and with a Hindu, a Muslim and a Sikh (P.K. Sehgal, Shah Nawaz, Gurbaksh Singh Dhillon) together in the first batch, unleashed a country-wide wave of protest. Nehru, Bhulabhai Desai and Tej Bahadur Sapru appeared for the defence, the Muslim League also condemned the trials, and on 20 November an Intelligence Bureau note admitted: "There has seldom been a matter which has attracted so much Indian public interest and it is safe to say, sympathy... this particular brand of sympathy cuts across communal barriers." A journalist (B. Shiva Rao) visiting the Red Fort prisoners on the same day reported that: "There is not the slightest feeling among them of Hindu and Muslim....A majority of the men now awaiting trial in the Red Fort is Muslim. Some of these men are bitter that Mr. Jinnah is keeping alive a controversy about Pakistan." The British were extremely nervous about the INA spirit spreading to the Indian army, and in January the Punjab Governor reported that a Lahore reception for released INA prisoners had been attended by Indian soldiers in uniform. A second issue was provided by the use of the Indian army in Vietnam and Indonesia; the impact this had on popular (at least urban) sentiments as well as on sections of the army bore vivid testimony to the tremendous advances in anti-imperialist consciousness brought about by the war. Meanwhile the usual post-war problems of high prices and retrenchment were being sharply aggravated by a major food crisis, with Wavell in January 1946 estimating a deficit of three million tons. A drastic cut in rations in February reduced the calorie value to 1200 per head, while even wartime London in 1943 had got over 2800 calories.

What the officials feared in the autumn of 1945 was another Congress revolt, a revival of 1942 made much more dangerous this time by the likely combination of attacks on communications with widespread agrarian revolt, labour trouble, army disaffection, and the presence of INA men with military expertise. Violent speeches by Congress leaders (Nehru above all, but also at first Patel and regional leaders in Bihar, CP, UP and elsewhere) initially aroused acute alarm, with their glorification of the heroes and martyrs of 1942, demands for stern punishment for official atrocities, and calls for immediate release of INA prisoners. The British began to realise fairly quickly, however, that this sabre-rattling was essentially election propaganda combined with the need to accommodate the popular mood. 1942 after all was the electoral trump card of the Congress, and as for the INA, Asaf Ali in a private conversation in October was reported to have explained that his party 'would lose much ground in the country" unless it took up their cause, but if the Congress came to power it would certainly remove the INA men from the army and might even put "some of them on trial". Another indication was the bitter campaign against the Communists, in which for the first time Nehru played a very active role, culminating in the expulsion of Communist AICC members in December. That much more was involved here than legitimate anger about the CPI's wartime role is indicated by the fact that there was no such concerted campaign against the Hindu Mahasabha, some of whose leaders had actually been in ministries in August 1942, while Rajagopalachari whose attitude on the Quit India and Pakistan issues had been very similar to that of the Communists, remained a top Congress leader. At the election meetings, reported an official source in November 1945, Congress speakers, "while condemning the invocation of religious issues by their Muslim rivals, concentrate upon the alleged atheist tenets of the Communists in their appeal to their audiences not to support them.

The crucial shifts, alike in British policies and Congress attitudes, came in the wake of three major popular explosions—in Calcutta on 21-23 November and again on 11-13 February, and in Bombay with the RIN revolt of 18-23 February. In Calcutta on 21 November, a Forward Bloc students' procession in Dharmtala street demanding release of INA prisoners was joined by communist students Federation cadres (so long considered their bitterest enemies) as well as by Islamia College students carrying the green flag of the League; and spontaneously the Congress, League and Red Flags were tied together, as symbol of all-in anti-imperialist unity. Police firing which killed a Hindu and a Muslim student was followed on 22 and 23 November by trouble all over the city: strikes by Communist-led tram workers, Sikh taxi-drivers, and in many factories, burning of police and army vehicles (150 were destroyed), crowds blocking trains, and veritable street fighting and barricades—"the crowds when fired on largely stood their ground or at most only receded a little, to return again to the attack". Order could be restored only after 14 cases of firing, which killed 33 and injured about 200. Calcutta erupted again between 11 and 13 February, in protest against the seven-year regorous imprisonment sentences passed on Abdul Rashid of the INA. This time the League student wing had given the initial strike call, and at least the appearance of total political unity was achieved by a mammoth Wellington Square rally on 12 February addressed by League leader Suhrawardy, Gandhian Congressman Satis Dasgupta, and the Communist Somnath Lahiri. But the real initiative in the strikes and street fighting, as in November, came from below, and to some extent from the Communists, described in an official account as "without doubt the most disruptive organisation concerned in the disturbances". The situation was "worse than that in November 1945", with a Communist-led general strike paralysing industrial Calcutta, all jute mills in the city and suburbs closed for two days, train services disrupted upto Chinsura and Naihati and bitter street clashes with the police and the army (two British and a Gurkha battalion had been deployed) which left 84 dead and 300 injured. As in November, the striking features were the total unity in the streets of Hindus and Muslims, students and workers, and violent anti-white feelings, with numerous attacks on *sahibs*, and attempts "to boycott everything European, to disaffect servants of Europeans and to prevent the sale of food to Europeans."

The greatest explosion of all was the naval mutiny in Bombay and the accompanying mass upsurge from 18 to 23 February 1946—one of the most truly heroic, if also largely forgotten, episodes in our freedom struggle. The RIN ratings' strike began on 18 February in the signals training establishment

Talwar as a protest against bad food and racist insults from white officers. It spread rapidly to Castle and Fort Barracks on shore and 22 ships in Bombay harbour, and, as in Calcutta in November, the tricolour, crescent, and hammer-and-sickle were raised jointly on the mastheads of the rebel feet. The demands as formulated by the elected Naval Central Strike Committee, combined service grievances with national political slogans: release of INA and other political prisoners, withdrawal of Indian troops from Indonesia, acceptance of Indian officers alone as superiors. Desperately seeking advice and help from national leaders but getting little or nothing, the ratings hesitated fatally on the borderline of peaceful strike and determined mutiny, and obeyed orders on the afternoon of 20 February to return to their respective ships and barracks only to find themselves surrounded by army guards. Fighting broke out next morning at Castle Barracks when ratings tried to break out of their encirclement, and there were remarkable scenes of fraternisation that afternoon as crowds thronged the Gateway of India with food for the sailors and shopkeepers invited them to take whatever they needed. The pattern of events in fact unconsciously echoed the course of the mutiny on the Black Sea Fleet during the First Russian Revolution of 1905, that, too, had begun over inedible food, and fraternising crowds had been shot down in a scene immortalised later on in the 'Odessa steps' sequence of Eisenstein's film classic *Battleship Potemkin*. On 22 February, the Bombay working-class, already restive over a recent ration-cut (3 mills at panel had gone on strike on this issue on 21 February), responded massively to a Communist call for a general strike, closing down all textile mills, railway workshops and city transport. There was bitter street fighting throughout the 22nd and 23rd, with crowds "erecting road blocks and covering them from nearby buildings," particularly in the proletarian districts of Parel and Delisle Road. Armoured cars and four military columns were needed to restore order, and official casualty figures were 228 civilians killed and 1046 injured (plus 3 police deaths and 91 wounded); 10 police outposts, 9 bunks, 10 post offices and 64 government grain shops had been attacked. The strike spread to naval bases all over the country, there were serious clashes also in Karachi, and throughout February there was considerable unrest in the airforce and army too. The Bombay ratings, however, surrendered on 23 February, not so much in face of British threats (though Admiral Godfrey had flown in bombers and warned that he was prepared to destroy the navy), but because Patel and Jinnah in a rare display of unanimity advised them to do so, giving an assurance that the national parties would prevent any victimisation—a promise soon quietly forgotten.

The RIN ratings, in sharp contrast to the men of the Azad Hind Fauj, have never been given the status of national heroes (they are yet to receive the pensions now being granted to all other freedom fighters) though their action involved much greater risk in some ways than joining the INA as alter-to an arduous life in Japanese POW camps. As in the Calcutta explosions a striking feature was total submergence of communal division—the Naval Central Strike Committee, incidentally, was headed by a Muslim, M.S. Khan. The last message of the Committee deserves to be remembered far better than it is: "Our strike has been a historic event in the life of our nation. For the first time the blood of men in the Services and in the streets flowed together in a common cause. We in the Services will never forget this. We know also that you, our brothers and sisters, will not forget. Long live our great people! Jai Hind!'

Even apart from the massive political strikes in Calcutta and Bombay, the winter of 1945-46 marked the beginning of an unprecedented wave of country-wide labour unrest as prices shot up and rations were cut. A glance through Wavell's *Journal* and the Mansergh documents immediately reveals how worried British officials had become, particularly in the context of repeated strike threats by all-India organisations of railway workers, postal employees, and Government clerical associations. The development of effective country-wide labour organisations strategic sectors gave a new muscle-power to the Indian trade union movement-strikes in the 1920s and 1930s had been mainly confined to single industrial centres, primarily Bombay or Calcutta textiles.

In the context of the present paper, the main significance of the Calcutta and Bombay explosions and labour militancy lies their impact on British and Congress attitudes. On 30 November 1945, a week after the Calcutta outburst, New Delhi informed London that while the original INA trails policy would have involved at least 200-300 accused and possibly 40 to 50 death sentences, it had to be recognised now that "abstract justice must to some extent give way to expediency." Future trains, it was announced on 1 December, would be "limited to cases of brutality and murder," instead of the sweeping charge of "waging war against the King" used in the first case, and imprisonment sameness passed against the first batch were remitted in January. By February 1946, Indian soldiers were being withdrawn from Vietnam and Indonesia. On 28 November the British Cabinet sub-committee on India decided on a Parliamentary delegation; on 22 January the much more significant decision was taken to send a Cabinet mission in March to negotiate with Indian leaders. Wavell meanwhile had started preparing a 'breakdown plan'. As presented to the Cabinet Mission on 30 May 1946, this visualised a withdrawal of the British army and officials to the Muslim provinces of NW and NE India, handing over the rest of the country to the Congress." While evidently reflecting a desire in some high official circles to make of Pakistan an Indian Northern Ireland, the 'plan' is still interesting evidence of the British recognition that it would be impossible to suppress any future Congress-led rebellion.

On the Congress side, there were indications from November 1945 onwards that the forces which had restrained militancy in the past were at work again, while Wavell on 31 December would recognise the Calcutta disturbances of 21-23 November as the "turning-point", which "caused at least a temporary detente". The point requires much further research, but it does seem that, as on some earlier occasions, business pressures played an important role here. The Governor of Sind on 3 November, Finance Member Rowlands on 17 November, and Secretary of State Pethick-Lawrence on 30 November independently referred to G.D. Birla as getting "alarmed at the virulence of Congress speeches" ". . .the strong capitalist element behind Congress . . . is becoming nervous about the security of its property", Wavell informed Pethick-Lawrence on

5 December. "There have recently been indications that the Congress leaders want to reduce the political tension by making it clear that there must be no mass movement until after the elections." And Birla himself next day conveyed an interesting assurance and explanation to a London official: "There is no political leader including Jawaharlal who wants to see any crisis or violence . . . popular impatience and the prevalent atmosphere are responsible for these strong speeches. Even leaders are often led. But I think unrestrained language will be heard less and less in the future".

In Calcutta on 21 November, Sarat Bose, so long adored as the brother of Subhas, refused to come to address the students squatting in Dharamtala street and later blamed the Communists for instigating violence. Patel at a Bombay election rally on 24 November condemned the "frittering away" of energies in "trifling quarrels" with the police, Gandhi began a fairly friendly dialogue with the Bengal Governor, and the Calcutta Working Committee session of 7-11 December strongly reaffirmed its faith in non-violence—insignificant contrast to the September AICC session where many members had glorified every aspect of the by no means non-violent 1942 struggle. During the February days in Calcutta, "the Indian National Congress, whatever individual members may have done, took no part . . . in the disturbance", while Suhrawardy's appearance at the Wellington Square meeting and the subsequent procession on 12 February was explained by the Police Commissioner in terms of his "intention of not committing the error of Sarat Bose who lost much popularity by not showing himself at Dhurrumtolla on the 21st November". An official situation Report on 13 February noted that there were by the riots and will bring pressure to bear to stop them. Congressmen are patrolling with loud speakers telling the people to get off the streets...".

In Bombay during the RIN upsurge, the Governor reported to Wavell that "the Congress leaders had decried any share in the mutiny, and had advised people to preserve order. I received a message from Vallabhbhai Patel to this effect on Thursday" (21 February). Next day messages came from Chundrigar and S.K. Patil, heads of the provincial League and

Congress units, "offering the help of volunteers to assist the police". An official telephone message from Bombay on 22 February reported that: "Congress were against today's hartal, and Vallabhbhai Patel was emphatic about this, but the Communists call for sympathy with the RIN ratings has won the day and the Congress Labour Union has been totally ineffective." Patel explained his attitude clearly in a letter to Andhra Congress leader Viswanathan on 1 March 1946. "...discipline in the army cannot be tampered with . . . . We will want Army even in free India." Against Patel's advice, Nehru accepted Aruna Asaf Ali's invitation to come to Bombay, but quickly allowed himself to be "restrained from inflaming the situation, as on arriving here he had been impressed by the necessity for curbing the wild outburst of violence"—though he did later on hail the RIN strike for breaking down the "iron wall" between army and people. Gandhi, it has to be noted, was as unequivocally hostile as Patel. On 22 February he condemned the ratings for setting 'a bad and unbecoming example for India", advised them to peacefully resign their jobs if they had any grievances, and made the very interesting statement that "a combination between Hindus and Muslims and others for the purpose of violent action is unholy...". Aruna Asaf Ali made the pertinent comment in reply to that; " It simply does not lie in the mouth of Congressmen who were themselves going to the legislature to ask the ratings to give up their jobs." She also made a tragically accurate prophecy that would be far easier to "unite the Hindus and Muslims at the barricade than on the constitutional front." It is tempting to set beside Gandhi's statement of 22 February Wavells' private comment of 30 May 1946; "We must at all costs avoid becoming embroiled with both Hindu and Muslim at once."

The Congress rationale behind firmly rejecting mass confrontations was the need to concentrate energies on fighting the elections. The Congress did win a massive victory, polling 91.3% of votes in the Central Assembly general constituencies, and winning majorities in every province except Bengal, Punjab and Sind. The Hindu Mahasabha and other rightwing groups were routed, while Communists could capture only 8 provincial assembly seats, all but one of them in constituencies reserved for labour (here they did put up a fairly tough fight, winning 112,736 votes against 321,607 of the Congress). The most significant feature of the elections, however, was the prevalence of communal voting, in sharp contrast to the sporadic but quite remarkable anti-British unity forged so often in these very same months in the streets of Calcutta, Bombay, or even Karachi. The League swept all the 30 Muslim seats at the centre, and won 442 out of 509 provincial Muslim constituencies—a very major advance as compared to 1937, though it still narrowly missed a majority in the Punjab, and was defeated in the NWFP.

Apart from the logic of separate electorates, it is possible that the extremely limited franchise (about 10% of the population in the provinces, less than 1% for the Central Assembly) may have had something to do with this stark contrast between united mass action and communal voting. The NWFP Governor reported to Wavell in February 1946 that Muslim officials and the "bigger Khans" or landlords were all for the League, but the Congress was still getting the support of the "less well-to-do" Muslims owing to its promises of economic reforms—promises, however, which Congress ministries did little to implement either after 1937 or in 1946-47. In this context, the tacit (and little-noticed) surrender by the Congress of its central slogan of the late-1930s—a Constituent Assembly elected on universal franchise—acquires crucial significance in understanding the course of events. Of all Indian political groups, only the Communists pressed this demand seriously in 1945-46, in their election manifesto, *For the Final Bid For Power* (1945), for instance, or in P.C. Joshi's meeting with the Cabinet Mission on 17 April 1946. Congress leaders, in contrast, quietly accepted the Cabinet Mission decision to have the Constituent Assembly elected by existing provincial legislatures based on limited voting rights. Much more was involved here than a mere question of abstract democratic principle. The League next year would win its demand for Pakistan without its claims to represent the majority of Muslims being really tested, either in fully democratic elections or (as Congress claims had been) in sustained mass movements in the face of official repression (as distinct from occasional communal riots not unaccompanied often by official complicity). It may not be irrelevant to recall here that the Congress after 1947 would go on winning all-India elections for 30 years, while the League was routed in East Pakistan in the very first vote held on the basis of universal franchise (1954), and would fail to provide political stability even in West Pakistan.

In the long and tortuous negotiations which went on from 24 March to 29 June 1946, the Cabinet Mission at times seemed to lean marginally towards the Congress, arousing grave suspicions in the mind of the Viceroy, who once, even accused its members—and particularly Nehru's old friend Cripps—of "living in the pocket of Congress". Yet this was due basically not to Labour pro-nationalist sympathies, but because, as Wavell himself pointed out in a note to the Mission on 29 March, the British had "an extremely difficult hand to play, owing to the necessity to avoid the mass movement or revolution which it is in the power of the Congress to start, and which, we are not certain that we can control." It is difficult to avoid the conclusion that the Congress leadership once again spiked its own guns in its eagerness for quick and easy power and desire at all costs to preserve social order. The spring and summer of 1946 marked the height of the greatest strike wave in the history of colonial India, and there is ample evidence that apart from disaffection in the armed forces, it was urban labour unrest which alarmed British officials most. Strikes in 1946 totalled 1629, involving 1,941,948 workers and a loss of 12,717,762 man-days in no previous year had stoppages exceeded 1000, or the workers involved 8 lakhs. There were widespread police strikes in April (in Malabar, Andamans, Dacca, Bihar and Delhi), threats of an all-India railway stoppage throughout the summer, a postal strike in July, and on 29 July—less than three weeks before the Great Calcutta Killing of 16 August—a total, absolutely peaceful and remarkably united *bundh* in Calcutta under Communist leadership in sympathy with postal employees. The Home Member pointed out in a note dated 5 April that in the case of a break with the League, "even if they fight, they would be beaten," but 'on the whole, I doubt whether a Congress rebellion could be suppressed." In such a situation, "by no means all units (of the army) could be relied on", "Police over a large area would be likely to crack," and "a call to a general strike would be widely obeyed . . . labour is amenable mostly to Communist and Congress leadership".

The Congress High Command, however, had already had already opted for a different policy. Congress President Azad on 3 March publicly welcomed the ration-cut (a major labour grievance) as "far-sighted", and declared that strikes were "out of place today", as the British were "now acting as caretakers" Patel's correspondence reveals desperate efforts by local Congress Labour leaders in May 1946 to prevent a strike ballot in the railways "since if a ballot is taken it will be in favour of the strike". In August, the Working Committee meeting at Wardha condemned "hasty or ill-conceived stoppage" and the "growing lack of discipline and disregard of obligations on the part of the workers".

There is some interesting evidence that fear of labour militancy, combined with a growing awareness of essential Congress moderation, played a crucial part in bringing about the next major shift in official policy: the decision to allow Nehru to form a purely Congress Interim Government on 2 September 1946. The brief agreement, always more apparent than real, between the Congress and the League in accepting the Cabinet Mission's long-term three-tier plan had broken down by the end of July, and Wavell had also failed in his efforts to set up a short-term coalition Government at the centre. On 31 July, with the postal strike still on and two days after the Calcutta *bundh,* the Viceroy wrote to Pethick-Lawrence: "I dislike intensely the idea of having an interim Government dominated by one party but I feel that I must try to get the Congress in as soon as possible. . . . If Congress will take responsibility they will realise that firm control of unruly elements is necessary and they may put down the Communists and try to curb their own Left wing. Also I should hope to keep them so busy with administration that they had much less time for politics." The Director of the Intelligence Bureau made the same point on 9 August—". . . the labour situation is becoming increasingly dangerous. . . . Until a responsible Indian Government is introduced at the Centre, there is little that can be done. The Communists are only part of a larger nettle which must be grasped. I am satisfied that a responsible Government, if one can be achieved, will deal more decisively with Labour than is at present possible." By an interesting coincidence, the D.I.B. note enclosed a militant leaflet by the Delhi Electric Supply and Traction Employees Union, which combined economic grievances with statements like: "We are soldiers of the RED FLAG . . . a part of the revolutionary army of the workers"; on 20 September Wavell would be "cynically amused" to note that the new Congress minister Sarat Bose's "first reaction to a threatened strike of the Delhi electricity workers had been to make a plan for troops to be flown to Delhi to take over essential services and to summon certain British technicians". By 5 August, Wavell had also received information that Patel was "convinced that the Congress must enter the Government to prevent chaos spreading in the country, and was even prepared to threaten resignation from the Working Committee if his views were not accepted".

From 16 August 1946 onwards, the whole Indian scene was rapidly transformed by communal riots on an unprecedented scale starting with Calcutta on 16-19 August, touching Bombay from 1 September, spreading to Noakhali in East Bengal (10 October) Bihar (25 October) Garmukteswar in the UP (November), and engulfing the Punjab from March 1947 onwards. The British, who as late as June 1946 had been making plans to bring five army divisions to India in the context of a possible Congress movement, made no much move while presiding over this awesome human tragedy. In Calcutta in August, in sharp contrast to November 1945 or February 1946, the army was called out only after 24 hours, though the Governor was reminded of his First World War experiences in course of his early morning tour of the city on the 17th. Two other examples, both taken from British sources, may suffice to indicate the extent of official passivity—if not deliberate connivance. Wavell commented on 9 November 1916 in the context of Bihar Muslim requests to use aerial bombardment to stop the riots "Machine-gunning from the air is not a weapon one would willingly use, though the Muslims point out, rather embarrassingly, that we did not hesitate to use it in 1942." In March 1947, the two main bazars of Amritsar were destroyed, while "not a shot was fired by the police "—and this, Penderel Moon pertinently recalls, was the city of the Jallianwala Bagh massacre.

The Interim Government of Nehru found itself presiding helplessly over this growing communal inferno. Collective functioning became all but impossible after Wavell had persuaded Jinnah to join the Government on 26 October without the League giving up its Direct Action programme, its rejection of the Cabinet Mission long-term plan, or its boycott of the Constituent Assembly. League obstructionism, in Congress eyes at least, included refusal to attend Nehru's 'tea-party Cabinets' (informal sessions to coordinate policies before meeting the Viceroy). And a rather demagogic budget moved in February 1947 by Liaquat Ali Khan imposing heavy taxes on (predominantly Hindu) big business—a "clever move", commented Wavell, since it "drives a wedge between Congress and their rich merchant supporters like Birla, while Congress cannot object to its provisions."

Confronted by Calcutta, Noakhali, Bihar and Punjab, the secular ideals of many within the Congress ranks and leadership tended to evaporate. If Nehru consistently denounced Hindu communalism in Bihar and elsewhere, and Azad blamed Wavell for not calling out troops promptly in Calcutta to suppress "the hooligans of Calcutta's underworld" unleashed by Suhrawardy, Patel sympathised with hostile Hindu reactions to Nehru's condemnation of Bihar. Communal riots, combined with the evident unworkability of the Congress—League coalition at the centre, compelled many by early 1947 to think in terms of accepting what had been unthinkable so far-Partition, and these came to include Nehru as well as Patel. The most insistent demands for this surgical solution had now started coming from Hindu and Sikh Communalist groups in Bengal and Punjab, alarmed by the prospect of compulsory grouping into Muslim-dominated Sections (the League interpretation of the Cabinet Mission plan) which might very well later form themselves into Pakistan, But Nehru, too, was telling Wavell in private by 10 March 1947: "... the Cabinet Mission plan was the best solution if it could be carried through ...the only real alternative was the partition of the Punjab and Bengal." A month later, Congress President Kripalani informed Mountbatten: "Rather than have a battle we shall let them have their Pakistan, provided you will allow the Punjab and Bengal to be partitioned in a fair manner."

To one man, however, the idea of a high-level bargain by which the Congress would attain quick power in the major part of the country at the cost of a partition on religious lines still seemed unimaginably shocking and unacceptable. Gandhi had taken little part in the tortuous negotiations since 1945, while he had also condemned the united anti-imperialist outbursts in 1945-46 as tainted with violence. Increasingly isolated from the Congress leadership, as well as from business leaders like Birla who had now developed closer ties with Patel, the old man of 77 with undiminished courage now staked his all in a bid to vindicate his life-long principles of change of heart and non-violence in the villages of Noakhali, followed by Bihar and then the riot-torn slums of Calcutta and Delhi, Gandhi's unique personal qualities and true greatness were never more evident than in the last months of his life: courage to stand against the tide, total disdain for all conventional forms of political power which could have been his for the asking now that India was becoming free, and a passionate anti-communalism which made him declare to a League leader a month after Partition, while riots were ravaging the Punjab: "I want to fight it out with my life. I would not allow the Muslims to crawl on the streets in India. They must walk with self-respect." At times the presence of Gandhi really seemed to work miracles, as when peace returned to Calcutta after a whole year on the eve of 15 August, renewed riots were abruptly halted by his fast-unto-death in early September, or, even in Delhi, when on 27 January 1948 he was invited by Muslims to speak from the platform of the Quwaat-ul-Islam mosque—just three days before his death at the hands of Hindu fanatic.

Intensely moving and heroic, the Gandhian way in 1946-47 could be no more than an isolated personal effort with a local and often rather short-lived impact. It is futile and dangerous to speculate on what might have been, but one might still argue that the only real alternative lay along the path of united militant mass struggles against imperialism and its Indian allies—the one thing which, as we have seem, the British really dreaded. Despite the obvious and major disruption caused by the riots, this possibility was by no means entirely blocked even in the winter of 1946-47.

Three months after the Calcutta riots, villages in many parts of Bengal (particularly Thakurgaon sub-division in Dinajpur and adjoining areas of Jalpaiguri, Rangpur and Malda in North Bengal, as well as pockets in Mymensingh, Midnapur and 24 Parganas) resounded to the slogans of *tebhaga chai* and *nij-khamare dhan tolo,* as sharecroppers responded to the call of the Communist-led Kisan Sabha to fight against the *jotedars* for the two-thirds share of the harvest promised by the Floud Commission (1940) but never implemented. Though Muslim majority South-East Bengal was largely untouched by *tebhaga,* and its strongest base was among low-caste semi-tribal groups like the Rajbansis, many Muslims did participate in the strong holds of the movement, producing leaders like Haji Muhammad Danesh, Niamat Ali, and even some *maulvis* who quoted the *Koran* to condemn *jotedar* oppression.

A second major outburst was in the Shertalai-Alleppey-Ambalapuzha area of Travancore state, where the close proximity of small-town industries with agricultural occupations made the formula of worker-peasant alliance more of a reality than in most areas, and where Communist coir-factory, fishermen, toddy-taper and agricultural labour unions had become powerful enough to control recruitment, establish arbitration courts, and even win the right to run their own ration shops. Economic grievances sharpened by acute food scarcity, coincided in the autumn of 1946 with national opposition, spearheaded by the Communists, to Dewan C.P. Ramaswami lyre's plans for an independent Travancore under an 'American-model' constitution which would have perpetuated his own power. Intense repression led to violent clashes and attacks on police camps in Punnapra and Vayalar on 24-27 October 1946, which left about 800 killed and ultimately vastly enhanced the prestige of the Communists in Kerala. The massacre prevented the alliance with the totally discredited Dewan towards which some right-wing Congress leaders had been moving, and Ramaswami Iyer next year accepted integration with India fairly easily, no doubt because he had realised that the alternative might well be a violent revolution. In this sense it was Punnapra-Vayalar which really brought about the integration of Travancore with India, blocking the road towards Balkanisation.

Where *tebhaga* and Punnapra-Vayalar had gone to the brink of armed struggle, but failed to cross it, Telengana in Hyderabad State between July 1946 and October 1951 saw the biggest peasant guerrilla war so far of modern Indian history, affecting at its height about 3000 villages spread over 16,000 square miles and a population of 3 millions. The beginning of the uprising is traditionally dated from 4 July 1946, when thugs employed by the *deshmukh* of Visunur (one of the biggest and most oppressive of Telengana's landlords, with 40,000 acres) murdered a village militant, Doddi Komarayya, who had been defending a poor washerwoman's mite of land. Unlike *tebhaga* and to a much a greater extent that in Travancore, the Communist-led agrarian revolt in Telengana against particularly gross form of feudal oppression retained, till the entry of the Indian army in September 1948, the broader dimensions of a national-liberation struggle to overthrow the Nizam and his Razakar hands and unite Hyderabad with India. Another decisive advantage was the very slack enforcement of the Arms Act in Hyderabad, where, as Sundarrayya recalls, "large numbers of country-guns . . . were available and . . . in common use," while till September 1948 arms could be collected more or less openly in the neighbouring Andhra districts of Madras, since everyone—including the Congress—wanted to block the Nizam's bid to set up an independent and autocratic Muslim-dominated state. Incidentally, though the urban Muslim population, including many workers, remained generally outside the Telengana struggle, the Communist-led peasant revolt also succeeded in defusing what might have been quite an explosive communal situation in Hyderabad State, where the first political movements in the 1930s had been under Arya Samaj and Hindu Mahasabha inspiration.

As Travancore and Hyderabad revealed, the situation in the princely states was full of radical possibilities, and 1946-47 in fact saw a major upsurge in States Peoples' movements a most everywhere. The Congress High Command, and particularly Sardar Patel, tackled the situation in what had become the standard practice of the party: using popular movements as a lever to extort concessions from princes, while simultaneously restraining radical elements (or even using force to suppress them once the prince had been brought to heel, as after 'police action' in Hyderabad). Thus in Kashmir in June 1946, after Nehru had chivalrously rushed off to get arrested on hearing the news of the detention of Sheikh Abdullah by the very unpopular and despotic Hindu Maharaja of a Muslim majority state, Patel assured Wavell that Nehru had gone against his advice, and soon began negotiations with Kashmir Prime Minister Kak to bring about a peaceful accession to India. "This alters the whole outlook for the States," the Nawab of Bhopal declared on hearing of the appointments of Patel and his civil servant friend V.P. Menon to head the new States Department. On 5 July 1947, Patel assured the princes: "the Congress are no enemies of the Princely Order, but on the other hand, wish them and the people under their aegis all prosperity, contentment and happiness." Between July 1947 and September 1948, Patel and Menon brought off first the "accession" and then the "integration" of the states through a skilful combination of threats of mass pressure and baits–'surrender' only of powers of defence, external affairs, and communications in the first phase, which the princes in any case had never enjoyed under British paramountcy, and generous offers subsequently of privy purses and offices of Rajpramukhs. The rapid unification of India is certainly Sardar Patel's greatest and very real achievement, but we must not forget the considerable role played here, too, by the existence or at least the potential presence of mass pressures—as well as the way socially radical possibilities were blocked by this speedy 'revolution' from the top.

Popular movements in urban areas were seriously disrupted by the riots, which began precisely in Calcutta and Bombay, the two main centres of the 1945-46 upsurge. Yet five months after the August riots, the students of Calcutta were again on the streets on 21 January 1947 in Hands off Vietnam' demonstrations against the use of Dum Dum airport by French planes, and all communal divisions seemed forgotten in the absolutely united and ultimately victorious 85-day tram strike under Communist leadership which began the same day, followed soon afterwards by port employees and Howrah engineering workers. January and February 1947 in fact saw a new strike wave, with 100,000 out in Kanpur textiles, a threat of a coal stoppage, and strikes in Coimbatore, Karachi and elsewhere due "largely to Communist agitation." "There are strikes everywhere—everybody wants higher wages and less work," Birla complained to Gandhi's secretary Pyarelal on 18 January.

The socially radical movements of which Telengana was the climax never coalesced into an organised and effective country-wide political alternative. The fear they undoubtedly inspired, however, helped to bring about the final compromise by which a 'peaceful' transfer of power was purchased at the cost of Partition and a communal holocaust. V.P. Menon reported to Wavell in the wake of the early 1947 strike wave "that Congress leaders were losing popularity . . . there were serious internal troubles in Congress and great fear of the Left Wing; and that the danger of labour difficulties was acute." A week later, Wavell's *Journal* recorded a conversation with Patel "about the danger of the Communists. I got the impression he would like to declare the party illegal' – a desire which the Home Minister would fulfil within a few months of independence, in March 1948. The British Government was also quick to come forward with a dramatic gesture when in February 1947 the League refused to join the Constituent Assembly and cooperate in Cabinet functioning led to a major political crisis, with the Congress demanding resignation of the League ministers and threatening to withdraw its own nominees from the Interim Government if its demands were not met. This was the immediate context of Attlee's famous speech in Commons on 20 February 1947, fixing June 1948 as deadline for transfer of power and announcing the replacement of Wavell by Mountbatten. The hint of possible Partition or even Balkanisation into numerous states was very clear in this policy statement, but the bait of complete transfer of power by a definite and fairly early data proved too tempting to be refused—particularly as the only real alternative for the Congress was to plunge into another mass confrontation, difficult in the context of communal riots and very dangerous socially in view of what appeared to be a growing Left menace.

Something like a cult had developed around Mountbatten, depicting him as super statement-cum-Prince Charming who solved the sub-continent's problems in record time through a combination of military forth-rightness, personality and tact. There is enormous exaggeration here. The formula of freedom-with-Partition was coming to be widely accepted well before Mountbatten took over charge, and the final draft of Wavell's 'breakdown plan in September 1946 had already envisaged complete British withdrawal by 31 March 1948. The working-out of the Mountbatten plan in fact revealed once again the potential strength of the Congress position, as well as the repeated failure of its leaders to use this fully due to their eagerness for quick and peaceful accession to power. Mountbatten's original Plan Balkan' had envisaged transfer of power to separate provinces, which—along with princely states rendered independent by the lapse of paramountcy—would then have the choice of joining India, Pakistan, or remaining separate. A single outburst by Nehru in Simla on 10 May was sufficient for Mountbatten to give this up completely. Mountbatten himself, as well as his admirers, have been full of praise for the decision, on an "absolute hunch", of showing this plan privately to Nehru on the eve of seeking Cabinet sanction for it. Historically the much more significant point surely is that Nehru's opposition was sufficient to make Mountbatten abandon a plan on which British officials had been working for several weeks. The alternative then adopted owed its inception, not to Mountbatten, but to V.P. Menon, who had suggested in January 1947 a transfer to two Central Governments, India and Pakistan, on the basis of grant of Dominion Status with a right of secession. Vallabhbhai Patel, significantly enough, had privately agreed with this idea, even though formally it meant a retreat from the Lahore resolution of 1929—since Dominion Status on the basis of existing political structures would obviate the need to wait for agreement in the Constituent Assembly, ensure a peaceful and very quick transfer of power, win for

India influential friends in Britain by pandering to British sentiments about Crown and Commonwealth, and allow for continuity in the bureaucracy and army. Unlike Plan Balkan, the revised scheme did guard against fragmentation of the country, but at the cost, it must be added, of blocking some interesting non-communal regional possibilities—moves towards a united, autonomous Bengal by Suhrawardy and Abul Hashem, which a few Congress leaders like Sarat Bose seemed prepared to consider, and the demand of Khan Abdul Ghaffar Khan for an independent Pathan state in the NWFP. The Frontier Congress leaders felt that only such a slogan could counter the League bid to capture the province for Pakistan, now that anti-Muslim riots in Hindu majority provinces had weakened the traditional Pathan identification with Indian nationalism. The Congress High Command in 1947 let the Pathans down very badly indeed, signally failing to use its position of strength to block the decision to have a plebiscite on the India-Pakistan issue alone, and that on the basis of the old limited electorate. The NWFP went to Pakistan, with the local Congress boycotting the plebiscite in protest, by the decision of just 9.52% of its total population. The Frontier Gandhi would later declare with justice that he and his movement had been "thrown to the wolves" by the Congress leadership.

IV

In conclusion, a few general comments may be attempted on two broad problems which emerge from the study of 1945-47 developments—the reasons behind the failure of the Left alternative, and the nature of the great but incomplete transition which was consummated on 15 August.

Within the Communist movement, a strong tendency had developed by late 1947 to attribute the Left failure to the allegedly reformist' policies of the leadership, and particularly of P.C. Joshi—and at the Calcutta Party Congress in February 1948 Joshi was unceremoniously ousted as General Secretary and replaced by B.T. Ranadive with his much more militant line. Judging from official comments and reactions. Communist actions at least at local levels were hardly lacking in militancy in the 1945-47 period. A glance through the Home Political

(Internal) files immediately reveals how completely the CPI had displaced the Congress as the Enemy No. 1 already by the end of 1945. It may also be argued that Communist militancy was often more effective during these years than in the "Ranadive period', which saw such complete fiascoes as the call for country wide railway strike and rebellion on 9 March 1949, as well as the gradual decline even of the Telengana armed struggle's. Party cadres and the leadership in fact showed unusual flexibility at times, as when the Students Federation joined the Forward Bloc demonstration in Calcutta on 21 November 1945, and their action was endorsed next day by P.C. Joshi's telegram: "Get all war-time understanding out of your heads —, new tactical line needed. Be with the people." A considerable lag is noticeable, however, at the level of theoretical formulation and general slogans. Here the persistent calls for Congress-League-Communist unity made little sense and even sounded rather pathetic at a time when the Congress and the League obviously had no intention at all of coming together, and in fact seemed to agree only in a common detestation of the Communists. Another example would be the curious passage in the CPI Election Manifesto which gave an assurance that the Party 'shall not touch the small zamindar or the rich peasant but shall open before them the prospect of becoming the best of the farmers and cattle-breeders, reputed members in their own village." Less than a year after this programmatic statement, the Party would be leading the Bengal sharecroppers in a struggle against the *jotedars*, who were not zamindars but big farmers.

As in other periods of 'united front', the central problem was to combine broad multi-class objectives with retention of initiative and independence. The Chinese Communists under Mao Tse-tung, as everyone knows, did this brilliantly during the anti-Japanese War; a lesser-known example would be the Bolsheviks, who up to the very eve of October 1917 had a very modest 'bourgeois-democratic' minimum programme (an 8-hour day, a democratic republic, and return to peasants of *Otrezki* lands seized by the gentry), but certainly never expected bourgeois parties like the Kadets to carry out this programme for them. In colonial India, too, substantial advances were made in regions like Kerala and Telengana by Communists taking over the initiative and leadership in the national struggle, as when P. Krishna Pillai, E.M.S. Namboodripad and A.K. Gopalan during the 1930s simultaneously built up the Congress, the CSP as legal cover, and the illegal Communist Party in Travancore and Malabar. But all too often united front came to mean a policy of waiting on bourgeois leaders and putting undeserved trust in their 'progressive' intentions—an attitude which in its turn repeatedly bred an equally disastrous release into ultra-Left sectarianism.

But failures of Communist leadership probably provide only a small part of the explanation for the Left defeat in the post-War years. The Communists, we must remember, were no more than a small, though in these years rapidly growing force at the national plane, with only scattered pockets of real influence. In addition, they still had to live down their 1942 reputation. The break within the Left over Quit India had pushed the Socialists much closer to the Congress High Command, and a *Fortnightly Report* from U.P. Noted with relief in November 1945 that: "Congress Socialists as such have not come much to notice, "since there was now "little difference in either the avowed objective or the outward means of attaining that objective between the Congress and the Congress Socialists," the British, as we have seen, were alarmed above all by the militancy of urban labour, but with a few short-lived exceptions (Calcutta in November 1945 and February 1946, Bombay in February 1946, Punnapre-Vayalar in October 1946), all the strikes of the period were on economic demands alone. This may have been partly the responsibility of a trade union leadership sunk in 'economism', but it remains more than a little dubious whether labour would have responded on a country-wide scale to a call for political action coming from the Communists alone (A joint Congress-Communist call would have been quite a different thing, as the British were well aware, but the Congress High Command had no intention of going in that direction). As for peasant movements, a crucial limitation here came from the marked, and growing, regional variations. All-in peasant unity against landlords was possible only on regions like Telengana, with its crude and blatant forms of feudalism. Regions like the Punjab or Gujrat, where considerable rich peasant development coincided with the absence of zamindari, had in sharp contrast kept largely aloof even from the 1942 rebellion, while Communists naturally found entry difficult for a time into the Quit India strongholds of Bihar or east UP. Poor peasants, sharecroppers, and agricultural labourers, often or low caste of tribal origin, still provided combustible material. But, as the experience of the later stages of *tebhaga*, 1948-49, and Naxalbari has repeatedly indicated, movements of such sections alone, however militant and heroic, tend to end in a self-defeating isolation in which guerrilla war degenerates into sporadic individual terrorism. The Telengana 'spark' thus failed to kindle a 'prairie fire'.

Controversies about Communist policies naturally lead on to the broader question of evaluating the real significance of August 1917. The problem lies in combining recognition of the very real and fundamental changes associated with the coming of freedom with an awareness of its equally real limits and contradictions. Perhaps some guidance can be sought from Antonio Gramsci's very interesting concept, developed in the context of his study of Risorgimento Italy, of 'passive revolution': 'passive' not in the sense of popular forces being inactive (as they were not, in 19th, century Italy and even less so during the Indian freedom movement), but because the privileged groups in town and country were able to successfully detach attainment of political independence and unity from radical social change. Gramsci explained this in terms of the success of the leading bourgeois group, the Moderates headed by Cavour, in asserting its hegemony through a process of 'trasformismo', bringing about "the gradual but continuous absorption. Of the active elements produced by allied groups- and even of those which came from antagonistic groups and seemed irreconcilably hostile". In Italy "the Action party (of Mazzini and Garibaldi) was in fact in directly led by Cavour", the Indian counterpart would be the subordination of Left elements within the Congress, best typified by Nehru and the CSP in the 1930s, to the basically Right-oriented High Command. Such 'hegemony' was, however, sharply distinct, according to Granmsci, from what he considered to have been the classic 'Jacobin' model of successful and through-going bourgeois revolution based on mobilisation of peasantry and total destruction of feudalism in the countryside. In Italy, despite unification and political independence, fullscale capitalist transformation proved very difficult to achieve, since the new ruling group was a bloc between Northern industrialists and Southern landlords established at the cost of peasant aspirations, and fundamental agrarian change remained a *'rivolutions mancata'* (a 'missing' or 'absent' revolution). One major consequence was the perpetuation and sharpening of regional disparities, the North flourishing at the cost of the South-modern Italy's persistent 'Southern Question'. Historical parallels can never be exact, and a number of differences are evident in the Indian context (e.g., the absence of a Piedmont, or of direct foreign help in overthrowing alien rule and the related much greater role of popular forces, which ensured establishment of democratic forms far more quickly than in Italy); it would be labouring the obvious, however, to list the similarities. It is interesting that Gramsci in 1933 made a passing reference to Gandhism as, a 'naive theorisation of the 'passive revolution' with religious overtones".

The millions who rejoiced throughout the subcontinent, thrilled to Nehru's midnight speech on India's 'tryst with destiny', and made of 15 August an unforgettable experience, had certainly not been entirely deluded, as subsequent developments abundantly proved. The Communist slogan in 1948-49 of 'Yeh Azadi Jhuti Hai' cut very little ice, for the new Indian Government certainly did not act as an imperialist puppet; 'a passive revolution' also implied fundamental, though slow and contradictory change. Yet it is possible to sympathize with the many to whom independence seemed a sorry thing if compared to the generous dreams of the freedom fighters, and it is well-known that Gandhi in great part shared this sense of disillusionment. The agony of many committed leftists was well expressed in the last two poems Samar Sen has written: "the battleship (of the R.I.N.) lie silent in harbour, immobilised by treachery", it Noakhali, Bihar, or Garhmuktesar, Hindus and Muslims find unity only after death; and "the passions of youth have become the just of again men".

Bibliography

CONTRIBUTORS TO SOUTH ASIA: THE JOURNAL OF SOUTH ASIAN STUDIES

Abeyagunawardena, D.S. S. Arasaratnam, *Sri Lanka after Independence: Nationalism, Communalism and Nation Building*, X: 1, p. 111.

Abeyagunawardena, D.S. B. Swan, *Sri Lanka Mosaic: Environment, Man, Continuity and change*, XII:2, p.112

Abeyasekare, S. D. Kantowsky, *Sarvodaya: The Other Development*, VI:1, pp. 61-63.

Adams, J. *Urbanism and Economic Development in Western India*, 1:2, pp. 1-10.

Agarwal, U. A.K.M. Farooque, *Roads and Communications in Mughal India*, 11: 1 & 2, pp. 198-200.

Ahmad, Q. *Medieval India: A Miscellany*, Vol. 1, No. 2, pp. 115-117.

Akhtar, M.S. C. Shackle, *Catalogue of the Punjabi and Sindhi Manuscripts in the India Office Library*, II:1 & 2, p. 151.

Alam, A.M.Q. *Privatisation Policy and the Problem of Industrial Development in Bangladesh*, XII: 2, pp. 49-68.

Alexander, H.M.L. Discarding the "Steel Frame": Changing Images Among Indian Civil Servants in the Early Twentieth Century, V:2, pp. 1-12.

Ali, A. *The 1915 Racial Riots in Ceylon (Sri Lanka): A Reappraisal of its Causes*, IV:2, pp. 1-20.

Ali, I. *Relations Between the Muslim League and the Punjab National Unionist Party*, 1935-1947, No. 6, pp. 51-65.

Allen, M. — C. Bougle, *Essays on the Caste System*, No. 2, pp. 109-110.

Allen, M. — L. Boulnois, *Bibliographic du Nepal, Vol. I: Sciences Humaines, references en langues europeennes. Suppliment* 1967-73, No. 6, p. 121.

Allen, M. — Buddhism without Monks: The Vajrayana Religion of the Newars of Kathmandu Valley, No. 3, pp. 1-14.

Allen, M. — J.E. Schwartzberg (ed.), *A Historical Atlas of South Asia*, III: 1, pp. 92-93 (from the perspective of Social Anthropoloty).

Allen, M. — M. Singer, *When a Great Tradition Modernizes: An Anthropological Approach to Indian Civilisation*, No. 6, pp. 130-132.

Ambirajan, S. — Academy of Sciences, USSR, *Oriental Countries of Today*;

R. Vedavalli, *Private Foreign Investment and Economic Development*;

S. Chishti, *India's Terms of Trade, 1930-68*; and

D. Nayyar, *India's Exports and Export Policies*, I: 2, pp. 143-145.

Ambirajan, S. — C.P. Bhambhri, *World bank and India*, VI: 2, pp. 80-81.

Ambirajan, S. — M.M. Deshpande and P.E. Hook (eds.), *Aryan and Non-Aryan in India*, IV: 1, pp. 81-82.

Ambirajan, S. — W.A. *Lewis, Dynamic Factos in Economic Growth*;

T. Singh, *India's Development Experience*;

C.N. Vakil and V.S.M. Rao (eds.), *Industrial Development of India Policy and Problems*; and

B. Dasgupta, *The Oil Industry in India, Some Economic Aspects*, No. 6, pp. 145-147.

Ambirajan, S. — Political Economy and Indian Famines, No. 1, pp. 20-28.

Ambirajan, S. — J.E. Schwartzberg (ed.), *A Historical Atlas of South Asia*, III: 1 pp. 87-89 (from the perspective of Economic History).

Ambirajan, S. — The Changing Attitudes Towards Business in India: A Long View, XII:1, pp. 1-28.

Ambirajan, S. — The Political Economy of Indian Economic Development, XII:2, pp. 1-12.

Amritmahal, R.	F.W. *Rawding, The Rebellion in India*, 1857, I:2, p. 123.
Amzad Hossein Main,	A.K.H. J.G. Williams, *the Art of Gupta India*, VII:2, pp. 92-94.
Appleyard, R.T.	J.E. Schwartzberg (ed.), *A Histrocial Atlas of South Asia*, III: 1, pp. 93-94.
	(from the perspective of Economic Demography).
Arasaratnam, S.	T. Abeyasinghe (ed.) *A Study of Portuguese Regimentos on Sri Lanka at the Goa Archives*, No. 5, pp. 106-107.
Arasaratnam, S.	M. Alam, *the Crisis of Empire in Mughal North India: Awadh and the Punjab, 1707-48* XI:1, pp. 110-112.
Arasaratnam, S.	Anisussaman (ed.) *Factory Correspondence and Other Bengali Documents in the India Office Library and Records*, VII:2, pp. 94-95.
Arasaratnam, S.	A. Das Gupta, *Indian Merchants and the Decline of Surat c. 1700-1750*, IV: 1, pp. 87-89.
Arasaratnam, S.	Factors in the Rise, Growth and Decline of Coromandel Ports *cira* 1950-1720, VII:2, pp. 19-30.
Arasaratnam, S.	T. Fernando and R.N. Kearney (eds.), *Modern Sri Lanka a Society in Transition;*
	M. Roberts (ed.) *Collective Identities and Protest in Modern Sri Lanka;* and *J. Jiggins, Caste and Family in the Politics of the Sinhalese*, III:2, pp. 91-94.
Arasaratnam, S.	J. Fisch, *Hollands Ruhm in Asien*, XI: 1, pp. 91-92.
'Arasaratnam, S.	H. furber, *Rival Empires of Trade in the Orient, 1600-1800, Vol. II*, 1:11, pp. 129-130.
Arasaratnam, S.	H.A.I. Goonetileke, *A Bibliography of Ceylon*, VI:1, pp., VI:1, pp. 60-61.
Arasaratnam, S.	Indian Commercial Groups and European Traders, 1600-1800: Changing Relationships in Southeastern India, 1:2, pp. 42-53.
Arasaratnam, S.	D. Kaushik, *The Indian Ocean. Towards a Peace Zone, No.4, p. 143.*
Arasaratnam, S.	D. Ludden, *Peasant History in South India, X:2*, pp. 98-100.
Arasaratnam, S.	C. Manogaran, *Ethnic Conflict and Reconciliation in Sri Lanka*, XI:2, pp. 126-128.

Arasaratnam, S. O. Prakash, *The Dutch East India Company and the Economy of Bengal 1630-1720*, IX:2, pp. 100-102.

Arasaratnam, S. D. Rothermund, *An Economic History of India*, XIII:1, pp. 116-117.

Arasaratnam, S. M. Roberts, *Facets of Modern Ceylon History Through the Letters of Jeronis Pieris*, No. 6, pp. 133-134.

Arasaratnam, S. J. Sarkar, *Fall of the Mughal Empire, Vol. 1, 1739-1754*, and *Anedotes on Aurangzib*, XIII:1, p. 136.

Arasaratnam, S. N. Steensgard, *Carracks, Caravans and Companies: European-Asian Trade in the Early Seventeenth Century*. No. 4, pp. 117-118.

Arasaratnam, S. The Politics of Commerce in the Coastal Kingdoms of Tamil Nadu, 1650-1700, No. 1, pp. 1-19.

Arasaratnam, S. A.J. Wilson, *The Break-up of Sri Lanka. The Sinhalese-Tamil Conflicet*, XIII:1, pp. 128-131.

Ardussi, J.A. S. Beyer, *The Cult of Tara: Magic and Ritual in Tibet*, No. 6, pp. 129-130.

Ardussi, J.A. E.M. Dargyay, *The rise of Esoteric Buddgism in Tibet*, II:1&2, pp. 188-189.

Ardussi, J.A. U. Schweinfurth and H. Schweinfurth-Marby, *Explorations in the Eastern Himalayas and the river Gorge Country of Southeastern Tibet-Francis K. Word (1885-1958)*, 1:1, pp. 148-149.

Arnold, D. C.J. Baker and D.A. Washbrook, *South India: Political Institutions and Political Change*, 1880-1940, No. 6, pp. 138-140.

Arnold, D. M.M. Bouton, *Agrarian Radicalism in South India*, IX:2, pp. 114-115.

Arnold, D. D. Chakrabarty, Rethinking *Working Class History Bengal, 1890-1940*, XII:2, pp. 96-98.

Arnold, D. Rs. Suntharalingam, *Politics and Nationalist Awakening in South India* 1852-1891, No. 5, pp. 120-121.

Arnold, D. The Gounders and the Congress: Political Recruitment in South India, 1920-1937, No. 4, pp. 1-20.

Athiyaman, P. and Venkatachalapathy, A.R., Debate: On Gandhi, Mayo and Emilsen XII:2, pp. 83-88.

Atkinson, D.W.	Tagore and Gandhi: The Poet and the Pragmatist, VI: pp. 1-14.
Aung-Thwin, M.	R.A.I.H. Gunawardana, *Robe and Plough: Monasticism and Economic Interest in Early Medieval Sri Lanka*, IV:1, pp. 75-80.
Aveling. H.	A.K. Ramanujan, *Hymns for the Drowning—Poems for Visnu by Nammalour*, VI:2, pp. 95-97.
Ayres, R.G.	R. Cashman, *Patrons, Players and the Crowd—The Phenomenon of Indian Cricket*, IX:1, p. 122.
Bader, J.	Gunther D. Sontheimer and Hermann Kulke (eds.), Hinduism reconsidered, XIII:2, pp. 117-120.
Bailey, G.	Debate: On the De-construction of Culture in Indian Literature: A Tentative Response to Vijay Mishra's Article, XII:1, pp. 85-102.
Bailey, G.	J.W. De Jong, *Buddhist Studies*, VI:2, pp. 91-92.
Bailey, G.	R.F. Gombrich (ed.), *Indian Ritual and its Exegesis*, XII:1, pp. 118-120.
Bailey, G.	H. Kulke, *Jagannatha-Kult and Griapati-Konigtum, ein Beitrgg zur Geschichte Religiose Legitimation Hinduistischer Herrscher*, VI:2, p. 90-91.
Bailey, G.	A. Oster, *The Play of the Gods*. Locality, Ideology, Structure and Time in the Festivals of a Bengali Town, V:1, pp. 61-62.
Bailey, G.	Puranic Notes: Reflections on the Myth of Sukesin, VI:2, pp. 46-61.
Bailey, G.	J. Schever, *Sive dans le Mahabharata; and* S. Kramrisch, *The Presence of Siva*, VI:1, pp. 72-74.
Bailey, G.	P. Schreiner and R. Sohnen, *Sanskrit Indices and Text of the Brahmapurana*, XII:1, pp. 125-126.
Bailey, G.	Secular and Religious in Indian Literature: A Comparison of Writings on the theme of Leve in the Gitagovinda and the Caurapancasika IV:1, pp. 1-14.
Bailey, G.	R. Sohnen, *Untersuchungen zur Composition von Reden and Gesprachen im Ramayana*, VI:2, pp. 76-77.
Bailey, G.	M. Taddei (ed.), *South Asian Archaeology 1977*, VI:2, pp. 102-103.
Baker, D.E.U.	J. Brown, *Gandhi's Rise to Power: Indian Politics 1915-1922*, No. 3, pp. 137-139.

Baker, D.E.U. The Swaraj Parties in the Central Provinces and Berar, India, 1924-26: An Essay in Regional Politics, II: 1&2, pp. 46-59.

Balasubramanian, K. P. M. Blaikie, *Family Planning in India: Diffusion and Policy*, II: 1&2, p. 182.

Balasubramanian, K. D.G. Mandelbaum, *Human Fertility in India: Social Components and Policy Perspectives*, II: 1&3, pp. 181-182.

Barrier, N.G. I. Ali, *The Punjab under Imperialism*, XII:2,pp.94-96.

Barrier, N.G. R. Jeffrey, *What's Happening to India? Punjab, Ethnic Conflict, Mrs. Gandhi's Death and the Test of Federalism*, IX:2, pp. 123-124.

Barrier, N.G. W.W. Reinhardt, *The Legislative Council of the Punjab, 1897-1912*, No. 2, pp. 120-121.

Bartley, C.J. L.M. Finn, *The Kulacudamani Tantra and the Vamakesvar Tantra with the Jayaratha Commentary*, X:2, pp. 86-87.

Bara, R.K. A Beginning in Prose: Some Steps in the Emergence of Modern Hindi Literature, V:1, pp. 5-15.

Barz, R.K. C.P. Agrawal (ed.), *Jaya Sankar Prasad Issue, Journal of South Asian Literature*, IV:1, pp. 60-62.

Barz, R.K. P. Gaeffke, *Hindi Literature in the Twentieth Century*, II:1&2, pp. 192-194.

Barz, R.K. K. Hazareesingh, History *of Indians in Mauritius*, 1:2, pp. 135 & 137.

Barz, R.K. B.B. Kachru, *Kashmiri Literature*, VI:2, pp. 89-90.

Barz, R.K. R.S. McGregor, *A New Voice for New Times*, VI:2, pp. 93-94.

Barz, R.K. R.S. McGregor, *Hindi Literature of the Nineteenth and Early Twentieth Centuries*, No. 6, pp. 134-135.

Barz, R.K. M.U. Memon (ed.), *Studies in the Urdu Gazal and Prose Fiction*, IX:1, pp. 100-101.

Barz, R.K. D. Rahbar, *Urdu Letters of Mirza Asadu'llah Khan Ghalib*, X:2, pp. 89-90.

Barz, R.K. The Cultural Significance of Hindi in Mauritius, III:1, pp. 1-13.

Basham, A.L. W.N. Nrown, *India and Indology—Selected Articles*, II: 1&2, pp. 185-187.

Basham, A.L.	P.S. Jaini, *The Jaina Path of Purification,* III:2, pp. 76-77.
Basham, A.L.	R.S. Sharma, (ed.) *The Indian Historical Review,* Vol.I, No.1, No. 6. pp. 121-122.
Basham, A.L.	A.K. Warder, *An Introduction to Indian Historiography,* No. 3, pp. 114-116.
Basham, A.L.	T. Zachariae, *Opera Minora, zur indischen Wortforschung, zur Geschichte der indischen Literature and Kultur, zur Geschichte der Sanskritphiologie,* II: 1&2, p. 152.
Baxi, U.	The Ultra-Modernity of Tradition: Some Comments on "the Modernity of Tradition" by Lioyd and Susanne Rudolph, No. 2, pp. 101-108.
Bedford, I.	B.R. Nanda (ed.), *Socialism in India,* No. 3, pp. 127-128.
Beer, D.R.	P. Addy, *Tibet on the Imperial Chesshored: The Making of British Policy Towards Lhasa, 1899-1925,* X:1, pp. 97-98.
Beer, D.R.	C.A. Bayly, *Imperial Meridian: The British Empire and the World, 1780-1830,* XII:2, pp. 91-92.
Begum, H.	Mass Media and Women in Bangladesh, IX:1, pp. 15-24.
Behera, K.S.	A. Boner, S.R. Sharma and R.P. Das, *New Light on the Sun Temple of Konarak: Four Unpublished Manuscripts Relating to Construction, History and Ritual of this Temple,* No. 6, pp. 127-129.
Bell, S.	B. Kapferer, *A Celebration of Demons: Exorcism and the Aesthetics of Healing in Sri Lanka,* IX:1, pp. 116-117.
Bell, S.	M. Roberts, *Caste conflict and Elite Formation: The Rise of a Karava Elite in Sri Lanka,* 1500-1931., VI:2, pp. 97-98.
Bennett, S.	Shikar and the Raj, VII:2, pp. 72-88.
Berwick, J.	M. Borthwick, *The Changing Role of Women in Bengal, 1849-1905,* IX:1, pp. 107-108.
Bharati, A.	L. Siegel, *Sacred and Profane Dimensions of Love in Indian Tratitions as Exemplified in the Gitagovinda of Jayadeva,* II: 1&2, pp. 189-190.
Bhattacharya, D.	F.R. Frankel, *India's Political Economy, 1947-77: The Gradual Revolution,* III:2, pp. 89-90.

Bhattacharya, S. The Indian Working Class and the Nationalist Movement, X:I, pp. 53-68.

Bilimoria, P. R. Champalakshmi, *Vaisnava Iconography in the Tamil Country*, VII:2, pp. 91-92.

Bilimoria, P. Mr. Hiriyanna, *Essentials of Indian Philosophy*, X:1, pp. 89-90.

Bilimoria, P. N.S. Junankar, *Gautama: The Nyaya Philosophy*, IV:1, pp. 73-75.

Birmingham, J. Chalcolithic and Early Iron Age Pottery in West Bengal, No. 2, pp. 1-23.

Biscrone, R. G.F. Dales, *Excavations at Nad-i Ali (Sorkh Dagh) Afghanistan*, II:1&2, pp. 184-185.

Bishop. D.H. G. Ramachandran and T.K. Mahadevan (eds.), *Quest for Gandhi*, No. 2, pp. 121-122.

Blackburn, S.H. The Kallars: A Tamil "Criminal Tribe" Reconsidered, 1:1, pp. 38-51.

Blake, S.P. The Hierarchy in North India During the Mughal Period of Indian History, VI:1, pp. 1-32.

Borchardt, D.H. V. Kumar, *Committees and Commissions in India, 1947-1973* No. 6, pp. 148-149.

Boreham, N. I. Talbot, *Provincial Politics and the Pakistan Movement. The Growth of the Muslim League in North-West and North-East India 1937-47*, XIII:1, pp. 104-107.

Borthwick, M. M.F. Franda, *India in the 70s; Indian in an Emergency: Bangladesh and India*, II:1 & 2, pp. 223-224.

Borthwick. M. R. Ghadially (ed.), *Women in Indian Society. A Reader*, XII:1, pp. 115-116.

Borthwick. M. V.C. Joshi (ed.), *Sri Aurobindo: An Interpretation*, 1:1, pp. 138-139.

Borthwick. M. D. Kopf, *The Brahmo Samaj and the Shaping of the Modern Indian Mind*, II:1 & 2, pp. 206-208.

Borthwick, M. I.J. Parekh and P.K. Garg, *Indian Women: An Inner Dialogue*, XIII:1, pp. 120-121.

Boxer, C.R. S. Arasaratnam, *Merchants, Companies and Commerce on the Coromandel Coast 1650-1740*, IX:2, pp. 102-104.

Boxer. C.R. S. Arasaratnam (ed.), *Selections from the Dutch Records of Sri Lanka. Memoir of J.S. van Gollenesse, Governor of Ceylon, 1743-51*, No. 5, pp. 107-108.

Bradley, D. M.C. Shapiro and H.F. Schiffman, *Language and Society in South Asia*, VI:2, pp. 98-100.

Bradley, D. G.A. Zograph, *Languages of South Asia: A Guide*, VI:1, pp. 80-82.

Brand, M. B. Baumer (ed.), *Kalatattvakosa:* A Lexicon of Fundamental Concepts of the Indian Arts. Vol. 1: Eight Selected Terms, XII:2, pp. 108-110.

Brass, P.R. Review Article: Indian Elections Studies, 1:2, pp. 91-108.

Brasted, H.V. M. Bose, *The Lost Hero: A Biography of Subhas Bose*, VI:1, pp. 56-57.

Brasted, H.V. V. Gautam, *Aspects of Indian Society and Economy in the Nineteenth Century (A Study Based on an Evaluation of the American Consular Records)*, No. 6, pp. 135-136.

Brasted, H.V. Irish Models and the Indian National Congress 1870-1922, VIII: 1 & 2, pp. 24-45.

Brasted, H.V. See Bridge, C.

Brasted, H.V. S. Sen, *Working Class of India: 1830-1970, 1:2, pp. 123-124.*

Brasted, H.V. D. Taylor and M. Yapp (eds.), *Political Identity in South Asia*, VI:1, pp. 78-79.

Brasted, H.V. and Bridge, C., The British Labour Party and Indian Nationalism, 1907-1947, XI:2, pp. 69-100.

Brasted, H.V. and Dounds, G. Passages to India: Peripatetic MPs on the Grand India Tour 1870-1940, II: 1 & 2, pp. 91-111.

Brennan, L. J.M. Brown, *Gandhi and Civil Disobedience: The Mahatma in India Politics, II: I 82, pp. 167-169.*

Brennan, L. A. Chaturvedi, *District Administration: The Dynamics of Discord*, XII:2, pp. 101-103.

Brennan, L. P. Robb (ed.), *Rural India: Land, Power and Society under British Rule*, IX:2, pp. 112-114.

Brennan, L., L.Heatheote, and A. Lucas, the Causation of Faminer: A Comparative Analysis of Lombok and Bengal 1891-1974, VII:1, pp. 1-26.

Brennan, L. The Local Face of Nationalism: Congress Politics in Rohilkhand in the 1920s, No. 5, pp. 9-19.

Brennan, L. E. Whitcombe, *Agrarian Conditions in Northern India*, No. 4, pp. 125-127.

Bridge, C. S.C. Ghosh, *Decision-Making and Power in the British Conservative Party: The Indian Problem, 1924-34*, No. 5, pp. 124-126.

Bridge, C. D.A. Low, *The Contraction of England*, X:2, pp. 106-107.

Bridge, C. G. Rizvi, *Linlithgow and India: A Study of British Policy and the Political Impasse in India 1936-43*, III:2, pp. 84-85.

Bridge, C. See Brashed, H. V.

Bridge, C. The Impact of India on British High Politics in the 1930s: The Limits of Cowlingism, V:2, pp. 13-23.

Bridge, C. K. Veerathappa, *British Conservative Party and Independence*, I:2, pp. 132-134.

Bridge, C. and Brasted, H.V. Anita Inder Singh, *The Origins of the Partition of India 1936-47*, XIII:2, pp. 131-135.

Brittlebank, K. Ambiguity an Multiple Causation: the Anthropological Use of Texts, with Special Reference to Flesh-Avoidance in Ancient India, XIII:2, pp. 1-16.

Broomfield, J.H. Four Lives; History as Biography No. 1, pp. 74-90.

Broomfield. J.H. R.J. Moore, *The Crisis of Indian Unity 1917-1940*, II: 1&2, pp. 165-167.

Brown J. Reply to review by D. Baker of *Gandhi's Rise to Power: Indian Politics* 19151922, No. 3, pp. 139-142.

Brown, I. A. Vickers, *Bali, A Paradise Created*, XIII:1, pp. 134-135.

Caldwell, J., and Caldwell, P., Family Planning in India: A Worm's Eye View from a Rural Area in South India, V:1, pp. 51-53.

Caldwell, P. See Caldwell, J.

Callahan, R. S. Chakravarty, *From Khyber to Oxus: A Study in Imperial Expansio*, I:1, pp. 133-134.

Callahan, R. V. Eyre, *Journal of an Afghanistan Prisoner*, I:1 pp. 132-133.

Callahan, R.	C. Hibbert, *The Great Mutiny: India 1857, II: 1&2, p. 203.*
Callahan, R.	J.P. Lawford, *Britain's Army in India: From its Origins to the Conquest of Bengal,* II: 1&2, p. 156.
Caplan, L.	L.E. Rose, *Nepal—Strategy for Survival,* No. 3, pp. 134-135.
Carrol, L.	Ideological Factions in a Caste(s) Association—the Kayastha Conference: Educationists and Social Reformers, I:2, pp. 11-26.
Cashman, R.	H. Fukazawa, *Studies in the Social and Economic History of India,* No. 4, pp. 116-117.
Cashman, R.	J. Lebra-Chapman, *The Rani of Jhasi: A Study in Female Heroism in India,* XI: 1, pp. 98-100.
Cashman, R.	J.R. McLane, *Indian Nationalism and the Early Congress,* VII:1, pp. 87-89.
Cashman, R.	A. Pant, *A Moment in Time,* No. 5, pp. 123-124.
Cashman, R.	R. Shears and I. Gidley, *Devi: the Bandit Queen,* IX:1, pp. 110-112.
Cashman, R.	K.R. Shirsat, *Kaka Joseph Baptista: Father of Home Rule Movement in India,* I:2, p.126.
Cashman, R.	R. P. Tucker, *Ranade and the Roots of Indian Nationalism,* 1:2, pp. 124-126.
Cassels, N.G.	Social Legislation under the Company Raj: The Abolition of Slavery Act V 1843, XI:1, pp. 59-88.
Catanach. I.J.	M.C. Carras, *The Dynamics of Indian Political Factions: District Councils in Maharashtra,* No. 4, pp. 131-132.
Catanach. I.J.	A.T. Carter, *Elate Politics in Rural India: Political Stratification and Political Alliances in Western Maharashtra,* I:1, pp. 158-159.
Catanach. I.J.	N. Charlesworth, *Peasants and Imperial Rule: Agriculture and Agrarian Society in the Bombay Presidency,* 1850-1935, X:2, pp. 97-98.
Catanach. I.J.	D. Hardiman, *Peasant Nationalists of Gujarat: Kheda District 1917-1934,* VII:2, pp. 99-100.
Catanach. I.J.	Z. Hasan, *Dominance and Mobilisation: Rural Politics in Western Uttar Pradesh 1930-1980,* XII:1, pp. 142-143.
Catanach. I.J.	A. Maddison, *Class Structure and Economic Growth: India and Pakistan Since the Moghuls,* No. 3, pp. 128-129.

Catanach. I.J.	C. Malamoud (ed.), *Debts and Debtors,* IX:1, pp. 113-114.
Catanach. I.J.	Poona Politicians and the Plague, VII:2, pp. 1-18.
Catanach. I.J.	P. Radhakrishnan, *Peasant Struggles, Land Reforms and Social Change Malabar,* 1836-1892, XIII:1, pp. 114-116.
Catanach. I.J.	H. Streefkerk, *Industrial Transition in Rural India: Artisans, Traders and Tibals in South Gujarat,* X:2, pp. 95-96.
Chakrabarty, D.	S. Dasgupta *et al., The Great Gherao of 1969,* I:1, pp. 159-160.
Chakrabarty, D.	E. Driver and A. Driver, *Social Class in Urban India: Essays on Cognitions and Structures,* XI:2, pp. 125-126.
Chakrabarty, D.	Open Space/Public Space: Garbage, Modernity and India, XIV:1, pp. 15-32.
Chakrabarty, D.	C.H. Philips and M.D. Wainwright (eds.), *Indian Society and the Beginnings of Modernisation c. 1830-1850,* II:1&2, pp. 157-159.
Charlesworth, N.S.	Ambirajan, *Classical Political Economy and British Policy in India,* II:1&2, pp. 203-205.
Coe, J.	Congress and the Tribals in Surat District in the 1920s, VIII: 1&2, pp. 59-70.
Colley, D.	G.S. Ghurye, *The Legacy of the Ramayana,* VI:2, pp. 84-86.
Comans, M.	Owen Cole and Piara Singh Sambhi, *A Popular Dictionary of Sikhism,* XIII:2, pp. 140-142.
Comains, M.	T.N. Madan, "*Non-Renunciation: Themes and Interpretations of Hindu Culture,* XII:2, pp. 106-108.
Comains, M.	H. Turskig (ed.), *Yantracintamani of Damodara,* XI:2, pp. 140-141.
Comains, M.	D. White, *The Bagavad Gita: A New Translation and Commentary,* XII:1, pp. 113-125.
Comains, M.	E. Zelliot and M. Berntsen, *The Expoerience of Hinduism: Essays of Religion in Maharashtra,* XI:1, pp. 94-95.
Conlon, F.F.	A.D.D. Gordon, *Businessmen and Politics: Rising Nationalism and a Modernising Economy in Bombay, 1918-33,* II:1&2, pp. 213-215.
Conroy H.	S. Bhattcharya, *Long Road to Peace,* II:1&2, p. 227.

Crocker, W. S.P. Cohen and R.L. Park, *India Emergent Power?*, II: 1&2, pp. 221-222.

Crocker, W. B.R. Nanda (ed.) *Indian Foreign Policy. The Nehru Years*, I:1, pp. 144-146.

Dale, S.F. The Mappilas During Mysorean Rule: Agrarian Conflict in Eighteenth-Centruy Malabar, No. 6, pp. 1-13.

Das Gupta, A. The Maritime Merchant and Indian History, VII:1, pp. 27-33.

Davies, A.J. P.R. Brass, *Caste, Faction and Party in Indian Politics Volume One, Faction and Party*, IX:2, pp. 117-118.

Davies, A.J. B.B. Misra, *the Indian Political Parties: An Historical Analysis of British Behaviour up to 1947*, I:1, pp. 141-142.

Davies, A.J. D.B. Rosenthal, *The Expansive Elite: District Politics and State Policy-Making in India*, III:2, pp. 90-91.

Davis, R. The Influence of the Irish Revolution on Indian Nationalism: The Evidence of the Indian Press, 1916-22. IX:2, pp. 55-68.

DeJong, J.W. G. Grimm, *Buddhist Wisdom: The Mystery of the Self*, II:1&2, p. 187.

DeJong, J.W. L. Joshi, *Studies in the Buddhistic Culture of India (During the 7th and 8th Centuries)*, II: 1&2, pp. 187-188.

DeJong, J.W. R.E.A. Joshnsson, *The Dynamic Psychology of Early Buddhism*, IV:1, pp. 83-84.

De Munck, V.C. The Economics of Love: An Examination of Sri Lanka Muslim Marriage practices, XI:1, pp. 25-38.

De Silva, C.R. The Portuguese and Pearl Fishing off South India and Sri Lanka, I:1, pp. 14-28.

Devalle, S.B.C. N.G. Barrier and V.A. Dusenbery (ed.), The Sikh Diaspora: Migration and the Experience beyond Punjab, XIII:2, pp. 120-122.

Devji, F.F. Gender and the Politics of Space: The Movement for Women's Reform in Muslim India, 1857-1900, XIV:1, pp. 141-153.

Dhanagare, D.N. Congress and Agrarian Agitation in Oudh, 1920-22 and 1930-32, No. 5, pp. 67-77.

Dhanagare, D.N.	L. Brennan, *Land Policy and Social Change in Northern India: Rohilkhand 1800-1911*, II: 1 &2, pp. 208-210.
Dias, H.D.	H. Marby, *Tea in Ceylon—An Attempt at Regional and Temporal Differentiation of the Tea Growing Areas in Ceylon*, No. 4, pp. 141-142.
Diehl, F.W.	E.L. Jones, *The European Miracle, Environments, Economics and Geopolitics in the History of Europe and Asia: and*
	E.L. Jones, Growth Recurring: *Economic Change in World History*, XII:1, pp. 137-140.
Digby, S.	D. Barrett, *Early Cola Architecture and Culpture:* 866-1014 A.D.; and
	J.C. Harle, *Gupta Sculpture, Indian Sculpture of the Fourth to Sixth Centuries A.D.*, No. 6, pp. 124-127.
Disney, A.	J.C. Boyajian, *Portuguese Bankers at the Court of Spain, 1626-1650*, VI:1, pp. 57-58.
Disney, A.	Commentary on the Papers by S. Arasaratnam and I.B. Watson (in the same issue), 1:2, pp. 65-66.
Disney, A.	T.R. De Souza, *Medieval Goa: A Socio-Economic History*, IX:1, pp. 101-103.
Disney, A.	M.N. Pearson, *Costal Western India: Studies from the Portugues Records*, IX:1, pp. 103-105.
Disney, A.	M.N. Pearson, *The New Cambridge History of India*, I.1. *The Portugues in India*, IX:2, pp. 128-132.
Disney, A.	R. Ptak, *Portuguese Asia: Aspects in History and Economic History (Sixteenth and Seventeenth Centuries)*, XI:1, pp. 89-91.
Disney, A.	H. Scholberg, *Bibliography of Goa and the Portuguese in India*, VI:1, pp. 74-76.
Disney, A.	G.D. Winius, *The Black Legend of Portuguese India*, X:1, pp. 91-93.
Douds, G.	See Brasted, H.V.
Douds, G.	The Indian Princes: Britain's Fifth Column? XI:2, pp. 57-68.
Drake, P.J.	A. Ambirajan, *Political Economy and Monetary Management India, 1766-1914*, IX:2, pp. 104-106.
Dua, B.D.	S. Gopal, *Jawaharlal Nehru: A Biography, vol. 2*, VII:2, pp. 104-105.

Dua, B.D.	V. Mehta, *A Family Affair: India Under Three Prime Ministers,* VI:1, pp. 69-70.
Dua, B.D.	S. Wolpert, *Jinnah of Pakistan,* X:1, pp. 102-104.
Dufty, N.F.	V.K. Jayawardena, *The Rise of the Labour Movement in Ceylon,* No.3, pp. 126-127.
Dunham, J.	N.N. Bhattacharyya, *Ancient Indian Rituals and their Social Contents,* No. 6, pp. 122-123.
Dunham, J.	H.G. Coward, *Bhartrhari,* II:1&2, pp. 152-154.
Dunham, J.	S. Iyangar, *The Hathayogapradipika of Svatmarama, with the Commentary lyotsna of Brahmananda,* No. 4, pp. 111-112.
Dunham, J.	Review Article: Irawati Karve's 'Yuganta', No. 1, pp. 132-135.
Dutta, D.K.	D.W. Attwood and B.S. Baviskar (eds.) *Who Shares? Cooperatives and Rural Development,* XIII:1, pp. 119-120.
Duyker, E.	C. Younger, The Anglo-Indians: Neglected Children of the Raj, X:2, pp. 93-95.
Ellinwood, D.C.	S.P. Cohen, *The Indian Army: Its Contribution to the Development of a Nation,* No. 2, pp. 119-120.
Embree, A.T.	R.D. Choksey, *Mountstuart Elphinstone: The Indian Years, 1796-1827.* No. 3, pp. 120-121.
Emilsen, W.W.	Debate: A Note on Mayo, Athiyaman, and Venkatachalapaty, XII:2, pp. 89-90.
Emilsen, W.W.	Gandhi and Mayo's 'Mother India', X:1, pp. 69-82.
Emmeneau, M.B.	*Proceedings of the Second International Conference Seminar of Tamil Studies,* No. 3, pp. 116-117.
Epstein, S.J.M.	The Breaking of the Money-Lender: Western India and the Commercialisation of Agriculture 1880-1930, IV:2, pp., 21-33.
Evans, B.	From Agricultural Bondage to Plantation Contract: Continuity of Experience in Southern India, 1860-1947, XIII:2, pp. 45-64.
Farmer, B.H.	E. Meyer, *Ceylan, Sri Lanka,* I:2, p. 111.
Farmer, B.H.	H.A.I. Goonetileke, *A Bibiliography of Ceylon,* No. 2, p. 109.
Farmer, B.H.	H.A.I. Goonetileke, *A Bibliography of Ceylon,* Vol.: III, 1:1, p, 120.

Feith, D.	C. Berkson, W. O'Flaherty and G. Michell, *Elephanta: The Cave of Shiva,* VI:1, pp. 55-56.
Ferrell, D.W.	Localisation of Nationl Issues: Non-Cooperation and the Delhi Municipal Elections of 1922, No.-5, pp. 20-31.
Fisher, M.H.	Robert W. Stern, *The Cat and the Lion: Jaipur State in the British Raj,* XIII:2, pp. 130-131.
Fitzgerald, J.L.	I. Proudfoot, *Ahimsa and a Mahabharata Story,* XIII:1, pp. 123-124.
Flora, R.	J. Auboyer, *et al., Oriental Art, a Handbook, of Styles and Forms,* VI:2, pp. 79-80.
Flora, R.	I. Srivastava, *Dhrupada, a Study of its Origin, Historical Development, Structure and Present State,* V:1, pp. 62-64.
Forbes, A.D.W.	Archives and Resources for Maldivian History, III:1, pp. 70-82.
Forbes, A.D.W.	Sources Towards a History of the Laccadive Islands, II:1&2, pp. 130-150.
Franco, E.	O. Qvarnstrom, *Hindu Philosophy in Buddhist Perspective,* XII:1, pp. 126-129.
Franklin, A.B.	T.W. Clark (ed.), *The Novel in India: Its Birth and Development,* No. 2, pp. 126-127.
Freitag, S.B.	Enactments of Ram's Story and the Changing Nature of 'the Public' in British India, XIV:1, pp. 65-90.
Freitag, S.B.	Introducton to "Aspects of the 'Public' in Colonial South Asia'. XIV:1, pp. 1-14.
Freitag, S.B.	"National Leaders", Administrators and Social Control: Communal Riots in the United Provinces, 1870-1925, I:2, pp. 27-41.
Freitag, S.B.	J.D. Rogers, Crime, *Justice and Society in Colonial Sri Lanka,* XI:1, pp. 112-114.
Frykenberg, R.E.	On Roads and Riots in Tinnevelly: Radical Change and Ideology in Madras Presidency During the 19th Century, IV:2, pp. 34-52.
Frykenberg, R.E.	Review Article: India as the Wheel Turns, I:1, pp. 110-113.
Fukazawa, H.	M. Malgonkar, *Chhatrapatis of Kolhapur,* No. 2, p. 118.

Furber, H.	C.R. Boxer, *Jan Compagnie in Oorlog en Vrede,* I:2, p. 112.
Furber, H.	M. Lipton *et al, The Erosion of a Relationship,* I:2, pp. 142-143.
Furedy, C.	S.U. Ahmed, *Dacca: A Study in Urban History,* X:1, pp. 95-96.
Furedy, C.	K. Ballhatchet and J. Harrison (eds.), *The City in South Asia—Pre-Modern and Modern,* IX:2, pp. 106-107
Furedy, C.	Centre for Science and Environment, *The State of India's Environment 1984-5,* XI:2, pp. 117-118.
Furedy, C.	K. Choudhuri, Calcutta: *Story of its Government,* I:1, pp. 150-151.
Furedy, C.	J.V. Ferreira and S.S. Jha (eds.), *The Outlook Tower: Essays on Urbanisation in Memory of Patrick Geddes,* I:1, pp. 149-150.
Furedy, C.	L.A. Gordon, *Bengal: The Nationalise Movement 1876-1840,* No. 5, pp. 119-120.
Furedy, C.	Lord Curzon and the Reform of the Calcutta Corporation, 1899: A Case Study in Imperial Decision-Making, I:1, pp. 75-89.
Furedy, C.	V.T. Oldenburg, *The Making of Colonial Lucknow 1856-1877,* IX:2, pp. 107-109.
Furedy, C.	Whose Responsibility? Dilemmas of Calcutta's Bustee Policy in the Nineteenth Centruy, V:2, pp. 24-46.
Gabard, W.M.	R.I. Crane (ed.), *Transition in South Asia: Problems of Modernisation,* No. 3, pp. 130-131.
Gaeffke, P.	E.C. Dimock, E. Gerow, C.M. Naim, A.K. Ramanujan, G. Roadarmel, and J.A.B. Van Buitenen, *The Literatures of India: An Introduction,* II:1&2, pp. 190-192.
Galla, A.	The Articulation of the Local Power Structure in Early South India, VII:2, pp. 31-46
Garlington, W.	Candravali and the Caurasi Vaisnavan Ki Varta, VII:1, pp. 77-86.
George, P.V.	B.M. Bhatia, *Indian Agricultur—A Policy Perspective,* XI:1, pp. 100-102.
George, V.	K.C. Mascarenhas, *A Strategy for Rural Development: Dairy Co-operatives in India,* XII:1, pp. 134-135.

Ghadially, R. — Veiling the Unveiled: The Politics of Purdah in a Muslim Sect, XII:2, pp. 33-48.

Ghosh, R.N. and Narayanan, N.S., *European Settlements: A Plan for Colonising India in 1823,* IV:2, pp. 53-62.

Ghosh, R.N. — C. Mukherjee, *Urban Growth in a Rural Area – A Case Study of a Town in West Bengal,* No. 4, p. 137.

Ghosh, R.N. — R. Sau, *India's Economic Development: Aspects of Class Relations,* IX:1, pp. 123-125.

Ghosh, R.N. — K.M. De Silva (ed.), *History of Ceylon, Vol III,* No. 5, p. 105.

Ghosh, R.N. — J. Toye, *Public Expenditure and Indian Development Policy, 1960-1970,* IX:1, pp. 123-125.

Ghosh, S.C. — A. Basu, *The Growth of Education and Political Development in India, 1898-1920,* No. 5, pp. 114-115.

Gillen, P. — R. Jayaraman, *Caste Continuities in Ceylon: A Study of the Social Sturcture of Three Tea, Plantations,* No. 6, pp. 151-152.

Gilmartin, D. — Democracy, Nationalism and the Public a Speculation on Colonial Muslim Pditics, XIV:1, pp. 123-140.

Gooneratne, B. — R.K. De Silva, *Early Prints of Ceylon (Sri Lanka),* X:1, pp. 93-94.

Gooneratne, Y. — G. Bandini (ed.), *South Asian Digest of Regional Writing, Vol. 9,* XIII:1, pp. 126-128.

Gooneratne, Y. — R. Mohan (ed.), *Indian Writing in English,* IV:1, pp. 62-63.

Gooneratne, Y. — Review Article: Blood in the Lotus-Pool: I Have Seen Bengal's Face: A Selection of Modern Bengali Poetry in English Translation, I:1, pp. 102-109.

Gordon, A.D. — H.L. Erdman, *Political, Attitudes of Indian Industry: The Baroda Business Elre,* No. 5, pp. 128-129.

Gordon, R.A. — A. Seal, *The Emergence of Indian Nationalism: Competition and Collaboration in the Later Nineteenth Century,* No.1, pp. 139-142.

Granda, P. — G.S. Ghurye, *Vedic India,* IV:1, pp. 80-81.

Granda, P. — M.H. Rama Sharma, *The History of the Vijayanagar Empire, Vol. I: Beginnings and Expansion (1308-1569),* IV:1, pp. 86-87.

Greenberger, A.J. E. Eden, *Up the Country: Letters Written to her Sister from the Upper Provinces of India, II:1&2*, pp. 159-160.

Gregorian, R. Unfit for Service: British Law and Looting in India in the Mid-nineteenth Century, XIII:1, pp. 63-64.

Guha, R. S. Islam (ed.), *Bangladesh District Records: Chittagong Vol. I, 1760-1787*, IV:1, pp. 90-91.

Guha, R. Review Article: The Mahatma and the Mob—"Essays on Gandhian Politics: The Rowlatt Satyagraha of 1919", edited by R. Kumar, No.3, pp. 107-111.

Gundara, J.S. Aspects of Indian Culture in Nineteenth Century Zanzibar, III:1, pp. 14-27.

Gunther, H.E. See Spate, O.H.K.

Gupta, S.K. Y. Etinger and O. Melikyan, *The Policy of Non-alignment*, No. 3, pp. 135-136.

Gurry, M. Neither Threat Nor Promise: An Australian View of Australian-Indian Relations Since 1947, XIII:1, pp. 85-101.

Hall, P.H. W.M. Callewaert and R. Kumar (eds.), *E.E.C. India Towards a Common Perspective*, X:1 pp. 112-113.

Haman, C. K. Thairani, *British Political Missions to Sind: 1799 to 1843*, pp. 109-111.

Hansen, K. Hindi New Cinema: Basu Chatterji's Sara Akash, IV:1, pp. 15-21.

Haq, S. See Khan, M.M.

Harcourt, M.V. K. Gough and H.P. Sharma (eds.), *Imperialism and Revolution in South Asia*, No. 5, pp. 130-132.

Hardiman, D. J. Breman, *Patronage and Exploitation: Changing Agrarian Relations in South Gujarat*, No. 5, pp. 129-130.

Hardiman, D. G. Shah, *Caste Association and Political Proess in Gujarat. A Study of Gujarat Kshatriya Sabha*, I:1, pp. 157-158.

Harnetty, P. "A Curious Exercise of Political Economy": Some Implications of British Land Revenue Policy in the Central Provinces of India 1861-c. 1900, No.6, pp. 14-33.

Harrex, S.C. A. Ahmad, *The Shore and the Wave,* No. 3 pp. 123-125.

Harrex, S.C. Review, Article: "Obstinately Minor": Poetry from India, III:2, pp. 63-74.

Harris, G.T. M.V. Nadkarni et al, *The Political Economy of Forest Use and Management,* XII:2, pp. 99-100.

Harris, G.T. K.N. Raj, A. Sen and C.H.H. Rao (eds.), *Dharm Narain, Studies on Indian Agriculture,* XIII:1, pp. 118-119.

Harrison, P. A. Yuyama (ed.), *Prajna-paramita-ratna-guna-samcaya-gatha (Sanskrit Recension A),* I:1, pp. 128-129.

Hasan, M. "Congress Muslims" and Indian Nationalism, Dilemma and Decline, 1928-1934, VIII:1&2, pp. 102-120.

Hasan, M. The Muslim Mass Contact Campaign: An Attempt at Political Mobilisation, VII:, pp. 58-76.

Hashmi, A. Some Directions of Contemporary Urdu Poetry in Pakistan: From 1965 to the present, 1:2, pp. 67-80.

Haynes, E.S. Comparative Industrial Development in 19th-and 20th-Century India: Alwar State and Gurgaon District, III:2, pp. 25-42.

Heathcote, L. See Brennan, L.

Heimann, J. Small Change and Ballast: Cowry Trade and Uswage as an Example of Indian Ocean Economic History, III:1, pp. 48-69.

Hellmann-Rajanayagam, D. The Concept of a "Tamil Homeland' in Sri Lanka Its meaning and Development, XIII:2, pp. 79-110.

Henningham, S. J.D. Hunt, *Gandhi in London,* II:1&2, pp. 210-211.

Henningham, S. The Contribution of "Limited Violence" to the Bihar Civil Disobedience Movement, II:1&2, pp. 60-77.

Henry, R. I. Stone, *Canal Irrigation in British India,* IX:2, pp. 109-111.

Heston, A. R. Agarwala, *An Econometric Model of India,* II:1&2, pp. 180-181.

Heston, A. S.B. Mukherjee, *The Age Distribution of the Indian Population: A Reconstruction for the States and Territories,* 1881-1961, pp. 160-161.

Higgott, R. M.M. Khan, *Bureaucratic Self-Preservation: Failure of Major Adminsitration Reform in the Civil Service of Pakistan,* III:2, pp. 94-95.

Hogan, W.P. I. Brecher and S.A. Abbas, *Foreign Aid and Industrial Development in Pakistan,* No. 3, pp. 129-130.

Hogan, W.P. L. Castle and C. Findlay (ed.), *Pacific Trade in Serivces,* XII:2, pp. 100-101.

Hogan, W.P. Exports of Manufactures: The South Asian Experience in the 1960s, No. 3, pp. 45-56.

Hogan, W.P. K. Markenstein, *Foreign Investment and Development,* No. 3, p. 130.

Holroyde, P. Film Australia, *India: 14 Films,* 1:2, pp. 154-155.

Huilgol, G. S.D. Gokhale (ed.), *Social Welfare,* 1:2, pp. 145-148.

Huilgol, G. Manu and Mother-right: Social Transformation in Antiquity, IV:1, pp. 22-34.

Husain, Z. Maulana Sayyid Abul a'la Maududi: An Apprasisal of his Thought and Political Influence, IX:1, pp. 61-82.

Ifeka, C. 'Spiritual' and 'Statistical' Models of the Sexes in British India, 1871-1931, V:1, pp. 16-28.

Inden, R.B. B. De (ed.), *Perspectives in Social Sciences I: Historical Dimensions,* II:1&2, pp. 196-197.

Inden R.B. D. Devahuti, *Harsha: A Political Study,* No. 4, pp. 115-116.

Irschick, E.F. Civil Disobedience in Tamil Nadu, 1930-32, No. 6, pp. 34-50.

Irwin, P.G. The Dairying Industry of Kaira, Western India, No. 1, pp. 123-131.

Islam, M.M. Irrigation and Punjab Agriculture, 1906-1945: Some Preliminary Notes, I:1, pp. 29-37.

Jacobs, M. G. Bouchon, *mamale de Conanor: un adversaire de l'Inde portugaise (1507-1528),*I:1, pp. 130-131.

Jacobs, M. D. Rothermud, *Grundzuge der Indischen Geschichte,* I:1, pp. 127-128.

Jacobs, M. K. Specker, *Weber im Wettbewerb. Das Sohicksal des sudindischen Textilhandwerks im 19-Jahrhundert,* IX:2, pp. 111-112.

Jayarajan, P.M.	Reply to review by T. Rahula of *History of the Evolution of the Sinhala Alphabet*, III:1, pp. 94-95.
Jayaraman, R.	B.V. Lal, *Girmitiyas: the Origins of the Fiji Indians*, IX:1, pp. 120-121.
Jayaraman, R.	T.N. Madan, *Doctors and Society: Three Asian Case Studies: India, Malaysia, Sri Lanka*, VI:1, pp., VI:1, pp. 66-67.
Jayawardena, C.	I. Ahmad (ed.), *Caste and Social Stratification Among the Muslims*, No. 5, pp. 117-119.
Jayawardena, C.	B.S. Cohen, *India: The Social Anthropology of a Civilisation*, No. 3, pp. 113-114.
Jeffrey, R.	A.K. *Gopalan, In the Cause of the People: Reminiscences;*
	E.M.S. Namboodiripad, *Conflicts and Crisis, Political India*; and
	E.M.S. Namboodiripad, *Indian Planning in Crisis*, No. 5, pp. 122-123.
	Government of India, *Census of India*, 1981;
	Jain, A.K. and Visaria, P. (eds.), *Infant Mortality in India: Differentials and Determinants;* and
	K. Mahadeven (ed.), *Fertility and Mortality: Theory, Methodology and Empirical Issues*, XI:2, pp. 120-123.
Jeffrey, R.	N.P. Mohamed; *Drift, Wood The Bull*, I:1, p. 157.
Jeffrey, R.	E.C. Multon, *Indian Studies in Conada*, IX:2, p. 93.
Jeffrey, R.	W.H. Morris-Jones, *the Government and Politics of India*, XI:1, pp. 92-94.
Jeffrey, R.	M. Roberts (ed.), *Documents of the Ceylon National Congress and Nationalist Politics in Ceylon, 1929-50*, II:1&2, pp. 212-213.
Jeffrey, R.	The Social Origins of a Caste Association, 1875-1905, No. 4, pp. 39-59.
Jeffrey, R.	Women and the 'Kerala Model: Four Lives, 1870s-1980s, XII:2, pp. 13-32.
Johnson, B.L.C.	Indian Council of Social Science Research, *A Survey of Research in Geography*, No. 4, pp. 142-143.
Johnson, B.L.C.	A. Robinson, *Economic Prospects of Bangladesh*, No. 5, p. 133.

Johnson, B.L.C. U. Schweinfurth et al., *Landschafts-okologische Forschungen auf Ceylon* No. 3, pp. 133-134.

Johnson, B.L.C. U. Schweinfurth, H. Flohn and M. Domros, *Studies in the Climatology of South Asia*, No. 2, pp. 113-114.

Johnson, B.L.C. *Yearbook of the South Asia Institute, Heidelberg University, 1968/69*, No. 2, pp. 112-113.

Jolley, L. E. Bishop and J.M. Waller (eds.), *International Co-operation in Orientalist Librarianship: Papers Presented at the Library Seminars, 28th International Congress of Orientalists, Canberra, 1971*, I:1, pp. 121-122.

Jones, G.W. B. Hartmann, *Reproductive Rights and Wrongs: The Global Politics of Population Control and Contraceptive Choice,* XI:2, pp. 123-125.

Jones, G.W. K. Mahadevan (ed.), *Fertility Policies in Asian Countries,* XII:2, pp. 105-106.

Jones K.W. P. Tandon, *Beyond Punjab: 1937-1960,* No. 2, pp. 128-129.

Jones K.W. P.H.M. van den Dungen, *The Punjab Tradition: Influence and Authority in 19th-Century India,* No. 5, pp. 112-113.

Jones, P. J.E. Jayasuriya, *Educational Policies and Progress During British Rule in Ceylon 1796-1948,* II:1&2, pp. 225-226.

Jones, P. J.P. Naik, *Policy and Performance in Indian Education,* I:2, pp. 149-150.

Jordens. J. K.W. Jones, *Arya Dharma: Hindu Consciousness in Nineteeth-Century Punjab,* I:1, pp. 139-140.

Jordens, J. G. Richards (ed.), *A Source-Book of Modern Hinduism,* X:1, pp. 94-95.

Jukes, G. S.U. Din, *Soviet Afghan Relations,* IX:2, pp. 122-123.

Kalupahana, D.J. Buddhism and Social Change, X:2, pp. 5-14.

Keenleyside, T.A. The Inception of Indian Foreign Policy: the Non-Nehru Contribution, IV:2, pp. 63-78.

Kemp, S.F. H.C. Dandekar, *Men to Bombay, Women at Home: Urban Influence on Sugao Village, Deccan Maharashtra, India 1942-1982,* X:1, pp. 104-105.

Kemper, S. T.N. Madan (ed.), *Way of Life: King, Householder, Renouncer,* XII:1, pp. 129-131.

Kenna, C. V.G. Vitsaxis, *Hindu Epics, Myths and Legends in Popular Illustrations,* IV:1, p. 58.

Kennedy. B. H. Scholberg and E. Divien, *Bibliographie des Francais dans l'Inde,* No. 4, p. 110.

Khan, M.M. and Haq. S.'D. Wright, Bangladesh: Origins and Indian Ocean Relations (1971-1975), XII:1, pp. 131-132.

Khan, M.M. and Mostafa, I.M. Paramanand, *Political Development in South Asia,* XII:1, pp. 132-133.

Khanna, S. The New Business Class, Ideology and State: The Making of a 'New Consensus', X:2, pp. 47-60.

Khondker, H.H. Famine Policies in Pre-British India and the Question of Moral Economy, IX:1, pp. 25-40.

Khondker, H.H. G. Murshid, *Reluclant Debutante: Response of Bengali Women to Modernisation,* 1849-1905, IX:1, pp. 108-110.

Kiernan, V.G. The Communist Party of India and the Second World War, X:2, pp. 61-74.

Kingston, B. P. Jeffery, *Frogs in a Well: Indian Women in Purdah,* III:2 pp. 85-86.

Klaiman, M.H. D.M. Wulff, *Drama as a Mode of Religious Realisation: The Vidagdhamadhava of Rupa Gosvami,* IX:1, pp. 97-100.

Klaiman, M.H. Religious Tradition and Religious Revolution: The Case of Vaishnavism in Bengal, VI:1, pp. 33-43.

Klein, I. Indian Nationalism and anti-Industrialisation: The Rootts of Gandhian Economics, No. 3, pp. 93-104.

Knight, L.A. The Mysore Grants, 1860: The Appeal of Tippu Sultan's Son, 1:1, pp. 63-74.

Knopf, D. G.R. Madan, *Western Sociologists Indian Society-Marx, Spencer,* VI:w, pp. 92-93.

Kondos, V. Nepalese Absolutism?, VII:2, pp. 47-71.

Kondos, V. B.C. Olschak and G. T. *Wangyal, Mystic Art of Ancient Tibet,* No. 4, pp. 112-113.

Kondos, V. H.R. Trivedi, *Scheduled Caste Women: Studies in Exploitation,* II:1&2, pp. 172-174.

Kopf, D. B. Chandra, *Nationalism an Colonialism in Modern India,* VI:2, pp. 81-83.

Kozlowski, G. The Power of Language and the Language of Power: A Study of Mawlana Muhammad Ali's Political Rhetoric, V:1, pp. 29-41.

Kulke, H. Kings without a Kingdom: The Rajas of Khurda and the Jagannatha Cult, No. 4, pp. 60-77.

Kumar, D. R. Jeffrey, *The Decline of Nayar Dominance,* I:2, pp. 128-129.

Kumar, R. I.J. Catanach, *Rural Credit in Western India, 1875-1930,* No. 4, pp. 124-125.

Kumar, R. Gandhi, Ambedkar and the Poona Pact, 1932, VIII:1&2, pp. 87-101.

Kumar, R. The Political Process in India, No. 1, pp. 91-108.

Lal, B.V. I.H. Van den Dreisen, *Indian Plantation Labour in Sri Lanka: Aspects of the History of Immigration in the 19th Century,* IX:1, pp. 118-120.

Lansbury, R.D. A.S. Singh, *Industrial Productivity: A Psychological Prespective,* XII:2, pp. 98-99.

Law-smith, A. Response and Responsibility: The Government of India's role in the Bengal Famine, 1943, XII:11, pp. 49-66.

Lawson, M. Suresh Chandra Ghosh, *Education Policy in India Since Warren Hastings,* XIII:2, pp. 135-138.

Leffrey, R. B.R. Joshi *Democracy in Search of Equality: Untouchable Politics and Indian Social Change,* VII-2, pp. 105-106.

Leiten, G.K. G. Adhikari, *Documents of the History of the Communist Party of India,* V:pp. 90-100.

Leiten, G.K. Review Article: When Communism Came to India, No. 5, pp. 90-100.

Lenneberg, C. G. Omvedt, *We Will Smash This Prison! Indian Women in a Struggle,* V: pp. 94-95.

Leonard, K. Punjabi Pioneers in California: Political Skills on a New Frontier, XII:2, pp. 69-82.

Leonard, K. Z. Yazdani, *Hyderabad During the Residency of Henry Russell, 1811-1820: A Case Study of the Subsidiary Alliance System,* IV:1, pp. 91-92.

Lewandowski, S. A.D. King, *Colonial Urban Development,* I:2, pp. 139-141.

Lewandowski, S. H. Spodek, *Urban-Rural Integration in Regional Development: A Case Study of Saurashtra, India 1800-1960,* I:1, pp. 138-139.

Lewandowski, S.	Urban Planning in the Asian Port City: Madras, An Overview, 1920-1970, II:1&2, pp. 30-45.
Loewald, K.	L.W. Bowman and I. Clark (eds.), *The Indian Ocean in Global Politics,* VII:2, pp. 109-110.
Loewald, K.	D.H. McMillan (ed.), *Asian Perspectives on International Security,* IX:1, pp. 125-127.
Lougheed, A.L.	See K.C. Roy.
Lucas, A.	See Brennan, L.
Ludden, D.	M.R. Barnett, Politics of Cultural Nationalism in South India, 1:2, pp. 129-131.
Ludden, D.	M.R. Barnett, *Politics of Cultural Nationalism in South India,* 1:2, pp. 129-131.
Ludden, D.	Ecological Zones and the Cultural Economy of Irrigation in Southern Tamilnadu, I:1, pp. 1-13.
Ludden, D.	G.L. Hart III, *Poets of the Tamil Anthologies: Ancient Poems of Love and War,* III:2, pp. 77-78.
Mabbett, I.W.	Cosmography, Architecture and Ritual in Hindu-Buddhist Culture, VI:1, pp. 44-53.
Mabbett, I.W.	A.L. Dallapiccola (ed.), *The Stupa—Its Religious, Historical and Arehitectural Significance,* VI:2, pp. 83-84.
Mabbett, I.W.	D. Lorenzen, *The Kapalikas and Kalamukhas,* No. 3, pp. 117-1118.
Mabbett, I.W.	D. Srinivasan, *Concept of Cow in the Rig Veda,* VI:2, pp. 101-102.
Maddern, M.	R. Tagore, *The Broken Nest,* No. 4, pp. 127-128.
Major, A.J.	Sikh Ethno-Nationalism, 1967-1984: Implications for the Congress, VIII:1&2, pp. 168-181.
Manor J.	M.H. Gopal, *Tipu Sultan's Mysore, An Economic Study,* No. 2, pp. 117-118.
Manor, J.	Kengal Hanumanthaiah in Mysore: The Style and Strategy of Individual Leadership in the Integration of a Region's Politics, No. 4, pp. 21-38.
Marshall. J.G.	I.E. Rose, *The Politics of Bhutan,* II:1&2, p. 221.
Marshall, P.J.	J.R. Seeley, *The Expansion of England,* No. 4, pp. 121-122.
Martell, W.H.T.	M.H. Rama Sharma, *The History of the Vijayanagar Empire, Vol. 2: Decline and Disappearance (1569-1679)* II:1&2, p. 77.

Martell, W.H.T. S.R. Wasti, *Biographical Dictionary of South Asia*, VI:2, p. 105.

Masica, C.P. A.J. Alston, *The Devotional Poems of Mirabai*, VI:2, pp. 78-79.

Masica, C.P. M. Juergensmeyer and N.G. Barrier (eds.), Sikh Studies—*Comparative Perspectives on a Changing Tradition*, VI:2, pp. 87-88.

Masselos, J. M. Archer, *Company Drawings in the India Office Library*, No. 3, pp. 122-123.

Masselos, J. Appropriating Urban Space: Social Constructs of Bombay in the Time of the Raj, XIV:1, pp. 33-64.

Masselos, J. Audiences, Actors and Congress Dramas: Crowd Events in Bombat City in 1930, VIII:1&2, pp. 81-86.

Masselos, J. Bombay in the 1870's: A Study of Changing Patterns in Urban Politics, No. 1, pp. 29-55.

Masselos, J. Change and Custom in the format of the Bombay Mohurrum During the Ninteenth and Twentieth Centuries, V:2, pp. 47-67.

Masselos, J. F.F. Conlon, *A Caste in a Changing World: The Chitrapur Saraswat Brahmans, 1700-1935*, IV:1, pp. 69-71.

Masselos, J. Hugh Owen: A Tribute, X:2, pp. 1-4.

Masselos, J. Introduction (to Indian National Congress Centenary Edition) Comity and Commonality: the Forging of a Congress Identity, VIII:1&2, pp. 1-4.

Masselos, J. D.S. Kharbas, *Maharashtra and the Marathas: Their History and Culture. A Bibliographic Guide*, No. 4, pp. 110-111.

Masselos, J. R. Lipsey (ed.), *Coomaraswamy 1: Selected Papers. Traditional Art and Symbolism;*

R. Lipsey (ed.), *Coommaraswamy 2: Selected Papers, Metaphysics; and*

R. Lipsey, *Coomaraswamy, His Life and Work*, II:1&2, pp. 163-165.

Masselos, J. I.W. Mabbett. *A Short History of India, 2nd ed.*, VII:2, p. 89.

Masselos, J. C. Markovits, *Indian Business and Nationalist Politics 1931-1939: The Indigenous, Capitaist Class and the Rise of the Congress Party*, XI:1, pp. 102-105.

Masselos, J. P.Z. Palsapure, *Industrial Development of Vidarbha;*
S.D. Punekar and A.R. Golwalkar, *Rural Change in Maharashtra: An Analytical Study of Change in Six Villages in Konkan;*
V.V. Borkar and M.V. Nadkarni, *Impact of Drought on Rural Life;* and
V. Subramaniam, *Parched Earth: the Maharashtra Drought, 1970-73,* I:1, pp. 151-153.

Masselos, J. Power in the Bombay 'Moholla", 1904-1915: An Initial Exploration into the World of the Indian Urban Muslim, No. 6, pp. 75-95.

Masselos, J. Pyarelal, *Mahatma Gandhi, Vol II The Discovery of Satyagraha—On the Threshold,* IX:1, pp. 112-113.

Masselos, J. Spare Time and Recreation: Changing Behaviour Patterns in Bombay at the Turn of the Nineteenth Century, VII:1, pp. 34-57.

Masselos, J. N.K. Wagle (ed.), *Images of Maharashtra: A Regional Profile of India,* VI:1, pp. 79-80.

Maxwell, N. J.G. Marshall, *Britain and Tibet 1765-1947: A Select Annotated Bibliography,* II:1&2, pp. 183-184.

Mayer, P.B. M.C. Carras, *Indira Gandhi in the Crucible of Leadership: A Political biography,* V:1, pp. 64-65.

Mayer, P.B. *Development, and Demise: The Congress as the Raj,* VIII: 1&2, pp. 182-197.

Mayer, P.B., J.E. Di Bona, *Language Change and Modernisation: The Development of a Hindi-English English-Hindi Glossary of Technical Terms in the Field of Education,* No. 3, pp. 131-132.

Mayer, P.B., R.G. Fox (ed.), *Urban India: Society, Space and Image,* No. 2, pp. 127-128.

Mayer, P.B. K. Gough, *Rural Society in Southeast India,* IX:1, pp. 114-116.

Mayer, P.B. V.M. Sirsikar, *Sovereigns Without Crowns: A Behavioural Analysis of the Indian Electoral Process,* No. 6, pp. 147-148.

Mayer, P.B. *Studies in Socio-Cultural Change in Rural Villages in Tiruchirapalli District, Tamilnadu, India*: No. 1-5 and *Studies on Agrarian Societies in South Asia,* VI:2, pp. 103-105.

Mayer, P.B. Support for the Principles of Democracy by the Indian Electorate, No. 2, pp. 24-32.

Mayer, P.B. — The Penetration of Capitalism in a South Indian District: The First 60 Years of Colonal Rule in Tiruchirapalli, III:2, pp. 1-24.

Mayer, P.B. — Myron Weiner, *Sons of the Soil: Migration and Ethnic: Conflict in India,* IV:1, pp. 71-73.

McAlpin D.W. — A. Dhamotharan, *Tamil Dictionaries: A Bibliography,* III:2, p. 75.

McDonald, G. — D.N. Dhamotharn, *Agrarian Movements and Gandhian Politics,* II:1&2, pp. 169-170.

McGuire, J. — S. Bose, *Agrarian Bengal: Economy, Social Structure and Politics,* 1919-1947, X:2, pp. 100-102.

McGuire, J. — L. Dube, *Sociology of Kinship: An Analytical Survey of Literature*; and R.B. Inden, *Marriage and Rank in Bengali Culture: A History of Caste and Clan in Middle Period Bengal,* I:1, pp. 153-155.

McGuire, J. — B. Hettne, *The Political Economy of Indirect Rule: Mysore 1881-1947,* VII:2, pp. 97-98.

McGuire, J. — M.M. Islam, *Bengal Agriculture 1920-1946: A Quantitative Study,* VII:2, pp. 100-101.

McGuire, J. — A. Kawai, "Landlords" and *Imperial Rule: Change in Bengal Agrarian Society* c. 1885-1940, XI:1, pp. 106-107.

McLean, M.D. — B. Candidasa (transl. by M.H. Klaiman), *Singing the Glory of Lord Krishna: The Srikrsnakirtana,* IX:2, pp. 98-99.

McLean, M.D. — I. Raeside (tr.) *Gadyareja; a fourteenth century Marathi version of the Krsna Legend,* XIII:2 pp. 114-116.

McLean, M.D. — David Seyfort Ruegg, *Buddha-nature, Mind and the Problem of Gradualism in a Comparative Perspective: On the Transmission and Reception of Buddhism in India and Tibet,* XIII:2, pp. 116-117.

McLean, M.D. — A. Sharma, *Women in World Religions,* X:2, pp. 92-93.

McLean, M.D. — Tradition and History in Isvarachandra Gupta's Biography of Bamprasad Sen, IX:2, pp. 69-80.

McLean, M.D. — K. Werner (ed.), *The Yogi and the Mystic Studies in Indian and Comparative Mysticism,* XIII:1, pp. 124-126.

McLeod, W.H. — Ahluwalias and Ramgarhias: Two Sikh Castes, No. 4, pp. 78-90.

McLeod, W.H. — B.N. Goswamy and J.S. Grewal, *The Mughals and the Jogis of Jakhbar. Some Madad-i-Ma'ash and Other Documents*, No. 1, pp. 138-139.

McLeod, W.H. — Inter-Linear Inscriptions in Sri Lanka, No.3, pp. 105-106.

McLeod, W.H. — E.C. Sachau and A.T. Embree, *Alberuni's India*, No. 2, pp. 114-115.

McLeod, W.H. — W. Shah, *The Adventures of Hir and Ranjha, and R.K. Kuldip, Waris Shah*, No. 4, pp. 113-115.

McLeod, W.H. — C. Vaudeville, *Kabir, Vol. 1*, No. 5, pp. 101-104.

McPherson, K. — A. Copley, C. *Rajagopulachari: Gandhi's Southern Commander*, X:2, pp. 105-106.

McPherson, K. — G. Minault, *The Khilafat Movement: Religious Symbolism and Political Mobilisation in India*, VII:2, pp. 98-99.

McPherson, K. — C.M. Naim (ed.), *Iqbal, Linnah and Pakistan: The Vision and the Reality*, V:1, pp. 66-67.

McPherson, K. — A. Roy, *The Islamic Syncretictic Tradition in Bengal*, IX:1, pp. 105-107.

McPherson, K. — F. Robinson, *Separatism Among Indian Muslims: The Politics of the United Provinces' Muslims*, 1960-1923, No. 5, pp. 116-117.

McPherson, K. — M. Shakir, Muslims in Free India;
M. Shakir, *Secularisation of Muslim Behavious;*
M. Shakiir, *Muslim Attitudes: A Trend Report and Biliography*; and
P. Dixit, *Communalism: A Struggle for Power*, I:1, pp. 142-143.

McPherson, K. — The Muslims of Madras and Calcutta: Agitational Politics in the Early 1920s, No. 5, pp. 32-47.

Meister, M.W. — H. Goetz, *Rajput Art and Architecture*, III:2, pp. 82-83.

Meister, M.W. — P. Rawson, Erotic Art of India, 1:2, pp. 115-116.

Metcalf, B.D. — T.N. Madan (ed.), *Muslim Communities of South Asia*, 1:2, pp. 136&137.

Miller, D.B. — A Genius-like Feeling for the Social Stuff, No. 6, pp. 112-120.

Miller, D.B. G.S. Ghurye, *I and Other Explorations*, No. 4, pp. 135-136.

Miller, D.B. Holi-Dulhendi: Licensed Rebellion in a North Indian Village, No. 3, pp. 15-22.

Miller, D.B. Review Article: The Brahman/Kshatriya Relationship in India and Bali V:1, pp. 55-60.

Miller, D.B. W. Wiser and C. Wiser, *Behind Mud Walls* 1930-1960, *with a Sequel: The Village in* 1970, No.3, pp. 118-119.

Miller, D.F. A. *George, Social Ferment in India*, X:1, pp. 105-107

Miller, D.F. *India: The Speeches and Reminiscences of India Gandhi, Prime Minsiter of India;*
H.A. Rizvi, *Crisis in India Democracy*: and
H.C. Hart (ed.), *India Gandhi's India*, I:1, pp. 147-148.

Miller, D.F. R.S. Khare, *Culture and Democracy: Anthropological Reflections on Modern India*, IX:2, pp. 118-120.

Miller, D.F. W.H. Morris-Jones, *Politics Mainly Indian*, II:1&2, pp. 222-223.

Miller, D.F. A. Nandy, *The Intimate Enemy: Loss and Recovery of Self Under Colonialism*, VI:1, pp. 70-72.

Miller, D.F. P. Oldenburg, Big City Government in India, I:2 pp. 141-142.

Miller, D.F. This Great Organisation of Ours': The Generations of Congress Discourse, VIII:1&2, pp. 141-153.

Miller, D.F. What Price Politics? – In India, No. 2, pp. 33-46.

Minault, G. Making Invisible Women Viible: Studying the History of Muslim Women in South Asia, IX:1, pp. 1-14.

Minault, G. S.A. Quraishi and U. Sims-William, *Catalogue of the Urdu Mansucripts in the India Office Library*, III:2, p. 75.

Mishra, V. Review Article: David Schulman and the Laughter of South Indian Kings and Clowns, X:1, pp. 83-88.

Mishra, V. The Centre Cannot Hold: Bailey, Indian Culture and the Sublime, XII:1, pp. 103-114.

Mishra, V.C. Two Truths Are Told: Tagore's Kabir, 1:2, pp. 80-90.

Moffatt, M.	M. Weiner, Sons or the Son: pp. 87-89.
Mojumdar, K.	S.D. Muni, *Foreign Policy of Nepal*, No. 6, pp. 144-145.
Moore, R.J.	N. Mansergh, *The Prelude to Partition: Concepts and Aims in Ireland and India*, II:1&2, p. 170.
Moore, R.J.	S.A. Mujahid, *Quaid-i-Azam Jinnah: Studies in Interpretation*, VII:1, p. 89.
Moore, R.J.	J. Nehru, Selected Works of Jawaharlal Nehru, No.4, p. 130.
Moore, R.J.	Review Article: The Transfer of Power: An Historiographical Survey, IX:1, pp. 83-96.
Moore, R.J.	R. Sisson and S. Wolpert (eds.) *Congress and Indian Nationalism: The Pre-Independence Phase*, XII:1, XII:1, pp. 133-134.
Morris-Jones, W.H.,	Idia 40 Years On, X:2, pp. 75-84.
Mostafa, I.M.	See Khan, M.M.
Moulton, E.C.	Hume and the Indian National Congress, A Ressessment, VIII:1&2, pp. 5-24.
Mukherjee, C.	D. Bhattacharya (ed.), *Focus on West Bengal: Problems and Prospects*, No. 4, pp. 134-135.
Mukherjee, S.N.	R.B. Inden and R.W. Nicholas, *Kinship in Bengali Culture*, II:1&2, pp. 175-177.
Murphy, E.	M. Holmstrom, *South Indian Factory Workers, Their Life and Their World*, I:1 pp. 155-157.
Murphy, E.	Labour Leadership and Politics in India: Profiles of Three South Indian Unionists, IV:2, pp. 79-93.
Nanda, B.R.	S. Ray (ed.), *Gandhi, India and the World: An International Symposium*, No. 2, pp. 122-124.
Nandakumar, P.	G.L. Hart III, *The Poems of Ancient Tamil: their Milieu and their Sanskrit Counterparts, No.* 6, p. 123.
Narain, I.	Robert Wade Village Republics: *Economic Conditions for Colective Action in South India*, XIII:2, pp. 125-128.
Narayanan, N.S.	See Ghosh, R.N.
Newell, W.H.	M.J. Akbar, *Riot After Riot, Reports on Caste and Communal Violence in India*, XII:1, pp. 140-142.
Newell, W.H.	G.D. Berreman, *Hindus of the Himalayas: Ethnography and Charge*, No. 3, p. 119.

Newell, W.H.	C. von Furer-Haimendorf, *Return to the Naked Nagas: An Anthropolgist's View of Nagaland* 1936-1970, I:1, p. 149.
Newell, W.H.	S.B. Ortner, *Sherpas Through Their Rituals,* II:1&2, pp. 178-179.
Newman, R.S.	A. Bhatt, *Development and Social Justice: Micro Action by Weaker Sections,* XII:1, pp. 135-137.
Newman, R.S.	G. Etienne *Food and Poverty: India's Half Won Battle,* XI:1, pp. 102-104.
Newman, R.S.	C. Maloney, *People of the Maldive Islands,* V:1, p. 68.
Newman, R.S.	P. Alexander, *Sri Lankas Fishermen: Rural Capitalism and Peasant Society,* VII:2, pp. 106-108.
Newman, R.S.	Green Revolution—Blue Revolution: The Predicament of India's Traditional Fishermen, IV:1, pp. 35-46.
Newman, R.S.	R.S. Khare and M.S.A. Rao, *Food, Society and Culture: Aspects in South Asian Foods Systems,* X:2, pp. 102-105.
Newman, R.S.	Konkani Mai Ascends the Throne: The Cultural Basis of Goan Statehood, XI:1, pp. 1-24.
Nugent, H.M.	The Communal Award: The Process of Decision-Making, II:1&2, pp. 112-129.
O'Neil, J.L.	D.S. Kharbas and R.N. Sharma, *Sanskrit Grammar: A Bibliography of Western Language Muterials,* No. 5, p. 101.
Oddie, G.A.	R.H.S. Boyd, *India and the Latin Captivity of the Church,* No. 5, pp. 133-134.
Oddie, G.A.	J.T.F. Jordens, *Dayananda Saraswati: His Life and Ideas,* III:2, pp. 83-84.
Oddie, G.A.	P.D. Reeves (ed.), *Sleeman in Oudh, An Abridgement of W.H. Sleeman's A Journey through the Kingdom of Oude in 1849-50,* No. 3, pp. 121-122.
Oddie, G.A.	Regional and Other Variations in Popular Religionin India: Hook-Swinging in Bengal and Madras in the Nineteenth Century, X:1, pp. 1-10.
Oldmeadow, P.	S.B. Ortner, *High Religion: A Cultural and Political History of Sherpa Buddhism,* XIII:2, pp. 143-144.

Omvedt, G.	*Science and Human Progress: Essays in Honour of late Professor D.D. Kosambi*, I:1, pp. 123-124.
Orr, K.	B. Grant, Gods and Politicians, VI:2, pp. 86-87.
Owne, H.F.	M. Gaborieau and A. Thorner (eds.), *Asie du Sud: traditions et changements,* III:2, pp. 95-97.
Owne, H.F.	Interactions Between the National and the Local in modern South Asia: A Note, No. 5, pp. 1-8.
Owen, H.F.	J.E. Schwartzberg (ed.), *A Historical Atlas of South Asia,* III:1, pp. 83-85.
	(from the perspectives of Modern History and Teaching).
Owen, H.F.	The Non-Brahmin Movements and the Transformation of Congress, 1912-1922, VIII-1&2, pp. 46-58.
Palmer, N.D.	J.W. Mellor (ed.), *India: A Rising Middle Power,* IV:1, pp. 63-65.
Palmer, N.D.	J.E. Schwartzberg (ed.), *A Historical Atlas of South Asia,* III:1, pp. 91-92.
	(from the perspective of Political Science).
Panikkar, K.N.	P. Rule, *The Pursuit of Progress: The Intellectual Development of R.C. Dutt,* 1948-88, II:1&2, pp. 205-206.
Parnaby, O.	K.L. Gillion, The *Fiji Indians,* III::2, p. 84.
Pearson, G.	B.R. Nanda (ed.), Indian Women, I:1, pp. 134-135.
Pearson, M.N.	S. Arasaratnam, *Francois Valentyn's Description of Ceylon*, IV:1, pp. 89-90.
Pearson, M.N.	C.E. Bosworth, *The Later Ghazznavids: Splendour and Decay. The Dynastty in Afghanistan and Northern India,* 1040-1186. pp. 194-196.
Pearson, M.N.	G. Bouchon, Regent of the Sea': Cannanor's Response to Portuguese Expansion 1507-1528, XI:2, pp. 132-134.
Pearson, M.N.	B.G. D'Souza, *Goan Society in Transition: A Study in Social Change,* I:1 pp. 131-132.
Pearson, M.N.	R.M. Eaton, *Sufis of Bijapur,* I:2, pp. 116-117.
Pearson, M.N.	R.G. Fox (ed.), *Realm and Region in Traditional India*; and
	A.R. Khan, *Chieftains in the Mughal Empire,* I:2, pp. 120-122.

Pearson, M.N. S. Gopal, *Commerce and Crafts in Gujarat, 16th and 17th Centuries: A Study in the Impact of European Expansion on Pre-capitalist Economy*, No.6, pp. 132-133.

Pearson, M.N. M. Hasan, Babur *Founder of the Mughal Empire in India*, X:1, pp. 90-91.

Pearson, M.N. R. Islam (ed.), A Calender of Documents on Indo-Persion Relations (1500-1750);

M.S. Akhtar (ed.), *The Majama' al-Shu'ara'-i Jahangir Shahi of Mulla Quati'i-i Herawai* (d.1024/1615); and R. Islam (ed.), *Mahmud b. Amir Wali Balkhi, The Bahr ul-Asrar, Travelogue of South Asia*, VII:1, p. 87.

Pearson, M.N. B.L. Jones, *The European Miracle: Environments, Economics and Geopolitics in the History of Europe and Asia*, VI:1, pp. 63-64.

Pearson, M.N. Shireen Moosvi, *The Economy of the Mughal Empire* c. 1595; *A Statistical Study*, X:2, pp. 87-89.

Pearson, M.N. Fernao Meandes Pinto, *The Travels of Mendes Pinto, ed.*, and trans by Rebecca D. Catz, XIII:2 pp. 113-114

Pearson, M.N. T. Raychaudhuri and I. Habib, *The Combridge Economic History of India* Vol.I, c. 1200-c 1750, V:1, pp. 69-71.

Pearson, M.N. J.F. Richards (ed.), *Kingship and Authority in South Asia*, II:1&2, pp. 197-198.

Pearson, M.N. J. Sarkar, *A Short History of Aurangzib*, V:1, p. 69.

Pearson, M.N. J. Sarkar, *Studies in Aurangzib's Reign (Studies in Mughal India, First Series)*, XIII:1, pp. 103-104.

Pearson, M.N. J.E. Schwartzberg (ed.), *A Historical Atlas of South Asia*, III:1, pp. 86-87.
(from the perspective of Medieval History).

Pearson, M.N. Tuti-Nama: *Tales of a Parrot;*

P. Chandra, Tuti-Nama: Tales of a Parrot; and

M.A. Simar (transl.), The Cleveland Museaum of Art's Tuti-Nama: Tales ofa Parrot, IV:1, pp. 59-60.

Pearson, M.N. L. Varadarajan (ed.), *India in the 17th Century: Social, Economic and Political Memories of Francois Martin* (1670-1694), V:1, pp. 71-72.

Pearson, M.N.	Wealt and Powȩr: Indian Groups in the Portuguese Indain Economy, No. 3, pp. 36-44.
Peiris, G.H.	The Current Land Reforms and Peasant Agriculture in Sri Lanka, No. 5, pp. 78-90.
Pettigrew, J.J.M.	The Growth of Sikh Community Consciousness 1947-1966, III:2, pp. 43-62.
Philips.J.	Private Profit and Imperlalism in Eighteenth Century Southern India: The Tanjore Revenue Dispute, 1775-1777, IX:2, pp. 1-16.
Possehl, G.L.	D.E. King, *A Comprehensive Bibliography of Pakistan Archaeology: Paleolithic to Historic Times*, I:1, pp. 120-121.
Potter, D.C.	The Last of the Indian Civil Service, II:1&2, pp. 19-29.
Proctor, J.H.	Scottish Missionaries in India: An Inquiry into Motivation, XIII:1, pp. 43-62.
Price, P.G.	Acting in Public versus Forming a Public Conflict Processing and Political Mobilisation in Nineteenth Century South India, XIV:1, pp. 91-122.
Raeside, I.	J. Dalvi *Chakra*, No. 6, pp. 149-150.
Rahula, T.	P.M. Jayarajan, *History of te Evolution of the Sinhala Alphabet*, 1:2, pp. 111-113.
Ramusack, B.N.	J. Manor, *Political Change in an Indian State: Mysore* 1917-55, II:1&2, pp. 217-219.
Rao, G.L.	S.P. Varma, I. Narain et al., *Voting Behaviour in a Changing Society* (A Case Study of the Fourth General Election in Rajasthan), No. 4, pp. 133-134.
Rawson, J.	R.A. Schermerhorn, *Ethnic Plurality in India*, II:1&2, pp. 177-178.
Ray, A.	A.K. Chattopadhyay, *Slavery in the Bengal Presidency*, 1:2, pp. 122-123.
Ray, S.	A. Mascarenhas, *The Rape of Bangla Desh*, No. 5, pp. 132-133.
Ray, S.	M. de Mellow, *Remembered Glory*, No. 5, p. 133.
Ray, S.N.	T. Banarjee, *Panchagram (Five Villages), Delhi*, 1973, No. 3, pp. 125-126.
Ray, S.N.	M. Bandopadhyaya, *Padma River Boatman*, No. 4, pp. 128-130.

Ray, S.N. L.A. Gordon and B.S. Miller, *A Syllabus of Indian Civilization*, No. 3, pp. 112-113.

Reeves, P. A.T. Harrison (ed.), *The Graham Indian Mutiny Papers*, VII:2, pp. 95-96.

Reeves, P. G. Winius and R. Ross (eds.) *Itinerario, vol.vii*, no. 1, IX:1, p. 97.

Reeves, P. The Congress and the Abolition of Zamindari in Uttar Pradesh, VIII:1&2, pp. 154-167.

Regmi, M.C. M.S. Jain, *The Emergence* ·*f a New Aristocracy in Nepal* (1837-58), No. 4, pp. 118-121.

Richards, J.F. R.J. Moore (ed.), *Tradition and Politics in South Asia*, III:2, pp. 80-82.

Richards, J.F. Review Article: The Islamic Frontier in the East: Expansion into South Asia, No. 4, pp. 91-109.

Rivett, K. Gandhi, Tolstoy and Coercion, XI:2, pp. 29-56.

Rivett, K. B. Parekh, *Gandhi's Political Philosophy: A Critical Examination*, XIII:1, pp. 107-110.

Rizvi, G. L. Collins and D. Lapierre, *Freedom at Midnight*, No. 6, pp. 140-141.

Rizvi, G. Review Article: Lord Linlithgow and the Reviewers, I:1, pp. 114-119.

Rizvi, S.A.A. B.C. Bush, *Britian, India, and the Arabs*, 1914-1921, No. 3, p. 126.

Rizvi, S.A.A. M. Hedayetullah, Kabir: *The Apostle of Hindu-Muslim Unity*, II:1&2, p. 198.

Rizvi, S.A.A. A.R. Kelkar, Studies in Hindi-Urdu I, *Introoduction and Word Phonology*, No. 4, pp. 123-124.

Rizvi, S.A.A. I.A. Khan, *The Political Biography of a Mughal Noble: Mum'im Khan-i Khanan*, No. 5, pp. 67-84.

Roberts, M. Apocalypse or Accommodation? Two Contrasting Views of Sihala-Tamil Relations in Sri Lanka, XII:1, pp. 67-84.

Roberts, M. From Southern India to Lanka: The Thaffic in Commodities, Bodies and Myths from the Thirteenth Century Onwards, III:1, pp. 36-47.

Roberts, M. Irrigation Policy in British Ceylon During the Nineteenth Century, No. 2, pp. 47-63.

Roberts, M. B.L.C. Johnson and M. Le M. Scrivenor, *Sri Lanka Land, People and Economy*, IX:1, p. 118.

Roberts, M. — Mobility of Karavá Families in Sri Lanka, IV:1, pp. 47-56.

Roberts, M. — Review Article: 1970 and Thereabout in Sri Lanka: The Politics of a General Election, I:1, pp. 90-101.

Roberts, M. — Review Article: "Our Duty to Act": Brown Sahibs in Universal Suits: A Review Article on the Abortive 1962 Coup in Sri Lanka, VI:2, pp. 62-77.

Rocher, L. — A.L.Basham (ed.), *A Cultural History of India*, I:1, pp. 125-126.

Rocher, L. — K.W. Bolle, *The Bhagavadgita: A New Translation*, III:2, pp. 78-79.

Rocher, L. — H. Brinkhaus, *Die altindichen Mischkastensysteme*, III:2, pp. 79-80.

Rocher, L. — J.D.M. Derrett, *The Death of a Marriage Law: Epitaph for the Rishis*, II:1&2, pp. 179-180.

Rocher, L. — W. O'Flaherty and J.D.M. Derrett (eds.), *The Concept of Duty in South Asia*, II:1&2, pp. 155-156.

Rocher, R. — R.K. Barz, *Introduction to Hindi and Urdu*, 1:2, pp. 113-114.

Rooksby, R.L. — W.H.R. Rivers and the Todas, No. 1, pp. 109-122.

Rothermund, D. — A. Das Gupta and M.N. Pearson, *India and the Indian Ocean*, 1500-1800, X:2, pp. 90-92.

Rothermund, D. — Freedom of Contract and the Problem of Land Alienation in British India, No. 3, pp. 57-78.

Rothermund, D. — J. Gallagher, G. Johnson and A. Seal (eds.), *Locality, Province, and Nation: Essays on Indian Politics*, 1870-1940; and

G. Johnson, *Provincial Politics and Indian Nationalism: Bombay and the Indian National Congress*, 1880-1915, No. 6, pp. 136-138.

Rothermund, I. — Gandhi and Maharashtra: Nationalism and the National Respoose, No. 1, pp. 56-73.

Roy, A. — M. Hasan, *A Nationalist Conscience M.A. Ansari, the Congress and the Raj*, XI:1, pp. 107-110.

Roy, A. — A. Jalal, *The Sole Spokesman: Jinnah, the Muslim League and the Demand for Pakistan*, X:1, pp. 98-102.

Roy, A. — O, Khalidi, *Dakan Under the Sultans* 1292-1724. *A Bibliography of Monographic and Periodical Literature*, XIII:2, pp. 128-129.

Roy, A. O. Khalidi (ed.), *Hyderabad: After the Fall*, XI:2, pp. 137-140.

Roy, A. D. Rothermound (ed.), *Hyderabad: After the Fall*, XI:2, pp. 137-140.

Roy, A. D. Rothermund (ed.), *Islam in Southern Asia. A Survey of Current Research*, No. 6, pp. 141-144.

Roy, A. Sexuality—An Islamic Hitorical Perspective with Special Reference to South Asia, XIII:2, pp. 17-44.

Roy, A. The Bengal Muslim Cultural Mediators' and the Bengal Muslim Identity in the Nineteenth and Early Twentieth Centuries X:1, pp.

Roy, A. The Social Factors in the Making of Bengali Islam No. 3, pp. 23-35.

Roy, K.C., and Lougheed, A.L., India's Foreign Aid Experience Since 1956: Some Observations, No. 6, pp. 66-74.

Rubinstein, R. M.S. Zurbuchen, *The Language of Balinese Shadow Theatre*, XIII:1, pp. 131-134.

Ryland, S. Edwin Montagu in India, 1917-1918: Polities of the Montagu-Chelmsford Report, No. 3, pp. 79-92.

Saini, B.S. S. Nilsson, *The New Capitals of India, Pakistan and Bangladesh*, No.4, pp. 137-139.

Samaraweera, V. Litigation and Legal Reform in Colonial Sri Lanka II:1&2, pp. 78-80.

Schweinfurth-Marby, H. R.N. Kearney. *Trade Unions and Politcs in Ceylon*, No. 2, pp. 129-130.

Scrase, T. K. Kumar, *Social Character of Learning*, XII:1, pp. 116-118.

Shah, A.M. The Rural-Urban Networks in India, XI:2, pp. 1-28.

Sharma, A. P. Bowes *The Hindu Religious Tradition: A Philosophical Approach*, IV:1, pp. 84-86.

Sharma, A. Fearlessness (Abhaya) as a Fundamental Category in Gandhian Thought and Practice, X:1, pp. 11-34.

Sharrad, P. Y. Gooneratne, *Silence, Exile and Cunning: The Fiction of Ruth Prawer Jhabvala*, VII:2, pp. 108-109.

Sharrad, P. M. Jamal (ed.), *The Penguin Book of Modern Indian Poetry*, X:1, pp. 111-112.

Shephard, A. M.J. Mazarr, *Missile Defences and Asian-Pacific Security*, XII:2, pp. 103-105.

Shepherd, R. A. Hashmi, *My Second in Kentucky*, IX:2, pp. 125-126.

Shepherd, R. R. Tagore, *Selected Poems*, IX:2, p. 125.

Sherlock, S. Which Union Makes Us Strong? Trade Unions in the Indian Railways in the 1960s, XI:1, pp. 39-58.

Shroff, M. Liberalisation of the Economy: The Indian Experience, XIII:1, pp. 1-18.

Silva, K.T. J. Jiggins, *Caste and Fanily in the Politics of the Sinhalese* 1947-1976, IV:1, pp. 66-68.

Simkin, C.G.F. A.L. Datar, *India's Economic Relations with the USSR and Eastern Europe*, 1953-1969, No. 4, pp. 139-141.

Simmons, C.P. Housing, Health and Educational Facilities in the Indian Coalfields During the Colonial Era, I:1, pp. 52-62.

Sinclair-Brull, W. J.N. Gray and D.J. Mearns (eds.), *Society from the Inside Out: Anthropological Perspectives on the South Asia Household*, XIII:1, pp. 121-123.

Singh. S.D. R. Maduro, *Artistic Creativity in a Brahmin Painter Community*, III:2, pp. 86-87.

Singh. S.D. J.E. Schwartzberg (ed.), *A Historical Atlas of South Asia*, III:1, pp. 85-86. (from the perspective of Ancient History).

Singh. S.D. H. Zimmer, *Artistic From and Yoga in the Sacred Images of India*, IX:2, pp. 95-97.

Smith, D.E. W.H. Morris-Jones (ed.), *The Making of Politicians*, I:2, pp. 148-149.

Smith, R.F.I. S.N. Jha, *Leadership and Local Politics: A Study of Meerut District in Uttar Pradesh*, 1923-1973, IV:1, p. 68.

Smith, R.F.I. I. Narain, *Twilight or Dawn: The Political Change in India* 1967-71, No. 3, pp. 132-133.

Smith, R.F.I. R.J. Vatikiotis (ed.), *Revolution in the Middle East and Other Case Studies, and G.F. Hudson* (ed.), *Reform and Revolution in Asia*, No. 4, pp. 136-137.

Smith, R.T. V.S. Srinivasa Sastri and the Moderate Style in Indian Politics, No. 2, pp. 81-100.

Soegito, I. A. Preibish, *Guide to South Asian Materials in the National Library of Canada*, IX:2, pp. 93-95.

Spate, O.H.K. and Gunther, H.E., J.E. Schwartzberg (ed.), *A Historical Atlas of South Asia*, III:1, pp. 90-91 (from the perspective of Cartography).

Spate, O.H.K. — J.E. Schwartzberg (ed.), *A Historical Atlas of South Asia*, III:1, pp. 89-90. (from the perspective of Geography).

Spodek, H. — A. Ashraf, *Government and Politics of Big Cities: An Indian Case Study*; and S.N. Mukherjee, *Calcutta; Myths and History*, II:1&2, pp. 21-220.

Staelin C.D. — J. Masselos, *Nationalism on the Indian Subcontinent*, No. 5, pp. 115-116.

Stenson, M. — S. Arasaratnam, *Indians in Malaysia and Singapore*, No. 2, pp. 130-131.

Stern, R.W. — R.W. Jones, *Urban Politics in India: Area, Power and Policy in a Penetrated System*, No. 5, pp. 127-128.

Stern, R.W. — G.K. Lieten, *The First Communist Ministry in Kerala*, 1957-1959, VII:2, p. 105.

Stern, R.W. — D.F. Miller, *Pervasive Politics: A Study of the Indian District*, No. 4, p. 135.

Stoddard, B. — K.V.N. Rao, *The Emergence of Andhra Pradesh*, No. 4, pp. 130-131.

Stoddard, B. — N.S. Ramaswami,*The Founding of Madras*, II:1&2, p. 157.

Stoddard, B. — P. Robb and D. Taylor (eds.), *Rule, Protest, Identity: Aspects of Modern South Asia*, II:1&2, pp. 161-162.

Stoddard, B. — S. Saraswati, Minorities in Madras State: Group Interests in Modern Politics, 1:1, pp. 143-144.

Stoddard, B. — The Unwanted Commission: National Agitation and Local Politics in Madras City, 1928, No. 5, pp. 48-66.

Stoddard, B. — D.A. Washbrook, *The Emergence of Provincial Politics: The Madras Presidency* 1870-1920; and

C.J. Baker, *The Politics of South India* 1920-1937, I:1, pp. 134-136.

Stokes, E. — The Return of the Peasant to South Asian History, No. 6, 96-111.

Subrahmanyam, S. — The 'Pulicat Enterprise': Luso-Dutch Conflict in South-Eastern India, 1610-1640, IX:2, pp. 17-36.

Sundrum, R.M. — J.N. Bhagwati and P. Desai, India: *Planning for Industrialisation*;

S.R. Lewis, *Pakistan: Industrialisation and Trade Policies; and*

I. Little, T. Scitovsky, and M. Scott, *Industry and Trade in Some Developing Countries–A Comparative Study*, No. 2, pp. 110-112.

Suntharalingam, R., The "Hindu" and the Genesis of Nationalist Politics in South India, 1878-1885, No. 2, pp. 64-80.

Tangri, S.S. E.W. Nafziger, Class, Caste and Entrepreneurship: *A Study of Indian Industialists*, IV:1, pp. 68-69.

Taylor, D.D. R.S. Khare, *The Changing Brahmans: Associations and Elites Among the Kanya-Kubjas of North India*, No. 3, pp. 119-120.

Taylor, R.H. N.R. Chakravarti, *The Indian Minority in Burma: Rise and Decline*, No.5, pp. 126-127.

Taylor, R.H. C.L. Keeton, *King Thebaw and the Ecological Rape of Burma; The Struggle Between British India and French Indo-China in Burma*, No. 5, pp. 111-112.

Tewari, L.G. Women's Fasts and Festivals from Uttar Pradesh: Their Art, Rituals, and Stories, V:1, pp. 42-50.

Thomas, D.A. Lucknow and Kanpur 1880-1920: Stagnation and Development under the Raj, V:2, pp. 68-80.

Thomson, M. Hind Swaraj and the Constructive Work Programme, IX:2, pp. 37-54.

Tinker, H. R.J. Moore, *Endgames of Empire: Studies of Britain's Indian Problem*, XII:2, pp. 92-94.

Tinker, H. Z.H. Zaidi (ed.), *Jinnah-Ispahani Correspodence*, 1:2, pp. 127-128.

Treloar, A. P. Bilimoria and P. Fenner, *Religions and Comparative Thoughts (Essays in Honour of Dr Lan Kesarcodi-Watson)*, IX:2, pp. 95-97.

Treloar, A. J. Peterfalvi and M. Biardeau, *Le Mahabharata*, IX:2, pp. 97-98.

Van den Dungen, P.G. Gaur, *Catalogue of Panjabi Printed Books Added to the India Officer Library*; and W.E. Gustafson and K.W. Jones (eds.), *Sources on Punjab History*, 1:2, pp. 110-111.

Van den Dungen, P. Reply to review by K.W. Jones of *The Punjab Tradition: Influence and Authority* in 19th-Century India, No. 5, pp. 113-114.

Van den Dungen, P. B.S. Singh, *The Jammu Fax: Maharaja Gulab Singh*, No. 5, pp. 108-109.

Van Schendel, W. Self-Rescue and Survival: The Rural Poor in Bangladesh, IX:1, pp. 41-60.

Varadarajan, L. Traditions of Indigenous Navigation in Gujarat, III;1, pp. 28-35.

Varady, R.G. North Indian Banjaras: Their Evolution as Transportiers, II:1&2, pp. 1-18.

Varma, C.B. F.J. Hoffman, *Rationality and Mind in Early Buddhism*, X:2, pp. 85-86.

Varma, C.B. P. Richman, *Women, Branch Stories, and Religious Rhetoric in a Tamil Buddhist Text*, XII:1, pp. 120-123. 113-125.

Vicziany, M. P.B. Desai, *Survey of Research in Demography;* and B. Kuppuswamy, *Population and Society in India*, I:1, pp. 150-154.

Voigt, J.H. F.G. Hutchins, *Spontaneous Revolution. The Quit India Movement*, No. 2, pp. 124-125.

Warrell, L. Conflict in Hierarchy: Jealousy Among the Sinhalese Buddhists, XIII:1, pp. 19-42.

Washbrook, D.A. D. Arnold, The Congress in Tamilnad, I:1, pp. 131-132.

Watson, I.B. Between the Devil and the Deep Blue Sea: Commercial Alternatives in India, 1707-1760, I:2, pp. 54-64.

Watson, I.B. K.N. Chaudhuri, *The Trading World of Asia and the English East India Company* 1660-1760, II 1&2, pp. 200-202.

Watson, I.B. M. Moir, *A General Guide to the India Office Records*, XII:2, pp. 114-115.

Watson, I.B. Premchand, *Deliverance and Other Stories*, XII:2, pp. 112-113.

Watson, I.B. O.V. Vijayan, *After the Hanging and Other Stories*, XIII:2, pp. 144-145.

Webb, A.D. Charles Edward Trevelyan in India: A Study of the Channels of Influence Employed by a Covenanted Civil Servant in the Translation of Personal Ideas into Official Policy, VI:2, pp. 15-33.

Weber, T. Gandhi and the Nobel Peace Prize, XII:1, pp. 29-48.

Weber, T. M.W. Sonnleitner, *Vinoba Bhave on Self-Rule and Representative Democracy*, XIII:1, pp. 110-111.

Webster, J.C.B. S. Manickam, *The Social Setting of Christian Conversion in South India: The Impact of the Western Methodist Missionaries on the Trichy-Tanjore Diocese with Speical Reference to the Harijan Communities of the Mass Movement Area* 1820-1947, IV:1, p. 95.

Wicks, P.C. C.M. Turnbull, *A History of Malaysia, Singapore and Brunei*, XII:2, pp. 110-112.

Williams, R.A. J.D. Smith, *The Visaladevarasa: A Restoration of the Text*, II:1&2, pp. 154-155.

Wilson, A.J. Y. Gooneratne, *Relative Merits: A Personal Memoir of the Bandaranaike Family of Sri Lanka*, X:1, pp. 107-111.

Wong, J.Y. Monopoly in India and Equal Opportunities in China, 1830-33: An Examination of a Paradox, V:2, pp. 81-95.

Woods, P. R. Jeffrey, et. al. (ed.), India: *Rebellion to Republic: Selected Writings*, 1857-1990, XIII:2, pp. 123-125.

Woods, P. M. MacMillan, *Women of the Raj*, XI:2, pp. 141-143.

Woods, P. P. Reeves & J. Wardrop (Comp.), *The Indian Nationalist Movement, c. 1912-1922, Leadership, Organisation and Philosophy, The Writings of Hugh Owen*, XIII:2, pp. 138-140.

Woods, P. P.G. Robb, *The Government of India and Reform: Policies Towards Politics and the Constitution* 1916-1921, I:1, pp. 140-141.

Wright, D. L. Blinkenberg, *India-Pakistan: The History of Unsolved Conflicts; and B.L.C. Johnson, Bangladesh*, I:1, pp. 146-147.

Wright, D. D.B. Forrester, *Caste and Christianity: Attitudes and Policies on Caste of Anglo-Saxon Protestant Missions in India*, VII:2, pp. 96-97.

Wright, D. Islam and Bangladeshi Polity, X:2, pp. 15-28.

Wright, D. B.L.C. Johnson, *India, Resources and Development, II*:1&2, pp. 224-225.

Wright, D. D.J. Johnson and J.E. Johnson, *Through Indian Eyes*, I:1, pp. 126-127.

Wright, D. M.M. Khan and J.P. Thorp (eds.), *Bangladesh: Society, Politics and Bureaucracy*, IX:2, pp. 120-122.

Wright, D. L. Lifschultz, Bagladesh: *The Unfinished Revolution*, VI:1, pp. 64-66.

Wright, D D.B. Mokashi, Palkhi: *An Indian Pilgrimage*, XI:1, pp. 97-98.

Wright, D. M. Rahman, *Emergence of a New Nation in a Multi-Polar World: Bangladesh*, IV:1, pp. 65.

Wright, D. D.P. Singhal, *A History of the Indian People*, VII:1, pp. 89-91.

Wright, D. Doris Meth Srinavasan (ed.), *Mathura: The Cultural Heritage*, XIII:2, pp. 111-113.

Wright, D. R. Thapar, *Ancient Indian Social History;*

M.J. Shendge, *The Civilised Demons; The Horoppans in the Rig Veda*; and

M. Stutley, *Ancient Indian Magic and Folklore: An Introduction*, VII:2, pp. 89-91.

Wright, D. L. Ziring, R. Braibanti and W.H. Wriggens (eds.), *Pakistan, the Long View*, II:1&2, pp. 171-172.

Wright, D.L. *Swartz of Thanjavur; A Missionary in Politics*, IV:2, pp. 94-105.

Wright, T.P. P. Hardy, *The Muslims of British India*, No. 4, pp. 122-123.

Yang, A.A. Disciplining 'Natives': Prisons and Prisoners in Early Nineteenth Century India, X:2, pp. 29-46.

Yarwood, A.T. H.I. London, *Non-white Immigration and the White Australia Policy*, No. 1, p. 142.

Younger, C. Racial Attitudes and the Anglo-Indians: Perceptions of a Community Before and After Independence, VI:2, pp. 34-46.

Zafarullah, H. Z. Hasan, S.N. Jha and R. Khan (eds.), *The State, Political Processes, and Identity: Reflections on Modern India*, XIII:1, pp. 112-114.

Zamora, M.D. and Zimmerman, L. S. Ahmad, *Class and Power in a Punjabi Village*; and

C.V. Wiser, *Four Families of Karmpur*, II:1&2, pp. 174-175.

Zamora, M.D. S. Vatuk (ed.), American Studies in the Anthropology of India, II:1&2, pp. 226-227.

Zimmerman, L. See Zamora, M.D.

INDEX OF BOOKS REVIEWED IN SOUTH ASIA (BY AUTHOR)

Note: there is only one entry for each book-thus only the rirst/primary author is listed alphabetically.

Bold face indicates a Review Article

Abeyasinghe, T. (ed.), *A Study of Portuguese Regimentos on Sri Lanka at the Goa Archives,* No. 5, pp. 106-107. (Arasaratnam, S.)

Academy of Sciences, *USSR, Oriental Countries of Today,* I:2, oo, 143-145. (Ambirajan, S.)

Addy, p. *Tibet on the Imperial Chessboard: The Making of British Policy Towards Lhasa,* 1899-1925, X:1, pp. 97-98. (Beer, D.)

Adhikari, G. *Documents of the History of the Communist Party of India,* V: pp. 90-100. (Leithen, G.K.)

Agrawal, R. *An Econometric Model of India,* II: 1&2, pp. 180-181, (Heston, A.)

Agrawal, C.P. (ed.) *Jaya Sankar Prasad Issue, Journal of South Asian Literature,* IV:1, pp. 60-62. (Barz, R.K.)

Ahmad, A. *The Shore and the Wave,* No. 3, pp. 123-125. (Harrex, S.C.)

Ahmad, I. (ed.) *Caste an Social Stratification Among the Muslims,* No. 5, pp. 117-119. (Jayawardena, C.)

Ahmad, S. *Class and Power in a Punjabi Village,* II:1&2, pp. 174-175. (Zamora, M.D. and Zimmerman, L.)

Ahmed, S.U. Dacca: *A Study in Urban History,* X:1, pp. 95-96. (Furedy, C.)

Akbar, M.J. Riot After Riot, *Reports on Caste and Communal Violence in India,* XII:1, pp. 140-142. (Newell, W.H.)

Akhtar, M.S. (ed.), *The Majma' al-Shu ara'-i Jahangir Shahi of Mulla Quati' i-i Herawai* (d. 1024/1615), VI:1, p. 61, VII:1, p. 87. (Pearson, M.N.)

Alam, M. *The Crisis of Empire in Mughal North India: Awadh and the Punjab,* 1707-48, XI:1, pp. 110-112. (Arasaratnam, S.)

Alexander, p. *Sri Lankan Fishermen: Rural Capitalism and Peasant Society,* VII:2, pp. 106-108. (Newman, R.S.)

Ali, I. *The Punjab under Imperialism*, XII:2, pp. 94-96. (Barrier, N.G.)

Alston, A.J. *The Devotional Poems of Mirabai*, VI:2, pp. 78-79. (Masica, C.P.)

Ambirajan, A. *Political Economy and Monetary Management:* India 1766-1914, IX:2, pp.104-106. (Drake, P.J.)

Ambirajan, S. *Classical Political Economy and British Policy in India*, II:1&2, pp. 203-205. (Charlesworth, N.)

Anisussaman (ed.) *Factory Correspondence and Other Bengali Documents in the India Office Library and Records*, VII:2, pp. 95-95. (Arasaratnam, S.)

Arasaratnam, S. *Francois Valentiin's Description of Ceylon*, IV:1, pp. 89-90. (Pearson, M.N.)

Arasaratnam, S. *Indians in Malaysia and Singapore*, No. 2, pp. 130-131. (Stenson, M.)

Arasaratnam, S. *Merchants, Companies and Commerce on the Coromandel Coast* 1650-1740, IX:2, pp. 102-104. (Boxer, C.R.)

Arasaratnam, S. (ed.) *Selections from the Dutch Records of Sri Lanka. Memoir of J.S. van Gollenesse, Governor of Ceylon* 1743-51, No. 5, pp. 107-108. (Boxer, C.R.)

Arasaratnam, S. *Sri Lanka after Independence Nationalism, Communalism and Nation Building*, X:1, p. 111. (Abeyagunawardena, D.S.)

Archer, M. *Company Drawings in the India Office Library*, No. 3, pp. 122-123. (Masselos, J.)

Arnold, D. *The Congress in Tamilnad*, 1:2, pp. 131-132. (Washbrook, D.A.)

Ashraf, A. *Government and Politics of Big Cities: An Indian Case Study*, II:1&2, pp. 219-220. (Spodek, H.)

Ashton, S.R. *British Policy Towards the Indian States*, 1905-1939, VI:1, pp. 54-55. (Copland, I.)

Attwood, D.W. and B. S. Baviskar (eds.), *Who Shares? Cooperatives and Rural Development*, XIII:1, pp. 119-120, (Dutta, D.K.)

Auboyer, J., et al. *Oriental Art, A Handbook of Styles and Forms*, VI:2, pp. 79-80. (From, R.)

Baker, C.J. and D.A. Wasnoroox, South India: Porricat Instructions and romman Change, 1880-1940, No. 6, pp. 138-140, (Arnold, D.)

Baker, C.J. The *Politics of South India* 1920-1937, I:1, pp. 134-136. (Stoddart, B.)

Ballhatchet, K. and J. Harrison (eds.), *The City in South Asia*–Pre Modern and Modern, IX:2, pp. 106-107. (Furedy, C.)

Banarjee, T. *Panchagram* (Five Villages), Delhi, 1973, No.3, pp. 125-126. (Ray, S.N.)

Bandini, G. (ed.) *South Asian Digest of Regional Writing*, Vol. 9, XIII:1, pp. 126-128. (Gooneratne, Y.)

Badopadhyaya, M., *Padma River Baotman*, No. 4, pp. 128-130. (Ray, S.N.)

Barnett, M.R. *Politics of Cultural Nationalism in South India*, I:2, pp. 129-131. (Ludden, D.)

Barrett, D. *Early Cola Architecture and Sculpture*: 866-1014 A.D., No. 6, pp. 124-127. (Digby, S.)

Barrier, N.G. *The Sikhs and their Liternature: A Guide to Books, Tracts and Periodicals* (1848-1919), No. 1, pp. 136-138. (McLeod, H.)

Barz, R.K. *Introduction to Hindi and Urdu*, I:2, pp. 113-114. Rocher, R.)

Basham, A.L. (ed.) *A Cultural History of India*, 1:1 pp. 125-126. (Rocher, L.)

Basu, A. *The Growth of Education and Political Development in India*, 1898-1920, No. 5, pp. 114-115. (Ghosh, S.C.)

Baumer, B. (ed.) *Kalatattuvakosa: A Lexicon of Fundamental Concepts of the Indian Arts*. Vol. 1: *Eight Selected Terms*, XII:2, pp. 108-110. (Brand, M.)

Bayly, C.A. *Imperial Meridian: The British Empire and the World*, 1780, 1830 XII:2, pp. 91-92. (Beer, D.)

Berkson, C. W, O. Flaherty and G. Michell, *Elphanta: The Cave of Shiva*, VI:1, pp. 55-56. (Feith, D.)

Berreman, G.D. *Hindus of the Himalayas: Ethnography and Change*, No. 3, p. 119. (Newall, W.H.)

Beyer, S. *The Cult of Tara: Magic and Ritual in Tibet*, No. 6, pp. 129-130. (Ardussi, J.A.)

Bhagwati, J.N. and P. Desai, India: *Planning for Industrialisation*, No. 2, pp. 110-112. (Sundrum, R.M.)

Bhambhri, C.P. *World Bank and India*, VI:2, pp. 80-81. (Ambirajan, S.)

Bhatia, B.M. *Indian Agriculture-A Policy Perspective,* IX:1, pp. 100-102, (George, P.V.)

Bhatt, A. *Development and Social Justice: Micro Action by Weaker Sections,* XII:1, pp. 135-137, (Newman, R.S.)

Bhattacharya, D. (ed.), *Focus on West Bengal: Problems and Prospects,* No. 4, pp. 134-135. (Mukherjee, C.)

Bhattacharya, N.N., *Ancient Indian Rituals and their Social Contents,* No. 6, pp. 122-123. (Dunham, J.)

Bhattacharya, S. *Long Road to Peace,* II:1&2, p. 227. (Conroy, H.)

Bilimoria, P. and P. Fenner, *Religions and Comparative Thoughts (Essays in Honour of Dr lan Kesarcodi-Watson),* XI:1, pp. 95-97. (Treloar, A.)

Bishop, E. and J.M. Waller (eds.), *International Co-operation in Orientalist Librarianship: Papers Presented at the Library Seminars, 28th International Congress of Orientalists, Canberra,* 1971, I:1, pp. 121-122. (Jolley, L.)

Blaikie, P. *Family Planning in India: Diffusion and Policy,* II:1&2, p. 182. (Balasubramanian, K.)

Blinkenberg, L. *India-Pakistan: The History of Unsolved Conflict,* I:1, pp. 146-147. (Wright, D.)

Bolle, K.W. *The Bhagavadgita: A New Translation,* III:2, pp. 78-79. (Rocher, L.)

Boner, A. S.R. Sharma and R.P. Das, *New Light on the Sun Temple of Konarak: Four Unpublished Monuscripts Relating to Construction, History and Titual of this Temple,* No. 6, pp. 127-129/ (Behera, K.S.)

Borkar, V.V. and M.V. Nadkarni, *Impact of Drought on Rural Life,* I:1, pp. 151-153, (Masselos, J.)

Borthwick, M. *The Changing Role of Women in Bengal,* 1849-1905, IX:1, pp. 107-108. (Berwick, J.)

Bose, M. *The Lost Hero: A Biography of Subhas Bose,* VI:a, pp. 56-57. (Brasted, H.)

Bose, S. *Agrarian Bengal: Economy, Social Structure and Politics,* 1919-1947, X:2, pp. 100-102. (McGuire, J.)

Bosworth, C.E. The Later Ghaznavids: *Splendour and Decay. The Dynasty in Afgghanistan and Northern India,* 1046-1186, II:1&2, pp. 194-196. (Pearson, M.N.)

Bouchon, G. 'Regent of the Sea': *Cannanor's Response to Portuguese Expansion* 1507-1528, XI:2, pp. 132-134. (Pearson, M.N.)

Bouchon, G. *Mamale de Cannanor: un adversaire de I'Inde portugaise* (1507-1528), I:1, pp. 130-131. (Jacobs, M.)

Bougle, C. *Essays on the Caste System,* No. 2, pp. 109-110. (Allen, M.R.)

Boulnois, L. *Bibliographie du Nepal, Vol. I: Sciences Humaines, references en langues europeennes.* Supplement 1967-73, No. 6, p. 121. (Allen, M.)

Buton, M.M. *Agrarian Radicalism in South India,* IX:2, pp. 114-115. (Arnold, D.)

Bowes, P. *The Hindu Religious Tradition: A Philosophical Approach,* IV:1, pp. 84-86. (Sharma A.)

Bowman, L.W. and I. Clark (eds.), *The Indian Ocean in Global Politics,* VII:2, pp. 109-110. (Loewald, K.)

Boxer, C.R. *Jan Compagnie in Oorlog en Vrede,* I:2, p. 122 Furber, H.)

Boyajian, J.C. *Portuguese Bankers at the Court of Spain,* 1626-1650, VI:1, pp. 57-58. (Disney, A.R.)

Boyd, R.H.S. *India and the Latin Captivity of the Church,* No. 5, pp. 133-134. (Oddie, G.A.)

Brass, P.R. *Caste, Faction and Party in Indian Politics: Volume One, Faction and Party,* IX:2, pp. 117-118. (Davies, A.J.)

Breman, J. *Patronage and Exploitation: Changing Agrarian Relations in South Gujarat,* No. 5, pp. 129-130. (Hardiman, D.)

Bridge, C. Holding India to the Empire: *The British Conservative Party and* the 1935 Constitution, XI:2, pp. 115-117. (Low, D.A.)

Brinkhaus, H. *Die altindischen Mischkastensysteme,* III:2, pp. 79-80. (Rocher, L.)

Brown, J. *Gandhi and Civil Disobedience: The Mahatma in Indian Politics,* II:1&2, pp. 167-169. (Brennan, L.)

Brown, J. *Gandhi's Rise to Power: Indian Politics* 1915-1922, No. 3, pp. 137-139. (Baker, D.)

Brown, J. *Modern India: The Origins of an Asian Democracy,* IX:2, pp. 81-82. (Copland, I.)

Brown, W.N. *India and Indology—Selected Articles,* II:1&2, pp. 185-187. (Basham, A.L.)

Bush, B.C. *Britian, India, and the Arabs,* 1914-1921, No. 3, p. 126. (Rizvi, S.A.A.)

Callewaert, W.M. and R. Kumar (eds.), *E.E.C. India: Towards a Common Perspective,* X:1, pp. 112-113. (Hall, P.H.)

Candidasa, B. (transl. By M.H. Klaiman), *Singing thne Glory of Lord Krishna:* The Srikrsnakirtana, IX:2, pp. 98-99. (McLean, M.D.)

Carras, M.C. India Gandhi in the Crucible of Leadership: *A Political Biography,* V:1, pp. 64-65. (Mayer, P.B.)

Carras, M.C. *The Dynamics of Indian Political Factions: District Councils in Maharashtra,* No. 4, pp. 131-132. (Catanach, I.J.)

Carter, A.T. Elite Politics in Rural India: *Political Stratification and Political Alliances in Western Maharashtra,* I:1, pp. 158-159. (Catanach, I.J.)

Cashman, R. Patrons Players and the Crowd—*The Phenomenon of Indian Cricket,* IX:1, p. 122. (Ayres, R.G.)

Castle, L. and C. Findlay (ed.), *Pacific Trade in Services,* XII:2, pp. 100-101. (Hogan, W.)

Catanach, I.J. *Rural Credit in Western India,* 1875-1930, No. 4, pp. 124-125. (Kumar, R.)

Catz, R.D. (ed. and tr.) *The Travels of Mendes Pinto,* XII:2, pp. 113-114, (Pearson, M.N.)

Centre for Science and Environment, *The State of India's Environment* 1984-5,XI:2, pp. 117-118. (Furedy, C.)

Chakrabarty, D. Rethinking Working-Class History: *Bengal,* 1890-1940, XII:2, pp. 96-98. (Arnold, D.)

Chakravarti, N.R., *The Indian Minority in Burma: Rise and Decline,* No. 5, pp. 126-127. (Taylor, R.H.)

Chakravarty, S. From Khyber to Oxus: *A Study in Imperial Expansion,* I:1, pp. 133-134. (Callahan, R.)

Champaiaksnmu, K., Varsnava (Bilimoira, P.)

Chandra, B. *Nationalism and Colonialism in Modern India,* VI:2, pp. 81-83. (Kopf, D.)

Chandra, P. Tuti-Nama: *Tales of a Parrot,* IV:1, pp. 59-6. (Pearson, M.N.)

Charlesworth, N. Peasants and Imperial *Rule: Agriculture and*

Agrarian Society in-the Bombay Presidency, 1850-1935, X:2, pp. 97-98. (Catanach, I.J.)

Chattopadhyay, A.K. *Slavery in the Bengal Presidency,* I:2, pp. 122-123. (Ray, A.)

Chaturvedi, A. District Administration: *The Dynamics of Discord,* XII:2, pp. 101-103. (Brennan, L.)

Chaudhuri, K.N. *The Trading World of Asia and the English East India Company* 1660—1760, II:1&2, pp. 200-202. (Watson, I.B.)

Chishti, S. *India's Terms of Trade,* 1930-68, I:2, pp. 143-145. (Ambirajan, S.)

Choksey, R.D. Mountstuart Elphinstone: *The Indian Years,* 1796-1827, No. 3, pp. 120-121. (Embree, A.T.)

Choudhuri, K. Calcutta: *Story of its Government,* I:21, pp. 150-151. (Furedy, C.)

Clark, T.W. (ed.) The Novel in India: *Its Birth and Development,* No. 2, pp. 126-127. (Franklin, A.B.)

Cohen, B.S. India: *The Social Anthropology of a Civilisaton,* No. 2, pp. 113-114. (Jayawardena, C.)

Cohen, S.P. and R.L. Park, India: *Emergent Power?,* II:1&2, pp. 221-222. (Crocker, W.)

Cohen, S.P. The Indian Army: *Its Contribution to the Development of a Nation,* No. 2, pp. 119-120. (Ellinwood, D.C.)

Cole, W.O. and Sambhi, P.S., *A Popular Dictionary of Sikhism,* XIII:2, pp. 140-142. (Comans, M.)

Collins, L. and D. Lapierre, *Freedom at Midnight,* No. 6, pp. 140-141. (Rizvi, G.)

Conlon, F.F. A Caste in a Changing World: *The Chitrapur Saraswat Brahmans,* 1700-1935, IV:1, pp. 69-71. (Masselos, J.)

Copley, A. C. Rajagopalachari: *Gandhi's Southern Commander,* X:2, pp. 105-106. (McPherson, K.)

Copley, A.R.H. *The Political Career of C. Rajagopalachari,* 1937-1954, VI:1, pp. 58-59. (Copland, I.)

Coward, H.G. *Bhartrhari,* II:1&2, pp. 152-154. (Dunham, J.)

Crane, R.I. (ed.) Transition in South Asia: *Problems of Modernisation,* No. 3, pp. 130-131. (Gabard, W.M.)

D'Souza, B.G. Goan Society in Transition: *A Study in Social Change,* I:1, pp. 131-132.. (Pearson, M.N.)

Dales G.F. *Excavations at Nad-i Ali* (Sorkh Dagh) Afghanistan, II:1&2, pp. 184-185. (Biscione, R.)

Dallapiccola, A.L.(ed.), The Stupa—*Its Religious, Historical and Architenctural Significance,* VI:2, pp. 83-84. (Mabbett, I.W.)

Dalvi, J. *Chakra,* No. 6, pp. 149-150. (Raeside, I.)

Dandekar, H.C. *Men to Bombay, Women at Home: Urban Influence on Sugao Village, Deccan Maharashtra, India* 1942-1982, X:1, pp. 104-105. (Kemp, S.F.)

Dargyay, E.M. *The Rise of Esoteric Buddhism in Tibet,* II:1&2, pp. 188-189. (Ardussi, J.A.)

Das Gupta, A. and M.N. Pearson, *India and the Indian Ocean,* 1500-1750, IV:1, pp. 90-92. (Rothermund, D.)

Das Gupta, A. *Indian Merchants and the Decline of Surat c. 1700-1750,* IV:1, pp. 87-89. (Arasaratnam, S.)

Dasgupta, B. *The Oil Industry in India, Some Economic Aspects,* No. 6, pp. 145-147. (Ambirajan, S.)

Dasgupta, S. et al. *The Great Gherao* of 1969, I:1, pp. 159-160. (Chakrabarty, D.)

Datar, A.L. *India's Economic Relations with the USSR and Eastern Europe,* 1953-1969, No. 4, pp. 139-141. (Simkin, C.G.F.)

De Jong, J.W. *Buddhist Studies,* VI:2, pp. 91-92. (Bailey, G.)

De Mellow, M. *Remembered Glory,* No.5, p. 105, (Ghosh, R.N.)

De Silva, R.K. *Early Prints of Ceylon* (Sri Lanka), X:1, pp. 93-94. (Gooneratne, B.)

De Souza, T.R. Medieval Goa: *A Socio-Economic History,* IX:1, pp. 101-103. (Disney, A.R.)

De, B. (ed.) Perspectrrves in

Derrett, J.D.M. The Death of a Marriage Law: *Epitaph for the Rishi,* II:1&2, pp. 179-180. (rocher, L.)

Desai, P.B. *Survey of Research in Demography,* I:2, pp. 150-154. (Vicziany, M.)

Deshpande, M.M. and P.E. Hook (eds.), *Aryan and Non-Aryan in India,* IV:1, pp. 81-82. (Ambirajan, S.)

Devahuti, D. Harsha: *A Political Study,* No. 4, pp. 115-116. (Inden, R.)

Dhamotharan, A. Tamil Dictionaries: *A Biblography,* III:2, p. 75. (McAlpin D.W.)

Dhanagare, D.N. *Agrarian Movements and Gandhian Politics,* II:1&2, pp. 169-170. (G. McDonald)

Di Bona, J. E. Language Change and Modernisation: *The Development of a Hindi-English English-Hindi Glossary of Technical Terms in the Field of Education,* No. 3, pp. 131-132. (Mayer, P.B.)

Dimock, E.C., E. Gerow,C.M. Naim, A.K. Ramanujan, G. Roadarmel, and J.A.B. Van Buitenen, *The Literatures of India: An Introduction,* II:1&2, pp. 190-192. (Gaeffke, P.)

Din S.U. *Soviet Afghan Relations,* IX:2, pp. 122-123. (Jukes, G.)

Dirks, N.B. *The Hollow Crown: Ethnology of an Indian Kingdom,* IX:2, pp. 101-116. (Copland, I.)

Dixit, P. Communalism: *A Struggle for Power,* I:1, pp. 142-143. (McPherson, K.)

Driver, E. and A. Driver, Social Class in Urban India: *Essays on Cognitions and Structures,* XI:2, pp. 125-126. (Chakrabarty, D.)

Dube, L. Sociology of Kinship: *An Analytical Survey of Literature,* I:1, pp. 153-155. (Mcguire, J.)

Dunham, J. *Sources for the Study of British India in the State Library of Victoria,* I:2, p. 109. (Crawcour, P.)

Eaton, R.M. *Sufis of Bijapur,* I:2, pp. 116-117. (Pearson, M.N.)

Eden, E. Up the Country: *Letters Written to her Sisten from the Upper Provinces of India,* II:1&2, pp. 159-160. (Greenberger, A.J.)

Erdman, H.L. Political Attidudes of Indian Industry: *The Baroda Business Elite,* No. 5, pp. 128-129. (Gordon, A.D.)

Étienne, g. Food and Poverty: *India's Half Won Bttle,* XI:1, pp. 102-104. (Newman, R.S.)

Etinger, Y. and O. Melikyan, *The Policy of Non-alignment,* No. 3, pp. 135-136. (Gupta, S.K.)

Eyre, V. *Journal of an Afghanistan Prisoner,* I:1, pp. 132-133. (Callahan, R.)

Farooque, A.K.M. *Roads and Communications in Mughal India,* II:1&2, pp. 198-200. (Agarwal, U.)

Fernando, T. and R.N. Kearney (eds.), *Modern Sri Lanka: a Society in Transition,* III:2, pp. 91-94, (Arasaratnam, S.)

Ferreira, J.V. and S.S. Jha (eds.), *The Outlook Tower: Essays on Urbanisation in Memory of Patrick Geddes,* I:1, pp. 149-150. (Furedy, C.)

Film Australia — India: 14 Films, 1:2, pp. 154-155. (Holroyde, P.)

Finn, L.E. — *The Kulacudamani Tantra and the Vamakesvar Tantra with the Jayaratha Commentary*, X:2, pp. 86-87. (Bartley, C.J.)

FIsch, J. — *Hollands Ruhm in Asien*, XI:1, pp. 91-92. (Arasaratnam, S.)

Forrester, D.B. — Caste and Christianity: *Attitudes and Policies on Caste of Anglo-Saxon Protestant Missions in India*, VII:2, pp. 96-97. (Wright, D.)_

Fox, R.G. (ed.) — *Realm and Region in Traditional India*, I:2, pp. 120-122. (Pearson, M.N.)

Fox, R.G. (ed.) — *Urban India: Society, Space and Image*, No. 2 pp. 127-128. (Mayer, P.B.)

Franda, M.F. — India in the 70s, *India in an Emergency; Bangladesh and India*, II:1&2, pp. 223-224. (Borthwick, M.)

Frankel, F.R. — *India's Political Economy* 1947-77: *The Gradual Revolution*, III:2, pp. 89-90, (Bhattacharya, D.)

Fukazawa, H. — *Studies in the Social and Economic History of India*, No. 4, pp. 116-117. (Cashman, R.)

Furber, H. — *Rival Empires of Trade in the Orient*, 1600-1800, Vol. II, I;1, pp. 129-130. (Arasaratnam, S.)

Gaeffke, P. — *Hindi Literature in the Twentieth Century*, II:1&2, pp. 192-194. (Barz, R.K.)

Gallagher, J.G. — Johnson and a. Seal (eds.), *Locality, Province, and Nation: Essays on Indian Politics*, 1870-1940, No. 6, pp. 136-138. (Rothermund, D.)

Gandhi, I. — India: *The Speeches and Reminiscences of Indira Gandhi, Prime Minister of India*, I:2, pp. 141-142. (Miller, D.F.)

Gaur, G. — *Catalogue of Punjabi Printed Books Added to the India Office Library*, I:2, pp. 110-111. (Van den Dungen, P.)

Gautam, V. — *Aspects of Indian Society and Economy in the Nineteenth Century (A Study Based on an Evaluation of the American Consular Records)*, No. 6, pp. 135-136. (Brasted, H.)

George, A. — *Social Ferment in India*, X:1, pp. 105-107, (Miller, D.F.)

Ghadially, R. (ed.), — *Women in Indian Society:* A Reader, XII:1, pp. 115-116. (Borthwick, M.)

Ghosh, S.C. *Decision-Making and Power in the British Conservative Party: The Indian Problem,* 1924-34, No. 5, pp. 124-126. (Bridge, C.)

Ghosh, S.C. *Education Policy in India:Since Warren Hastings,* XIII:2, pp. 135-138. (Lawson, M.)

Ghurye, G.S. *I and Other Explorations,* No. 4, pp. 135-136. (Miller, D.B.)

Ghurye, G.S. *The Legacy of the Ramayana,* VI:2, pp. 84-86. (Colley, D.)

Ghurye, G.S. *Vedic India,* IV:1, pp. 80-81. (Granda, p.)

Gillion, K.L. *The Fiji Indians,* III:2, p.84. (Parnaby, O.)

Goetz, H. *Rajput Art and Architecture,* III:2, pp. 82-83, (Meister, M.W.)

Gokhale, S.D. (ed.), *Social Welfare,* I:2, pp. 145-148. (Huilgol, G.)

Gombrich, R.F. (ed.), *Indian Ritual and its Exegesis,* XII:1, pp. 118-120. (Bailey, G.)

Gooneratne, Y. Relative Merits: *A Personal memoir of the Bandaranaike Family of Sri Lanka,* X:1, pp. 107-111. (Wilson, A.J.)

Gooneratne, Y. *Silence, Exile and Cunning: The Fiction of Ruth Prawer Jhabvala,* VII:2, pp. 108-109. (Sharrad, P.)

Goonetileke, H.A.I., *A Bibiliography of Ceylon,* No. 2, p. 109. (Farmer, B.H.)

Goonetileke, H.A.I., *A Bibiliography of Ceylon,* VI:1, pp., VI:1, pp. 60-61. (Arasaratnam, S.)

Goonetileke, H.A.I., *A Bibiliography of Ceylon,* Vol. III:1, p. 120. (Farmer, B.H.)

Gopal, M.H. *Tipu Sultan's Mysore, An Economic Study,* No.2, pp. 117-118. (Manor, J.)

Gopal, S. Commerce and Crafts in Gujarat, 16th and 17th Centuries: *A Study in the Impact of European Expansion on Pre-capitalist Economy,* No. 6, pp. 132-133.. (Pearson, M.N.)

Gopal, S. Jawaharlal Nehru: *A Biography, vol.* 2, VII:2, pp. 104-105. (Dua, B.D.)

Gopalan, A.K. *In the Cause of the People Reminiscences,* VII:2, pp. 105-106. (Jeffrey, R.)

Gordon, A.D.D. Businessmen and Politics: *Rising Natonalism and a Modernising Economy in Bombay,* 1918-33, II:1&2, pp. 213-215. (Conlon, F.F.)

Gordon, L.A. and B.S. Miller, *A Syllabus of Indian Civilisation*, No.3, pp. 112-113. (Ray, S.N.)

Gordon, L.A. Bengal: *The Nationalist Movement* 1876-1940, No. 5, pp. 119-120. (Furedy, C.)

Goswany, B.N. and J.S. Grewal, *The Mughals and the Jogis of Jakhbar, Some Madad-i-Ma'ash and Other Documents*, No. 1, pp. 138-139. (McLeod, H.)

Gough, K. and H.P. Sharma (eds.), *Imperialism and Revolution in South Asia*, No. 5, pp. 130-132. (Harcourt, M.V.)

Gough, K. *Rural Society in Southeast India*, IX:1, pp. 114-116. (Mayer, P.B.)

Government of India, *Census of India*, 1981, XI:2, pp. 120-123. (Jeffrey, R.)

Grant, B. *Gods and Politicians*, VI:2, pp. 86-87. (Orr, K.)

Gray, J.N. and D.J. Means (eds.), *Society from the Inside Out: Anthropological Perspectives on the South Asia Household*, XIII:1, pp. 121-123. (Sinclair-Brull, W.)

Grimm, G. *Buddhist Wisdom: The Mystery of the Self*, II:1&2, p. 187. (De Jong, J.W.)

Gunawardana, R.A.L.H., *Robe and Plough: Monasticism and Economic Interest in Early Medieval Sri Lanka*, IV:1, pp. 75-80. (Aung-Thwin, M.)

Gustafson, W.E. and K.W. Jones (eds.), *Sources on Punjab History*, I:2, pp. 110-111. (Van den Dungen, P.)

Hardiman, D. *Peasant Nationalists of Gujarat: Kheda district* 1917-1934, VII:2, pp. 99-100. (Catanach, I.J.)

Harle, J.C. Gupta Sculpture: *Indian Sculpture of the Fourth to Sixth Centuries* A.D., No. 6, pp. 124-127. (Digby, S.)

Harrison, A.T. (ed.), *The Graham Indian Mutiny Papers*, VII:2, pp. 95-96. (Reeves, P.)

Hart, G.L. (III) Poets of the Tamil Anthologies: *Ancient Poems of Love and War*, III:2, pp. 77-78. (Ludden, D.)

Hart, g.L. (III) The Poems of Ancient Tamil: *their Milieu and their Sanskrit Counterparts*, No. 6, p. 123. (Nandakumar, P,)

Hart, H.C. (ed.) *India Gandhi's India*, I:1, pp. 147-148. (Miller, D.F.)

Hartmann, B. Reproductive Rights and Wrongs: *The Global Politics of Population Control and Contraceptive Chocie*, IX:2, pp. 123-125 (Jones, G.W.)

Hasan, M. A Nationalist Conscience: M.A. Ansari, the *Congress and the Raj,* XI:1, pp. 107-110. (Roy, A.)

Hasan, M. Babur: *Founder of the Maghal Empire in India,* X:1, pp. 90-91. (Pearson, M.N.)

Hasan, Z. *Dominance and Mobilisation:* Rural Politics in Western Uttar Pradesh 1930-1980, XII:1, pp. 142-143. (Catancach, I.J.)

Hasan, Z., S.N. Jha and R. Khan (eds.), *The State, Political Processes, and Identity: Reflections on Modern India,* XIII:1, pp. 112-114. (Zafarullah, H.)

Hashmi, A. *My Second in Kentucky,* IX:2, pp. 135&137, (Barz, R.K.)

Hazareesingh, K. *History of Indians in Mauritius,* 1:2, pp. 135&137. (Barz, R.K.)

Hedayetullah, M. Kabir: *The Apostle of Hindu-Muslim Unity,* II:1&2, p. 198. (Rizvi, S.A.A.)

Hettne, B. *The Politial Economy of Indirect Rule:* Mysore 1881-1947, VII:2, pp. 97-98. (McGuire, J.)

Hibbert, C. *The Great Mutiny*: India 1857, II:1&2, p. 203. (Callahan, R.)

Hiriyanna, M. *Essentials of Indian Philosophy,* X:1, pp. 89-90. (Bilimoria, P.)

Hoffman, F.J. *Rationality and Mind in Early Buddhism,* X:2, pp. 85-86. (Varma, C.B.)

Holmstrom, M. *South Indian Factory Workers, Their Life and Their World,* I:1, pp. 155-157 (Murphy, E.)

Horowitz, D.L. *Coup Theories and Officers'Motives. Sri Lanka in Comparative Perspective,* VI:2, pp. 62-67, (Roberts, M.)

Hunt, J.D. *Gandhi in London,* II:1&2, pp. 210-211. (Henningham, S.)

Hutchins, F.G. Spontaneous Revolution. *The Quit India Movement,* No. 2, pp. 124-125. (Voigt, J.H.)

Inden, R.B. and R.W. Nicholas, *Kinship in Bengali Culture,* II:1&2, pp. 175-177. (Mukherjee, S.N.)

Inden, R.B. *Marriage and Rank in Bengali Culture: A History of Caste and Clan in Middle Period Bengal,* I:1, pp. 153-155. (McGuire, J.)

Indian Council of Social Science Research, *A Survey of Research in Geography,* No. 4, pp. 142-143. (Johnson, B.L.C.)

Institute for the Study of Languages and Cultures of Asia and Africa (Tokyo), *Studies in Socio-Economic Change in Rural Villages in Tiruchirapalli District, Tamilnadu, India*, Nos. 1-5, VI:2, pp. 103-105, (Mayer, P.)

Islam, M.M. Bengal Agriculture 1920-1946: *A Quantitative Study*, VII:2, pp. 100-101, (Mcuire, J.)

Islam, R. (ed.) *A Calendar of Documents on Indo-Persian Relations* (1500-1750), ii, VI:1, p. 61;VII:1, p. 87. (Pearson, M.N.)

Islam, S. (ed.) *Mahmud b. Amir Wali Balkhi. the ul-Asrar. Travelogue of South Asia*, VI:1, p. 61; VII:1, p. 87. (Pearson, M.N.)

Islam, S. (ed.) *Bangladesh District Records Chittagong* Vol. 1, 1760-1787, IV:1, pp. 90-91. (Guha, R.)

Jyangar, S. *The Hathayogapradipika of Svatmarama, with the Commentary Jyotsna of Brahmananda*, No. 4, pp. 111-112. (Dunham, J.)

Jain, A.K. and P. Visaria (eds.), *Infant Mortality in India: Differentials and Determinants*, XI:2, pp. 120-123 (Jeffrey, R.)

Jain, M.S. *The Emergence of a New Aristocracy in Nepal* (1837-58), No. 4, pp. 118-121, (Regmi, M.C.)

Jaini, P.S. *The Jaina Path of Purification*, III:2, pp. 76-77. (Basham, A.L.)

Jamal, M. (ed.) *The Penguin Book of Modern Indian Poetry*, X:1, pp. 111-112, (Sharrad, P.)

Jansson, E. India, Pakistan or Pakhtunistan? *The Nationalist Movements in the North-West Frontier Province*, 1937-47, VII:2, pp. 101-104. (Copland, I.)

Jayarajan, P.M. *History of the Evolution of the Sinhala Alphabet*, 1:2, pp. 111-113. (Rahula, T.)

Jayaraman, R. *Caste Continuities in Ceylon: A Study of the Social Structure of ThreeTea Plantations*, No. 6, pp. 151-152. (Gillen, P.)

Jayasuriya, J.E. *Educational Policies and Progress During British Rule in Ceylon* 1796-1948, II:1&2, pp. 225-226. (Jones, P.)

Jayawardena, V.K. *The Rise of the Labour Movemet in Ceylon*, No. 3, pp. 126-127. (Dufty, N.F.)

Jeffery, P. Frogs in a Well: Indian Women in Purdah, III:2, pp. 85-86. (Kingston, B.)

Jeffrey, R. *The Decline of Nayar Dominance,* I:2, pp. 128-129. (Kumar, D.)

Jeffrey, R. *What's Happening to India? Punjab, Ethnic Conflict, Mrs. Gandhi's Death and the Test of Federalism,* IX:2, pp. 123-124. (Barrier, N.G.)

Jeffrey, R., et. al. (ed.), India: *Rebellion to Republic: Selected Writings,* 1857-1990, XIII:2, pp. 123-125 (Woods, P.)

Jha, S.N. *Leadership and Local Politics: A Study of Meerut District in Uttar Pradesh,* 1923-1973, IV:1, p. 68, (Smith, R.F.I.)

Jiggins, J. *Caste and Family in the Politics of the Sinhalese* 1947-1976, IV:1, pp. 66-68. (Silva, K.T.)

Jiggins, J. *Caste and Family in the Politics of th Sinhalese,* III:2, pp. 91-94. (Arasaratnam, S.)

Johansson, R.E.A. *The Dynamic Pshychology of Early Buddhism,* IV:1, pp. 83-84, (De Jong, J.W.)

Johnson, B.L.C. and M. Le M. Scrivenor, *Sri Lanka: Land, People and Economy,* IX:1, p. 118. (Roberts, M.)

Johnson, B.L.C. *Bangladesh,* I:1, pp. 146-147. (Wright, D.)

Johnson, B.L.C. *India, Resources and Development,* II:1&2, pp. 224-225. (Wright, D.)

Johnson, D.J. and J.E. Johnson, *Through Indian Eyes,* I:1, pp. 126-127. (Wright, D.)

Johnson, G. Provincial Politics and Indian Nationalism: *Bombay and the Indian National Congress,* 1880-1915, No. 6, pp. 136-138. (Rothermund, D.)

Jones, E.C. Growth Recurring: *Economic Change in World History,* XII:1, pp. 137-140. (Diehl, F.W.)

Jones, E.C. *The European Miracle, Environments, Economics and Geopolitics in the History of Europe and Asia,* VI:1 pp. 63-64. (Pearson, M.N.)

Jones, K.W. Arya Dharma: *Hindu Consciousness in Nineteeth-Century Pubjab,* I:1, pp. 139-140. (Jordens, J.)

Jones, R.W. *Urban Politics in India: Area, Power and policy in a Penetrated System,* No. 5, pp. 127-128. (Stern, R.W.)

Jordens, J.T.F. *Dayananda Saraswati: His Life and Ideas,* III:2, pp. 83-84. (Oddie, G.A.)

Joshi, B.R. *Democracy in Search of Equality: Untouchable Politics and Indian Social Change* VII:2, pp. 105-106 (Jeffrey. R.)

Joshi, L. *Studies in the Buddhistic Culture of India (During the 7th and 8th Centuries)*, II:1&2, pp. 187-188. (De Jong, J.W.)

Joshi, V.C. (ed.) *Sri Aurobindo: An Interpretation*, I:1, pp. 138-139. (Borthwick, M.)

Juergensmeyer, M. and N.G. Barrier (eds.) *Sikh Studies; Comparative Perspectives on a Changing Tradition*, VI:2, pp. 87-88. (Masica, C.P.)

Junankar, N.S. *Gautama: The Nyaya Philosophy*, IV:1, pp. 73-75. (Bilimoria, P.)

Tuti-Nana: Tales of a Parrot, IV:1, pp. 59-60. (Pearson, M.N.)

Kachru, B.B. *Kashmiri Literature*, VI:2, pp. 89-90m (Barz, R.K.)

Kantowsky, D. *Sarvodaya: The Other Development*, IV:1, pp. 61-63 (Abeyasekare, S.)

Kapferer, B. *A Celebration of Demons: Exorcism and the Aesthetics of Healing in Sri Lanka*, IX:1, pp. 116-117. (Bell, S.)

Karve, I. Yuganta: *The End of an Epoch*, No. 1, pp. 132-135. (Dunham, J.)

Kaushik, D. The Indian Ocean. *Towards a Peace Zone*, No. 4, p. 143. (Arasaratnam, S.)

Kawai, A. "Landords" and Imperial Rule: Change in Bengal Agrarian Society c. 1885-1940, pp. 106-107. (Mc Guire, J.)

Kearney, R.N. *Trade Unions and Politics in Ceylon*, No. 2, pp. 129-130. (Schveinfurth-Marby, H.)

Keer, D. Shahu Chhatrapati, *a Royal Revolutionary*, I:1, pp. 136-138. (Copland, I.)

Keeton, C.L. *King Thebaw and the Ecological Rape of Burma: The Struggle Between British India and French Indo-China in Burma*, No. 5, pp. 111-112. (Taylor, R.H.)

Kelkar, A.R. Studies in Hindi-Urdu I, *Introduction and Word Phonology*, No. 4, pp. 123.124. (Rizvi, S.A.A.)

Khalidi, O. (ec.), *Hydrabad: After the Fall*, XI:2, pp. 137-140. (Roy, A.)

Khalidi, O. *Dakan Under the Sultans 1292-1724. A Biliography of Monographic and Periodical Literature*, XIII:2, pp. 128-129. (Roy, A.)

Khan, A.R. *Chietains in the Mughal Empire,* 1:2, pp. 120-122. (Pearson, M.N.)

Khan, I.A. *The Political Biography of a Mughal Noble: Mun'im Khan-i Khanan,* No. 5, pp. 105-106. (Rizvi, S.A.A.)

Khan, M.M. and J.P. Thorp (eds.), *Bangladesh: Society, Politics and Bureaucracy,* IX:2, pp. 120-122. (Wright, D.)

Khan, M.M. Burmucratic Self-Preservation: *Failure of Major Administrative Reform in the Civil Service of Pakistan,* III:2, pp. 94-95. (Higgott, R.)

Kharbas, D.S. and R.N. Sharma, Sanskrit Grammar: *A Bibliography of Western Language Materials,* No. 5, p. 101, (O'Neil, J.L.)

Kharbas, D.S. *Maharashtra and the Marathas: Their History and Culture, A Bibliographic Guide,* No. 4, p. 110-111. (Masselos, J.)

Khare, R.S. and M.S.A. Rao, Food, Society and Culutre: *Aspects in South Asian Foods Systems,* X:1, pp. 102-105. (Newman, R.S.)

Khare, R.S. *Culture and Democracy: Anthropological Reflections on Modern India,* IX:2, pp. 118-120. (Miller, D.F.)

Khare R.S. The Changing Brahmans: *Associations and Elites Among the Kanya-Kubjas of North India,* No. 3, pp. 119-120. (Taylor, D.D.)

King, A.D. *Colonial Urban Development,* 1:2, pp. 139-141, (Lewandowski, S.)

Kind, D.B. *A Comprehensive Bibliography of Pakistan Archaeology: Paleolithic to Historic Times,* I:1, pp. 120-121. (Possehi, G.L.)

Kopf, D. *The Brahmo Samaj and the Shaping of the Modern Indian Mind,* II:1&2, pp. 206-208. (Borthwick, M.)

Kramrisch, S. *The Presence of Siva,* VI:1, pp. 72-74. (Bailey, G.)

Kuldip, R.K. *Waris Shah,* No. 4, pp. 113-115, (McLeod, H.)

Kulke, H. *Jagannatha–Kult and Gajapati–Konigtum, ein Beitrag zur Geschichte Religioser Legitimation Hinduistischer Herrscher,* VI:2, pp. 90-(Bailey, G.)

Kumar, K. *Social Character of Learning,* XII:1, pp. 116-118 (Scrase, T.)

Kumar, R. (ed.) *Essays on Gandhian Politics: The Rowlatt Satyagraha of* 1919, No. 3, pp. 107-111. (Guha, R.)

Kumar V. *Committees and Commissions in India,* 1947-1973, No. 6, pp. 148-149. (Borchardt. D.H.)

Kuppuswamy, B. *Population and Society in India,* I:2, pp. 150-154. (Vicziany, M.)

L. Brennan Land Policy and Social Charge in Northern India: Rohilkhand 1800-1911, II:1&2, pp. 208-210. (Dhanagare, D.N.)

Lal, B.V. Girmitiyas: *The Origins of the Fiji Indians,* IX:1, pp. 120-121. (Jayaraman, R.)

Lawford, J.P. *Britain's Army in India From its Origins to the Conquest of Bengal,* II:1&2, p. 156, (Collahan, R.)

Lebra-Chapman, J., The Rani of Jhansi: *A Study in Female Heroism in India,* XI:1, pp. 98-100. (Cashman, R.)

Lewis, S.R. *Pakistan: Industrialisation and Trade Policies,* No. 2, pp. 110-112. (Sundrum, R.M.)

Lewis, W.A. *Dynamic Factors inEconomic Growth,* No. 6, pp. 145-147. (Ambirajan, S.)

Lieten, G.K. *The First Communist Ministry in Kerala,* 1957-1959, VII:2, p. 105. (Stern, R.W.)

Lifschultz. L. Bangladesh: *The Unfinished Revolution,* VI:1, pp. 64-66. (Wright, D.)

Lipsey, R. (ed.) Coomaraswamy 1: Selected Papers. *Traditional Art and Symbolism,* II:1&2, pp. 163-165. (Masselos, J.)

Lipsey, R. (ed.) Coomaraswamy 2: *Selected Papers. Metaphysics,* II:1&2, pp. 163-165. (Masselos, J.)

Lipton, M., M. et al. *The Erosion of a Relationship,* I:2, pp. 142-143. (Furber, H.)

Little, I., T. Scitovsky, and M. Scott, *Industry and Trade in Some Developing Countries – A Comparative Study,* No.2, pp. 110-112. (Sundrum, R.M.)

London, H.I. *Non-white Immigration and the White Australia Policy,* No. 1, p. 142. (Yarwood, A.T.)

Lorenzen, D. *The Kapalikas and Kalamukhas,* No. 3, pp. 117-118. (Mabbet, I.W.)

Low, D.A. *The Contraction of England,* X:2, pp. 106-107. (Bridge, C.)

Ludden, D. *Peasant History in South India,* X:2, pp. 98-100. (Arasaratnam, S.)

Manor, J. — *Political Change in an Indian State: Mysore* 1917-55, II:1&2, pp. 217-219. (Ramusack, B.N.)

Mansergh, N. — *The Prelude to Partition: Concepts and Aims in Ireland and India,* II:1&2, p. 170 (Moore, R.J.)

Marby, H. — Tea in Ceylon —*An Attempt at Regional and Temporal Differentation of the Tea Growing Areas in Ceylon,* No. 4, pp. 141-142. (Dias, H.D.)

Markenstein, K. — *Foreign Investment and Development,* No. 3, p. 130. (Hogan, W.P.)

Markovits, C. — *Indian Business and Nationalist Politics* 1931-1939: *The Indigenous Capitalist Class and the Rise of the Congress Party,* XI:1, pp. 102-105. (Masselos, J.)

Marshall, J.G. — Britain and Tibet 1765-1947: *A Select Annotated Bibliography,* II:1&2, pp. 183-184. (Maxwell, N.)

Mascarenhas, A. — *The Rape of Bangla Desh,* No. 5, pp. 132-133. (Ray, S.)

Mascarenhas, K.C. — A Strategy for Rural Development: *Dairy Co-operatives in India,* XII:1, pp. 134-135 (George, V.)

Masselos, J. — *Nationalism on the Indian Subcontinent,* No. 5, pp. 115-116. (Staelin, C.D.)

Mazarr, M.J. — *Missile Defences and Asian-Pacific Security,* XII:2, pp. 103-105. (Shephard, A.)

McAlpin, M.B. — Subject to Famine: Food Crises and Economic Change in 1860-1920m VI:1, pp. 67-69. (Copland, I.)

McGregor, R.S. — *A New Voice for New Times,* VI:2, pp. 93-94. (Barz, R.K.)

McGregor, R.S. — *Hindi Literature of the Nineteenth and Early Twentieth Centuries,* No. 6, pp. 134-135. (Barz, R.K.)

McLane, J.R. — *Indian Nationalism and the Early Congress,* VII:1, pp. 87-89. (Cahman, R.)

McMillan, D.H. (ed.) *Asian Perspectives on International Security,* IX:1, pp. 125-127. (Loewald, K.)

Medieval India: *A Miscellany,* Vol. 1, No. 2, pp. 115-117. (Ahmad, Q.)

Mehta, V. — A Family Affair: *India Under Three Prime Ministers,* VI:1, pp. 69-70. (Dua B.D.)

Mellor, J.W. (ed.) — India: *A Rising Middle Power,* IV:1, pp. 63-65. (Palmer, N.D.)

Memon, M.U. (ed.) *Studies in the Urdu Gazal and Prose Fiction*, IX:1, pp. 100-101. (Barz, R.K.)

Metcalf, T.R. *Land, Landlords and the British Raj: Northern India in the Nineteenth Century*, IV:1, pp. 92-94, (Copland, I.)

Meyer, E. Ceylan, Sri Lanka, I:2, p. 111. (Farmer, B.H.)

Miller, D.F. *Pervasive Politics A Study of the Indian District*, No. 4, p. 135. (Stern, R.W.)

Minault, G. The Khilafat Movement: *Religious Suymbolism and Political Mobilisation in India*, VII:2, pp. 98-99. (McPherson, K.)

Misra, B.B. The Indian Political Parties: *An Historical Analysis of British Behaviour up to* 1947, I:1, pp. 141-142. (Davies, A.)

Mohmed, N.P. *Drift Wood/The Bull*, I:1, p. 157, (Jeffrey, R.)

Mohan, R. (ed.) *Indian Writing in English*, IV:1, pp. 62-63. (Gooneratne, Y.)

Moir, M. *A General Guide to the India Office Records*, XII:2, pp. 114-115 (Watson, I.B.)

Mokashi, D.B. Palkhi: *An Indian Pilgrimage*, XI:1, pp. 97-98. (Writht, D.)

Moore, R.J. (ed.) *Tradition and Politics in South Asia*, III:2, pp. 80-82. (Richards, J.F.)

Moore, R.J. *Endgames of Empire: Studies of Britain's Indian Problem*, XII:2, pp. 92-94. (Iinker, H.)

Moore, R.J. *The Crisis of Indian Unity* 1917-1940, II:1&2, pp. 165-167. (Broomfield, J.H.)

Moosvi, S. *The Economy of the Mughal Empire* c. 1595; *A Statistical Study*, X:2, pp. 87-89. (Pearson, M.N.)

Morris-Jones, W.H. (ed)*The Making of Politicians*, I:2, pp. 148-149, (Smith, D.E.)

Morris-Jones, W.H. *Politics Mainly Indian*, II:1&2, pp. 222-223. (Miller, D.F.)

Morris-Jones, W.H. *The Government and Politics of India*, XI:1, pp. 92-94 (Juffrey, R.)

Multon, E.C. *Indian Studies in Canada*, IX:2, p. 93, (Jeffrey, R.)

Mujahid, S.A. Quaid-i-Azam Jinnah: *Studies in Interpretation*, VII:1, p. 89. (Moore, R.J.)

Mukherjee, C. *Urban Growth, in a Rural Area – A Case Study of a Town in West Bengal*, No. 4, p. 137, (Ghosh, R.N.)

Mukherjee, S.B. *The Age Distribution of the Indian Population: A Reconstruction for the States and Territories*, 1881-1961, II:1 &2 pp. 160-161. (Heston, A.)

Mukherjee, S.N. *Calcutta: Myths and History*, II:1&2, pp. 219-220. (Spodek, H.)

Muni, S.D. *Foreign Policy of Nepal*, No. 6, pp. 144-145. (Mojumdar, K.)

Murshid, G. *Reluctant Debutante: Reponse of Bengali Women to Modernisation*, 1849-1905, IX:1, pp. 108-110. (Khondker, H.H.)

Nadkarni, M.V. et al. *The Political Economy of Forest Use and Management*, XII:2, pp. 99-100. (Harris, G.T.)

Nafziger, E.W. *Class, Caste and Enterpreneurship: A Study of Indian Industrialists*, IV:1, pp. 68-69, (Tangri, S.S.)

Naik, J.P. *Policy and Performance in Indian Education*, I:2, pp. 149-150. (Jones, P.)

Naim, C.M. (ed.) *Iqbal, Jinnah and Pakistan: The Vision and the Reality*, V:1, pp. 66-67. (McPherson K.)

Namboodiripad, *E.M.S.,Conflicts and Crisis. Political India*, VII:2, pp. 105-106. (Jeffrey, R.)

Nambodiripad, E.M.S., *Indian Planning in Crisis*, No.5, pp. 122-123. (Jeffrey, R.)

Nanda B.R. (ed.) *Indian Foreign Policy:* The Nehru Years, I:1, pp. 144-146. (Crocker, W.R.)

Nanda B.R. (ed.) *Indian Women*, I:2, pp. 134-135. (Pearson, G.)

Nanda B.R. (ed.) *Socialism in India*, No. 3, pp. 127-1283. (Bedford, I.)

Nandy, A. *The Intimate Enemy: Loss and Recovery of Self Under Colonialism*, IV:1, pp. 70-72. (Miller, D.)

Nayyar, D. *India's Exports and Export Policies*, I:2, pp. 143-145. (Ambirajan, S.)

Nehru, J. *Selected Works of Jawaharlal Nehru*, No. 4, p. 130. (Moore, R.J.)

Nilsson, S. *The New Capitals of India, Pakistan and Bangladesh*, No. 4, pp. 137-139. (Saini, B.S.)

O'Flaherty, W. and J.D.M. Derrett (eds.), The *Concept of Duty in South Asia*, II:1&2, pp. 155-156. (Rocher, L.)

Oldenburg, P. *Big City Government in India*, I:2, pp. 141-142. (Miller, D.F.)

Oldenburg, V.T. *The Making of Colonial Lucknow* 1856-1877, IX:2, pp. 107-109. (Furedy, C.)

Olschak, B.C. and G.T. Wangyal, *Mystic Art of Ancient Tibet*, No. 4, pp. 112-113. (Kondos, V.)

Omvedt, G. *We Will Smash This Prison! Indian Woen in a Struggle*, VI:2, pp. 94-95. (Lenneberg, C.)

Ortner, S.B. High Religion: *A Cultural and Political History of Sherpa Buddhism*, XIII:2, pp. 143-144. (Oldmeadow, P.)

Ortner, S.B. *Sherpas Through Their Rituals*, II:1&2, pp. 178-179. (Newell, W.H.)

Oster, A. *The Play of the Gods, Locality, Ideology, Structure and Time in the Festivals of a Bengali Town*, V:1, pp. 61-62, (Bailey, G.M.)

Palsapure, P.Z. *Industrial Development of Vidarbha*, I:1, pp. 151-153. (Masselos, J.)

Pandey, B.N. (ed.) *Leadership in South Asia*, II:1&2, PP. 211-212. (Crance, R.J.)

Pant, A. *A Moment in Time*, No. 5, pp. 123-124. (Cashman, R.)

Paramanand *Political Development in South Asia*, XII:1, pp. 132-133. (Khan, M.M. and Mostafa, I.M.)

Parekh, B. *Gandhi's Political Philosophy: A Critical Examination*, XIII:1, pp. 107-110. (Rivett, K.)

Parekh, I.J. and P.K. Garg, Indian Women: *An Inner Dialogue*, XIII:1, pp. 120-121. (Borthwick, M.)

Pearson, M.N. Coastal Western India: *Studies from the Portuguese Records*, IX:1, pp. 103-105. (Disney, A.R.)

Pearson, M.N. *Merchants and Rulers in Gujarat*, I:2, pp. 117-120. (Misra, S.C.)

Pearson, M.N. *The New Cambridge History of India*, 1.1. The Portuguese in India, XI:2, pp. 128-132. (Disney, A.)

Pereirs, J. *Monolithic Jinas*, I:2, pp. 114-115. (Masselos, J.)

Peterfalvi, J. and M. Biardeau, Le *Mahabharata*, IX:2, pp. 97-98. (Treloar, A.)

Philips, C.H. and M.D. Wainwright (eds.), *Indian Society and the Beginnings of Modernisation* c. 1830-1850, II:1&2, pp. 157-159. (Chakrabarty, D.)

Pinto, F.M. R.D. Catz, (ed.), *The Travels of Mendes Pinto*, XIII:2, pp. 113-114. (Pearson, M.N.)

Prakash, O. *The Dutch East India Company and the Economy of Bengal* 1630-1720, IX:2, pp. 100-102. (Arasaratnam, S.)

Prasad, R.C. *Early English Travellers to India: A Study in the Travel Literature of the Elizabethan and Jacobean Periods with Particular Reference to India*, IV:1, p. 90. (Copland, I.)

Preibish, A. *Guide to South Asian Materials in the Natioanl Library of Canada*, IX:2, pp. 93-95. (Soegito, I.)

Premchand *Deliverance and Other Stories*, XII:2, pp. 112-113. (Watson, I.B.)

Proceedings of the Second International Conference Seminar of Tamil studies, No. 3, pp. 116-117. (Emmeneau, M.B.)

Proudfoot, I. *Ahimsa and a Mahabharata Story*, XIII:1, pp. 123-124. (fitzgerald, J.L.)

Ptak, R. *Portuguese Asia: Aspects in History and Economic History (Sixteenth and Seventeenth Centuries)*, XI:1, pp. 89-91. (Disney, A.)

Punekar, S.D. and A.R. Golwalkar, *Rural Change in Maharashtra: An Analytical Study of Change in Six Villages in Konkan*, I:1, pp. 151-153. (Masselos, J.)

Pyarelal Mahatma Gandhi, Vol. ii: *The Discovery of Satyagraha-On theThreshold*, IX:1, pp. 112-113. (Masselos, J.)

Quraishi, S.A. and U. Sims-Williams, *Catalogue of the Urdu Manuscripts in the India Office Library*, III:2, p. 75. (Minault, G.)

Qvarnstrom, O. *Hindu Philosophy in Buddhist Perspective*, XII:1, pp. 126-129. (Franco, E.)

Radhakrishnan, P., Pasant Struggles, *Land Reforms and Social Change: Malabar*, 1836-1892, XIII:1, pp. 114-116. (Catanach, I.J.)

Raeside, I (tr.) Galyaraja; a fourteenth century Marathi version of the Krsna Legend, XIII:2, pp. 114-116. (McLean, M.D.)

Rahbar, D. Urdu Letters of *Mirza Asadu'llah Khan Ghalib*, X:2, pp. 89-90. (Barz, R.)

Rahman, M. *Emergence of a New Nation in a Multi-Polar World: Bangladesh*, IV:1, pp. 65. (Wright, D.)

Raj, K.N., A. Sen and C.H.H. Rao (eds.),Dharm Narian. *Studies on Indian Agriculture*, XIII:1, pp. 118-119. (Harris, G.T.)

Rama Sharma, M.H., *The History of the Vijayanagar Empire*, Vol.: 1, pp. 65 (Wright, D.)

Rama Sharma, M.H., *The History of the Vijayanagar Empire, Vol. 2, Decline and Disappearance* (1569-1679), VI:1, p. 77. (Martell, W.H.T.)

Ramachandran, G. and T.K. Mahadevan (eds.), *Quest for Gandhi*, No. 2, pp. 121-122. (Bishop, D.H.)

Ramanujan, A.K. *Hynns for the Drowning-Poems for Visnu by Nammalvar*, VI:2, pp. 95-97. (Aveling, H.)

Ramaswami, N.S., *The Founding of Madras*, II:1&2, p. 157. (Stoddart, B.)

Ramusack, B.M. *The Princes of India in the Twilight of Empire*, 1914-39, II:1&2, pp. 215-217. (Copland, I.)

Ranu, G. N. *Family Structure and Fertility: Emerging Patterns in an Indian City*, XI:2, pp. 119-120. (Edmundson, W.)

Rao, K.V.N. *The Emergence of Andhra Pradesh*, No. 4, pp. 130-131. (Stoddard, B.)

Rawding, F.W. *The Rebellion in India*, 1857, I:2, p. 123. (Amritmahal, R.)

Rawson, P. *Erotic Art of India*, I:2, pp. 115-116. (Meister, M.W.)

Ray, B. *Hyderabad and British Paramountcy* 1858-1883, XI:2, pp. 135-137. (Copland, I.)

Ray, S. (ed.) *Gandhi, India and the World: An International Symposium*, No. 2, pp. 122-124. (Nanda B.R.)

Ray, S. and Maddern, M. (eds.) *I Have Seen Bengal's Face: a Selection of Modern Bengali Poetry in English Translation*, I:1, pp. 102-109. (Gooneratne, Y.)

Raychaudhuri, T. and I. Habib, *The Cambridge Economic History of India*, Vol., c. 1200-c. 1750, V:1, pp. 69-71. (Pearson, M.N.)

Reeves, P. & Wardrop, J. (Comp.), *The Indian Nationbalist Movement*, c. 1912-1922, *Leadership, Organisation and Philosophy, the Writings of Hugh Owen*, XIII:2, pp. 138-140. (Woods, P.)

Reeves, P.D. (ed.), Sleeman in Oudh, *An Abridgement of W.H. Sleeman's A Journey through the Kingdom of Oude* in 1849-1850, No. 3, pp. 121-122. (Oddie, G.A.)

Reinhardt, W.W. *The Legislative Council of the Punjab*, 1897-1912, No. 2, pp. 120-121. (Barrier, N.G.)

Richards, G. (ed.), *A Source-Book of Modern Hinduism*, X:1, pp. 94-95. (Jordens, J.)

Richards, J.F. (ed.), *Kingship and Authority in South Asia*, II:1&2, pp. 197-198. (Pearson, M.N.)

Richman, P. *Women, Branch Stories, and Religious Rhetoric in a Tamil Buddhist Text*, XII:1, pp. 120-123, 113-125, (Varma, C.B.)

Rizvi, G. *Linlithgow and India: A Study of British Policy and the Political Impasse in India* 1936-43, III:2, pp. 84-85, (Bridge, C.)

Rizvi, H.A. *Crisis in Indian Democracy*, 1:2, pp. 141-142. (Miller, D.F.)

Robb, P. (ed.) Rural India: *Land, Power and Society under British Rule*, IX:2, pp. 112-114. (Brennan, L.)

Robb, P. and D. Taylor (eds.), *Rule, Protest, Identity, Aspects of Modern South Asia*, II:1&2, pp. 161-162, (Stoddart, B.)

Robb, P.G. *The Government of India and Reform, Policies Towards Politics and the Constitution* 1916-1921, I:1, pp. 140-141, (Woods, P.)

Roberts, M. (ed.) *Collective Identities and Protest in Modern Sri Lanka*, III:2, pp. 91-94. (Arasaratnam, S.)

Roberts, M. (ed.) *Documents of the Ceylon National Congress and Nationalist Politics in Ceylon*, 1929-50, II:1&2, pp. 212-213. (Jeffrey, R.)

Roberts, M. *Caste Conflict and Elite Formation: The Rise of a Karava, Elite in Sri Lanka*, 1500-1931, VI:2, pp. 97-98. (Bell, S.)

Roberts, M. *Facets of Modern Ceylon History Through the Letters of Jeronis Pieris*, No. 6, pp. 133-134. (Arasaratnam, S.)

Robinson, A. *Economic Prospects of Bangladesh*, No. 5, p. 133, (Johnson, B.L.C.)

Robinson, F. *Separatism Among Indisan Muslims: Politics of the United Province's Muslims*, 1860-1923, No. 5, pp. 116-117. (McPherson, K.)

Rogers, J.D. *Crime, Justice and Society on Colonial Sri Lanka*, XI:1, pp. 112-114, (Freitag, S.B.)

Rose, L.E. *Nepal—Strategy for Survival*, No. 3, pp. 134-135. (Caplan, L.)

Rose, L.E. *The Politics of Bhutan*, II:1&2, p. 221, (Marshall, J.G.)

Rosenthal, D.B. *The Expansive Elite; District Politics and State Policy-Making in India*, III:2, pp. 90-91, (Davies, A.J.)

Rothermund, D. (ed.), *Islam in Southern Asia. A Survey of Current Research*, No. 6, pp. 141-144. (Roy, A.)

Rothermund, D. An Economic History of India, XIII:1, pp. 116-117, (Arasaratnam, S.)

Rothermund, D. *Grundzuge der Indischen Geschichte*, I:1, pp. 127-128. (Jacobs, M.)

Roy, A. *The Islamic Syncretistc Tradition in Bengal*, IX:1, pp. 105-107, (McPherson, K.)

Ruegg, D.S., *Buddha-nature, Mind and the Problem of Gradualism in a Comparative Perspective. On the Transmission and Reception of Buddhism in India and Tibet*, XIII:2, pp. 116-117, (McLean, M.D.)

Rule, P. *The Pursuit of Progress: The Intellectual Development of R.C. Dutt*, 1948-88, II:1&2, pp. 205-206. (Panikkar, K.N.)

Sachau, E.C. and A.T. *Embree, Alberuni's India*, No. 2, pp. 114-115. (McLeod, H.)

Saraswati, S. *Minorities in Madras State: Group Interests in Modern Politics*, I:1, pp. 143-144. (Stoddart, B.)

Sarkar, J. *A Short History of Aurangzib*, V:1, p. 69. (Pearson, M.N.)

Sarkar, J. *Fall of the Mughal Empire*, Vol.1, 1739-1754, and *Anecdotes on Aurangzib*, XIII:1, p. 136. (Arasaratnam, S.)

Sarkar, J. *Studies in Aurangzib's Reign (Studies in Mughal India, First Series)*, XIII:1, pp. 103-104. (Pearson, M.N.)

Sarjkar, S. *Modern India* 1885-1947, IX:2, pp. 81-92.

Sau, R. *India's Economic Development: Aspects of Class Relations*, IX:1 pp. 123-125, (Ghosh, R.N.)

Schermerhorn, R.A.,*Ethnic Plurality in India*, II:1&2, pp. 177-178. (Rawson, J.)

Scheuer, J. *Siva dans le Mahabharata:*, VI:1, pp. 72-74, (Bailey, G.)

Scholberg, H. and E. Diven, *Bibliographie des Francais dons l'Inde,* No. 4, p. 110. (Kennedy, B.)

Scholberg, H. *Bibiography of Goa and the Portuguese in India,* VI:1, pp. 74-76. (Disney, A.R.)

Schreiner, P. and R. Sohnen, *Sanskrit Indices and Text of the Brahmapurana,* XII:1, pp. 125-126. (Bailey, G.)

Schwartzberg, J.E. (ed.), *Historical Atlas of South Asia,* III:1, pp. 85-86 (from the perspectives of Modern History and Teaching). (Owen, H.F.)

Schwartzberg, J.E. (ed.), *Historical Atlas of South Asia,* III:1, pp. 85-86 (from the perspectives of Ancient History). (Singh, S.D.)

Schwartzberg, J.E. (ed.), *Historical Atlas of South Asia,* III:1, pp. 86-87 (from the perspective of Medieval History). (Peasonn M.N.)

Schwartzberg, J.E. (ed.), *Historical Atlas of South Asia,* III:1, pp. 87-89 (from the perspective of Economic History). (Ambirajan, S.)

Schwartzberg, J.E. (ed.) *Historical Atlas of South Asia,* III:1, pp. 89-90 (from the perspective of Geography), (Spate, O.H.K.)

Schwartzberg, J.E. (ed.), *Historical Atlas of South Asia,* III:1, pp. 90-91 (from the perspective of Cartography). (Spate, O.H.K. and Gunther, H.E.)

Schwartzberg, J.E. (ed.), *Historical Atlas of South Asia,* III:1, pp. 91-92 (from the perspective of Political Science). (Palmer, N.D.)

Schwartzberg, J.E. (ed.), *Historical Atlas of South Asia,* III:1, pp. 92-93 (from the perspective of Social Anthropology). (Allen, M.)

Schwartzberg, J.E. (ed.), *A Historical Atlas of South Asia,* III:1, pp. 93-94 (from the perspective of Economic Demography), (Appleyard, R.T.)

Schweinfurth, U. and H. Schweinfurth-Marby, Explorations in the *Eastern Himalayas and the River Gorge Country of Southeastern Tibet-Francis K. Ward* (1885-1958), I:1, pp. 148-149. (Ardussi, J.A.)

Schweinfurth, U. Et al. *Landschafts-okologische Forschungen auf Ceylon,* No. 3, pp. 133-134. (Johnson, B.L.C.)

Schweinfurth, U., H. Flohn and M. Domros, *Studies in the Climatology of South Asia,* No. 2, pp. 113-114 (Johnson, B.L.C.)

Science and Human Progress: Essays in Honour of late Professor D.D. Kosambi, I:1, pp. 123-124. (Omvedt, G.)

Seal, A. The Emergence of Indian Nationalism: *Competition and Collaboration in the Later Nineteenth Century,* No. 1, pp. 139-142. (Gordon, R.A.)

Seeley, J.R. *The Emergence of England,* No. 4, pp. 121-122. (Marshall, P.J.)

Sen, S. *Working Class of India:* 1830-1970, I:2, pp. 123-124. (Brasted, H.V.)

Shackle, C *Catalogue of the Punjabi and Sindhi Manuscripts in the India Office Library,* II:1&2, p. 151. (Akhtar, M.S.)

Shah, G. *Caste Association and Political Process in Gujarat. A Study of Gujarat Kshtriya Sabha,* I:1, pp. 157-158. (Hardiman, D.)

Shah, W. *The Adventures of Hir and Ranhja,* No. 4, pp. 113-115.. (McLeod, H.)

Shakir, M. Muslin Attitudes: *A Trend Report and Bibliography,* I:1, pp. 142-143. (McPherson, K.)

Shakir, M. *Muslims in Free India,* I:1, pp. 142-143. (McPherson, K.)

Shakir, M. *Secularisation of Muslim Behaviour,* I:1, pp. 142-143. (McPherson, K.)

Shapiro, M.C. and H.F. Schiffman, *Language and Society in South Asia,* VI:2, pp. 98-100. (Bradley, D.)

Sharma, A. *Women in World Religions,* X:2, pp. 92-93. (McLean, M.D.)

Sharma, R.S. (ed.), *The Indian Historical Review,* Vol.1, No.1, No. 6, pp. 121-122. (Basham, A.L.)

Sher, I. and S.A. Abbas, *Foreign Aid and Industrial Development in Pakistan,* No. 3, pp. 129-130. (Hogan, W.P.)

Shears, R. and I. Gidley, Devi, *The Bandit Queen,*IX:1, pp. 110-112. (Cashman, R.)

Shendge, M.J. *The Civilised Demons:* The Harappans in the Rig Veda, VII:2, pp. 89-91. (Wright, D.)

Shirsat, K.R. Kaka Joseph Baptista: *Father of the Home Rule Movement in India,* I:2, p. 126. (Cashman, R.)

Shulman, D.D. *The King and the Clown in South India Myth and Poetry,* X:1, pp. 83-88. (Mishra, V; XII:1, pp. 85-102. (Bailey, G. Mishra, V.)

Siegel, L. *Sacred and Profane Dimensions of Love in Indian Traditions as Exemplified in the Gitagovinda of Jayadeva,* II:1&2, pp. 189-190. (Bharati, A.)

Simsar (transl.), M.A. *The Cleveland Museaum of Art's Tuti-Nama: Tales of a Parrot,* IV:1, pp. 59-60. (Pearson, M.N.)

Sohnen, R. *Untersuchungen zur Composition von Reden und Gesprachen im Ramayana,* VI:1, pp. 76-77. (Bailey, G.)

Speacker, K. Weber im Wettbewerb. *Das Schicksal des sudindeischen Textilhandwerks im* 19. Jahrhundert, IX:2, pp. 111-112. (Jacobs, M.)

Spodek, H. Urban-Rural Integration in Regional Development: *A Case Study of Saurashtra, India* 1800-1960, I:2, pp. 138-139. (Lewandowski, S.)

Srinavasan, D.M. Mathura: *The Cultural Heritage,* XIII:2, pp. 111-113. (Wright, D.)

Srinivasan, D. *Concept of Cow in the RigVeda,* VI:2, pp. 101-102. (Mabbett, I.W.)

Srivastava, I. Dhrupada, *a Study of its Origin, Historical Development, Structure and Present State,* V:1, pp. 62-64. (Flora, R.)

Steensgard, N. Carracks, Caravans and Companies: *European-Asian Trade in the Early Seventeenth Century,* No. 4, pp. 117-118. (arasaratnam, S.)

Stern, R.W. The Cat and the Lion: *Jaipur State in the British Raj,* XIII:2, pp. 130-131. (Fisher, M.H.)

Stone, I. *Canal Irrigation in British India,* IX:2, pp. 109-111. (Henry, R.)

Streefker, H. Industrial Transition in Rural India: *Artisans, Traders and Tibals in South Gujarat,* X:2, pp. 95-96. (Catanach, I.J.)

	Studies in Socio-cultural Change in Rural Villages in Tiruchirapalli District, Tamilnadu, India: Studies on Agrarian Socieities in South Asia, VI:2, pp. 103-105. (Mayer, P.)
Stutley, M.	*Ancient Indian Magic and Folklore: An Introduction,* VII:2, pp. 89-91. (Wright, d.)
Subramaniam, V.	Parched Earth: *The Maharashtra Drought,* 1970-73, I:1, pp. 151-153. (Masselos, J.)
Suntharalingam, R.	*Politics and Nationalist Awakening in South India,* 1852-1891, No. 5, pp. 120-121. (Arnold, D.)
Suntharalingam, R.	*Indian Nationalism: An Historical Analysis,* IX:2, pp. 81-92. (Copland, I.)
Swan, B.	Sri Lanka Mosaic: *Environment, Man, Cotinuity and Change,* XII:2, p. 112. (D.S. Abeyagunawardena)
Taddei, M. (ed.)	*South Asian Archaeology* 1977, VI:2, pp. 102-103. (Bailey, G.)
Tagore, R.	*Selected Poems,* IX:2, p. 125. (Shepherd, R.)
Tagore, R.	*The Broken Nest,* No. 4, pp. 127-128. (Maddern-m.)
Talbot, I.	*Provincial Politics and the Pakistan Movement. The Growth of the Muslim League in North-West and North-East India* 1937-47, XIII:1, pp. 104-107. (Boreham, N.)
Tandon, P.	*Beyond Pubjab:* 1937-1960, No. 2 pp. 128-129 (Jones K.W.)

Taylor, D. and M. Yapp (eds.), *Political Identity in South Asia,* VI:1, pp. 78-79. (Brasted, H.)

Thairani, K.	*British Politcal Missions to Sind:* 1799 to 1843, pp. 109-111. (Hamann, C.)
Thapar, R.	*Ancient Indian Social History,* VII:2, pp. 89-91, (Wright, D.)
Thompson, E.	*The Making of the Indian Princes,* II:1&2, pp. 215-217. (Copland, I.)
Toye, J.	*Public Expenditure and Indian Development Policy,* 1960-1970, IX:11, pp. 123-125. (Ghosh, R.N.)
Trivedi, H.R.	*Scheduled Caste Women: Studies in Explotation,* II:1&2, pp. 172-174. (Kondos, V.)
Tucker, R.P.	*Ranade and the Roots of Indian Nationalism,* I:2, pp. 124-126. (Cashman, R.)

Tumbull, C.M. *A History of Malaysia, Singapore and Brunei*, XII:2, pp. 110-112, (Wicks, P.C.)

Turstig, H. (ed.) *Yantracintamani of Damodara*, XI:2, pp. 140-141. (Comans, M.)

Vakil, C.N. and V.S.M. Rao (eds.) *Industrial Development of India Policy and Problems*, No. 6, pp. 145-147. (Ambirajan, S.)

Van den Dreisen, I.H., *Indian Plantation Labour in Sri Lanka: Aspects of the History of Immigration in the 19th Century*, IX:1, pp. 118-120. (Lal, B.V.)

Van den Dungen, P.H.M., *The Punjab Tradition: Influence and Authority in 19th—Century India*, No. 5, pp. 112-113. (Jones, K.W.)

Varadarajan, L. (ed.), *India in the 17th Century: Social, Economic and Political Memoirs of Francois Martin* (1670-1694), V:1, pp. 71-72. (Pearson, M.N.)

Varma, S.P., I. Narain et al. *Voting Behaviour in a Changing Society (A Case Study of the Fourth General Election in Rajasthan)*, No. 4, pp. 133-134. (Rao, G.L.)

Vatuk, S. (ed.) *American Studies in the Anthropology of India*, II:1&2, pp. 226-227. (Zamora, M.D.)

Vaudeville, C. *Kabir*, Vol. 1, No. 5, pp. 101-104. (McLeod, H.)

Vedavalli, R. *Private Foreign Investment and Economic Development*, I:2, pp. 143-145. (Ambirajan, S.)

Veerathappa, K. *Brirish Conservative Party and Independence*, I:2, pp. 143-145. (Bridge C.)

Vickers, A. Bali, *A Paradise Created*, XIII:1, pp. 134-135. (Brown, I.)

Vijayan, O.V. *After the Hanging and Other Stories*, XIII:2, pp. 144-145. (Watson, I.B.)

Viasaxis, V.G. *Hindu Epics, Myths and Legends in popular Illustrations*, IV:1, p. 58, (Kenna, C.)

Von Furer-Haimendorf, C., *Return to the Naked Nagas: An Anthropologist's View of Nagaland* 1936-1970, I:1, p. 149, (Newell, W.H.)

Wade, R. Village Republics:*Economic Conditions for Collective Action in South India*, XIII:2, pp. 125-128. (Narain, I.)

Wagle, N.K. (ed.) *Images of Maharashtra: A Regional Profile of India*, VI:1, pp. 79-80. (Masselos, J.)

Warder, A.K. *An Introduction to Indian Historiography*, No. 3, pp. 114-116. (Basham, A.L.)

Washbrook, D.A. *The Emergencde of Provincial Politics: The Madras Presidency* 1870-1920, I:1, pp. 134-136. (Stoddart, B.)

Wasti, S.R. *Biographical Dictionary of South Asia,* IV:2, p. 105. (Martell, W.H.T.)

Weiner, M. Sons of the Soil: *Migratiòn and Ethinic Conflict in India,* III:2, pp. 87-89. (Moffatt, M.)

Weiner, M. Sons of the Soil: *Migration and Ethnic Conflict in India,* IV:1, pp. 71-73. (Mayler, P.B.)

Werner, K. (ed.) *The Yogi and the Mystic: Studies in Indian and Comparative Mysticism,* XIII:1, pp. 124-126. (McLean, M.D.)

Whitcombe, E. *Agrarian Conditions in Northern India,* No. 4, pp. 125-127. (Brennan, L.)

White, D. *The Bhagavad Gita: A New Translation and Commentary,* XII:1, pp. 113-125. (Comans, M.)

Williams, J.G. *The Art of Gupta India,* VII:2, pp. 92-94. (Amzad Hossein Mian, A.K.H.)

Wilson, A.J. *Electoral Politics in an Emergent State,* I:1, pp. 90-101. (Roberts. M.)

Wilson, A.J. The Break-up of Sri Lanka. *The Sinhalese-Tamil Conflict,* XIII:1, pp. 128-131. (Arasaratnam, S.)

Winius, G. and R. Ross (eds.), *Itinerario vol.*vii, no. 1, IX:1, p. 97. (Reeves, P.)

Wintus, G.D. *The Black Legend of Portuguese India,* X:1, pp. 91-93. (Disney, A.)

Wiser, C.V. *Four Families of Karimpur,* II:1&2, pp. 174-175. (Zamora, M.D. and Zimmerman, L.)

Wiser, W. and C. Wiser, *Behind Mud walls* 1930-1960, with a Sequel: The Village in 1970, No. 3, pp. 118-119. (Miller, D.B.)

Wolpert, S. *Jinnah of Pakistan,* X:1, pp. 102-104. (Dua, B.D.)

Wright, D. Bangladesh: *Origins and Indian Ocean Relations* (1971-1975), XII:1, pp. 131-132. (Khan, M.M. and Haq, S.)

Wulff, D.M. *Drama as a Mode of Religious Realisation:* The Vidagdhamadhava, (Klaiman, M.H.)

Yazdani, Z. *Hyderabad During the Residency of Henry Russell, 1811-1820: A Case Study of the Subsidiary Alliance System,* IV:1, pp. 91-92. (Leonard, K.)

Yearbook of the South Asia Institute, Heidelberg

University, 1968/69, No. 2,pp. 112-113. (Johnson, B.L.C.)

Younger, C. The Anglo-Indians: Neglected Children of the Raj, X:2, pp. 93-95. (Duyker, E.)

Yuyama, A. (ed.) *Prajna-paramita-ratna-guna-samcaya-gatha* (Sanskrit Recension A), I:1, pp. 128-129. (Harrison, P.)

Zachariae, T. *Opera Minora, zur indischen Wortforschung, zur Geschichte der indischen Literatur and Kultur, zur Geschichte der Sanskritphilogie*, II:1&2, p. 152. (Basham, A.L.)

Zaidi, Z.H. (ed.) *Jinnah-Ispahani Correspondence*, I:2, pp. 127-128. (Tinker, H.)

Ziring, L., R. Braibanti and W.H. Wriggens (eds.), *Pakistan, the Long View*, II:1&2, pp. 171-172. (IWright, D.)

Zograph, G.A. *Languages of South Asia: A Guide*, VI:1, pp. 80-82. (Bradley, D.)

Zurbuchen, M.S. *The Language of Balinese Shadow Theater*, XIII:1, pp. 131-134. (Rubinstein, R.)